Studies in Halakhah and Rabbinic History

MAGGID

Rabbi Eitam Henkin

STUDIES IN HALAKHAH AND RABBINIC HISTORY

Edited by
Chana Henkin
In collaboration with
Rabbi Dr. Eliezer Brodt

Maggid Books

Rabbi Eitam Henkin, *Hy"d*
Studies in Halakhah and Rabbinic History

First Edition, 2021

Maggid Books
An imprint of Koren Publishers Jerusalem Ltd.

POB 8531, New Milford, CT 06776-8531, USA
& POB 4044, Jerusalem 9104001, Israel
www.maggidbooks.com

The publication of this book was made possible
through the generous support of *The Jewish Book Trust.*

ISBN 978-1-59264-581-7, *hardcover*

Printed and bound in the United States

We are humbled and privileged to be partners in spreading the Torah and scholarship of Rav Eitam Henkin Hy"d.

Nicole and Raanan Agus and family
New York and Jerusalem
2021

May the Torah in this volume
be a source of comfort to the family of
Rav Eitam and Naama Hy"d,
and of light and strength to all those privileged to study it.

Pamela and George Rohr

Dedicated in memory of

Rabbi Eitam and Naama Henkin H"yd

&

Rabbi Yehuda Henkin ztz"l

It is an honor and privilege
to support the continuation of their good work for future generations,
may their memory be a blessing.

And יבדל"א *in honor of*

Rabbanit Chana Henkin

whom we are proud to partner with in her remarkable vision
and appreciate our warm friendship.

Jay and Jeanie Schottenstein
Joey and Lindsay
Jonathan and Nicole
Jeffrey

The remarkable legacy of Rav Eitam and Naama Henkin
will be a light unto the world
through the publication of his writings contained in

"STUDIES IN HALAKHAH AND RABBINIC HISTORY."

May their memories be a blessing and comfort to all.

Amy & Bob Book

Other Books Authored by R. Eitam Henkin *Hy"d*

Lakhem Yihyeh L'Okhlah, Kiryat Arba, 2011.

L'Hakot Shoresh (co-author: R. Avraham Wasserman), Jerusalem, 2012.

Esh Tamid: Hilkhot Shabbat; Ḥidushim U'Be'urei Dinim al Seder Shulḥan Arukh U'Mishnah Berurah, Jerusalem, 2015.

Ta'arokh Lefanai Shulḥan, Jerusalem, 2019.

Contents

PART III: RABBI YOSEF ELIYAHU HENKIN

Editor's Preface

This book contains a sampling of our son's halakhic and historical works. He began publishing in rabbinic journals at age twenty-one. At that point, he was married, with his first child on the way. In the ensuing decade until his death, he published more than forty articles and three books. Another book and some ten articles were published posthumously from material found on his computer, with additional material presently in various stages of preparation for publication. His works were published in a uniquely diverse range of venues, from the ḥasidic *Bet Aharon V'Yisrael* of Karlin-Stolin, to *Yeshurun, Yerushatenu* and *Ḥitzei Giborim, HaMa'ayan, Ḥakirah, Alonei Mamreh, Teḥumin, Emunat Itekha, Tzohar, Akdamot,* and *Tziyon* of The Historical Society of Israel.

The idea for the present volume came from R. Moshe Rosenberg and R. Elli Fischer. Shortly after our family arose from *shivah,* R. Rosenberg requested our permission to organize volunteer translators from among those who had followed our son's works and now sought an appropriate response to our son R. Eitam's and our daughter-in-law Naama's deaths *Hy"d* at the hands of murderous foes of Israel. Our family expresses deep appreciation to Rabbis Rosenberg and Fischer and the other translators. In particular, I must mention Michael Appel, who was responsible for, and did marvelous work on, no fewer than seven chapters of this book. We felt that the inconsistencies in style resulting from the work of different translators were a small price to pay for this expression of the solidarity of *Am Yisrael.* I ask the translators' forgiveness for the liberties I took in editing their work. I ask my son's forgiveness, and take sole responsibility, for any errors in the text.

Thanks to a teenage prank, two of our children were able to unlock our son's computer following *shivah*. Years earlier, he and a friend had scaled an abandoned water tower, the tallest structure in our neighborhood, upon which they hung a sheet painted with the *gematria*, numerical equivalent, of their names. Our daughter Taama and our son Yagil guessed correctly that that would have been their brother's code. They found meticulously organized files of Torah writings in various stages of completion, including *ḥiddushim* on four sections of *Shulḥan Arukh*.

Two of our son's friends, R. Shmaryah Gershuni and Oz Bluman, together with our son Dr. Yagil Henkin, catalogued the files. In addition, Nomi Englard-Schaffer and Hannah Spellman assisted in organizing the files. My late husband *ztz"l* carefully reviewed each file. From that point, R. Dr. Eliezer Brodt took over the task of bringing our son's writings to the publication stage. He spent endless hours with our son's computer, insisting on painstakingly comparing files and notes to verify the latest and best formulation. Many times, we spoke several times a day. With his quick mind, he typically could solve a problem in minutes. If not for his patient guidance, wisdom, skill, brilliance and wide-ranging knowledge, readers would not be holding this book, nor the additional works that are planned.

I express heartfelt appreciation as well to our publisher, Matthew Miller, and to R. Reuven Ziegler, Caryn Meltz, and Debbie Ismailoff of Maggid Books, Koren Publishers, for their guidance, encouragement, and patience; and to Rachelle Emanuel for reading and correcting the manuscript, and finessing the language, with extraordinary skill. She typically knew the right word, and turned a good sentence into a sparkling one.

Our son *Hy"d* was a kollel student in his early twenties when he and Professor David Assaf began an exchange of articles that each had written. Professor Assaf was astonished to find a wunderkind with no academic training, producing the work of a seasoned scholar. The two were of different stripes religiously and politically, but there developed between the two a genuine affection and appreciation. We are indebted to Professor Assaf for his mentorship of our son.

The bond between R. Eitam and his father was unique, and my revered husband *ztz"l* went to his grave grieving for his son. Our son had one *rav*, and that was his father. It was he who walked to and from pre-school with the young Eitam, and who taught him halakhah along the way – a tradition that Eitam continued with his own sons. It was his father who taught him to read, in Hebrew and then in English, and who taught him to ride a bicycle and eventually to play the guitar. It was his father who set the standard for learning and writing. Similarly, my husband had one *talmid* who grasped the totality of his halakhic and hashkafic legacy, and that was his son. Beyond the Shabbat-table conversations, R. Eitam read every *teshuvah* and article that his father wrote, and his father did likewise as soon as Eitam began to write; and they discussed their writings together. Shortly after he married, Eitam edited and, with his silver pen, rewrote his father's commentary on the Torah, which eventually was published as *Mahalakhim Bamikra.* R. Eitam was the rabbinic *yoresh,* heir, and that was clear to all. Although R. Eitam would protest the comparison with his father and with his saintly great-grandfather, R. Yosef Eliyahu Henkin *ztz"l,* one cannot fail to note the similarity of incisive mind, integrity, and self-effacing nature. He also shared with both an unwillingness "to quit the battlefield in the midst of a conflict," as was said of his great-grandfather, the Gaon.

One characteristic illustration of our son's generosity of spirit was in correspondence shown to me by R. Moshe David Chechik. A Ben-Gurion University professor, who had headed two departments at the university, was among the scores of scholars in touch with our son. This professor heard through the grapevine that our son was collecting documents relating to Maharil Diskin, and asked to see something. Our son responded, "Truth be told, I felt more than a twinge when I received your request…The topic itself (the tension between traditionalism and modernity in Orthodox leaders, in particular those considered as zealots) is of much interest to me…and I have for several years been collecting material on the topic, though not methodically, and have been planning to use this material for a full-scale article. However, I don't find much benefit in *kin'at sofrim,* academic jealousy; and as you are ahead of me and have already begun to write…the academic world will certainly benefit from your work as with your previous work. Therefore I will be happy to send you the materials in my possession." Our son modestly added that the professor didn't need his bibliographical assistance, but he was appending a list of primary sources that had "landed in his fishing net," with good wishes for an excellent article.

I thank HaShem that this book benefited from the irreplaceable guidance of my husband *ztz"l,* and that we had the comfort of working together on this book. I close with thanksgiving to HaShem that our son merited a rare and extraordinary partnership with our beloved daughter-in-law, Naama *Hy"d,* his *ḥavera* and *eshet brit.* They "ascended in a storm" to the heavens together, on the third day of Ḥol HaMo'ed Sukkot, 2015. May their souls repose peacefully together in *Gan Eden* until the time when the *tzaddikim* will arise once again.

Chana Henkin
Jerusalem 2021

Introduction

Still vivid in my mind's eye are the horrific events that transpired on that fateful third night of Ḥol HaMo'ed Sukkot 2015, when I received the email informing me of R. Eitam's and his wife Naama's murder, *Hy"d*. I kept staring at my screen and repeatedly hitting refresh, hoping all the while that the heartrending news was not true. To my deep despair, this was not the case. My disbelief had in part to do with being someone who knew R. Eitam and had been following his writings for so long. I felt that the gaping void created upon his untimely death would never be in any way filled.

Almost immediately, already during the *shivah*, people reached out to me, asking what was to become of R. Eitam's voluminous writings. Simultaneously, HaShem's many other messengers were working on some form of preserving his writings. One group of volunteers from all over the world embarked upon a project to enlist help in translating his many works into English. Others offered help in publishing his works. His parents immediately turned their attention to publishing his work on *Hilkhot Shabbat, Esh Tamid*, which was in its final stages prior to his murder.

At the time, however, no one had really gauged the extent of his literary legacy, still preserved in his computer's hard drive. It was following the *shivah*, when his brother and some close friends began cataloging his hard drive, that it became quite clear that R. Eitam's legacy included a plethora of print-worthy material. Eventually, I was invited to help out with this endeavor by processing what exactly was on the hard drive. As I perused the many files, I quickly discovered numerous, nearly-complete articles; a manuscript of his book about the *Arukh HaShulḥan*, and much more. Slowly some of the articles and materials started being prepared for print. At the same time, R. Eitam's father, R. Yehuda Henkin *ztz"l* – a unique, first-rank *talmid ḥakham* and *posek*, and his mother, Rabbanit Henkin, and I began working full force on publishing his book on the *Arukh HaShulḥan,* titled *Ta'arokh Lefanai Shulḥan*. Barukh HaShem, in 2018 the book was printed by Maggid Books.

Next, we restarted the translation project, with the intent of publishing a selection of R. Eitam's essays in book form. After carefully deciding which essays would be most valuable for an English audience, the volunteers were contacted, to ascertain whether their offers to translate some of R. Eitam's material, gratis, still stood; and many responded in the affirmative. In layman's terms, the significance of such an offer is two-fold; first, translating is time-consuming, and a team working together would cut time significantly. Second, translation can cost as much as several thousand dollars per article. Our translators willingly waived their fees, performing a tremendous *ḥesed* for the Henkin family, *l'zekher nishmot* R. Eitam and Naama.

When the translations were completed, R. Eitam's parents vigorously scrutinized each essay for accuracy, and his mother devoted months to making numerous necessary adjustments throughout the book, as needed.

R. Eitam *Hy"d* published his articles in various Torah journals, starting from around 2006. Over time his writing gained renown for its comprehensiveness, clarity, high quality, and at times, exciting new discoveries from manuscripts. His readership ran the full spectrum of society; from far right to far left.

In general, R. Eitam's writings demonstrate a stellar command of both the halakhic and historical aspects of the topics he undertook. His many Torah articles and full-fledged halakhic works stand alongside his many first-rate historical essays. He was a unique combination of an outstanding *talmid ḥakham* and historian, who was also blessed with exceptional research and writing skills. A unique quality of R. Eitam's extraordinary writing skills was his inimitable ability to craft bibliographic essays, generally perceived as boring, into fascinating reads, of interest to the general reader.

One facet that cannot be overstated is R. Eitam's deep-seated *yirat Shamayim* which shines through his biographical essays, written with tremendous respect for the personality on whom the essay focuses. He was a seeker of truth, who carefully evaluated the evidence he gathered, devoid of any intent to seek out scandal and eschewed slandering anyone.

This volume contains a veritable smorgasbord of R. Eitam's writings. The first section is comprised of halakhic essays, focusing upon areas related to *Hilkhot*

Shabbat and *Yoreh De'ah*. Noteworthy is his article discussing checking strawberries for insect infestation, a subject on which R. Eitam dedicated a full-length book called *Lakhem Yihyeh L'Okhlah*.

The second section, titled *Studies in Rabbinic History*, includes historical essays, starting as far back as R. Akiva, on to the era of the *Rishonim* with Maharam of Rothenberg's captivity, as well as more current topics. This section also has two of his essays about *shemitah*, a topic R. Eitam was very fond of and wrote much about. In addition, several essays relate to R. Kook, yet another personality he devoted much time to, studying about and discovering new facets of this towering luminary. Indeed, given the volume of material published yearly regarding R. Kook, R. Eitam's discoveries are an extraordinary feat. Of these, some are essays regarding R. Kook's students and how they related to his legacy upon his passing. Some of the above, unknown material was found only upon thoroughly examining R. Eitam's hard drive.

Additionally, a few of the chapters were translated into English from his work on the *Arukh HaShulḥan*. One final, fascinating essay relates to the *ḥerem* on R. Yeḥiel Mikhel Pines in Jerusalem of the 1880s. At the time, this controversy rocked the rabbinical world and involved many great Torah personalities including, among others: R. Shmuel Salant, R. Dovid Karliner, R. Yehoshua Leib Diskin, and R. Mordekhai Gimpel Yafeh. This article is a mere sampling of a topic which R. Eitam devoted a great deal of time researching and writing about, thereby providing a new understanding of the affair and its impact on the *Yishuv Hayashan*.

The final section contains an essay dedicated to R. Eitam's great-grandfather, R, Yosef Eliyahu Henkin, one of the greatest and most important American *poskim* in the past century. This essay, based on an essay written by his father, R. Yehuda Henkin, very carefully documents the gaon R. Yosef Eliyahu Henkin's life story. The second essay in this section deals with R. Yosef Eliyahu Henkin in relation to the well-known Langer Affair and R. Goren.

Eliezer Brodt

The family of R. Eitam and Naama Henkin *Hy"d*
expresses heartfelt appreciation to our translators

Michael Appel
Rena Bar-David
Dr. Yocheved Cohen
Ilana Elzufon
Rachelle Emanuel
R. Elli Fischer
Meshulam Gotlieb
Shimon Lerner
R. Moshe Rosenberg
Simi Peters and the team at Academic Language Experts

בצר הרחבתם לנו

Part I

Studies in Halakhah

Chapter 1

"What You Permitted, We Prohibited":[1] The Kosher Status of Strawberries

BACKGROUND

Strawberries must be cleansed before eating because they are naturally infested by various insects. This fact has been mentioned by several halakhic authorities of recent centuries.[2] In our time, the issue has re-emerged in books devoted to the problem of bugs in food, foremost among them R. Moshe Vaye's *Bedikat HaMazon*

1. Editor's note: From the *Viduy* (confession) of R. Nissim Gaon (990–1057), recited by Sephardim on Yom Kippur, and by Ashkenazim on Yom Kippur Katan: *"For I was as a rebellious son before You, doing what is evil in Your eyes, as a slave rebelling against his master, as a disciple differing with his rabbi... What you permitted, I prohibited; what You prohibited, I permitted... Where You were lenient, I was stringent; where You were stringent, I was lenient... I pray for Your forgiveness."*
This chapter initially appeared in the author's *Lakhem Yihyeh L'Okhlah* (Kiryat Arba, 2011) as a chapter entitled "*Kashrut Tutei HaSadeh*" (pp. 121–28). It has been supplemented with as yet unpublished material written after the book's publication. We have divided the supplement into two parts in this chapter: first, our opening, "Background," and afterward as the final portion of this chapter, beginning with the section entitled "New Developments and their Halakhic Analysis." Finally, we added a previously-published section, called "Afterword," from *Lakhem Yihyeh L'Okhlah*, 137–38. Translation by R. Elli Fischer.
2. *Responsa Ḥinukh Bet Yehudah* 55b (cited in *Pitḥei Teshuvah, Yoreh De'ah* 84:7); *Darkei Teshuvah, Yoreh De'ah* 84:93 (citing R. David Pardo's *Mizmor L'David*); R. Yisrael Meir Mizraḥi, *Pri Ha'Aretz* 2:13; and R. Eliezer Papo, *Pele Yo'etz*, the beginning of the entry for *bedikot* (I thank R. Ravid Azulai for bringing this source to my attention). For a fuller treatment of these sources, see *Lakhem Yihyeh L'Okhlah*, 147–48. See also R. Ḥayim David HaLevi, *Mekor Ḥayim* 260:12.

K'Halakhah.[3] R. Vaye describes thrips and other insects found in strawberries, and explains the (complicated) cleansing methods to be used before they may be eaten. It would seem that many people, even those who are meticulous about what they eat, were not previously aware of this problem and would eat strawberries without examining them sufficiently.

In 2008 or thereabouts, a ruling that completely prohibits eating strawberries began to gain popularity. It was based on investigations undertaken by various parties (first in the United States, then in Israel), which concluded that the insects on strawberries – whose presence, as noted, has long been known[4] – remain even after cleansing. This ruling garnered the attention of the kashrut-observant public, and, as a result, much of the community ceased eating strawberries unless they are mashed or peeled.

In some respects, the scientific investigations undertaken in modern laboratories have stretched the boundaries of the prohibition beyond the requirements of halakhah.[5] Because of this, four years ago, I published my book *Lakhem Yihyeh*

3. R. Moshe Vaye, *Bedikat HaMazon K'Halakhah* (Jerusalem, 1998–2007).
4. Contrary to the popular belief that this is a new type of infestation. In actuality, all that changed was that they concluded that the methods of cleansing that were originally thought to be effective are not, in fact, effective. That is, those who relied on an expert opinion to eat corn or strawberries over the years (for example, see the responsum of the rabbis of the Torah V'ha'Aretz Institute from 2003, responsum 18579 on the Moreshet website) inadvertently violated the prohibition of eating *sheratzim* (insects) according to those who later prohibited it. This being the case, we might wonder: How are we supposed to know whether, and which of, today's expert rulings will turn out to be mistaken?
5. From *Lakhem Yihyeh L'Okhlah*, 16–17: "Even in the past generation, and occasionally nowadays, there are public declarations that something that rabbis and experts heretofore thought was permissible is in fact prohibited, because there turns out to be some phenomenon that had not previously been detected, because some method of cleaning that they had been relying on is ineffective, or the like. However, in my humble opinion, these matters, and those like them, should attest to the contrary – namely, that there is a problem of method, and that some of these investigations have stretched the boundaries of the prohibition beyond their limits. Indeed, according to the aforementioned experts, it emerges that the instance of 'a pest jammed inside a legume' – which was permitted by some of the greatest *Rishonim* and *Shulḥan Arukh* on the grounds that it does not creep – almost never actually occurs, and thus Heaven forfend that these authorities throughout the generations permitted something that is actually forbidden! (See what *Tola'at Shani* 1, p. 38, states: "Therefore, in my humble opinion, all insects found in legumes should be prohibited" except those found in rice!) Should we not be concerned about casting aspersions on all the early authorities who permitted this very thing!? Rather, in my opinion, it is simply certain that, even given the ascertained facts that in laboratory studies they found that at birth the insect is smaller than the hole it creates around itself and is capable of crawling inside the hole, and only later matures and fills the entire hole, perforce this is not called 'creeping' as far as halakhah is concerned (according to the permissive opinions). **On such matters, we follow halakhic definitions, not scientific definitions. The Torah was not given**

L'Okhlah regarding bug infestation in foods, including a chapter dealing extensively with the kashrut of strawberries. Following a detailed clarification of the facts and the halakhah, the chapter concluded with the permissibility of eating strawberries following removal of the leafy cap and rinsing under a stream of running water, while it is initially desirable to soak them for a few minutes in soapy water. This *heter,* permissible ruling, is based on the ruling of my master and teacher, R. Dov Lior *shlit"a.*

CLARIFYING THE FACTS

The facts pertaining to strawberries were investigated in a recently published comprehensive study undertaken by the Makhon L'Mitzvot Hateluyot Ba'Aretz, under the leadership of R. Shneur Zalman Revaḥ.[6] In this study, almost 500 strawberries from eight different sources of cultivation in Israel were inspected. The method of inspection, in most cases, was comprised of four stages:

1. Cutting off the cap and part of the flesh
2. Visual inspection
3. Soaking and stirring in soapy water
4. Examining the water with a fine strainer (plus a second visual inspection of the fruit)

The official results of the study were that there was a 17% infestation rate (79 of 471 strawberries). However, close scrutiny of the details yields findings whose implications deviate from the overall, ostensibly uniform, results.

In the first place, the study inspected strawberries in base units of 50, sometimes more. This quantity is more than double the quantity of strawberries in commercially available boxes, which is the base unit of inspection from the consumer's perspective. Secondly, for some reason, the details of the study contain no description of the second visual inspection, following the soaking. Had such an inspection not taken place, it could call into question the validity of the study's findings, if there is concern that even after the soaking, insects may remain on the strawberry itself. However, when I inquired about this (on 22 Sivan 2009), R. David Ben-Yosef, the supervisor of the study, clarified that the second visual inspection after soaking had indeed taken place. The reason that it does not appear

---

to ministering angels, nor was it given to laboratory researchers capable of distinguishing between grains of flour, identifying germ colonies with the naked eye, tracing the hatching of eggs, and the like, even if they do not use specialized equipment."

6. Printed in *Tenuvot Sadeh* 85 (Av–Elul 5769/2009): 29–33.

in the study's documentation is that the result in [almost] every instance was that the strawberries were completely insect-free![7]

Secondly, the distribution of findings across the different batches of strawberries was not uniform. As noted, strawberries from eight different growers were inspected. More than one-third of the insects (30 of 79) were found in the strawberries from a single source ("random market purchase"), from which only about 20% of the total number of strawberries came (90 of 471). With regard to the remaining strawberries, it turns out that those from two sources – both of which are Arab growers – had a significantly higher infestation rate than those from Jewish-owned sources (22 of 115 strawberries). If we separate the findings related to these three growers, where there was an exceptionally high infestation rate relative to the others, and examine only the strawberries from Jewish-owned sources, it emerges that the incidence of insects drops to 10% – 27 insects in 266 strawberries. In fact, even within this group, 14 of the insects were found in strawberries from one bio-organic source. With respect to most of the Jewish-owned sources – four out of five – the average incidence was a mere 6% (13 insects in 216 strawberries). It therefore seems necessary to conduct a second study, of the same magnitude, focusing exclusively on strawberries from Jewish-owned sources. If the results are consistent with the above, it will demonstrate that a different conclusion should be reached for this specific subset (which represents, it seems, a considerable proportion, if not the majority, of strawberries sold in stores in Israel).

In conclusion, the study's declared outcome of a 17% infestation rate is not evenly distributed. In half of the sources investigated (the Arab and bio-organic growers), the prevalence of insects was relatively high, about 30%; in the other half, the non-organic Jewish-owned sources, the prevalence was very low, about 6%. At the same time, it was demonstrated that a superficial visual inspection does not reveal all of the insects liable to be found on the strawberry.

As for the effectiveness of soaking in soapy water and then rinsing – even if this method, on rare occasions, does not completely eliminate the presence of

7. It should also be noted that in strawberries from two of the growers investigated, there was a second soaking and straining (following the initial soaking and straining). In one case, the results were completely clean; and in the second case, a single larva was found among 66 strawberries, the presence of which seems merely incidental. It should further be noted that one of the two groups was rinsed in a special industrial machine, after which nothing was found, neither during visual inspection nor through straining, except for half a book louse. Additionally, all of the achenes ("seeds") were removed from a different batch of 20 strawberries, whereupon nothing was found.

insects – there is, in my opinion, no need to be concerned about the presence of insects after soaking and rinsing, at the very least with respect to strawberries from Jewish-owned sources.[8] As noted, these conclusions need further support in more focused research. Our ensuing discussion will focus on the theoretical case wherein even after inspection and soaking, experts say that there may sometimes be additional insects hidden on the surface of the strawberry, which are impossible to remove during the inspection.[9]

DETECTING AND IDENTIFYING INSECTS, AND THEIR PROHIBITION

The recent public discussion about the kashrut of strawberries was incorrectly diverted to the question of whether insects invisible to the naked eye are

8. The study concludes that in general, rinsing and soaking are adequately effective, even if it is recommended to rub the strawberry manually, with a brush, or the like: "It seems clear that, with proper rinsing, it is sufficient, certainly if accompanied by manual rubbing of the entire surface of the strawberry. It is not necessary to require peeling [of the strawberry].... Even though there are rare cases of [the insects] burrowing, this minority case does not generate a requirement of peeling." Regarding what R. Avraham Rubin wrote (*Bet Hillel* 7:1 [2006]: 118–20) – namely, that after the different steps of cleaning, an additional visual inspection is required; and only then will the presumption of prohibition (*ḥezkat isur*) be removed from the strawberry – I do not understand his reasoning. Firstly, a substantial minority (*mi'ut hamatzuy*) is not a basis for presuming prohibition; in fact, the opposite is the case. Secondly, the *poskim* state explicitly that a thorough cleaning is the equivalent of a visual inspection. In the case of strawberries, in fact, a thorough cleaning is superior to a visual inspection. If it has been determined to be effective, what need is there for visual inspection? (R. Moshe Vaye writes similarly in *Bedikat HaMazon K'Halakhah*, 124.)
9. In this context, it is worth noting what was reported in the name of R. Yehudah Amiḥai in the newspaper *B'Sheva* (May 27, 2009), 8, that after a single rinse there is still a 30% infestation rate, and after two additional rinses the infestation rate is only 8%–10%. He therefore concludes, "We permitted eating strawberries after two thorough rinses and after crushing, though some rabbis did not permit even this." However, according to the detailed research of the Makhon L'Mitzvot Hateluyot Ba'Aretz, this level of infestation (even before rinsing) exists only in some of the produce in the market. Likewise, their own investigation showed that rinsing and soaking are effective (for instance, two rinses). Compare this to the figures from the Makhon L'Ḥeker HaḤakla'ut al pi HaTorah, reported in brief in *Bedikat HaMazon K'Halakhah* (vol. 2, 555), according to which the inspection of forty samples from various sources during a single season found all to be infested. In the least infested sample, there were two insects per kilogram, and in the most heavily infested there were twenty-two insects per 250 grams. This data is too general and not broken down, but it does not deviate from the findings of the study by the Makhon L'Mitzvot Hateluyot Ba'Aretz, according to which some sources were almost completely insect-free (with the average weight of a box of strawberries being about 500 grams), while others were heavily infested. In any event, after removing the cap of the strawberry, infestation seems uncommon enough to be considered a *mi'ut hamatzuy* (ibid., 559, footnote).

prohibited. Some researchers in the field claimed that "all insects, of any size, that live on plants are identifiable while they are crawling – even the smallest of insects."[10] Nevertheless, there are grounds to discuss, in principle, the prohibition of indiscernible insects, and this will clarify several points that are important for the present discussion.

R. Moshe Vaye[11] makes a straightforward distinction between insects that cannot be detected at all without optical enhancement and are not prohibited; and insects that are **visible** to the naked human eye – as tiny black specks, for instance – but can only be **identified** as insects, and not as dirt, for example, with some sort of optical enhancement. In this latter case, according to R. Vaye, the insects are prohibited. Therefore, he does not rule out – indeed, he requires – using magnification devices to identify the insects. R. Yitzḥak Yaakov Fuchs reiterates this view in his book, *HaKashrut*.[12]

The truth, however, must be told: We find no such distinction in the statements of all the *poskim*, who permit insects that are visible only by means of a magnifying glass or the like;[13] on the contrary, the principle implied by their statements is that anything that one cannot know by natural means to be an insect is not prohibited – irrespective of categories such as "detection" or "identification." R. Vaye's main proof for the distinction between detection and identification is the discussion among many latter-day authorities [*Aḥaronim*] concerning an insect called *milbin* – which R. Vaye identifies as a mite. They offer several grounds to permit it, but not because it is difficult to identify. However, it should be self-evident that these *poskim* were discussing a creature that could be identified without any optical instruments.[14]

10. R. Shneur Zalman Revaḥ, in a letter to R. Shlomo Amar dated 10 Iyar 5769 (May 4, 2009; published in *Tenuvot Sadeh* [above, n. 6], pp. 22–28). However, aside from the fact that larvae eggs are prohibited even though they cannot be discerned while crawling, and the fact that the eggs of certain genera (especially thrips) are indiscernible without magnification, R. Revaḥ himself (*Tola'at Shani*, vol. 1, pp. 137, 184) mentions insects that are indiscernible to the naked eye.
11. *Bedikat HaMazon K'Halakhah*, p. 102, as well as pp. 58, 66–67, and 200.
12. R. Yitzḥak Yaakov Fuchs, *HaKashrut* (Ḥemed, 2002), 327, n. 8.
13. As R. Elyakim Schlanger notes in *Halikhot Sadeh* 51 (p. 35). See also *Emunat Itekha* 31 (5769/2009): 38. (I have found only a single source, in *Responsa Pri HaSadeh* 3:80, which states that small creatures ["*milbin*"] are considered discernible because they can be identified with a magnifying glass.) Of course, we are not discussing the inability to discern an insect due to camouflage, hiding, motionlessness, or the like (these have implications vis-à-vis nullification at the *d'Orayta* level, but not vis-à-vis the fundamental prohibition); rather, we are discussing tiny specks that can be seen with the naked eye but not identified as insects.
14. R. Vaye cites *Responsa She'elat Ya'avetz* (New York, 1961) as mentioning examination under a magnifying glass, but that proves nothing for our discussion, as the magnifying glass was

R. Vaye brings support for his view from a lone contemporary *posek* when he writes in the name of R. Shlomo Zalman Auerbach that if an average person sees only a black speck, but an expert says it is a worm, it is prohibited from that point forward. However, in my opinion, this evidence should be weighed in light of what R. Auerbach states elsewhere. *Shemirat Shabbat K'Hilkhatah*[15] states in his name, as a matter that is obvious, that the prohibition of worms does not include citrus aphids (even if they are visible as small specks) "since the eye of an **average person** does not discern when they crawl."[16] Moreover, in the second edition of *Shemirat Shabbat K'Hilkhatah*,[17] the same thing was written with a similar formulation: "If they cannot reach a stage where it will be possible to discern that they live and move, they cannot be called *sheretz hashoretz*, 'any creeping thing that creeps'" (Vayikra 11:43). However, he adds that it had been made known to him that in actuality, before they enter the pupal stage (when their movement is indiscernible), "Even with normal vision, one can sense their movement somewhat."

---

mentioned as an aid to help the examiner find insects more easily, not as an instrument without which it would be impossible for the examiner to identify the insect (as R. Vaye himself notes, p. 102); see also *Shu"t Shevet HaLevi* 4 (Bnei Brak, 2001), 142:b. Indeed, in the very next responsum (*She'elat Ya'avetz* 2:125), R. Yaakov Emden attests that his eyesight is weak and it is difficult for him to see the *milbin* without a magnifying glass. Moreover, some *Aḥaronim* contested this statement of R. Emden. See R. Shlomo Kluger, *Tuv Ta'am VaDa'at* 2 (Lwow, 1852), *Kuntres Aḥaron* 53:

> Examination by means of a magnifying glass, which you write in the name of R. Yaakov Emden, makes no sense to me, for examination cannot be other than something that anyone can do. That which is only possible by the exceptional means of this instrument is not considered an examination that is grounds to permit. There is support for this in the Sages' statement in the second chapter of Pesaḥim [37a]: "They will say, 'All shaped [matzah] is prohibited, but the shaped [matzah] of Baitos is permitted.'"

Thus far, one might posit that R. Kluger disagrees with R. Emden only when it comes to rendering something permitted, but when it comes to finding something prohibited, he concurs. However, he continues:

> Further evidence: The experts say that if we look at water under a magnifying glass, worms would be visible in all water. And if we look at any slaughtering knife, we would find flaws in the knife. Given that we have never taken this into consideration, perforce that seeing something with a device is not considered seeing that would warrant stringency, and so certainly it is not considered seeing that warrants leniency. Thus, using this device is not considered an examination.

15. *Shemirat Shabbat K'Hilkhatah* (Jerusalem, first edition, 1965) ch. 3, n. 46.
16. The author adds that he later learned that Ḥazon Ish was stringent about this, but it is not clear whether this means that Ḥazon Ish was stringent with respect to detection and identification, or that he felt that citrus aphids are forbidden. (Incidentally, the aforementioned citation by R. Fuchs of *Shu"t Shevet HaLevi* that appears below states that there is no obligation to examine a tiny black speck; thus, R. Fuch's statements contradict themselves.)
17. Ch. 3, n. 105.

In other words, practically speaking, these aphids belong in the category of "any creeping thing that creeps" and are therefore prohibited.

However, it is also clear that R. Auerbach requires only the eyes of an average person, not those of an expert. It is likewise explicit in R. Auerbach's words that there could be situations in which small specks are visible but not identifiable as insects (without a magnifying glass or a similar device), and in such instances, there is no prohibition.[18] This being the case, we should say that the meaning of the statement attributed to R. Auerbach in *Bedikat HaMazon K'Halakhah* is that in a case where an expert explains to someone that a particular speck is actually a worm, the person himself can now identify it as a worm, even if earlier he thought it was only a black speck.[19]

R. Shmuel Wosner *(Shu"t Shevet HaLevi* 7:122) likewise wrote explicitly that if someone sees a black speck and does not identify it as a worm, he has no obligation to examine it under a magnifying glass. He explains that in such a case it is not the seeing of the eye that causes the stringency, but the magnifying glass; this being the case, it is not prohibited. He likewise clarifies the issue of average vision versus the vision of an expert: "Examination applies only to what is visible to **most people**." That is, even if there is someone with exceptional vision who can see that the specks are creatures, they are not prohibited. R. Wosner mentions the words of R. Shlomo Kluger (above, n. 13), "for examination cannot but be **something that anyone can do**. That which is only possible by the exceptional means of an instrument is not considered...." However, R. Wosner later qualifies his statement and says that one must be concerned about things that people with acute vision can see, even if those with average vision cannot

18. It is obvious to me that the positions brought in the name of R. Auerbach in *Shemirat Shabbat K'Hilkhatah*, which were presented to him for review on three occasions (the first edition in 1965, the second edition in 1979, and in the edition of "addenda et corrigenda" in 1993) and left as they were, should be preferred over hearsay testimony that was published after R. Auerbach's death, in 1998. Accordingly, we can also infer that the view attributed to R. Auerbach in *Halikhot Sadeh* (p. 42), "The Torah did not forbid a worm that is so small that the eye of a person with the finest vision cannot detect it," is not referring to an expert with particularly rare vision, but to an average person, who must be someone with "the best vision," that is, twenty-twenty vision, vision that is in no way even somewhat defective. (There is thus no need for what R. Vaye and R. Zev Weitman wrote about this in *Emunat Itekha* 38 [5761/2001]: 28, 32.)
19. Just as in the case of citrus aphids, which R. Auerbach ultimately prohibited because the **experts** found that an **average person** can discern their movements. Similarly, see *Ḥokhmat Adam* (38:28) regarding water bugs that are discernible as worms by those familiar with them, even without assistance of an optical device, but to someone who has never been shown them, they will not be discernible until they are removed and placed separately. At that point, even such a person will see with his own eyes that they are insects.

(7:125:b). He also writes there that experts make things clearer for the public, but this is something that the public is capable of clarifying for themselves with proper training, as we have explained.

Similarly, R. Shlomo Amar wrote at length, in a responsum dated Nisan 5769 (2009) (*Tenuvot Sadeh* 85 [Av–Elul 5769], 9–21), that if one sees a speck on the body of the strawberry, but it is impossible to discern whether it is a worm or dirt, and this can only be clarified with some optical device, then:

> Since it is not possible to determine its identity without specialized devices, it has not yet reached the status of a living creature, and is not forbidden. We can further say that even if they examined the speck and say that it is certainly a worm, it remains permitted.... Even if he saw the speck and there is great concern that it is an insect, one is nevertheless not obligated to examine it.... Since to a regular eye it does not have the form of a worm or any other form, but simply looks like a speck, not crawling at all, but simply staying where it is, motionless, there is no need to be concerned about it.

I also asked *mori v'rabi* R. Dov Lior (on 17 Iyar 2009), and he responded that, indeed, as long as the insect cannot be discerned naturally, it is not prohibited, even if we see a small black speck; in such a case, there is no requirement to use a magnifying glass. He spoke of all people, not only about experts.[20]

R. Naḥum Eliezer Rabinovich likewise wrote (*Responsa Si'aḥ Naḥum, Yoreh De'ah* 45) that even if "the semblance of small specks of fine dust" are visible, if they are not recognized as insects by the naked eye, and their motion is indiscernible, they are permitted.

R. Asher Weiss likewise ruled incisively (*Minḥat Asher* 1:41, p. 130) that we base ourselves on the average person with respect to all the laws of the Torah, and the average person may rely on his senses and need not seek out an expert to identify worms, especially if there is uncertainty about whether there are even worms present.

In sum, if one detects a small black speck or the like, which is not crawling, such that the vast majority of people with good vision cannot determine with the naked

20. See also the last paragraph of R. Meir Mazuz's approbation to *Lakhem Yihyeh L'Okhlah* (p. 12):
> Our custom on the night of Rosh Hashanah was to take dried figs and visually examine them thoroughly.... One whose eyesight is weak should use a magnifying glass, but there is no need to look under a microscope that magnifies an insect on a strawberry 450 times! A person can go only on what **his eyes** see!

eye whether it is an insect, there is no prohibition. There is no validity to findings that use methods of optical enhancement or people with exceptionally rare vision.

THE HALAKHIC IMPLICATIONS OF THE FINDINGS

Let us now summarize the halakhic status of strawberries, in light of the issues we discussed throughout *Lakhem Yihyeh L'Okhlah*:

Nullification at the Level of the Torah Prohibition (*bitul mid'Orayta*)[21]

The concern about strawberries is that even after cleansing, insects that are hard to detect and remove will remain hidden on the surface of the strawberry. However, based on our discussion, if no insects can be found through close observation of the exterior of the fruit, or if identifying the insect requires a great deal of effort, the insects are nullified at the Torah level according to all opinions.

An Intact Creature (*beriya*)[22]

According to the opinion that an intact creature is nullified in the concentration of circa one per mil (i.e., one to a thousand), which, we suggested, can be combined as an uncertainty (*safek*, in order to reach a lenient ruling), it is not clear that this leniency can be applied in practice to strawberries; for it is possible that small strawberries are not one thousand times the bulk of the insects found on them. We can only apply the leniency of "uncertainty" in the case of large strawberries.[23] However, the position that the status of *beriya* does not apply in such

21. Translator's note: A key question that arises whenever a forbidden food, or a food item containing forbidden mixtures, becomes mixed with permitted food is whether the prohibited food is considered halakhically nullified (*batel*) by a majority of the permissible food. A secondary question is, in cases where there is no nullification, whether the resulting prohibition is forbidden at the level of a Torah commandment (*mid'Orayta*) or at the rabbinic level. Stated differently, the question is whether, at the Torah level, nullification indeed takes place (*bitul mid'Orayta*), but not at the rabbinic level. The halakhic differences between foods that are rabbinically prohibited and foods that are prohibited *mid'Orayta* are manifold. This issue is treated at length in *Lakhem Yihyeh L'Okhlah*, 23–41.

22. Ed. note: The general principles of nullification do not apply to a *beriya*, a wholly intact item or creature. In *Lakhem Yihyeh L'Okhlah*, 103–7, the author cited one view that even a *beriya* can be nullified when it is only one in about one thousand items, and another view that a creature must have some intrinsic significance to be considered a *beriya* that cannot be nullified.

23. On the other hand, we cannot definitively say that small strawberries do not have one thousand times the bulk of the insects, for the primary problem with strawberries is the larvae of thrips, which are only about half the size of the achenes on the surface of the strawberry. It is therefore necessary to take real measurements, as this is considered, in my opinion, *ḥisaron yediya*, a lack of information [Ed. note: which can be remedied by measuring the size of the thrip and the strawberry] and nothing more. [Ed. note: Since the reality can be clarified by measuring, the

cases, either because the bugs are tiny and repulsive or because they will never be alone as single units and therefore have no independent significance, certainly applies even to small strawberries – and perhaps the halakhah follows this position. In either case, since, in reality, it is uncertain that there is an insect upon the specific strawberry being considered (and on the contrary, in most cases the strawberries are clean), we are thus dealing with an uncertainty at the rabbinic level, on which we rule leniently (after examining whatever possible).

A Substantial Minority (*mi'ut hamatzuy*)[24]

In principle, it seems that the risk of infestation should be calculated for each individual strawberry, for they are commonly eaten one by one. That is, even if we assume that the threshold of a "substantial minority" for the purpose of calculating a *mi'ut hamatzuy* is as low as 10%, it means that insects must be found on at least one in every ten strawberries in order for the infestation to be considered a substantial minority. This applies to insects found on the body of the strawberry, not its cap, which is generally removed. Our analysis of the studies shows that fruits from the relatively clean sources do not reach this level of infestation. Moreover, since the obligation to examine in such cases is rabbinic, and a significant proportion of produce on the market is from the clean sources, if the consumer is uncertain whether the strawberries in his possession come from one of the cleaner sources or one of the more infested sources, and he cannot easily clarify this, he may be lenient. In addition, we have seen that when it comes to bugs and when there is nullification at the level of *d'Orayta*, it is not clear that there are grounds for being stringent and equating the threshold of a *mi'ut hamatzuy* vis-à-vis bugs with the threshold of 10% that applies to *treifot* (animals rendered non-kosher by terminal conditions).

In practice, however, it stands to reason that the presence of insects should be calculated with respect to the quantity that a person would eat at a single sitting. Therefore, in the case of strawberries (as opposed to larger fruits such as peaches), since several fruits are eaten in one sitting, the insects are indeed present as a *mi'ut*

---

author does not tend to apply *safek bitul* here.] This is not the same situation as the question that the *poskim* discuss, of whether a cherry contains sixty times the bulk of a worm that infests it (see Maharshal, *Yam Shel Shlomo*, Ḥulin 3:102; *Shakh* on *Yoreh De'ah* 84:30); for it is clear that in that case, they are discussing a worm that is much larger than the aforementioned larva (see *Responsa Maharil HaḤadashot* 78:2; *Terumat HaDeshen, siman* 172).

24. Translator's note: The general principles of nullification do not always apply to a "substantial minority." The questions of what constitutes a "substantial minority," how it is calculated, and when the general rules of nullification do not apply to it are addressed in *Lakhem Yihyeh L'Okhlah*, 53–81.

hamatzuy, and so *l'khatḥilah*, preferably, an examination should be performed. However, after a regular examination (and in such cases, cleansing is superior to visual inspection), it is no longer necessary to be concerned, and they are permitted even without the need to take further uncertainties into account. It goes without saying that in such cases, the Sages did not require one to peel or mash the strawberries.

PRACTICAL CONCLUSION

In conclusion, it is not clear that a "substantial minority" of store-bought strawberries are infested and, consequently, that they must be inspected, because in many sources of cultivation, the incidence of insect infestation is very low (and if one does not know whether the fruit comes from one of the sources with a higher infestation rate, he may, as stated, be lenient, because the uncertainty is whether there are insects present [*safek matzuy*], not whether there is a presumption of prohibition [*safek muhzak*]). Moreover, there is rabbinic disagreement [*plugta de-rabbanan*] about how to define the quantitative unit that one would be obligated to examine. Nevertheless, *l'khatḥilah*, an examination should be done, as long as it is not too troublesome. After a regular examination (by cleansing the fruit, as per below), it is all but certain that no insects will remain, if there ever were any. At this point, even if there are insects that remain hidden in the fruit, they are nullified *mid'Orayta* according to all opinions. As for the question of *beriya*, since this is an uncertainty regarding a rabbinic prohibition, we rule leniently; and to this we can add the view of those who maintain, for various reasons, that the prohibition of *beriya* does not apply at all in such cases.

Therefore, with respect to strawberries from a source that is not generally known to be infested (and preferably not from a bio-organic source or from Arab growers), one should remove the leafy caps together with a bit of flesh and then rinse the strawberries under running water – and ideally they should be soaked in soapy water and the like for a few minutes – and then they may be eaten.[25] One who is scrupulous should undertake the stringency of rubbing each strawberry in addition to rinsing it; such practice is praiseworthy.[26] On the other hand, one

25. Unless one sees with his own eyes that there remain worms on the strawberry (in which case, if one cannot remove them, there is nothing to be done; and if one finds three such strawberries in a box, the entire box is prohibited until all uncertainty is completely removed. On this, see the responsum of my father and teacher, R. Yehuda Herzl Henkin, in *Responsa Bnei Banim* 1:8 [Jerusalem, 1981], 34–37). However, for most strawberries, according to all opinions, one need not even be concerned with a supposition of such a phenomenon.

26. Those who are especially scrupulous may take upon themselves the method of examination detailed by R. Vaye (*Bedikat HaMazon K'Halakhah* 2, 559–61), which is very burdensome, entails the loss of some of the fruits, and takes into account *insubstantial minorities*. Some are

should not object to those who are lenient and eat strawberries after removing the cap and rinsing, even without soaking, for they have much upon which to rely. This is the practical ruling of my teacher, R. Dov Lior (on 24 Iyar 2009).[27]

NEW DEVELOPMENTS AND THEIR HALAKHIC ANALYSIS

In the years following the publication of *Lakhem Yihyeh L'Okhlah*, some of the institutes, in fact, altered their rulings, whether because the underlying facts changed, or because they changed their halakhic opinions, or, as seems to be the primary reason, because they looked into the statistics and measured more comprehensively and methodically than previously. Thus, even though R. Yehudah Amiḥai, head of the Torah V'ha'Aretz Institute, had not previously permitted strawberries unless each berry was rubbed with an abrasive pad,[28] beginning in 5773 (Tishrei 2012), he permitted them after soaking two or three times and rinsing – without any need to rub.[29] Nevertheless, others still require scrubbing with a brush after soaking,[30] and some still do not permit without peeling or mashing.

All of the halakhic institutes, with their various rulings, rely on investigation conducted in-house. Some of them, for whatever reason, do not publish their results in detail, but only issue their bottom-line rulings, which does not allow others – even the greatest *poskim* – to express an independent view.[31] Nevertheless, several institutes publish their results as well, especially the Makhon L'Mitzvot Hateluyot

---

so strict that they do not eat strawberries unless they are peeled or mashed, but there is no end to this; see *Arukh HaShulḥan, Yoreh De'ah* 39 and 65:46, based on *Leḥem HaPanim* cited in *Ḥagorat Shmuel, s.v. v'haklal hasheni*) – and let us suffice with this.

27. R. Lior reiterated his support in a letter to R. Moshe Bigel on 3 Nisan 2014 and in a letter to R. Meir Lubin from the winter of 2012 (published in *Responsa Dvar Ḥevron, Yoreh De'ah* 2:46). I can add that I know that on several occasions, R. Lior was asked to give his approbation to prohibitive rulings about strawberries, and he declined to do so. See also R. Meir Mazuz's approbation to *Lakhem Yihyeh L'Okhlah* cited in n. 20 above.
28. See n. 9 above, as well as responsum no. 35516 on the Yeshiva website and nos. 111716 and 149545 on the Moreshet website.
29. See responsum no. 156341, from September 11, 2013, on the Moreshet website (requiring two soakings), and the responsum on the Torah V'ha'Aretz Institute website, dated 14 Shevat 5775/2015 (requiring three soakings).
30. The bulletin of the Koshrot organization, winter 2013 (no. 269253 on the Arutz 7 website) and the instructions that the same organization sent out, which appeared in *Emunat Itekha* 107 (Iyar 5775/2015): 157. It should be noted that the initial instructions mandated soaking for five minutes, and the later instructions, three minutes.
31. When my friend, R. Michael Machlouf, asked a leading Torah sage in the spring of 2011 about the facts with respect to eating strawberries, he replied, "I am a complete ignoramus in this regard!" The facts pertaining to insects (prevalence, the possibility of removal, etc.) are not part

Ba'Aretz. Therefore I wish to revisit the question of eating strawberries in light of data that was published after my book came out.

DATA FROM 2012

The laboratory of the Makhon L'Mitzvot Hateluyot Ba'Aretz reported in Shevat 2012 that there was a 12.7% infestation rate at first rinsing, a 3.6% infestation rate after a first rinsing, and an infestation rate of only 1.2% after a second rinsing.[32] This apparently means that the basic infestation rate of the strawberries is 12%, a figure that is generally accepted as a "substantial minority" that would mandate an examination, yet significantly lower than the basic infestation rates of strawberries in earlier years. In light of these findings, R. Amiḥai *shlit"a* was asked why a simple rinse of the strawberries in insufficient. He answered:

> When there is a 12% infestation rate, it means that there is a substantial minority, and it cannot be eaten without examination. As long as you have not examined them, you may not eat them. Rinsing alone lowers [the rate of infestation], but an examination of most is not sufficient for an infested species, only an examination of all. Therefore, there is a need for two soakings of the strawberries in water (and rinsing), and then rubbing with a sponge, abrasive pad, or the like.[33]

In other words, since an infestation rate of 12% is a substantial minority that mandates an examination, and since the obligation to examine applies to each fruit/berry independently, in keeping with the ruling of Rashba cited by Rema,[34] one should now do whatever is necessary to bring the rate of infestation down to zero, literally 0%.

---

of the curriculum of the kollelim, so even the greatest of sages cannot express an opinion unless those who investigate the facts deign to share their findings and not just their conclusions.

32. This was published on the Kosherot website (no. 49660). However, the leaflet "*Otzar HaTorah V'ha'Aretz L'Tu B'Shvat*," which was likewise published in 2012, reported that the infestation rate "after a first rinsing" is 9% (no data was provided about infestation prior to rinsing) and "after a second rinsing, there is a dramatic drop" to 1.4%. The use of terminology in these parallel publications, as well as all other publications of the Makhon L'Mitzvot Hateluyot Ba'Aretz below, is not clear ("rinsings" in this context seems to mean "soakings"), nor is it uniform (it is not always clear whether the initial examination was done before or after any cleansing action). This, of course, is in addition to the change in the data itself in this case. It is possible that the Tu B'Shvat publication reflects interim results only.
33. Responsum no. 149545 on the Moreshet website, dated 30 Shevat 5772/2012.
34. *Yoreh De'ah* 84:8 (see also *Lakhem Yihyeh L'Okhlah*, 78).

In my opinion, however, this is incorrect. Rashba's statement means that if there is a group of individual items [i.e., fruits, berries, etc.] that must be examined out of concern for a substantial minority, one may not examine only some or even most of them, because the concern applies equally to each piece. If each item must be examined on its own, how does examining its fellow items benefit the item that was not examined? But this does not pertain to our situation, where each strawberry, without exception, has been cleaned. Here, the question is otherwise: If the chosen method of examination is proven to be effective for most, but not all, of the pieces (in the present case, rinsing that lowers the rate of infestation from 12.7% to 3.6%), can it be relied upon when before that rinsing, the original conditions were those of a substantial minority?[35]

The Sages instructed us to be concerned for a minority even though, according to Torah law, we follow the majority. Nevertheless, they did not instruct us to be concerned for a minority of a minority. Therefore, when someone takes several strawberries to eat, since according to the accepted position there are insects in a substantial minority of the strawberries, he must examine them, even though according to the aforementioned data (that one in eight is infested on average), it is most likely that the strawberries in his hand are clean. The person takes a step to separate the prohibited from the permitted – that is, he rinses the strawberries, whereupon (according to the above data) the infestation rate of the strawberries drops to only one in 28. Thus, concern that the strawberries in his hand were not only initially from the infested 12.7%, but that they are also among the 1/28 that remain infested after rinsing (or the 1/83 that remain infested after a second rinsing) is, *prima facie*, the classic case of worrying about the minority of a minority.[36] Likewise, in any case where someone takes a fruit that is infested in a substantial minority of cases, and takes an action that effectively cleans it in

35. This is in contrast to fruits that are presumed to be infested. On whether examinations that only partially clean the item are effective, and under what conditions, see chapter 4 of *Lakhem Yihyeh L'Okhlah.*

36. Moreover, there is no end to this, for the larger the breadth of the investigation, the greater the chances that some infestation will be found after all the cleansing. To illustrate, based on the 2015 study (below), R. Amiḥai ruled that one must soak the fruit three times, since after this procedure, all of the dozens of boxes examined were found to be completely insect free. However, what if in all those boxes a single, solitary insect was found even after a third rinsing. In such a case, would he issue a ruling for the public to perform four soakings from now on, in order to remove this far-fetched concern for infestation even after three rinses!? If the answer is affirmative, then, as said, there is no end to this. If the answer is negative, then we must discuss where the boundary runs.

most cases, the percentage that remains infested is, *prima facie*, the minority of a minority, about which we do not worry.[37]

Nevertheless, it seems that this issue hinges on how a unit of measurement is calculated with regard to a substantial minority. The aforementioned case was where one person took several strawberries, as is customary. But in the case of a family intending to serve an entire box of strawberries, it would seem – though by no means definitively – that the entire box should be treated as one unit, especially if its contents are chopped up and mixed together on a plate or the like.[38] If this is correct, then (according to the 2012 data) an individual who wants to eat strawberries must rinse them once in running water, and a family that wants to eat an entire box should soak them again.

This is true all the more so according to the data reported a year later by the insect research lab of the Torah V'ha'Aretz Institute,[39] according to which there was a 6% infestation rate at first rinsing, a 3% infestation rate after a first rinsing, and an infestation rate of only 0.3% after a second rinsing – figures that at each stage are many times lower than what has taken hold of the public imagination since the declaration that strawberries are forbidden! Although these rates are not fixed – on the contrary, we see that they fluctuate from year to year – they show that at certain times not even a substantial minority of strawberries are infested (according to most views), and, more importantly, rinsing is consistently effective at cleaning most, but not all, of the strawberries.

DATA FROM 2015

According to the data published in Shevat 2015 by R. Amiḥai[40] regarding research conducted by the research lab of the Torah V'ha'Aretz Institute, dozens of boxes

37. See chapter 3 of *Lakhem Yihyeh L'Okhlah* (especially p. 55), where I demonstrate with respect to a substantial minority that we do not maintain that requiring the examination of a fruit means that it will not be permissible until any shadow of a doubt about its infestation has been eliminated.
38. See *Lakhem Yihyeh L'Okhlah*, ch. 3, section 6.
39. Published on the Koshrot website, no. 57002. This data is based on the examination of 386 strawberries, not at one time, but over the course of several years (a situation that raises questions about the validity of the data and its relationship with the different seasons of the year). The Torah V'ha'Aretz Institute also published an update on 15 Shevat 5774/2014 (on the Yeshiva website, article/200), according to which 540 strawberries were examined. However, for some reason, the results were reported relative to boxes ("as supplied"), not to individual strawberries. At first rinsing, all boxes were infested. After a first rinsing 60% of boxes were infested, after a second rinsing, 20% of boxes were infested, and after a third rinsing, no infestation was found.
40. *Emunat Itekha* 107 (Iyar 5775/2015): 45–46.

("as supplied") of strawberries, each containing thirty to forty-five strawberries, were examined as follows: First, the leaf and some flesh were removed from every strawberry, and an initial examination was conducted. Then they were soaked in soapy water three times, while the water was vigorously stirred. After each soaking, another examination was conducted.

After the description of the process, the report provides specific examination results for ten boxes. Presumably, the full list of results, for all the dozens of boxes, was not published due to space considerations. However, there is no indication as to why these ten boxes were selected, nor whether or how they are representative of the overall average. In any case, the results are as follows:

1. In each box, between six and seventeen insects were found initially.[41] That is, the base rate of infestation fluctuates, **on average**, around 30% of the strawberries if we assume that each insect was on a different berry, which, of course, is not necessarily the case. In any event, these figures are significantly higher than the figures from 2012–2013 (5772).
2. In each case, one rinsing (soaking) did not render the box completely clean, but there was a significant drop in the rate of infestation – to an average of three insects, or 8%.[42]
3. A second rinsing effectively rendered the boxes almost completely insect free; in six of the ten boxes, no insects remained, and in the other four boxes, there were still a few isolated insects. The total average rate of infestation was less than 2%.[43]
4. After the third rinsing, as expected, no insects were found in any box.[44]

In keeping with his policy, R. Amiḥai's conclusion based on these findings is that after removing the leafy cap and part of the flesh, one should rinse (i.e., soak) them **three times** in order to obtain a 0% infestation rate, and then rinse them in running water to remove the soap. However, based upon what I have written, the

41. It was recorded that fifteen sloughed exoskeletons were found. These (which do not have the status of a *beriya* which is not nullified) are presumably rinsed off easily.
42. This data does not indicate the degree of effectiveness of rinsing under running water after a single soaking (which is simpler than a second soaking, and possibly nearly as effective).
43. That is, we can say that each rinsing (soaking) eliminated more than three-quarters of the insects that were there before that rinsing.
44. It should be noted that in three boxes, more insects were found in the second examination than in the first (!), or different kinds of insects were found. It is not clear why this happened, and it raises questions about the validity of the examinations as a whole. I raised this and other questions with the researchers, but have not yet received a response.

halakhah requires only one soaking, as this effectively cleans three-quarters of all infested strawberries,[45] since even at the outset, only a minority of strawberries were infested. However, it is possible that with such borderline statistics (i.e., where there is still 8% infestation after one cleansing), one should nevertheless perform a rinse after the soaking.

AFTERWORD[46]

We have now completed our halakhic inquiry with the help of the Almighty. With regard to relying *l'khatḥilah* on permissive rulings, let us bring the words of R. Shlomo Kluger (Maharshak),[47] which were cited in our time by R. Yosef Shalom Elyashiv[48] and earlier by R. Mordekhai Brisk,[49] who wrote: "This gaon of blessed memory [Maharshak] is himself worthy of being relied upon, even when circumstances are not pressing." R. Kluger permitted whole chickpeas, a substantial minority of which were infested by maggots with no external sign of infestation, on several grounds. He added that even if, in general, one should not rely on these rationales *l'khatḥilah*, only *bedi'avad*, nevertheless, this case – where there would be no other way to eat the chickpeas (except by cutting each pea in half, which is very tedious) – is a *sha'at hadeḥak*, pressing circumstance. Maharshak writes: "To prohibit the entire species – there is no greater loss than that," and in such a case, one may act *l'khatḥilah* on the basis of a leniency that applies *bedi'avad*, because, "*kol sha'at hadḥak k'di'eved dami*, any pressing circumstance is treated as *bedi'avad*; and prohibiting the entire species is worse than one who transgressed and cooked one time without inspecting. If food that was cooked one time in this fashion [i.e., without the requisite inspection] is permitted *bedi'avad*, then certainly an entire species should not be prohibited." The author of *Korban Netanel* wrote similarly:[50] "Regarding your objection, namely, that permissibility based on a double uncertainty (*sfek sfeika*) is only *bedi'avad*, when they have already been cooked, but not *l'khatḥilah* – I say that since it will come to prohibit the entire species of food to the Jewish people… it is considered *bedi'avad*."

---

45. This figure is consistent through all examining described here.
46. The author's *Divrei Siyum* in *Lakhem Yihyeh L'Okhlah* (137–38), has been appended here, as the fitting ending for this chapter.
47. *Tuv Ta'am VaDa'at* III (Lwow, 1852), *siman* 158.
48. *Bedikat HaMazon K'Halakhah*, 177.
49. *Shu"t Maharam Brisk* 1 (Tasnád, 1939), 88.
50. *Shu"t Torat Netanel*, 38.

One who is scrupulous about observance may ask: So what? Why not avoid chickpeas? They are certainly not a staple food. Moreover, why did R. Shlomo Kluger define this as prohibiting "the entire species"? They could have made the effort to cut each pea in two and inspect it for infestation, and if it was not infested, they could eat it! This person would also have to ask why Rema writes (*Yoreh De'ah* 96:1, at the end) that in a place where the only radishes in the market were cut with knives of non-Jews, one may purchase them and rely on the view that permits them, *bedi'avad*, after removing the place of the cut: Why couldn't they simply refrain from eating radishes? There is no existential need to eat radishes, so why not follow *ikar hadin*, the basic halakhah, namely, that *l'khatḥilah* the entire radish is forbidden?

However, it is not the way of the Torah to completely forbid things to the public when a practice has been established and when it is possible to find grounds for leniency, even using a *bedi'avad* approach (as *Taz, Yoreh De'ah* 96:8, states: "Since one cannot find other [radishes], the *l'khatḥilah* is treated like *bedi'avad*"). Furthermore, even if there is another way but which is extremely tedious, we see that people prefer to simply refrain altogether. This would be tantamount to requiring that which is impossible and to prohibiting an entire species; and it is therefore proper to endeavor to find grounds to permit and justify the established practice, even *l'khatḥilah*. See what we wrote[51] concerning R. Ḥayim Yitzḥak Ḥasid,[52] who likewise deems such conditions "impossible", and once he found grounds to permit, he concluded that one should not cast aspersion upon an established practice unless the prohibition [of the said practice] has been adopted by the entire Jewish people. Additionally, he writes, if it is a "decree that most of the public cannot tolerate," we should rule permissively. He wrote thus even though one cannot say about sweet cherries and the like that prohibiting them is a "decree that most of the public cannot tolerate" (for these are not staple foods); nevertheless, where there is a permissive established practice, that practice should not be prohibited.

It is surely a great act of piety and asceticism to refrain from eating anything questionable, even after inspection. However, it is clear that such practice is not the black-letter law and should not be applied to the public (see *Ḥatam Sofer, Yoreh De'ah* 77, at the end; *She'elat Ya'avetz* 2:124–25; *Shu"t Baḥ Haḥadashot,* 23).[53] "It

51. *Lakhem Yihyeh L'Okhlah,* 62–63.
52. *Ohel Yitzḥak, Yoreh De'ah* 5.
53. R. Avigdor Nebenzahl, in a letter (reproduced in *Lakhem Yihyeh L'Okhlah,* 11), writes that even if something is halakhically permitted, there are other reasons for concern: First, we are stricter about danger than we are about prohibitions; and second, desensitization of the heart (*timtum halev*). In truth, throughout *Lakhem Yihyeh L'Okhlah,* I did not mention the grave issue of *tim-*

is enough that we have found a reasonable explanation for the practice of the disciples of prophets [i.e., the Jewish people]."

tum halev due to forbidden foods even once – because in virtually all rabbinic responsa from past eras, from the greatest *Rishonim* and *Aḥaronim,* who dealt with practical questions of the laws of maggot infestation, I have not found a single instance where *timtum halev* is invoked as a reason to be stringent above the letter of the law. Rather, they dealt only with halakhic parameters. It is apparent that their silence about this indicates simply that where something is halakhically permitted, there is no concern for *timtum halev.* The Sages state explicitly: "*Transgression* desensitizes the heart" (Yoma 39a, commenting on Vayikra 11:43), meaning, because it is a transgression, it causes *timtum halev,* not because of any natural properties (see the explanation of Maharal of Prague, *Tiferet Yisrael,* ch. 8). Our subject is no different from other laws governing mixtures, and we do not find – neither in *Shulḥan Arukh,* nor in its commentaries, nor in the works of other *poskim* – that even where a prohibited foodstuff is *batel* (nullified) one should be stringent out of concern for *timtum halev.* (The dispute among *Rishonim* about whether a prohibited foodstuff that is nullified by a majority in a dry mixture is actually transformed into something permitted, discussed in *Yoreh De'ah* 109, has no bearing on the present inquiry.) Rather, it is only when something is prohibited according to the laws of prohibited foodstuffs, and is actually a prohibited food, but may be eaten for some extraneous reason – for example, to save a life – that we find concern for *timtum halev.* (See *Yoreh De'ah* 81:7, in Rema and commentaries, and this is also the intent of *Meshekh Ḥokhmah* on Devarim 6:11.) With regard to danger, in my humble opinion, there is no clear conclusion about the present case, for although Shabbat 90a mentions a dangerous maggot that infests figs, Avodah Zarah 30b mentions concern for puncture marks (indicating the potential presence of snake venom in the fig) but not this type of maggot. This is because the question of danger hinges on time and place, and nowadays we know of no such dangerous maggot infesting figs. So too, according to Rabbenu Ḥananel, lettuce is dipped in *ḥaroset* (Pesaḥim 115b) because there is concern for a dangerous maggot. Many *Rishonim* followed this interpretation, and *Taz* cites it as well. However, *Mishnah Berurah* and *Arukh HaShulḥan* omit this interpretation, apparently because nowadays this dangerous maggot no longer infests lettuce. Certainly, then, there is no obligation to be concerned about types of danger that are not mentioned in the Gemara and which go against medical consensus (as reported in the name of my great-grandfather, R. Yosef Eliyahu Henkin, on *Yoreh De'ah* 70:2 and 87:6, in *Yeshurun,* vol. 21 [Jerusalem, 2009], 519, 522; on the relationship between danger and prohibition, see also *Zivḥei Re'ayah* [R. Kook's commentary on Ḥulin] 9b, p. 45 [in the 1985 edition]).

Chapter 2

Are Tests and Experiments Significant with Regard to Absorbance and Emission in Modern-Day Utensils?[1]

In the past year (2013), we learned of a number of scientific experiments that were conducted to measure the degree of *bli'ah* and *plitah*, absorbance and emission, in various materials that occurs in cooking, in order to reach conclusions about the status of modern-day metal utensils in the laws of kashrut. A preliminary experiment was conducted decades ago by R. Dr. Yisrael Meir Levinger *shlit"a*, and its findings published, among other places, most recently in *HaMa'ayan*.[2] R. Levinger opened a debate on this topic in subsequent issues, including a thorough article by R. Ro'i Siton.[3] An additional, thorough and up-to-date experiment was performed recently

1. Translated by R. Elli Fischer. This chapter initially appeared in *HaMa'ayan* 54:2 (Tevet 5774).
2. R. Dr. Yisrael Meir Levinger, "*Bli'ah U'Plitah*," *HaMa'ayan* 53:1 (Tishrei 5773), 85–89.
3. R. Yaakov Ariel, R. Neriyah Glick, R. Dr. Dror Fixler, and the response of R. Y. M. Levinger, "*Od B'Inyan Bli'ah U'Plitah B'Kelim*," *HaMa'ayan* 53:2 (Tevet 5773/2013), 90–97; R. Ro'i Siton's article in *HaMa'ayan* 53:3 (Nisan 5773), 37; R. Shmuel HaKohen in *HaMa'ayan* 53:4 (Tamuz 5773), 65; and R. Shaul Bar Ilan, ibid., 28.

by R. Yair Frank *shlit"a*.[4] It is the analyses of R. Ro'i Siton which I wish to examine here in detail.

THE HALAKHIC VALIDITY OF THE SCIENTIFIC EXPERIMENTS

At the outset, we must ask: To what extent is it possible to assign halakhic validity to the aforementioned experiments and investigations? It is patently obvious to me, and I am not aware of any opposing argument, that these experiments can only have any halakhic significance at all if the experimental method can also test metal utensils that were produced by older technologies,[5] and yield the finding that the degree of their absorbance and emission is **greater** than one-sixtieth.[6] If this does not turn out to be the case, it will mean that there is no way, using that experimental method, to make sense of the words of *Ḥazal* and the *Rishonim* even in context of conditions pertaining in their times (and presenting the issue as a new reality resulting from a change in the method of manufacturing metals in our times could prove misleading). It goes without saying that this conclusion is utterly unacceptable; it would amount to disagreeing with *Ḥazal* regarding basic halakhic categories and principles. That leaves us with the task of continuing the

4. I am grateful to R. Yair Frank who provided me with the draft of the research. It is a comprehensive, thorough work (about a hundred pages), whose first three chapters analyze the halakhah with regard to all the issues related to this question, and the next two discuss the scientific research that has been performed and the question of its halakhic ramifications. The work also includes comments and criticisms of the parallel experiments of Rabbis Siton and Glick. See also n. 14 with regard to additional halakhic analysis on this topic.
5. Apparently, in several places in the world, there are still utensils similar to those that were common in the times of the *Rishonim*.
6. It should be noted that R. Frank indeed performed a comparative analysis (using various methods) of the degree of absorbance of earthenware and of a variety of metals and modern materials. In the first method of analysis (by weight) it was found that earthenware has a greater degree of absorbance, but this was performed only for the **first** cooking and not with regard to the degree of absorbance of earthenware after it was already sealed by water following the first cooking (which cannot be measured by weighing). In the second method of analysis (using acidity), which was indeed performed also for an additional cooking, the results were not uniform: With exposure to an alkaline environment the change in most of the materials was about one-quarter to one-third of earthenware, while with exposure to an acidic environment the change in Pyrex was about one-half (!) of that of earthenware. Only in the third method of analysis (absorbance and emission of a fluorescent substance) a clear and unambiguous difference was found between the measurements of earthenware and other materials, but it would appear that one must then determine whether the results are dependent on the type and properties of the substance, and one must also explain the disparities between the results of the different experiments. In addition to all this, one must conduct experiments (in my humble opinion, as noted) with old metal utensils as well.

endeavor to clarify how *Ḥazal* viewed reality and defined it with regard to this halakhah. The only faithful conclusion in this case would be that those methods and those experiments that were performed are devoid of halakhic meaning, whether for leniency or stringency, since this is not the way in which we are supposed to relate to reality (in this area) according to the Torah – and there is nothing further to say.[7]

WHAT HAS CHANGED SINCE THE TIME OF *ḤAZAL*

Now we come to the substance of the issue. In my humble opinion, the reason we assume as a given that contemporary utensils do not absorb or emit flavor, is not because the method of manufacture has changed (which, of course, it has), but that *our sense of taste has weakened* compared with the days of *Ḥazal,* at least with regard to sensing flavor that was absorbed or emitted. As proof of this, note that the average person cannot sense absorbed or emitted flavor, not only from an iron utensil – but, generally, even from a wooden utensil, even though we see and understand that wooden utensils absorb and emit, and there has been no substantive difference in the nature of wooden utensils or in their method of manufacture since antiquity. Most people, to the best of my knowledge, will not be able to identify if the soup in their pot was stirred with a dairy or meat wooden spoon, even if that spoon was used within twenty-four hours and even if the pot did not contain sixty times the volume of the spoon, or close to that amount.

Apropos of the experiments described by R. Siton, I will describe a small experiment of my own: I took a wooden spoon (an old one, like utensils in the average kitchen) and for about half a minute I used it to stir milk that had been boiled in a glass cup. I then washed the spoon well, and then stirred with it, also for a half minute, about half a cup of tea which had been boiled in a small metal pot (a cezve). At the same time, I stirred the same amount of tea using a new metal

7. I presented these thoughts to R. Dov Lior *shlit"a* (on 2 Kislev 2014), that it would appear that in order to grant halakhic meaning to the results of the experiments that were presented to him regarding stainless steel, a comparative analysis would need to be performed in the same way with old iron utensils – or at least earthenware utensils; and likewise, regarding the method of measurement in question, the principles of absorbance and emission would need to be matched with those discussed by *Ḥazal;* since if this is not the case, this method would not be salient to the thinking of *Ḥazal,* and thus it would not be possible to rule according to its results. R. Lior *shlit"a* said that indeed it would appear that one should perform this analysis (and added that he would convey this to the authors of the study), and that in general, the remarks in his letter (which was published recently in *Emunat Itekha* 101 [Tishrei 5774/2013]: 150) relate to the finding that stainless steel utensils do not absorb, but he was not commenting on the research method itself. He also emphasized that he was relating only to stainless steel but not iron utensils – even modern ones.

spoon. I tasted it myself and gave it to my family to taste (as *mesiḥim lefi tumam*, without knowledge of the experiment) and no one could discern **any** difference in taste between the cups. Even when the family members were asked to guess which of the two cups was "dairy," the success of the guesses wavered as expected at around 50%.[8]

To me it is thus clear that even if R. Siton used in his experiments an iron utensil manufactured by erstwhile methods, he would most likely be unable to detect the emission of taste. This can shed light, as an interim conclusion, on the value of these kind of experiments as relates to our topic.[9] The fundamental issue, as stated, is not that the utensils changed. Rather, it seems, that our sense of taste has weakened in this regard.[10]

---

8. It is, however, possible that very sensitive tasters would be capable of discerning the difference in this sort of experiment – but not the majority of people, and certainly not with methods that are less precisely measured. Similarly, it is possible that if the wooden spoon were larger than the volume of tea (e.g., we were tasting directly from it) an average person might taste the milk – but again not with less precise a measure, which is obviously the way utensils are generally used.
9. This brings us back to our claim at the beginning of the article, that for the various experiments to have halakhic credence, they need also to be performed on metal utensils that were manufactured by earlier technologies (not necessarily utensils from ancient times; since the laws were agreed upon by the *Rishonim*, it is sufficient to test utensils from their times, or which were manufactured in our time with the same methods) and to find a degree of absorbance or emission in them greater than one in sixty.
10. As stated, the basic support for our argument is the fact that the average person today generally has difficulty sensing absorbed taste in utensils even when the utensil absorbs or emits, while for *Ḥazal* there was no doubt that emission of taste by utensils was an obvious reality that everyone sensed. Indeed, it appears that we can point to additional proofs that changes have occurred over many generations in the intensity of the sense of taste: With regard to undiluted wine, there is a debate in the Gemara if one recites the blessing *borei peri hagefen* (Berakhot 50b), and Rashi explains, "Since their wine was very strong and it was not potable without water"; this is also the explanation of Rambam (in *Peirush HaMishnayot*), and Ra'avan (*Sefer Ra'avan, Pesaḥim* 108b, n. 74) even wrote that it was "dangerous to drink." This is with regard to the wine of *Ḥazal*'s time, whereas "our wine which is not so strong, it is good to drink it undiluted" (Mordekhai, Pesaḥim 611 and Ra'avan there). It was not suggested that diluting the wine was to prevent their becoming intoxicated by drinking too much, since if that were the case, they would not have discussed the blessing. Rather, it is clear as was suggested, that without diluting, their wine was not good for drinking. See also *Bet Yosef, Oraḥ Ḥayim* 272. Recently Prof. Zohar Amar explained that actually, wine in Israel contains two or three times the amount of alcohol as wine in France; but it was also found that there is an upper limit to the concentration of alcohol that is naturally possible in wine, about 16%, and the average wine in our time has close to this concentration, just as in the time of *Ḥazal*, and even so it is considered definitely potable even without being diluted. Thus, nature has changed with regard to sensitivity of taste as well. However this is not a definitive proof, either because one

THE POSITION OF SCHOLARS OF ASHKENAZ: SOURCES, NOT SENSES

Here we ought to note that which is, in my humble opinion, a consistent and clear position of most of the *poskim* of Ashkenaz: that with regard to taste in mixtures, we are unable to rely simply on our senses, but rather we operate within the guidelines of *Ḥazal*, without deviation.[11] This is the reason that with regard to glass utensils (as R. Siton noted), most of the *Rishonim* of Ashkenaz did not discuss at all its degree of absorbency by themselves testing its absorbance or taste, but rather by comparing glass to another material discussed by *Ḥazal* – earthenware. The same is true regarding bone china (again, as noted by R. Siton), where those who prohibited them – in accordance with whom Rema rules regarding both bone and glass utensils – evaluated them not with reference to the senses but based on inferences in the Gemara from the Torah, which suggest, in their view, that bone absorbs. That is, the position of the scholars of Ashkenaz is that we make our evaluation based on the sources, not on the senses. This was the methodology of those *poskim* of Ashkenaz who permitted bone utensils, as discussed below, and not as argued by R. Siton.

Indeed, R. Siton did not mention the fact that those who prohibited these two classes of utensils did not base themselves on a taste test, nor on an objective reality, but rather on halakhic reasoning and a halakhic reality. R. Siton tried to prove from R. Yeḥiel of Paris, who was stringent regarding glass but lenient regarding bone china, that there is no schematic reasoning, but rather an analysis of each material. However, on the contrary, his examples prove precisely the reverse, since in neither case did R. Yeḥiel of Paris analyze the degree of actual absorbance[12] but rather the source of the laws: he compares glass to earthenware because they are both made from sand,[13] as opposed to bone utensils for which

can argue that this is a function of sensitivity to alcohol and not necessarily the sense of taste, or because even today, some homemade wines (which are more similar to wine in the time of *Ḥazal*) are also considered difficult to drink straight.

11. Both leniently and stringently; obviously not in the way which has been presented, as if "we relate to any material as if it has definitely absorbed" [as expressed by R. Siton in his article in *HaMa'ayan*. With regard to the idea that according to *poskim* of Ashkenaz one should not rely upon experiments or the like, *Sedei Ḥemed* already discussed this (*Asifat Dinim*, letter *hei*, "*hekhsher kelim*," 21); I was alerted to his discussion by the work of R. Y. Frank, though he explained it differently from what I have suggested here.

12. Practically, I cannot understand at all the assumption that he came to his conclusions on these laws based on the criterion of taste: Is there any possibility of explaining, based on taste, that bone utensils absorb **less** than glass utensils?

13. This has nothing to do with a test based on the senses, but is *dimuy milta l'milta*, a comparison of one thing to another, which is common in halakhah, as explained in *Hagahot Rabbenu Peretz*

he did not find a source to prohibit them in the statements of *Ḥazal*, and therefore was lenient with regard to them. (This is the meaning of his language: "We have not found any absorbance or prohibition for it.")[14]

The additional salient example in the position of the *poskim* of Ashkenaz of non-reliance on the senses with regard to absorbance and emission, is that Ashkenazim – following the ruling of Rema (and practically, also Sephardim) – do not rely on the tasting of a gentile cook, a law that, very surprisingly, R. Siton did not mention at all.[15] And based on what I wrote earlier, it appears that there is a clear explanation for this: Over time, the *poskim* of Ashkenaz sensed that the results of routine tests based on the senses in these areas did not correlate with the words of *Ḥazal*, and that the reason for this, as noted, was probably that over the course of time, sense of taste had weakened, so that it was no longer possible to sense emitted or absorbed taste well; and therefore they taught us not to rely any longer on the tasting of a gentile cook since "we are not experts in this,"[16]

---

on *Semak* (mitzvah 222).

14. Similarly *Or Zaru'a*, who cited R. Yeḥiel of Paris and ruled like him, did not even mention implicitly that he was lenient based on the senses but analyzed the issue at length based on the discussions in Ḥulin to prove from them that *Ḥazal* were not concerned with absorbance in bone (*Piskei Avodah Zarah* 297). And Mordekhai who argued with this (Pesaḥim 582) also did not analyze the issue with respect to the criterion of taste but based on the implication of the verses about the utensils of Midyan (Bemidbar 31:22–23).

15. As a side note, R. Siton mentioned the responsum of Rashba on glass utensils (1:233), and wrote that "Rashba did not mention at all the *midrash* in *Avot D'Rabi Natan*, but analyzed glass utensils based on the core issue, and ruled based on his opinion…" With apologies to him, this is mistaken, as one who looks inside will discover, since in his opening words Rashba explicitly cites *Avot D'Rabi Natan*. Upon a cursory examination, I have not found any *Rishonim* who were lenient about glass who did **not** cite the statement in *Avot D'Rabi Natan*, even though it is true that in addition to this they also explained the issue based on recognition of the senses. See *Raviyah* (end of *siman* 464) who learns from *Avot D'Rabi Natan* that glass utensils do not absorb and only afterward explains that this is because they are smooth (and even according to the phrasing of Mordekhai in Pesaḥim 574, "that glass utensils are smooth and do not absorb, as we say regarding the heart, and there is a proof based on *Avot D'Rabi Natan*," it is not implied that he would have said this himself without the proof of *Avot D'Rabi Natan*). Similarly *Kol Bo* (*siman* 48, s.v. *kli ḥeres*) questioned those who prohibit glass, based specifically on what is written in *Avot D'Rabi Natan*.

16. This phrase appears in Rema's *Torat Ḥatat* 61:1; it is also in *Ḥidushei Ḥatam Sofer* to Gittin 52b, and other *Aḥaronim*. There is however a debate among the *poskim* of Ashkenaz if one can still rely on the tasting of a Jew (where this is permitted), and the main proof for our discussion is from the opinion that we do rely on this at all. That said, it should be noted that even for those who rely on the tasting of a Jew, according to many *poskim* this is only *bedi'avad* (as explained in *Shakh, Yoreh De'ah* 96:5 and *Minḥat Yaakov* 61:3), and thus it does not apply to permitting a utensil *l'khatḥilah* – and in this vein R. Y. Frank commented in his work (ch. 5) with regard to

but rather to take *Ḥazal*'s statements at face value. And in truth if we are correct, how can one be lenient in this regard in something that is bound to change in one way or another over the generations just as it changed in the past?[17] Based on this approach it is clear, therefore, that although we cannot sense absorbance or emission in metal utensils, there is no room to deviate from the established halakhic rulings in their regard, as R. Uriel Eisenthal *shlit"a* wrote in his book *Megilat Sefer.*[18]

ASHKENAZ VERSUS SEFARAD

This is, as noted, the position held by all Ashkenazim who abide by Rema. But with regard to Sephardim, who were lenient regarding glass and the like largely based on the senses, and also rely on the opinion of a gentile cook, and also hold like *Shulḥan Arukh* with regard to permitting cooking in a utensil when it is unable to create taste (*Yoreh De'ah* 99:7), in that case indeed it appears that the issue veers in the direction proposed by R. Siton, that in our day there is little need to be concerned for taste absorbed in or emitted by utensils, since if the principle in these laws is based on taste that can be sensed, then if there is no sensation of taste, there is no concern. But this is all only at first glance, since in practice the issue is not clear at all, as we see that the Sephardi *poskim* analyzed most cases based on the reasoning behind the laws and their sources just as the Ashkenazi scholars did, and only in certain specific and limited situations did they analyze issues using reality tests. This is true also of relying on the tasting of a gentile cook. Additionally the Sephardi scholars, in the dozens and hundreds of cases and disputes in these areas, did not consider settling disputes between the great *poskim* based on experiments of taste alone. If we were inclined to rely in an extreme fashion on experiments to resolve questions about absorbance, we would have to

---

nullifying a prohibition *l'khatḥilah* – and in any case the issue returns to our comment at the beginning of the article.

17. This is in contrast to new issues which *Ḥazal* did not rule on at all, for which one should not be stringent due to doubt such as this; such as the taste of animal fat in olive oil discussed in *Responsa HaRema* 54, similarly see also *Responsa Mekom Shmuel, siman* 74, and see also *Responsa She'elat Ya'avetz* 2:142 and *Responsa Ein Yitzḥak* beginning in *Oraḥ Ḥayim* 19:4. (The aforementioned responsum of Rema has served as a major foundation in the article of R. Yitzchak Dvir, "*Beliyat Keilim B'Yameinu*" in *Emunat Itekha* 101 [Tishrei 5774/2013]: 134–49, but in my humble opinion it does not provide a proof for our issue and its conclusions are limited to that area. Our article was written and completed before the publication of R. Dvir's article; other than this footnote, our article is not to be viewed as a response to him.)
18. As the editor of *HaMa'ayan shlit"a* noted [in *HaMa'ayan* 53:3 (Nisan 5773), 46, n. 5]; similarly R. Aharon Pfeiffer already wrote as such in a letter in his book *Derekh Kokhav* (Bnei Brak, 1995), 310–11 (mentioned also by R. Y. Frank in his work).

cross out entire *simanim* in the laws of *ta'arovot*, mixtures; and it is clear that not one of our *poskim*, from Sepharad or Ashkenaz, entertained the notion of doing so. Not to mention that with this approach, there will ultimately be findings that contradict the teachings of *Ḥazal* themselves, as noted at the outset.

There is much to elaborate on this last issue, but this is not the place. It appears clear that there is a solid imperative of our *poskim* (mostly in Ashkenaz – but also in Sepharad) not to rely in these areas on a test of the senses alone. In any case, scientific experiments in these areas can only have halakhic value if they are performed in the manner described above – through comparison of the absorbance and emission of today's utensils with the utensils of old.

Chapter 3

Waiting Five-Plus Hours Between Meat and Milk[1]

As is known, according to halakhah, one is required to wait six hours between meat and milk. The basis of this law is in the behavior of Mar Ukva in the Talmud, who waited between meat and milk "from one meal to another."[2] Most *Rishonim* understand this to mean waiting the amount of time from one meal to the next, which is approximately six hours.[3] This interpretation is reflected, as well, in the ruling of the *Shulḥan Arukh* and all of the *Aḥaronim,* later authorities,[4] and stands in contradistinction to the view of some *Rishonim,* who understood the words to mean not a waiting period, but the conclusion of the meal and/or

1. Translated by R. Moshe Rosenberg. This chapter initially appeared in *Bet Aharon V'Yisrael* 24:3 (Shevat–Adar 5769).
2. Ḥulin 105a.
3. According to Rambam, *Hilkhot Ma'akhalot Asurot* 9:28. This duration is also mentioned by *Ba'al HaMa'or* (*Ma'or HaGadol,* Ḥulin 37a, s.v. *v'of,* although he rules leniently). Following in their wake are *Itur* (*Sha'ar* 1, *Hekhsher HaBasar* 13a), Rashba (*Torat HaBayit Ha'Arokh, Bayit* 3, *Sha'ar* 4, and also in *Torat HaBayit HaKatzar* and *Mishmeret HaBayit, Torat HaBayit Ha'Arokh, Bayit* 3, *Sha'ar* 4, and in his comments to Ḥulin 105a), the students of Rabbenu Yonah (on the *Rif,* Berakhot 40b, s.v. *lo shanu*), Rabbenu Yeruḥam (*Toldot Adam V'Ḥava, Netiv* 15:5, p. 137a), Rabbenu Peretz (in his glosses to *Semak,* Commandment 213:8), the author of *Hagahot Oshri* (to the *Rosh,* Ḥulin, ch. 8, end of *siman* 5), *Orḥot Ḥayyim, Agur,* and additional *Rishonim,* who explicitly mentioned a duration of six hours (Rabbenu Ḥananel, Rif, Rashi, Ra'avan, Roke'aḥ, and other *Rishonim* mention that one must wait the length of a meal, but do not specify what that length is).
4. *Yoreh De'ah,* 89:1.

washing one's hands and/or cleansing one's mouth with a food that neutralizes the taste [of the meat].[5]

Yet there are those, including my own family, whose custom is to wait five hours and a fraction of a sixth hour from the end of a meat meal until the next meal. This custom requires clarification, as R. Yisrael Isserlein, author of *Terumat HaDeshen*,[6] writes: "Who dares protest" the behavior of those who make their own compromise and wait only one hour, since a group of *Rishonim* permit the consumption of dairy after nothing more than completing the meat meal, washing one's hands and cleansing one's mouth! Nevertheless, it would appear that the majority of *Aḥaronim* follow Maharshal, R. Shlomo Luria's reading of *Terumat HaDeshen*, that only regarding common folk can we not protest, "but it is proper to protest this behavior when practiced by *bnei Torah*, learned people, and to scold them not to be lenient in this matter." Maharshal concludes, "That is how anyone who bears the fragrance of Torah should conduct himself."[7] In fact, *Terumat HaDeshen* himself concludes that "refined people (*tzenu'in*) refrain from being lenient in this matter,"[8] and his words are the basis for the rulings of Rema and *Levush*.[9] It

5. As per *Behag* (*Hilkhot Berakhot*, ch. 6, p. 76). Following him were *Ba'al HaMor* (ibid.), Ra'avan HaYarḥi (*Sefer HaManhig, Hilkhot Se'udah*, 216–18), Rabbenu Tam (*Sefer HaYashar*, novellae 472), Tosafot (Ḥulin 105a, s.v. *l'se'udata*), Raviyah (Ḥulin, 1:108), Rabbi Eliezer of Metz (*Sefer Yere'im* 63; *Yere'im HaKatzar* 149), R. Yaakov Or Zaru'a (vol. 1, *Hilkhot Basar V'Ḥalav*, end of *siman* 460), Mordekhai (Ḥulin 687), *Ra'ah* (*Bedek HaBayit* on Rashba, *Torat HaBayit Ha'Arokh, Bayit* 3, *Sha'ar* 4, p. 86b), and one of Rashi's students (*Siddur Rashi, siman* 577). To be precise, there are two opinions here as well – some require a formal conclusion to the meal, while others only require washing and cleansing the mouth, even within the same meal.
6. In his glosses to *Sha'arei Dura*, 76:2.
7. *Yam Shel Shlomo*, Ḥulin 8:9. This is quoted by *Shakh* (*se'if katan* 2) and *Taz* (*se'if katan* 1), and others. See the author of *Me'il Tzedakah*, who warns not to rule leniently (*Kanfei Yonah* on *Shulkhan Arukh, Yoreh De'ah* 89:1, p. 65a–b), Similar is Rabbi Ḥayim ben Atar (*Pri Toar* on *Shulkhan Arukh, Yoreh De'ah* 89:1, *se'if katan* 5).
8. In fact, this was his personal practice, as recorded by his student in *Leket Yosher* I, p. 35, *siman* 2. However, his language "refrain from being lenient in this matter" refers to waiting one hour. He does not address waiting into the sixth hour. In truth, even Maharshal, *Shakh*, *Taz*, and their supporters, who wrote in favor of rebuking those who are lenient, referred to those who rely on the opinion not to wait at all (and simply add the one-hour wait). In that case, they would also agree that there is no reason to rebuke those who are accustomed to waiting five-plus hours, because this also is derived from the opinion to wait six hours, but is just calculated differently. See also the following note.
9. Although one must differentiate between them and Maharshal and his followers. The former group clearly believes that it is an absolute requirement to wait the length of a meal, and therefore, we should rebuke those who are lenient. However, the formulations of *Terumat HaDeshen*, Rema, and his student, *Levush*, indicate that they did not adjudicate between the two opinions (as seen in *Semag*, *Semak*, *Or Zaru'a*, *Hagahot Maimoniyot*, and other *Rishonim*, who

is clear that their positions were formulated even against a prevailing custom. In other words, the fact that there was one or another custom is insufficient; one must find a source for it in the *poskim*.

This is especially so since it would appear that the custom of waiting five-plus hours is even less defensible than the custom to wait only one hour. Those who wait one hour are adopting the view of those *Rishonim* who do not require waiting at all, but suffice with ending the first meal. In fact, they are being stricter than that view requires.[10] Moreover, they are following a view that is mentioned by the *poskim*. However, those who wait five-plus hours seem to be following the position that requires a six-hour wait, yet not following that view properly, Heaven forbid.

But after researching the matter, God granted me the privilege to find a clear source and reasoning for this custom of waiting five hours plus a fraction of an hour. Although my results cannot dislodge the opinion of the majority of later authorities, and those who observe six hours should certainly not deviate from their custom, nevertheless, the next paragraphs can buttress the custom of those who wait only five-plus hours, and show that that position is firmly rooted in halakhah.

---

mentioned both opinions without choosing between them), but only advised that stringency is appropriate. Therefore, there is no reason to rebuke those who are lenient. This is borne out by the wording of *Terumat HaDeshen* (ibid.), Rema ("there are those who are stringent… and this is correct behavior"), and even more in *Levush* ("and those who are stringent… will be blessed"). This is also explicit in *Minhagei Maharil*, who writes that the custom is to wait one hour, and that waiting six hours is a pious custom, *minhag ḥasidim* (*Sefer Maharil, Hilchot Isur V'Heter* in *Sha'arei Dura*, end of *siman* 8). See also *Isur V'Heter Ha'Arokh* 40:4, which cites this custom with no equivocation. This is what *poskim* rely upon when they allow a sick person to wait an hour when necessary, after he recites grace after meals and cleanses his teeth (*Ḥokhmat Adam* 40:13; *Arukh HaShulḥan* 89:7).

10. See *Torat Ha'Asham* (by the author of *Tosafot Yom Tov*), *klal* 75–76, end of *siman* 1, who gives a reason for the one-hour wait (as opposed to *Terumat HaDeshen*, who believes that this was a "deliberate compromise." See *Pri Ḥadash* and *Gra* on *se'if katan* 6, who base this custom on the *Zohar*; and *Kereiti U'Fleiti*, *se'if katan* 3, who dismisses this and gives a different reason, writing, "it's almost a logical reason." See also *Hagahot Zer Zahav* on *Isur V'Heter Ha'Arokh* mentioned above, *siman* 2). Parenthetically, I will mention a surprising idea from the book *Isur V'Heter* attributed to Rabbenu Yeruḥam (Livorno, 1882), *siman* 39. He writes that the duration to wait for the taste of meat to dissipate (according to Rashi) is three hours; I have not found any corroborating opinion among the *Rishonim* (and perhaps it is a scribal error, and this requires further study).

SIX HOURS – UNTIL THE SIXTH HOUR

As mentioned above, the Talmud states that Mar Ukva waited *l'se'udata aḥarita,* from one meal to the next. Rambam, who was the first to deal with the time interval, writes that the amount of time is "like (*k'mo*) six hours." From where, one can ask, does Rambam derive that the period between one meal and the next is six hours? It would seem to be more plausible to say that the time for one meal is in the morning and for the next, in the evening.[11] *Leḥem Mishneh*[12] explains that Rambam's source for the interval of six hours between one meal and the next comes from the words of *Ḥazal* that the first meal of scholars is in the sixth hour of the day.[13] "And six hours from then would be the time for the next meal." In other words, the *se'udah aḥarita,* the next meal, would be in the twelfth hour of the day.

According to these words of *Leḥem Mishneh,* it is impossible to deduce (from Rambam's language the requirement of) waiting six full hours from the end of one meal to the beginning of the next,[14] nor even waiting six full hours from the conclusion of the first meal until the commencement of the next,[15] for if the first meal begins in the sixth hour, and continues into it, while the next meal begins in the twelfth hour, then from the end of former until the beginning of the latter, we have no more than five hours and a fraction. This point was made by the author of *Kereiti U'Fleiti,*[16] who personally holds that one must wait a full six hours and not be lenient, yet noted that according to Rambam, scholars eat at the end of the sixth hour, and therefore the interval until their next meal, according to Rambam, is in fact only "about five hours."

However, one can deflect this proof [for the 5-plus position] as several Talmudic passages clearly state that the second meal of a *talmid ḥakham* is actually in

11. As per *Rosh* in Ḥulin 105a (ch. 8, end of *siman* 5). Similar is *Ritva* (ibid., s.v. *basar*). *Ra'viyah* (*siman* 1108) even adduces a verse, "In the evening meat to eat, and bread in the morning" (Shemot 16:8). However, see Tosafot Pesaḥim 2a, s.v. *v'ka'or,* which claims that anything up to the sixth hour of the day is called "morning."
12. Also *Gra* on *Shulḥan Arukh, Yoreh De'ah* 89:1, *se'if katan* 2.
13. Pesaḥim 12b; Shabbat 10a. To begin eating later is considered "throwing a rock into a jug." It seems obvious from here that Mar Ukva began his meal before the seventh hour (albeit, he might have tasted something in the morning, see the Gemara's reference there; either way it says that *talmidei ḥakhamim* are accustomed to eat in the sixth hour).
14. According to *Arukh HaShulḥan, Yoreh De'ah* 89:4 (end of the *siman*).
15. According to *Dagul MiRevava* on *Shulḥan Arukh, Yoreh De'ah* 89:1, and so for many *Aḥaronim.*
16. On *Shulḥan Arukh, Yoreh De'ah* 89:1, *se'if katan* 3 (although he concludes with, "but it is difficult").

the first hour of the night (i.e., thirteen hours from the beginning of the day),[17] in which case, the interval from the end of the first meal to the beginning of the second is a full six hours. And while the *Kereiti U'Fleiti* might still sidestep this difficulty by pointing out that the scholar can still begin his meal in the twelfth hour,[18] we have not yet arrived at a satisfying explanation of the five-plus custom.

SIX "DAYLIGHT" HOURS

But there is a far more powerful proof that can be brought to support the five-plus position. From the passage in Pesaḥim (and its parallel in Tractate Shabbat), which according to Leḥem Mishneh and the Gaon of Vilna is Rambam's source for the six-hour figure, it is crystal clear that the Talmud is speaking of *sha'ot zemaniyot*[19] ['daylight' hours, which are calculated by dividing the day into twelve equal parts]. A group of *Aḥaronim,* later authorities, headed by Pri Ḥadash,[20] hold thus. Since

---

17. See Berakhot 2b, "From when the poor person enters to eat, etc." and Rashi s.v., *misheha'ani.* See also Berakhot 4b. According to Rabbenu Yonah, Rosh, Rashba, and other *Rishonim,* it is even forbidden to eat a half hour before the time for recitation of *Shema* (although this is not an issue for Mar Ukva), and this is the accepted ruling (see *Shulḥan Arukh, Oraḥ Ḥayim* 235:2).
18. See responsa of *Terumat HaDeshen, siman* 1. In his time, it was customary to pray the evening service and recite the *Shema* several hours before nightfall, and he agreed to this, as long as it was after *plag haminḥah.* Even though this is not the forum for a discussion of this topic, we see that under these circumstances, it was possible to eat the evening meal in the twelfth hour of the day, and he also heard that at least in one place, all the great rabbis behaved this way. In the wake of *Raviyah*'s opinion (above, n. 11), we can base this on the verse, "In the evening you will eat meat and in the morning you will be satiated with bread" (Shemot 16:12). The Gemara records in the name of Abaye that one who has a meal should only eat it during the day (Yoma 74b, although the reason is that a person should see his food. Therefore the same law pertains to a nighttime meal by candlelight, as per Maharsha there in *Ḥidushei Aggadot,* s.v. *lo.* But see *Pnei Yehoshua* on Berakhot 2b, s.v. *v'khol,* who appears to understand "*yemama* [twenty-four-hour day]" in the plain sense of the word). However, it is difficult to say that this was the custom during the time of Mar Ukva (carefully read Rashi mentioned above). According to the stricter opinion, one would have to see it from the opposite perspective, that if the final meal was at the thirteenth hour, then Mar Ukva's wait would have been more than six full hours, even closer to seven. But nobody entertains this (however, the aforementioned *Kereiti U'Fleiti* does feel that there is a basis to be strict).
19. See Pesaḥim 12b. This is universally accepted with respect to the times for eating and burning ḥametz on the eve of Pesaḥ. Rambam himself writes that all hours mentioned in the Mishnah – including the aforementioned discussion and certainly the *baraita* – are "relative hours," *sha'ot zemaniyot* [daylight hours of the particular day, divided into twelve equal "hours"] (Commentary to the Mishnah, Berakhot 1:5).
20. On *Shulḥan Arukh, Yoreh De'ah* 89:1, *se'if katan* 2 and *se'if katan* 6. (Cited by *Leḥem HaPanim* 1 on *Shulḥan Arukh* 89:1, *siman* 5, and in *Ikarei HaDat* [also called *Ikarei Dinim*] by R. Daniel Tirani, 10:5, and the glosses of R. Shlomo Eiger on *Shulḥan Arukh* 89:1). See Ḥida (*Birkei Yosef* and *Shiyurei Berakhah* on *Shulḥan Arukh* 89:1, *se'if katan* 3) who defended his position before

the position of the Gaon of Vilna and Ba'al HaTanya is that "daylight" hours are calculated from sunrise to sunset, each such hour in winter in Israel will be no longer than fifty minutes. In other words, those six complete daylight hours will amount to no more than five clock hours. It is clear, then, that according to Rambam and the authorities who follow him in calculating six hours, it is possible for one's mouth and teeth to be clear of meat after five hours and a fraction of the sixth. It therefore surprises me that many *Aḥaronim* who discuss the interval of six hours, and assume that it means six sixty-minute hours, base their conclusions on reasoning alone, and make no reference to the view of the Rambam.[21]

I also came across the view of R. David Pardo,[22] cited in *Darkei Teshuvah*,[23] who concludes that *Pri Ḥadash*, who said that we are dealing with *zemaniyot* hours, is the source for the custom to wait all year long the minimum amount of time for six *zemaniyot* hours. In other words, if that amount of time suffices in the winter, then it is clear that the taste of meat dissipates from the mouth and any strands of meat caught between one's teeth are considered neutralized within that interval all year long, for the rabbis make no distinction between times of the year. This is exactly what I have been arguing, and the reverse of those who have claimed that we are dealing with sixty-minute hours. The proponents of the sixty-minute hours ask: How can one wait less time between meat and milk in winter? Is meat digested more rapidly in the winter months because the days are shorter? In fact, no one[24] ever suggested that one would wait longer in summer than in winter. The *zemaniyot* hours school merely argued that five hours plus (i.e., six *zemaniyot* hours) is sufficient all year round, with the term "six hours"

---

his many disputants (although, practically, he ruled stringently), and also adduced proof from *Solet L'Minḥah* by the author of *Shevut Ya'akov* who also upheld the ruling of *Pri Ḥadash*, writing that "the lenient one does not lose anything, as this is only the stringency of the scrupulous ones."

21. See the glosses by the author of *Knesset HaGedolah* on the *Tur*, *Yoreh De'ah* 89 (*siman* 6), who writes that these are certainly regular hours and not *sha'ot zemaniyot*. After all, it is not feasible to say that in the short days of winter, meat is digested more quickly. In a similar fashion, R. Hayim Elgazi rejected the *Pri Ḥadash* (*Ba'ei Ḥayai* on *Shulḥan Arukh*, *Yoreh De'ah* 89:1, p. 39b). As mentioned, most of the *Aḥaronim* held this position (see R. Ḥayim Pinḥas Luriah, *Petaḥ HaDa'at* [Piotrkow, 1911] on *Hilkhot Basar V'Ḥalav*, *Masakh HaPetaḥ*, *siman* 19, who elaborates on this topic). But for us, we see that Rambam's source in the Gemara is referring to *sha'ot zemaniyot*, specifically in light of the later analysis by *Aḥaronim* that Rambam's "like (*k'mo*) six hours" is not to be taken precisely (see below, n. 27).
22. 89:6.
23. In *Mizmor L'David*, p. 61a (where he mentions the three-hour custom).
24. Besides *Ikarei HaDat* mentioned earlier (consistent with his view, he is stringent in the summer months to wait six full *sha'ot zemaniyot*, even though this is longer than six "fixed" hours).

being approximate,[25] and indicating that what is required is at least six *zemaniyot* hours according to the winter clock. R. Pardo concludes that this view has "some substance on which to rely."

EXPLICIT IN THE WORDS OF ME'IRI

All of the above was my own understanding, following the way several *poskim* understood the position of Rambam. But when I discussed my understanding with my revered father, R. Yehuda Herzl Henkin *shlit"a* [*ztz"l*], he replied that my approach is found explicitly in the words of one of the early authorities, none other than R. Menaḥem Hame'iri. After mentioning those who would eat cheese immediately after fowl, Me'iri comments, "But we are strict and wait six hours or five, equivalent to the amount of time between one meal and the next, just as the law requires regarding animal meat [and dairy]."[26] His words explicitly reflect our custom, i.e., that the amount of time to wait between meat and milk is not precisely six hours, but "six hours or five," namely five-plus hours. He reiterates this point, as well, writing further, "For [after eating] any meat dish, whether from beast or fowl, one may not subsequently eat cheese until the passage of six hours or five, which is the amount of time between one meal and another." One should not misconstrue his words to mean that a majority of the sixth hour must pass because, in one place, he actually stipulates a mere five as sufficient: "For even the meat between the teeth is considered meat until one has waited five hours, which is the interval for digestion." The basis for his words can be understood in light of what we have written above,[27] and thus our position finds ratification.

---

25. For this reason, the interval is not mentioned in the Gemara, and even Rambam wrote "like six." This is also the view of some of the "stringent" *poskim*, such as the author of *Peraḥ Shoshan* (*Yoreh De'ah, klal* 1) who writes that six-hour interval is because "four is the mealtime for everyone." On most days, this will result in more than six "fixed" hours before the evening meal. Therefore six hours are always required – in the manner of clock hours of a *lo plug* stringency [to create a set measure rather than a variable one]. And the lenient ones believe in a *lo plug* on the lenient side. (But see *Torat Ha'Asham, klal* 75–76, *siman* 1, who explains the six-hour measure more clearly.) *Peraḥ Shoshan* also tried to say that if Rambam meant *zemaniyot* hours he would have specified this explicitly – but we see across all of *Mishneh Torah* that it was not his way to specify this. In my humble opinion, it is also not a problem to rebut the other arguments of *Peraḥ Shoshan*.

26. *Magen Avot* by Me'iri, beginning of *inyan* 9. He takes a similar approach in *Bet HaBeḥirah* to Ḥulin 105a: "The interval between one meal and the next is six hours, or close to it." Even though in that reference, he does not mention the word "five."

27. It is apparent to me that his basis is the Rambam's phrase, "like six hours." In *Solet L'Minḥah* by the author of *Shevut Ya'akov*, mentioned above in the words of Ḥida, there is an exact reading of Rambam: "'Like six hours' – shows that is not intended to be precise." Other *Rishonim* express

VIEWS OF CONTEMPORARY *POSKIM*

After writing the above, I turned my attention to what contemporary *poskim* have written on the subject. I discovered that R. Ovadiah Yosef *shlit"a* [*ztz"l*][28] examined the topic and was inclined toward waiting only five and a half hours. Aside from some sources I cited and others that he added, R. Yosef relied on the principle that less than a half hour is considered "near" (*samukh*), while more than that is considered "distant" (*muflag*). He considered, as well, that in the time of the Talmud, timepieces were not common, and therefore people had to depend upon their own approximations. His conclusion was that one may be lenient in case of pressing need, especially with respect to dairy after fowl, in which case one may even be lenient *l'khatḥilah*.[29] In a second responsum[30] he added that *Mateh Ephraim* (R. Ephraim Ardit) wrote to calculate the interval from the end of the first meal until the beginning of the next, which would amount to fewer than six hours, along the lines of the *Kereiti U'Fleiti*, as we explained.

Likewise, the Rebbe of Sanz-Klausenberg *ztz"l*[31] defended the local ḥasidic practice of waiting five hours in cases where meat was consumed during the day and dairy only after nightfall,[32] adding that the custom was not specifically to wait

---

it similarly, albeit not consistently (see Rashba in *Torat HaBayit HaKatzar*, 3:4, and also *Torat HaBayit Ha'Arokh*; and in *Agur*, *Hilkhot Se'uda* 223 and *Hilkhot Isur V'Heter* 242; and in *Orḥot Ḥayim*, *Hilkhot Isurei Ma'akhalot* 73; and in *Kol Bo* 106; all of them use the phrase "like six hours" at least once, while at other times writing "six hours").

28. *Shu"t Yabi'a Omer* I, *Yoreh De'ah*, end of *siman* 4.

29. In a short responsum printed in the journal *Or Torah* (14:9, p. 469), R. Yosef wrote that there is sufficient basis to rely on the lenient view, *l'khatḥilah*, to wait five-plus hours even after meat from cattle. More from contemporary rulings: R. Yisrael Stein heard from R. Shlomo Zalman Auerbach *ztz"l* that one who is lenient and waits less than six hours, relying on the language of Rambam, does not need to wait five hours plus another half hour or longer, because, based on Rambam's formulation, five-hours-plus-something is sufficient (*Moriah*, 20:10–12, p. 79). R. Yaakov Yitzḥak Fuchs quoted R. Yosef Shalom Elyashiv *shlit"a* [*ztz"l*] saying that this is the basic law, and it is only a custom to be stringent in waiting the full six hours (*HaKashrut*, p. 273, n. 76). Moreover, I saw in *HaMa'ayan* 19:2 (Tevet 5739), 33 (R. Yitzḥak Adler, "*Minhagei HaRav ztz"l V'Hanhagotav*") that the descendants of the gaon R. Yitzḥak Dov HaLevi Bamberger of Wurtzberg have a tradition that their ancestor had the personal practice to only wait five-plus hours between meat and dairy (and the author further wrote that it is said in the name of R. Ḥayim of Brisk that he read the source in Rambam in the same way. However, it is difficult to rely on this type of hearsay).

30. *Shu"t Yabi'a Omer* III, *Yoreh De'ah* 3:9.

31. *Shu"t Divrei Yatziv*, volume of collected material and addenda, *siman* 69.

32. A similar custom is followed by students of Ḥatam Sofer. See *Shu"t Siaḥ Yitzḥak* (Jerusalem, 1995), *siman* 399. Also see R. Menasheh Klein, *Mishneh Halakhot* 12 (New York, 2000), *siman* 11, where he documents this custom being followed in Sanz (and see *Mikdash Yisrael* on Sefirah and Shavuot, pp. 307–9, where he collects many testimonies from the Sanz dynasty that they

only five hours, but that once the sixth hour began, people did not pay attention to the clock, to complete the hour. He brought support from the Gemara which said that a person can err by one hour or more,[33] and concluded that apparently, in case of need, authorities were lenient based on all of these factors, and "in any event, after five hours they were not so precise."

My revered father and teacher supplied me with a responsum he penned several years ago, (which was not published in his volumes of *Responsa Bnei Banim*). Aside from the reasons to be lenient in cases of need listed above,[34] he added, "Were I not afraid, (I would say that) the mere fact that we now eat three meals a day, as opposed to the two that were commonly consumed during the periods of the Talmud and *Rishonim,* establishes our situation as somewhat of 'a case of need', since we have become accustomed to more frequent meals and it is known that hunger is connected to habits and eating patterns." There is explicit support for this idea in the *Orḥot Ḥayim,* which states that some do not wait a full six hours to eat cheese on Shavuot following *Minḥah* [after the meat meal in the morning] because "if one is hungry for another meal, it is clear that the meat has been digested."[35] According to this, my father wrote, there would be room for leniency in an institution or the army, etc., when two meals are scheduled six hours apart, even when the second begins only five-plus hours after the end of the first. This is especially so because one is dealing with the needs of many (*tzorkhei rabim*). Nevertheless, this leniency concerns primarily a meal, based upon the language of the Gemara ("from one meal to another"), as opposed to merely eating a snack.[36]

---

waited less than the full six hours; however, see above, end of n. 29). See also *Da'at Torah* by Maharsham, *Yoreh De'ah* 89:1, where he tends toward leniency during the transition from night to day. Similarly is *Da'at Kedoshim* (by the author of *Eshel Avraham* from Buczacz [Abraham David b. Asher Anshel Wahrman], *Yoreh De'ah* 89:2.

33. See Pesaḥim 12b – this is, in fact, the source of Rambam's "like six hours."

34. Like the issue of approximation described above. My father *shlit"a* [*ztz"l*] added: "In this situation, the principle '*Ein danim efshar mi'i efshar,* we do not derive the possible from the impossible,' is not invoked; for in earlier times without clocks they could not be precise with times. This is not the case today where we can be exact with six full hours (similar to how *Tiferet Yisrael* explains Mishnah Sanhedrin 5:20, that today, even if two witnesses disagree on time, even with a difference of one hour, their testimony is null and void because everyone has watches…). In my humble opinion, even today not everyone wears a watch. Even one who does is not always looking at it, or might misread the time (and even if you want to uphold the position of *Tiferet Yisrael,* this has no bearing on our instance because capital cases require a higher threshold of coordinated testimony due to the Biblical injunction, '*The* [*court*] *shall save*')."

35. *Orḥot Ḥayim, Hilkhot Ma'akhalot Asurot* 73, s.v. *v'yesh* (which concludes that those who wish to be lenient should at least clean their teeth well). Similar is *Kol Bo, siman* 106, s.v. *v'aḥar.*

36. In R. Meir Yehoshua Rosenberg, *Kur HaMivḥan* on *Hilkhot Basar V'Ḥalav* (Springfield, 1932), which my father *shlit"a* [*ztz"l*] used when studying with his grandfather, HaGaon R. Yosef

SUMMARY

The upshot of our discussion is that the concept of waiting only five-plus hours between meat and dairy appears explicitly in the words of Me'iri, and is implied in the words of Rambam (who is, in fact, the original source for the interval of six hours), as understood by the *Kereiti U'Fleiti*, *Orḥot Ḥayim*, and other *Aḥaronim*, who inferred that "like – *k'mo* – six hours" means not exactly six hours. Additionally, the view of *Pri Ḥadash* and *Solet L'Minḥah*, as well as other *Aḥaronim* is that the six hours are six *sha'ot zemaniyot*, "daylight hours," and as R. David Pardo explains, that since during the winter months (and at the latitude of Eretz Yisrael, that works out in winter to five clock hours) an interval of about five hours is sufficient to dissipate the substance and taste of the meat, therefore that same interval was adopted for the entire year. Additional factors were added by contemporary authorities, all adding up to the conclusion that the custom is founded on a clear halakhic basis.

One might be tempted to refute my conclusion by asking why it matters that a few authorities may have accepted the practice of five-plus hours. After all, an entire group of prominent *Rishonim* accepted the idea that one need only conclude the first meal and not wait at all, but that did not stop Maharshal from castigating learned people who followed that view, and the *Aḥaronim* agreed with him that one should be strict. But in fact, that situation is not analogous to ours. One who adopts the view that no wait is required is being lenient against the mainstream interpretation of the Gemara that requires waiting the amount of time until the next meal, an interval estimated to be (about) six hours. It is against such a leniency that the *poskim* wrote that we must fulfill both reasons given in the Talmud, as well as both interpretations of Mar Ukva's behavior. Our custom of five-plus hours, on the other hand, upholds both interpretations of the Gemara (finish the meal and wait until the next), only differing in the method of defining the interval that satisfies the "next meal" requirement.

Blessed be the Merciful One for His assistance.

Eliyahu Henkin *ztz"l*, he annotated in the margin something he heard from his grandfather in *Yoreh De'ah* 89: "Some say that five-plus hours is like six, and there is no reason to pile on stringencies ('my grandfather'). But I heard from him on another occasion that he does not agree with this." (Perhaps the difference is between the basic law in which one should behave strictly, and one who is following a family custom). See above, n. 29, for the opinions of other *gedolim*.

Chapter 4

Demarcations of the Shabbat Prohibition Concerning Electronic Doors and Other Sensors – A Response[1]

Issue 104 of the periodical *Emunat Itekha* (Tamuz 2014): 54–65) featured an essay, "*Hafalat Hayshanim B'Shabbat*," by R. Dror Fixler and R. Eli Reif, published with the endorsement of their mentor the gaon R. Naḥum Eliezer Rabinowitz *shlit"a* [*ztz"l*] (pp. 66–68). Their essay dealt with the halakhic parameters of electronic sensors and their use on Shabbat, primarily with the example of automatic doors.

Truth be told, the discussion itself is not new, as approximately fifty years ago the *poskim* began addressing the question of automatic doors operated by a photoelectric sensor and similar devices.[2] Despite interim technological

1. Translated by Shimon Lerner. Ed. note: This article is part of a discussion of electronic sensors which appeared in the journal *Emunat Itekha* 105 (Torah V'ha'Aretz Institute), 5775.
2. R. Yehoshua Neuwirth, *Shemirat Shabbat K'Hilkhatah*, first edition, ch. 18:51; *Yesodei Yeshurun* 5, pp. 160–61; see also in the index of R. E. Weissfish, *HaḤashmal BaHalakhah* 2 (Jerusalem, 1981), s.v. *ta foto electri* (Note: I was unable to find the passage quoted there in the name of *She'arim Metzuyanim BaHalakhah*).

advances,[3] it is well known that the vast majority of recent *poskim,* if not all, did not distinguish between these devices and other electrical items, as far as using them on Shabbat is concerned. Activation of electrical sensors, such as by opening an electronic door, is considered clearly forbidden, as noted in *Shemirat Shabbat K'Hilkhatah.*[4] With the endorsement of my father and mentor R. Yehuda Herzl Henkin *shlit"a* [*ztz"l*], I wish to elaborate on my understanding that there is no difference between activating an electronic device by hand or via sensors.

ACTIVATION OF A DEVICE VIA SENSORS

The essence of the claim made by the gaon R. Naḥum Rabinowitz *shlit"a* [*ztz"l*] and his *talmidim* can be boiled down to two main points:

1. Activation via automatic sensors is fundamentally different from the other modes of operating electric appliances.
2. Any action which is a byproduct of someone innocently going on his way and walking as usual cannot be considered a *melakhah* (prohibited Shabbat violation).

Regarding the first point, in my humble opinion, the claim made regarding sensors – that the person does not himself activate the mechanism, but rather that the mechanism activates itself, and only "utilizes" the person to trigger the timing of operation – is baffling. Is it possible to picture an electronic device as having an autonomous identity to which we can ascribe its actions irrespective of the person acting upon it?

Moreover, in my opinion the actual details of how the sensors work are irrelevant from a halakhic point of view. As Rambam writes when describing a *psik reisha* (an action which necessarily causes a specific outcome) in the opening chapter of the laws of Shabbat:

---

3. Most of which have also been previously addressed. See *Responsa Ma'aseh Ḥoshev* 1:12 (referring to an electromagnetic or infrared sensor), and *Ma'arkhei Lev* by R. Prof. Ze'ev Lev pp. 387–88, among others. It should be noted as well that not every technical or scientific detail is necessarily important from a halakhic point of view; as stated by the gaon R. S. Z. Auerbach, *Minḥat Shlomo* I (Jerusalem, 1999), 11:2 and 12:3, stating that despite the fact that the state electricity consists of an alternating current at a rate of fifty times per second, "we can only deal with that which we see." Since our impression is of a continuous current, we can not consider it as starting anew. This logic is analogously applicable in our situation.
4. *Shemirat Shabbat K'Hilkhatah,* ch. 23:53 (1979 edition; 23:62 in the new edition). See also R. Moshe Levy, *Menuḥat Ahava* I (Bnei Brak, 1992), 24:17, and R. Yitzḥak Yosef, *Yalkut Yosef, Shabbat* 3 (Jerusalem, 2012), 318:28.

> When one performs an action that results in the performance of a forbidden labor, **and it is a certainty that this action will cause that labor to be performed,** one is liable [i.e., *mid'Orayta*] even though one did not intend [to perform the forbidden labor]. **For it is known to all that it is impossible that the labor will not come to be performed.** (1:6)

This means that the very reason a *psik reisha* is forbidden is because it is clear that the forbidden act will occur together with the undertaken action, and they are therefore considered one single action and ruled upon together. There is no indication whatsoever in the words of Rambam that we must find the underlying reason for this causal connection and figure out why these two actions are linked to one another. The salient fact is that this is the reality, that performing one act will cause the other to occur.

Thus, for example, if we were to imagine a restroom contraption that turns on the incandescent lighting every time a paper towel is removed from the dispenser, this would be considered a classic *psik reisha,* given that it is impossible to remove the paper towel without performing the *melakhah* (turning on the lights). As Rambam sets down, it does not at all matter whether the contraption works via a mechanical spring, light-sensitive sensor, or any other mechanism. No matter what, it will be considered a *psik reisha* and the only question left to discuss will be whether it is wanted/convenient (and obviously whether the prohibition is *mid'Orayta* or rabbinic in nature).

Furthermore, in my opinion, specifically according to this claim by Rabbis Fixler and Reif, it is not clear what is the new aspect of the electronic sensors that was not present in previous generations of devices, foremost among them the simple thermostat, responsible for activating refrigerator compressors. This same thermostat, discussed in the halakhic literature over the last eighty years, is for our purposes no more than an electronic sensor whose mode of operation can be described in the same terms: "not being acted upon by man – but rather it acting on man" (of its own accord). It "feels on its own" the changes generated in ambient temperature and responds accordingly, activating the system on its own without any human intervention. Nevertheless, it is clear even from all the *poskim* who permitted opening the refrigerator door on Shabbat, that were it the case that opening the door would immediately lead to the activation of the compressor, this action would be completely forbidden. It is only because this is not the case that they found room for leniency because of *grama* [ed. note: an indirect cause], *safek psik reisha* [a possible *psik reisha*], etc. Based on what we have written, it is easy to understand why both those forbidding and even those allowing thermostat operation saw no need to inquire as to the exact mechanism by which the thermostat is activated (beyond an elementary understanding of how it functions) and why no one even considered claiming that it consists of an automatic system whose actions are of its own accord and should not be attributed to the person influencing it.

ACTIVATION OF A DEVICE VIA WALKING

It has thus been determined that the method in which modern sensors are activated is not relevant to the discussion of whether or not they are forbidden as a *psik reisha*. What is left to discuss is whether or not this actively constitutes the "**performance of an action**" (in the words of Rambam). Without this prerequisite, the discussion whether or not the "action" is considered a *psik reisha* cannot get off the ground.

This brings us to the second point made by the authors, that no prohibition applies to the activation of an electronic door (for example) via sensor, due to the fact that the subject is simply going about his own business and not actively "performing an action."[5]

However, this claim too eludes my understanding, for as distinct from the refrigerator (or the paper towel contraption described above), in the case of an electronic door the subject is directly interested in the act of opening, and this is the desired result. A person does not walk straight into a glass wall; he is well aware that his walking will trigger the sensor to open the door. This is his will and intent as he approaches. It is not an uncommon sight to observe people who, upon realizing that the door has not yet opened, deliberately move this way or that as they approach in order to activate the sensor. Additionally, should the sensor be out of order, they of course stop and do not continue walking. It is thus impossible to claim that there is no "performance of an action." The walking itself is not "innocent" and devoid of context, but rather done with the intention of activating the sensor.[6] It is no different from extending one's hands in front of an electronic faucet for the purpose of using it.

5. Presumably, according to this claim, the permissibility of the sensors does not specifically depend on their method of activation (as described), but even if we were to construct a stairwell in which the act of placing one's weight on the stairs activates the lighting in the hallway (a case similar to that which is forbidden by *kal vaḥomer* in the sources we have brought above), this should ostensibly be permissible since the person is not intending to perform a *melakhah* but only innocently walking and minding his own business.
6. It would appear as if the authors have come to the conclusion that it is not possible for the act of walking to be considered an "action" regarding the Shabbat prohibitions. However, is it possible

Furthermore, in similar fashion to what is proven by the discussion in the *poskim* regarding a refrigerator, here too we can use as proof the discussion in the *poskim* regarding the Shabbat elevator. The main focus of the debate regarding the Shabbat elevator revolves around the effect of the additional weight of the person entering the elevator. This is seemingly even more innocuous than walking, as it does not require moving any limbs and consists purely of standing even without any other movement at all. The activation is achieved through body weight alone and therefore would it not be absurd to apply Shabbat prohibitions to standing in place? Indeed, within the discussion some have addressed the meaning of such an assertion and inquired into the relationship between standing in place, the added weight, and the final outcome. Regardless, it is clear even from the position of the gaon R. Shlomo Zalman Auerbach and many others who permit the elevator's use, that if the reality were that entering the elevator would actually activate it, and if the added weight were the direct cause of functions that would not occur otherwise, then entering the elevator would be strictly prohibited.[7] The simple reason behind it being that, like it or not, the person entering would be the direct cause of these actions, and not only are they beneficial to him, but in fact they are his direct intention and purpose upon entering the elevator. Much more so in the case of the electronic door where the person is not only standing but actively participating using his body.

REGARDING THE *POSKIM*

Before closing, I would like to address the proofs from the *poskim* discussed in the original essay. First, the proof brought from *Shevet HaLevi,* and his explication of the difference of opinions between Rashba and Ran: Regarding this, it must be noted that *Shevet HaLevi* explicitly states that the absence of a prohibition is only when the action is performed completely as usual without any special intention or any additional act whatsoever. If there exists any intention whatsoever, it

---

to assert that if we were to build a "carousel" belt that turns grindstones when one walks on it; and one were to walk upon and activate it, could this in any way be considered minding one's own business? In n. 45 of their article, they assert that we cannot compare our situation to someone walking on the planks at the olive press, for that instance is considered the usual way of performing the *melakhah.* I do not understand this distinction; the electronic door too is specifically meant to be activated in this particular way. Moreover, see *Mishnah Berurah, siman* 336, *se'if katan* 24–25 and *Arukh HaShulḥan, siman* 336, *se'if* 21, regarding walking on grass which could cause some of it to be uprooted – clearly not the usual way to cut such grass – permitted solely because it is not a *psik reisha,* neither of these *poskim* being aware of the "novel ruling" that it should be permissible anyway considering that it is merely a man walking along innocently.

7. See discussion at length in *Shemirat Shabbat K'Hilkhatah,* ch. 23:49 in the footnotes, and *Responsa Minḥat Shlomo* I, 91:10.

becomes worse than a *psik reisha*. In his words (vol. 9, *siman* 69), the claim that "the person is not doing anything but only walking along innocently as usual and does not even add a single movement in service of the *melakhah*" is only applicable "so long as he does not consider walking there in order to turn on the light." Hence, *Shevet HaLevi* continues, this *heter* has no connection "to the widespread current situation in which doors are opened via an electronic eye by the one who enters, for in this case, the one who enters has a very clear vested interest in the door opening for him, and it is prohibited."[8]

Regarding the proof brought from the *sugya* of innocent trampling of dangerous pests (where the term "walking innocently" was first coined), according to most *Rishonim* this has no bearing on our case. This is because since the initial prohibition of a *melakhah she'einah tzerikhah l'gufah*[9] is of rabbinic origin, and the rabbinic prohibition was not extended to the case of dangerous pests. Nevertheless, we still require the action to be done as innocently as possible, to remove it as far as we can from the prohibited scenario.[10] Rambam, on the other hand, holds that a *melakhah she'einah tzerikhah l'gufah* is prohibited *mid'Orayata*. Accordingly, there is discussion among the commentaries as to the reason, in keeping with Rambam's position, for the permission to continue walking in this case. It may be due to *safek pikuaḥ nefesh*, a possibly life-threatening situation [ed. note: of poisonous snakes and scorpions], and thus treading upon the dangerous pests would be permissible even intentionally.[11] Alternatively, the permission comes solely from the fact that the consequences are unintended. Namely, it is permitted

8. This is what he also writes there in responsum 68. It is strange that the authors themselves expressed surprise over his words in n. 44 of their article, ignoring the difference between an action which is "convenient" as opposed to "intended." Instead they unnecessarily shifted his interpretation far afoot "that he has adopted hazy terminology leaving an opening" (?), while there is nothing ambiguous or unclear in his language, as explained above. (Even without this argument I find it difficult to contend that someone approaching an electronic door does not add any movement in order to cause the outcome, this being another reason to prohibit such an action.)
9. Ed. note: According to Tosafot, this is a *melakhah* performed for purposes other than the original purpose in the *Mishkan*. Other *Rishonim* explain *melakhah she'einah tzerikhah l'gufah* otherwise.
10. *Kol kama d'efshar l'shinuyei meshaninan*. As stated in Rashba, Ritva, and Ran, and similarly in Me'iri, Shabbat 221b; see also *Bet Yosef*, *siman* 316 (and not for the reason of *mar'it ayin* [suspicious looking activity] as stated by *Levush* and copied into *Mishnah Berurah)*. In my opinion it is tenuous to try to fit this into the opinion of Rambam from the words of Ramban that it is permissible even if there is explicit intention (see the addendum by the gaon R. Rabinowitz), which only fits according to Ramban's opinion that *melakhah she'einah tzerikhah l'gufah* is of rabbinic origin, in contrast to the position of Rambam.
11. *Leḥem Mishneh*, *Hilkhot Shabbat* 11:11 based on *Maggid Mishneh* (it does raise the question what then is meant by the term "innocently").

to walk innocently – without explicit intention to trample – and one need not worry about trampling [the snakes and scorpions], since there is no intention to do so. Either way, the bottom line is that even according to Rambam, this cannot be used to support the case where one has normal deliberate intentions.

It therefore seems clear that even according to the principles established in the article, the permissive stance can only be applicable to situations similar to walking through the hallways of hotels and activating decorative lighting, etc., but not for electric doors and the like. Furthermore, according to many opinions, one should *l'khatḥilah* refrain from traversing even decoratively lit hallways due to *psik reisha* (and all the more so in the case of actual, not decorative, illumination); neither of these cases being similar to what my esteemed great-grandfather the gaon R. Yosef Eliyahu Henkin wrote regarding *psik reisha,*[12] because in our instance the activation happens immediately, before our eyes. Nevertheless, in the case of street cameras and the like, it is acceptable to be lenient as expressed by R. Y. E. Henkin (ibid.), for if the *melakhah* is not at all apparent at the moment of activation, it cannot be considered as meeting the requirements for *psik reisha.* In any case it is not relevant to our case in which we are discussing intentional actions.[13]

Further on in their article (sections 3–4) the authors noted the words of the gaon R. Ovadiah Yosef, who rules leniently in the case of a rabbinic *psik reisha;* however it is widely known that Ashkenazim rule more strictly (see *Mishnah Berurah* 314:11), especially in the case where the consequence is "convenient" where even in *Responsa Be'er Yitzḥak* (cited in the article) the final ruling is to forbid. This is in contrast to the portrayal in the article where it seems that the common approach is to be lenient "with no room for stringency."[14]

---

12. See R. E. Y. Henkin, *Responsa Gevurot Eliyahu* (Lakewood, 2012), *Oraḥ Ḥayim* 91:3.
13. As far as the discussion regarding a recognizable action (see addendum of R. Rabinowitz), this is indeed dependent on the observer's perception and understanding. Just as in the case when someone calls out to an animal and it approaches, no one has ever doubted that this constitutes a recognizable action, despite it being merely a distant sound that does not touch the animal, because everyone understands the mechanism at play, so too it would seem here; everyone understands that approaching the electronic sensor is what causes the door to open. Only when someone walks by the door without noticing it at all would we be able to say that it is not even a *psik reisha* and only an utter byproduct (*mit'asek*) as if someone were talking to a friend and a nearby animal happened to hear and approach, which is seemingly not considered a prohibited action at all.
14. Additionally, they did not make mention of the addendum to the gaon R. Ovadiah Yosef's opinion, appearing in his *Responsa Yabia Omer* 6, *Oraḥ Ḥayim* 35:8: "Regarding halakhic practice, we rule more stringently in the case of a rabbinic *psik reisha,* at least when it is considered convenient" and the *heter* is specifically in a case of great need or in conjunction with additional mitigating circumstances. Similarly, in section 4 of the article, the authors state that although

Finally, with regard to what appears at the end of the article concerning the definition of "mundane (weekday-like) activities": According to Rambam, I cannot discern why this should make any difference. Even if we accept that the term "mundane (weekday-like) activities" according to Rambam applies only to actions similar to those prohibited as a *melakhah*, even so, according to Rambam, there are additional prohibitions emanating from the obligation to "respect (Shabbat) by refraining from your business, *me'asot derakhekha*" (which can be called "disrespecting Shabbat" as noted in the article cited there), so why should it make any difference whether Rambam forbids it under one name or another?

SUMMARY

Based on our above analysis, there appear to be a number of different levels regarding Shabbat prohibitions relating to electronic devices activated by various types of sensors:

1. Any activation that is unintended and we are entirely indifferent to its occurrence – e.g., walking down a street that activates street cameras – is permissible according to most opinions.
2. Any activation that is unintended but the protagonist benefits from the outcome – e.g., streetlights that light up as pedestrians pass by – a few authorities permit but most *poskim* prohibit (especially if the lighting is beneficial and not just decorative).
3. Any activation that is directly intended with the outcome and its benefits in mind – e.g., walking toward an electronic door or moving one's hand toward an electronic faucet – is prohibited by all; and the lone opinion permitting this (in the case of a door) requires much further study.

ADDENDUM[15]

The response of the authors *shlit"a* (*Emunat Itekha* 105 [Tishrei 2014]: 86–87) overlooks our fundamental point that we are dealing with a *davar hamitkaven,*

most of the *Aḥaronim* have ruled in favor of *Even Ha'ozer* and against *Magen Avraham* regarding the prohibition of water-activated millstones, several have nonetheless upheld *Magen Avraham*'s opinion; but is this reason to rule like them *l'khatḥilah*? (However, when the opposite is the case, i.e., the majority rule leniently, they were not so quick to point out the divergent stricter opinions – see n. 40 therein). In my opinion there is much room to distinguish between the scenarios, but that shall be left for another forum.

15. This addendum was prepared by R. Eitam *Hy"d* and was found on his desk after his ascent in a tempest to the heavens. In *Emunat Itekha*, 105:81–85, R. Eitam *Hy"d* responded to R. Dror Fixler and R. Eli Reif's article on "Operating Sensors on Shabbat" (*Emunat Itekha*, 104:54–65). The

a premeditated act, and not a *psik reisha,* an inevitable consequence. They write that "in our generation there is a total disconnect between a person's actions and their effect, even greater than in the case of the thermostat which was itself already deemed permissible in previous generations." Besides it not being clear to me that there indeed exists a greater disconnect, the primary reason previous generations permitted the opening of a refrigerator door is that the mechanism activated via the thermostat is not instantaneous but rather graduated and indirect – unlike the case of electronic doors and the like.

The one point which I would like to further clarify concerns the position of Rambam. I do not presume to rule on my own against *Leḥem Mishneh* and *Maggid Mishneh;* however, if we are to rely on many other commentators on Rambam, they are unanimous in saying that the meaning of *lefi tumo,* innocently, is exactly as it sounds: devoid of any intention to perform the forbidden action. As to the authors' question, how is this achieved in practice, this has already been addressed by Rashi (Shabbat 121b, s.v. *lefi tumo*):

> Not that he stand beside it and plainly kill it; but if he happens to be walking along innocently and there is a snake or scorpion in his path, he does not need to avoid it but may step upon it as he walks; and if it dies from this, so be it, since that was not his intention. For unintended actions are, according to R. Yehudah, only prohibited rabbinically; and in the case of harmful pests, they did not decree a prohibition.

Meaning, even if he does step on them, it is not certain that they will die; and in any case, he is not intending this outcome. Radbaz (responsa 5:149) explains in this fashion the position of Rambam, at great length. Regarding the dissenting opinions of Ramban and other *Rishonim* who disagree with Rashi, and hold that the Talmud is referring even to intentional trampling – I have already written that this is specifically in light of their position that a *melakhah she'eina tzerikha l'gufa* is only prohibited *mid'rabbanan,* as they state explicitly. I therefore do not understand how their position can be used to support Rambam [as he holds that a *melakhah she'eina tzerikha l'gufa* is prohibited *mid'Orayta*]. Furthermore, one who wishes to make the claim that "there is no hint whatsoever in the words of Rambam" regarding one certain specific detail, must also admit, in my opinion, that there is likewise nothing in the opposite direction to hint that he is talking about a case of clear intention. On the contrary, the language used: "and if he

authors responded to his response. The addendum brought here was written as a final response, and was published in *Emunat Itekha* 110 (Shevat 5776/2016): 7–8.

trampled them" (as appears in the more accurate manuscripts, and not "if he tramples them") seems to indicate the opposite.

Likewise, the authors' attempt to support their reading of Rambam by mentioning *Mirkevet Hamishneh* is puzzling. They are most likely referring to his quote "and the matter of innocently trampling mentioned by *Rabbenu* (Rambam), it seems to mean that it is permissible to intentionally walk on them and trample them." However, in his very next sentence *Mirkevet Hamishneh* writes:

> And to crush and thereby weaken them, as he is walking in a manner that is not a *psik reisha*, meaning that he does not intend to kill or trample them with such a force capable of killing them. Therefore even if he does kill them it is still permissible as it is an unintended action...

This is exactly in line with the words of Rashi above and as Radbaz explained, completely refuting the authors' own argument. Incidentally, this is all according to the opinion of Rambam. There are of course many other *Rishonim* around – what shall we do with their opinions?

Bottom line, the far-reaching position taken by the authors and written as *halakhah l'ma'aseh*, practical halakhic guidance, is in complete opposition to the decades-long ruling found in *Shemirat Shabbat K'Hilkhatah* and accepted as binding, in practice, by all observant communities. Excluding the gaon R. Naḥum Eliezer Rabinowitz *shlit"a* [*ztz"l*], there has to this day not been any prominent *posek* who has given a *heter* in this matter, despite the fact that the core practical issue has been around and recognized for a number of decades. And the source they wish to depend upon, *Shevet HaLevi,* states explicitly that it is forbidden; and therefore we are left to conclude that the lone permissive opinion requires much further study.

Chapter 5

Two Clarifications on the Prohibition of *Lo Teḥonem*[1]

DOES THE PROHIBITION APPLY TO ALL GENTILES, OR JUST TO IDOLATERS?

Rambam's Position in *Sefer HaMitzvot*

In setting forth the law of *lo teḥonem,* Rambam writes in *Sefer HaMitzvot* (*lo ta'aseh* [negative commandment] 50):

> He has exhorted us not to have mercy on idolaters nor to enhance objects that are designated for them, and this is the meaning of His words *lo teḥonem* [Devarim 7:2]. [And the Sages] received an oral tradition explicating [the verse as]: Do not show them favor (*ḥen*).

1. Translated by Michael Appel. This chapter originally appeared in *HaMa'ayan* 216 (5776). Translator's Note: We have deliberately left the phrase *lo teḥonem* untranslated throughout this article because its interpretation is the subject of dispute in the Gemara. The phrase appears in Devarim 7:1–4:

> When HaShem your God brings you to the land that you are about to enter and possess, and He dislodges many nations before you – the Hittites, Girgashites, Amorites, Canaanites, Perizites, Hivites, and Jebusites, seven nations more populous and stronger than you – and HaShem your God delivers them to you and you defeat them, you must destroy them utterly: make no pact with them and ***lo teḥonem***. Do not intermarry with them: do not give your daughters to their sons or take their daughters for your sons. For they will steer your son away from Me to worship other gods, and HaShem's anger will blaze forth against you and He will promptly wipe you out. (adapted from JPS Translation)

In the following commandment (*lo ta'aseh* 51), Rambam writes of another prohibition, that "*they shall not dwell in your land*" [Shemot 23:33] and writes that this applies to idolaters:

> But if he [the gentile] accepts upon himself not to practice idolatry, then it is permitted, and he is called a *ger toshav*[2] according to our Sages. ... However, an idolater may not dwell among us, we do not sell him land nor rent it. We have received the oral tradition: "Do not provide them dwelling (*ḥanaya*) on the ground."

Rambam tells us here that the prohibition of *lo teḥonem* applies only to idolaters.[3] However, the question begs: The prohibition of *lo teḥonem* is addressed in the previous commandment (*lo ta'aseh* 50), while this commandment (*lo ta'aseh* 51) relates to "*they shall not dwell in your land.*" Why mention *lo teḥonem* here? Also, the **rental** of land is not a *d'Orayta* prohibition, and is even sometimes permitted *l'khatḥilah,* such as when it is not rented for the purpose of domestic living.[4] It would be a stretch to say that it is mentioned here just to be all-inclusive even though it is not an integral part of this prohibition and, in fact, belongs with the previous commandment.

In my humble opinion, both questions can be answered with one simple solution. Rambam here is following the Talmud Yerushalmi on *lo teḥonem.* In the Talmud Bavli (Avodah Zarah 20a), the primary derivation from the verse of *lo teḥonem* is that we are not to give them any land rights. This, according to the Talmud Bavli, is the plain meaning of the word *teḥonem* as written (as opposed to [the alternate explanations] "showing favor" or "free gifts," in which the grammar would call for alternative vowelizations of the word), and this is demonstrated by the *baraita* brought by the Bavli:

---

2. Perhaps he only intends to use the term *ger toshav* with regard to permitting him to dwell in the land, as he writes, "For he is a *ger* only in the sense that he may live in the land," meaning that we are not also commanded to support him, etc. However, see *Hilkhot Isurei Bi'ah* 14:7.
3. We should mention regarding the *Maggid Mishneh* on *Hilkhot Shabbat* (20:14): "Certainly, a pagan [slave] does not even have a single day's grace period and we do not keep him. Rabbi Yishmael did not disagree as far as allowing an idolater in his home, because even any dwelling in the land is prohibited to them..." However, whether he is referring specifically to an idolater, this depends upon the question of whether or not his cessation from idolatry can classify him as a *ger toshav*. Plainly speaking, he must commit to upholding all the seven Noahide commandments (see Rambam, *Hilkhot Milah* 1:6), but the matter is undecided with respect to our topic. See *Ma'aseh Roke'aḥ*. If so, this requires further study.
4. See R. D. Kokhavi, *Sefer HaBatim* (Jerusalem, 1983) here, where it seems that he learns from this that, given that in our times Jews have no dominion over them, and it is therefore not possible to fulfill "*they should not dwell in your land,*" then even a sale would be prohibited only rabbinically. This requires further study.

a. *Lo teḥonem* – Do not give them a foothold in the land
b. An alternative, *lo teḥonem* – Do not show them favor
c. Another alternative, *lo teḥonem* – Do not give them free gifts

This indicates that the first explanation (a) is the main one, even though two additional secondary interpretations are given. Also, only the first one is the halakhah expounded upon in the Mishnah there. However, the parallel Yerushalmi text (Avodah Zarah 1:9) reverses the order:

a. *Lo teḥonem* – Do not show them favor
b. *Lo teḥonem* – Do not give them free gifts
c. *Lo teḥonem* – Do not give them a foothold in the land

From here, the primary teaching would be about not showing them favor.

And this is precisely what Rambam wrote; for in mitzvah 50 regarding the prohibition of *lo teḥonem,* he mentioned only not showing them favor:

> And this is the meaning of His words *lo teḥonem.* [And the Sages] received an oral tradition explicating [the verse as]: Do not show them favor (*ḥen*). He concludes explicitly: "At the end of tractate Avodah Zarah in the Yerushalmi, they said 'Do not show them favor' as a negative commandment."

See also *Sefer HaḤinukh,* mitzvah 426, who followed Rambam in this approach and did not mention land rights at all in the prohibition of *lo teḥonem.*[5] This explains why Rambam mentioned land rights in *lo ta'aseh* 51. Even though it belongs with the law of *lo teḥonem* in *lo ta'aseh* 50, he wanted to mention there only the core prohibition of showing favor. He then placed the prohibition of granting land rights together with the prohibition of "*they shall not dwell in your land*" because it fits within the same topic (*Sefer HaḤinukh* does the same in mitzvah 94). This also explains why Rambam added the prohibition against rentals. Even though the Bavli considers this a rabbinic prohibition, the Yerushalmi holds that renting a field constitutes a *d'Orayta* prohibition because the gentile often derives blessings from there (see *Pnei Moshe* there). Presumably

5. And likewise *Semak* (mitzvah 135). However, it is possible that he omitted land rights because they only apply in Eretz Yisrael (similar to Rabbenu Yonah in *Sha'arei Teshuvah,* 3:57). But it is mentioned in *Hagahot Rabbenu Peretz.* In *Semag, lo ta'aseh* 48, land rights are mentioned first in accordance with the Bavli (while *Sefer Yerei'im* does not count *lo teḥonem* at all).

Rambam is referring to a field: "We should not sell him land, nor rent it." If so, this is a detail of the commandment as recorded in the Torah. Either way, we see that Rambam in *Sefer HaMitzvot* takes the position that selling land to a gentile is only prohibited to an idolater (see also *Zohar HaRakia* by R. Shimon b. Tzemaḥ Duran, *ot* 83).

However, practically speaking, this is irrelevant. It is clear that in *Mishneh Torah* (*Hilkhot Avodah Zarah* 10:3–4) Rambam retracted and ruled like the Bavli in all respects. The main prohibition is granting land rights, and secondary additions were prohibitions against showing favor and giving free gifts. Therefore, only selling land is prohibited *mid'Orayta*, and rental is a rabbinic preventive enactment [*seyag*]. The same is true regarding what he first wrote in *Sefer HaMitzvot*, limiting the prohibition to idolaters. Here too, we must rely on the formulation in *Mishneh Torah*, where the plain meaning includes all gentiles.[6] *Kaftor VaFeraḥ* (ch. 10) echoes this position explicitly: "It stands to reason since, as a result of our sins, the land is controlled by Ishmaelites, one may even rent a place suitable for dwelling to an Ishmaelite, for the renter is not a pagan who would bring in idolatry… But to sell them houses or fields in the Land of Israel, categorically no, due to the prohibition of *lo teḥonem*, as per Rambam *z"l*."

The Position of Tosafot

The straightforward meaning of the text is that the commandment *lo teḥonem* refers to the seven Canaanite nations:

> …seven nations more populous and stronger than you … destroy them utterly; do not make a pact with them and *lo teḥonem*. Do not intermarry with them… because they will steer your son away from Me, etc. (Devarim 7:1–3)

This is noted by *Semag* in *lo ta'aseh* 38. Based on this reading of the text, Tosafot (Avodah Zarah 20a, s.v. *d'amar*) ask why the Mishnah and Gemara apply this to all gentiles. They answer that each phrase of the verse must be understood independently, on its own ground:

1. "Do not intermarry" certainly does not apply to all gentiles, who are allowed to intermarry upon conversion. This is not true with respect to *lo teḥonem*,

6. To distinguish it from "*they shall not dwell in your land,*" at the end of the chapter. See what I wrote about this in *HaMa'ayan* 52:2 (Tevet 5772), 116–18.

where there is no reason to distinguish between the seven nations and any other gentiles.

2. Similarly, "Do not make a pact with them" – Because we are dealing with conquest and there is a requirement to destroy them, then of course it would be prohibited to strike a treaty with the seven nations. But this does not apply to *lo teḥonem* (whose purpose is the reverse of a treaty, not to give them a new foothold in the land). Alternately, one could say that the seven Canaanite nations are more steeped in idolatry than other gentile nations (so there would be more reason not to establish treaties with them). This is the substance of Tosafot's words.

At first glance, the position of Tosafot is difficult to understand. Even if we assume that the seven nations are steeped in idolatry to a greater extent than others, how do we know that the reasoning would not still apply to other pagan nations? Has the Torah supplied a yardstick to measure the threshold for idolatry? One would have to answer that, since the Torah has already stated that the seven nations must be utterly destroyed, it goes without saying that they cannot be granted any land rights. So we are forced to conclude that *lo teḥonem* applies to the *other* gentile nations. And the reason for the extra command not to strike a treaty with the seven nations after being told to destroy them is to preclude the possibility of striking a peace treaty as a substitute for destroying them, as a treaty would remove them from the definition of "enemy."[7]

But the question remains: Since the prohibition against intermarriage is specific to the seven nations, what reason would there be for *lo teḥonem* to apply broadly to all other nations? If we have no reason to make a distinction, then we should explain the verse based on its straightforward meaning and its context. Why remove it from its straightforward meaning for no reason? In my humble opinion, Tosafot here, when mentioning "other gentile nations," is referring to idolaters as well,[8] because during the era of the Sages, all gentile nations were idolaters (as were the surrounding nations during the time and place of the Tosafists). This is borne out in the conclusion of Tosafot, "The seven Canaanite nations are more steeped in idolatry than other gentile nations." We see from here that Tosafot considered all the other gentile nations to also be idolaters, perhaps not as fervently so. This nullifies the question, as the verse deals entirely with exhortations to distance ourselves from idolatry. In truth, there is no reason to distinguish between the seven Canaanite nations and any other idolaters with regard to the prohibition

7. See Rambam, *Hilkhot Melakhim* 6:5, and Ramban on Devarim 20:11.
8. See *Ḥidushei Mahardam* on *Sefer HaMitzvot, lo ta'aseh* 51.

against giving free gifts, etc.[9] On the contrary, there is no reason to believe that Tosafot would apply the prohibition of *lo teḥonem* to nations that are not idolaters. It is impossible to claim that the Torah did *not* intend to distinguish between idolaters and non-idolaters, as the text expressly stipulates idolaters.

One might also ask in the same manner: Didn't the Torah already teach us [regarding the pagan nations], "Do not allow them to dwell in your land lest they cause you to sin because you will worship their gods" (Shemot 23:33)? If so, why the additional need for *lo teḥonem*!? It must be that *lo teḥonem* applies to the other nations! However, one might deflect this answer and say that the prohibition in Shemot only applies when one sells land to a gentile who will actually dwell there. If not, then he would not cause you to sin (and when we are stronger than them, we can prevent them from dwelling on the land that they purchased). *Lo teḥonem* is required to teach all the additional prohibitions in addition to the prohibition of their "dwelling on your land," such as showing favor, etc.

To conclude, it seems, in my humble opinion, that according to Tosafot in Avodah Zarah, the prohibition of *lo teḥonem* only applies *mid'Orayta* to idolaters.[10] However, Rambam holds that it applies to all gentiles based on the straightforward sense of the prohibition, and this is the position of most of the *Rishonim*.[11]

The Position of *Mizbaḥ Adamah*

There is, however, an opinion among the *poskim* that the prohibition of *lo teḥonem* is limited to idolaters, and that is the position of the *Mizbaḥ Adamah* (*Yoreh De'ah* 151),[12] who wrote that we have seen that the leading great rabbis Moharsha and Maharam"m sold houses, presumably because the prohibition of "*They shall not dwell in your land*" only applies to idolaters, and does not apply to Ishmaelites,

---

9. See Tosafot to Yevamot 23a, s.v. *hahu*. (However, from the text version reading "*umot ovdei avodat kokhavim*" we can conclude nothing. See *Tosafot HaRosh* there.)

10. Here, I retract what I had previously written on this subject in *HaMa'ayan*, 52:2 (Tevet 5772), p. 117. I group the opinion of Tosafot with that of Rashba (*Shu"t Oraḥ Ḥayim, siman* 8) and Me'iri (Avodah Zarah 20a, etc.), who are explicit that *lo teḥonem* only applies to idolaters, as cited in R. Shmuel Vozner, *Shu"t Shevet HaLevi* 4 (Bnei Brak, 2002), 213 and R. Eliezer Waldenberg, *Shu"t Tzitz Eliezer* 15 (Jerusalem, 1983), 47:5. (Also see the sources that I bring in *HaMa'ayan*, 52:2 (Tevet 5772), p. 114.)

11. Specifically Ramban and Ran in Gittin 38b, where it is conclusively shown that *lo teḥonem* is not dependent on idolatry, as there it refers to a Canaanite slave (see Rashba there). Until now we have only discussed Tosafot in Avodah Zarah. But Tosafot in Eruvin 64b, s.v. *v'lamadnu* (and *Tosafot HaRosh* there), implies that there is no distinction between idolaters and other gentiles, as the laws of a gentile's leavened products on Pesaḥ in that discussion are certainly not dependent on the issue of idolatry. See also *Shu"t Radbaz* 5, *siman* 314.

12. *Mizbaḥ Adamah*, p. 12a.

as Rambam wrote in *Hilkhot Avodah Zarah* and in *Sefer HaMitzvot*, and as codified (in a different context) in *Shulḥan Arukh, Ḥoshen Mishpat* 175:40–41. And in the Talmud, this is said specifically referring to idolaters. And *Kaftor VaFeraḥ* has already written that, in our day, it is permitted to rent homes to Ishmaelites. And when he writes, "But to sell them houses or fields in the Land of Israel, categorically no, due to the prohibition of *lo teḥonem*," this is only with reference to idolaters. And even though *Bet Yosef* (*Ḥoshen Mishpat* 249) prohibits giving free gifts to anyone not considered a *ger toshav*, this is not a proof regarding a sale in which the [Jewish] seller benefits. This is the gist of what *Mizbaḥ Adamah* wrote.[13]

In my humble opinion, most aspects of this position are very difficult to support. Like what we cited above, his citation from *Kaftor VaFeraḥ* says exactly the reverse of the point he wants to make, permitting only rentals, while prohibiting any land sales, even to Ishmaelites, due to *lo teḥonem*. The ruling of *Shulḥan Arukh* in *Ḥoshen Mishpat* has to do with the laws regarding abutting property lines; and neither the Gemara nor *Rishonim* make reference here at all to *lo teḥonem*. And with respect to our Talmud's use of the term "idolater," we already know that this was due to the censor (see Baḥ, *Ḥoshen Mishpat*, ibid.), and that the correct original language is "gentile." And regarding the distinction between a sale, which generates benefit to the seller, and a free gift: This is not so simple. After all, it is true of any sale, that the seller benefits. Nevertheless, we learn that "we do not sell them houses." The prohibition against giving them land rights stems from the law of *lo teḥonem*, and there is no proof to rebut it from the law of "*They shall not dwell among you*." (And we have already explained the position of Rambam above.)

We are left after all this with the report of house sales by Moharsh"a and Maharam"m. In our generation, R. Meir Mazuz has shown (in *Et HaZamir*, p. 304)[14] that the reference is apparently to R. Shlomo Elgazi and R. Meir Mizraḥi, respectively, who we know left Israel for the Diaspora [ed. note: and presumably sold their homes to local Arabs]. We can say that they were following the permissive ruling of *Kaftor VaFeraḥ* (explained below) and not necessarily because they agreed with the position of *Mizbaḥ Adamah*. And further, *Shemen HaMor*, that was published in Eretz Yisrael in the generation following the *Mizbaḥ Adamah*, deals with land sales to gentiles at length (*siman* 4, p. 33b) and never

13. See the continuation of his responsum. R. Hayim Palagi followed a similar line of reasoning in *Shu"t Nishmat Kol Ḥai, siman* 54. However, I do not understand his question (s.v. *u'k'she'ani*) on the *Aḥaronim* who wrote that *lo teḥonem* applies to all gentiles when Rashba seems to indicate the opposite. It is simply that the other *Rishonim* disagree with Rashba, as mentioned.

14. "*Ḥidushim V'Hagahot al Masekhet Kiddushin*" in Meir Zamir, *Et HaZamir* (Bnei Brak, 2009).

once hints at the notion that this might be limited to idolaters – we see that he never had a permissive tradition in this matter, contrary to those who wrote that the practice in Israel was to follow the ruling of *Mizbaḥ Adamah*.

The Position of Netziv

Another opinion among the *Aḥaronim*, opposing the position that the prohibition of *lo teḥonem* applies only to idolaters, is often brought today in the name of Netziv. In his treatise on *shemitah* (*Shu"t Meishiv Davar* 2, *siman* 56, part 2) he writes:

> In reality, the aforementioned author escaped the wolf, only to be snared by the lion. He attempted to avoid the prohibition of *shemitah*, which most *poskim* believe to be rabbinic today, and was ensnared in the prohibition of selling land in Israel to idolaters, which all agree is a *d'Orayta* prohibition.

He means that even a sale to Ishmaelites would be prohibited *mid'Orayta*. Ridbaz cites this in his own treatise on *shemitah*, in which he argues against those who wanted to sell land in Israel to Ishmaelites [ed. note: i.e., Muslims] on the grounds that they are not considered idolaters: "This opinion has already been nullified by the great gaon, Netziv *ztz"l*, and he is correct that they [Muslims] are not included in the category of *ger toshav*."[15] Ḥazon Ish also alluded to this: "On the contrary, the *shemitah* prohibition today is rabbinic, while the sale is a *d'Orayta* prohibition just like *tereifah* and *basar b'ḥalav* [non-kosher foods], etc. And so it is written in *Meishiv Davar*, *siman* 5[6]…"[16]

However, in recent years, it has become clear that the second half of the *shemitah* treatise in *Meishiv Davar*, in which this passage appears, was not authored by Netziv. It was written by a contemporary of his and erroneously published among Netziv's writings.[17] Today, we can show that Netziv held exactly the opposite position. In his own treatise on *shemitah*, which we can prove that he authored (that is, the first half of the *siman* in *Meishiv Davar*, mentioned above), he agreed with the position that *lo teḥonem* would not apply to the sale of land to Ishmaelites because they are not idolaters. However, he then added that this would not provide a solution to the *shemitah* prohibition:

15. *Kuntres HaShemitah LaRidbaz* (1909), p. 12a.
16. *Ḥazon Ish, Shevi'it, siman* 24:4. Also see R. Yehonatan Abelman, *Kuntres Torat Yehonatan* (Jerusalem, 1973), ch. 8.
17. See my article in *HaMa'ayan* 50:3 (Nisan 5770), 102–4, (and in the following issue, 50:4 [Tamuz 5770]: 71–72), and to this specific point, see my article in *HaMa'ayan* 55:4 (Tamuz 5775), 34–35.

> Even to sell to a gentile, where it is possible to avoid the prohibition of *lo teḥonem* because the Arabs are not idolaters, [would not help] because a Jew is prohibited from plowing any land, even land owned by a non-Jew..."

This is also the opinion of his contemporary, R. Alexander Moshe Lapidot.[18]

PROOF THAT A TEMPORARY SALE IS NOT PROHIBITED

Selling a Field to a Gentile *L'Khatḥilah*

In Mishnah Gittin (4:9) we find: "One who sells his field to a gentile, and it is subsequently purchased by a Jew, the purchaser must bring first fruits (*bikurim*) because of *tikkun olam*.[19] Rashi explains, "so that it will not become commonplace to sell land in Israel to gentiles." However, the Mishnah at the end of the second chapter of Avodah Zarah teaches that we do not sell them houses, not to mention fields, and the Gemara there explains that this is because of *lo teḥonem*. We seem to have a contradiction: How can the Mishnah in Gittin casually mention land sales to gentiles when there is a *d'Orayta* prohibition of *lo teḥonem*?

Additionally, Rashi's explanation in Gittin begs clarification. Is it not sufficient that the sale [of land in Eretz Yisrael to a gentile] violates a *d'Orayta* prohibition, that there is additional need or purpose in a rabbinic requirement to bring *bikurim* after the prohibited sale? This is addressed in *Ḥidushei HaRamah V'Shitat HaKadmonim* (also published in the name of Ritva), who wrote explicitly regarding Rashi's approach: "The rabbis fined the seller by forcing him to repurchase the first fruits from the gentile... lest each and every person sell his field to gentiles, thereby violating *lo teḥonem* – not giving them a foothold in the land." According to this, we would be forced to conclude that, for some reason, people were not scrupulous about observing the exhortation of *lo teḥonem* alone and relied on the fact that the land retained its holiness. Therefore, *Ḥazal* enacted legislation as described in the Gemara (47b). But we can still ask regarding a close read of Rashi's expression, "that it not become **commonplace**, etc." – would it be proper

18. He is the one mentioned in the quote from Netziv. See *Sefer Torat R. Alexander Moshe*, 128–29. Based on all this, it is clear why R. Avraham Yitzḥak Kook brought this view as an additional support for the *heter* in highly straitened times; see *Mishpat Kohen* (Jerusalem, 1966), *siman* 58 and *simanim* 60–61 (just as R. Yitzḥak Elḥanan Spektor did, see his language in *Sefer HaShemitah* of R. Yeḥiel Mikhel Tukachinsky [Mossad HaRav Kook, 1973], part 2, ch. 11. However, outside of highly straitened times, R. Spektor did not agree to permit even the position of *Kaftor VaFeraḥ* (see below), as I wrote in *HaMa'ayan* 52:2 (Tevet 5772): 113–15.
19. The Jew is fined by being required to separate *bikurim* from produce that grew while under the gentile's ownership.

to sell land as long as one does not do so regularly? Furthermore, in 41a, the Gemara states that when one sells his house to a gentile, the money received is forbidden for use. Rashi there explains that this is because the seller has violated *lo teḥonem*. Me'iri and Ritva take this to mean that this is a fine (the commentators on Rambam did not see their words). This strengthens our question: Why, in our case, was a regulation of *bikurim* required when, even without this, the fine prohibits benefit from the funds of the sale? (Even if one were to limit the case to sale of a house and not a field, then the same fine should be imposed on the field, and no further measure would be necessary.)

Either way, the original question remains: Why did the Mishnah phrase the sale of a field to a gentile using *l'khatḥilah* language, as if to say that this is permitted? Even according to Rambam's Commentary to the Mishnah, whose version of the Talmudic text relates only to the buyer and not to the seller[20] – the question still stands, because the first part of the Mishnah still seems to indicate that one is permitted to sell a field to a gentile in the Land of Israel. This requires further study.

Explanation of *Kaftor VaFeraḥ*

I searched the commentators and the only one I found to address this question explicitly was *Kaftor VaFeraḥ* (ch. 10). He proves from here that there is an instance in which one is permitted to sell land to a gentile without violating *lo teḥonem*. This is similar to the case in Gittin 44a [where a gentile has seized the home of a Jew, the Jew is able to receive payment for it after the fact] where he is permitted to document and register it as a sale in their courts, because he is doing so only to prevent them from stealing his money. *Kaftor VaFeraḥ* writes as follows:

> It stands to reason that this would be the case for one who lives in a town in Israel that is populated entirely by gentiles and desires to move to another town. He may sell his house there to gentiles out of concern that, otherwise, they will destroy it, or that they will squat there and live in it against his will.

20. See further in Me'iri, and in *Mirkevet HaMishneh* (*Hilkhot Terumot* 1:10). With respect to the *baraita* on folio 44 mentioned above, Rambam explains consistently that this results from wages of idolatry (See *Hilkhot Avodah Zarah* 9:13); *Or Same'aḥ* and others point out that this is explicit in a *Tosefta*; see *Ma'aseh Roke'aḥ*. With respect to *Ḥidushei Ḥatam Sofer* (Gittin 47a), that from here we learn that if gentiles are raising prices, we are permitted to suspend a *mitzvah d'Orayta* in order to stabilize the market price, he is referring to *bikurim*. His reasoning is that enriching the gentile runs afoul of *lo teḥonem*. (I regret that I do not understand the logic. If it referred to a free gift, then I would understand. But to purchase from him, even if he raises prices when we have no control [over him], how does *lo teḥonem* apply?) See also *Zera Yitzḥak* who explains that the Torah is concerned for the resources of the Jews.

> Similarly, this would apply if he is in a town populated by a majority of Jews and is under monetary duress, and there is no Jew who will buy his house, even at a discount. The prohibition on selling houses to gentiles only applies when these conditions are not present... It stands to reason that this also applies to a field, as it is taught at the end of chapter 4 of Gittin, "One who sells his field to a gentile must purchase and bring the first fruits because of *tikkun olam.*" Rashi explained this to mean so that one not become used to selling them land in Israel. We can say that this man was forced to sell his field due to one of the reasons we have enumerated. This is the case for all instances where land sales in Israel to a gentile are mentioned... Therefore, we see that it is permitted for a Jew to sell land in Israel to a gentile under duress, based on one the reasons we have given, or something similar.

Until this point, it would appear that *Kaftor VaFeraḥ* is discussing situations of such extreme pressure that they fall into the category of *oness*, intolerable duress, such as when a person wishes to move or sell his home and can find no Jew to purchase it.[21] However, in continuation, he implies that it would also be permitted to sell to gentiles in situations of great financial loss or the like. He adduces support from the Talmud Yerushalmi on the topic of *lo teḥonem*, "However in places where it is customary to sell, he may sell." He adds that the *Ba'al HaHashlama* wrote that the Yerushalmi appears to differ with the Bavli. But *Kaftor VaFeraḥ* resolves this by explaining the Yerushalmi's statement ("where it is customary to sell") as being limited to cases where the sale is under duress, whereas the Bavli refers to a situation that does not involve duress. The reason that the Yerushalmi refers to it as a "custom" is because there were places where it was customary not to sell, even when under duress. He cites the *Itur* who upholds the Yerushalmi and writes, "This is how we do it." And *Kaftor VaFeraḥ* adds: "And if he can sell at a high price to a gentile, but sells at a lower price to a Jew, then he is to be praised," meaning that one is not required to do so.[22]

Mirkevet HaMishneh (Terumot 1:10) seems to adopt this view: "After the first enactment, **one who was destitute and forced to sell** would not make an effort

21. This reasoning was upheld in R. Avraham Borenstein, *Shu"t Avnei Nezer, Yoreh De'ah* (Piotrkow, 1912), 458:18, who permitted selling land to gentiles in circumstances where they would otherwise take the field by force (adding that it would be less problematic if they found a way afterward to repurchase from the gentile, when it was generally agreed-upon practice to do so).
22. *Kuntres Torat Yehonatan* deduced the same from his words in ch. 9 (section 60) [holding that the *d'Orayta* prohibition only applies when done for the gentile purchaser's benefit, but not when the seller benefits himself]. See the following footnotes.

to redeem it and it would remain in the hands of gentiles. For this reason, they stood up and enacted [ed. note: that they must bring *bikurim*] as per Torah law," implying that the sale in this fashion was permitted (and this also seems to explain Rashi's position).[23] Regarding the reasoning of *Kaftor VaFeraḥ*, although the Bavli's discussion about writing and registering a document in gentile courts was only in regards to recovering the value of the house that the gentile had already seized by force, it follows that it would apply to any similar duress regarding property loss. If the seller had no permitted recourse, then he would lose his money or property. Therefore, once the Talmud has concluded that one who recovers his assets from them is not prohibited under *lo teḥonem*, this would extend to other forms of loss or great duress.[24]

But this opinion of *Kaftor VaFeraḥ* is a radically novel idea, one that we do not find permitted anywhere among the *Rishonim*.[25] It is one thing to say that when a man wishes to move to another city that the Torah does not force him to remain – on the contrary, it is better for him not to live among gentiles – so by taking money for his home, he is only preventing a foregone theft upon his departure, thereby saving his funds. This is not relevant to the prohibition of giving gentiles a dwelling place.[26] It is quite another thing to claim that the same would apply to one trying to sell a house while remaining in the city, because he needs funds and no Jew wishes to buy it. Just because he wants to sell now, should we allow him to transgress *lo teḥonem*? Let him wait until he can find a Jewish buyer! And the discussion in Gittin 40a is irrelevant here, because it refers to a case where the gentile has already seized the house, and therefore already has a "dwelling" in the land. The Gemara there only relates to the recovery of his funds.

With regard to the Yerushalmi cited by *Kaftor VaFeraḥ*, all of the *Rishonim* who bring the Yerushalmi[27] explain the issue not with respect to *lo teḥonem*, but to

23. And I recently found that *Ḥokhmat Adam, Sha'arei Tzedek* (*Sha'ar Mishpetei Ha'Aretz* 11:16) also brings down *Kaftor VaFeraḥ* as halakhah.

24. I later saw that the author of *Yisa Berakhah* explained the *Kaftor VaFeraḥ* similarly, explaining that the monetary loss is equivalent to *oness*, intolerable duress, in this regard (*Shu"t Ma'aseh Ish, Yoreh De'ah, siman* 2, p. 9a).

25. See what I wrote about this topic in *HaMa'ayan* 52:2 (Tevet 5772), p. 120. Also see R. David Friedman of Karlin in his treatise on *shemitah*, published at the end of *Shu"t She'elat David* 1, dealing with the position of *Kaftor VaFeraḥ*. From his words too, it is apparent that this is a minority opinion.

26. In truth, Me'iri also rules leniently in a similar way in the passage in Gittin. If he was compelled and cannot recover his property in any way, "he may sell it *l'khatḥilah* and collect the money," and this does not violate *lo teḥonem*.

27. Tosafot Avodah Zarah 21a; *Sefer HaTerumah, Hilkhot Avodah Zarah* 144; *Or Zaru'a, Piskei Avodah Zarah* 137; and Ramban, Rashba, Ran, and other commentators there.

the prohibition, *"Do not bring a to'evah [abomination] into your house,"* and that is specifically regarding land outside of Eretz Yisrael.[28] This is certainly what the *Itur* meant when he said, "This is how we do it," because it was not his practice to discuss customs of Eretz Yisrael.[29] The same goes for the *Hashlama*. The version of the *Hashlama* that we have (end of the first chapter of Avodah Zarah) reads as follows: "Yerushalmi: In a place where it is customary to rent, he may even rent out a home. This seems to contradict our Mishnah." He is only discussing the Yerushalmi's dispensation for renting land, even for a home. But he never mentions the issue of sale, in which logic says he would agree with the other *Rishonim*.

Are We Dealing with Sinners?

According to the rest of our *poskim*, what can we say about the question under discussion? How can we explain the Mishnah in Gittin that implies that there is a way that *l'khatḥilah*, the sale of land in Eretz Yisrael to a gentile is permitted? It is possible that the commentators relied on the Bavli in 47b, in which Rav Ashi holds there were two successive rabbinic enactments. At first, people would routinely sell their fields to gentiles, thinking (according to Rashi) that because the holiness of the land remains intact, there is also no prohibition on the sale. To counter this, the original enactment forbade bringing *bikurim* from these fields in order to prevent the sales.[30] But when the Sages saw that this had an opposite effect – namely that the original owners were no longer diligently seeking to redeem their fields from the gentiles (see Rambam's Commentary to the Mishnah), the Sages restored the original Torah law [ed. note: obligating the seller to bring *bikurim* from the field that was sold to a gentile]. According to this, our

28. After writing this article, I found that *Pe'at HaShulḥan* (*Hilkhot Eretz Yisrael*, ch. 1, *Bet Yisrael*, section 40) already posed this challenge to *Kaftor VaFeraḥ* and rejected his position.

29. I saw in *Kuntres Torat Yehonatan* (9:60) that he writes in the wake of *Kaftor VaFeraḥ* that we do not have the authority to oppose the *Itur* because the ruling based on local custom in the Yerushalmi applies to *oness*, duress, and not only outside the Land of Israel. This is difficult, in my opinion, because all the other *Rishonim* hold that this is not the case. Based on what I have written, without this, there is no proof from the *Itur*.

30. Similar to the fine that one who leases a field from a gentile is required to separate *ma'aser* (Demai 6:2). According to Rambam in his Commentary to the Mishnah, this was enacted so that the field remain in the gentile's hands until he is forced to sell it to a Jew, as we were commanded "*lo teḥonem* – and the Oral Law teaches: 'Do not give them settlement in the land.' Therefore we pressure them so they are unable to lease out the field until they are forced to sell it." (Rambam also ruled this way in *Mishneh Torah, Hilkhot Ma'asrot* 6:12; see *Mahar"i Kurkus* there). Also see *Rut Rabba* 7:11, "R. Yosei bar Avin said, when anyone sold his field to a gentile, his relatives would bring barrels full of roasted grain and nuts. They would break them in front of the children, who would collect them and say, 'so-and-so has been cut off from his ancestral land.' If he got it back, they would say, 'so-and-so returned to his ancestral land.'"

entire discussion has been about sinners and, therefore, there is no proof from their actions that such sales are permitted activities.

However, this answer was already raised by Rama"h (based on Rashi), which we have considered to be insufficient. After all, the language of the Mishnah addresses the seller of a field *l'khatḥilah* and how he should behave. If we were dealing with sinners, it would have been more appropriate for the Mishnah to begin by stating that it is prohibited to sell a field to gentiles. Or at least to word it as a post facto (*bedi'avad*) ruling, saying that "one who sold his field to a gentile must purchase and bring *bikurim*."[31]

The Gemara in Gittin 47a presents the case of a Jew who purchased a field from a gentile before a third of its produce had grown, and then sold it back to the gentile after a third of the produce had grown. Maharsha questions why the first half of the story is necessary, because the halakhah is only derived from the second half, in which the Jew sells the field to the gentile after a third of the produce has grown. So why the need for the first half?

> Because it is prohibited to sell land in Eretz Yisrael to a gentile, the Gemara did not wish to begin the case with a Jew committing this sin by selling land to a gentile. But in the case where the Jew first purchased the field from the gentile and then sold it back to him, it is possible that there is no prohibition.

This seems extremely difficult to comprehend. Right above this discussion, on the same page, we have a Mishnah that uses this exact formulation of a sale to a gentile, even *l'khatḥilah*![32]

The Means to Permit – A Temporary Sale

Therefore, it seems to me, in my humble opinion, that we have none other than the straightforward meaning of the text, that there is a circumstance in which selling land in Eretz Yisrael to a gentile does not violate *lo teḥonem*. Seeing that most *Rishonim* do not agree with *Kaftor VaFeraḥ* (as per above), the only option

31. As Rambam writes in *Hilkhot Terumah* 1:10, "When a gentile purchases land in Israel from a Jew, it does not become exempt from mitzvot… Therefore, if the Jew repurchases… He brings *bikurim*…" However, in *Hilkhot Bikurim* 2:15, Rambam copied the exact language of the Talmud: "If ones sells his field to a gentile and repurchases it, he brings *bikurim*." See R. Ḥayim Kaniyevski, *Derekh Emunah, Terumot* (Bnei Brak, 1994), 1:10 at the end of the discussion on *lo teḥonem*. But he does not explain why Rambam uses the wording of the Mishnah in Gittin in *Hilkhot Bikurim* with any rationale for how such a sale could have been permitted.
32. See *Tiferet Yaakov*, who rejected Maharsha for several reasons, but none that need concern us here.

remaining is the opinion of R. Yizḥak Elḥanan Spektor and his followers that a temporary sale does not fall within the purview of *lo teḥonem.*[33] I believe that a proof can be brought from our Mishnah, based on the version that most *Rishonim* had: "One who sells his field to a gentile, and then the Jew acquires it, the Jew brings…" This is precisely our situation. The Jew sold the field to a gentile for a limited time which terminated, and then [the seller] returned and reacquired it (it does not say "returned and repurchased"). Even though this does not fall under the category of *lo teḥonem,* and the Jew has not violated any prohibition, the Sages still fined him by obligating him to bring *bikurim* from the fruits that ripened during the gentile's possession of the field.[34]

The reason for the fine is that this sale harms *yishuv ha'Aretz,* settlement of Eretz Yisrael. *Ḥazal* made many similar decrees in order to strengthen settlement of Eretz Yisrael. (And if you ask: then the Mishnah should have said "… because of settlement of the Land of Israel," this would be a challenge to Rashi's interpretation in any case.) Another possible reason for the fine is that, as land sales to gentiles [in Eretz Yisrael] are generally forbidden, even though in this instance it is permitted, *Ḥazal* wished to discourage forbidden sales and therefore enacted this fine. This fits well with Rashi's explanation, "So that it will not become **commonplace** to sell land in Eretz Yisrael to gentiles." In other words, even though this particular sale might be permitted, it well might lead to prohibited sales in the future.[35]

---

33. See *Sefer HaShemitah* by R. Yeḥiel Mikhel Tukachinsky, section 2, ch. 11; *Shu"t Har Tzvi, Zera'im* 2:48; *Shu"t Mishpat Kohen* 65; article by Meir Stolovitz from Khaslavich in *Kovetz Sha'arei Zion,* 18:4–7 (Tevet–Adar 2, 1938): 39–42; *Ma'adanei Eretz* by R. Shlomo Zalman Auerbach, *Shevi'it* (Jerusalem, 1944), 1:11; Ridbaz, *Kuntres Hora'ot Sha'ah,* ch. 30; R. Yisrael Yehoshua Trunk, *Shu"t Yeshuot Malko* (Piotrkow, 1927), *Yoreh De'ah* 56–58. The source for this is already found in the *Rishonim* in *Ḥinukh* (339) quoting Ramban in his response to *Sefer HaMitzvot, lo ta'aseh* 227, "… we will not leave it to them through a final sale…." See a contrary opinion in *Shu"t Bnei Tziyon* vol. 1:2, sections 101–3, and section 107. Also see R. Betzalel Zolty, below n. 35, who rules on the question of a temporary sale. See also *Ḥazon Ish* (*Shevi'it* 24).
34. Since there is a permissible method of selling, the temporary sale mentioned above (or a sale with stipulation to repurchase), the Mishnah did not need to write explicitly in what fashion such a sale was permitted, because this is not relevant to what it is coming to teach here. And do not think that perhaps the Mishnah agrees with the position that *lo teḥonem* does not apply to a sale to a non-idolatrous gentile. If the Mishnah is referring to a sale to a specific permitted buyer, then the simplest explanation would be that it is referring to a *ger toshav.* Also, when the Gemara mentions gentiles generically, it refers to idolaters. This is not true for a sale to a non-specific buyer, where many parameters exist, and there is no need to spend time on all of them.
35. Similar to how Rashi explained the prohibition against gentile cooking: "So that the Jew does not become habituated to visit him for food and drink, where he might be fed something non-kosher."

One way or another, this is the reason behind the first enactment in the Gemara. People became habituated to selling, in a permissible fashion, and believed that since the holiness of the land was not impacted, nothing was amiss. So the Sages enacted the ban on bringing *bikurim* from those fields. Only when they saw that this caused the sellers to sell fields on a permanent basis and that the fields passed completely to gentile hands, did they revert to the original Torah law.[36]

SUMMARY

With the Almighty's help we have explained Rambam's position in *Sefer HaMitzvot* with regard to the laws of *lo teḥonem* and "*they shall not dwell in your land*," that he follows the Yerushalmi. In *Mishneh Torah*, he reverted to rule like the Bavli in prohibiting sale of land in Eretz Yisrael to all gentiles. Against this, we saw the position of Tosafot in Avodah Zarah that limited the prohibition, in my humble opinion, to idolaters. Most decisors rule like Rambam,[37] although several *Aḥaronim* ruled in accordance with the second opinion, or was inclined in that direction; and this was used as an additional reason to be lenient when faced with pressing circumstances.

Next, in another fashion, we found in Tractate Gittin land sales to gentiles in Eretz Yisrael treated as *l'khatḥilah*. After clarification, I proposed that this follows the opinion of those *Aḥaronim* who hold that *lo teḥonem* does not apply to temporary sales (or sales that are conditioned upon reversal). On the other hand, we saw that the opinion of *Kaftor VaFeraḥ*, that sale to a gentile is permitted when the seller is under duress or pressed for funds and cannot find a Jewish purchaser, is a singular opinion among the *Rishonim*, even though we have found a few *Aḥaronim* who agreed with him.

It goes without saying that everything I have written here is meant to be for the purpose of study alone, and is not intended as a practical halakhic ruling.

(Avodah Zarah 38a, s.v. *mid'rabbanan*). In other words, it will end up that way. See also Shabbat 13a.

36. After writing this, I saw that R Betzalel Zolty *ztz"l* already dealt with this issue (*Kerem Tzi'on, Shevi'it,* and in other places). He also deduced from the Mishnah that there must be a permissible method of sale – but he holds like the author of *Torat Ḥesed* that the permission is to swap fields with a gentile who already owns land in Israel. Since it was common for gentiles to own land in Israel, the Mishnah's default position was to refer to it as a permissible sale (see *Kovetz Mori'ah,* 16:11–12 (Av 5749/1989): 93, comment from R. Binyamin, *av bet din* of Wilkomierz, father of *Aderet,* who challenged Rabbi Avraham Aveli of Vilna who wrote that there is no violation of *lo teḥonem* with a land swap). In my humble opinion, what I wrote above is more in line with the Mishnah's formulation.

37. As ruled by *Pe'at HaShulḥan, Hilkhot Eretz Yisrael* 1:19.

Chapter 6

Washing Before Kiddush[1]

Editor's Introduction

In the 16th century, R. Moshe Isserles (Rema) wrote that washing before kiddush was the prevailing Ashkenazi custom, and in his Darkhei Moshe *gloss on the Tur he wrote that he had never seen otherwise. That had been the ruling of leading Tosafists in France, as well as Rashba and Rosh in 13th-century Spain. Baḥ, in 16th to 17th century Eastern Europe, cited the practice as the "universal custom." It remained the prevailing custom at least through the days of Ba'al HaTanya in the 18th century. But by the 19th century, the Ashkenazi custom had begun changing, so that today it remains associated in the minds of many only with German Jewry. Besides explicating the practice of washing before kiddush, this chapter hints at what may have caused the change.*

ESH TAMID, SIMAN 271

Rema writes succinctly regarding the laws of kiddush that it is desirable *l'khatḥilah* to follow "the widespread custom" and wash before kiddush. The *Mishnah Berurah* brings[2] the *Eliyah Rabbah* to explain Rema's reasoning: If we don't have wine, we recite kiddush on challah; and in that case, we have no choice but to wash before kiddush. Therefore it is desirable always to wash before kiddush, in order to maintain consistency in religious practice.

In our opinion, this explanation, of maintaining consistency in religious practice, is not sufficient to explain Rema's ruling, for it is unusual to make kiddush

1. Translated and adapted by the author's mother, from *Esh Tamid: Hilkhot Shabbat; Ḥidushim U'Be'urei Dinim al Seder Shulḥan Arukh U'Mishnah Berurah* (Jerusalem, 2015), 75–78. Any errors are the translator's.
2. *Mishnah Berurah* 271:61, based on the first reason given by *Eliyah Rabbah,* 271:27.

on bread. Additionally, it does not explain what the *Mishnah Berurah* writes[3] in the name of *Magen Avraham*, that members of the household who do not recite kiddush may wash before kiddush since, according to all opinions, there is no *hefsek* on their part between washing and eating. This implies that such a practice is desirable *l'khatḥilah*, and not merely because of the chance situation that one may, at some point, need to recite kiddush over bread.

Indeed, Tosafot[4] and Rosh[5] explain otherwise, that the reason for washing before kiddush is that kiddush must take place where the meal is eaten, *bimekom se'udah*. Their explanation is cited by *Olat Shabbat* and *Tosafot Shabbat* and other *poskim*. Moreover, Rema, following Maharil's position, writes[6] that one must eat immediately in the place where kiddush has been recited; and if there was an interruption, the person who recited kiddush did not fulfill the mitzvah even *bedi'avad*, post-factum. All the more so, then, if he planned the interruption between kiddush and the meal in advance! *Magen Avraham* writes[7] that there should not be even a momentary interruption; and *Bi'ur Halakhah*[8] brings many *Aḥaronim* who explain that this holds true even *bedi'avad*. Although many *Aḥaronim* disagree, and *Mishnah Berurah* himself states that, *bedi'avad*, we need not be stringent here, certainly *l'khatḥilah* we should follow the opinion not to make even a brief interruption. In his *Mishnah Berurah*,[9] he writes that *l'khatḥilah* one should take great care not to have even a short break.

Therefore, in keeping with all of the above, it is certainly preferable to wash before kiddush and avoid leaving the place of the meal following kiddush for another room, but rather begin the meal immediately after kiddush. And although washing itself is not an interruption – since it is for the purpose of the meal – nevertheless, washing following kiddush often results in a *hefsek*. While waiting for family members to wash, and especially when there are guests, people are easily diverted, or speak regarding other matters, and lose concentration on the kiddush. *Bigdei Yesha* cautions against this, saying that one should not "go outside between kiddush and washing," and relates that he himself "saw many times that this happens, and the kiddush is thus rendered not *bimekom se'udah*." Although *bedi'avad*, we can deem the mitzvah to have been fulfilled, certainly

3. 271:58.
4. Tosafot, Pesaḥim 106b, s.v. *mekadesh*.
5. Rosh, Pesaḥim 10:16.
6. *Oraḥ Ḥayim* 273:3.
7. Ibid., 5, based on Maharil's opinion which was cited above.
8. 273:3.
9. Ibid., 12.

l'khatḥilah it is preferable because of all the above to wash before kiddush, in accordance with Rema.

WHAT CONSTITUTES A *HEFSEK?*

Tur citing Tosafot, and Rosh, Ritba, Rabbenu Yeruḥam, and especially Ran and Mordekhai,[10] all maintain that bringing a small table – as was the custom in the days of the Talmud, that those partaking of a meal reclined on couches, with portions served on small "end tables" – does not represent an interruption between kiddush and the meal. However, bringing a large table would constitute a *hefsek*; and even regarding small tables, we can assume that those were brought by members of the family, while the *ba'al habayit* who recited kiddush remained in his place. *Levushei Serad,*[11] following *Magen Avraham,* writes that filling the wine cup with warmed water[12] is an interruption. Similarly, anything which is not needed for kiddush and for the challah – even that which is comparable to bringing a small table – would constitute an interruption.

BIMEKOM SE'UDAH

Rema's ruling to wash before kiddush is consistent with his opinion that it is preferable to sit during kiddush, and the *Mishnah Berurah*[13] cites *Levushei Serad* in the name of *Kolbo*[14] that the reason is so that kiddush will be more precisely *bimekom se'udah.* Likewise, *Levush* writes: "So that it will be apparent that we sat down for the meal." According to this, kiddush must be strictly continuous with the meal, and there should not be an interruption by rising (and certainly not for blessing children and the like); for if this were not the case, why would there be a need to recite the kiddush while seated, if it is followed by leaving the table?

Bet Yosef justifies his position of washing hands following kiddush by explaining that contrary to *Kolbo*'s opinion, standing at the table is considered *bimekom se'udah.* He brings proof from Rambam,[15] that on the first night of Sukkot, kiddush is recited while standing – but this is puzzling, for then we stand of

10. Tosafot, Pesaḥim 100b, s.v. *she'ein*; Rosh, ibid. 10:3; Ritva, ibid; Rabbenu Yeruḥam, *netiv* 12, part 1; Ran, Shabbat 44b, s.v. *ner*; Mordekhai, Pesaḥim, *siman* 611.
11. 271:12.
12. Ed. note: Magen Avraham writes that this is because of the need to measure carefully the quantity of warmed water needed to dilute the wine, as was their custom; and *Levushei Serad* comments that kiddush is considered *l'tzorekh se'udah* and not a *hefsek* since we cannot eat without kiddush.
13. *Mishnah Berurah* 271:46.
14. *Siman* 31. This is found likewise in *Orḥot Ḥayim, Hilkhot Havdalah,* ch. 27.
15. *Hilkhot Sukkah* 6:12.

necessity.[16] However, afterward, *Bet Yosef* again brings *Kolbo*: "If others drink while he still sits in his place [he needn't repeat the kiddush], but... if he rises from his seat, he must recite the kiddush again." This phrasing, taken from the Ge'onim, as quoted by R. Isaac Guiat,[17] and *Sefer Ha'Itim*[18] and other *Rishonim*, demonstrates that it is necessary to sit during kiddush in order for the kiddush to be considered *bimekom se'udah*.[19] This seems to me to be compelling proof. *Kolbo*, following this opinion, holds that we must sit during kiddush in order for it to be considered *bimekom se'udah*, but the *Bet Yosef* in the beginning of his gloss refutes this; however, at the end of this gloss, he brings this opinion without commenting otherwise, and this requires substantial additional study.

IS KIDDUSH A *HEFSEK*?

Regarding the crux of the matter, those who hold that washing must follow kiddush in order that there not be an interruption between washing and eating – should consider: Why should the concern about a *hefsek* between washing and eating carry greater weight than the concern for a *hefsek* between kiddush and the *se'udah*? The *Tur*, cited by the *Mishnah Berurah*,[20] writes that the cup of kiddush wine is part of the meal and therefore is included in *birkat hamazon* said for the bread. If so, kiddush does not constitute an interruption between washing and *hamotzi*. Parenthetically, we might wish to argue otherwise from the *Shulḥan Arukh*'s stating[21] that if a person was seated at a meal on Friday afternoon and the time for kiddush arrived, following the kiddush he must again recite *hamotzi*. Although the *Mishnah Berurah* explains[22] that this is the rule because the kiddush was an interruption – it is not the kiddush per se that constituted the interruption, but rather that once Shabbat began, it became forbidden to continue the meal without kiddush, and the meal was thus interrupted by the arrival of Shabbat and the prohibition to eat before kiddush. Moreover, at the outset of the meal, there was no intention to recite kiddush midway through the meal, and the meal was indeed interrupted.[23] On the contrary, this *din* proves that kiddush does not constitute an interruption. This is certainly the case, as *Taz* explains, according

16. Ed. note: To avoid sitting in the sukkah before saying the blessing "*leishev basukkah*" for the first time.
17. *Hilkhot Kiddush*, p. 11.
18. P. 142.
19. Their reservations apply to another matter, and not to the matter of kiddush *bimekom se'udah*.
20. *Tur, Oraḥ Ḥayim* 272; *Mishnah Berurah* 272:37.
21. *Oraḥ Ḥayim* 271:4.
22. *Mishnah Berurah* 271:17, following the *Aḥaronim*.
23. See *Mishnah Berurah*, beginning of 272:21.

to the *yesh omrim* in the *Shulḥan Arukh,*[24] that even if the kiddush was recited on wine, a second *hamotzi* is not made following kiddush. But even according to the first opinion in the *Shulḥan Arukh* there, that in the event that the kiddush was recited on challah, we would not recite a second *hamotzi* following kiddush. The *Aḥaronim* explain that this is because when wine is unavailable and therefore the person interrupting his meal would recite kiddush over bread, *hamotzi* is said in lieu of *borei pri hagafen* before the *berakhah* of kiddush [ed. note: that is, following the verses of *vayekhulu,* and before the body of the kiddush itself]. This demonstrates that kiddush does not constitute an interruption before eating. If so, it is untenable that kiddush over wine, which permits us to eat, constitutes an interruption between washing the hands and *hamotzi,* as *Levush* wrote.[25] Indeed, even recitation of *havdalah* between washing and *hamotzi* does not constitute an interruption, even though it is entirely unrelated.[26] From all the above, it is clear that we need not be concerned that we are causing a *hefsek* by reciting kiddush following washing the hands.

BET YOSEF AND REMA ON RULING OF ROSH AND *HAGAHOT MAIMONIYOT*

The *Bet Yosef* argues that even Rosh and *Hagahot Maimoniyot* did not require us to wash before kiddush regularly. This is a difficult reading of their words, and it is contested by Rema in his *Darkhei Moshe;*[27] and *Ma'amar Mordekhai*[28] wrote explicitly that *Bet Yosef*'s reading of Rosh is forced. Also, regarding that which *Bet Yosef* wrote, to prove from the responsum of Rashba[29] "that although he wrote that today it is customary to wash the hands before kiddush, and wrote that none refrain from doing so [other than on Pesaḥ night] – that implies that they did not do so consistently, but rather occasionally wash their hands and afterward recite the kiddush" – not only is this not the obvious interpretation, especially in light of the comment of *Rishonim* that specifically on Pesaḥ night, we need to refrain from that practice.[30] Indeed, Rashba wrote explicitly: "In these countries, it is the

24. 271:4.
25. 271:5.
26. See *Magen Avraham* 174:6, and *Mishnah Berurah* 174:11 and 14.
27. Rema's glosses on the *Tur*. See the long version (printed at the back of the *Tur* in most editions, 271:4).
28. 271:16.
29. Part 1, responsum 752.
30. See *Ma'amar Mordekhai,* 271:15 who expresses surprise at *Bet Yosef*'s words, for the straightforward understanding of Rashba is precisely the reverse; and today, we have [in print] the words of a disciple of Rashba as well as Maharam Ḥalawah in his rulings, Pesaḥim 106b, proving this beyond doubt.

custom to wash before kiddush."[31] This proves that he was referring to consistent behavior, and the fact that the *Bet Yosef* does not mention this is truly puzzling.

BOLSTERING THE CUSTOM OF ASHKENAZ

I should add that it is not my intention to oppose the custom of washing following kiddush. The ruling of the *Bet Yosef* is based on Rambam[32] and is in accordance with *Shibolei HaLeket* in the name of R. Isaiah d'Trani, Ra'avan, Roke'aḥ, *Sefer Ha'Itur*, and *Sefer Ha'Itim*;[33] and such was the custom of Maharam Rothenburg;[34] and see also the Vilna Ga'on who upheld the view of the *Shulḥan Arukh*, and others. Rather, my aim is to bolster the foundation of the custom of Ashkenaz as Rema ruled, following Rabbenu Tam, Rosh, and Mordekhai[35] as well as *Hagahot Maimoniyot*, Raviyah, *Semag* and Rashba;[36] and see also *Machzor Vitri*[37] and *Ohel Mo'ed*.[38] Indeed, this was the universal custom in Ashkenaz, except for Maharam Rothenburg – as described in *Minhagei Maharil*, *Minhagei De'vei Maharam*, Mahari Tirna, and *Agur*.[39] *Darkhei Moshe* wrote that he never saw anyone do otherwise; and likewise *Baḥ* wrote that "such is the universal custom" (read carefully so as not to err!), and *Levush* wrote that such is the widespread custom, which one may not change. See also *Magen Avraham*, who mentions in passing "and as is our custom that we wash hands before kiddush."[40] Such was the custom until the days of *Shulḥan Arukh HaRav*, as is mentioned in 271:23; and only afterward did this change.[41] This continues to be the practice in our family, following the custom of our forebear the Ga'on R. Yosef Eliyahu Henkin – but in our time this halakhah has almost been forgotten, to the extent that those who see it assume that this is a special custom, and they don't know that such is the ruling of Rema, in principle and in practice.

---

31. *Responsa Rashba*, part 4, end of *siman* 279.
32. *Hilkhot Shabbat* 29:6.
33. *Shibolei HaLeket, Inyan Shabbat, siman* 69; Ra'avan, Berakhot, *siman* 188; *Sefer Rokeaḥ, siman* 52; *Sefer Ha'Itur, Hilkhot Matza V'Maror*; and *Sefer Ha'Itim, siman* 150.
34. Cited in *Tashbatz, siman* 15.
35. Pesaḥim, ch. 10.
36. *Hagahot Maimoniyot, Hilkhot Shabbat* 29:6; Raviyah, Pesaḥim, *siman* 517, see his reasoning; *Semag, Mitzvat Aseh* 29; and Rashba, cited above.
37. *Hilkhot Pesaḥ, siman* 56, in contrast with *siman* 150.
38. *Hilkhot Kiddush V'Havdalah, derekh* 1, *netiv* 4.
39. *Minhagei Maharil* (*Seder HaHagadah, siman* 8) and *Minhagei De'vei Maharam* (*Seder Kabbalat Shabbat*), and Mahari Tirna (*Minhag Shel Shabbat*, 33), and *Agur* (*siman* 378).
40. 249:6.
41. *Arukh HaShulḥan* in 271:33 already wrote that for several generations, we do not know of this custom, and he himself wrote to follow the *Shulḥan Arukh*.

(*Arukh HaShulḥan*'s mention of Baḥ, *Taz,* and *Magen Avraham* as differing with Rema is puzzling; for Baḥ wrote explicitly that the custom should not be changed, only that since *Bet Yosef*'s reading of R. Bruna's position in the Gemara seems more precise, it is best to compromise: that the one making kiddush should wash following kiddush, while other family members should wash before kiddush. This suggestion was endorsed by the *Magen Avraham* and *Ateret Zekenim,* but in practice we do not find that this was practiced. *Maḥtzit HaShekel* and *Tosafot Shabbat* suggest that as a result of this opinion, it became the custom for all members of the family to wash following kiddush, because of the sense that it is proper for all present to recite kiddush quietly, word for word, with the one reciting kiddush. However, since today we do not practice this, we ought to revert to the original practice, *v'dok*![42] And *Taz* wrote only that one who fears[43] and wishes to wash following kiddush should not be stopped, as he is acting correctly. Therefore, none ruled to abolish the custom, even though their basic ruling is otherwise.[44])

BLESSING THE CHILDREN

In any event, I am surprised by those who bless their children following kiddush and before the meal. How can they justify this, after the *Mishnah Berurah* ruled that one does not fulfill the mitzvah even *bedi'avad* with an interruption that is not for the purpose of the meal? Also, as we cited above, in his opinion a delay and a loss of focus on connecting the kiddush with the meal, constitute a *hefsek*.[45] Certainly one should take this into account, and not bless the children between kiddush and the meal, but rather before kiddush, as this blessing is not part of the meal.

However, some justification (*limud zekhut*) for their practice comes from another quarter. For the *Arukh HaShulḥan* was more lenient regarding the *din* of *hefsek,* and wrote that when, for instance, people change clothing for the meal following kiddush, it is not considered a *hefsek,*[46] and according to him, blessing the children following kiddush is easier to justify. When the *Arukh HaShulḥan* wrote there, "I saw someone who did not explain thus, and it is not clear to me," perhaps he was referring to the *Mishnah Berurah*.

42. Ed. note: *V'dok*: *v'dakdek u'metza kushta,* "examine closely and you will find this is true."
43. Ed note: One who fears deviating from the plain meaning of the words of R. Bruna in Pesaḥim 106b, that he who washes should not recite kiddush.
44. See further *Shulḥan Arukh HaRav,* 271:23 and *Pri Megadim* citing the *Eliyah Rabbah*.
45. 273:14.
46. 273:4 According to the view of *Eshel Avraham* there, even napping is not considered an interruption between kiddush and the meal, similar to the law of napping during the meal.

Part II

Studies in Rabbinic History

Chapter 7

Tu b'Av – The Dances and the Festival[1]

THE PARADOX OF THE FESTIVAL AND THE STANDARD EXPLANATION

Tractate Ta'anit of the Talmud concludes with a well-known *mishnah* on customs practiced on two days of the year:

> Rabban Shimon b. Gamliel said: No days were as festive for Israel as the fifteenth of Av and Yom Kippur, when the maidens of Jerusalem would go out in borrowed white garments, so as not to shame whoever did not have.... The maidens of Jerusalem would go out and dance in the vineyards. What did they say? "Young man, lift up your eyes and see what you choose for yourself: Look not at beauty, look at family. 'Grace is a lie and beauty is fleeting, a woman who fears God, she is to be praised' [...] and thus it says: Go out, daughters of Zion, and see King Solomon."[2]

In recent years, questions have been raised about these proceedings:

The Question of Propriety. People wonder, how could an event of this sort have taken place? Girls dancing in the vineyards and boys gazing at them – wasn't this a

1. Translated by Ilana Elzufon and condensed somewhat for this volume. The original article appeared in *Alonei Mamre* 122 (2009).
2. Ta'anit 4:8.

blatant breach of modesty and the values toward which we educate? All this, when the Temple stood, and Rabban Shimon b. Gamliel himself praised the custom. Likewise, the practice itself is surprising: to select a bride based upon dance? The entire story is exceedingly strange.

The Conflict Between the Dance Festival and Yom Kippur. An event of this sort took place on Yom Kippur?! The holiest day of the year, devoted to prayer, fasting, and repentance, whose apex was the Temple service – on this day they would hold a mass matchmaking "happening" in the vineyards? Even if the proceedings conformed to rigorous standards of modesty, holding such an event on a day meant for prayer and supplication is odd and negates the essence of Yom Kippur as we know it today. Imagine the uproar that would ensue if someone, in the spirit of "renew our days as of old," were to institute such a custom today!

These questions – combined with the assumption that no convincing response to them is to be found – provide support for those who challenge halakhah as it is determined and practiced today, especially regarding relations between the sexes and the laws of modesty. This chapter will attempt to explain Tu b'Av as it appears in the sources, with the goal of addressing these difficulties.

THE STANDARD EXPLANATION: GREATER HOLINESS

The standard answer asserts that during the period of the Second Temple, the spiritual and ethical level of the nation was so elevated that there was no breach of modesty, no evil inclination, but in fact the reverse: Couples sought to establish a home in Israel in purity and with fear of Heaven. This explanation first appears in Ritva, who wrote that the white garments teach us "that the *yetzer hara* was removed from them and they were free of sin; and this is why the maidens of Israel would say: 'Young man, lift up your eyes and see…' and they were not concerned about temptation."[3] His words were cited with variations in *Yalkut Me'am Lo'ez*: "The *Tanna* demonstrates how pure and free of the *yetzer hara* they were… and on the august and holy day they would go out to dance in the vineyards in order to establish families in Israel."[4]

In this spirit, we can further explain that the Mishnah's phrase "look at family" does not refer to the girl's lineage and her parents' status, as is typically understood, but rather, the family that the young man and young woman are about to establish. Likewise "look not at beauty," which is not vital for establishing a

3. Bava Batra 121a.
4. On Shoftim 21.

home in Israel, since "grace is a lie and beauty fleeting" but rather "at family,: i.e., examine the traits beneficial for home and family. These are, of course, the girl's personal qualities, her character, and her fear of God; for "a woman who fears God, she is to be praised."[5] This also explains the white garments, which symbolize the holiness and purity of Yom Kippur, as *Yalkut Me'am Lo'ez* continues: "And this is why it was said that they wore white garments, as a hint to what is written, 'at all times let your clothing be white'[6] ... to imply that we are like angels" – innocent of sin and the evil inclination. According to this explanation, it is clear that today, with the "decline of the generations," we are not able to hold an event of this sort with holiness and purity as in years past.[7]

DIFFICULTIES WITH THIS EXPLANATION

In practice, it is difficult to accept this explanation. First, because it is unclear how dances led to the choice of a righteous marriage partner. Did the boy indeed see her qualities and personality this way or recognize her fear of Heaven?

Moreover, it is difficult to accept the claim that the spiritual and moral level of the Jewish people was so elevated at that time that such things only occurred with holiness and purity, with no taint of sin. The words of the Sages point actually to the reverse:

On the night of Yom Kippur, "the notables of Jerusalem would not sleep the entire night, in order that the *kohen gadol* would hear the voices and not doze off. It is taught, Abba Shaul says: Even outside of Jerusalem they would do likewise, as a remembrance of the Temple – but they would sin."[8] Rashi comments there: "They would sin – men and women would enjoy themselves together, and come to sin." There is no room to claim that this refers only to a handful of sinners while the rest of the people behaved otherwise, for the Talmud describes this as a norm in Nehardea – a city of Torah and Torah scholars with numerous yeshivot and a large Jewish population. Furthermore, the Talmud relates that they had good intentions – to perform a mitzvah in remembrance of the Temple – but stumbled because "sin crouches at the door,"[9] and as Rashi explains: "The *yetzer hara* caused them to sin involuntarily" – despite their desire to perform a mitzvah.

---

5. Mishlei 31:30.
6. Kohelet 9:8.
7. For a comprehensive explanation of this approach, see R. Eliyahu Kitov, *The Book of Our Heritage* (Feldheim, 1994), "The Fifteenth of Av," sections "Tu b'Av like Yom Kippur" and "Restrictions of Holiness and Modesty."
8. Yoma 19b.
9. Bereshit 4:7. See Yoma 20a.

Me'iri explains that "they came to sin because of their sexual laxity."[10] He seems to mean that they were guilty of sexual misconduct, behaved without restraint, scorned matters of modesty, and therefore sinned. But his words can also mean not that they were sexually lax, but that in this one case, they breached the bounds of modesty by holding a mixed event and ended up sinning. In a similar vein, Maharsha explains that they sinned because they let their guard down, assuming they were immune to sin since they were engaged in a mitzvah. "By not sleeping in their homes at night and socializing together, and thinking they were performing a mitzvah in memory of the Temple – this brought them to sin."[11] Meaning, they came to sin precisely with mitzvah-intent, and through their confidence that the mitzvah shielded them from sin,[12] and certainly not with deliberate intention. Either way, the conclusion is the same: even in their times, there was no guarantor against sexual misconduct,[13] and people were not free of the *yetzer hara* even when intending to perform a mitzvah.

We read in Tractate Pesaḥim of a similar phenomenon, again specifically on Yom Kippur: "Where they were accustomed to light a lamp on Yom Kippur night – they should light, and where they were accustomed not to light – they should not light."[14] Rashi explains there: "Those who were accustomed to light and those who were accustomed not to light – both had the same intention: to avoid marital relations." Meaning, there were places where they worried lest they sin on the night of Yom Kippur, when the Torah forbids marital relations – and therefore it was necessary to employ various methods in order to distance themselves from temptation. As in the previous case, here too the Mishnah speaks of Yom Kippur, a day when there would seem to be no need for great concern about violating a serious Torah prohibition. Yet such concerns existed, to the point where it was necessary to take practical steps in order not to falter.

10. Me'iri, *Bet HaBeḥira*, Yoma 19b.
11. *Ḥidushei Aggadot*, Yoma 20a.
12. It is reasonable to explain the words of the Maharsha in this fashion, for since the intent of the people of Nehardea was for a mitzvah, we can ask: How, in truth, did they end up going from a mitzvah to a sin? The answer is that they assumed that on Yom Kippur the *yetzer hara* has no power, or is weakened, as is brought in the continuation of the Gemara (Yoma 20a), that Satan is not permitted to prosecute on Yom Kippur, and certainly when they are engaged in a mitzvah, they need not be concerned about sin. Thanks to this reasoning, they were lax and breached the boundaries of modesty, and in the end came to sin.
13. Tosefta Ketubot 1:9, Ketubot 13b. In truth, this is completely obvious, to the point where one could question the basic reasoning of Ritva and *Yalkut Me'am Lo'ez*, were it not for the single source of the words of R. Yoḥanan cited below.
14. Pesaḥim 53b (Mishnah).

Similarly, the Mishnah recounts that at the *simḥat bet hasho'eva* festivity, the Sanhedrin enacted "an important measure"[15] whose nature is specified in the Gemara: "R. Elazar said ... They decreed that the women sit above and the men below... They expounded ... : If in the future, when they will be occupied with eulogies and the *yetzer hara* will not rule over them – [nevertheless] the Torah stipulated that men and women should be separate – now, when they are occupied with rejoicing and the *yetzer hara* rules over them, how much more so!"[16]

During a mass celebration, there can be laxity and enticements. Therefore, the Sanhedrin had to enact regulations separating men and women to prevent frivolity and, from there, sin. Clearly, there was a concern about the *yetzer hara*, even within the Temple itself, and even when rejoicing for mitzvah purposes. Rambam ruled similarly, based on the teaching of *Ḥazal*: "Bet Din are obliged to station lookouts during festivals, to patrol the gardens and orchards and river banks, so that men and women not congregate there to eat and drink, and come to sin. They should caution the public against this, so that men and women not celebrate together in homes, and not be drawn to wine, lest they come to sin."[17]

A SOURCE FOR THE STANDARD EXPLANATION, AND ITS REFUTATION

There is one source in the Gemara implying that during the Second Temple period great holiness and piety generally prevailed, obviating the need for concern about temptation: "R. Yoḥanan said, I remember when a boy and girl of sixteen or seventeen would go for a stroll together in the market and they did not sin."[18] *Yalkut Me'am Lo'ez* brings these words to prove his point regarding the great piety that protected the revelers in the vineyards, for the words of R. Yoḥanan demonstrate that at that time, people were immune to

15. Sukkah 5:2.
16. Sukkah 51b.
17. *Hilkhot Shevitat Yom Tov* 20:20. Parenthetically, the explanation of *Yalkut Me'am Lo'ez*, that we learn from the *mishnah* in Ta'anit of the extent to which people of that period were free of temptation, is contradicted by his own words. For he goes on to write that the custom of dances and matchmaking on that day came about so that people should be married and not sin: "so that men and women should not remain without a partner and possibly reach the point of wantonness" – that is to say, they were indeed concerned about temptation. This is difficult to reconcile with his own words, and requires further study.
18. Bava Batra 91b.

temptation and sin. These words appear to describe a state of affairs contrary to the sources we have cited until now.[19]

A close reading of the words of R. Yoḥanan provides a possible resolution: R. Yoḥanan said: "I remember when...," meaning, "I remember that there [once] was," implying that "today," i.e., at the time these words were said, it was no longer so. When did the state of affairs that he recounts take place? When was there no concern for sin? This cannot have been in the time of R. Yoḥanan, the first generation of *Amora'im,* because the story in Nehardea – wherein people did reach the point of sin – took place during the period of the *Tana'im,* as the one who relates it is Abba Shaul, who lived at the same time as R. Akiva. Therefore, it seems reasonable that the anecdote took place long before the days of R. Yoḥanan, and even before the time of Abba Shaul. If so, what period is R. Yoḥanan speaking of? Maharsha responds to this question:

> When he said, "I remember when a boy and girl... and they did not sin," he meant to say that the generations had declined day by day since the time of the Destruction.[20]

R. Yoḥanan, however, spoke about the situation at the time when the Temple stood, when it is told that people did not sin in such circumstances,[21] due to the greatness of that generation and the protective 'umbrella' of the Temple. After the destruction, the protection and merit of the Temple were lost and the

19. It would be difficult to say that the difference stems from the fact that *metayelin,* strolling, refers to a different type of activity, which might be less likely to lead to sin. For the meaning of "stroll" is "enjoying themselves" (*mesaḥakim,* Rashbam there), and this is precisely the term used about the event in Nehardea. If so, how is it that in Nehardea they reached the point of sin, while here they did not sin?
20. Bava Batra 91b.
21. "In such a situation" – of boys and girls strolling in the marketplace, as opposed to a mass celebration such as the *simḥat bet hasho'eva* or the Festival of Dances. In such cases the atmosphere and circumstances were different, and therefore in such a setting, even in the days of the Temple, there was concern, as we will explain below.
It should also be noted regarding the textual variant in Tractate *Kalla Rabbati* (2:9), where the word "naked" is added, i.e., that the boy and girl were apparently walking in the market unclothed. This is of course inconceivable. According to this textual variant it appears that R. Yoḥanan is not talking about an actual case that happened, but is using an allegorical description to illustrate the greatness of the people of the Second Temple Period, by saying that even had they walked this way they would not have sinned – but he did not mean that they actually did this, for in practice, even in their time, they were concerned about temptation, as we have said. Therefore, specifically according to this textual variant, it is clear how these words can be reconciled with the principle "there is no guarantor for sexual immorality."

generations declined, and therefore this situation no longer prevailed at the time of R. Yoḥanan. However, Maharsha's words are somewhat unsatisfactory, since the expression "I remember" indicates that R. Yoḥanan recounted something he witnessed with his own eyes. However, in truth, even if R. Yoḥanan spoke of what he himself saw when he was young, he referred only to an innocent situation in a city square, which is not similar to that mixed gathering in Nehardea or to the mass rejoicing in the Temple, and certainly not to a situation such as the Festival of Dances. Either way, R. Yoḥanan clearly did not mean to claim that during that time there was no need for precautions against temptation, for even in the days of the Temple, with its protection and the merit of the generation, the *yetzer hara* still ruled, as the Gemara in Sukkah says: "The *yetzer hara* ruled over them."[22]

ANOTHER PROOF OF GREATER HOLINESS, AND ITS REFUTATION

It would seem that our claim – that during this period there was no exceptional piety protecting against temptation – can be challenged from another direction: there are several places in the Talmud that tell of Sages of Israel who were lenient in certain laws of modesty:

R. Gidel would sit at the entrance to the mikveh when women came out following immersion, for reasons brought in the Talmud. When the Sages questioned whether he did not fear the *yetzer hara*, he replied that for him women were like white geese, i.e., they had no effect upon his desires. R. Yoḥanan acted similarly.[23]

R. Aḥa carried a bride on his shoulders at her wedding, and when they asked him a similar question, he replied that carrying the woman was for him like carrying a wooden beam.[24] Similarly, it is told of Ulla, that he would kiss his sister (as a greeting, similar to a handshake) over her heart: "on her bosom."[25]

---

22. It is possible that the Festival of Dances continued to take place in some fashion after the destruction of the Second Temple, as indicated by the Talmud at the end of Ta'anit, which includes the burial of the remains of those killed at Betar among the reasons for the celebration – an event that took place long after the destruction of the Temple, at the end of the Bar Kokhba rebellion, which was during the time of Abba Shaul. Even so, it is reasonable to assume that the festival took place in a limited fashion, and not in its original full format as during the time of the Temple (see *Mishnah Berurah* 131:30), and this is the reason why the *mishnah* in Ta'anit mixes past and present tense.
23. Berakhot 20a.
24. Ketubot 17a.
25. Avodah Zarah 17a.

These *Amora'im* acted as they did because they were not greatly concerned about temptation, and therefore permitted themselves to be lenient with certain laws of modesty. The obvious conclusion, it seems, is that in those days there was apparently less concern for the *yetzer hara*. How does this square with the sources we cited above?

There are several answers to this. The simplest is that these anecdotes concern only a handful of great rabbis, who were so holy that they were not concerned about temptation – and certainly do not constitute a precedent for the community at large, since the Talmud itself cites these cases as rare and exceptional. Another answer is that most of the Sages did not approve of these practices, for the Talmud relates that they were puzzled by these actions. Regarding Ulla, it is even said that his actions contradicted his own words, since he said elsewhere that even mere closeness is forbidden – and how much more so an act of this sort. Similarly, we can cite the Talmud at the end of Kiddushin, where it is related that some of the greatest *Tanna'im* – such as R. Akiva, R. Tarfon, R. Meir, and more – nearly transgressed sexual prohibitions, or confessed that, despite their greatness, even for them there is no guarantor against sexual misconduct[26] – "watch me carefully on account of my daughter-in-law."[27] We can infer that even then, a person's greatness was no guarantee of immunity from temptation, and even the great rabbis were concerned about this, with the exception of a few individuals who attained an exceptional level of piety. All the more so, one cannot say that the entire generation was on such a level that there was no need for concern about temptation.

In light of the above, it is clearly impossible to accept the standard explanation of exceptional piety protecting those celebrating in the vineyards from thoughts of sin. To address the question of how the Jewish people could have celebrated this festival and the questions we posed above, we will need to get to the roots of the Festival of the Dances.

THE ROOTS OF THE FESTIVAL AND THE CELEBRATION

At first glance, it would seem that the joy of the fifteenth of Av and of Yom Kippur stemmed from the dances and the matches in the vineyards. However, the Talmud

26. Not necessarily "despite," for the Sages taught that whoever is greater than his fellow – his inclination [to sin] is greater (Sukkah 52a). See Ya'avetz (Kiddushin 81b) who asked regarding R. Meir's statement "watch me carefully on account of my daughter," for it is said that a person need not be concerned about relatives, and answered that whoever is greater than his fellow, his [evil] inclination is greater!

27. Kiddushin 81a–b.

in Ta'anit[28] shows that this is not the case, but rather that there were other, unrelated reasons for the celebration:

> No days were as festive for Israel… This is reasonable regarding Yom Kippur, wherein there is forgiveness and atonement, and which is the day on which the second tablets were given. But what is the fifteenth of Av?
>
> R. Yehudah said in the name of Shmuel: The day on which the tribes were permitted to intermarry with each other…
>
> R. Yosef said in the name of R. Naḥman: The day on which the tribe of Binyamin was permitted to marry into the community…
>
> Rava bar bar Ḥanna said in the name of R. Yoḥanan: The day that the deaths in the desert ceased…
>
> Ulla said: The day on which Hoshea son of Elah abolished the guards that Yerovam son of Nevat had stationed on the roads to prevent Israel from going up [to Jerusalem] for the pilgrimage festivals…
>
> R. Matana said: The day on which those killed at Betar were permitted to be buried…
>
> Rava and R. Yosef both said: The day that they stopped cutting trees for the woodpile [on the altar]…

If so, these were festive days for Israel not because of the celebration in the vineyards, but the reverse: because these were *already* days of great rejoicing for Israel, the daughters of Israel joined in the celebration with their dances. The Mishnah describes the dances in order to portray the rejoicing on these days, rejoicing that was the *result* of their being festive days, and not a reason for their being so.[29]

---

28. 30b.
29. See Ḥida's words on the matter (*Ḥayim Sha'al* 51). We will also point out the words of Rashbam (Bava Batra 121b), who emphasizes that the *Amora'im* who cited different reasons for the festival are not disputing with each other. Each emphasized one reason more than the others, based on what he received from his teacher (or as he understood the festival's meaning). The fact that the festival preceded the dances is supported by the language of the Mishnah, where Rabban Gamliel begins in the past tense: "There **were** no festive days in Israel…" and concludes in present tense: "and the daughters of Jerusalem **go out and dance** in the vineyards." These

Most of the reasons cited by the *Amora'im* for the joy of the festival are plausible, save the last: Why should "the day that they stopped chopping wood for the woodpile [of the altar]" be reason for rejoicing? The commentators give two reasons for this – fulfilling the mitzvah on the one hand, and freeing up time for Torah study on the other:

1. That day when they stopped, they rejoiced, because on that day they completed a great mitzvah.[30]
2. When they chopped wood for the woodpile on the altar, they were idle from Torah study; but on that day they stopped, and made it a festive day, because from here on they were engaged with Torah.[31]

In this context, we should note that as opposed to the **five** events that occurred on Tisha b'Av, the Sages cited **six** events that took place on Tu b'Av – which falls **six** days after Tisha b'Av – thus illustrating that the joy of the Jewish people is greater than the sorrow. The Talmud Yerushalmi relates regarding the first fortuitous event on Tu b'Av, the day on which the deaths in the desert ceased:

> R. Levi said: Every Tisha b'Av eve, Moshe would send out a herald to proclaim throughout the camp: Go out and dig. And they would go out and dig graves for themselves and sleep in them; and in the morning they would arise and find themselves missing fifteen thousand and more. In the last year, they did so and arose and found themselves complete. They said: Perhaps we erred in calculating [the date]? And thus on the tenth, eleventh, twelfth, thirteenth, and fourteenth. Once they reached the fifteenth of Av and the moon was full, they said: It seems that God has annulled this harsh decree. They arose and celebrated.[32]

Why was the festival eventually celebrated in the vineyards? The commentators provide three principal answers:

---

days became festive due to past events, but the celebrations themselves also take place in the present.

30. Rashbam, Bava Batra 121b. *Nimukei Yosef* wrote likewise. See also *Megilat Ta'anit,* s.v. *b'ḥamisha asar b'Av.*
31. Rabbenu Gershom there. This interpretation seems supported by the continuation of the Gemara, which recounts that from that date onward an obligation to add Torah learning at night was in effect, just as Rashi explains in Ta'anit: "From the fifteenth of Av onward, one who adds nights to the days – occupying himself with Torah at night – adds life to his life. One who does not increase hours of Torah study at night, may his mother bury him – i.e., may he die before his time."
32. Yerushalmi Ta'anit 4:7.

1. Tu b'Av falls at the height of the grape harvest, making it natural to combine the joy of the festival with the agricultural celebration. "We cause merit to fall on a meritorious day."[33]
2. Tu b'Av is the last day of the year when a sapling that is planted belongs for matters of *orlah*-fruit to the outgoing year. On Rosh Hashanah, that sapling will be considered a year old, and thus one "saves" a full year of *orlah*.[34] Likewise it is the last day on which planting of trees is permitted before the sabbatical year; and thus, it is a milestone in the agricultural-religious calendar.
3. One of the reasons for the festival – permitting the tribe of Binyamin to marry into the community of Israel – actually took place in the vineyards, as is recounted in Shoftim chapter 21. As stated there, before that event, the Jewish people already held celebrations in vineyards – because of the two previous reasons.

In light of the words of the *Amora'im*, we may wonder why this festival and its customs were lost over the course of the generations. Aside from the obvious cause of Israel's exile from our land, R. Tzadok HaKohen of Lublin[35] wrote that none of the reasons cited in the Talmud justified a festival for all generations:

> The reasons for Tu b'Av mentioned in the Talmud were "local," for that generation alone.... If so, why should we today celebrate a festival on account of those events for all the Jewish people?

Writing in the late nineteenth century, R. Tzadok spoke of his times. But in truth, his words apply as well to the days of Rabban Shimon b. Gamliel, when the holiday was still celebrated to some extent. It is possible that R. Tzadok's reasoning applies principally to the straightforward "historical" reasons, which were not perceived as relevant to subsequent generations. However, the connection to matchmaking and marriage – the permission for the tribes to intermarry with each other and for the tribe of Binyamin to marry into the community – were likely seen as worthy of celebration not just in their time, for they impacted the continuity of the Jewish people. This is also almost certainly the reason that one of the central customs of the holiday is connected to matchmaking.[36]

---

33. Ta'anit 29a.
34. Rambam, *Hilkhot Ma'aser Sheni* 9:10.
35. Died 1900. In his book *Pri Tzaddik* – Devarim, "Fifteenth of Av" (following *Parashat Va'etḥanan*).
36. *Sha'agat Aryeh* in his book *Gevurot Ari* (Ta'anit 30b, and also see *Responsa Reshit Bikurim* p. 90) raises a difficulty, that after the division [of the Land of Israel], the tribes were permitted

THE MODESTY PROBLEM

The questions raised by the festivities were discussed already by the *Rishonim*. The author of *Kol Bo* asks how the Sages could have approved the dances and the matchmaking: "Heaven forbid, it would seem that the daughters of Israel were unprotected and available for the taking!" His answer: "This custom was for girls whose fathers couldn't afford to marry them off, and they might sit [unmarried] until their hair grew white if not for this custom."[37]

That is to say, according to *Kol Bo*, the practice was only a last resort. One who could marry off his daughter in a more respectable fashion certainly would not permit her to be part of the dances. However, Rabban Shimon b. Gamliel's language in the Mishnah is undeniably otherwise, and likewise the Talmud's description of the day's customs.

There emerges a distinctly favorable picture of the festivities from the Talmud and *Rishonim*. Aside from the joy associated with the historical events enumerated in the Talmud, the day was a sort of centralized matchmaking day[38] with numerous Jewish homes established then: "The maidens of Israel went out and danced in the vineyards… [and] whoever did not have a wife, would go there"[39] – with the objective of meeting someone, in a manner not foreign to ours today. Each of the sides described their good qualities: "Those among them [the women] who were beautiful would say…," and the young men would also describe their advantages, according to the commentary of *Korban Netanel* on the Rosh:[40] "And likewise he would say: 'Cast your eyes upon the young men who learn Torah'" – and thus they would meet each other. If indeed two young people appealed to each other, they would "inform their families after they returned, and reach agreements and be betrothed" according to the law of Moshe and Israel, in the words of Me'iri.[41]

---

to intermarry with each other; but this does not contradict the fact that the day on which this permission took effect became a day of celebration.

37. *Kol Bo* 62 (attributed to *Ra'a MiLunel*, author of *Orḥot Ḥayim*).
38. Which took place specifically on this date, on which two events connected to matchmaking and marriage took place: the tribes were permitted to intermarry, and the tribe of Binyamin was permitted to marry into the community (as explained by the author of the *Bnei Yisaskhar, "Betula Be'maḥol,"* part 2).
39. Ta'anit 31a.
40. Ta'anit 4:90.
41. Ta'anit ibid. We can deduce that all customs of the holiday conformed to halakhah from the decree that all the garments required immersion [in a mikveh]. Had the community not followed halakhah strictly during the festival, there would not have been place for *Ḥazal* to enact so detailed a decree. Rambam explains that "they were required to immerse all gar-

On the other hand, the dances in the vineyards appear in the sources as part of the day's festivity, and not as a "display" through which a young man would choose his life partner. Furthermore, a close reading seems to indicate that there was no direct connection between the custom of the dances and the custom of the matches, which was a separate part of the day's festivity! There are many proofs for this:

1. From the account at the end of the book of Shoftim,[42] in which we first hear of the custom of the dances, it is clear that the girls of Shilo were going out to dance in the vineyards with no connection to matches, and only in that instance did the men of Binyamin take advantage of the opportunity to seize women from among the celebrants in order to marry them.
2. In light of this, *Yalkut Me'am Lo'ez* (cited above) explains that seizing daughters of Israel from the dances was an emergency measure, so that a tribe of the Jewish people would not be cut off, and therefore after the kidnap, the elders commanded the men of the tribe to "go to the Land of Binyamin" – in order that "the daughters of Shilo would not halt the custom of the dances out of fear."
3. Some of the commentators went to the trouble of seeking a separate reason for the custom of the dances, as an expression of joy and thanksgiving to God – with no connection to matchmaking. Ran writes that the verse "go out and see"[43] that is brought in our *mishnah* "meaning that they go out and dance," and see "King Solomon" – that is, God – for this is a

---

ments, because they mingled together and no doubt among those many women, some were not ritually pure" (*Commentary on the Mishnah*, end Ta'anit), and Rashi wrote, "They require immersion: before they wear them, because not everyone knows whether her friend might be *niddah*" (Rashi Ta'anit 26b). If so, why did they require even folded garments stored in a box to be immersed (Ta'anit 31a)? Me'iri wrote that it was so as not to shame those whose garments required immersion. *Kol Bo* no. 62 wrote likewise, and the same is implied by Rashi; but their explanations do not apply to new garments: "Lest the owner of the garment wore it while *nidda*, but would be uncomfortable admitting this to the questioner; therefore they required all garments to be immersed, so that those who were *nidda* would not be shamed, or lest they be refused when they sought to borrow." However the Talmud Yerushalmi (above) explains that the Sages required immersion for all the garments – even those stored in a box – in order that, as a result of taking them out for immersion, they would not be tempted to "protect" the garments and be unwilling to lend them. But one can explain that the Yerushalmi's rationale was intended only to extend the decree to clothing stored in a box, but all agree that the reason for immersing clothing that was worn was for reasons of *niddah*.

42. 21:17–23.
43. Shir HaShirim 3:11.

"Festival of God."[44] Tosafot Yom Tov also comments thus,[45] that the one who said "go out and see" was none other than Rabban Gamliel himself, who called the daughters of Israel to go out and celebrate the festival of God with dances; while matchmaking was a separate part of the character of that day.

4. This is also implied by the girls' words, "Look not at beauty": Were there only a dance, is there something to gaze at other than beauty? And what is the meaning of "lift up your eyes and see what you choose?" If this refers to watching the dances, it would have been enough to say "see what you choose," while "lift up your eyes" would have been obvious; from this it also seems that the dances were unconnected to the matchmaking (for the meaning of the statement "lift up your eyes," see below).

If so, what is the meaning of the girls' words "lift up your eyes and see what you choose"? Maharsha explains that the intent was not the gazing at the dances, but rather the meeting between the couple, as the Sages said, "a man is forbidden to betroth a woman before he has seen her"[46] – for a person clearly needs to see and know whom he is meeting.[47] Therefore, it was necessary to say "lift up your eyes," so that he not refrain from looking at her out of modesty. The phrase "see what you choose for yourself" can be interpreted not just as "choose" (*livror*) but also as "clarify" (*l'varer*) – the young man needs to investigate and look into the young woman's qualities.

On the contrary, from the custom of the dances we can learn about the strict modesty of the festival. As said, the book of Shoftim relates that the girls of Shilo were accustomed to go out and dance in the vineyards every year, and the elders took advantage of one of these occasions and advised the men of Binyamin to hide in the vineyards in order to take wives from among the dancers. *Arukh HaShulḥan* asks why the elders didn't instruct the men to mingle and join with the dancers. He replies that this is certainly prohibited, and if the fathers of Shilo had seen the men of Binyamin preparing to mingle in the vineyards, they would not have

44. Shoftim 21:19.
45. Ta'anit 4:8.
46. Kiddushin 41a; see the words of Rabbenu Yehonatan there, that this does not refer to simply seeing but to the need to get to know her personality and qualities, her family, etc. (see also Ritva).
47. Maharsha in Ta'anit there, also the author of *Responsa Binyamin Ze'ev* (305), a contemporary of Maharsha, and similarly the words of Maharshal (*Yam Shel Shlomo*, Gittin 1:18).

allowed their daughters to participate.[48] Therefore, the men of Binyamin were forced to hide to succeed in acquiring wives.

This explanation solves the problem of immodesty in the dances, but an additional question remains: As we are speaking of a festival of joy for all Israel, why did only girls go out to dance in the vineyards, as the Mishnah recounts and as is described in the book of Shoftim? Maharsha explains[49] that the dances were held in the vineyards as that is where the tribe of Binyamin were permitted to marry into the community; and this was joyful especially for the daughters of Israel, for it was the women who were prohibited from marrying into the tribe of Binyamin – "And the men of Israel swore at Mitzpa saying: no man from among us will give his *daughter* to Binyamin for a wife."[50] The men of Israel could have taken for themselves wives from Binyamin, so in practice the prohibition fell on the women of Israel (who could not marry men from Binyamin) and not on the men. Therefore, when the tribe was permitted to marry into the community of Israel, it was the women primarily who rejoiced, for from that day on they could marry their heart's choice, even from the tribe of Binyamin.

However, Maharsha's explanation is bound to a particular time. Yet the dances took place even before the tribe of Binyamin were permitted to marry into the community, so it is difficult to explain the dances of the women in this fashion. However, if the dances were to celebrate the harvest, we can explain that the men were the ones who worked in the vineyards and harvested the vines, and following the completion of the grape harvest, the daughters of Israel took part in the celebration in their own special way.

THE FESTIVAL WAS NOT IN JERUSALEM

From the description in the Mishnah that "the maidens of Jerusalem would go out and dance in the vineyards," one gets the picture of numerous crowded vineyards, broad agricultural areas to which the young girls of Jerusalem went out in great

48. *Arukh HaShulḥan, Even Ha'ezer* 22:3. Similarly, the author of *Responsa Zikhron Yosef* wrote (339) – "The girls of Shilo went out: From the fact that it is not written "with the young men" or "boys," we infer that only the maidens danced together, and not with the young men." Maharshal writes likewise (*Yam Shel Shlomo*, Gittin 1:18), and the author of *Responsa Binyamin Ze'ev* deduces from the verse "the girls of Shilo went out to dance" that the girls went out alone, and men were not usually found there: "And what happened with the men of Binyamin, as it is written 'if the girls of Shilo go out to dance in the dances,' it is clear that there were no men there..." (*Responsa Binyamin Ze'ev* 305).

49. Bava Batra 121a.

50. Shoftim 21:1.

numbers for the dances. However, the historical records, as well as agricultural findings, do not support the existence of large vineyards in Jerusalem during the Second Temple period. Winepresses from that period were found only at a distance of five kilometers and more from the border of ancient Jerusalem, and the large concentrations of vineyards, appropriate to the description of the Mishnah, were and still are in the area of the Hebron mountains and around Shilo.[51] If so, how could the young girls of Jerusalem go out to the vineyards?[52]

We can't resolve the contradiction between Jerusalem and vineyards, except to conclude that the word "Jerusalem" that appears before us has its source in a corrupted version of the text of the Mishnah. In fact, many variant texts indeed do not write "maidens of Jerusalem" but "maidens of Israel!"[53] According to the version "maidens of Israel," it is obvious that the center of the Festival of Dances was not in Jerusalem – but presumably in Shilo, the area known as one of the great centers of viniculture in the country, and where at the end of the book of Shoftim we already hear that the Festival of Dances took place: "They said, now is a festival of God in Shilo from days of yore… and see, if the maidens of Shilo come out to dance in the dances, come out of the vineyards and each man abduct a wife for himself…"[54] The events described in these verses are similar to the celebration described at the end of Ta'anit, and it is reasonable to assume that the festival that took place during the Second Temple period and afterward, as Rabban Shimon b. Gamliel relates, was none other than a renewal and continuation – inspired by the words of the prophet – of the festival that had taken place since "days of yore" in Shilo and other vineyard-rich areas in the land of Israel,[55] of which Jerusalem is not one.

---

51. We cannot interpret *kerem* as referring to olive groves, since the unmodified term *kerem* in the Mishnah refers specifically to a vineyard. (See Berakhot 35a: It is called an "olive-*kerem*," not just a *kerem*.)
52. Rashi interprets the "maidens of Jerusalem" of Shir HaShirim: "Maidens of Jerusalem – these are Israel, who fear and are whole with God" (Rashi, Shir HaShirim 3:10). However, it is difficult to extrapolate from Rashi's commentary on Shir HaShirim, which is written entirely as a literary allegory, to our Mishnah. And in fact, Rashi himself did not interpret our Mishnah as referring to "all Israel" as he did with Shir HaShirim.
53. Thus in Yerushalmi within the Talmud, and in the Petiḥta to Midrash Eikha, and in Rif and Me'iri and Rosh on Ta'anit, and in *Sefer Ha'Eshkol*, and in Radak on Shoftim 21, and more. See more below regarding the explanation of *Shita Mekubetzet* on the reason for the textual variation.
54. Shoftim 21:19–21.
55. The fact that the celebration described at the end of Ta'anit is a restoration of the festival that took place at Shilo is indicated in a manuscript cited in *Ohel David Sasson* (p. 57) in the name of R. Sherira Gaon and R. Hai Gaon, and thus explained Radak (Shoftim, above), and the

WHITE GARMENTS – THE CUSTOM OF JERUSALEM

Having seen the existence of alternative texts of the Mishnah, let us compare the printed text with versions preserved in other variant texts, and note the implications of the differences between the versions:

> Rabban Shimon b. Gamliel said: No days were as festive days for Israel as the fifteenth of Av and Yom Kippur, when the **people of [*bnei*] Jerusalem would go out** in borrowed white garments, so as not to shame whoever did not have. All the garments require *tevila,* immersion [in a mikveh]. And the **maidens [*benot*] of Israel**[56] would go out and dance in the vineyards. And what would they say? Young man, lift up your eyes and see what you choose for yourself: Look not at beauty, look at family. "Grace is a lie and beauty fleeting, a woman who fears God, she is to be praised."

The text "the people of Jerusalem would go out," (and not: "the maidens...would go out," as in the printed versions) is the version of the Mishnah brought in the Talmud Yerushalmi and in additional sources.[57] This means that all people of Jerusalem observed the custom of white garments, not just the maidens of the city![58] Even Rambam preferred the text of the Yerushalmi, for he interpreted the Talmud's words "all the garments require immersion," to mean that the women's garments required immersion out of concern for menstrual impurity, and the men's garments also required immersion out of concern for other types of impurity: "and thus with men who are not pure."[59] That is to say, the custom to wear white garments was indeed shared by all people of Jerusalem, men and women alike.

---

author of *Be'er Moshe* (on the Yerushalmi in Ta'anit). There are however differences in the manner that the day was celebrated in the time of the Judges and in that of the Mishnah. The words of the Talmud, "Whoever did not have a wife turned to there" indicate that this was not a local festival, but a festival observed by all Israel, as in the version of the Yerushalmi (Ta'anit 4:7) "Bnei Israel" and not only "*Benot,*" and of course – "festive days for Israel." By contrast, in the story in Shoftim we hear only that "the girls of Shilo went out" (although there as well, Radak comments "daughters of Israel"); and apparently in that period the festival had not yet spread to all Israel, and was observed primarily by the people of Shilo; see *Metzudat David* on Shoftim 21:20.

56. And not the maidens of Jerusalem, as we demonstrated above.
57. See *Dikdukei Soferim* on Ta'anit 26a (pp. 163–64, *simanim* 300 and 1).
58. For "daughters [*banot*] are included in the category of children [*banim*]," as is known, in the language of the author of *Melekhet Shlomo* on the Mishnah there.
59. Rambam's *Commentary on the Mishnah,* Ta'anit, ibid.

In truth, it makes sense that the people of Jerusalem, where the Temple stood, adopted such a custom of *hiddur* (beautification of a mitzvah) for themselves.[60]

However, one can ask regarding this text and its implications: If the custom of white garments was common to men and women, why, when the Talmud explains the details of the custom, does it deal only with women? "The daughter of the king borrows from the daughter of the *kohen gadol,* the daughter of the *kohen gadol* from the daughter of the deputy [*kohen gadol*], the daughter of the deputy from the daughter of the [*kohen*] anointed for war, the daughter of the [*kohen*] anointed for war from the daughter of an ordinary *kohen*"[61] – which seems to imply that this custom was only for the maidens! However, we can interpret the words of the Talmud inclusively, that it was not necessary to mention the garments of the men, as men tend toward greater uniformity and less color in clothing, and therefore there was little novelty in their dressing in white. By contrast, the fact that all women – even the most distinguished or wealthy – wore simple, identical white garments borrowed from friends, is a departure from the norm, justifying mention in the Talmud.[62] The language of the Talmud indeed proves that the white garments were common to the entire house of Israel – both women and men – for the *baraita* opens in the masculine and plural: "and all

---

60. It is even possible that the Ashkenazi custom to wear a white *kittel* on Yom Kippur is a remnant of the custom of the people of Jerusalem on this day during the time of the Temple – a sort of "remembrance of the Mikdash," as explained in Ritva: "In white garments ... and in the midrash they said that it is fitting to wear white garments on Yom Kippur for this reason" (Ritva, Bava Batra 121a). Indeed, the reason given in various sources for the *kittel* – in order to resemble angels (Baḥ, *Oraḥ Ḥayim* 18) – is precisely the reason given in *Yalkut Me'am Lo'ez* (Shoftim 21) for wearing white clothing on that festival: "... and from here is also derived the custom to wear white garments on Yom Kippur, to say that we resemble angels." Also, the second reason for wearing white clothing on Yom Kippur – that it is a day of forgiveness and atonement (ibid.) – is identical to the explicit reason in the Gemara itself (Ta'anit 30b). See further in *Otzar Dinim U'Minhagim,* s.v. *kittel,* and also in the encyclopedia *Otzar Yisrael* under that entry, and in the Rema, *Shulḥan Arukh, Oraḥ Ḥayim* 610.
61. Ta'anit 31a.
62. It seems that over the course of the generations the custom of wearing similar and simple white garments on Yom Kippur was neglected among women, to the point where, in the opinion of Tosafot (Megilla 31a), the reason for reading the portion [of the Torah] about sexual prohibitions at *minḥa* on Yom Kippur, connects to the tendency of women to adorn themselves specially on that day, to the extent that there was a need to caution the men not to falter (see also *Mishnah Berurah* 610: 16, which reinstated the custom of women wearing white on Yom Kippur).

Israel borrowed one from another (*sho'alin zeh mizeh*) so that whoever did not have (*ein lo*) would not be shamed (*yitbayesh*)."[63]

If so, the custom described in the Mishnah of white garments was common to all residents of Jerusalem, both men and women, and not only the "maidens." Even the second mention of the "maidens of Jerusalem" refers to all "maidens of Israel" and not just "Jerusalem." Based on these textual variants, we can resolve the difficulty of the author of *Shita Mekubetzet*, R. Betzalel Ashkenazi, who asked: Why does the Mishnah mention twice "maidens of Israel/Jerusalem" – it would have been sufficient to write this once? The answer is that the first reference is to "Jerusalem" and the second time to "Israel," and therefore both mentions are necessary.[64]

THE FESTIVAL OF DANCES – ON TU B'AV ONLY

According to a literal reading of the Mishnah, "*... and as Yom Kippur, when the maidens of (Jerusalem) [Israel] would go out*," the Festival of Dances in the vineyards took place on two calendar dates – on Tu b'Av and again, on Yom Kippur. This is surprising in itself: Where do we find a festival that takes place on two separate dates, with identical format, content, and customs? Additionally, the reason for dances in the vineyards specifically on Tu b'Av, at the end of the grape harvest, is clear; but what does Yom Kippur have to do with going out to vineyards?

Furthermore, as we mentioned, the content and customs of the festival are inconsistent, to put it mildly, with the character of Yom Kippur. From the Talmud's description, the festival would have necessitated various *melakhot* (forbidden work).[65] Second, and primarily, as we noted at the beginning of the chapter, the

---

63. In practice, the printed text of the Mishnah also hints at the textual variants, since it says "so as not to embarrass he who does not have" (*mi she'ein lo*) – and not "she who does not" (*she'ein lah*).

64. His words are cited in *Shinui Nusḥa'ot* on the Mishnah ("*Perushei HaRishonim V'ha'Aḥaronim*," published by Me'orot). The author of *Dikdukei Soferim* gave a similar explanation, but decided in favor of the opposite variant: "Israel" the first time and "Jerusalem" the second time. We prefer the variant that places "Jerusalem" first, for many reasons that have been made clear above, and it should be noted that this is also the variation of the Mishnah found in the Talmud Bavli: first "Jerusalem" (as in the Yerushalmi and in the Mishna), and at the end "Israel" (as in *Dikdukei Soferim* and Rif and *Sefer Ha'Eshkol*).

65. It is more than reasonable to assume that the practices of the festival would require practices prohibited on Yom Kippur including carrying musical instruments. See, for example, *Metzudat Tzion* (Shoftim 21:21) on the word *meḥolot*: "...it is called *maḥol* because it is normally accompanied by flutes (*ḥallilim*)." This would have involved carrying on Yom Kippur in a public domain, for the vineyards were no doubt outside the city, as Radak deduced from the language "went out." He writes: "the dance ... was outside the city of Shilo... beside the vineyards of

difficulty in connecting the Festival of Dances to Yom Kippur derives from the very essence of Yom Kippur: It is a day of holiness, repentance, and prayer, a day of fasting and affliction[66] – what room is there for joy?[67] The author of *Tiferet Yisrael* raised this difficulty: "On Yom Kippur, it is not fitting that they should sing 'young man lift up…' for would it even occur to you that the holy nation of Israel would occupy themselves on the awesome and holy day with matchmaking?!"[68] Tractate Yoma is devoted to the day's service, describing the awesome majesty of the Temple and its surroundings on that day: the service, driving away the scapegoat, uttering the ineffable name of God, the prostration of the *kohanim* and the nation, and more. True, all this took place only in Jerusalem,[69] but it is unreasonable to assume that only in Jerusalem were the Jewish people focused on the service of Yom Kippur, while elsewhere they were partying.[70]

It might seem possible to explain the dissonance between Yom Kippur and the Festival of Dances in that Yom Kippur as we know it, as a day of prayer and supplication, was enacted by the Men of the Great Assembly. We might be tempted

---

Shilo… and they told them [the men of Binyamin] to lie in ambush in the vineyards" (Shoftim 21:19; see also *Encyclopedia Mikra'it*, 4, p. 321). It should be noted that the Mishnah also uses the term "go out." Also, the Sages decreed that "all the garments require immersion," and Rashi explains "before they wear them," meaning – immersion that same day. It is also understood from Rambam that the borrowing of garments took place on that same day – "because they would mingle with each other and without doubt among all those many women some were not pure," so of course the immersion needed to be on the same day. This is also understood from the *Pnei Moshe* (Yerushalmi Ta'anit 4:7, s.v. *mitokh she'ata oseh ken*). How could they immerse garments on Yom Kippur, something that is not possible according to halakhah (see further *Responsa Ḥayim Sha'al* 1:21).

66. Shemot 23:27.

67. This difficulty has already been raised in the book *Gevi'a HaKesef*, which answered that because matchmaking is a mitzvah, we do not worry about excess joy. But this explanation does not solve our problem: Yom Kippur is not a day of joy, and not "even" the joy of matchmaking, which can be postponed for another day. Ḥida, in his book *Birkei Yosef* (*Oraḥ Ḥayim* 141:4), explains, in an original fashion, that the festival took place not on Yom Kippur but "*b'motza'ei Yom HaKippurim*." But it is unlikely that the dances in the vineyards took place at night; and if by "*motza'ei Yom HaKippurim*" he meant the eleventh of Tishrei, this contradicts Rabban Gamliel's statement in the Mishnah. In any case, no one else explains it this way.

68. *Yakhin*, Ta'anit 4:8, 63.

69. According to the traditional version, in which the Mishnah says "maidens of Jerusalem," the difficulty is even greater. Tractate Yoma describes all Jerusalem as united on Yom Kippur around the holy service in the Temple. Whenever referring to the public, the term "nation," or "Israel" is used in the singular; there is no need to elaborate further.

70. [Translator's note: the Hebrew original for "partying" is *oskim b'ḥinga'ot.*] *Targum Onkelos* translates *ḥag HaShem* (festival of God) in Shoftim (21:21) as *ḥingya*, and elsewhere (Shemot 15:20), he also translates *meḥolot* (dances) as *ḥingin* (see further Rashi, Beitzah 33b s.v. *ḥinga*).

to posit that when the Temple was standing, prayers had not yet been enacted as a communal obligation, and therefore – outside of the Jerusalemites, who were concentrated around the Temple – the rest of the Jewish people were not occupied with prayers and the like. However, this line of thinking does not solve anything, for even if we assume that at the time of the Temple, the communal prayers were not yet instituted,[71] it is still clear that Yom Kippur was a day of penitence and self-affliction, and not a day of joy.[72] This is the essence of the day as prescribed in the Torah: "And you shall afflict your souls." It is clear that people did not spend this day idly or with various occupations, even for purposes of a mitzvah – but in repentance, prayer, and supplication.[73]

71. This assumption is fuzzy, to put it mildly. The *amida* and other prayers were established mostly by the Men of the Great Assembly, who lived at the beginning of the Second Temple period; that is to say, the primary prayers were in existence for the entire Second Temple period. See, for example, the words of R. Yehoshua b. Ḥananya about the *simḥat bet hasho'eva*: "When we rejoiced at the *simḥat bet hasho'eva*, our eyes saw no sleep. How so? The first hour – the morning *tamid* sacrifice. From there – to prayer. From there – to the *musaf* sacrifice. From there – to the *musaf* prayer. From there – to the *bet midrash*. From there – to eating and drinking. From there – to the *minḥa* prayer. From there – to the afternoon *tamid* sacrifice; from then on to the *simḥat bet hasho'eva*" (Sukkah 53a), and his description as written in plural teaches us that this was the custom of the entire community.
72. See, for example, Sforno: "On the tenth of the month is Yom Kippur: For a man to confess and lament his sins, and it is not joy and pleasure but a day of affliction" (Vayikra 23:27). His words are similar to the Talmud: "It atones for those who repent, but it does not atone for those who do not repent" (Shevu'ot 13a), and therefore Rabbenu Yonah wrote that it is a mitzvah to repent on Yom Kippur itself. Common sense mandates that Yom Kippur was never a day of sitting idly, and certainly not a day of joy and celebration – but a day of repentance and supplication, even before the public prayers were instituted by the Men of the Great Assembly. Nor can one claim that since, in the time of the Temple, Yom Kippur atoned for all sins, therefore the Jewish people were less occupied with repentance; for the Talmud says: Yom Kippur "atones for those who repent and does not atone for those who do not repent," and obviously "sins between a person and his fellow – Yom Kippur does not atone until he appeases his fellow" (Yoma 85b). Aside from this, regarding joy, the Sages taught that "there is no joy without [eating] meat… there is no joy without [drinking] wine" (Pesaḥim 109a, Rambam, *Hilkhot Shevitat Yom Tov* 6:17), and these are of course not compatible with Yom Kippur.
73. Aside from this, one cannot attribute the differences in the character of the day to the existence of the Temple, since the festival described in the Mishnah took place both before and after the destruction of the Temple. Before, as is explicit in Shoftim 21; and after, as we have seen, the Talmud mentions the burial of those killed at Betar as one of the reasons for the day; and see for example the words of R. Nissim Gaon, that "R. Matana told us that the matter that led to making Tu b'Av a celebration is the burial of these people who were killed" (Commentary of R. Nissim Gaon on Berakhot 48b).

REREADING THE LANGUAGE OF THE MISHNAH

In light of all we have said, the question begs: Did the Festival of Dances really take place on Yom Kippur? The only source – indeed, apparently a clear and explicit one – for the celebration of the Festival of Dances on Yom Kippur is the Mishnah at the end of Tractate Ta'anit: "No days were as festive for Israel as the fifteenth of Av and Yom Kippur, when..."[74] But in this source itself, does the event described at the **end** of the Mishnah, the celebration of the dances in the vineyards, necessarily refer to Yom Kippur? It would seem, ostensibly, from the language *shebahen* [in which], that everything said in the Mishnah applies both to Tu b'Av and to Yom Kippur. However, we wish to argue that there is a different way to understand this *mishnah* and the word *shebahen* in particular:

> No days were as festive for Israel as the fifteenth of Av and Yom Kippur, **on which (*shebahen*): [on Yom Kippur]** the people of Jerusalem would go out in borrowed white garments.... And [**on the fifteenth of Av**] the maidens of Israel would go out to the vineyards...

That is to say, the word *shebahen* is a general heading for two topics – Yom Kippur and its customs, and Tu b'Av and its customs. This reading is consistent with the approach of the Talmud Bavli, which first discusses why Yom Kippur is a festival, and afterward discusses why Tu b'Av is a festival – and then returns to the custom to wear white garments, which is among the customs of Yom Kippur, and afterward to going out to the vineyards, which is among the customs of Tu b'Av.

According to this explanation, which divides the words of the Mishnah between Tu b'Av and Yom Kippur, there is a question: Why in the first part of the Mishnah is Tu b'Av mentioned before Yom Kippur, while in the second part, Yom Kippur comes before Tu b'Av? The answer to this is learned from the words of the Sages in the beginning of Tractate Nazir, where the principle "hold on to the latter expression" is defined, and which mentions several *mishnayot* where this rule

74. There seems to be an additional hint to the festival taking place specifically on Yom Kippur, from the story in Shoftim on which it is told that the day on which the girls of Shilo went out to dance in the vineyards was a "Festival for God" – and what is a Festival for God, if not a holiday mandated by the Torah. (The possibility of linking the Shilo festival to Yom Kippur is considered by Radak in Shoftim 21:19, but only following a list of alternative dates that also includes Pesaḥ, Sukkot, and others.) However, in truth the expression "Festival for God" is also used in the Prophets to refer to a mass gathering of the people, a meeting or assembly (as noted in the commentary *Da'at Mikra* on Shoftim 21:19; see there), and not specifically to the accepted connotation of "holidays of God" (Vayikra 23:2).

is applied.[75] For example: "With what may we light and with what may we not light? We may not light...:" Since the Mishnah's first part concluded with "may we not light," the Mishnah "held on" to that expression and discussed it first in the second part, even though it opened with "with what may we light." Thus also our Mishnah – since its first section concluded with Yom Kippur, it immediately began to discuss Yom Kippur and its customs, and only afterward returned to deal with the customs of Tu b'Av.

It becomes clear, then, that wearing white garments was customary only on Yom Kippur,[76] while going out to vineyards was customary only on Tu b'Av – and not on Yom Kippur. Indeed, that is precisely the opinion of R. Sherira Gaon and R. Hai Gaon: The celebration of the dances in the Mishnah was only on Tu b'Av.[77] This is also the meaning of Rambam's words in his *Commentary on the Mishnah* (end of Ta'anit), where he does not mention Yom Kippur at all in the matter of a "day of joy," and this is also implied in the words of other commentators.[78] In truth, even the Talmud can be understood this way, for as we said, the Gemara differentiates between the reasons for these two days and their content – white clothing apart, and the dances apart. From the Yerushalmi as well,[79] there is no implication of any connection between Yom Kippur and the dances mentioned in the continuation of the *baraita*, and it is certainly reasonable that they are two separate matters. And even from the book of Shoftim, it seems clear that

75. See there (Nazir 2a), and see an identical concept at the beginning of Tractate Berakhot (2b): "The *Tanna* began with *arvit*...," and more.

76. This also emerges from *Tosafot Yom Tov's* variant of the Mishnah text, which reads: "[...] and on Yom Kippur, on which they would [...] go out in white garments" – meaning, that the going out in white garments was specifically on Yom Kippur, and so also wrote the author of *Sha'agat Aryeh* (*Gevurot Ari*, Ta'anit 30b). This is clear on its own in light of the reasons for white clothing, as we explained above, at length.

77. As cited in the manuscript in *Ohel David Sasson*, part 1, p. 57. Indeed, Abravanel comments that the Festival of Dances was on Sukkot (as is one of the possibilities raised by Radak, as mentioned above). But see *Da'at Sofrim* (ibid., v. 19) who explains that even according to Abravanel's opinion this festival is connected specifically to Tu b'Av, because the decision to snatch the women was made on Tu b'Av.

78. See the words of the *Pnei Moshe* on the Yerushalmi (halakhah 7), who mentions "joy and dances" only regarding Tu b'Av and not Yom Kippur – implying that on Yom Kippur there indeed were not dances and joy; also according to the opinion of *Be'er Moshe*, the festival was specifically on Tu b'Av – "and the fifteenth of Av in Shilo was the place where all Israel gathered annually to celebrate" (*Be'er Moshe*, Shoftim 21), and thus also comments the author of *Hilḥeta Gevirta* (printed at the end of *Mishnayot Ta'anit, "Perushei HaRishonim V'ha'Aḥaronim,"* Me'orot edition), who indicates that "during the time of the Temple Tu b'Av was a day of joy" – Tu b'Av specifically, and not Yom Kippur.

79. Ta'anit 4:11; see there.

the dances did not take place on Yom Kippur; and their location specifically in the vineyards lends credence to their being held in the summer, at the season of the grape harvest.[80]

THE INTERPRETATION OF *TIFERET YISRAEL*

R. Yisrael Lifshitz, author of *Tiferet Yisrael* on the Mishnah, also reached the conclusion that our *mishnah* should be divided between Tu b'Av and Yom Kippur, and that the dances were only on Tu b'Av. He reaches his conclusion in a different and interesting fashion that deserves its own mention. First, he raises the conceptual difficulty that we mentioned above, of the dissonance between the customs of the festival and the spirit of Yom Kippur. He explains that the dances were held on Tu b'Av, while on Yom Kippur they would *sing* to God rather than dance. How could they sing on Yom Kippur, which is not a joyous day? He answers, that this is similar to the Ashkenazi custom to sing the *vidui*, confession, with a melody – because the sins have already been forgiven and been transformed into merits, and it is appropriate to sing of merits:

> "And thus it says...." that on Yom Kippur they were referring to God, who is called a young man all through Shir HaShirim... and it seems to me that for this reason as well the custom of Israel is to sing the "*Ashamnu bagadnu*" on Yom Kippur – should it not be a lament?! Rather, this hints that all [the sins] have become merits, and it is fitting to sing about them as about merits.

He likewise explains the words of the dances in this spirit:

> "Young Man" – this is God, as it is said "a young man like cedars." "Lift up Your eyes ... what You choose for Yourself" – meaning: Where is there a nation in the world as holy as this nation! "Do not look at loveliness" – although they have sinned before You, "look at family" – they are Your children, the sons of Your proven servants, the sons of Avraham, Yitzḥak, and Yaakov. "Grace is a lie" – the grace of the other nations...

And in this fashion, he continues to explain all that is said in our Mishnah.

---

80. The only source explicitly connecting Yom Kippur with the Festival of Dances is the Targum of *Megilat Eikha*, on the verse "her maidens grieve": "Her maidens lament that they have ceased to go out on the fifteenth day of Av and on Yom Kippur... to celebrate" (Eikha 1:4 – from a close reading of the language, it seems clear that this source is based on our Mishnah and aims to explain it). The author of *Korban Ha'Edah* followed this in his commentary to the Yerushalmi (Ketubot 2a). Likewise *Naḥal Eshkol* by R. Tzvi Binyamin Auerbach (*Hilkhot Tu b'Av*, but his words in fact require further study, since our Mishnah refers to single women and not married women).

CONCLUSION: TU B'AV – A FESTIVAL OF LOVE OF ISRAEL

The linking of the borrowed white garments to Yom Kippur requires clarification: The reason for white clothing on Yom Kippur is clear; but why lent garments? The Talmud says: "so as not to shame whoever did not have." But what does this have to do with Yom Kippur, and with it being a festive day for Israel?

It can be explained as follows: On this day, on which all wear white and resemble angels and all Jerusalem was united around the service of the day, the fact that they all dressed alike, and in fact, each person wore his friend's garment – this symbolized modesty, purity, and primarily unity, which were so great on this day that there were no more festive days for Israel than it.[81] As we have explained, it seems that this custom had been unique to the people of Jerusalem; however, at the time when the Temple stood, Jerusalem represented the heart of the Jewish people, and therefore this custom was accepted by the entire Jewish community.

Tu b'Av is also the festival of the Jewish people – most of the reasons brought in the Talmud revolve around this, as do the customs of the day. "Rabban Shimon b. Gamliel said: No days were as festive *for Israel* as the fifteenth of Av and Yom Kippur." For the nation, in a societal sense, there were indeed no days more festive than these, for on these two days the people were more united than at any other time, and there is no greater joy than the unity of the Jewish people.

These are the words of Ritva,[82] who asks: How can it be said that there were no days more festive for Israel than these, as we know that "whoever has not seen the *simḥat bet hasho'eva* (festivity of the water drawing on Sukkot) has never seen joy in his days,"[83] implying that this was a greater joy? He answers: Only those with prestigious lineage took part in the *simḥat bet hasho'eva* – while the remainder of the population participated in the event only as spectators, but did not take an active part in the festivity. On Tu b'Av, the festivity was, by contrast, of the masses.

Love of Israel also breaks forth from the reasons for the festival, as the author of *Siftei Tzaddik* expounded, on granting license for the tribe of Binyamin to marry into the congregation: "On that day they attained a heightened understanding, and realized that it was preferable to draw the tribe of Binyamin near.... And this is the festive day, when they merited a higher knowledge, that the essence is love of Israel."

81. Yom Kippur is considered a Yom Tov (festival), according to the Talmud, because it is a "day of forgiveness and atonement" – and according to our explanation, we can sharpen the meaning – that the intent is both for forgiveness and atonement between a person and God, and also between a person and his fellow – as is in fact the case.
82. Bava Batra 121b.
83. Sukkah 51a–b; see also 53a.

Chapter 8

The Mysterious "Bruriah Episode"[1]

INTRODUCTION

The first chapter of Avodah Zarah relates the events leading up to the pursuit of R. Meir by the Roman authorities, forcing him to flee to Babylonia: "He arose, fled, and came to Bavel."[2] The Talmud gives two explanations for his flight: either because of R. Meir's entanglement with the authorities, as described beforehand – or because of the Bruriah Episode. What is the Bruriah Episode? The Talmud does not specify. The first to do so, hundreds of years later, was Rashi:

> Once, she mocked the adage of the Sages that "women's minds are easily swayed (lit. lightweight)." He said to her, "By your life, you will come to agree with their words." And he commanded one of his disciples to seduce her into sin. He [the disciple] persisted for many days until she consented. And when she discovered the truth, she strangled herself, and R. Meir fled due to shame.

1. Translated by Michael Appel. This chapter initially appeared in *Akdamot* 21 (2008).
2. Avodah Zarah 18b, according to the printed version. In some of the early "textual witnesses" the word "*ata*" or the word "*kam*" is missing.

Rashi's words received little attention over the course of successive generations, and when they did, they were referenced for their halakhic implications.[3] However in our time, this has changed, with the Bruriah Episode receiving much attention in both the Torah and academic worlds. In light of the shift in the status of women in Jewish society and, more broadly, in the modern world at large, the rare figure of Bruriah – the lone woman to attain a status parallel to the *Tanna'im* – has received much attention, and even served as an educational model in the revolution of women's Torah learning of the past several decades.[4]

By contemporary standards, Bruriah is perceived without doubt as an exceptional role model, either as one of the Sages of the Oral Law whose words are quoted as halakhah, or as an exceptional woman Torah scholar, serving as an emblem of female success in Torah study. Either way, the strange story of the Bruriah Episode clouds this image, casting a heavy shadow on her behavior and the way she ended her life. It is therefore no surprise that the Torah world today attempts to soften the Bruriah Episode for educational purposes, explaining it in a manner which fits what is known about R. Meir and Bruriah from all other Talmudic references.[5] Religious feminists have similarly sought to negate

3. See R. Yaakov Reischer, *Shvut Yaakov* 2:111; R. Yehoshua Falk, *Pnei Yehoshua* (Or HaḤokhma edition, 1998), *Berakhot* 31b; R. Ḥayim Yosef Azulai, *Responsa Tov Ayin*, no. 4; R. David Tawil, *Responsa Naḥalat David* no. 26. Contemporary *poskim* also address this story. See R. Eliezer Yehudah Waldenberg, *Responsa Tzitz Eliezer* (1977) 9:3; R. Yehuda Herzl Henkin, *Responsa Bnei Banim* (Jerusalem, 1981), 2:40; R. Menashe Klein, *Responsa Mishneh Halakhot*, 9:238. For a different perspective, Ḥida, in *Mar'it Ha'Ayin* (p 94) cites Rema MiFano in the name of R. Israel Saruk, who wrote that Bruriah was the reincarnation of Bat Sheva, and the student was the reincarnation of Uriah the Hittite, and he [Uriah] was responsible for her death – measure for measure (this is also cited by R. Yehiel Halperin, *Sefer HaDorot* II (Warsaw 1882), 87.
4. This is well-known; however, we will mention, for example, that the first institution in Israel for Torah study for women was named for her: Midreshet Bruriah (1976; today, known as Midreshet Lindenbaum).
5. See article by Bruriah ben Shachar, "*Demuta Shel Bruriyah U'Mashma'uta LeDorot*" [Bruriah's Image and Its Historical Implications], *Shirat Alamot* (Jerusalem, 2004), 260–65; she debates how one can accept the story as described, and despite this, derive from it educational lessons. See also R. Shlomo Aviner, "*Bruriyah V'Limud Torah*" [Bruriah and Torah Study], *Iturei Kohanim*, 223 (2003), 25–29; he accepts the Bruriah Episode as written, but attempts to soften its implications in various ways, most of them problematic; and he admits, "nevertheless, we have not escaped the argument, and the Lord has the answers." Also see the references in n. 21.

the negative implications of the episode that are liable to be associated with women's learning.[6]

Before dealing with the Bruriah Episode itself, I wish to address several hypotheses, problematic both factually and methodologically, that have been advanced by feminist academics regarding the source and purpose of the story. It is widely claimed that the Sages used this story to delegitimize women's Torah study and Bruriah's exceptional accomplishments in this area.[7] Were this true, we would have found the Bruriah Episode in the Talmud itself or in a Midrash of the Sages, and not in Rashi's commentary alone. Not merely is this not the case, but precisely the reverse, the Sages often praise Bruriah and learn from her behavior.[8] Over two hundred years ago, the Ḥida raised the possibility that "from what occurred to Bruriah in the first chapter of Avodah Zarah, the Sages conceded to the position of Rabbi Eliezer" who forbade the teaching of Torah to women – and immediately rejected such speculation, because we have no discernible proof that the Sages concluded this from the story or saw it as a representative episode: "From that which happened once to Bruriah, we are not permitted to extrapolate a halakhic precedent, so long as we haven't seen this in [the words of] the Sages."[9]

---

6. See Brenda Bacon, "How Should We Learn the Story of Bruriah's Death" in *To Be a Jewish Woman* II (Jerusalem, 2002), 121–30. Bacon surveys the major feminist ideas stemming from the story and its source, evaluates them, and adds her own opinion from an educational-feminist perspective. An interesting discussion of this article, incorporating the approaches of researchers including Avraham Grossman, appears on the website "Kolekh" beginning on 13 March 2007, at http://www.kipa.co.il/kolech/show.asp?id=18654. For another source dealing with this story, see n. 73.
7. Prominent examples include: Rachel Adler, "Character and Context in the Legend of Bruriah," *Tikkun*, 3 (1988), 103–4, and the analysis of Daniel Boyarin, *HaBasar SheBaru'ach* (Jerusalem 1999), 185–94, especially p. 190. Avraham Grossman dismissed Boyarin's view, calling it "a radical conclusion," that is so far from the straightforward meaning of the text (Avraham Grossman, *Ḥasidot U'Mordot* [Jerusalem, 2001], 270–71).
8. For example, Pesaḥim 62b: " Bruriah, the wife of R. Meir, the daughter of R. Ḥananyah b. Tradyon, studied daily three hundred traditions of three hundred Sages, and even she did not fully digest the work [*Sefer Yuḥasin*] in three years; and you wish to study it in three months?!!!"
9. *Responsa Tov Ayin*, no. 4. Avraham Grossman pointed out (*Ḥasidot U'Mordot*, 270) that Boyarin's claim had already been raised by Aharon Heyman, who mentioned the Bruriah Episode and wrote that "R. Meir proved the wisdom of the Sages who had said in Mishnah Sota 20a, "One who teaches Torah to his daughter, it is as if he taught her *tiflut*, licentiousness [alternative translation according to Rambam: nonsense]" (Aharon Heyman, *Toldot Tanna'im V'Amora'im* I [Jerusalem, 1964], 295). Grossman failed to notice that the first time this argument is raised is by the Ḥida (op cit.), over one hundred years before Heyman.

Another claim is that Rashi himself invented the Bruriah Episode, constructing a hybrid of motifs in Talmudic literature, in order to establish that Bruriah's end bears out the ruinous path on which she set out.[10] It goes without saying that anyone versed in Rashi's methodology and commentaries knows that this cannot be true. A brief quote from Rashi himself will suffice: "It is hard for me to say thus, as I have never heard this tradition."[11]

MAJOR QUESTIONS ABOUT THE STORY

Despite our dismissal of the aforementioned claims, the reliability of the Bruriah Episode is worthy of clarification. Rashi's source is unknown to us. The story does not appear anywhere in Talmudic literature, it is not mentioned in Ge'onic writings, nor do we find even a single mention of it in the period of the *Rishonim*, except for Rashi[12] (and, in his wake, Menorat HaMa'or and Maharil, as we shall

---

10. Tal Ilan, *Integrating Women into Second Temple History* (Tubingen, 1999), 189–94, also cited by Bacon (see n. 6 above).
11. Pesaḥim 86b, s.v. *talmud lomar* (regarding an interpretation he heard from someone, but about which he had no handed-down tradition; compare Shabbat 85b). Space is insufficient to record the number of times Rashi humbly admits "I don't know," or "I didn't hear this." And there is not even one instance where it possible to prove that Rashi brought a story on his own and not from a transmitted tradition. See R. Yehudah Leib Maimon, *Sefer Rashi* (Jerusalem, 1956), 31–114, who counts nearly forty works of the Sages that Rashi had before him, close to a fifth of which are unknown to us. In the words of Avraham Grossman (in relation to the discussion referenced in n. 6), "Heaven forbid for that righteous man, for whom truth was his beacon, to have invented so horrific a story on his own."
12. This fact, on its own, is not that unusual. We have other instances of stories that the Talmud references without details, where Rashi fills in the blanks: The episode of a rat and pit (Ta'anit 8a, Rashi s.v. *miḥulda*); the episode of Nathan Tzutzita (Shabbat 56b, Rashi on Sanhedrin 31b); the episode of the tax collector (Sanhedrin 44b, Rashi s.v. *d'ba'aya*), etc. However, these stories differ substantially from the Bruriah Episode: First, in most cases, Rashi is not alone among the *Rishonim* to mention the incident; the episode of the rat is also cited by *Sefer Ha'Arukh* of R. Natan bar Yeḥiel, (Lemberg, 1870) (entry "ḤLD") and by Tosafot (Ta'anit 8a, s.v. *b'ḥulda*, following Rashi's interpretation). The episode of Natan is cited in an expanded and different presentation in *Menorat HaMa'or* of R. Israel Alnekave, (New York, 1929), 127–29; and compare with Rashi and Tosafot on Shabbat 56, s.v. *Natan d'Tzutzita*). And the tax collector incident is cited in a different version by Yerushalmi (Sanhedrin 6:6 and Ḥagiga 2:2) and in *Midrash Aseret HaDibrot*, 41 (in *Otzar Midrashim* [New York, 1915], 460–61), et al. Second, in some instances, Rashi himself tells us which source he used. For instance, regarding the episode of the rat and pit, he says "it is found in the aggadah"; and in the Natan Tzutzita episode, he says "I found in *Sefer Ha'Aggadah*." Most importantly, all these examples portray relatively simple stories that do not contain dubious and troubling elements that contradict what is known to us about the personalities involved from other sources (as we will further explain).

presently see). The story is singular and improbable, casting two exceptional Talmudic figures in a most problematic light.

From a human perspective, the story presents an extreme picture: Is it logical that because of a single instance of mockery ("one time") of the Sages by Bruriah, Rabbi Meir would place her in a position to be seduced by another man?![13] This is not the behavior of a level-headed man, certainly not one of the greatest *Tanna'im*. The description also does not fit with Rabbi Meir's own activities in promoting *shalom bayit*, marital harmony,[14] and it contradicts what we know about the exemplary relationship that Rabbi Meir and Bruriah had.[15] Similarly, the episode is problematic halakhically: How could Rabbi Meir allow his disciple to seduce a woman into adultery, a sin for which both the man and woman are obligated

---

13. The point that her mocking was a one-time occurrence weakens the attempts to claim that R. Meir acted properly to "educate" Bruriah in light of her debased behavior (see, for example, R. Aviner, n. 5 above, that despite the student's behavior violating halakhah, "R. Meir was not concerned with this because he wanted to put his wife in her place"!). Negating such a claim may have been the intent of Ḥida (*Responsa Tov Ayin* no. 4), who writes, "We are not permitted to extrapolate a halakhic precedent from that which happened once to Bruriah." In other words, this was not a representative occurrence. In this vein, R. Barukh Epstein (1860–1942) records in his memoirs a particularly interesting conversation between himself and the wife of Netziv of Volozhin regarding women's Torah study:

> I remember, when she mentioned Bruriah, wife of R. Meir, I said to her: "After all, she had a character defect in mocking the Sages for their dictum that 'women are easily tempted'; and in the end, she came to her end by that very temptation, as told in the story by Rashi..." And she answered me by saying: "Although I am familiar with this story, did the Sages blame all men for Aḥer, who strayed from the proper path. Moreover, Bruriah did not 'mock' in the sense of contemptuous jeering. She felt that the Sages had not fully grasped the nature of women; and in her opinion, women could be resolute, that's all" (*Mekor Barukh* [Vilna, 1848], part 4, p. 1953).

14. Yerushalmi Sota 1:4 (see also *Vayikra Rabba* 9:9), where R. Meir preferred to suffer even an extreme insult rather than cause a quarrel between husband and wife. Gittin 52a relates how R. Meir once tarried at length in a certain city in order to make peace between a husband and wife who were quarreling. We can cite further instances demonstrating that R. Meir was proactive in helping women, as told in Sanhedrin 11a, for example, where R. Meir forwent his honor to help a woman receive her *get*. Also see *Yalkut Shimoni*, end of *Shelakh* (par. 550), regarding a harlot who came to R. Meir's *bet midrash* to convert. (In Menaḥot 44a, this story is told about R. Ḥiya. However, see Tosafot there, s.v. *l'vet midrasho shel R. Ḥiya*, who prefer the version of Tosefta associating the story with R. Meir.)
15. *Midrash Mishlei* 31:10, that opens and closes with the words "A woman of valor, who can find." See also Berakhot 10a. It is important to emphasize as well that all of R. Meir's troubles with the Roman authorities, described prior to the Bruriah Episode, stemmed from his attempt to rescue Bruriah's sister. This alone demonstrates the strength of the bond between R. Meir and Bruriah, for R. Meir was prepared to endanger his own life to save her sister.

to give up their lives before violating? This doubly confounding problem was addressed by Rabbi Israel Lifshitz, the Tiferet Yisrael:

> Because [R. Meir] knew that he [the student] was God-fearing and would not actually commit the sin, even after she acquiesced, as she did. Heaven forbid that R. Meir would cause her to sin. Such is my humble opinion.[16]

In other words, the story does not refer to actual adultery – lest one think that Rabbi Meir would instruct his student to commit adultery with a married woman – but with tempting and seducing alone. However, this answer of Tiferet Yisrael raises new questions: How could R. Meir rely upon his student not to sin, after all, "There is no guardian against sexual sin."[17] In fact, the Talmud in Kiddushin relates that R. Meir himself nearly succumbed to the temptation of Satan, who appeared before him as a woman.[18] Besides, the student would certainly have sinful thoughts, themselves prohibited, so how could R. Meir allow that? Ben Ish Ḥai, Rabbi Yosef Ḥayim of Baghdad, asks this question:

> An even stronger question on R. Meir Ba'al HaNes: How did he permit his student to perform this act of seduction without concern that the student

16. Tiferet Yisrael on Rashi, printed in Vilna edition at the end of Avodah Zarah (*Hagahot V'Ḥidushim* [Tal-Man edition], 36). R. David Sperber, one of the great Romanian rabbis of the past generation, leaned toward this position, because, "Heaven forbid that the act would actually be committed. Do not even mention that R. Meir would cause such a thing to occur. Such sin would not befall a righteous man" (*Responsa Afarkasta D'Aniya* [Brooklyn, 2002], 4: 334. R. Sperber wrote this in response to a rabbi who wrote that concerning R. Meir's student it is written, "Cursed is he who seduces a woman to commit adultery." Even though the student acted at the behest of his rabbi, he behaved wrongly). The first who attempted to soften the difficulties raised by the story was the author of *Shalshelet HaKabalah*, R. Gedalia b. Yosef ibn Yaḥya, who lived in the generation following R. Yosef Karo. In his version (*Shalshelet HaKabalah* [Warsaw, 1928], entry "R. Shimon b. Gamliel II," p. 15a), he wrote that Bruriah "wrote in her book" that the dictum 'women are easily tempted' did not apply to herself. His intent was thereby to say that her mockery was a regular occurrence, as opposed to what we wrote (see n. 13 above). He also adds that R. Meir changed places with the student at the last moment, so that Bruriah would not actually commit adultery. It goes without saying that there is no hint of these details in the original story.
17. Tosefta Ketubot 1:9; Ketubot 13b. Note there that this principle was already in place several generations before R. Meir.
18. In order to make the point that one should not disparage people who fail in their struggle with their evil inclination, as this is a great trial (Kiddushin 81a). R. Meir was also wont to say "Be vigilant with me – even as regards my daughter" (ibid., 81b). In any event, this is not the only difficulty, as we shall see presently.

> would think improper thoughts at the time he carried out his seductive conversations with her?

And he answers:

> In my humble opinion, this student was a eunuch, and had no sinful thoughts or desires. And she was unaware, because there are natural eunuchs from birth who are not recognizable from without, either in their features or facial hair.[19]

In other words, according to Ben Ish Ḥai, R. Meir sent on this mission a student who had no chance of sinful thoughts, and certainly no chance of the sin itself. This answer, however, has no foundation in Rashi's words. Moreover, even according to the explanations of Tiferet Yisrael and Ben Ish Ḥai, it is almost certain that the student would have needed to violate the prohibitions against secluding oneself with a married woman, itself a Torah violation (according to most opinions), and might even be considered *avizaraihu d'gilui arayot*, acts leading to adultery, for which one is obligated to give up one's life to avoid.[20] Besides, the questions regarding R. Meir's behavior arise not only as regards his disciple, but also Bruriah herself – as he seemingly transgressed several biblical prohibitions regarding his wife, including placing a stumbling block before her and causing her pain. My father [R. Y. Henkin] asked thus regarding the answer of Ben Ish Ḥai:

> It is difficult, in my humble opinion. Is the problem only vis-à-vis the disciple? No lesser a question begs, how R. Meir could have allowed himself to sin against his wife, tempting her thus, and transgressing, "Do not put a stumbling block before the blind!"[21]

---

19. Ben Yehoyada on aggadot of the Talmud, Avodah Zarah 18b.
20. Ben Ish Ḥai proceeds to describe how the episode played out: Not only did Bruriah refrain from actual sin, she even refused to be seduced. It only appeared thus to onlookers. However, even though his description of the events has no basis in the story itself, his version of the episode still contains a violation of grave prohibitions. And his question – "This is most astonishing, how this righteous and holy woman was seduced into adultery!" – remains.
21. *Responsa Bnei Banim* (above, n. 3), vol. 4, essay 4, n. 4. R. Yigal Ariel arrived at the same point: "The story, as it appears before us, is strange, impossible from a halakhic perspective, contradicts what is written beforehand in the Talmud, and does not fit the character of the protagonists." (R. Yigal Ariel, *Arapeh Meshuvatam* [Ḥispin, 1998], 365, n. 148). Similarly, R. Baruch Efrati poses a list of questions on the Bruriah Episode and concludes, "I have not found an answer to any of these questions, and I will thank anyone who can settle my mind in this matter." ("Bruriah,

Another equally disturbing question can be directed at Bruriah herself:[22] How could such a supremely learned woman permit herself to commit suicide?[23] Against these questions, my father surmised that the Bruriah story is not from the Sages but rather a folk tale:

Therefore the story is not reasonable, in my humble opinion.... This story is not found in Talmudic literature and its source is unknown, and the other *Rishonim* do not mention it. Perhaps it is rooted in some tale or source into which Bruriah's name became inserted. We have no complaint with Rashi, as he simply recorded what he heard. And even though we cannot compare Rashi with the *Aḥaronim*, we see something similar in Tiferet Yisrael at the end of Mishnah Kiddushin (note 67) where he relates a strange story about Moses,

---

the *Tanna'it* – Perspectives on her Personality," *Iturei Kohanim*, 223 [2003]: 34, n. 9). Despite this, he accepts the story as written, since it is brought in Rashi.

22. As far as the sin itself is concerned, many are inclined to reduce the severity of Bruriah's transgression by explaining how difficult it is for anyone to withstand prolonged temptation. After all, some of the greatest *Tanna'im* almost succumbed to lesser temptations (see Kiddushin 80b–82a). According to this reasoning, the story even highlights Bruriah's steadfastness, as she stood strong for "many days" against the student's entreaties. This is certainly correct (and not in keeping with Grossman, who suggests that "the point of the story is to show how difficult it is for a woman to withstand the seduction of men" (above, n. 7, p. 271). However, this only shifts the question of Bruriah's behavior from one side to the other: How could Bruriah allow a situation, in which a man constantly propositioned her, to persist for an extended time? Why didn't she chase him away and publicize his actions or inform his rabbis? From this perspective, the temporary weaknesses of the other *Tanna'im* are more understandable.
    My father and teacher justified Bruriah in this respect and wrote that a grain of truth to possibly glean from this story is that Bruriah did not have many people to discourse with, "as there were no other learned women, while her husband and the other Sages were always in the *bet midrash*. Therefore she was willing to be visited often by the student." (*Responsa Bnei Banim*, vol. 4, p. 105). He also raised a different possibility, that the dictum "women are easily tempted," can mean that they are liable to err in judgment by relying on their "*bina yeteira*, deeper understanding." This is why Bruriah allowed the student to visit her frequently, "and did not chase him away, assuming that he would not influence her, and this is why she succumbed" (*Responsa Bnei Banim* 2:40, p. 157 in the notes).
23. Ben Ish Ḥai also dealt with this question and answered in keeping with his approach, "She did not transgress the prohibition of suicide because she was not sane and acted in a fit of madness. And her husband fled to Babylonia because he accepted upon himself the punishment of exile in atonement for what he caused." However, notwithstanding the fact that Rashi clearly states that R. Meir fled due to "embarrassment" and not as atonement, and the fact that it is difficult to square this line of reasoning halakhically – as any person who commits suicide is somewhat deficient in sanity, and Shvut Yaakov (2:111) declares that Bruriah was guilty of transgressing the prohibition against suicide – we still can pose the question: How could R. Meir have allowed himself to trigger a series of events that would result in his wife's insanity?

but since then, it has become clear that the story's source is a popular gentile tale about Aristotle.[24]

This solution is also undeniably problematic. It is difficult to assert that Rashi – the greatest Talmudic interpreter – naively inserted a story that he heard from questionable sources, especially a story so unusual and illogical. However, the suggestion that the source of the story is not in rabbinic literature is reasonable.

THE EPISODE THAT NEVER HAPPENED

On the basis of this conclusion, I wish to suggest a different answer to the source of the Bruriah Episode. As my father stated, the story indeed reached us via questionable sources. However, in my humble opinion, it is not Rashi who wrote it down, but someone else whose words made their way into Rashi's commentary.

To understand how this came about, we need recourse to the manner in which manuscripts were handled in the Middle Ages. Until the advent of the printing press (and for some time afterward), a person who wanted to note comments and corrections on the content of a manuscript, would not normally do so on a separate piece of parchment, which was an expensive commodity. Instead, he would write notes in the margins and, sometimes, if space was unavailable, between the lines of text itself. So it is not surprising that when a scribe copied the manuscript, he could easily confuse the main body of the text with the comments. As a result, additions to a text were copied as if they were part of the original content. We know of many examples of paragraphs and sentences that entered in this fashion into various commentaries, and even into the Talmud itself. Ge'onic responsa already address several places in the Talmud where Savora'im had written full

24. *Responsa Bnei Banim* 4, essay 4, n. 5. Regarding the insertion of Moses' name into a story about Aristotle, there is a similar example closer to our topic, where R. Meir's name is inserted into a story of adultery no less strange than the Bruriah Episode. In the *Midrash Aseret HaDibrot* (Bnei Brak, 1977), 24–25, a story is told in connection with the commandment, "Do not commit adultery," in which R. Meir was molested by the wife of his host who got him drunk. When he discovered what had transpired, he asked to be punished, and his teacher decreed that he be devoured by lions in the forest. However, his merit protected him, and the lions did not harm him. This story is cited by *Seder HaDorot* (p. 264, no. 8) in the name of "a certain small book." R. M. D. Gross identified this story (in *Avot HaDorot* 3 [Tel Aviv, 1971], 873) with "an ugly tale about R. Meir," and pointed out that "the Vilna Gaon already hollered in protest that this story has absolutely no foundation in the Talmud or midrashim." It should be noted that another version associates this tale not with the famed *Tanna* R. Meir, but rather with "a certain sage, who also happened to be called R. Meir" (*Otzar Midrashim* [New York, 1915], above, n. 12, entry "Meir," p. 277). This is also the opinion of the editor of the S. Katzin edition who identifies the story with another "R. Meir" as "the details are problematic."

sentences in the margins, and the scribe mistakenly brought the notes into the main body of the Talmudic text.[25]

Rashi himself testifies in several places that a sentence in the Talmud that he had before him came from a mistaken student who wrote a marginal comment: "This version written in the books is flawed, written by commentators who were not well-versed in the tradition, and placed an incorrect explanation within the text."[26] Likewise, "this text in *elu hein halokin* is the correct version, but a mistaken student who had difficulty understanding wrote it down [here] in his copy."[27]

If the Talmud itself suffered from these mistakes, it is not surprising to find not a few sentences and phrases in Rashi's commentary that he himself never wrote, but were inserted by students of the Tosafists. For example, in one place Rashi says, "This is my opinion, but in a copy I found...," and concludes, "And I say that this is a scribal error."[28] On this, R. Yoel Sirkis (Baḥ) points out that "it is a plain fact that a mistaken student wrote this in the margin." In another place, Baḥ writes that certain comments attributed to Rashi were not written by Rashi himself, rather they originated in the glosses of Rabbenu Tam and were mistakenly inserted into Rashi's words.[29] And many others have pointed out the same phenomenon in various places. The phenomenon of mistaken additions to a text continued through the Tosafists' time, as Rabbenu Tam points out in one source: "and this answer of the Riva, he never answered this way and did not author that Tosafot. The copyists attributed it to him, but do not rely on them, because most of them are mistakes."[30]

Is it plausible that an insertion of this sort occurred in the Rashi we are discussing? Rashi's writings were in the hands of the greatest of the Tosafists (foremost among them, Rashi's own grandchildren) for many years. They explained and often argued with Rashi across the entire Talmud. When they felt Rashi's

25. *Teshuvot HaGe'onim* (Jerusalem, 1967), Bava Metzia, *Ḥelek HaPeirushim*, no. 3.
26. Rashi, Keritot 4a, s.v. *v'hakha*. In some places, Rashi's comments have been inserted into the Talmud itself, as pointed out by R. Betzalel Ashkenazi, author of *Shita Mekubetzet*: "... And this is the interpretation of Rashi, but the copyists inserted it into the Gemara" (*Shita Mekubetzet* [Berlin, 1859], Ketubot 31a).
27. See Shevu'ot 3b, s.v. *kushya*, for the full explanation. See also Shabbat 71b, end of s.v. *hakhi garsinan*, etc. Also see R. Rafael Halperin, in *Atlas Etz Ḥayim* 3 (Jerusalem, 1980), 258–68, where he collects all the instances where Rashi points out the same.
28. Mo'ed Katan 19a, s.v. *v'ein olin*.
29. Baḥ, Avodah Zarah 66a (note *gimel* in Vilna Shas edition).
30. R. Yaakov b. Meir (Rabbenu Tam), *Sefer HaYashar* (Jerusalem, 1981), *ḥidushim* no. 316 (288 in Vienna edition).

comments were questionable, they never shied away from saying so. More than once, they highlight instances where Rashi's sources were unknown to them.[31] It would be only natural to find some question on their part regarding the Bruriah Episode, seeing how the episode is rife with questions from beginning to end. Compounding this is the fact that Rashi's commentary is the first and only source for the story.

However, the Bruriah Episode is not mentioned at all, or even hinted at, in all the compilations and commentaries of the Tosafists! In fact, there is no reason to believe that they were even familiar with the story. The first text that bears witness to the story appears in the early fourteenth century, some two hundred years after Rashi's death, in Menorat HaMa'or of R. Isaac Abohav:

> We have already found that the greatest of women who mocked the saying of the Sages that "women's minds are easily swayed" (lit. lightweight), went astray in the matter, as is written in the first chapter of Avodah Zarah, that "R. [Meir] went and fled to Babylonia, some say because of the Episode of Bruriah," and Rashi comments: "That once she mocked…"[32]

Another reference to the Bruriah Episode appears several decades later in the responsa of Maharil:

> For Bruriah, her end casts light on her beginnings: for some say she did not rely upon the Sages who said that women's minds are easily swayed. And the greatest of all wise men, King Solomon, said: "I will take many [wives] and I will not be swayed and I will not founder etc." And here too, she relied upon her righteousness, that she would not founder, by means of [her] learning.[33]

---

31. "Rashi explained in his commentary on the Torah that the Sages of Israel argued… but we do not find this argument in our Talmud" (Menaḥot 96b, s.v. *lo*). "This is difficult because we have not found this in the entire Talmud… it is difficult because this is missing from the book" (Avodah Zarah 17a, s.v. *ma'ot*). "Rashi comments … And this is surprising, for where is his source for this entire matter?" (Sukkah 48b, s.v. *kemin*). "And also, from where does he know that Aḥer expounded before Ḥananya? This is not written in any *baraita*!" (Ḥagiga 14b, s.v. *vehatanya*). Note that in the last two examples, Tosafot discount the possibility that Rashi based himself on a Talmudic source that was unknown to them.
32. R. Isaac Abohav, *Menorat HaMa'or, ner* 1, *klal* 2, part 3, end of ch. 6, p. 79 in the Mossad HaRav Kook edition. Little is known about the book's author; however most scholars agree that he wrote during the first part of the fourteenth century.
33. R. Jacob Molin, *Responsa Maharil*, no. 199. Following Maharil, the next mention of the Bruriah Episode was about one hundred years later, in *Sefer Yuḥasin HaShalem*: "And the

These two sources are the only references during the period of the *Rishonim* for the existence of the Bruriah Episode in Rashi, and both were written decades after the conclusion of the period of the Tosafists. What accounts for the silence of the Tosafists? Could this episode have passed silently through their study halls without stirring up a single question? Logic dictates that had the story been known to them, they would have commented on it. On the very page of the Talmud where the Bruriah Episode appears, there are many comments by the Tosafists on Rashi's words, some pertaining to his version of the text,[34] and some comparing his positions with those of R. Ḥananel and other commentators[35] and with positions of several great Tosafists: Rabbenu Tam, Ri, and Rabbenu Elḥanan.[36] How is it possible that in just this one instance, precisely the problematic Bruriah Episode, there is not a single word uttered by any of the Tosafists?

Moreover, one of comments by the Tosafists on that very page addresses the issue of when a person is allowed to end his own life.[37] And, lo and behold, this very question arises in the Bruriah story on the same page! The Tosafists should have clarified their position in light of Bruriah's suicide, but instead, they bring a Talmudic source from another tractate, as if the Bruriah Episode simply did not exist.

We can safely conclude that this story was never seen by the Tosafists because, as we have suggested, Rashi never wrote it; it is, rather, the work of an anonymous student from a later generation. It stands to reason that the student found the story in a baseless source and chose to accept it for lack of any alternative explanation for the Bruriah Episode. The student even copied the story in the margin of Rashi's commentary. Thereafter, the scribe who copied the manuscript mistakenly inserted the story into the body of Rashi's words. From there, it spread

wife [of R. Meir] the scholar Bruriah, and the entire Bruriah Episode at the beginning of Tractate Avodah Zarah, and when his wife died, he went down to Babylonia out of shame for his wife; and there are those who say because of religious persecution" (R. Avraham Zacuto, *Sefer Yuḥasin HaShalem* [London, 1857], 43; see also p. 59, that Bruriah was mentioned "in the other places in a praiseworthy fashion, and in one place, in an unflattering fashion").

34. Tosafot, Avodah Zarah 18a, s.v. *l'hitlamed.*
35. Ibid., s.v. *hogeh haShem*; s.v. *v'khi shalmi mai i'avid.*
36. Ibid., 18b, s.v. *shelo*; s.v. *shemezablin,* and see previous note. Also, in the surrounding pages, Tosafot have abundant commentary on Rashi on a variety of topics, including a questioning of his source for one of his interpretations (Avodah Zarah 17b, s.v. *ma'ot*), clarifying the text variant that Rashi used (Avodah Zarah 19b, s.v. *higi'a*), and others (see Avodah Zarah 17b, s.v. *raban*, ibid., s.v. *ziburta*).
37. *Avodah Zarah* 18a, s.v. *v'al.* Rabbenu Elḥanan's language invites even more making a connection to the Bruriah Episode: "And R. Yaakov [Tam] says that injuring oneself and committing suicide out of fear that the gentiles will force him … to violate the Torah is permitted (Tosafot R. Elḥanan, Avodah Zarah, ibid. [Kreuzer: Bnei Brak 2003], 105).

to other versions of Rashi's commentary until, by the time of the Maharil (and perhaps earlier), the story was assumed to have originated with Rashi himself.[38]

However, our idea, as with many instances where a "mistaken student" is invoked, is based on logical inferences and not conclusive facts, as we do not have unequivocal proof from manuscripts. The single surviving manuscript of Rashi's commentary to Avodah Zarah is the Parma manuscript,[39] dated to circa 1300, the end of the Tosafist era and after the compilation of Tosafot to Avodah Zarah.[40] In this manuscript, the Bruriah story does indeed appear. However, this manuscript was written many years after the deaths of the greatest of the Tosafists and around two hundred years after Rashi's death. This large gap in time is sufficient to make possible the sequence of events that we have described.

THE PARMA MANUSCRIPT OF RASHI, AND R. NISSIM GAON

By way of our mention of the Parma manuscript, we will highlight the major differences between the manuscript and the printed versions. These differences have significant implications for the content of the story.

The fundamental differences are as follows:

1. The expression used by the Sages: "women's minds are easily swayed" [*nashim da'atan kalah aleihen*] is in the manuscript edition correctly, according to the words of the Sages themselves and in Rashi,[41] and not in the incorrect form contained in the printed version [*nashim da'atan kalot hen alayhu*].
2. The extra term in the manuscript, "that she acceded to him" [*shenitratzet lo*], sharpens the situation described in the story: the seduction to sin was not just

38. The speed and ease of the spread [of the Bruriah Episode] can be understood in light of the fact that this is the only existing explanation for the substance of the Bruriah Episode. This would give a copyist a good reason, when seeing a copy of Rashi's manuscript with the story, to insert it into his own copy, believing it to be a superior copy than one missing the story. Therefore, by the beginning of the fourteenth century the story had already spread far and wide: to Italy in the south (the manuscript), to Spain in the east (*Menorat HaMa'or*), and then to Germany in the west (Maharil). See also n. 56.
39. Bibliotech Parma, plate 3155, De Rossi 1292. Of course, the first printed Rashi on the Talmud contains the story.
40. E. E. Urbach, in his book, *Ba'alei HaTosafot* (Jerusalem, 1968), 507, proves that the editing of the Tosafot printed on Avodah Zarah was completed before the end of the thirteenth century, based on the writings of R. Elḥanan from the end of the twelfth century.
41. See Shabbat 33b; Pesaḥim 88b; Kiddushin 80b. And in Rashi, Kiddushin ibid.; Kohelet 7:28. This proves without a doubt that the manuscript version is superior to the printed versions.

in principle, but in actuality. In other words, seducing her into actual adultery and not stopping short at the point of agreement.

3. The printed version which says "And when she became aware" [*u'kheshenoda lah*] shows that she committed suicide in the wake of her discovery of her husband's subterfuge which proved the righteousness of his claim. But the manuscript version, "and when the matter became known" [*u'kheshenoda hadavar*] implies that she committed suicide due to the public humiliation of her sin becoming widely known, also attesting to an actual sin. This also implies that the "shame" [*kisufa*] which caused R. Meir to flee to Babylonia was not just that people knew his wife had committed suicide, but that she had succumbed to temptation and had an adulterous affair.[42]

This analysis yields several conclusions. First, the manuscript version shows that Bruriah actually sinned and did not merely agree to sin (unlike the explanations of *Aḥaronim* to the contrary) which serves to underscore the implausible nature of the story. Second, the consistent differences between the manuscript and printed versions raise the following suspicion: Perhaps over the course of time, a deliberate correction was made to the story, maybe in light of the fact that any formulation which implied actual adultery must have been mistaken.[43] In any event, we remain convinced that this story is apocryphal, of dubious provenance, which was inserted into Rashi's commentary by a scribe mistakenly copying the words of a student.

Our conclusion is strengthened by the position of R. Nissim bar Yaakov of Kairouan, R. Nissim Gaon, who lived in the generation preceding Rashi. In his work, *Ḥibur Yafeh MeHayeshu'a*, he brings many accounts of the Sages and comments upon them. In our case, he interprets the Talmudic statement, "he arose and fled to Bavel" as follows: "He went, **took his wife** and all his belongings, and moved to Iraq."[44]

---

42. Another meaning implicit in the phrase, "when the matter became known," is that R. Meir's role also became known, and this was perhaps the reason that he fled. This depends on how far one expands the definition of "the matter" that became known.

43. It should be noted that the version quoted by *Menorat HaMa'or* that was close in time to the manuscript (see note 32 above; even though it was first printed in Constantinople in 1514) is very close to the printed versions. It is also interesting that the version of Rashi brought by *Ein Yaakov* (Avodah Zarah 18a) is contemporary with the printed versions and is a mixture of both versions together.

44. R. Nissim bar Jacob Gaon (R. Nissim Gaon), *Ḥibur Yafeh MeHayeshu'a* (Jerusalem, 1970), 30. Grossman sees in the words of R Nissim Gaon "a different tradition that explains the Bruriah Episode in another way" (above n. 7, p. 271). In truth, however, R. Nissim Gaon does not interpret the Bruriah Episode at all, but rather "this Episode" that is brought before it (however, see below, n. 73).

Besides the fact that R. Nissim Gaon does not hint at the story attributed to Rashi at all, he even writes that R. Meir escaped to Babylonia together with Bruriah, contradicting the version attributed to Rashi, in which R. Meir flees in the wake of Bruriah's death. We should point out that R. Nissim Gaon's commentary most often reflects not only his own views, but also the tradition received by his teacher, R. Hai Gaon and the other Babylonian Ge'onim.[45]

"The Rav Papa Episode" – A Comparison

At this stage, we wish to proffer a new chapter, a literary one, to the body of research about the Bruriah Episode. This is not the only personal story that the Talmud relates without detailing its content. The last chapter of Pesaḥim tells of the deathbed charge of R. Yehudah HaNasi concluding with the phrase, "Do not sit on the bed of an Aramean woman." The Talmud offers several reasons for this statement and concludes, "Some interpret this to mean an actual Aramean woman, because of the Rav Papa Episode."[46] What is the Rav Papa Episode? Here, too, as with the Bruriah Episode, the Talmud leaves out the details. However, in contrast to the Bruriah Episode about which we know nothing other than what is found in Rashi, the Ge'onim were privy to a tradition regarding the particulars of the Rav Papa Episode. In fact, there are many versions of the episode brought by the early *Rishonim* that seem to be based on an early common source.

As we have been dealing with Rashi, we will begin with his version of the Rav Papa Episode:

> There was an Aramean woman who owed him [Rav Papa] money and he entered her home every day to collect [the debt]. One day, she strangled her son and left him on the bed. When Rav Papa entered, she said to him, "Sit here while I go bring your money." He did so. When she returned, she exclaimed, "You killed my son!" and he fled the city.[47]

A simple comparison between this story and the Bruriah Episode reveals that they bear a clear resemblance to one another. Both stories deal with an undisclosed incident in the Talmud, introduced by the phrase, "And some say it was because

45. Grossman, above, n. 7.
46. Pesaḥim 112b.
47. In contrast to the Bruriah Episode, these words are certainly those of Rashi. Rashi's grandson, Rashbam, also maintains Rashi's version (in his commentary to Pesaḥim), and as we will see, Rashi refers to this story in Berakhot 8b as well. In general, the Rav Papa story is free of startling elements that contradict all that we know, unlike the Bruriah Episode.

of the matter of..."[48] Both stories begin with the tale of a woman. Both describe a regular series of encounters between a man and this woman, both feature death by strangulation, and both feature a similar outcome, namely, a flight to another land.

The literary comparisons exist not only in motif, but also in structure:

1. "One time she [Bruriah] mocked," in the Bruriah Episode parallels "There was one Aramean woman" in the Rav Papa Episode.
2. "He urged her day after day" parallels, "He entered her home every day."
3. "And when she found out, she strangled herself" parallels "One day she strangled her son."
4. "R. Meir escaped to Bavel" parallels "He fled the city."

An examination of the alternate versions of the Rav Papa Episode sharpens the connection between Rashi's version of it and the Bruriah Episode. Besides Rashi and Rashbam, who present the version of the Rav Papa Episode of the French scholars, there are four additional scholars of the same period who present an entirely different version of the story. R. Ḥananel and R. Nissim Gaon, who lived in North Africa in the generation prior to Rashi, bring a version that they received from their teachers. Thus writes R. Nissim Gaon:

> It is related that Rav Papa lent money to a gentile man. When Rav Papa began to press him to repay the loan, the gentile decided to libel him, to avoid repayment. What did he do? He took a dead baby, placed it on his bed, and covered it with clothing so that nobody would detect it. Then he said to Rav Papa, "Come to my house with me and I will give you the money I owe you." Rav Papa went with him and entered the house. The gentile said, "Sit on the bed." Rav Papa took notice of the things on the bed before sitting down and discovered the dead baby hidden among the clothing. He realized that he was being set up for a false accusation.
>
> And this episode was transmitted to me by my teacher, the holy sage, Rabbenu Ḥushiel, head of the rabbinical academy, of blessed memory. And I also found it in responsa of the Ge'onim.[49]

---

48. It should be noted that these are the only two places in the Talmud Bavli where this sentence appears.
49. The explanation of R. Nissim Gaon (from his *Sefer HaMafte'aḥ* [Vilna, 1847]), printed in the Vilna Shas on Berakhot 8b.

According to R Nissim Gaon, Rav Papa's debtor was a man who took the body of an anonymous child and attempted to frame Rav Papa with it, but R. Papa sensed the plot. The version of R. Ḥananel, the son of R. Ḥushiel, is similar to R. Nissim Gaon's, but told tersely:

> That an Aramean man owed him [Rav Papa] money, and he went to the man's house to collect. This Aramean had a child who had died and was lying on the bed. When Rav Papa entered, the man instructed him, "Sit on the bed." When Rav Papa sat down, the man shouted, "You killed my son!"[50]

The prime difference between this version and that of R. Nissim Gaon is that this was not an anonymous child, but the child of the debtor (similar to Rashi's version), and the debtor was able to successfully frame Rav Papa with the child's death. This also appears in the version of Ra'avan (R. Eliezar bar Nathan), the preeminent rabbi of Ashkenaz at the end of Rashi's generation:

> He [Rav Papa] came to the house of a gentile who owed him money. The gentile's dead son was on the bed and he seated Rav Papa on the same bed. He then framed Rav Papa for killing his son and fined him.[51]

This story is identical to R. Ḥananel's with the exception being the detail brought by Ra'avan that Rav Papa was forced to pay the gentile a fine. Similarly, R. Nathan bar Yeḥiel, author of the *Arukh,* who lived in Rome at the time of Rashi, cites a similar version which is distinguished by the fact that it is written in Aramaic, and also adds a twist: that the gentile brought witnesses against Rav Papa:

> A certain Aramean owed [Rav Papa] money. He went to collect. When he reached the house, the man said, "Sit on the bed." There was a dead child there. The man brought witnesses and when they found Rav Papa sitting on the bed, he said to Rav Papa, "You killed him!"[52]

It is evident that these are four versions of the same core story that developed over the years from the original version. Rashi's version, however, is an entirely different story, with four new elements that do not appear in any of the other versions:

---

50. Pesaḥim 112b.
51. R. Eliezer bar Natan, *Sefer Ra'avan* (S. Z. Erenreich edition, 1926), Berakhot no. 134.
52. *Sefer Ha'Arukh* (op cit., n. 12), entry "*Aram Alef.*"

1. The debtor was a woman, not a man.
2. Rav Papa visited her home to collect the debt on a regular basis.
3. Her son did not die naturally, but she strangled him.
4. As a result of the incident, Rav Papa was forced to flee to another land.

In other words, the four new elements in Rashi's version of the Rav Papa Episode are identical to the common motifs shared by the Bruriah Episode!

In my opinion, the numerous parallels between the story elements cannot be coincidental. It is hard to know the definitive source of these parallels, but it is possible to offer the following explanation: The Talmud describes two incidents introduced by the phrase, "Some say," which go on to describe personal stories whose details are unknown. With respect to the Rav Papa Episode, there is an ancient Ge'onic tradition. But with respect to the Bruriah Episode there is no information whatsoever. This lacuna triggered an attempt to fill in the gaps in the Bruriah story. It is possible that over the course of time, this gave rise to the Bruriah narrative, as influenced by the details of the better-known Rav Papa Episode and its central themes.[53]

We cannot conclude our discussion of the Rav Papa Episode without mentioning that, in the Talmud (Berakhot) there is a third version of the story, cited as a directive from Rava:[54]

---

53. Alternatively, it is possible that the two episodes were written or constructed by the same author, which would account for the similarities between them. According to this hypothesis, it makes sense to speak of an early collection of stories from which Rashi chose to take his version of the Rav Papa Episode; and then, over time, it made its way from there into his interpretation of the Bruriah Episode, which is far more dubious and without parallels in the works of the Ge'onim.

54. Some *Aḥaronim* have wondered about this, that in Pesaḥim this teaching is brought as R. Yehudah HaNasi's will, while in Berakhot it is brought as Rava's. R. Ḥ. Kohut was inclined to emend the Talmud so that "Rava" is also written in Pesaḥim (R. Natan bar Yeḥiel, *Arukh HaShalem*, Levov, 1878, p. 290, *hagahah b'guf hadevarim*). However, his suggestion seems mistaken, for only one out of four directives [in the will] is identical in the two places. Maharatz Ḥayot (printed in the Vilna edition at the end of Tractate Berakhot, *Hagahot V'Ḥidushim* in the Tal-Man edition, p. 20) brought another explanation in the name of *Responsa Mekom Shmuel*: R. Yehudah HaNasi warned not to sit on the bed of an Aramean woman only when she did not lift the bed, while Rava comes to add that even if the bed was raised and it appears clear that there is no dead body beneath it – nevertheless it is forbidden to sit there. However this explanation is also illogical, because in Pesaḥim too the Talmud attributes the law to the Rav Papa Episode, and it is certainly referring to the same episode. Therefore, we need to explain differently: First, illustrating the teaching of a *Tanna* with a story about an *Amora* is not anachronistic, for the Talmud's intention is to show that R. Yehudah HaNasi was correct in his directive, and that is

> Rav Papa went to an Aramean woman. She took out the bed and said to him, "Sit." He replied to her, "I will not sit until I lift up the bed." He lifted up the bed and found a dead child there.[55]

As many have already noted, it is almost certain that this version is not an original part of the Talmud, but was inserted during the period of the *Rishonim*. It does appear in some printings and manuscripts. However, as noted by R. Raphael Nathan Rabinowitz, author of *Dikdukei Sofrim*, in the Munich manuscript, the story is surrounded by parentheses and the margin contains the comment, "This is not from the language of the Talmud, and is a commentary." Also, in the Paris manuscript, the story is entirely absent.[56] There is also proof from R Nissim Gaon's introduction to *Sefer HaMafte'aḥ*, in which he shows that the Talmud sometimes records stories that "are not from our Talmud nor the Talmud of Eretz Yisrael." The examples he cites include "that which is said in Berakhot and Pesaḥim regarding not to sit on the bed of an Aramean woman because of the Rav Papa Episode."[57] Here is clear-cut evidence that, during the transition period between the Ge'onim and the *Rishonim*, the Rav Papa Episode was not found in the Talmud. This is also evident from R. Nissim Gaon's commentary on the Talmud itself, which concludes with the words, "And this incident is known through a tradition from my teacher, our master, the holy rabbi, R. Ḥushiel, head of the academy, of blessed

---

proven by the Rav Papa Episode. Second, Rava's repeating R. Yehudah HaNasi's directive is not surprising, as he sought to emphasize the importance of this matter in his eyes. This is similar to the dictum of Shmuel HaKatan who said "Do not rejoice upon the downfall of your enemies" (*Avot* 4:19), while in fact this is a verse from Mishlei (24:17, and see Rambam's commentary on *Avot* there).

55. Berakhot 8b. This story is similar to the version of R. Nissim Gaon, who speaks of an anonymous baby, and of a failed attempt to incriminate Rav Papa; and, on the other hand, the version is similar to Rashi's in that it speaks of a woman and not a man. However, in many editions, this incident is brought without focusing specifically on a woman: "He went to a gentile woman, they brought out a bed, they instructed him to sit upon it, he told them ... " (see R. Refael Natan Rabinovitch, *Dikdukei Sofrim* [Munich 1865], Berakhot, p. 32). This entirely matches R. Nissim Gaon's version. Of greater note is that in the Gemara's version, the basic fact, which serves as the framework of the story – that this Aramean woman owed money to Rav Papa – is missing.
56. MS Munich – *Dikdukei Sofrim, Berakhot*, p. 32; MS Paris – ad loc., p. 384. Also in MS Firenze (II.1.7 BNC, p. xv) the story is missing from the body of the Gemara, and appears only as a note in the margin of the scroll. These three stages – first, a notation in the margin of the scroll; afterward the note appearing in parentheses in the text itself; and finally as an inseparable part of the text – can serve as an informative illustration of the fashion in which, in our hypothesis, the Bruriah Episode made its way into Rashi's text.
57. Rabbenu Nissim bar Yaakov (R. Nissim Gaon), *Sefer HaMafte'aḥ* (Vilna, 1847), with notes of Be'er Yaakov, p. 4.

memory. And I have also found it similarly in the responsa of the Ge'onim."[58] To use the phrase of the redactor of the *Sefer Ha'Arukh HaShalem*, R. Ḥanoch Kohut, "Because of this, there is no doubt that the story of the Rav Papa incident is not brought in any fashion in either Berakhot or Pesaḥim."[59]

A NEW IDENTITY FOR THE BRURIAH EPISODE

We are left with one question: What is, in fact, the Bruriah Episode? And why did the Talmud refer to the incident without explaining what the issue was, as if it were obvious to all?[60]

Thus far, we have related to the Bruriah Episode as yet another instance wherein the Talmud references a matter obliquely without detailing its content.[61] We have also been working under the assumption that the only one of the *Rishonim* who addressed the Bruriah Episode was Rashi (and, in his wake, *Menorat HaMa'or* and Maharil). However, in fact, there is an additional reference to the Bruriah Episode among the *Rishonim*, albeit minimal in nature. Perhaps for this reason,

---

58. Op cit., p. 13, and according to what Y. Goldenthal raised, that these words prove "that the episode which is found in the Talmud was added by one of the *Aḥaronim*, and was not there from the beginning."

59. *Arukh HaShalem* (op cit., n. 54), p. 290, a note in the body of the text. In any case, it is obvious that also before Rashi, this version was not in the Talmud (as A. M. Lifshitz and A. Aptowitzer noted, *Sefer Rashi* [above, n. 11], p. 231, n. 25, and p. 301, n. 19). This answers the question of many *Aḥaronim*, who wondered how Rashi's commentary on Pesaḥim can be reconciled with the Gemara in Berakhot (see *Masoret HaShas* on the page in Berakhot; "*hafla'ah shebe'arakhin, erekh adam*" [p. 21], and more).
Nevertheless, it is still difficult why Rashi did not mention in Berakhot (s.v. *ma'aseh d'Rav Papa*) that the son was killed by his mother, and simply writes: "and her son died"; and why he omitted the fact that the plot succeeded and Rav Papa was incriminated. We should note that one of the Spanish sages, who lived some two generations after Rashi, R. Zekharia bar Yehudah, brings Rashi's above commentary in his book in a kind of composite combination of our Talmud with our Rashi. In this construction, it is filling in the missing detail that the gentile woman "committed this deception in order to avoid returning her loan or to gain money" (R. Zekharia bar Yehudah, *Sefer HaNer* [Jerusalem, 1958], 11, on Berakhot 8b); however it is not clear to what extent his words are a quote of Rashi, and it is possible that they are an addition by the one who made the citation.

60. Some claim that the story in Rashi can be proven from the Talmud's silence in this matter, for it stands to reason that the Talmud did not wish to relate the episode in detail so as not to disgrace Bruriah and R. Meir (and see Rashi on Kiddushin 33b, s.v. *k'de'ita*). However this argument is not compelling, because there are additional instances in which a Gemara mentions an episode without detailing its content – for example the Episode of Rav Papa – even when there is no shame involved. And on the other hand, there are many stories in the Talmud involving an element of shame to the subject of the story, and the Sages did not refrain from relating them.

61. Some of these instances are mentioned in n. 12.

the reference was overlooked by most of those who have addressed the Bruriah Episode. But I believe that buried within this reference is an important key to our issue.

R. Judah bar Kalonymos of Speyer, who was the teacher of the Rokeaḥ, R. Elazar of Worms, and lived in the generation after Rashi, authored a work entitled "Genealogy of the *Tanna'im* and *Amora'im*." R. Judah's book systematically presents the life and works of the Talmudic Sages. One of the entries is devoted to Bruriah, detailing her halakhic activities. At the end of the entry, R. Judah lists some acts of Bruriah mentioned in the Talmud: "And the Bruriah Episode in chapter 1 of Avodah Zarah; and in Eruvin chapter 5 where she expounded...."[62]

A close reading of R. Judah of Speyer's words reveals that in mentioning the Bruriah Episode, he sends the reader to the first chapter of Avodah Zarah. It goes without saying that nearly all Talmudic manuscripts of his time did not include Rashi's commentary. In other words, in his opinion, the story of the Bruriah Episode is contained in the Talmud itself![63]

As we know, the Talmud ends the story with R. Meir's flight to Bavel and with the phrase, "Some say it was because of this episode [*hai ma'aseh*], while others say it was due to the Bruriah Episode [*ma'aseh d'Bruriah*]." The common assumption has been that "*hai ma'aseh*" ["this episode"] refers to the entire sequence of

62. R. Yehudah bar Kalonymos of Speyer, *Yiḥusei Tanna'im V'Amora'im* (Jerusalem, 1963), 33. Grossman did note the words of R. Y. of Speyer, but wrote that "he did not add any meaningful insights into the Bruriah Episode." We will argue otherwise shortly. R. Yigal Ariel also relates to this, and he explains that the Bruriah Episode that the Talmud in Avodah Zarah is referencing, is the incident in Eruvin: He writes, "Their intention apparently was to [reference] Bruriah's active involvement in shaping the character of the students... her extreme and excessive involvement in halakhic ruling, and her active mixing-in, in directing the students and their education aroused opposition, and in the end, hurt her as well as R. Meir's standing." (*Arapeh Meshuvatam* [above, n. 21], 366–67). Surprisingly, Boyarin also arrives at a very similar identification (*HaBasar SheBaru'aḥ* [above, n. 7], 193), although he claimed much and proved little, and his words are less thought-out. R. Y. Ariel's argument itself is implausible (Where did Bruriah exhibit "extreme involvement in halakhic rulings"? In his book *Aggadah Shel Mishpaḥah* [Ḥispin, 2006], 148 in the footnote, R. Ariel uses a gentler formulation, "excessive involvement," but the claim is still odd). Furthermore, R. Ariel's argument is based on a very selective quote of R. Judah of Speyer; and following the reference to Eruvin, he continues and refers to Bruriah's quarrel with a heretic in Berakhot, implying that this too is part of the Bruriah Episode, that in his opinion aroused the opposition of the Sages.

63. Ed. note: The reader is referred to the original Hebrew for the content of this footnote, which has an extensive discussion of three additional ways to read the words of R. Judah of Speyer, and the downside of each, leading R. Eitam to his reading. https://eitamhenkin.wordpress.com/2011/06/14/[תעלומת-מעשה-דברוריא-הצעת-פיתרון]

events brought immediately prior, from beginning to end. However, based on the words of R. Judah of Speyer, we can read the Talmudic passage with a different assumption, dividing the long sequence into two separate episodes, as we shall presently see.

Where does the "Bruriah Episode" appear in the Talmud? The answer is simple: "Bruriah the wife of R. Meir, was the daughter of R. Ḥanina b. Tradyon. She said to him, 'My sister's captivity in a brothel is a shame upon me.' R. Meir took a purse of coins and went...."[64] – This is the Bruriah Episode!! Although most of the story deals with the actions of R. Meir, the Talmud does not open by saying, "R. Meir was the son-in-law of R. Ḥanina b. Tradyon, whose daughter was captive in a brothel." Rather, it establishes Bruriah as the focus of events. Bruriah is the thread connecting the characters in the story: She is R. Meir's wife, R. Ḥanina b. Tradyon's daughter, and she is the one with a sister who needs to be rescued. Bruriah is the protagonist who initiates the developments: She directs her husband to set out on the rescue mission in order to redeem the family's honor – *her* family.

And what is "*hai ma'aseh*, this episode"? Apparently, "this episode" refers to the second half of the story, which takes place sometime afterward.[65] This second narrative describes how the guard is interrogated and reveals R. Meir's actions to the Romans. They search and eventually find him, but he eludes them via quick thinking and by miraculous intervention.

This reading of the Talmud not only makes sense of the Bruriah Episode but also stands on its own merits, for several reasons:

1. The conclusion, "he arose, fled, and went to Bavel." The flight concludes the narrative, with the implication that it was precipitated by the events described. It stands to reason that the Bruriah Episode is part of this unhappy chain of events vis-à-vis the Romans, and not a completely separate episode (as in the commentary attributed to Rashi) with no connection to the preceding events.

64. Avodah Zarah 18a. And indeed, R. Yehudah Leib Maimon as well, in his edition (*Yiḥusei Tanna'im V'Amora'im*, 33) and also R. Refael Netta Rabinovitch (*Dikdukei Sofrim*, [Munich, 1879], 11) chose to note on this page the Bruriah Episode that R. Y. of Speyer mentioned, and not on the following page on which Rashi's commentary is found. It also may be that in our identification of the Bruriah Episode as that which appears in the Talmud itself, that R. Ḥayim Palagi already preceded us, in "*Derush L'Hesped*" in *Zekhirah L'Ḥayim* 2 (Izmir, 1890), 26b: "like the Bruriah Episode that is brought there..."

65. As in the language of the Talmud: "*lesof ishtama milta*" (Avodah Zarah 18b), in other words, sometime following the first incident.

2. Splitting the story into two episodes makes sense from a literary perspective. The first half opens with Bruriah, deals with her efforts to rescue her sister, and ends happily – the captive sister is returned. At this point, the chronology of the story jumps ahead, Bruriah's sister exits the story, and the Bruriah Episode ends. The second half of the story, "this episode," continues from a later point in time, no longer revolving around the rescue of Bruriah's sister, but rather around the rescue of R. Meir himself. Although the incident underlying "this episode" – namely, R. Meir's rescue of Bruriah's sister – does not itself appear in the second story but rather in the Bruriah Episode which precedes it, so too the incident underlying the Bruriah Episode – namely that her sister was held captive in a brothel – does not appear in the Bruriah narrative, but rather in the story which precedes it in the Talmud, which deals with the execution of Bruriah's parents, R. Ḥanina b. Tradyon and his wife, and the placing of their captive daughter in a brothel.[66]
3. The notion that the Talmud places before us two separate episodes is also hinted at in the Talmud itself, in the words of the guard to the investigators, "such and such was the episode" – in other words, the prior episode, the Bruriah Episode.
4. What is the difference between R. Meir fleeing due to "this episode" and him fleeing due to the Bruriah Episode? The Bruriah Episode presents the family's entanglement with the Roman authorities, who were after Bruriah's family, and R. Meir as well due to his marriage into the family,[67] as well as his efforts to rescue his sister-in-law from their clutches. To escape their net, he was forced to flee to another land, not under Roman rule.[68] By contrast, a different element is at the core of the second episode, that of shame.[69] To

66. "... Immediately they decreed for him to be burned [at the stake] and for his wife to be put to death, and for his daughter to be placed in a brothel" (Avodah Zarah 17b).
67. Her father died by their hands under torture, his wife was killed together with him, and his daughter was forced into a brothel (Avodah Zarah 17b–18a, and see *Sifri Devarim*, 307). His son too did not die a natural death but was killed by bandits (Tractate Smaḥot 12:13, and compare to *Eikha Rabba* [Vilna], 3:6).
68. Grossman already offered a similar explanation, that the Bruriah Episode is connected to her family's being pursued by the Romans ("On the Parsha of Bruriah," *Kolekh* 40 [Kislev 2002]; see also his words in connection with n. 6); but unlike our explanation, he does not connect this to the story that was brought in the Talmud.
69. The reason for the escape "because of shame" ("*mishum kisufa*"), is already known to the reader, from the episode brought in Rashi. It is interesting to note that this reason appears in another incident related to R. Meir, in which it is told that he fled (*arak*) from the *bet midrash* (Yerushalmi Beitzah 5:2). This is how R. Yosef Karo explained the reason for his fleeing: "Since Rebbi responded thus to him, R. Meir knew that they were performing the act indirectly and

> escape the Romans pursuing him, R. Meir was forced to simulate eating non-kosher food or embracing a prostitute, and likewise he was seen publicly entering a brothel. Although his behavior was justifiable and not forbidden, and although he did not actually engage in forbidden acts but merely appeared to do so, it would have been difficult to explain this to the public, and could have caused a desecration of God's name [*ḥilul HaShem*].[70] To prevent this, R. Meir was forced to flee far away to Babylonia where people would not have heard the story, and R. Meir would not be associated with these acts.[71]

Even if we ourselves would not have read the Talmud thus of our own accord, R. Judah of Speyer paved the way for us. According to his position, the Bruriah Episode was right in front of the reader's eyes the entire time. This reading fits well with the version of R. Nissim Gaon that we cited earlier, in which R. Meir fled to Babylonia with his wife.[72] Whether the escape was due to Roman pursuit

---

therefore it was permitted; and he fled out of shame, because it became known that he had chastised them inappropriately" (*Bet Yosef, Oraḥ Ḥayim* 339:3, and so too in *Kesef Mishneh* on Rambam, *Mishneh Torah, Hilkhot Shabbat* 23:5).

70. A similar idea was raised already by the Maharal of Prague, who wrote that according to the explanation that R. Meir was observed as if he had eaten food cooked by gentiles, *ḥilul HaShem* (desecration of God's name) was involved, for people could identify him (Maharal, *Ḥidushei Aggadot* 4 [Henig edition, 1980], 45 on Avodah Zarah 18a). A similar explanation was put forth even earlier by R. Yisrael Isserlein, author of *Terumat Hadeshen*, who connected the flight to the concern lest people who witnessed the acts identify R. Meir afterward, thereby causing a *ḥilul HaShem*: "And furthermore, there is reason for concern, perhaps those who witnessed the acts would identify R. Meir afterward, and it would be a *ḥilul HaShem* retroactively" (*Responsa Terumat Hadeshen*, no. 196, end) – and *the ḥilul HaShem* would obviously be a great shame to a man of R. Meir's stature.
71. Perhaps also, the danger to R. Meir abated following this episode – for the Romans concluded (in their opinion) that the person they were pursuing was not R. Meir. And perhaps they removed his image that they had etched beside the gates of the city – and if so, what remained at the end of the episode was the reason for the shame. This sharpens the difference between the two opinions regarding the reason for the escape. One should also note that the versions of the Gemara indeed hint to the two opposite ways of the transition to Bavel: a hasty escape, "*arak*," or a routine arrival, "*ata*."
72. It should be noted that many parts of the writings of R. Nissim Gaon were seen by R. Y. of Speyer (see *Yiḥusei Tanna'im V'Amora'im*, Mossad HaRav Kook edition [op cit., n. 62], introduction, pp. 20, 24); and it is not inconceivable that he was acquainted with the version of R. Nissim Gaon on the topic. One should also note that in the introduction to *Sefer HaMafte'aḥ*, R. Nissim Gaon writes "It should be mentioned that occasionally there will be mentioned matter that is neither in our Talmud nor in the Talmud of Eretz Yisrael" (*Sefer HaMafte'aḥ* with notes of Be'er Yaakov [above, n. 49], p. 4), and he notes a number of instances of this sort – including the Rav Papa Episode – but he does not mention the Bruriah Episode (although perhaps this is just chance, for his intention was not to count all instances of this sort but rather to give examples).

of R. Meir, Bruriah and her family, or whether it was to prevent embarrassment and desecration of God's name, either way it would have been natural for R. Meir to flee together with Bruriah and not alone.[73]

SUMMARY AND EDUCATIONAL CONCLUSIONS

In conclusion, let us summarize the main points of this article for the reader:

1. The episode as it appears in Rashi contains a large number of peculiar details that are inconsistent with Talmudic sources. Because of this, and due to the complete silence of Tosafot as well as a lack of evidence that the story was known to their generation, there is leeway to conclude that the story was not written by Rashi, but later on, and was inserted into Rashi's commentary as a result of a scribal error.
2. The Bruriah Episode is parallel to the Rav Papa Episode, both in its Talmudic foundation and in their central themes. The parallels are sharpened when comparing the Bruriah Episode to Rashi's version of the Rav Papa Episode, as opposed to the other versions of that period. We cannot establish the source of the parallels with certainty, but it is reasonable that it is not coincidental and that the Bruriah Episode was composed with the inspiration of the Rav Papa Episode.

---

73. After concluding writing our article, Dalia Hoshen's book appeared: Dalia Hoshen, *Beruria the Tannait: A Theological Reading of a Female Mishnaic Scholar* (Lanham, 2007), with the fourth chapter dedicated to the Bruriah Episode (see mainly pp. 69–73). Some of her work overlaps with parts of our thinking, although she shortens many matters and elaborates on others. Nevertheless, it should be noted that she raised the possibility that "this Episode" (*hai ma'aseh*) and the "Bruriah Episode" are presented together in the Talmud before us (p. 71), and so too the hypothesis that the source of this story is not Rashi but rather in a collection of unauthoritative midrashim, and from there, the story made its way into Rashi's commentary over the course of years (pp. 72–73). However, we should note that in order to back up this hypothesis, she relies on the absence of the "Bruriah Episode" in a number of books of commentary and mussar from the period of the *Rishonim*, from *Maḥzor Vitri* and up to *Magen Avot* of Rashbatz, with the assumption that all who deal with the meeting between Bruriah and R. Yossi on the way to Lod would also deal with the Bruriah Episode in Rashi's commentary ("Had they recognized this story about Bruriah, they certainly would not turn to her as an icon of modesty," p. 72). This is surprising for a number of reasons: first, this assumption itself is questionable. Second, Rashbatz's mention proves the reverse, for during his time – the end of the fourteenth century and first half of the fifteenth century – there is no doubt that the Bruriah Episode already existed in Rashi's commentary. And finally, for some reason, she does not notice at all the fact, which is several times more salient, that even in the writings of Ba'alei HaTosafot, there is no mention of this story.

3. R. Judah of Speyer implies that the Bruriah Episode is in the Talmud itself. Therefore it seems that the lengthy narrative should be divided into two sections: the Bruriah Episode and "this episode." This reading is not in sync with the generally accepted understanding of this passage, but many details fall far better into place as a result. And especially, the nature of the Bruriah Episode becomes apparent in a way that articulates with the Ge'onic versions as brought by R. Nissim Gaon.

Let us now return to where we started, to the hashkafic questions that the Bruriah Episode raises in our generation in both the Torah world and the religious-feminist world. Practically speaking, we are no longer forced to accept the story in Rashi as part of Bruriah's life history, and those who wish to delve into her background now have a concrete basis for ignoring this story.[74] For educators who reach this passage in the Talmud and are deliberating how to teach it, we now have the version of R. Judah of Speyer, which allows us to locate the Bruriah Episode in the Talmud itself. In this way, the educational dilemma can now be put to rest.

---

74. We will note that many of the later lexicons of the Sages of the Talmud already did so, even if intuitively and not on a reasoned foundation. See: R. M. D. Gross, *Avot HaDorot* 2 (above, n. 24), p. 151; Mordekhai Margaliot (ed.) *Encyclopedia of the Sages of the Talmud and the Ge'onim* 1 (Tel Aviv, 1995), 76–77; Ze'ev Yavetz, *Toldot Yisrael* 6 (Tel Aviv, 1963), 155–57; Tzvi Kaplan, entry: "Bruriah," *Hebrew Encyclopedia*, vol. 9, p. 578. All of these left the Bruriah Episode out of their account, and some explicitly preferred "this Episode" as the explanation of the flight to Bavel. More complex is the account of Shlomo Berman, who one hundred years ago authored pamphlets on the sages of Israel which were collected afterward into the volume *MiGiborei Ha'Umah* (Jerusalem, 1955). In the entry "R. Meir," Berman referred to Bruriah with contradictory references testifying to his confusion about her. First, he writes that on the heels of Roman harassment, R. Meir "and his household [ed. note: i.e., his wife] fled to the land of the Partim" (p. 151; like the words of R. Nissim Gaon); but then he writes that apparently "his dear wife Bruriah did not live long, and died during her husband's lifetime" (pp. 152–53); and later he explicitly references the "Bruriah Episode," and comments that the reason R. Meir fled is unclear. Some say it was because the Roman authorities sought to kill him… and some say because of an infamous incident in his family that shamed him; but he rejects these theories and suggests R. Meir fled because of rivalry with R. Shimon b. Gamliel (p. 159. Regarding this conflict, see Horayot 13b).

Chapter 9

R. Akiva's Development: The Whole Story[1]

INTRODUCTION: OPINIONS REGARDING R. AKIVA'S LIFE

One who comes to set forth R. Akiva's life story, relying on contemporary works, will quickly find himself in a maze. Almost all those who attempt to write a history of R. Akiva end up producing differing pictures, as there is almost no detail on which opinions concur.[2] Some say that R. Akiva had only one wife, while others list four different wives; some believe he had, at most, one daughter and two sons, while others write that he had at least three daughters and six sons. According to certain views, R. Akiva married at the age of forty, while others have him already married at twenty, and so on.

A description of R. Akiva's life – and particularly his marriage to the daughter of Kalba Savua and his early Torah study – appears in different rabbinic texts, with each recounting a similar, yet different, story, with numerous discrepancies between the accounts. No wonder that the commonly held academic view

1. Ed. note: The bulk of this chapter was written in 2005, with later additions being mainly in the form of bibliographical references and notes in the introduction. It was originally published in *Alonei Mamre* 123 (2011). Translated by Perry Zamek.
2. Compare, for example, Y. S. Ben-Zuri, *Rabbi Akiva* (Jerusalem, 1924), ch. 1; A. Heimann, *Toldot Tanna'im V'Amora'im* 3 (Jerusalem, 1964), 988–1008; M. D. Gross, *Avot HaDorot* (Tel Aviv, 1971), 108–24; B. Z. Segal, *Encyclopedia L'Ḥakhmei HaTalmud V'haGe'onim* (Tel Aviv, 1970), 725–34; H. E. Kulitz, *Rosh LaḤakhamim* (Tel Aviv, 1980), ch. 1; R. Halperin, *Atlas Etz Ḥayim* 3 (Jerusalem, 1980), 275–78; Y. M. TaShma, "Rabbi Akiva," in *HaEncyclopedia HaIvrit* 27 (Jerusalem, 1975) 96–99.

maintains that the rabbinic sources fail to provide an accurate description and that the truth of the matter cannot be determined, as the rabbinic texts are no more than inspirational fables. The Sages, it would seem, attempted "to forge for R. Akiva the biography of a model scholar, a paradigmatic martyr, and an ideal husband"[3] – and so the stories about him should primarily be subjected to literary analysis.[4]

This conclusion is, of course, not limited to R. Akiva. It derives from skepticism toward descriptions and narratives in rabbinic literature. There is even a literary-interpretive school that argues that the stories of the Sages, and particularly those in the Talmud Bavli, lack any historical significance.[5] Although this argument is not necessarily accepted by most scholars, it allows far-reaching conclusions to be drawn regarding the life of the "real" R. Akiva.[6]

---

3. T. Ilan, *Masekhet* 3 (Jerusalem, 2005), 103–12. See also M. Wachsman, *Morei HaDorot* (Tel Aviv, 1971), 22–25. He holds that rabbinic sources are merely "parables," some contradictory and others exaggerated, and which only evidence "the extent to which the personality of this sage was exceptional, in the eyes of both his contemporaries and later generations." Indications of such an approach in relation to the life of R. Akiva can already be found in B. Z. Becher's *Aggadot HaTanna'im*, translated from the German eighty-five years ago (Jerusalem, 1921), A2:24–80, but its chief application to the life of R. Akiva was made by S. Safrai in his *Akiva ben Yosef – Ḥayyav U'Mishnato* (Tel Aviv, 1971), 9–64. See also his work *Eretz Yisrael V'Ḥakhameha BiTekufat HaMishnah V'haTalmud* (Tel Aviv, 1984), 172–75.
4. See, for example, the treatment by A. Shinan, "Rabbi Akiva's Three Wives," in: *Masekhet* 2 (Jerusalem, 2004), 11–25. Shinan is careful to label his analysis as a "literary examination" only, while setting aside the question of historicity. According to him, each of the stories about R. Akiva was formulated in isolation from the others, and so he concludes that Rachel and the daughter of Kalba Savua are not the same individual: one is a "Babylonian wife" while the other is a "wife from the Land of Israel." In addition to these two, he finds a third wife, a "Roman wife." This approach was adopted by R. B. Lau, who described Shinan's argument as "strongly research-based"; see his *Ḥakhamim* II: *Yemei Yavneh ad Bar Kokhva* (Tel Aviv, 2007), 314–16, and n. 89 there, and also pp. 181–85. For a further response to Shinan's article, and for a rather speculative suggestion regarding the "Roman wife," see T. Ilan's article (n. 3, above). Further on in this article, we will address the question of how many wives R. Akiva did in fact have (see nn. 14, 17, 74).
5. Among the best known proponents of this school is Y. Frenkel. See his textbook *Midrash VaAggadah* 2 (Tel Aviv, 1997), 365–75. For a faithful representation of this approach in a biography of *Ḥazal*, see: A. Meir, *R. Yehudah HaNasi* (Tel Aviv, 2002), particularly the introduction, pp. 11–15. For the more commonly accepted approach, and its application on the same topic, see A. Oppenheimer, *R. Yehudah HaNasi* (Jerusalem, 2007).
6. See, for example, E. Steinman, *Be'er HaTalmud* 2 (Tel Aviv, 1963), 9–42. Although this work does not purport to be a scientific essay, and does not utilize academic research on rabbinic literature, its author does grant himself very broad literary license regarding the life story of R. Akiva, with a rather creative interpretation of the various sources, apparently on the basis of veiled assumptions that these sources are in any case not exact.

What is common to most of the above and the widely accepted approach in literary research is, inter alia, the fundamental assumption that, if there exist in the rabbinic texts parallel stories with different details, then this necessarily represents a contradiction between different traditions, or two independent stories, neither of which is faithful to the truth. The tendency is then, to give preference to one of the sources and to declare it more reliable than the others, or, to treat all of the sources merely as "belles lettres."

However, the failure to reconcile contradictory sources does not necessarily justify the determination that things are not as they appear,[7] or that some of the stories are untrue. A new attempt may indeed be successful in reconciling the sources. Let me state at the outset that it is not my intention to indulge in apologetics, nor to engage in polemics with scholars regarding R. Akiva's life, nor to address more broadly academic approaches to rabbinic texts.

My purpose in this article is to focus on R. Akiva himself, and to suggest an alternative sequence to his life story, one that seeks to reconcile the variant sources in a consistent manner, without inaccuracies or contradictions.[8] In this way, I would like to demonstrate that it is possible to obtain a clear, trustworthy, and contradiction-free picture from the rabbinic sources regarding the life of one of the greatest of the *Tanna'im*.

---

7. Y. Frenkel (*Midrash VaAggadah* 1:183–89) analyzes incisively and in line with the best of the literary and hermeneutic tools to be found in academic research, the various approaches that developed over the years in interpretation of midrashic sources, and describes, inter alia, the difference between allegory, which involves the overt or tacit intention of the author, and allegoristics, which interprets allegorically sources in which there is no hint of their having an allegorical meaning. It would be difficult to assume that he did not sense that his own interpretations of "stories of the Sages" and their meaning was clearly allegoristic! (And that, despite its being shaped with literary tools.) Here is not the place to discuss this at length.
8. An approach of this type already appeared about 150 years ago, in R. Eliyahu Medliatich's commentary on *Avot D'Rabi Natan*, entitled *Ben Avraham* (Vilna, 1833; reprinted in Jerusalem, 1971). To the best of my knowledge, he was the first to deal systematically with the differences between the various sources on R. Akiva, attempting to reconcile them and assemble from them a complete story (see also Addendum B to Version A of *Avot D'Rabi Natan*, ch. 8; limitations of space prevent us from discussing this at length). However, he did not write this as an organized monograph, but rather as a commentary on the Mishnah – a commentary that did not make it into the popular Vilna Shas edition, but was published as a book in its own right, and was doomed to a certain anonymity and lack of influence. In the context of the present article, see the analysis by R. Yigal Ariel in his book, *Arapeh Meshuvatam* (Ḥispin, 1998), 291–333. Although his treatment of R. Akiva's life is not essentially biographical, most of what he writes is consistent with our own approach, as will be set out below.

REASONS FOR THE DISCREPANCIES BETWEEN RABBINIC SOURCES

Stories about the life of R. Akiva abound in rabbinic literature. The best known, and most detailed, among them deal with the period commencing with his marriage and ending with his attaining preeminence as a Torah scholar, and it is here that we find most of the discrepancies and contradictions. Hence, we will focus on that period. There are three principal texts detailing the life of R. Akiva before he achieved greatness:

1. **Talmud Bavli, Ketubot 62b–63a**[9] (henceforth: Ketubot). Abstract: R. Akiva was a shepherd for Ben Kalba Savua. His employer's daughter set her heart on him, and became betrothed to him on condition that he study Torah. In response, her father expelled them from his home and excluded them, under oath, from benefiting in any way from his property. R. Akiva went off to study, returning after twelve years. However, as a result of hearing his wife's words, he goes off for a further twelve years. Upon his return, as one of the leading Sages of the time, he releases Kalba Savua from his vow.
2. **Talmud Bavli, Nedarim 50a** (henceforth: Nedarim). Abstract: R. Akiva becomes betrothed to the daughter of Kalba Savua, who expels them from his home and takes a vow not to allow them any benefit from his property. The two marry. They live together in dire poverty, until certain events lead R. Akiva's wife to send him to the *bet midrash*. He goes off to study, returning after twelve years, but as a result of hearing his wife's words, he goes off again for twelve years. When he returns, as one of the leading scholars of the age, he releases Kalba Savua from his vow.
3. ***Avot D'Rabi Natan* 6:2**[10] (hereinafter: *Avot D'Rabi Natan*). Abstract: R. Akiva was forty years old, but had not yet learned anything. As a result of the incident of a stone hollowed out by water, he took upon himself to study. Initially

9. *Yalkut Shimoni* (Mishlei, *siman* 948), which is later than the rest of the sources and based on some of them, brings a story identical to that in Ketubot, apart from minor differences. We will mention the most significant of them.
10. *Avot D'Rabi Natan,* Version A, which is the more commonly printed version. In Version B (ch. 12), the story is told somewhat differently, but parallel in most respects: (a) R. Akiva began to learn as a result of the episode of the stone. (b) This occurred when he was forty years old. (c) Initially he studied alongside his son. (d) During his studies he supported himself from the sale of wood. (e) His wife suffered with him during the period of study. The principal biographical differences are the mention that he had twenty-four thousand students, and the omission of his wife's name.

he studied alongside his young son, later going to study with R. Eliezer and R. Yehoshua, until he became one of the leading scholars of the age. The text concludes by mentioning that his initial period of study was twelve years, and that his wife Rachel played an important role in this.

In our opinion, the different details in parallel stories are not evidence of inaccuracy or of a "well-developed imagination" on the part of the Sage who relates the episode. Rather, the differences lie in the context in which they are brought.[11] If we compare the stories carefully, while setting aside the paradigmatic assumption of contradictory information, we will note that there is not one fact that necessarily contradicts any other fact. Each of the stories emphasizes certain details and ignores others. The reason for this is the general context within which each story is cited.[12]

To wit: The Gemara in Ketubot deals with scholars who left their homes and their wives for extended periods of time – twelve years, or twice that; hence it focuses on this aspect and its (in this case, positive) outcome.

The Gemara in Nedarim discusses those Sages who lived with their wives in great poverty, but eventually became wealthy. It therefore dwells in detail upon the poverty of R. Akiva and his wife, and then his departure to study Torah – which in the end led to his wealth, as the Gemara concludes there.

The *baraita* in *Avot D'Rabi Natan* brings stories of *Tanna'im* who were ignoramuses in their early lives, but afterward became leading scholars of their generation. Hence, the marriage of R. Akiva and his wife's assistance are mentioned in passing, incidentally as it were, while there is extensive detail regarding his first steps in Torah study and the difficulties that he faced.

My approach in constructing R. Akiva's biography will be to integrate the different sources, weaving them together until the various occurrences become one all-encompassing story, in which each detail has its proper place, based

---

11. And as pointed out by Maharsha (in Nedarim). Those who argue otherwise will have to explain, inter alia, why and how the right hand, as it were (which edited Ketubot), was not aware of what the left hand (which edited Nedarim) was doing, to the point that the same story, appearing twice in the Talmud Bavli itself, "mixed" different details into the two parallel passages, details that ostensibly contradict one another.
12. That is, we accept the view that the stories of the Sages were all brought for a specific purpose – depending on context – but contrary to the claim that the creators of the story invented details at will, we believe that the Sages chose, from the tradition that they had before them, the details relevant to their narrative, without bringing those facts that were not important for the specific purpose of those passages.

upon the assumption that each text reflects only some of the events. Following is the chronological sequence of the sources: initially the story of the betrothal (Ketubot), then the story of married life (Nedarim), followed by the story of the beginning of studies and their continuation (*Avot D'Rabi Natan*), and finally the story of the return home and the subsequent events up to the annulment of the vow (Ketubot and Nedarim).

FACTS THAT CONTRADICT THE COMMONLY HELD NOTION OF R. AKIVA

As a preface to R. Akiva's life story, let us present a number of facts that do not match the commonly held view of him, and which touch principally on three issues: his age upon marriage to the daughter of Kalba Savua, his life from his marriage till he departed to undertake Torah study, and the reason that he did not study Torah till the age of forty:

1. R. Akiva married the daughter of Kalba Savua when he was at most thirty-three years old, and apparently younger. We learn this from the *baraita* in *Avot D'Rabi Natan*, which relates that at the age of forty, R. Akiva already had a son who was a pupil of the local *melamed*. This son was at least six years of age, since that was the age of instruction, and at this age children are sent to the local *melamed*: "And they are enrolled at age six or seven [...]; before age six they are not accepted, from then on they are accepted"[13] – hence R. Akiva was married at least seven years beforehand, and apparently even longer.[14] This detail can also be gleaned from the continuation of the *baraita*, which states that one who did not study Torah cannot argue, in his defense, that he was burdened with the care of his children, since at the time that R. Akiva

13. Bava Batra 21a, and as explained there, this was enacted prior to R. Akiva's time. See also Ketubot 50a.

14. As the son with whom R. Akiva studied was not necessarily his firstborn. There are those who, on this basis, wished to prove the statements of Rashi and of the students of Rabbenu Gershom (Bekhorot 58a and elsewhere, followed by *Arukh*: s.v. *kere'aḥ*; Rashbam: Pesaḥim 112b; Ri Hazaken: Bava Batra 113a; and Rid: Shabbat 150a) that R. Yehoshua b. Korḥa was the son of R. Akiva – and, according to our calculations, the opposing view of Tosafot is disputed. But even if we were able to resolve matters from a chronological perspective (something not at all easy), this does not rule out Rabbenu Tam's statement, in which he wonders how the Gemara could refer to R. Akiva by a derogatory name, and why R. Yehoshua b. Korḥa never mentions his lineage (see Sanhedrin 110b, where R. Yehoshua b. Korḥa mentions R. Akiva by name, and nothing more). See also Rabbenu Nissim (quoted in Tosafot Bekhorot, 58a, followed by Rabbenu Yehudah of Speyer, the teacher of Rokeaḥ: *Erkei Tanna'im V'Amora'im*, s.v. *R. Yehoshua b. Korḥa*) who states that the bald person referred to by Ben Azzai is not R. Akiva.

commenced learning, he already had "sons and daughters" – the plural indicating at least two.[15] Thus it may be assumed that there were at least two sons and two daughters[16] – and again it would seem that his marriage to Rachel took place many years before he began studying in an organized manner.[17]

2. Following his marriage to the daughter of Kalba Savua, R. Akiva remained at home and did not immediately depart for twelve years of study. This is gleaned from the repetition in the Gemara,[18] which initially states "she sent him," but then recounts that the bride's father heard of the betrothal and expelled her from his home, and only then does it state "he went." Hence, he

---

15. In the words of Ibn Ezra (Vayikra 5:24), based on the rule coined by the Sages (see Sifra, Metzora, *Parashat Zavim*, *Parashah* 5, and in numerous places in the Talmud and Midrash). See also *Hagahot HaGriv* (*Avot D'Rabi Natan*) and others, whose version of the text reads "many sons and daughters."
16. When one counts the number of known offspring of R. Akiva, we indeed find two sons and two daughters. Two sons: R. Shimon, who was married off by R. Akiva (Yerushalmi Berakhot 6:8, cf. Bavli Shabbat 112a) and died during his father's lifetime; and two daughters: one daughter who was married to R. Yehoshua b. Kefusai (Shabbat 147a), and it is apparently this daughter for whom a miracle occurred on her wedding night (Shabbat 156b), and an additional daughter to whom Ben Azzai was betrothed, but he apparently did not marry her (Ketubot 63a, Tosafot there). However, it is possible that both instances refer to the same daughter – who initially became betrothed to Ben Azzai, but when he did not marry her, she married R. Yehoshua b. Kefusai. We also learn from elsewhere in the Gemara (Mo'ed Katan 21a) that along with R. Shimon, another son of R. Akiva passed away (apparently an unmarried son, since R. Akiva's words, "even two sons, bridegrooms," implies married. However, compare with the language in *Semaḥot* ch. 8, but in any case the name of an additional son is not mentioned. Even taking both these possibilities together, the number of R. Akiva's offspring is not less than four.
    Y. Kanovitz, in his book *Rabbi Akiva* (Jerusalem, 1965), 28, lists three additional sons, but he erred in that he included in his list anyone whose father's name was Akiva; indeed, there are other Sages whose name was Akiva (see Yerushalmi Yevamot 2:12, 16:5, and elsewhere), and it is unlikely that the Gemara would simply say "son of Akiva" without giving the honor due to R. Akiva and without hinting at the son's lineage. Furthermore, in many variants these individuals are called "son of Akavya," and not "son of Akiva." And even though, in a number of sources, R. Akiva is also mentioned as Rabbi Akavya (see, for example, *Yalkut Shimoni*, *Tetzaveh*, 282), it is clear that these are copyists' errors, apart from a single mention of an unknown sage.
17. In line with our approach that R. Akiva married Rachel at a relatively young age, there is no need for the implausible explanation quoted by R. Y. Halperin in *Seder HaDorot* (Warsaw, 1882, s.v. *Rabi Yehoshua b. Korḥa*) and in *Binyan Yeshoshua* (*Avot D'Rabi Natan*. This view was followed by Heiman, Gross, Kulitz, and Halperin. For their source, see Tosafot on Megilla 28a, and Shabbat 127b), that R. Akiva may have had another wife prior to the daughter of Kalba Savua, and it was she who bore Rabbi Yehoshua b. Korḥa; and particularly since there is no evidence for the existence of such a wife. See also *Hagahot HaGra* (ibid.) who connects all of R. Akiva's children to Rachel.
18. In Ketubot.

did not go immediately upon her sending him, and various other events took place.[19] At this point the Gemara in Nedarim takes over the tale: It recounts that, after Kalba Savua's daughter had been expelled from her father's home, R. Akiva completed the marriage to her, and it subsequently describes their married life during this period of poverty – again indicating that he was at home following the marriage. This is consistent with what was written in the previous paragraph, that a period of seven to ten years passed following the marriage, during which R. Akiva had not yet learned Torah.

3. During the years between his marriage and his departure to study for twelve years, R. Akiva apparently attempted a number of times to fulfill his promise to his wife and to go and learn, but he was not successful. He *tried*, both since it was on this condition that his wife agreed to be betrothed to him, and since, as we wrote above, following the marriage his wife sent him, which implies that he went. He was *not successful* – as we have seen, it was only after some seven to ten years that he finally set himself down to learn. There are many proofs of these attempts to study without success:

   a. Following the appearance of Eliyahu at R. Akiva's home, his wife again said to him, "Go to the House of Study."[20] This repeated request implies that, during those years in which R. Akiva was at home, his wife would press him to fulfill his promise to study Torah.

   b. When R. Akiva ultimately went to study Torah, the Mishnah[21] uses the term *ḥazar* – he returned – meaning that he had already been there previously, that is, he had already attempted to settle down there and study.[22]

   c. The story of the release of Kalba Savua from his vow indicates that, at the time of his marriage, R. Akiva was perceived as someone who did not even

---

19. And as explained by Maharsha (Nedarim), that R. Akiva did not go after the betrothal and before she married him (unlike Tosafot, Shabbat 150a, s.v. *v'Rabi*).

20. Nedarim. The implication of "again" is that this was in addition to her having sent him to study following their betrothal ("sent him"; Ketubot).

21. In *Avot D'Rabi Natan*. This was also sensed by Safrai, whose comments on the matter are similar to ours. Ben-Zuri also outlines a similar approach, particularly in relation to what we said above, on the years that R. Akiva spent at home following his marriage but prior to his period of studies.

22. This is also stated almost explicitly in Version B of *Avot D'Rabi Natan*: first it states "that he sought to learn Torah; only after that was the incident of the well, which caused him to take the final decision to study (although it is possible to read that sentence as a prologue to the story, and then there is no proof from here. However, the straightforward meaning tends toward our view).

know one verse,[23] whereas at the time that he finally decided – at the age of forty – to learn Torah, he was considered as already knowing some verses and midrashim by heart.[24] This too indicates that even before starting his studies, R. Akiva had attempted to learn at a certain level. Apparently, he had initially given up, since nonetheless it is said of him in *Avot D'Rabi Natan* that "he was forty years old [...] and had not learned anything."

4. This evidence, and the fact that R. Akiva was an *am ha'aretz,*[25] seems to indicate that R. Akiva was slow-witted, and therefore was unsuccessful in learning. However, this is in no way possible, since when R. Akiva ultimately decided to learn, he grew to towering Torah stature. He displayed razor-sharp analytical ability, until he had overtaken all his teachers. This can hardly be said of someone with learning disabilities. It is almost certain that R. Akiva was, by his nature, sharp-witted – and righteous – and there is extensive evidence of this:
   a. R. Akiva was not an ordinary *am ha'aretz,* in the negative sense, but rather a humble individual of fine character.[26] His being defined as an *am ha'aretz* relates solely to his level of knowledge of Torah, and not to his Torah potential.[27] Despite the fact that he was devoid of Torah knowledge, R. Akiva was pleasant with others and pleasant before God (which is the straightforward meaning of the expression *tzanua uma'alei*; see Maharsha, who relates R. Akiva's humility to the verse "and walk humbly with the Lord your God").
   b. Tosafot[28] explain that R. Akiva's hatred of the Sages[29] did not come from ignorance or derision of the Torah itself – but from a consistent, logical

23. Ketubot, and in *Yalkut Shimoni*: "Even one chapter or even one law or even one verse." Regarding the vow, see n. 73.
24. See *Avot D'Rabi Natan,* and as pointed out in *Binyan Yehoshua* there, based on statements made by R. Akiva when he decided to learn Torah. However, his addition that R. Akiva already knew Tanakh and Midrash is surprising, since the text clearly states that R. Akiva went to study with the teacher of the young children, and subsequently went on to learn Sefer Vayikra.
25. As he himself attested in Pesaḥim 49b. Similarly: "R. Akiva was ignorant for forty years" (*Bereshit Rabba, siman* 100).
26. Ketubot. Hence the mention of his name with the description of *amei ha'aratzot* (ignorant persons), in Pesaḥim (49b) is only incidental to his harsh statement and his attitude to the Sages.
27. And as the verse "Wisdom is with the humble" is applied to him by Maharsha in Ketubot.
28. Tosafot, Ketubot, s.v. *dehavah.*
29. See Pesaḥim 49b.

worldview; hence, in spite of this hatred, R. Akiva was observant of the commandments, and even meticulous in his observance.[30]

c. When he made his final, decisive choice to study Torah, R. Akiva revealed, in his words, that the reason for his not having learned stemmed not from the mind but from the heart: "The words of Torah will penetrate my heart"[31] – hence the source of the matter lay in his desire, and not in his ability.

In light of this evidence, it may well be suggested that the fact that R. Akiva was an *am ha'aretz* and unschooled derived from a fierce inner opposition to schooling and to scholars;[32] to the point that, despite his genius, R. Akiva did not even bother to learn the alphabet. There seems not to exist a direct source that sheds light on the reason for his anti-scholastic bent, but various hypotheses may be raised based on statements he made after he had become a Torah giant.[33]

5. Even after R. Akiva finally decided to study, he did not leave home immediately. During his initial period of study – when he learned to read and continued on to study the entire book of Vayikra[34] – he was still with his family.[35] Apparently only after he had acquired a firm foundation in Torah did he leave his home to study for a continuous period of years.

---

30. Tosafot, ibid. As may be understood from the statements of the Sages in Eruvin (see 21b, "in his childhood"; however, see *Avot D'Rabi Natan,* Version A, ch. 21).
31. *Avot D'Rabi Natan,* and more clearly stated in Version B (ch. 12) – "Is my heart harder than stone? I will go and learn one passage from the Torah. He continued to study, until he had learned the whole of the Torah" – and as we explained (see next note) the meaning is something like this: "If water can penetrate stone, then certainly my disposition can be changed through the study of Torah; I will go and try to learn one passage, and I will certainly change."
32. This explains why – in spite of the fact that over the course of his life and under the influence of his wife R. Akiva attempted on a number of occasions to go and study, as we have shown – he had failed: his inner resistance was apparently too strong for these attempts to succeed. It was only after many years, in which his wife's view was slowly internalized, and after the powerful encounter with the well and the water, that R. Akiva understood that neither he, nor the world, could exist without Torah, as Ben-Zuri puts it; see further below.
33. See for example the suggestion by R. Uriel Touito, in his "On the Character of R. Akiva," in *Mesilot* (Karnei Shomron, Tamuz 5764/2004), 149–52. Although his article is primarily homiletical, it should be noted that he too saw the main points that we established above, that R. Akiva married Rachel before he reached the age of forty, attempted to go and study, but was not successful (p. 144).
34. As recounted in *Avot D'Rabi Natan.*
35. Since, as we have seen, he initially went to study alongside his son, and it was only after he had learned all of Sefer Vayikra that it says that "he went" (*Avot D'Rabi Natan*). Furthermore, one source (Yerushalmi Shabbat 6:1) states that his wife provided for him during the time that he studied, while another source (*Avot D'Rabi Natan*) tells us that he earned his own living while

EVENTS OF R. AKIVA'S LIFE, IN CHRONOLOGICAL ORDER

Let us proceed to a suggested recounting of the events in the order in which they took place, beginning with R. Akiva's marriage to Kalba Savua's daughter and ending following his twenty-four years of study. That which is explicit in the sources will be written without brackets, while what is implied or can be extrapolated will appear in brackets.

Part One[36]

R. Akiva worked as a shepherd for one of the members of Kalba Savua's family,[37] [his age then being less than thirty-three]. Rachel,[38] the daughter of his employer, saw he was modest and of outstanding character, and decided to marry him, on condition that he go to study Torah.[39] R. Akiva agreed,[40] and Rachel became betrothed to him privately,[41] and sent him to study.

Part Two[42]

[Notwithstanding his hatred for scholars, R. Akiva went and attempted to study Torah, as he had promised his betrothed; but this study was nonetheless contrary

---

studying. Thus, it seems that the first referred to the period during which he was still with his family, while the second speaks clearly of the period in which he was already studying before R. Eliezer and R. Yehoshua.

36. This part appears in Ketubot.
37. "The son of Kalba Savua" – thus the text in Ketubot (and in *Yalkut Shimoni*), as well as some of the variants in Nedarim; and it appears from some places (see Ta'anit 4b, "the family of Kalba Savua," and *Bereshit Rabba* 98:8, "the household of Kalba Savua") that Kalba Savua was the name of a rich family, apparently named for the progenitor of the family (one might compare this with the present-day "Rothschilds"; see n. 74), and here it refers to one of its members. It is possible that this son's residence was close to Lod, since that is the location of most of the major events in R. Akiva's life. As recounted in *Avot D'Rabi Natan* (Version B, ch. 12), R. Akiva was located (and apparently lived) in the neighborhood of Lod when he began to study, and this was also where his teachers resided: R. Eliezer's yeshiva was in Lod, Naḥum of Gimzo dwelt near Lod (and R. Yehoshua's yeshiva was also located there, according to most approaches); R. Akiva's own yeshiva was in Bnei Brak, not far from there, and similarly the Sanhedrin was located in Yavneh and in the upper chamber of Nitzeh's house (in Lod).
38. Her name is given explicitly in *Avot D'Rabi Natan*, and also alluded to in Ketubot – "Raḥela [Aramaic for sheep, but also an allusion to the name Rachel] went after the sheep."
39. It may be assumed that this condition was because Rachel saw R. Akiva's enormous potential (see Maharsha on Ketubot), but did not share his attitude toward Torah study and Torah scholars, and based on her faith in his ability to change, she conditioned their marriage on his going to learn Torah.
40. Primarily because he wished to marry her, and it may be that he believed that it would not be difficult for him to go and learn from the Rabbis, notwithstanding his hatred of them.
41. Apparently because she was afraid of what her family and those around her might say regarding the fact that she became betrothed to an *am ha'aretz*. See also n. 62.
42. This part appears in Nedarim.

to his spirit, and so he returned.] Rachel's father heard that she had become betrothed to R. Akiva, and he expelled her from his home, vowing that she would not benefit from his possessions.[43] R. Akiva and Rachel proceeded to marry.

They lived in great poverty, so much so that in winter they slept in a hayloft, and R. Akiva would pick the straw from Rachel's hair.[44] [He saw that she was sad,] and said to her: Were I able, I would purchase for you a "Jerusalem of Gold!" [but she was not consoled]. Eliyahu HaNavi appeared to them in the guise of a poor man. He knocked at their door, and called out: Give me a little straw, for my wife has given birth, and I have nothing on which to have her sleep. R. Akiva said to his wife: Do you see, there are those who don't even have straw! [and thus we should rejoice in our lot. When Rachel saw that he thought that she was again saddened by their poverty, she revealed that she was not saddened by their financial state, but because he had not gone to study Torah as promised,[45] and] she again requested: Go to the *bet midrash* [and learn Torah]!

Part Three[46]

[It seems that he listened to her, and again went to the *bet midrash* in that locality, but once again was unable to bring himself to value study. In any event, he would orally recite those verses and midrashim that were taught to the ignorant.[47] Meanwhile, some years passed.] At this stage, he was already forty years old, and had four or more children.

Once, he saw a stone that had been worn away by water, and asked people: Who wore the stone away? They replied: The water wore it away. [This explanation seemed most strange to him,] and he expressed his astonishment,[48] whereupon they asked him: Do you not recite the verse "Stones – the water wore them away"?![49] [It was then that R. Akiva suddenly comprehended the potential

43. In Ketubot as well.
44. Maharsha, and before him the commentator in Nedarim, understood that she would also pick the straw from his hair, and that is likely (apart from those interpretations that state that he was bald, of course; see n. 62 below) in addition to what we have said to explain his later promise to purchase an adornment for her.
45. This is apparently what she told him, since otherwise we cannot understand why the Gemara would connect his two attempts at comforting her to her request that he go to study, and where that request came from.
46. This part is in *Avot D'Rabi Natan*.
47. As we have seen above, that when he finally decided to study, he already knew a few verses and midrashim.
48. See the emendation of the Vilna Gaon.
49. Iyov 14:19.

of Torah, for if water has the potential over time to penetrate and transform a stone] then how much more would protracted Torah study be able to penetrate [and transform] one's heart [and all that is needed is patience, just as in the case of water wearing down a stone. He then decided to] return to the *bet midrash*.

Initially he went to study with his son's *melamed*, sitting together with him to master the alphabet [with great patience]. He learned *alef* and *bet*. He learned from *alef* to *tav* [and continued diligently, until he had learned all of *Torat Kohanim*.] During this period of study [when, as we have stated, he was still with his family], Rachel provided for him [including] by selling the hair of her head.[50]

Part Four[51]

[Once he had mastered the basics, he went and fulfilled his promise to his wife] leaving [his town] to study Torah [with total devotion] for twelve years.[52] Initially he studied alone.[53] During this period there occurred a certain incident, in the wake of which he understood the importance of apprenticing himself to *talmidei ḥakhamim*,[54] without which, even if he were to cover the whole Torah, he would still be considered an *am ha'aretz*.[55] [Therefore] after studying the entire Torah on his own,[51] he went and sat before R. Eliezer b. Horkenos and R. Yehoshua b.

50. Yerushalmi Shabbat 6:7. And it appears that this was R. Akiva's intention in saying (*Avot D'Rabi Natan*), "She suffered with me a great deal in [learning] Torah," that is, not just during those years in which she was alone with their children, out of her desire that he learn Torah.
51. This part is in Ketubot and Nedarim.
52. There are a variety of explanations for this number (see, for example, *Iyun Yaakov* on Ketubot 62a, which quotes the Gemara in Ḥulin 24a that states that three years are required for one to see blessing [progress] in one's studies, and connect that with the statement in Kiddushin 30a, that there are four areas of study – Tanakh, Mishnah, halakhah, and aggadah – and so twelve years are required to cover these topics and see progress in them). The principal explanation is based on the statement (Ketubot 50a, q.v.), "A man must bear with his son up to twelve years," which implies that twelve years is the customary length of time – as it is in the present day – for the basic period of studies, from the beginning of the age of education until "at eighteen one marries." This is also the fact underlying the stories quoted in the Gemara (Ketubot 62a) prior to that of R. Akiva, which mention other individuals who went to study for twelve years; this appears to have been the customary term of study in those days, and it was even the practice to make an agreement with a bridegroom that he would undertake studies for that period of time, in return for his father-in-law ensuring his livelihood (q.v.). This would refute the view of Safrai and others, who viewed the number as being merely symbolic or typological.
53. *Avot D'Rabi Natan*.
54. See Yerushalmi Nazir 7:1, and *Derekh Eretz Zuta* (ch. 8), and compare with Semaḥot (4:34, and see Tosafot on Ketubot 17a).
55. As he states later, in Berakhot 47b.

Ḥananya,[56] receiving their traditions and serving them.[57] Throughout those years, he supported himself by gathering wood (alternatively, thorns), half of which he used for himself and the other half he sold to provide for the rest of his needs.[58]

Part Five[49]

After twelve years, R. Akiva returned to his town. He was already so great in Torah, that the Gemara demonstrates this by saying that [as it were] he brought twelve thousand students with him.[59] When he arrived home, he heard, as he passed behind his house, a wicked old man[60] saying to Rachel: Your father was justified in treating you as he did! First, for having married someone who is unlike you,[61] and furthermore, that he left you a living widow for all these years![62] For how long will you conduct yourself as a living widow?[63] She replied: Were he to lis-

56. *Avot D'Rabi Natan,* Nedarim. And specifically before them, since it was because of them that he initially went to serve scholars, as explained in the Yerushalmi (n. 53 above).

57. See Pesaḥim 36a.

58. *Avot D'Rabi Natan,* and as *Binyan Yehoshua* explains the word *hitkashet.*

59. Ketubot. This is the only detail in the entire story that is necessarily interpreted non-literally – based on the sources themselves (*Avot D'Rabi Natan,* Yerushalmi Pesaḥim 6:3), which state that it was only in the thirteenth year of his studies that R. Akiva began teaching Torah to others. Indeed, the Gemara in Nedarim does not state that he brought students with him on this visit. And this is how the difference (described in Nedarim) between his two returns to his hometown is explained: On his first return, no public honor was shown to him, and he arrived home alone, while on his second return all of the townspeople came out to welcome him, so much so that his wife had to push her way through the crowds to reach him. This occurred, as on this second occasion R. Akiva was already famous as one of the leading scholars of the generation, who had thousands of students. See also n. 67.

60. In Nedarim, "wicked person"; in Ketubot, "old man"; and in *Yalkut Shimoni,* which is neutral in terms of its context, "a certain person." The three sources are, of course, speaking of the same individual; the different emphasis regarding his character and what he said derives from the different point of reference to his words, depending on the context of the story, since the context of the story in Nedarim is the life of the Sages with their wives, while in Ketubot the context is the Torah study of the Sages, and so the different approaches are appropriate.

61. In two senses: he is unlike her in appearance, since he is bald (Nedarim 58a and commentaries, Tosafot Pesaḥim 112a), while she has such luxuriant hair that she was able to use it to provide for her husband; and in lineage, since he is the descendant of converts (Rambam, introduction to *Mishneh Torah, Dikdukei Soferim* on Sanhedrin 96b; see also *Menorat HaMa'or,* ch. 3, fifth candle, principle 3, part 2; R. Avraham Zacuto, *Sefer Yuḥasin,* s.v. *Rabi Akiva,* and elsewhere) from the offspring of Sisera (R. Nissim Gaon, Berakhot 27b, and see also Berakhot 27b and Yerushalmi Berakhot 4:1, which indicate that R. Akiva lacked the merit of his forebears), while she was from a family of wealth and distinguished lineage. The second of these differences was already indicated by Maharsha in Ketubot.

62. Nedarim.

63. Ketubot.

ten to me, he would go and sit in study for an additional twelve years! R. Akiva heard this, and said to himself: Since my wife has given me permission, I shall return [to the yeshiva].

He went and sat in study for a further twelve years. He continued to study with R. Eliezer and R. Yehoshua. [In contrast to the previous twelve years, when he only absorbed their Torah but did not open his mouth to challenge them, at this point] R. Akiva began to demonstrate his virtuosity in Torah already in the first year.[64] [Later] R. Yehoshua ordained him.[65] R. Akiva continued to grow greater in Torah until he disputed his teacher's words,[66] and from the status of disciple he became for them a disciple-colleague (*talmid-ḥaver*).[67]

Part Six

At the end of these twelve years, he returned to his town, and by now he had twenty-four thousand students.[68] All of the town's residents came out to honor him.[69] Rachel too was about to go out, but her neighbors said to her: You should borrow [attractive] clothes from us and wear them. To this she responded with the words of the verse, "The righteous one knows the spirit of his animal."[70] [After

64. Yerushalmi Pesaḥim 6:3.
65. Yerushalmi Sanhedrin 6a.
66. *Avot D'Rabi Natan.*
67. *Kalla Rabbati* ch. 2.
68. Nedarim. The Gemara does not state that these students accompanied him – something that is of course not plausible. See also Yevamot 62b, that these twenty-four thousand students were not concentrated in a single locality, but rather scattered between Gevat and Antipatris; and *Bereshit Rabba* 95, regarding those of his students who hailed from afar. This massive number presumably includes "students" with varying levels of closeness to R. Akiva (and as Heiman and others explain the passage in *Tanḥuma*, Ḥayei Sarah 6, regarding three hundred disciples, that they were direct disciples), and apparently this includes all of the students in the various *batei midrash* that had adopted his opinions and approach, even if they had not heard those directly from him. Regarding the text in Ketubot, see n. 58 above.
On the same matter: The meaning of the expression "twenty-four thousand pairs" (Nedarim) is that there were twenty-four thousand disciples, in two paired groups of twelve thousand each. This is the impression in the story regarding the doubling of the number of disciples. This impression is also preserved in slightly different form in Yevamot 62b.
69. Nedarim.
70. Ketubot. The verse itself is from Mishlei 12:10. According to the commentators, Rachel quoted this verse either because she knew that she would not be humiliated before her husband, and by this verse she referred to his time as a poor shepherd (Maharsha), or to say that, even were it some other righteous individual and not her husband, it may be assumed that a righteous person will not humiliate others. R. Nissim Gaon and *Shita Mekubetzet* quote her as saying [to her neighbors] the verse, "The righteous takes knowledge of the cause of the poor" (Mishlei 29:7).

that,] that same wicked [neighbor] came to her and said to her: You, where are you going? She replied to him in the same manner as she had replied to her neighbors: "The righteous knows the spirit of his animal."[71] She came to the crowd surrounding R. Akiva, and sought to come close, but the Sages pushed her away.[72] [Nonetheless,] she was able to reach R. Akiva, at whose feet she fell, whereupon his attendants [also] pushed her away.[73] R. Akiva saw this and said to them: Leave her be! That which is mine, and that which is yours – it is hers!

Subsequently Rachel's father became reconciled with them, and he was released from his vow; the Gemara in Nedarim states further that he[74] was one of the six sources from which R. Akiva became wealthy[75] during the second half of his life. After becoming wealthy, R. Akiva fulfilled his promise and purchased a *Yerushalayim Shel Zahav* for Rachel.[76]

---

71. Nedarim. This time her intention was apparently to hint to the continuation of the verse: "And the mercies of the wicked [i.e., the wicked neighbor] are cruel"; or to say to him that, unlike the righteous, who understand even the spirit of their animals, you are insensitive to the spirit of your neighbor.
72. Nedarim.
73. Ketubot.
74. Safrai and others argue that the story of R. Akiva being enriched by Kalba Savua is merely a tale, since according to the accepted chronology of events, this incident took place following the Temple's destruction, in which Kalba Savua lost his wealth (as recounted in *Eikha Rabba* 1 and parallel sources). This argument can be deflected based on what we have written in n. 38: Just as titles such as "Baron Rothschild" do not belong to one person only, but to members of the same family, so too, we are not dealing with the same Ben Kalba Savua whose storehouses in Jerusalem were burned prior to the Temple's destruction, but to another member of the same wealthy family, who was not a resident of Jerusalem, and some of whose property evidently survived even after the Temple's destruction.
75. The fifth source of his riches was the wife of Turnus Rufus. Rashi, Tosafot, and Ran write (based on Avodah Zarah 20a) that at some point she converted and married R. Akiva. This seems to have followed the death of Rachel, for a number of reasons. Among them, R. Akiva lived a long life, and it is likely that Rachel died many years before him. Moreover, we do not find any of the *Tanna'im* who had two wives, and so striking a halakhic situation, should it have occurred, would not have gone unremarked. It may be that this is why the wife of Turnus Rufus is listed almost last in the list of sources of his wealth – to indicate that this portion of his wealth came after the rest (apart from that from Keti'a bar Shalum).
76. Shabbat 59b, Yerushalmi Shabbat 6:7, *Avot D'Rabi Natan.*

Chapter 10

Reassessing the Imprisonment of Maharam of Rothenburg and His Ransom for Burial[1]

One of the better-known chapters in the history of the *Rishonim* is the account of the captivity of R. Meir son of R. Barukh of Rothenburg (Maharam), his death in prison, and the ransom of his body to be brought to a Jewish grave.[2] The main details are as follows: Maharam attempted to flee Germany with his family to escape persecution and the harsh edicts against the Jewish people. During his attempted escape, as he neared the German border on the fourth day of Tamuz in the year 1286, he was seized by soldiers of King Rudolf I of Habsburg, who imprisoned him and demanded an enormous ransom for his release. Maharam remained imprisoned for nearly eight years. During that time he continued to learn Torah, to write his novellae and responsa, and even to teach and communicate

1. Translated by Rena Bar-David. This chapter initially appeared in *Yerushatenu* 5 (2011).
2. A comprehensive review of this story and most of its sources, with the elimination of unfounded speculation, was undertaken by E. E. Urbach for his work *Ba'alei HaTosafot* (Jerusalem, 1986), part 2, 541–46. Note that the knowledge, traditions, and fragments of information about this incident that were shared orally and in writings from previous generations, were collected some 250 years ago by R. Y. Halperin and recounted quite accurately and thoroughly in his work *Seder HaDorot* (Karlsruhe, 1769), 58b.

with students who were regularly permitted to enter his cell.[3] On the 19th day of Iyar of the year 5053 (1293), Maharam left this world while in captivity. Even after his death, the ruler refused to release his body for burial. Another fourteen years would elapse before his remains would be brought to a Jewish grave on the 4th day of Adar, 1307, following the intervention of a benefactor named Alexander (Susskind) son of R. Shlomo Wimpfen. Wimpfen, who lived in Frankfurt am Main and settled in Worms later in life, paid an enormous sum for this noble cause.[4]

However, the best-known fact about the imprisonment of Maharam is his refusal to be ransomed for the exorbitant sum demanded by the authorities, based on the principle that "we do not ransom captives for more than their value, for the sake of public good." This was noted by Maharshal, in his discussion in Tractate Gittin on ransoming captives:

> I heard about our teacher and rabbi, R. Meir of Rothenburg, may his memory be for a blessing, who was held captive in the fortress at Ensisheim for a certain number of years, and the ruler demanded from the communities an exorbitant ransom, and the communities wished to pay but he [R. Meir] did not allow this. He said that it is not permitted to ransom captives for more than their worth. I am flabbergasted, as he was an exceptionally great Torah scholar, and there was none like him in Torah and piety in his generation, and it is permissible to ransom him for all the money in the world.[5] If due to his humility, he did not consider himself to be an

3. See article by R. Yona Emanuel, "Teachings of Maharam of Rothenburg During His Captivity," *Hama'yan* 33:3 (Nisan 5753): 1–9. Also see the responsum in *Responsa of Maharam of Rothenburg*, Prague edition, *siman* 119, which Maharam concluded with the following: "a craftsman without his tools is merely a layman, what's more for a layman like myself without books and commentaries available to me..." (See Maharshal, below).
4. The dates mentioned here all appear on the gravestone of Maharam: "This is the grave of the foremost rabbi and teacher, Meir son of R. Baruch, who was seized by a Roman king on the fourth day of the month of Tamuz in the year 46 of the sixth millennium, and died in captivity on the nineteenth of Iyar in the year 53, but was not buried until the fourth day of the month of Adar in the year 67 of the sixth millennium. May his soul be bound in the bonds of life with the righteous people of the world in *Gan Eden*, Amen Amen" (copied by L. Levinson, *Nefashot Tzaddikim* [Frankfurt am Main, 1855], 35). The benefactor passed away less than one year after the burial of Maharam on Yom Kippur in the year 68 (the inscription on his gravestone is copied here as well; see n. 28), and earned his place alongside Maharam. Their graves remain side by side in the ancient cemetery of Worms to this very day.
5. As already noted by Ramban, the great Torah scholar of the same generation as Maharam of Rothenburg: "A great Torah scholar is to be redeemed for all of the money in the world, and there is no consideration either of impoverishing [the community] or that others might be seized; because if the people of Israel lose their money or die at the hand of their enemies, there

> exceptionally great Torah scholar, at any rate he should have considered the amount of Torah learning that would be lost – as he himself wrote, that he sat in darkness without Torah and light; and he lamented his lack of the works of the *poskim* and Tosafot; and how could he not have considered the sin of loss of Torah, since the public needed him. Clearly, his opinion was that if they ransomed him, one need fear lest all of the rulers take the greatest Torah scholar of the generation into captivity for ransom so great that the means of the Diaspora communities would not be sufficient to ransom them, and the Torah would be forgotten from Israel. I also heard that the same evil ruler wanted to seize his student, Rosh [Rabbenu Asher]. He got wind of this and fled to Tulitila and was saved by God's compassion and mercy.[6] Because of this, the pious one [Maharam] said that it is better that a little wisdom be lost from Israel than the total loss of all Torah scholarship. And this is the sign [that he was correct], that at that time they ceased seizing the Diaspora sages.[7]

There have been recent attempts to challenge this tradition brought by Maharshal, arguing that this is a later tradition that was unknown to the generations that followed Maharam.[8] Two primary supports have been brought in favor of this argument:[9]

---

are many others like them, but there are not many Torah scholars at that level, and a Torah scholar is redeemed before a king, as it says in Tractate Horayot (13a); therefore one should not covet silver or gold [and refrain from freeing] him (*Ḥidushei HaRamban*, Gittin 45a, and also see Rosh, Gittin 4:44, *siman* 44).

6. These words about Rosh were displaced from their original place and inserted into the beginning of the paragraph in nearly every edition of *Yam Shel Shlomo* (since Prague 1812), and were finally returned to their proper place in the corrected editions published in recent years.
7. *Yam Shel Shlomo*, Gittin 4:66. Based on the interpretation of Maharshal as to why under certain circumstances a great Torah scholar should not be redeemed, it is clear that a case of this sort is unrelated to *Responsa Ridbaz* (1:40) who explains the practice of redeeming captives even for more than their worth because "the seizers do not intentionally seek Jews, rather anyone they can find." For if they redeem a very great scholar for an exorbitant sum, the seizers will be encouraged to seize others like him (see Ridbaz there).
8. See the article by S. Pachter and A. Aloni in *Makor Rishon* on 28 Tishrei 2010, *Shabbat* magazine, p. 11, and my response there on 12 Ḥeshvan 2010, *Shabbat* magazine, p. 10 (where I noted some of the information below).
9. With the exception of more marginal and less convincing explanations, such as the expectation that the concise wording on Maharam's gravestone would mention incidents from the time of his captivity, or the argument that Maharam's refusal was not mentioned by any of his students or by those who followed them, including Rosh and Tur when discussing the Talmudic passage of "not redeeming captives for more than their worth." This is a proof whose refutation comes with it, for even if Maharam had agreed to be redeemed for more than his worth, this would be

A. THE DESCRIPTION IN THE WILL OF R. YEHUDAH B. HAROSH

The communities' attempt to ransom Maharam, and Rosh's involvement, is related in R. Yehudah b. HaRosh's will, with no mention of Maharam's refusal to be ransomed, though a fact of this sort would certainly have been worthy of mention:

> And the reason for the departure of my master and father, of blessed memory, was the seizure of R. Meir of Rothenburg, who was imprisoned by the lord of the city, and the congregations of Ashkenaz ransomed him for a great fortune. The ruler refused to accept any guarantor other than my master and father, of blessed memory, who was forced to guarantee a large sum. And before the sum was divided among the communities, R. Meir of Rothenburg died in captivity and the ruler falsely accused my master and father, of blessed memory, saying that since he died in captivity before he could be released from prison, he [my father] was responsible when his death occurred, and that he and the communities must pay the money. And he fled from him and went to a different city, and because of his fear of the authorities fled Ashkenaz.[10]

B. A DOCUMENT FOUND IN THE YEAR 1616 WITHIN THE WALL OF AN OLD SYNAGOGUE IN WORMS

This document describes the captivity of Maharam, his death, and the redemption of his body by the benefactor. It does not contain any mention of Maharam's refusal to be redeemed for an exorbitant sum:

> Our teacher, R. Meir of Rothenburg son of R. Baruch of blessed memory, set out to cross the sea, he and his wife and his daughters and his son-in-law and all of his belongings. And he arrived at a city situated between the tall mountains that are called "Lombardische Gebirge" in the German language, and he thought to settle there until all of those traveling with him

a precedent important enough to merit mention in the writings of his students (according to this approach), but not a word was written. This is surprising, but in any case this is not proof of either approach.

10. *Zikhron Yehudah* (Makhon Yerushalayim edition, 2005), 180. The manner in which the details of this description square with the tradition of Maharshal and with the other sources about the captivity of Maharam, have already been discussed by E. E. Urbach (see n. 2). He concluded that the king originally demanded an exorbitant sum and Maharam initially refused to be released. However, over the years, the communities continued to negotiate with the king until an agreement was finally reached and the Rosh became a guarantor, etc., but Maharam had already died. One explanation for the fact that more successful negotiations eventually began is that in the summer of the year 1291, Rudolph I, the captor of Maharam, died himself.

> would gather there. And suddenly the thief and evil bishop of Basel, may his name and memory be obliterated, rode down from Rome through that city, accompanied by an apostate Jew named Kneppe, may his name and memory be obliterated. He saw and recognized our teacher and reported to the bishop, and caused Count Meinhard of Görz, lord of that city, to seize him on the 4th day of Tamuz in the year 46 of the sixth millennium and deliver him to King Rudolph.
>
> And because of our many sins, he died in captivity on the nineteenth day of Iyar in the year 53 of the sixth millennium and did not receive a proper burial until the year 67 of this millennium, on the fourth of Iyar, when a generous spirit entered the heart of one benefactor in the holy community of Frankfurt, home to the benefactor Susskind Wimpfen, who spent an exorbitant sum until he was able to bury Maharam with his forefathers in the holy community of Worms. And the benefactor died afterward, and secured his resting place at his side. May their souls be bound in the bonds of life with the other righteous men and women in *Gan Eden*, Amen.[11]

However in my opinion, this evidence does not suffice to prove that Maharam agreed to be redeemed for an excessive ransom, contrary to the tradition related by Maharshal. First, doubting the credibility of Maharshal's rendition of the events and describing it as merely "hearsay" is unjustified, not only because Maharshal was generally known for his very sharp critical thinking and also because he had in his possession important traditions and rare historical documents regarding the sages of Ashkenaz,[12] but especially because he includes another piece of "hearsay" in the same rendition of how the bishop who seized Maharam attempted to seize his student, Rosh, as well. We now know that this is indeed a fact, as this is precisely how the events were described in the last will and testament of R. Yehudah

11. This document was first copied in *Nefashot Tzaddikim*, p. 36 (and a hint to its content can be found in R. Avraham Zacuto, *Sefer Yuḥasin*). In our generation, it was printed again from the original manuscript in R. Judah Löw Kirchheim of Worms' *Customs of Worms* (Jerusalem, 1987), 252.
12. Such as the well-known entry in *Responsa Maharshal, siman* 29. Despite all of the corrections pointed out in research, it remains one of the most important chronicles of the history of the Franco-German rabbis, and as noted by Prof. I. M. Ta-Shma in *Knesset Meḥkarim*, 1: *Ashkenaz* (Jerusalem, 2004), 126. Another illustration related to Maharam himself and his years in captivity, is the wording of the Enactments of the Rhine Communities (*Takanot Shu"m*, 1223) as copied by Maharam and cited in *Yam Shel Shlomo*, Yevamot 4:18, where he proves that this was written while Maharam was in prison. (This document was cited earlier in *Responsa Maharam Minz*, Responsa 10, but a comparison of the wording shows that Maharshal's conclusions were based on a different source, as he wrote "I found in an old book.")

b. HaRosh. Maharshal never actually saw this will, which was printed less than 130 years ago from the single extant manuscript![13] Therefore, although the source for Maharshal's information about these events remains unknown, it was undoubtedly a reliable one that even stated correctly that after the Rosh escaped to Spain "there was a cessation of seizing the sages of the Diaspora."

Regarding the rendition that appears in the will of R. Yehudah b. HaRosh, which would seem to be very strong evidence,[14] note that in this description, there is conspicuous missing information. The will relates that Rosh was forced to flee to Spain immediately following and as a result of the death of Maharam – "And he escaped from him and went to a different city, and left Ashkenaz because of his fear of the authorities." However it is well established that Maharam died in 1293, as noted, while Rosh left Spain only ten years later, in 1303![15] Therefore, since it is clear that when R. Yehudah b. HaRosh drafted his will, he lacked knowledge about the precise circumstances of his father's escape from Ashkenaz to Spain, we certainly cannot draw decisive conclusions from the absence of other information that would have been less significant to him on this subject.

Regarding the document from Worms, I believe that it was written in order to glorify the benefactor who successfully arranged for Maharam's remains to receive a proper Jewish burial;[16] for this document does not provide any information whatsoever about Maharam's long years in prison, and it does not even allude to the attempts made to ransom Maharam during his lifetime. Instead, immediately after recounting the circumstances of his capture, the document proceeds directly

---

13. It was quoted earlier, with apparent mistakes, in *Shalshelet HaKabala* which was printed during the generation after Maharshal, in Venice in 1586 (60a–b). See the preface to the will in *Responsa Zikhron Yehudah*, p. 171.
14. Ḥida already raised questions arising from this description of Maharshal's tradition. See *Shem HaGedolim, Ma'arekhet Gedolim*, letter Mem, Maharam (Cracow edition, 19005), 66b. However, Ḥida had only the corrupt version of *Shalshelet HaKabala*.
15. See A. H. Freimann, *The Rosh* (Jerusalem, 1986), 26–29. Note that it appears from the account in the will that R. Yehudah b. HaRosh was also unaware that Maharam was imprisoned for more than seven years.
16. The document should actually be divided into two parts. The first half provides a meticulously precise description of events lasting no more than several weeks – the seizure of Maharam and his transfer to the king. This half is most likely based on an older document that was most probably written when the events occurred. The second half, on the other hand, bears a very strong resemblance to the writing on Maharam's gravestone (which was most likely written, at least in part, by the benefactor who redeemed his body!) – in the order of the events, in the facts that are noted, and in the style and wording. The difference is that it elaborates on the identity of the benefactor, his actions and his death. I refer to this half, which was written separately from the first half and apparently at a later time, when I speak of this tendency to greatly praise the benefactor.

to his death, followed by the act of kindness by the benefactor: "When a generous spirit entered the heart of one benefactor in the holy community of Frankfurt, home to the benefactor Susskind Wimpfen, who spent an exorbitant sum until he was able to bury Maharam with his forefathers in the holy community of Worms." The document goes on to provide information related not to Maharam's imprisonment, but rather to the benefactor: "And the benefactor died shortly afterward, and secured his resting place at his side. May their souls be bound in the bonds of life with the other righteous men and women [in *Gan Eden*]."

As the objective of the author of this document was to describe the generosity and good deeds of this benefactor, it is perfectly clear why he chose not to mention Maharam's refusal to be redeemed for an excessive sum (assuming that this information was available to the author). A refusal of this kind could raise serious questions about the benefactor's willingness to "spend an exorbitant sum" (!) in order to bury Maharam's remains, and readers may have wondered whether Maharam himself would have objected to the redemption of his remains for an excessive sum, had he been able to do so.

Left: The gravestone of the Maharam. Right: The gravestone of R. Alexander (Susskind) son of R. Shlomo Wimpfen. Photo credit: Dietrich Krieger.

Now, in the following section of the article, I will attempt to strengthen the conclusion that I presented in the previous section, and to elaborate on the halakhic problem encountered by those who sought to ransom Maharam's remains from the gentiles who held it hostage. The truth is that in the writings of the *Rishonim*, we find a direct and explicit reference to this precise scenario.

One of the leading *Rishonim* tells of "one of the great Torah scholars in his generation" who was seized by the ruler and held in captivity (in prison) until his death. The ruler "kept him in captivity in order to collect great sums of money for him." This leading *Rishon* stated that it was prohibited to accede to the ruler's demands, for the sake of the public good, as is written in *Gittin* that "captives shall not be ransomed for more than their worth." Thus, we have an explicit ruling that states that even a great Torah scholar shall not be ransomed for an excessive sum, for the sake of public good. Were the source of this ruling not known to us, we would likely have assumed that it referred to the famous incident involving Maharam of Rothenburg. However, this story is brought by R. Yitzḥak b. R. Shmuel (Ri HaZaken), one of the Ba'alei HaTosafot, who died over one hundred years before Maharam!

This ruling by R. Yitzḥak b. R. Shmuel HaZaken, which had already been alluded to by Tosafot[17] and copied by the Ra'ah,[18] was well known to all of the *Rishonim* in Ashkenaz and in Spain, and was quoted many times from the generation of Maharam of Rothenburg and onward: in Spain by the students of Rabbenu Yonah,[19] Rashba, and Ritva,[20] as well as Rabbenu Yeruḥam;[21] and in Provence by Me'iri[22] and Orot Ḥayim;[23] and by German authorities such as the students of Maharam, the Mordekhai,[24] and later by Rosh[25] followed by his son, Tur[26] and others.

However all of these references bring this incident in context of the laws of mourning, and copied only an abridged version of the story while including only the details necessary for that specific context, without mentioning the importance of the captive who died or the precise reason for being unable to ransom

17. Berakhot 18a, end of the commentary, s.v. *v'eyno*.
18. Berakhot, ibid.
19. Berakhot 11a, Rif, s.v. *kol*.
20. *Ḥidushim* on Berakhot 18a.
21. *Toldot Adam V'Ḥava*, Netiv 28, part 1.
22. Berakhot 18a, and see n. 27 below.
23. *Hilkhot Eivel*, *siman* 11.
24. Mo'ed Katan, *siman* 898; compare with Berakhot, *siman* 58.
25. Mo'ed Katan 83, *siman* 55, Berakhot 83, *siman* 3.
26. *Yoreh De'ah* 341.

his body. These are precisely the details that are germane in our investigation. In the cases of certain *Rishonim*, and particularly the earliest ones such as Rabbenu Yonah and the Mordekhai, it is clear that they had access to the full story. Regarding others, and especially the later *Rishonim*, they apparently had access only to secondhand accounts that did not include most of the circumstances of the incident and in many cases, some of the details were even distorted. The only source to preserve the entire story, accurately copying the response of Ri HaZaken word for word, was Ramban, in his work *Torat Ha'Adam*.[27]

Ramban is not only the earliest source among all available *Rishonim* to refer to the responsum by Ri HaZaken, but, as we noted above (n. 4), he is also apparently the first who explicitly wrote that the ruling that "one does not ransom captives for more than their worth" does not apply to great sages who are needed by the public. This ruling was the basis for Maharshal's challenge and response regarding the tradition that Maharam refused to be redeemed from prison. However it goes without saying that the rationale of Ramban does not apply after the great sage had died, as at that point he could no longer teach Torah to the public. If we were to argue that his body should be redeemed for more than its worth out of respect for his Torah, and similar considerations, the answer given by Ri HaZaken, as cited by Ramban, indicates that there is no such permissibility, and we do not find after him any authorities who disagreed.

In my humble opinion, it is possible to find somewhat of a hint of this halakhah in the description of Maharam's imprisonment, in the will of R. Yehudah b. HaRosh. He relates that when Maharam died in prison, it was following an agreement that was reached for his release (in exchange for an unknown sum), and after his death, the lord of the city demanded that his father, Rosh (the guarantor), and the communities pay the sum as agreed; and therefore Rosh "fled from him and went to a different city." Why didn't Rosh continue to collect funds from the communities for the exalted purpose of redeeming the *body* of Maharam? This proves that an exorbitant sum may not be paid for a body, even that of a great sage, even when paying such a sum for a living person would be permissible.[28] And, at the very

27. Ch. 15 (Ramban was later quoted in *Bet Yosef, Yoreh De'ah* 341, and this was the ruling of Levush, ibid., *siman* 4, and in brief by *Shakh*, ibid., subsection 15, and others). In addition to Ramban and the following generation, Me'iri too brought the details of the full story, though in brief (*Bet HaBeḥira*, Mo'ed Katan, 29a).

28. Meaning that although the sum would not have been considered excessive for a living person, this was not the case for the body of a deceased individual. Another hint to this halakhah, in a different case, can be found in my opinion in a question that appears in *Responsa Rosh*, 27:8.

least, there would be no obligation to pay such a sum, and therefore it would not be possible to compel such payment by the communities.

Thus, when the benefactor from Frankfurt, R. Alexander Wimpfen, sought to redeem the body of Maharam for "an exorbitant sum" that was greater than the body's worth, approximately a dozen years after Maharam died in prison, this was more than 130 years after Ri HaZaken wrote his responsum. Copies of this responsum were shared over the course of the years and even reached Spain in the southwest, where Ramban copied it into his work more than a full generation before Maharam was buried. It is even likely that Maharam himself was familiar with this ruling by Ri HaZaken. Does this mean that had the benefactor consulted with the great halakhic authorities of his generation from his own area, such as the Mordekhai who was a student of Maharam – and had he asked whether to redeem Maharam's body for the fortune that was demanded by the authorities, he would have been instructed not to do so but rather to "pray for God's salvation so that he puts into the mind of the ruler to release the body for burial for a smaller fee"?[29]

I have no intention, Heaven forbid, to judge the actions of that benefactor, of blessed memory, who was praised by the people of his generation for his noble act, as is written on his tombstone "...who had the heart and opportunity to do a great mitzvah and to redeem our teacher and our leader, R. Meir b. R. Baruch from the prison where he was held following his death for several years."[30] It is also possible that when he ransomed the body of Maharam of Rothenburg, there no longer existed the concern that caused Maharam to refuse to be redeemed for an exorbitant price, namely the concern that this would encourage further attempts to seize great Torah scholars, which indeed happened to his student, Rosh.

This is important to note, considering how during these devastating times in the history of Germany, the land was gradually becoming emptied of its great Torah scholars. Maharam died in prison in the year 1293. Five years later, two of his great disciples, R. Mordekhai b. R. Hillel, and his brother-in-law R. Meir HaKohen, author of *Hagahot Maimoniyot,* died as martyrs in the Rindfleisch massacres of 1298. Five years later, in 1303, his greatest disciple, Rosh, left for Spain as described

---

For the Maharam's own ruling concerning redeeming captives and a captive who refuses to be redeemed, although not in this specific context, see *Responsa Maharam Rothenburg* (Prague edition, 1608), *siman* 39.

29. As written by Rosh and mentioned above (n. 24) based on the words of Ri HaZaken.

30. *Nefashot Tzaddikim,* 39–40.

above. Although some other disciples of Maharam remained in Ashkenaz,[31] nevertheless, as most of the saintly people left the city, its "glory and radiance" left with them. This was the situation in 1307 when R. Alexander Wimpfen ransomed the body of Maharam. At this time, sadly enough, there was no need for concern that the ruler would seize another Torah scholar of a stature equal to him.

Within a period of only fifteen years, the first and greatest Golden Age of the sages of Ashkenaz came to an end, after nearly three hundred years, from the days of Rabbenu Gershom Me'or HaGolah and his peers of the generation preceding the year 1040. Following this, two to three generations were to pass before the glory of Ashkenaz Judaism would be revived by Maharil, his teachers and his disciples, members of his generation and the generation that followed, as recounted in the "books of chronicles."

31. Such as R. Moshe of Rothenberg, author of *HaParnas,* and R. Ḥayim b. R. Yitzḥak Or Zaru'a. Just a few years later, R. Alexander Zusslein, author of *Sefer Ha'Aguda* became active in Frankfurt.

Chapter 11

The Mussar Controversy[1]

THE DEVELOPMENT OF THE MUSSAR MOVEMENT AND ITS OPPOSITION: BACKGROUND

In 1897, Orthodox Jewry in Lithuania and White Russia was not preoccupied with the first Zionist Congress held that year in Basel. A completely different issue was at the forefront of their concerns: the controversy over the Mussar Movement and its educational institutions, and in particular, over the character and activity of one energetic individual, R. Yosef (Yozel) Horowitz, known as the Alter of Novardok,[2] after the yeshiva that he founded there.

A socio-scholastic movement, the Mussar Movement's primary emphasis was on *tikkun hamiddot,* cultivating one's character traits, and on the spiritual ennoblement of the individual.[3] The movement's beginnings are generally identified with the

1. Translated by Rachelle Emanuel. The chapter initially appeared in the author's *Ta'arokh Lefanai Shulḥan* (Jerusalem, 2018).
2. In accordance with the classical division of the Mussar Movement's yeshivot into three schools of thought from the end of the second generation onward, known by the names of their leaders: the Alter of Kelm, R. Simḥa Zissel Ziv; the Alter of Slobodka, R. Nosson Tzvi Finkel; and the Alter of Novardok, R. Yozel Horowitz. In fact, it is chronologically and conceptually more correct to say that the Kelm school of thought, with R. Simḥa Zissel at its head, served as the foundation for the other two. For the principal differences between them, see Tzvi Kaplan, *Shitin: Ma'amarim U'Reshimot* (Tel Aviv, 1953), 280–81; Zeitchik, *HaMe'orot HaGedolim* (New York, 1953), 230:164. See also Noam Green, "*Sheva Yipol Tzadik V'Kam,*" *Akdamot* 22 (5769/2009): 144, n. 4. For more on the Slobodka school of thought, see Tikochinsky, "*Gadlut Ha'Adam V'Shiflut Ha'Adam,*" *Hinukh VaDat* (2011), 223–26.
3. R. Dov Katz devoted five volumes of his *Tenu'at HaMussar* (Tel Aviv, 1958–1963) to the subject. The material is organized in a series of monographs of the movement's prominent personali-

start of R. Yisrael Salanter's public activity in the mid-nineteenth century (from 1849) in Vilna and Kovno. A group of followers who later became known in their own right crystallized around him. Among them were R. Yitzḥak Blaser, R. Simḥa Zissel Ziv, and R. Naftali Amsterdam. Their educational activity had already begun during his lifetime, with its first phase chiefly associated with R. Simḥa Zissel Ziv, founder of the Kelm yeshiva. Toward the end of the nineteenth century (the early 1880s – the exact date is not clear), the movement's focus moved to the second generation, to R. Yisrael's younger disciples and their disciples, with R. Nosson Tzvi Finkel, the head of the Slobodka yeshiva, among the most prominent.

The movement was already attracting attention within Orthodox Jewry in Russia at the beginning of the 1880s. Researchers differ on whether the Mussar Movement arose as an alternative to Ḥasidut's innovative theology, or as the continuation of the social teachings of the Vilna Gaon's followers, or as a powerful reaction to the spread of the *Haskalah* movement among Russian Jews.[4] Regardless, the movement threatened the scholastic theosophy of Lithuania's yeshiva world, on the one hand, and the ideology of the Russian *maskilim*, on the other. As with all of Judaism's social movements following Shabtai Tzvi, dissension was not long in coming.[5]

Opposition to the new doctrine had already begun during R. Yisrael Salanter's early activities, when he established "mussar houses" and developed innovative, educational, and psychological techniques for character improvement. At this

---

ties during the hundred years of its existence in Eastern Europe (1840–1940). For critical and up-to-date research on the movement's first days see Immanuel Etkes, *R. Yisrael Salanter U'Reishita Shel Tenu'at HaMussar* (Jerusalem, 1984); Mordekhai Pakhter, *Kitvei R. Yisrael Salanter: Drushim, Ma'amarim, Igrot* (Jerusalem, 1973), introduction, 7–68. See also R. Yeḥiel Yaakov Weinberg's series of articles on the Mussar Movement and its leaders in R. Avraham Abba Weingort (ed.), *Lifrakim* (Jerusalem, 2003), 3–84. [Editor's comment: See also Binyamin Braun, *Tenu'at HaMussar HaLita'it: Ishim V'Ra'ayonot* (Tel Aviv, 2014)].

4. Besides the research mentioned in the previous footnote, see Gedalia Alon, "*Yeshivot Lita,*" in *Knesset: Divrei Sofrim L'Zekher H. N. Bialik*, 8 (Tel Aviv, 1943–1944), 90–94 [also found in *Meḥkarim B'Toldot Yisrael B'Yemei Bayit Sheni U'Vitekufat HaMishnah V'HaTalmud*, I (Tel Aviv, 1957), 7–11]; Tzvi Kurtzweil, "*R. Yisrael MiSalant VeHatnu'a HaMussarit,*" *Sinai* 47 (1960): 100–112; Yona Ben Sasson, *Hagut Yehudit B'Mivḥan HaDorot* (Jerusalem, 1994), 183–201; Ḥagai Samet, "*Tenu'at HaMussar Shel R. Yisrael Salanter V'HaIdeologia HaMitnagedet: Hemshekh O Mahapekha?*" *Mikhlol* 14 (1997): 87–95; Breuer, *Oholei Torah*, 57–60.
5. R. Dov Katz devoted a separate volume, *Pulmus HaMussar* (Jerusalem, 1972), to the polemics surrounding the Mussar Movement, in which he incorporated most of the relevant documents published in the contemporary newspapers. See his long apologetic introduction (pp. 5–7, 17–20) where he explains his occupation with the subject as having been, inter alia, encouraged by R. Yeḥiel Yaakov Weinberg and R. Yeḥezkel Sarna.

stage, however, one cannot yet speak of a movement, but rather of the activity of a single individual together with a few associates.[6] Even the opposition to the educational institutions founded by his disciple R. Simḥa Zissel Ziv was local and not a reaction to the developing ideology of the new movement.[7]

The first public criticism of mussar as a social movement came from the *maskilim* in Russia, particularly from the centers in Kovno and Petersburg. Their opposition was part of a social and ideological struggle waged against those within Jewish society whom the *maskilim* perceived as regressive and reactionary. The opposition surfaced in 1883 as a result of the growing popularity of two institutions: the kollel for married students founded by R. Yisrael Salanter and R. Yitzḥak Elḥanan Spektor and now headed by R. Yitzḥak Blaser in Kovno, and the yeshiva headed by R. Nosson Tzvi Finkel in the neighboring suburb of Slobodka. Initially, the yeshivot ignored the charges leveled against them.[8] It was only seven years later, in 1890, that the opposition reverberated significantly in the local Jewish press. By virtue of his local rabbinic authority, R. Yitzḥak Elḥanan Spektor, rabbi of Kovno, was considered responsible for what was taking place in the mussar institutions in Kovno-Slobodka, especially in the Kovno kollel under his patronage. When allegations concerning financial irregularities in these institutions repeatedly appeared in the Jewish Russian press, R. Spektor published a detailed denial of the allegations.[9] A series of sharp exchanges then appeared in the press between R. Spektor and the opponents of the mussar institutions, led by Aleksander Zederbaum (Erez), editor of the daily *HaMelitz*.[10] The publicity in the press brought a group of well-known rabbis to address the issue for the first time. One of these rabbis, who alongside thirteen others signed a declaration supporting R. Spektor, was R. Yeḥiel Mikhel Epstein of Novardok, author of *Arukh HaShulḥan*.[11]

6. See Etkes, *R. Yisrael Salanter*, 208–14; Katz, *Tenu'at HaMussar* I, 155–56; *Pulmus HaMussar*, 21–23. See also R. Meir Heilprin, *HaGadol MiMinsk: R. Yeruḥam Yehudah Leib Perelman* (Jerusalem, 1994), 29–34.
7. See *Pulmus HaMussar*, 24; *Tenu'at HaMussar* II, 213–18.
8. *Pulmus HaMussar*, 25–29. As Katz notes, R. Yozel Horowitz's name was mentioned already then following his seclusion in a closed house in Slobodka, an act which drew much attention and criticism (as in the polemic of 1890, ibid., p. 51 inter alia). Although this was not the reason for the *maskilim*'s criticism, from their perspective it illustrated the social and personal damage that this movement could cause.
9. Ibid., 32–35.
10. Ibid., 36–51. As Katz points out (p. 52) Zederbaum's personal involvement in the matter prevented the letters of support for R. Spektor from being published in *HaMelitz* (which would have been considered the natural platform in other contexts). They were, instead, published in the Warsaw newspaper, *HaTzefira*.
11. *Pulmus HaMussar*, 52–57.

Ultimately, the controversy of 1890 did not manage to infiltrate into the intra-Orthodox sector, where most of the Mussar Movement's activity took place. Although the criticism of Aleksander Zederbaum and his associates brought about a change in the administration of the Kovno kollel,[12] the conflict at this stage was limited to rabbis versus *maskilim*. It was only seven years later, in 1897, that matters changed. This change was linked directly to the personality and activities of R. Yozel Horowitz, founder of the mussar yeshiva in Novardok. We will preface our description of the controversy with a short review of relevant details of R. Yozel's biography.[13]

---

12. For a detailed discussion of the Kovno kollel and these events, see Stampfer, *HaYeshiva HaLita'it B'Hit'havutah* (Jerusalem, 2005), 360–81. Katz does not elaborate on the topic and just mentions that it caused "a split between members of R. Spektor's family and R. Yitzḥak Blaser," after which the latter left the kollel's directorship in 1891. None other than R. Spektor's son-in-law, R. Tzvi Hirsch Saltzovsky, who was considered an opponent of the Mussar Movement, was appointed in his place (*Pulmus HaMussar*, 59–60, 121; *Tenu'at HaMussar* II, 250–51; compare *HaYeshiva HaLita'it B'Hit'havutah*, 380. See also the words of R. Spektor's associate, R. Yaakov Lifshitz, concerning R. Saltzovsky, "who in recent years was able to calm our rabbi and to serve as his right-hand man in organizing one of the more prestigious charities for the benefit of the Torah," Lifshitz, *Toldot Yitzḥak* (Warsaw, 1897), 49. For more about him and his role in managing the kollel, see the announcement published upon his death: *Hed HaZeman*, January 29, 1910 [4:18], 3). However, R. Yitzḥak Blaser continued to hold on to his role in the kollel's educational leadership until the 1897 controversy, when he finally left due to pressure by R. Spektor's son and by his successor in the Kovno rabbinate, R. Tzvi Hirsch Rabinowitz (the head director of the kollel until his appointment as rabbi of Mitava in 1880). R. Rabinowitz also opposed the Mussar Movement and had a major role in the dispute. In consequence, the kollel ceased being connected to the Mussar Movement (as Katz himself notes, *Pulmus HaMussar*, 257), and became an asset belonging to the Spektor family (compare the 1910 announcement of R. Hayim Soloveitchik and others in support of the kollel: Gerlitz (ed.), *Ḥidushei HaGraḥ HaShalem, Bava Kama* [Jerusalem, 2004], 346).
13. Sources: *Tenuat HaMussar* IV, 179ff. (particularly pp. 179–96); Zeitchik, *HaMe'orot HaGedolim*, 134–204 (approximately two hundred facts and anecdotes about R. Yozel from various sources). I have made limited use of the first detailed biography of R. Yozel, "*MiGedolei Yisrael: HaRav HaTzaddik R. Yosef Yozel Horovitz z"l*," published throughout the summer of 1935 in the World Agudath Israel's journal *Darkeinu*, whose author used the pseudonym "HaRav A. M. Mussari." (The articles are distinctly hagiographic in nature and incorporate some baseless details, such as the "fact" that, as a young child, R. Yozel attended the great yeshivot in Lithuania [37:10], as well as descriptions that chiefly reflect the author's outlook. However, it is possible to glean some important information from the work. Another article from that period, which lacks significant historical value, is that of Shabtai Don Yiḥye [Daniel], "*R. Yozel Ba'al HaḤorim*," *HaTor*, November 3, 1932 [12:3]: 3–6.) In the case of contradictions between sources, I have generally preferred Katz's later and more systematic version.

R. YOZEL HOROWITZ AND THE 1897 CONTROVERSY

R. Yozel was born circa 1848 in Plungiany, northern Lithuania, and grew up in the small village of Kurtuvenai (approximately 90 kilometers east of Plungiany) near Shavli (Šiauliai), where his father was rabbi. His beginnings were prosaic enough. He married the daughter of one Yaakov Stein of Sveksna (approximately 60 kilometers south of Plungiany), where he lived after his marriage, dealing mainly in trade and doing some local teaching. In his mid-twenties he became acquainted with R. Yisrael Salanter, while on business travel to Memel (known today as Klaipeda). Memel was a port city where R. Yisrael lived. The meeting between the two changed R. Yozel's life completely. However, R. Yozel's transformation was more revolutionary than what R. Yisrael Salanter desired. During this period, signs of R. Yozel's erratic personality emerged. He decided to leave his family and business and to turn his back upon his father in order to devote himself fully to study of Torah and mussar. He began his new path within the circle of R. Yisrael Salanter's followers in Kovno (approximately 190 kilometers southeast of Sveksna), and in 1875 he spent some time in the village of Rumshishki.[14] He returned to study in the Kovno kollel, which had been established in the late 1870s. There he was influenced by, among others, R. Yitzḥak Blaser, who had been appointed head of the kollel in 1880. R. Yozel reunited with his family who came to live with him in Kovno, while advancing along the path of mussar. In the early 1880s (circa 1882), after his wife died in childbirth, R. Yozel took another drastic step, scattering his children among foster families and secluding himself for almost two years in a locked house in Slobodka. The house was surrounded by a fence, and the only contact he had with others was through small openings, and via written notes.[15] Despite his extreme seclusion, or in fact, because of it, his name became known to the general public. He received financial support from the Berlin philanthropist Ovadiah Laḥman, all the while being the object of public criticism on the pages of *HaMelitz*. As a result, several well-known rabbis, including R. Yitzḥak Elḥanan Spektor, attempted to persuade him to come out of seclusion.

14. *Tenu'at HaMussar* 4, 184–85. According to one testimony, R. Shimon Yitzḥak HaLevi Finkelstein (1861–1947), later rabbi of Brownsville, New York, stayed with him in Rumshishki. In the introduction to *Seder Tefila: Im Biur Si'aḥ Yitzḥak* (Jerusalem, 1968), 15, his son relates: "My father learned with him [R. Yozel] between the ages of 14 and 17 [1875–1878] in a small Lithuanian village, Rumsasag (Rumshishki)." However, R. Finkelstein himself writes in the introduction to *Ein Shimon* (New York, 1935) that after his bar mitzvah he studied in Kovno and then, between the ages of 16 and 19, he studied alone.
15. See n. 22 below.

Following intervention by the local police (among others), R. Yozel resumed his public appearances (approximately in 1884). He continued his Torah studies, and his name spread further among followers of mussar. He later married his host's daughter, as the story goes, following the grief she and her family suffered when her previous engagement was broken. While maintaining contact with several prominent members of the Mussar Movement, R. Yozel soon returned to his reclusive lifestyle. He finally (circa 1886) moved into an isolated hut in a forest near Dyatlovo, a small village thirty-five kilometers southwest of Novardok in southern Lithuania, and 250 kilometers southeast of Kovno.[16] He remained there till circa 1895, when, under the influence of R. Simḥa Zissel Ziv, he suddenly abandoned his reclusive lifestyle. For the first time since he had come under the influence of the Mussar Movement twenty years earlier, he began to spread the doctrine of mussar among kollel fellows and students of Torah.

The first initiative R. Yozel undertook was the establishment of kollelim, institutions for Torah study for married men. It is related that his intention was to train the students to found yeshivot in the spirit of the Mussar Movement throughout Russia.[17] The financial resources required were provided by the

16. R. Yehudah Leib Nakritz ("*Yeshivot Bet Yosef D'Novardok*," 249), R. Ḥayim Efrayim Zeitchik (*HaMe'orot HaGedolim*, 195 in footnote), and R. Dov Katz (*Tenu'at HaMussar* 4, 192–93, 333) agree that the forest belonged to a certain Gershon Tzurinsky (whom R. Zeitchik mistakenly calls Zalman), who lived on an estate named Zoshen. Nakritz notes that the estate was near Dzyatlava (Zhetel), west of the Novoyelnya train station. Katz also writes at first that Zoshen was near Novoyelnya, and adds in a footnote that the said forest was close to Zoshen. However, later he twice specifies that the forest was adjacent to the village Delyatichi, and relates several anecdotes in that context. (Zeitchik makes the same error. See *HaMe'orot HaGedolim*, 198:50.) It seems that he was not aware that Novoyelnya and Delyatichi are tens of kilometers apart, on either side of Novardok! In fact, that forest near Zoshen was undoubtedly in the environs of Dzyatlava. In contemporary newspapers, we find the residents of Delyatichi expressing their admiration for the work of "the esteemed philanthropist [...] R. Gershon Tzirinsky who lives on the Zoshen estate adjacent to our town. Tzirinsky is the owner of innumerable forests..." (*HaLevanon*, November 4, 1874 [11:12], 94). The nature, therefore, of Katz's stories about Delyatichi is uncertain. It should be noted that there was a village with a small Jewish population some thirty kilometers southeast of Novardok by the name of Tsirin, which was probably Gershon Tzirinsky's place of origin.
17. There is an interesting, if subjective and extremely hostile, description of a failed attempt to establish a branch of R. Yozel's institutions in Minsk in 1900. The writer, Ḥayim David Rosenstein of Minsk (editor of the *Shira Ḥadasha* prayer book and father of the lexicographer Avraham Even Shoshan), described the arrival in town of a young married man "dressed in rags" who, refusing to reveal his identity, asked to be accepted into the local "Shomrei Torah" organization. Rosenstein related that the same young man appeared later dressed in elegant clothes together with a young boy, and joined up with another emissary of the Mussar Movement, who had already been active in the city. After a few days they succeeded in gathering a few boys and

charitable fund of the aforementioned philanthropist, Ovadiah Laḥman, and were supervised by R. Yitzḥak Blaser. Within a short time, an unstoppable R. Yozel with the help of R. Yitzḥak Blaser established a network of kollelim. Most of them were in the area of R. Yozel's last place of residence, Novardok (Lubecz, Dzyatlava, Lida), and some were in the area of his childhood home in northern Lithuania (Shavli, Dvinsk). According to a later estimate, in the summer of 1896 the kollel network consisted of about fifty students.[18] Once these institutions were operating, R. Yozel decided to establish a yeshiva for older youth, which would attract students from different regions, and would constitute a potential reservoir of students for the kollelim and for additional yeshivot for both older and younger students. R. Yozel decided on Novardok as the location for the new yeshiva, which he intended to be the pinnacle of his educational enterprises.

---

organizing a group of students to study mussar. "It then became known that the young man was the son-in-law of R. Yozel 'of the holes,' who had been sent here as a missionary...." (*HaMelitz*, January 26, 1900 [40:11], front page). Rosenstein later related that the son-in-law tried to bring boys who had already studied in R. Yozel's institutions to the town, and that R. Yozel himself once came there. However, they did not succeed in establishing anything significant (*HaMelitz*, January 29, 1900 [40:13], front page; Rosenstein, *Ketavim*, 99–106). Chronologically speaking, the son-in-law can only be R. Yisrael Yaakov Lubchansky. It should be noted that in the booklet of letters in favor of the mussar yeshivot (see n. 33 below), which were copied in the winter of 1900, as confirmed by R. Yeḥiel Mikhel Epstein on the last page, the name "Minsk" was added to the list of institutions at the front of the booklet (as was Babruysk). Already at the end of 1897 R. Yaakov Meir Grodensky wrote in a letter from Minsk, "Many of them [boys from mussar yeshivot] also learn in our town" (*Booklet of Letters*, 30a), but an attempt to open an official branch was apparently only made in 1900.

18. Nakritz, "*Yeshivot Bet Yosef D'Novardok*," 251. Katz writes (*Tenuat HaMussar* IV, 195) that institutions were established during this time also in Odessa in southern Russia, Berdichev (in present-day Ukraine), and Warsaw (present-day Poland). It is hard to believe that within such a short time it was possible to establish institutions over such a wide geographic area, and this is probably an anachronistic error. R. Nakritz's description ("*Yeshivot Bet Yosef D'Novardok*," 249, 253), which places them in a later period, seems more likely. Confirmation of R. Nakritz's assumption can be seen in the declaration of the rabbis who supported the Mussar Movement in the 1897 controversy. There institutions are mentioned in "the towns of Novardok, Lida, Lubecz, Dzyatlava, Dvinsk, and Shavli" (see below, n. 30). R. Epstein too, in his manifest in December 1896, only mentions institutions existing in those towns as well as in Iwye and Slonim, towns in the environs of Novardok, but not in areas further afield (*Kitvei Arukh HaShulḥan, siman* 68; see also below). Here we have to correct R. Nakritz (p. 254), who places the establishment of the institutions in Shavli and Iwye at a later date. It is true that there is evidence that not all the institutions associated with that period existed in practice. Even though R. Epstein mentions the kollel in Slonim already in the winter of 1897, its official opening with ten students was only a year later (See *HaMelitz*, January 11, 1898 [37:289], 4).

R. Yozel's surge of activity in founding institutions in the spirit of the Mussar Movement took place simultaneously with another initiative by R. Nosson Tzvi Finkel of Slobodka. In the fall of 1896, R. Finkel sent R. Isser Zalman Meltzer, a member of the staff of his yeshiva, together with a select group of Slobodka students, to establish a new yeshiva. The location decided upon was also far from northern Lithuania, in the town of Slutsk, about a hundred kilometers south of Minsk and 125 kilometers southeast of Novardok. The one responsible for this initiative was the rabbi of Slutsk, R. David Wilowski (the Ridbaz). Despite the fact that the yeshiva was founded at his request and operated under his auspices, the general public linked the move with the Slobodka yeshiva, which had already drawn attention in the Jewish press.[19] The combined impact of R. Yozel's network of kollelim around Novardok and the branch of Yeshivat Slobodka in Slutsk – and the resulting wide geographical spread of the mussar yeshivot, created the impression that this was an organized educational revolution which would likely change the face of the yeshiva world in Russia. This impression led to the outbreak of opposition to the Mussar Movement.

As R. Dov Katz describes, the controversy initially arose around the yeshiva in Slutsk. Not all of the town residents were pleased with the opening of the new yeshiva. A group formed round R. Meir Feimer (son of R. Yosef Feimer, the previous rabbi of Slutsk), who was at that time involved in a personal clash with the Ridbaz, the one who had brought in the new yeshiva, regarding succession to his father's position. In Adar I/February 1897, R. Meir Feimer published in *HaMelitz* a stinging attack against the mussar yeshivot. He rejected the change in classical methods of study, while also leveling allegations against the yeshiva's directors and students.[20] Numerous reactions to his article appeared in the press, some in favor and some opposing the mussar approach. For the first time, some of these were authored by well-known rabbis.[21] The controversy quickly turned against the

19. See *Pulmus HaMussar*, 61–63. For more on the establishment of the yeshiva in Slutsk see *Tenuat HaMussar* III, 41–42; Meltzer, *B'Derekh Etz HaḤayim* I, 87–91; Hillel Zeidman, "*Yeshivat Etz Ḥayim B'Kletzk*," in Mirsky (ed.), *Mosdot Torah B'Eiropa*, 229–30. An announcement in the press in the fall of 1897 testifies to how fast the Slutsk yeshiva throve despite the lack of sufficient finances: "As the yeshiva's [financial] situation is not yet stable, and as many more young men than we could accept came last semester, we are unable this semester to accept new [students] who are in need of support" (*HaTzefira*, October 3, 1897 [24:214], 1066).
20. *Pulmus HaMussar*, 63–66. Ironically, a few years later, in 1903, R. Feimer himself attempted to open a yeshiva fundamentally different from the classic model, introducing secular subjects into the curriculum. See R. Yosef Eliyahu Henkin (a student in Slutsk), *Lev Ivra* (New York, 1957) 89.
21. *Pulmus HaMussar*, 65–88.

yeshiva in Slobodka, and with the help of a group of students and staff members who opposed R. Nosson Tzvi Finkel and demanded his dismissal, local rabbis became involved. These rabbis included R. Moshe Duschinsky of Slobodka and R. Tzvi Hirsch Rabinowitz of Kovno, who turned out to be opponents of the mussar approach. As a result, the yeshiva split into two separate yeshivot: Knesset Yisrael and Knesset Bet Yitzḥak.[22]

At the same time, the polemics in the press became increasingly strident on both sides. In May 1897 a lengthy and sharp condemnation of the Mussar Movement and its yeshivot was signed by a group of known rabbis, all from towns in northern Lithuania: R. Tzvi Hirsch Rabinowitz, R. Moshe Duschinsky, R. Yitzḥak Yaakov (Itzele) Rabinowitz of Ponevezh, R. Avraham Aharon Burstein of Rietavas, R. Tzvi Yaakov Oppenheim of Kelm, R. Abba Yaakov Borokhov of Viekšniai, and more. Following the proclamation, additional well-known rabbis joined the opposition to mussar.[23]

From this point, R. Avraham Aharon Burstein, one of the signatories on the first proclamation, led the attack. In an exceptionally caustic article, published at the end of May – even before the aforementioned manifesto – R. Burstein attacked every aspect of the mussar yeshivot, explicitly naming some of the yeshivot: "They have built houses for their clique in Novardok, Slutsk, Dzyatlava, and Lubecz." He ended with a call "to expel the infamous 'master of the holes' and his coterie from taking shelter in God's territory."[24] 'The master of the holes' was none

22. For details see *HaYeshiva HaLita'it B'Hit'havutah*, 295–98, and compare with *Pulmus HaMussar*, 89–91, 96–100, and in greater detail 260–70; *Tenuat HaMussar* III, 43–55. See also R. Henkin, *Lev Ivra*, 89.
23. *Pulmus HaMussar*, 101–116. There is a two-month (!) difference between the date of signing the manifesto (May 10) and the date of publication in the press (*HaMelitz*, July 9, 1897). The reason for this becomes clear upon studying the dates of the letters expressing their assent to the manifesto: All were written in May, but the publication of the manifesto and the letters was postponed by the organizers who wanted to collect further signatures (see *Pulmus HaMussar*, 119–20). Moreover, the counter manifesto of the Mussar Movement's supporters, printed in *HaMelitz* on August 11, was signed on July 2, *before* the publication of the opponents' manifesto (but after R. Burstein's article; see below). It is clear that the manifestos and letters were distributed by mail even before they were published in the press. (Similar to the way the letters of the pamphlet "*Or LaYesharim*" would be distributed. See Henkin, "*MiHibat Tziyon L'AntiTziyonut: R. David Friedman KeMikreh Mivḥan.*")
24. *Pulmus HaMussar*, 122–25. Date of publication: *HaTzefira*, May 27. These words of attack were quoted a second time by R. Borokhov (see below, n. 29). R. Burstein's opposition to the mussar yeshivot and R. Itzele Rabinowitz's signature on the aforementioned manifesto carried significant weight in light of the fact that just a few years earlier, around 1890, both had served (though not together) as lecturers in Yeshivat Slobodka (as noted by R. Borokhov and others.

other than R. Yozel Horowitz of Novardok, who was so called on the pages of *HaMelitz* as early as 1883 when he withdrew from society in Slobodka and communicated with the outside world through holes in the wall. The story goes that there were two holes: one for dairy and one for meat.[25] The brunt of the storm which was initially centered on the Slutsk yeshiva and then moved north to Slobodka, returned southward after the split in the Slobodka yeshiva, with the new focus of the attack on the Mussar Movement being R. Yozel, to whose network three of the four institutions mentioned by R. Burstein belonged (Novardok, Dzyatlava, and Lubecz).[26]

R. YEḤIEL MIKHEL EPSTEIN'S ROLE IN THE CONTROVERSY

In 1890, the accusations against the kollel in Kovno led R. Yitzḥak Elḥanan Spektor, under whose wings the kollel operated, to step to the forefront in defense of the Mussar Movement. A similar phenomenon occurred in 1897, when R. Yozel and the students in his yeshivot became the targets of caustic allegations, and R. Epstein, rabbi of Novardok, entered the public fray against the movement's opponents.[27] The yeshiva that R. Yozel established in Novardok

---

See *Tenu'at HaMussar* III, 32; *HaYeshiva HaLita'it B'Hit'havutah*, 290). R. Burstein's brother later related that his brother left Slobodka as "the result of disagreements between him and the yeshiva's administration" (R. Reuven HaKohen Burstein, *Divrei Radbakh* [Warsaw, 1927], 5–6; this source completely ignores his brother's participation in the mussar polemic).

25. See *Pulmus HaMussar*, 27. Even if there were two holes, the reason for keeping them separate for meat and dairy is unclear (even though R. Dov Katz accepts it unquestioningly, and after him R. David Zaritsky, *Torat HaMussar* [Tel Aviv, 1959], 85; R. Betzalel Landau, "*Anak Loḥamei HaMussar BeDor HaAḥaron*," *Bet Ya'akov* 48–49 [Jerusalem, Sivan 5723/May–June 1963], 10; even as critical a researcher as Noam Green accepts the anecdote: "*Sheva Yipol Tzaddik V'Kam*," 144, n. 6. By contrast, R. Meir Bar-Ilan does not exclude the possibility of their being "more than a little exaggeration" – *MiVolozhin ad Yerushalayim* [Jerusalem, 1971], 264).

26. An additional expression of the tendency of the movement's opponents to attribute its development after R. Yisrael Salanter's death to the activity of "the recluse, R. Yozel, and his faction in Slobodka," and to identify the main rabbinic opposition in the 1897 controversy as being directed "against the new mussar approach of R. Yozel," can be found in an article published close to the climax of the controversy (*HaMelitz*, May 26, 1897 [37:109], 2). The rabbis who rejected the criticism of the opponents also understood that, from the midpoint of the dispute onward, the opposition was particularly directed against R. Yozel's institutions "in the community of Novardok and the adjacent towns," more than against the older institutions in Kovno and its environs. See letter of R. Ben Zion Sternfeld of Bielsk Podlaski, *HaTzefira*, August 27, 1897 (24:178), 882–83 (R. Dov Katz was not aware of this letter, and it does not appear in *Pulmus HaMussar*).

27. R. Epstein had, in fact, already written a public letter in support of Yeshivat Novardok at the end of the winter: "I find myself obliged to announce publicly that, as a result of our sins, the tents of Torah were deserted, and the sound of learning was not heard in our study halls. But

was under R. Epstein's direct auspices, and logistically and financially could only exist with the support of the town's leadership (see below). It was therefore natural that they were the address of R. Burstein's demand to "expel the infamous 'master of the holes' and his coterie."

Sure enough, the response of R. Epstein and Novardok's dignitaries was not long in coming. In a public letter dating from the beginning of June and signed by six of the dignitaries, it was written that "our town is in turmoil" as a result of R. Burstein's attack:

> He placed young men who have been studying in our town for about two years, and those nearby, on the pillar of disgrace. [...] There is no band here, no cult, just Torah scholars sitting and diligently studying [...] and all the residents of our town are pleased with them. It is not out of blindness that we distribute large sums of money weekly to support them. We know that the heads [of the yeshiva] are Torah greats.

Below the letter, R. Yeḥiel Mikhel Epstein, the local rabbi, added the following:

> Woe to a generation in which such a thing has occurred; that one who purports to be a halakhic authority speaks heresy. It would have been better had he not come into this world. As honorable laymen here testify, and as our own eyes see and rejoice in the joy of Torah and fear of God, would that scholars like these increase in Israel. Anyone who speaks ill of them, we say to him: "Out, out!"

R. Mordekhai Shlofer, a *dayan* in R. Epstein's rabbinical court, joined him in his protest, and demanded a public apology from R. Burstein.[28]

---

now, to our joy, for more than a year some young men, great in Torah, are studying here in the study hall, and their diligence in studying Torah, Talmud, and halakhah, by day and night, has lit up our eyes. And now there are also laymen who set aside time for Torah, and also some local young men who had stopped studying but now ... they too have returned to Torah learning, and the voice of Jacob is once again being heard in our study halls. [...] Also in the towns surrounding us, where there are young married men, they are all going along this path. I bear faithful witness to this" (*HaMelitz*, April 9, 1897 [37:73], front page; date of signature: March 30). Paradoxically, this letter did not receive any attention in the mussar controversy (and is not mentioned in Katz's book) because the dispute then revolved around Kovno-Slobodka in the north, and around Slutsk. It was only at the end of the spring that the opponents began to focus on R. Yozel's institutions in Novardok and its environs.

28. *Pulmus HaMussar*, 126–27. Date of publication: *HaTzefira*, June 25, 1897. Similarly, there were also those in Kovno who protested R. Burstein's words together with R. Yitzḥak Blaser (*Pulmus*

In contrast to R. Shlofer's relatively restrained response (considering the circumstances), and the factual style of the Novardok dignitaries, R. Epstein's language was blunt, and directed at R. Burstein personally. R. Meir Bar-Ilan, R. Epstein's grandson, later testified:

> Some years later, when my grandfather found out who R. Burstein was, and how great he was in Torah, he regretted having written so sharply. He would repeat this to the members of his household.[29]

This is an expression of the impulsive nature that in certain situations characterized R. Epstein's actions, when he did not consider some of the possible consequences. In this case, one can assume that it stemmed from the need to protect the yeshiva under his auspices and its founders from attack.

Whatever the case may be, the scathing attack upon R. Burstein proved to be a tactical error, prompting the rabbis who supported R. Burstein's position, or who knew him personally, to stand up in his defense with greater vigor and to intensify their accusations against the members of the Mussar Movement. In a joint letter published by R. Tzvi Hirsch Rabinowitz and R. Moshe Duschinsky of Kovno-Slobodka, they wrote:

> We are very sorry about those from Novardok who wrote and signed, and the honored gaon, head of the rabbinical court [i.e., R. Epstein], who, not knowing the true greatness of the gaon, head of the rabbinical court of Rietavas [i.e., R. Burstein], unintentionally blasphemed a most distinguished personage.

They then continued to set down in detail their support for R. Burstein's position.[30] This criticism of R. Epstein was moderate, with utmost care being taken not to dishonor R. Epstein. R. Abba Yaakov Borokhov's response was much stronger:

> I never imagined, that a rabbi as great in Torah as the gaon, the head of the Novardok rabbinical court, could publicize something so inaccurate.

HaMussar, 128–29). However, the vast majority of counter responses to the protests referred mainly to R. Epstein and his townsmen's letters; see below.

29. *MiVolozhin ad Yerushalayim*, 267. He adds that "even stronger words might have been published, but those on the editorial board of *HaTzefira* interested in protecting my grandfather's honor, returned material that had been submitted for publishing."

30. *Pulmus HaMussar*, 129–31. Date of publication: *HaTzefira*, July 18, 1897.

> Although I have never made his acquaintance, by the very fact that he is rabbi of the respected town of Novardok, he must be God-fearing and great in Torah [...]. And following him, a rabbinic authority of the town [R. Shlofer] lawlessly opened his mouth, speaking fiery words fit to be said of sinners, God forbid. [...] Has anything like this ever happened, that a rabbi and a halakhic authority openly slander a great rabbi, making out that he speaks heresy? [...] Do you imagine that by starting to use the weapons of the inquisitors and sentencing a great rabbi as a heretic, you can threaten honest witnesses not to reveal the truth, and that they will withhold their testimony?[31]

R. Yeḥiel Mikhel Epstein understood that leaving the platform of the press to the opponents of the Mussar Movement might endanger the existence of the yeshiva in Novardok and R. Yozel's other institutions. He therefore did not make do with publicizing the protest against R. Burstein,[32] but took additional steps. At a meeting held in Baranowicze (about sixty kilometers south of Novardok), apparently convened at the initiative of R. Epstein himself, about twenty rabbis of communities in the area signed a manifesto under the heading "For the Sake of Truth." The manifesto attested to the purity and integrity of the motives of the students and heads of the mussar yeshivot, together with a plea to the public not to believe the allegations of the opponents. Among the signatories were: R. Eliyahu David Rabinowitz-Teomim (the Aderet) of Mir, R. Yosef Shlopfer of Slonim, R. Yitzḥak Yaakov Reines of Lida, and of course, R. Yeḥiel Mikhel Epstein, who copied the manifesto in order to publicize it. Below the signatures, together with R. Mordekhai Tzvi Slutzky, a *dayan* in his rabbinical court, and a third *dayan* from Lida, he added: "This copy is identical word for word to the original. I, the young man of the House of Levi, was present with these [Torah] giants, and everything they say is holy of holies."

---

31. *Pulmus HaMussar*, 131–37. Because of the length, this was published late and in two parts: *HaTzefira*, August 30–31, 1897. This protest against R. Epstein's attack on R. Burstein, who is described by R. Borokhov as being of greater rabbinical stature than his opponent, can be considered preposterous, seeing that R. Burstein was only thirty years old at the time, almost forty years younger than R. Epstein.
32. Besides the circumstantial evidence for this (see below), we should note the words of R. Aharon Shmuel Tameret, who denounced those who met in Baranowicze "and the rabbi of Novardok at their head, who incited all of them" (*HaMelitz*, September 16, 1897 [37:201], 7; in my estimation, R. Tameret took the strongest stand expressed during the controversy against the Mussar Movement, but because of his relative anonymity, it did not have much effect). Mention of the planned meeting, even before it was held, appears in a letter of R. Zevulun Leib Barrit of Plungiany (*Pulmus HaMussar*, 151).

After approving the copy, R. Epstein attached a list of thirty rabbis from throughout Eastern Europe, "who agreed to write certificates… [in favor of] the young men studying in the towns of Novardok, Lubecz, Lida, etc., etc." Among them were R. Samuel Zanvil Klepfish of Warsaw, the Ridbaz of Slutsk, R. Avraham Yitzḥak HaKohen Kook of Bauska, R. Meir Atlas of Salant, R. Ben Tziyon Sternfeld of Bielsk, R. Eliyahu Feinstein of Pruzhany, R. Yitzḥak Blaser, and others. R. Epstein concluded: "All this has been copied word for word without any change. I hereby sign on the eve of Rosh Ḥodesh Av [July 29, 1897], here in Novardok."[33]

The letters of these rabbis began to be collected even before the outbreak of the mussar controversy, from November 1896, at the joint initiative of R. Epstein and R. Yitzḥak Blaser. They organized the letters in a pamphlet, opening with their own letters of support. The pamphlet seems originally to have been intended to help R. Yozel's institution raise money. However, before any public use was made of these letters, which could have toned down the opposition to the Mussar Movement, the storm erupted. As a result, R. Epstein had no choice but to change the purpose of the letters from fundraising to defense of the mussar yeshivot, which he did by publicizing the names of the prominent rabbis who wrote the letters in support of the mussar institutions.[34]

We can safely say that the turning point in the dispute, the moment when the tides began to shift in favor of the mussar yeshivot supporters, was when R. Epstein entered the picture: First, when he protested the words of R. Burstein, then at the meeting in Baranowicze, and finally when he published the names of tens of

33. *Pulmus HaMussar*, 144–48. Date of publication: first in *HaMelitz*, August 11, 1897, and then with R. Epstein's full version, in *HaTzefira*, August 15.

34. Only the names of the signatories were publicized in the press at the time, but the pamphlet with all the letters has been preserved until today, in apparently more than one copy. See Harel Cohen, "*Igrot Ha'Ra'ayah L'Temikha B'Kibutzei Talmidei Ḥakhamim*," *Me'Avnei HaMakom* VII (1993): 16. A copy of the booklet found in the Frankfurt library has recently (2011) been publicized as a digital file: http://nbn-resolving.de/urn:nbn:de:hebis:30:2-10558. At the end of this copy, R. Epstein added in his handwriting: "To know and to make known that all the thirty-one letters from contemporary rabbis have been copied word for word without any change. Signed on *Purim Katan* (February 13, 1900), Yeḥiel Mikhel HaLevi Epstein, author of *Arukh HaShulḥan*." (The next chapter will deal with the content of some of the letters.) It should be noted that in an additional letter R. Eliyahu David Rabinowitz Teomim (the Aderet) wrote: "I am obligated to join our friend, the great rabbi and glory of our generation, the head of the Novardok rabbinical court, in going forth to support…." The letter is not dated, but seems to have been written later in 1897, and therefore was not included in the pamphlet (I thank R. Betzalel Deblitzky who gave me a photocopy). [Editor's comment: The letter was recently published in "*Igrot Rabanei Lita Odot Kibbutz HaLomdim B'Novardok*," *Min HaGenazim* V (2015): 131–53.]

rabbis who supported the Mussar Movement. The fact that many first-rank rabbis came out in favor of the mussar yeshivot and their community forced most opponents to recognize that this was not a subversive and dangerous phenomenon at the fringe of Orthodoxy, as they initially had claimed, but a legitimate socio-religious stream.[35]

Nevertheless, allegations, articles, and responses by publicists and various writers continued to appear. Among these were Mikha Yosef Berdichevsky, Leon Rabinowitz (the editor of *HaMelitz*), and Naḥum Sokolov. When matters concerned a specific episode, well-known rabbis, such as R. Malkiel Tzvi HaLevi Tennenbaum of Lomza, joined in the debate.[36] Exchanges between rabbis concerning the ways of the Mussar Movement, or even concerning its very existence, were still heard in winter 1897. Some were in response to the manifesto of the Baranowicze meeting, but in the vast majority of cases the writers were not the first-rank rabbis of the time.[37] The opposition of the great rabbis ceased to be heard after the concentrated effort of R. Epstein and his colleagues in July and August 1897, and thus, they no longer needed to address the issue in public. The topic continued to occupy the minds of East European Jewry for some time, but the die was cast regarding the religious legitimacy of the Mussar Movement, its members, and its institutions.

35. Compare R. Nakritz ("*Yeshivot Bet Yosef D'Novardok*," 252): "Seeing that the rabbi, who is great in Torah, and the town dignitaries stood firmly in favor of the students of the yeshiva and its founder, the allegations of the opponents were of no avail." Reverberations of the Baranowicze manifesto found expression in letters of rabbis who joined the supporters of the mussar yeshivot (see, for example, R. Ben Tziyon Sternfeld, n. 25 above).

36. *Pulmus HaMussar*, 159–70, 194–210. The controversy took place basically within Orthodox circles, and Berdichevsky had to justify his involvement in the case on the grounds that "we are all Jews, according to our tendencies and perception of our world, and we are all allowed to listen to the needs of our spirit..." (ibid., 199). Even though their opinions reached the Orthodox world, the extent of their potential and practical influence on the future of the Mussar Movement was minimal.

37. See ibid., 171–87, 215–28. In winter 1898 there was an exchange of private letters concerning the topic, but this was among rabbis who lived far away and echoes of the case reached them at a later date. See ibid., 152–57.

Chapter 12

The Mussar Yeshiva in Novardok[1]

THE FOUNDING OF THE YESHIVA IN NOVARDOK

In 1895, R. Yozel Horowitz began to establish a network of kollelim for married men under the direction of R. Yitzḥak Blazer. One of these was located in Novardok. A short time later, in 1896, R. Yozel decided to establish a yeshiva for younger, unmarried students, affiliated with the new kollel. At R. Yozel's behest, Novardok's rabbi, R. Yeḥiel Mikhel Epstein (author of *Arukh HaShulḥan*), and the town notables agreed to support the new yeshiva,[2] and not long afterward, Yeshivat Novardok was established. Initially, about ten boys studied in the old *bet midrash* in the courtyard of the town's great synagogue, and by one estimate, by 1897 there were already about sixty students in the yeshiva.[3]

R. Yozel had come to Novardok about ten years earlier while living in the nearby forest. Why Novardok? The Mussar Movement had aroused considerable opposition in northern Lithuania ever since R. Yisrael Salanter's founding days. R. Yozel

1. This chapter was first translated by Rachelle Emanuel. It was adapted and abridged by the author's mother from a lengthy article in the author's recently published *Ta'arokh Lefanai Shulḥan* (Jerusalem, 2019). Those seeking greater detail, particularly in footnotes, are referred to the original piece.
2. R. Nakritz ("*Yeshivot Bet Yosef D'Novardok*," 251) writes that the *mashgiaḥ* (spiritual supervisor) of the yeshiva "would distribute monies that he received from the rabbi and the town council each week." Additional support came from Ovadiah Laḥman (Ovesi, *Ma'amarim U'Reshimot* [New York, 1883], 124). As was customary in those days, the students had their meals in the homes of the townspeople (Yaffa, *B'Ghetto Novogrodek* [Tel Aviv, 1988], 63).
3. "*Yeshivot Bet Yosef D'Novardok*," 250–51.

himself was denounced already in 1883, when he lived in seclusion in Slobodka. The rabbis of southern Lithuania, on the other hand, knew very little about the mussar methods and, for them, R. Yozel was an unknown. In addition, northern Lithuania already housed numerous yeshivot, including Telz, Kelm, and Slobodka; while in the Minsk district, the only yeshiva was in Mir, leaving room for a new institution.[4]

Concerning R. Yozel's choice of Novardok itself from among the towns of southern Lithuania, there is apparently one principal answer: the town rabbi, R. Yeḥiel Mikhel Epstein. R. Epstein became acquainted with R. Yozel when the latter was living in the forest near Slobodka, and R. Yozel was even a guest at R. Epstein's Shabbat table.[5] R. Yozel grasped the potential significance of R. Epstein's support for his planned yeshiva. As R. Meir Bar-Ilan sums up: "R. Yozel, who was clever and understood people, realized that my grandfather's [R. Epstein's] approval would be of help to him in case of controversy. He was correct." In all probability, R. Eliyahu Dov Barkovsky (1865–1943), who was *mashgiaḥ* (spiritual supervisor) of R. Yozel's yeshiva for its first ten years, helped win R. Epstein's support. R. Epstein had encountered R. Barkovsky while the latter was still learning in the Volozhin yeshiva, and, in 1891 bestowed *semikhah* upon him.[6] R. Epstein, therefore, would have seen nothing enigmatic in the character of the newly formed yeshiva staff.

From the 1920s, Yeshivat Novardok became identified exclusively with R. Yozel. However, during R. Epstein's lifetime, it was R. Epstein who was the yeshiva's patron, and the yeshiva was known by R. Epstein's name.[7] Some contemporaries even attributed the yeshiva's establishment to R. Epstein.[8] It was not uncommon in Eastern Europe in the second half of the nineteenth century for a yeshiva to be established under the wings of the local rabbi. Such was the case of the

4. For an overview of Lithuanian yeshivot before World War I, see Kalivansky, *HaYeshivot HaLita'iot B'Mizraḥ Eiropa* (henceforth: *HaYeshivot HaLita'iot*) (Tel Aviv, 2009), 31–52. See also Tikochinski, *Darkei HaLimud B'Yeshivot Lita* (henceforth: *Darkei HaLimud*) (Jerusalem, 2004), 104–5.
5. *Tenu'at HaMussar* 4:196.
6. See Moshe Tzinovitch, "*Rabbanim Yelidei Lubetz*," in Hillel [ed.], *Lubetz V'Dlatitz: Sefer Zikaron*, 256–58. According to the author, in the 1890 controversy R. Blazer sent R. Barkovsky to gather rabbinic signatures for the manifesto published then in defense of R. Yitzḥak Elḥanan Spektor and the mussar yeshiva in Slabodka. One of the signatories was R. Epstein, and this is probably how they became acquainted.
7. *Tenu'at HaMussar* 4:196.
8. See Gottlieb, *Ohalei Shem*, 153, written in about 1912, as well as R. Dov Arye Kelig, *Lev Arye* (Lwow, 1936), 6: "After that I traveled [in 1905] to study in the town of Novardok with the renowned rabbi R. Yeḥiel Mikhel Epstein, of blessed memory [...], because there was a large group of boys and many married men who were studying there...." See also Eisenstadt, *L'Toldot Yisrael B'America* I (Ashdod, 1997), 46. These sources describe a group of students under the sole auspices of the town rabbi, with no hint of an additional educational figure heading the institution.

kollel established by R. Yisrael Salanter in Kovno together with the town's rabbi, R. Yitzḥak Elḥanan Spektor, and with the yeshiva in Slutzk, founded by R. Isser Zalman Meltzer and disciples of R. Nosson Tzvi Finkel at the initiative and with the efforts of the town rabbi, the Ridbaz.[9]

R. Dov Katz adds that many students were drawn to Novardok, knowing full well that they would receive *semikhah* from R. Epstein, a document of great worth in the world of the rabbinate.[10] Numerous rabbis ordained by R. Epstein became acquainted with him while studying in Novardok, and some readily admitted that their choice of Novardok was in order to get to know R. Epstein.[11]

The combined impact of R. Epstein's role, together with the hullaballoo surrounding the Mussar Movement, ironically led to the yeshiva and its founder's becoming widely known within Russian Jewry. It is said that three years after the yeshiva's establishment in 1899, it already numbered about two hundred students and sixty married men,[12] although these numbers are probably exaggerated. In 1900, following a visit to Novardok, R. Yitzḥak Nissenbaum wrote of seventy students in the yeshiva and ten in the kollel.[13] The identical number appears in a letter from R. Epstein in 1901, noting "about eighty excellent scholars" in Novardok.[14] These are, presumably, the more correct figures.

THE NATURE OF YESHIVAT NOVARDOK DURING ITS FIRST PERIOD

R. Epstein's biographers picture an ambivalent relationship with Yeshivat Novardok and its founder. During the 1897 controversy, R. Burstein and other well-known rabbis from towns in northern Lithuania had signed a biting

9. One of the first yeshiva students, R. Yosef Eliyahu Henkin, wrote in his notebook: "I studied in Slutsk at the yeshiva of the Ridbaz, and learned Torah from one of the rabbis of the yeshiva, R. Isser Zalman Meltzer." (Entry from 1923 approx.) brought in my article: "*Mara D'Atra Shel America: HaGriya Henkin, Toldot Ḥayav, Demuto, U'Fo'alo,*" *Yeshurun* 20:131, n. 23. See n. 13 in ch. 23 below.) Over the years, however, R. Meltzer became one of the great *rashei yeshiva* of the first half of the 20th century, and the yeshiva came to be known by his name.
10. *Tenu'at HaMussar* 4:196. On study at Lithuanian yeshivot with the aim of training for the rabbinate and being ordained by the head of the yeshiva, see Breuer, *Oholei Torah*, 386–88; Stampfer, *HaYeshiva HaLita'it B'Hit'havutah*, 110–12.
11. See below, n. 47. Rabbinic ordination was, in fact, an integral part of the original aims of the kollel in Novardok.
12. *Yeshivot Bet Yosef D'Novardok*, 252; *Tenu'at HaMussar* 4:197.
13. "*Maḥshavot Retzutzot,*" *HaMelitz*, October 26, 1900 (40:223), 2. R. Nissenbaum also wrote that besides R. Yozel there was a *mashgiaḥ* – R. Eliyahu Dov Barkovsky, and that the group in Novardok was like a "central office" for the smaller groups under the leadership of R. Yozel.
14. *Kitvei Ha'Arukh HaShulḥan, siman* 72.

condemnation of the Mussar Movement.[15] In response, R. Epstein issued a scathing counterattack against R. Burstein. R. Meir Bar-Ilan, the most balanced of R. Epstein's biographers, describes his grandfather's counterattack thus:

> Unfortunately, my grandfather did what he did under the influence of R. Yozel, whom he perceived as a perfect tzaddik [...] Later, my grandfather got to know R. Yozel and did not always agree with his ways. But the joy that, despite all the difficulties, there existed in Novardok a large group of Torah scholars, among them outstanding kollel students who later left to go out in the world, remained with him till his last days. This also led him to admire R. Yozel for his tireless energy.[16]

In other words, R. Epstein held R. Yozel in high regard for his enterprise in sustaining the yeshiva, and for this he was ready to overlook the qualities which he liked less. R. Yehudah Leib Maimon, on the other hand, gives a fanciful description according to which R. Epstein did not get involved in the dispute or take sides, but "deep in his heart he was very troubled by them [the mussar practitioners]."[17] Others chose simply to avoid any mention of the controversy and R. Epstein's role in it.[18]

The factor responsible for this historiographical wrangling is the problematic reputation of Yeshivat Novardok and R. Yozel Horowitz in particular. The unconventional educational and psychological tools developed and practiced in R. Yozel's yeshiva aroused opposition even within the Mussar Movement, and to this day Novardok is described – and rightly so – as being most extreme in

15. See previous chapter, end of section B.
16. *MiVolozhin ad Yerushalayim*, 266–67; compare *Tenu'at HaMussar* 4:196.
17. R. Y. L. Maimon, *Sarei HaMe'ah* 6 (Jerusalem, 1950), 118. R. Maimon's distaste for Yeshivat Novardok is expressed elsewhere: "I spent about two years in Novardok and got to know the town and its zealous inhabitants. Only in Novardok was it possible to establish the well-known mussar yeshiva, which brought no honor to Israel, neither to its Torah, nor to Jewish ethics" (*L'Ma'an Tziyon Lo Eḥasheh*, 88).
18. See R. Nissan Wachsman, "*HaGaon Ba'al Arukh HaShulḥan*." The most extreme description was written by a native of Novardok, Eliezer Yerushalmi, in his belletristic book *MiYa'arot HaTzafon* (Tel Aviv, 1962), 94: "The elderly town rabbi [R. Epstein] was also unhappy with these practices, but being a modest and quiet individual, he did not fight R. Yozel. He merely kept his distance from him and his yeshiva, and never had any sort of involvement with the head of the yeshiva or the students." Yerushalmi was only five years old when R. Epstein died, and his family left Novardok around 1911. This faulty description illustrates the problematic nature of most of his book, at the very least concerning the period of his childhood and youth.

Eastern Europe's yeshiva world in the generation before the Holocaust.[19] However, in truth, treating the Novardok yeshiva throughout its history as a monolithic entity, and R. Yozel – the man and his educational philosophy – as being devoid of development, is nothing less than anachronistic.[20] This methodological fault is still found in many of the hagiographic and critical discussions of R. Yozel and Yeshivat Novardok to this very day.[21]

The most recent historical discussion is based on a large variety of sources, which can be divided into two main categories. The first consists of authentic contemporary documentation: official records, newspaper articles, diaries, letters, and various documents. The second consists of later, retrospective pieces: descriptions, testimonies, and memories that were documented at a later stage. This later documentation is an important genre which, in some respects, has no substitute. However, one must take into account the chronological gap between the events and their appearance in writing. This is especially the case regarding Yeshivat Novardok, where the mass of memoirs is greater and better known than the authentic documents.

Furthermore, a large portion of the documentation deals only with the period following R. Yozel's death, during the interbellum period in Poland and ending with the Holocaust. In my opinion, this period stands alone as an independent unit. In other words, to understand the history of the yeshiva during the twenty-five years in which R. Yozel stood at its head, when the yeshiva was for the most

19. See in detail Fishman, *"Musar and Modernity: the Case of Novaredok"*; Green, *"Sheva Yipol Tzaddik Vakam"* (henceforth: *Sheva Yipol Tzaddik*). To this day no well-organized historical research has been conducted on R. Yozel and his yeshiva. The research on Lithuanian yeshivot has been mainly devoted to those in Volozhin, Telz, and Slobodka (See *HaYeshiva HaLita'it B'Hit'havutah*; *Darkei HaLimud*, inter alia).

20. A good example of this can be found in Tzvi Sharfstein, *Toldot HaḤinukh B'Yisrael BaDorot Ha'Aḥaronim* I (Jerusalem, 1960), 369–72. See also Hillel Goldberg, "The World Is a Very Narrow Bridge"; Noam Green, *"Ḥinukh Ha'Adam V'Yiudo B'Tefisat HaRav Yosef Yozel Horvitz,"* in *Hagut BaḤinukh HaYehudi* 8 (2008), 13–36, especially 21–23; and recently to a certain extent *"Gadlut Ha'Adam VeShiflut Ha'Adam,"* 227–28. Even in R. Dov Katz's books one can find anachronistic descriptions at times.

21. Most critical works on development of the thought of members of the Mussar Movement have been philosophical rather than historical. See Binyamin Brown, *"Gadlut Ha'Adam V'Haktanato: Tmurot B'Shitat HaMussar Shel Yeshivat Slabodka,"* in Etkes (ed.), *Yeshivot U'Vatei Midrashot* (Jerusalem, 2006), 243–72; Tamar Ross, *HaMaḥshava Ha'Iyunit B'kitvei Mamshikhav Shel R. Yisrael Salanter B'Tenuat HaMussar,* PhD thesis in philosophy (Hebrew University, Jerusalem, 1986); Mordekhai Pakter, *"Tefisat HaTeshuvah B'Mishnat R. Yisrael Salanter U'Tenuat HaMussar,"* in Ish Shalom and Rosenberg (eds.), *Yovel Orot: Haguto Shel HaRav Avraham Yitzḥak HaKohen Kook* (Jerusalem, 1988), 257–76. For our purposes, Brown's summary in *"Gadlut Ha'Adam V'Haktanato"* (269–71) is significant, as it relates to phenomena in Yeshivat Novardok.

part in Novardok, one must delete from the discussion those sources that refer to the period between the two World Wars. This includes Ḥayim Grada's famous work, which is not relevant to the period of R. Yozel's lifetime.

In processing the sources, we need to differentiate between three periods, each distinguished from the others in regard to the yeshiva's character and the conditions under which it operated. The first: from the yeshiva's establishment in 1896 until R. Epstein's death in 1908 (with an interim period beginning at the end of the 1905 Russian Revolution). The second: from then until the yeshiva's exile during World War I (1915). The third: from then until R. Yozel Horowitz's death in winter 1919 (with an interim period ending with the move to Poland in 1922). As we shall see, each one of these periods was unique with regard to the material conditions of the yeshiva, and the nature of the yeshiva itself.

In sorting through the raw material, it quickly becomes evident that the vast majority of descriptions, memoirs, and testimonies regarding Yeshivat Novardok and its leaders belong to the second and third periods – after R. Epstein's death, and in particular after the yeshiva moved to Gomel (and later to Kiev) at the beginning of World War I. This is the case for most of the testimonies that can be dated in R. Ḥayim Efrayim Zeitchik's book, *HaMe'orot HaGedolim*, as well as the memoirs collected by Etkes and Tikochinski,[22] and those of R. Yozel's many followers who only came to Novardok after R. Epstein's death.[23] Moreover, all of R. Yozel's written "Torah" in our possession, in the pamphlets *Madregat Ha'Adam*, were written when the yeshiva was in exile during World War I, when he was about seventy years old. These writings represent only his later thinking.[24] Great care needs to

22. *Yeshivot Lita: Pirkei Zikhronot*, 361–422 (one from the third period and two from the interbellum period). Recently, additional memoirs of the network of Novardok yeshivot from the interbellum period have been published: Ben Zion Gold, "Mussarniks," in Assaf and Rappaport (eds.), *Yashan Mipnei Ḥadash: Shai L'Immanuel Etkes* I (Jerusalem, 2009), 103–8.

23. Among others: R. Yitzḥak Orlansky, R. David Budnik, R. David Bliacher, R. Yitzḥak Elḥanan Waldstein, R. Hillel Vitkind, R. Aharon Weinstein, etc. Even R. Avraham Yoffen, R. Yozel's oldest son-in-law, only joined the family in 1913 (R. S. Elberg [ed.], *HaPardes* 42:8 [1970], 40; Surasky, *Marbitzei Torah U'Mussar* 4:122). Prominent followers of R. Yozel who were in Novardok also in the first period are his son-in-law R. Yisrael Yaakov Lubchansky, R. Yoel Branchik, and R. Avraham Zalmans. R. Shmuel Weintraub falls chronologically between these two groups.

24. The pamphlets, containing the written version of his talks from this period, were printed between 1918 and 1924 in Poltava and Piotrkow. Eventually, they were collected in the New York edition, 1947. R. Aharon Ben Zion Shurin (*Keshet Giborim* 2:75) claims that R. Yozel's manuscripts from an earlier period were preserved by his followers. He is probably referring to writings such as drafts that were printed recently in (no editor given) *Shmuel Bekorei Shemo: Toldot Ḥayav Shel R. Shmuel Weintraub* (Bnei Brak, 1991), 100–103, and in (no editor given) *BeSufa U'Vesa'ara*, 360–62. These drafts contain brief notes that R. Yozel wrote for himself in preparation for talks

be taken when utilizing these sources to describe R. Yozel's educational doctrine and the character of Yeshivat Novardok at an earlier point.[25]

The sources at our disposal show clearly that Yeshivat Novardok was not static and unvarying from beginning to end. Over the years the yeshiva underwent significant social, educational, and even administrative changes. True, some minor aspects of the yeshiva's character were determined close to its founding – such as not appointing instructors[26] – but the vast majority of behaviors and rituals that gave Novardok its radical reputation had not yet come into being during the yeshiva's first decade.

This is explicit in the memoir literature: The writer Yehoshua Ovesi who, according to his testimony, studied in Novardok circa 1900 (during the "first period"), divides the followers of the mussar approach into two schools. The first consists of those "who are completely detached from life, behaving in a strange and shocking fashion, degrading themselves in front of all." This

---

he would give on the High Holidays in two different years (dates unknown). To date no writings of greater significance have been published.

In this connection: In the past there were testimonies regarding the existence of a few halakhic writings of R. Yozel. In 1935, it was related that during his period of seclusion in the forest he authored "glosses on *Oraḥ Ḥayim* and *Ḥoshen Mishpat* which are still in the hands of his son-in-law R. Avraham Yoffen" (Musari, "*Migedolei Yisrael*," *Darkeinu* 2:37 [1935], 10). There is a later report that another son-in-law, R. Yisrael Yaakov Lubchansky from Baranowicze, had a volume of *Ḥoshen Mishpat* with R. Yozel's annotations. See R. Asher Katzman (a Baranowicze graduate), "*Di Musar Bavegung Fun di Navardeker Yeshivos*," *Dos Idishe Vort* 238 (New York, May–June 1983), 28. Apparently these volumes were lost in the Holocaust, but R. Yozel's brother-in-law, R. Yehoshua Zelig Tarshish, preserved many halakhic quotations from them in his book, *Ein Tarshish* I (Kovno, 1932), 34–35, 47–48, 78–96 (according to the identifications of R. Shlomo Yosef Zevin, *Sofrim U'Sefarim* [Tel Aviv, 1959], 367).

25. David Fishman and Noam Green have already commented on the drawback of relying on *Madregat Ha'Adam* as the only source for understanding R. Yozel's approach. Green claims that later in R. Yozel's life, when he gave these talks, he may have changed, or at least toned down, some of his radical ideas as a result of years of experience ("*Sheva Yipol Tzaddik VaKam*," 146). He probably came to this conclusion because of the absence of significant antinomian expressions in *Madregat Ha'Adam*. However, all the historical documentation proves the opposite: As the years passed, R. Yozel's educational radicalism became more pronounced, reaching its climax during World War I.

26. See *Tenu'at HaMussar* 4:197–99. He even describes the division of the yeshiva into small study groups according to age and level, headed by *avrekhim* and prominent students (as a result of which the institution was often defined as a "*kibbutz*" rather than a yeshiva) as having existed from the founding of the yeshiva. He also says that R. Yozel was the sole educational authority. I tend to doubt this, in light of the fact that R. Eliyahu Dov Barkovsky served as the *mashgiaḥ* side by side with R. Yozel, as mentioned above. Although it is clear that R. Yozel had seniority, he did not have exclusive authority until after R. Barkovsky left circa 1907.

description matches the common image of Novardok students, based on the concepts of "man's lowliness" and "breaking one's character traits." By contrast, the second school consists of those who "ostensibly went along with the rest, behaved politely...paid attention to their appearance, and were socially integrated." In other words, students who matched the widely held image of Slobodka, based on the concept of "the greatness of man." Lo and behold, Ovesi himself explicitly says: "The Novardok group in my time, belonged to the second category!"[27]

Indeed, when R. Yozel's institutions were at the focus of the 1897 controversy and received letters of support from rabbis and laymen, Novardok was pictured as a conventional yeshiva, without exceptional features:

> There is no band here, no cult, nor [special] approach, just Torah scholars sitting and learning Talmud with tremendous diligence. [...] They are polite and well-mannered, and all the residents of our town are pleased. Not out of blindness do we distribute large amounts of money every week to sustain them. [...] The young married students, precious as gold, study God's Torah, Talmud, and halakhah both by day and at night. They are God-fearing, their behavior and good and honest character are pleasing in the eyes of God and man.[28]

True, this defense was intended to counter the criticism of the mussar yeshivot, but there is no reason to doubt the picture reflected therein.[29] Had the yeshiva already been eccentric, it is hard to imagine its success in marshalling the active support of public figures in Novardok.[30]

---

27. *Ma'amarim U'Reshimot*, 121. However, even with reference to the first group, he claims that "they hid the gnawing worm inside them, deep within their souls."
28. Pronouncement of representatives of the Novardok community and the halakhic authority R. Mordekhai Shlofer.
29. The limited extent of mussar study in Novardok appears, as well, in later testimony, unrelated to any controversy. R. Nissenbaum wrote in 1900, following a visit to Novardok, that the day was primarily devoted to Talmud, and only between *minḥa* and *ma'ariv* did they gather in a small room and study mussar. Ovesi (*Ma'amarim U'Reshimot*, 120) noted likewise. See also "*Yeshivot Bet Yosef D'Novardok*," 250.
30. Katz's descriptions of mussar being studied for hours at a time (*Tenu'at HaMussar* 4:273–74) are clearly anachronistic; compare, for example his use of Grada's writings to illustrate R. Yozel's talks (ibid., 276–78). The long hours of mussar study only developed toward the end of the following decade. See below.

The above, and similar laudatory words by R. Epstein,[31] emphasize classic Torah study, with no mention of mussar. R. Avraham Ashkenazi of Vselyub, who was friendly with R. Epstein, wrote in a similar vein in a letter of support for R. Yozel's institutions:

> We saw with our eyes, when we came to the large *bet midrash* in Novardok, how young men and excellent youth, distinguished in Torah and fear of God, sit in rows ... learning Torah and halakhah with great diligence, sharpening each other's minds.[32]

Later, in the Baranowicze manifesto, the amount of time devoted daily to mussar study in R. Yozel's institutions was described as "merely a half hour before *ma'ariv*"[33] – as was customary in Slobodka and its branches. In the spring of 1897, R. Epstein wrote:

> And because I hear people saying that they will grow only in mussar, I testify that that is false. They look in some mussar books, one in this book and one in that, for just half an hour between *minḥa* and *ma'ariv*; but they study Talmud and halakhah all day and night.[34]

Similar descriptions of mussar study for half an hour are repeated in the letters of many rabbis supporting R. Yozel's institutions during 1897.[35]

These descriptions, and especially those written by residents of Novardok (R. Epstein, R. Shlofer, and community notables), all emphasize the conventional behavior of the yeshiva students. Phenomena such as entering a pharmacy

31. *Kitvei Ha'Arukh HaShulḥan, siman* 68. The date of the declaration coincides with the first signs of the outbreak of the mussar controversy.
32. *Kuntres HaMikhtavim*, 34a. An advertisement for R. Dovid (Karliner) Friedman's book *Piskei Halakhot* provides additional corroboration for the conventional image of Novardok institutions during those first years: "Torah scholars who cannot afford it, such as those learning in the kollel in Kovno and Novardok," will receive a discount upon purchasing the book (*HaMelitz*, December 29, 1898 [38:280]). R. Friedman's mention of Novardok is ostensibly surprising considering that during the mussar controversy R. Friedman took a negative stand on the new movement, stating that traditional Torah study is the essence (*Pulmus HaMussar*, 116–19). The mention of the Kovno kollel in one breath with Novardok is striking, seeing that Kovno was already no longer part of the Mussar Movement. Clearly, the public considered the Novardok kollel, known to be under the supervision of R. Epstein, as a completely standard institution.
33. *Pulmus HaMussar*, 144–45.
34. *HaMelitz*, April 9, 1897 (37:73), front page.
35. See *Kuntres HaMikhtavim*, 10a, 12a, 14a, 17a, 24a, 27a.

and asking for nails, total sharing of personal property, and intentional unkempt appearance did not exist then.[36] Furthermore, there are no reliable testimonies of mussar study in Novardok for several hours a day until after R. Epstein's death.[37] R. Dov Katz likewise writes that as a rule "during the first years of the yeshiva, no great differences between [R. Yozel's] yeshiva and other mussar yeshivot were apparent." Only in time did his yeshiva become "extreme and zealous."[38]

Even the famed "bourse" (*birzhe*) – a mutual examination between a pair of students each delving into the moral character of the other – considered a trademark of the Novardok yeshiva, did not come into being during the first decade of the yeshiva. This practice began at the earliest in 1905, inspired by the street meetings of the revolutionaries during the 1905 revolution, which were called "bourses."[39]

Indeed, as has already been noted, a major milestone in the yeshiva's radicalization was the unsuccessful anti-tsarist revolution from 1905 to 1907, which broke out, among other reasons, as a result of Russia's defeat by Japan in 1905. Many young Jews were swept up by the socio-ideological currents of the time: the Bund

36. See *HaTzefira*, October 3, 1911 (37:216), 3 for a description claiming that Novardok students degrade themselves by walking in the streets wearing their clothes inside out, wearing winter clothes in summer, etc. Compare: *MiYa'arot HaTzafon*, 93–94; *Tenu'at HaMussar* 4, 255–60, and Silberg's memories from the period of World War I in Etkes and Tikochinski (eds.), *Yeshivot Lita: Pirkei Zikhronot*, 361–62, 365–68. See also *HaYeshivot Halita'iot*, 262–67.
37. See the reports of the yeshiva and its ways in *Hed HaZeman* 1910 (below, n. 80), and in *HaTzefira*, 1911 (previous footnote). They describe, with a few differences, three to four hours a day being devoted to mussar study: one hour in the morning from books, sometime in the middle of the day for the "bourse," between *minḥa* and *ma'ariv* for a study session, and short periods of time during the day for seclusion and studying alone. Compare *MiYa'arot HaTzafon*, 93–96. It should be noted that the tendency of these sources – independent of each other, but equally hostile to the yeshiva and its ways – was to write extremely colorful descriptions of the yeshiva; thus it is likely that the more moderate descriptions are the most accurate.
38. *Tenu'at HaMussar* 4:198. See also Surasky, *Marbitzei Torah U'Mussar* I:50.
39. See *Tenu'at HaMussar* 4:292–94; R. Ben Zion Bruk, *Gevilei Eish: Siḥot, Mussar, V'Divrei Hagut*, (Jerusalem, 1973), 15. On the "bourse" see also Silberg's memories in *Yeshivot Lita: Pirkei Zikhronot*, 362–63; Dov Rafel, "*HaḤinukh V'haLimud B'Yeshivot Novardok*," in A. Weiser (ed.), *Sefer Sanhedrai*, (Tel Aviv, 1972), 440–44. Katz in *Tenu'at HaMussar*, thought that the 1905 revolution just provided the inspiration for founding the ritual, and that R. Yozel thought of the analogy with the financial bourse. Actually, the revolutionaries themselves called their street meetings "bourse." Ber Borokhov, for example, in a letter from Warsaw in May 1905 wrote: "The Bundists have a 'bourse' here on one of the streets. The Bundists gather together in the 'bourse,' that is to say on the wide sidewalks of that street, and discuss their matters" (M. Mintz [ed.], *Igrot Ber Borokhov* 1897–1917 [Tel Aviv, 1989], 152).

and other socialist workers' movements.[40] This phenomenon affected R. Yozel's yeshiva and its students as well,[41] leading R. Yozel to develop a new educational approach that would be sufficiently radical to compete successfully with increasingly popular revolutionary trends. "This development did not appear suddenly in the yeshiva, but rather over the years [...] R. Yozel mainly found it necessary to strengthen the yeshiva's elan following the uprising in Russia in 1905, which swept up many of the yeshiva's students."[42]

The process of radicalization in the Novardok yeshiva from the 1905 revolution led to changes in the yeshiva staff. In 1906, about ten years after the yeshiva's establishment, R. Eliyahu Dov Barkovsky left his position as *mashgiaḥ,* and was appointed rosh yeshiva and *mashgiaḥ* in the yeshiva of R. Yitzḥak Reines in Lida. According to a later explanation, this move took place as a result of R. Barkovsky's discomfort with "the extreme mussar-regimen [...] which was not to his liking."[43] Sometime later, apparently in winter 1907–1908, a clash occurred – the first of several – between R. Yozel and one of his sons-in-law, R. Alter Shmuelevitz, who served as the head of a group of students in the yeshiva. R. Shmuelevitz was learning Talmud with his students to a greater extent than what began to be practiced at that time, at the expense of the hours designated in the new schedule for mussar (and which previously had been allocated to Talmud study). Because of the threat to the character of the yeshiva, and despite the family relationship, R. Yozel publicly dismissed his son-in-law.[44]

40. This was felt in many Lithuanian yeshivot. See Shulman, "*HaRuaḥ HaMahapakhanit B'Yeshivot (Telz VeShadov BeShanim 1906–1909)*," *Ha'Ever* 12 (5725/1965), 133–37; *HaYeshiva HaLita'it B'Hit'havutah,* 301; Breuer, *Oholei Torah,* 382; *Tenu'at HaMussar* 4:200; *HaYeshivot HaLita'iot B'Mizraḥ Eiropa,* 31 in footnote. On the place of Russian Jews in the 1905 revolution, see Eliyahu Feldman, *Yehudei Russia B'Yemei HaMahapeikha HaRishona V'haPogromim* (Jerusalem, 1999), 244–52; Yehudah Slutzky, "*Shenat 1905 B'Ḥayehem Shel Yehudei Russia,*" *Ha'ever* 22 (1937), 3–23.
41. *Tenu'at HaMussar* 4: 200. A later episode brought by R. Ḥayim Efrayim Zeitchik probably refers to this period. "Once, during a certain time, several unrespectable boys infiltrated his yeshiva," and R. Yozel made them leave. "After that there was a change for the better in the development of his doctrine" (Zeitchik, *HaMe'orot HaGedolim,* 204:75, see also 234:177). For more on the revolution in the town of Novardok, see Harkavi, *Novardok,* 47–48; *MiYa'arot HaTzafon,* 35.
42. It should be noted, however, that some of the Novardok rituals which Fishman ("Musar and Modernity: The Case of Novardok") interprets as imitating the activities of bund members in the 1905 revolution, only came into existence at a later date; the information we have concerning many of them relate to the interbellum period.
43. Moshe Tzinovitch, "*Rabbanim Yelidei Lubetz,*" in Hillel [ed.], *Lubetz V'Dlatitz: Sefer Zikaron,* 256–58.
44. *Tenu'at HaMussar* 4:329; Kol, *Eḥad B'Doro* I, 75. The date of winter 1907–1908 is clear as one of those present was R. Yosef Shlomo Cahaneman, who studied in Novardok from summer 1907 until spring 1908. Katz gives a third-hand account of a confrontation between R. Yozel

In short: The radicalization of the Novardok yeshiva, which began toward the end of the first decade of the twentieth century, should be seen, among other factors, as a direct reaction to the winds of change at the time and the influence of revolutionary ideas among Jewish youth, particularly following the 1905 revolution.[45] The radical nature of the yeshiva, which became increasingly more pronounced (against the backdrop of World War I and the 1917 revolutions), was closely connected to prevailing trends among young Jews at the time. For this reason, the phenomenon of Novardok never spread beyond its time and place. Even when

---

and his son (!), who was not a mussar devotee; for fear of damaging the yeshiva's spirit, the father refused to give the son a position in the yeshiva (*Tenu'at HaMussar* 4:329; according to Katz, the son was forced to emigrate to America, where he disappeared completely). According to another anonymous and undated narrative, one of the younger teachers recommended a student to the local rabbi for ordination without first consulting R. Yozel, and was promptly dismissed for breaching the yeshiva's conventions (ibid., 324).

45. We cannot avoid mentioning an unfortunate error in the memoirs of Zalman Shazar, *Kokhavei Boker* (Tel Aviv, 1966). Shazar etches in detail the character of the poet and writer Yaakov Shalom Katzenelenbogen (Yashak). Yashak was born in 1877 into a rabbinical family (the Ḥazon Ish was his cousin) but left religion and emigrated to London. Shazar relates (*Kokhavei Boker* 115, 117) that Yashak came to his town, Stowbtsy, "because he had staged an uprising, in which they would call out 'shah,' in R. Yozel's school of mussarniks in Novogrodek, and left the yeshiva and fled home." Further on (119–20) Shazar describes how Yashak told him about "the 'rebellion' which he was part of in the mussar yeshiva in Nowogrodek, and about the 'shah' they staged there for R. Yozel 'of the holes,' the rosh yeshiva, the hermit who hounds Zionism in his yeshiva [...] I did not know R. Yozel, and I never studied in that group of 'mussarniks,' but I felt with all my soul the tempest of rebellion that my esteemed teacher brought with him [...] the agitated young men shouting one tremendous, long 'sha-aah' into the expanse of the yeshiva in the middle of a night of study. [...] Those conversations that my teacher, the poet Y. S. Katzenelenbogen, had with me, when he related with fervor the 'shah' he had just organized against R. Yozel the ascetic hermit, the head of the mussar yeshiva in Novogrodek." This long description was brought by Hillel Goldberg in "The World Is a Very Narrow Bridge," 34, and adopted also by Holtzman (*Ahavot Tziyon: Panim B'Sifrut Ha'Ivrit HaḤadasha* [Jerusalem, 2006], 93), who added that Yashak left Novardok because "his soul was sick of the extreme, ecstatic and ascetic approach to learning that they had in the yeshiva." However, as explained above, at that time, Novardok was an entirely conventional mussar yeshiva with no extreme customs, and no internal rebellion occurred there. Even if Yashak had wanted to associate himself with those who opposed R. Yozel within Yeshivat Novardok, he could not have done so at a time when there were still no such opponents. Moreover, a remarkably similar rebellion against mussar study did occur at that time, during which the "shah" ritual (also called "hopka") took place – but this was not in Yeshivat Novardok, but in Yeshivat Telz! (See R. Yeruḥam Warhaftig's detailed memories in the introduction to *Shalmei Yeruḥam* [Jerusalem, 1941]; B. Z. Dinur, *B'Olam Sheshaka* [Jerusalem, 1958], 70–71; *HaYeshiva HaLita'it B'Hit'havutah,* 303ff.) Shazar, when he wrote his memoirs many years later, undoubtedly erred and exchanged R. Eliezer Gordon's yeshiva in Telz with R. Yozel's in Novardok, which later became much better known as a symbol of extreme mussar than Telz.

the network of yeshivot was flourishing between the two World Wars, Novardok did not manage to establish itself abroad, in America. Even its yeshivot in Eretz Yisrael were never as radical as those in Eastern Europe. The phenomenon was only possible in an unstable situation, whose present as well as whose future was uncertain. Later, following the Shoah and the establishment of the State of Israel, when the yeshiva world stabilized, virtually no institution authentically continued R. Yozel's pedagogical-behavioral practices.[46] Apparently, the Mussar Movement appealed to the yeshiva's benefactors and graduates only at that point in time.

R. YEḤIEL MIKHEL EPSTEIN'S ROLE IN SHAPING THE YESHIVA

The above explains the success of the unusual educational philosophy that developed in Yeshivat Novardok. However, even taking into account the amenable historical environment, this approach would probably never have taken root if not for its founder, R. Yozel Horowitz. His radical personality was evident long before he established the yeshiva. Nevertheless, in the yeshiva's first decade, it operated as a conventional institution, not essentially different from the other mussar yeshivot. How can this be explained? Why was Yeshivat Novardok, in its earliest stage, not operated in the style of R. Yozel, its head?

In my opinion, R. Yeḥiel Mikhel Epstein, the town rabbi and author of *Arukh HaShulḥan*, was a moderating and restraining factor in the face of radical trends that were to develop following his death. R. Epstein looked favorably upon the Mussar Movement and upon R. Yozel; but his style of learning belonged to the traditional rabbinic model of the nineteenth century and, as a result, both his direct and indirect influence upon the yeshiva kept it in the traditional bent.

There were many expressions of R. Epstein's presence in the yeshiva life: As mentioned above, the yeshiva was known by his name, and many students, so it appears, chose Novardok, not because of R. Yozel and the mussar environment but because of R. Epstein's presence.[47] These were not young men seeking

---

46. See Tikochinski, *"HaRav Ḥayim Zaichik V'Likḥei HaShoah,"* 138; *Yeshivot Bet Yosef D'Novardok*, 280–90. The "Ohr Yosef" network, established near Paris by R. Gershon Liebman, was considered as a sort of continuation from the organizational and ideological aspects. See David Shneor, *Ish al Diglo* (Jerusalem, 1998), 13–20, 73–74; Shurin, *Keshet Giborim*, 79–83.
47. Many of those who studied in Novardok during its early years and were ordained by R. Epstein had no connection to the Novardok ideology: R. Shmuel Levine, R. Yaakov Levitsky, R. Yisrael Livertovsky, R. Yeshaya Marcus, R. Dov Berel Svirsky, R. Moshe Yitzḥak Sokolovsky, R. Ozer Palei, R. Eliyahu Falksman, R. Ben Zion Tzvik, R. Yaakov Yisrael Kref, R. Shlomo Yehoshua Krumer, R. Yisrael Rosenberg, R. Naḥum Duber Reznik. Some came because of R. Yozel, but

social radicalization. The stereotype of a Novardok yeshiva student, if it existed at all, matched only a fraction of the yeshiva's population. The scholarly activity surrounding R. Epstein gave the yeshiva its image as a mainstream institution.

Moreover, during the first years R. Epstein was directly involved in admitting students to the kollel and yeshiva. He was the one setting goals and standards at the start. At least at the beginning, R. Epstein's support of R. Yozel's institutions was on condition that the kollel train rabbis and halakhic authorities. R. Epstein himself was the one to ordain these students.

His involvement in admissions was in both the kollel and the yeshiva. We learn this from an announcement by R. Epstein at the end of winter 1898: "This past summer [a yeshiva] was founded here in Novardok by God-fearing benefactors, who love Torah, to support excellent students.... Any prospective student should bring a recommendation from his local rabbi that he has superlative abilities in Torah."[48] At R. Epstein's insistence, financial support of the townspeople was dependent upon meeting a set minimum standard of scholarship, a condition customary in most Lithuanian yeshivot at the time.

R. Epstein was likewise involved in the yeshiva's fundraising. Not only did R. Epstein sign appeal letters,[49] he himself was the address for donations for the yeshiva.[50] This involvement contributed to R. Epstein's ability to influence the yeshiva's character both directly and indirectly. Moreover, for the majority of its years in Novardok, the yeshiva had no building of its own. Studies took place in *batei midrash* scattered throughout the town – strengthening R. Epstein's authority, as he was responsible for public religious buildings.[51]

---

in fact became closer to R. Epstein, including R. Yeruḥam Warhaftig and R. Yosef Shlomo Cahaneman. For others, R. Epstein was the reason for choosing Novardok: R. Yeḥezkel Abramsky, R. Menaḥem Mendel Burstein, R. Dov Arye Kelig, and R. Arye Leib Kaplan.

48. *HaTzefira*, June 2, 1898 (25:112), 620, and again on June 7 (issue 116), 640. Date of signature: March 18. The statement "This past summer [a yeshiva] was founded here" does not refer to the actual establishment of the yeshiva, but to the decision of "benefactors" to set aside financial support for the yeshiva boys, and not just for the kollel students (as above). This advertisement also appeared in a slightly shorter version in *HaMelitz*, May 25, 1898 (38:105), 4, and again on May 30 (issue 107), 6; June 5 (issue 112), 6; June 17 (issue 122), 8.
49. *Kitvei Ha'Arukh HaShulḥan, siman* 75, with a garbled transcript of the signature.
50. An illustration can be found in a small announcement of donations collected for the *yishuv* in Eretz Yisrael at a wedding in Petersburg. Mentioned there is also "the sum of 7.50 rubles for the Novardok kollel, sent to R. Yeḥiel Mikhel, head of the rabbinical court there" (*HaMelitz*, May 21, 1899 [39:60], 8, written by Zalman Noah Kleinstein of Vilna).
51. See *Tenu'at HaMussar* 4: 202.

All these factors establish R. Epstein as a central player in shaping the conventional norms that were dominant during the yeshiva's first years. Moreover, even after the radicalization began toward the end of R. Epstein's life, the *lamdanut* that continued to exist was a continuation of the character of the yeshiva shaped by R. Epstein.

Even when the yeshiva's radicalization was at its apex, in his fundraising R. Yozel chose to portray the yeshiva as mainstream, downplaying or concealing its radical character. In a letter to R. Moshe Avigdor Haikin in London in winter 1913, R. Yozel wrote that "great rabbis emerged from here to serve as *dayanim* in large communities." He described "men young in years, but great in Torah and fear of God, whose only wish and aim in life is to be under the banner of Torah."[52] In an earlier letter to R. Eliyahu Klatzkin of Lublin in 1911, R. Yozel described the yeshiva students as "diligently studying Talmud and halakhah, who will become Torah greats, excelling in their Torah and pure fear of God."[53]

R. Yozel's avoidance of any hint of innovative and radical features in the yeshiva, or even its association with mussar, was no doubt because potential donors were not necessarily of an inclination to support the Mussar Movement or Yeshivat Novardok. The graduates described as "great rabbis" serving in "large communities" were probably all ordained by R. Epstein. This association enabled R. Yozel to receive financial aid outside the limited circle of his supporters even during the second, radical period of the yeshiva.

THE MOTIVES FOR R. EPSTEIN'S SUPPORT OF R. YOZEL AND HIS YESHIVA

We will now attempt to trace the motives for R. Epstein's support of the Novardok yeshiva. This support is inextricably linked with the personal admiration he felt for R. Yozel. R. Epstein's letters show that he not only admired R. Yozel's enterprises, as R. Meir Bar-Ilan claimed, but also his character. In a declaration of support from December 1896, R. Epstein states: "Even in our generation God has given us men of great worth, righteous ones who are concerned about the honor of the Torah [...] Great are the deeds of the gaon, the famous and righteous R. Yosef Yozel, may God protect him [...] in whose merit [yeshiva students] have increased and settled in many towns."[54] In a private solicitation, R. Epstein describes R. Yozel

52. Heiman, "*M'Arkhiyono Shel HaRav Moshe Avigdor Haikin*," 175.

53. Ze'ira (ed.), *Shenot Dor VaDor* 1: 168–69.

54. *Kitvei Ha'Arukh HaShulḥan, siman* 68. The title "*gaon*" is a routine title of respect, common in letters of Lithuanian rabbis in the second half of the nineteenth century; whereas the adjective "righteous" was usually only given to one considered fitting for such a title.

as "a righteous man of stature, who has no financial benefits from this."[55] There is also mention of R. Epstein's admiration for R. Yozel in various memoirs. One such testimony tells that he said of R. Yozel, "There is no wise man like him in the whole world."[56] To a student who complained to R. Epstein about R. Yozel's practices, R. Epstein responded, "Cease speaking, and leave! ... He is unique in our times."[57] Besides the fact that the two rabbis were acquainted during the period of R. Yozel's seclusion, and that the latter was occasionally a guest at R. Epstein's home on Shabbat, R. Katz writes that each Purim R. Epstein would send R. Yozel *mishloaḥ manot*.[58]

All this is inconsistent with R. Bar-Ilan's description of R. Epstein's attitude toward R. Yozel as ambivalent. As R. Yozel's biography demonstrates, the turbulent aspects of his character came to the fore many years prior to the establishment of the yeshiva in Novardok. Although the yeshiva's radicalization began gradually, we find eccentric behavior of its founder as soon as he came to Novardok. This was especially pronounced with regard to his family. During his first years in the town, R. Yozel did not live with his wife and children, who remained in Slobodka. Because of "his reticence to benefit from the yeshiva, he did not hold to his commitment to support his wife. She earned their keep by baking and lived a sad and lonely life." Only later, under pressure of R. Yitzḥak Blazer, did R. Yozel bring the family to Novardok.[59] It is hard to imagine that R. Epstein was unaware

55. Ibid., *siman* 72; a letter from April 1901 to Avraham Eliyahu Harkavi.

56. R. Shlomo Zalman Bloch, *HaTzaddik Rabbi Shlomo*, 10.

57. *Tenu'at HaMussar* 4:196–97, related by R. Avraham Yoffen in the name of R. Yisrael Yaakov Lieder of Kapyl "who was present."

58. Ibid., related by R. Avraham Yoffen in the name of his father-in-law. Katz suggests that R. Epstein may have done this in order to elevate his own standing and influence in the yeshiva.

59. *Tenu'at HaMussar* 4: 206–7. Ovesi (*Ma'amarim U'Reshimot*, 124) relates that R. Yozel would take from the yeshiva's fund, but only for his vital needs. Compare Yerushalmi, *MiYa'arot HaTzafon*, 95, who relates that R. Yozel's daughter "would come sometimes to Shmuelik's mother [Yerushalmi's mother], and would complain about the constant poverty in their home." To some extent this illustrates the problematic nature of the radical stream of the Mussar Movement, which preferred moral perfection of the individual over relationships between people: "He acted with cruelty to his family when he withdrew to a life of Torah and seclusion. When deciding to leave his business and devote himself to Torah ... he did not take into account how they would live, and abandoned them without support. Despite the opposition of his own father, rabbis, and friends, he was firm as a rock in his decision ..." (*Tenu'at HaMussar* 4:327–28). Katz goes on to mention additional acts of indifference on the part of R. Yozel toward his family, in the spirit of one of the opinions in the Talmud (Eruvin 22a), that Torah survives in one "who acts as cruelly as a raven to his children and his household." Katz concludes: "He apparently felt that he had a weakness for his family [...] and went to the other extreme, to uproot it completely."

of these facts, and that his admiration for R. Yozel as "elevated and righteous" included anomalous acts such as these.

On the other hand, although these radical aspects of R. Yozel's lifestyle were evident for all to see, there is no hint of any attempt on his part to integrate them into the yeshiva's ideology during its early years. It would seem that at this stage he believed that an extreme lifestyle was only for exceptional individuals. Only later, as a result of external currents, did he conclude that this was the proper path for young people of the time. The absence of radical features in R. Yozel's educational doctrine during the first period allowed R. Epstein to ignore some of his unconventional personal behavior.

Whatever the case may be, the sum total of R. Yozel's character and behavior – which on other levels certainly reflected an exemplary figure[60] – led to R. Epstein's regarding him as a legitimate model of a "righteous" person. The significance of this should not be underestimated: After all, R. Epstein was the individual outside the Mussar Movement most sympathetic to R. Yozel. His endorsement was instrumental in the yeshiva's success in its first years and even afterward.

Was there a decline in R. Epstein's support for R. Yozel and his yeshiva at the end of this period, when R. Yozel began to integrate eccentric behavior into his educational doctrine? How did R. Epstein react to changes, such as the "bourse," that were gradually introduced into the yeshiva after the 1905 revolution? All the aforementioned testimonies regarding R. Epstein's high regard for R. Yozel refer to the earlier period, or are undated. However, the dates on his letters of recommendation for Yeshivat Novardok show that such letters continued to be written till shortly before his death.[61] He also continued to be in contact with the yeshiva and its students. It seems that R. Epstein did not sever his connection with R. Yozel and continued supporting the yeshiva through the end of his days. But does this mean that the changes in the yeshiva's character were to his liking? He certainly saw the goal of the Novardok kollel as training young men as rabbis and *poskim*, and at the very least, as a framework for traditional Torah study, with the study of mussar just an extra. There is no reason to assume that

60. See *Tenu'at HaMussar* 4:315–22. In this connection one should note the warmth which R. Yozel exhibited toward people. This stands in contrast to his turbulent image and the stories abounding in his lifetime (see ibid., 330–31). See for example Moshe Silberg (in *Yeshivot Lita: Pirkei Zikhronot*, 363–64); R. Moshe Shurin (brought by his son in *Keshet Giborim* II, 243); *Ma'amarim U'Reshimot*, 121, and more. Even some of R. Yozel's sharpest critics agree that he was a remarkable figure (see *Hed HaZeman*, June 27, 1910 [4:32], 3).

61. See *Kitvei Ha'Arukh HaShulḥan*, *siman* 75, Ḥeshvan 5667/October 1907.

increasing the portion of mussar, and the gradual radicalization of this study, would have met with his approval.

However, whereas in the first decade of the yeshiva's existence R. Epstein served as a moderating factor, in the last three years of his life, his ability to be involved in the institution declined. From 1905, at about the same time as the 1905 revolution, there was a noticeable deterioration in R. Epstein's health, especially his eyesight. He referred to this repeatedly in his letters. It may be assumed that, under the circumstances, R. Epstein found it difficult to continue active involvement in the yeshiva.[62] Moreover, health problems forced him to be away from home for long periods for medical treatment. We know, for example, that in summer 1905 R. Epstein was in faraway Petersburg for more than three months for eye surgery.[63] This was not his only extended trip. This situation certainly made it easier for R. Yozel to make significant changes in the yeshiva (such as the "bourse"), without incurring criticism from the yeshiva's patron who, upon his return, was faced with a fait accompli.

Yeshivat Novardok's radicalization beginning in the early twentieth century benefited from a combination of two factors. The dominant, external factor was the new Geist among Jewish youth in Russia in the aftermath of the 1905 revolution, and R. Yozel's resulting educational doctrine, which matched his own revolutionary personality. The internal factor was the gradual removal of the moderating force of the patronage of the town's rabbi, R. Yeḥiel Mikhel Epstein.

YESHIVAT NOVARDOK AFTER THE DEATH OF ITS PATRON

The significance of R. Epstein's involvement during Yeshivat Novardok's early years is striking when compared with the hostility of the town's rabbinic leadership following R. Epstein's death in winter 1908. After a transitional period of about nine months,[64] none other than R. Avraham Aharon Burstein of Tauragė was chosen as rabbi. He had been the fiercest opponent of the mussar yeshivot in the 1897 controversy. R. Dov Katz writes that he was chosen against R. Yozel's wishes. He writes that following R. Epstein's death:

62. Indeed, from mid-1905 we do not find him publishing any notices in the press on behalf of the yeshiva, as he had done previously. I was unable to locate even one notice between 1905 and his death in 1908.

63. See Kelig, *Lev Arye,* 6, and compare *Kitvei Ha'Arukh HaShulḥan, siman* 146 and *siman* 41.

64. During the first month, R. Yosef Shlomo Cahaneman served as rabbi, after which various candidates were considered (see n. 66 below).

> R. Yozel was much involved in the choice of a new town rabbi. He considered this a vital question for the yeshiva, as the local rabbi was to be the patron of the yeshiva ... The town residents chose R. Aharon Burstein, who would later serve as rabbi of Tauragė, but as he was among the best-known opponents of the Mussar Movement, and had signed the "manifesto" against its members, R. Yozel opposed his candidacy. Many obstacles were placed in his path until he was forced to leave.[65]

How was R. Burstein elected as rabbi of Novardok? According to R. Nakritz, the residents of Novardok were of two minds with regard to R. Burstein. Some supported him (and they presented him with a letter of appointment), while others opposed him, mainly because he was perceived as the foe of their previous rabbi, R. Epstein.[66] His outlook on the Mussar Movement was not the primary factor in the town residents' positions. R. Burstein's strong opposition to the Mussar Movement most probably weakened over the years, but he still could not be expected to support the yeshiva. His choice as rabbi by the heads of the community reflects a dramatic change in their earlier support for R. Yozel and his yeshiva, most likely because of the radicalization that the yeshiva was undergoing during those years.[67]

---

65. *Tenu'at HaMussar* 4:202. As we shall see below, one cannot accept R. Meir Bar-Ilan's claim that R. Burstein's appointment demonstrated that controversy did not leave scars in Novardok (*MiVolozhin ad Yerushalayim*, 267). R. Volbrinsky and Markovitz (authors of *L'Korot Ir Novardok V'Rabbaneha*) entirely ignore R. Burstein's appointment, as does R. Reines. Even R. Burstein's brother, who wrote a short biography in the preface to his book *Divrei Radakh*, makes no mention of this unpleasant episode.
66. *Yeshivot Bet Yosef D'Novardok*, 254. Compare Yerushalmi's claim (*Miya'arot HaTzafon*, 91–92) that his father was the one who proposed "his colleague from the yeshiva," R. Burstein, for the office of rabbi of the town, whereas others in the town did not agree. R. Nissan Wachsman writes that R. Burstein was elected at the behest of R. Cahaneman, R. Epstein's disciple and the acting rabbi immediately following R. Epstein's passing (Wachsman, *HaGaon Ba'al Arukh HaShulḥan*, 428). However, there is contradictory testimony suggesting that R. Cahaneman opposed the appointment of R. Burstein, lest his fierce struggle with the Mussar Movement provoke conflict (Surasky, *HaRav MiPonevezh*, 48). In my opinion, it is doubtful that R. Cahaneman was at all involved in R. Burstein's appointment, seeing that he left Novardok about six months before R. Burstein's arrival.
67. Further corroboration of the change in the townspeople's position on R. Yozel's yeshiva is found in a letter written by R. Avraham Yitzḥak HaKohen Kook (then rabbi of Jaffa, Israel) on September 18, 1908 – exactly six months after R. Epstein's death. R. Kook mentions that R. Yitzḥak Yaakov Rabinowitz of Ponevezh had left his town in order to serve as rabbi of Novardok (R. B. Z. Shapira [ed.], *Igrot LaRa'ayah*, [1990 edition], 296. R. Rabinowitz, a colleague of R. Burstein from their days in Slobodka, had signed the manifesto against the mussar yeshivot during the 1897 controversy. We have no other source testifying to R. Rabinowitz's involvement in the appointments to the Novardok rabbinate, but if the

R. Burstein's appointment against R. Yozel's diehard opposition caused R. Yozel to act with the objective of making R. Burstein's life miserable.[68] R. Katz writes sparingly, only saying that after about a year R. Burstein was forced to leave his position because of opposition from students of Yeshivat Novardok.[69] R. Moshe Frankel, son-in-law of R. Burstein,[70] gives the following very different picture: "When he was in the town, he discovered that a small minority opposed him. He therefore tried to leave town, but did not succeed because the wagon drivers there unanimously decided not to take him anywhere. He therefore left by foot at night."[71] This innocent description, implying that R. Burstein was surprised by the discovery that he had opponents in Novardok, is unlikely. However, it is probable that he did not expect such powerful opposition. In an unusual move following R. Burstein's appointment, most of the

information is correct, it can explain the gap of nine months between R. Epstein's death and R. Burstein's arrival.

68. See *MiYa'arot HaTzafon*, 96 and R. Nathan Kaminetzky, *Making of a Godol* (Jerusalem, 2002) pp. 1210–1213 (which I saw thanks to a reference by Noam Green, *Sheva Yipol Tzaddik VaKam*, p. 144). See, for example, what is related there by R. Zelig Starr, a Novardok yeshiva student at that time. However, the excerpt from R. Bialovlotzky's article, that R. Yozel first agreed to R. Burstein serving as head of the yeshiva in matters of halakhah and Talmud, is completely baseless. See also Mordekhai Gizbar's description: "I knew the author of *Arukh HaShulḥan* and the circumstances of his community in Novardok, and I still remember the *ḥilul HaShem* [profanation of God's name] that occurred in that community after the death of R. Mikhel Epstein, and the blood of two great rabbis, the rabbi of Kalisz and the rabbi of Tauragė, shed by those who carried the flag of mussar from R. Yozel's yeshiva in Novardok (*Ma'ariv*, July 20, 1964 [17:6059], 15). The author's memory erred in connection to the rabbi of Kalisz. He, and probably also Bialovlotzky, were most likely referring to R. Menaḥem Krakowsky; see below.
69. *Pulmus HaMussar*, 281. He adds that following this, R. Burstein's "hostility toward the mussar followers increased," and only at the end of his life did this change (R. Dov Katz heard this from him in 1925). However, R. Katz himself writes (*Tenu'at HaMussar* 3: 69–70) that when R. Burstein returned to Tauragė and established there a '*kibbutz*' of Torah students, he asked R. Nosson Tzvi Finkel to send him a group of students from the mussar yeshiva in Slobodka! This is also related by R. Yisrael Zissel Dvoratz, *Tevuna* (Jerusalem, 1958), 82, as proof that R. Burstein already then "subdued his opposition to the mussar doctrine," and he even sees this as an indication of the dying embers of the opposition to the Mussar Movement in Lithuanian yeshivot. Whatever the case may be, it is interesting that R. Nosson Tzvi Finkel and his followers attended R. Burstein's funeral after his death in 1925 in Jerusalem (*HaTor*, December 11, 1925 [6:3], 14).
70. R. Frankel did not know his father-in-law, as he married R. Burstein's daughter a few weeks after her father's death. See *Do'ar HaYom*, December 20, 1925 (8:75), front page.
71. Introduction to R. Burstein's book, *Ner Aharon* (Jerusalem, 1940). He adds that after it was discovered, the townspeople attempted to prevent his wife and children from leaving, "so that he would return." Ḥayim Zaks gives a different explanation for R. Burstein's departure at night (in his memoirs, "Der Alter fun Navardok"). According to him, R. Burstein escaped secretly because of severe ill-treatment by the yeshiva students. Compare: *MiYa'arot HaTzafon*, 96–97.

yeshiva's students were temporarily transferred to the small town of Dzyatlava (Zhetl), about thirty-five kilometers southwest of Novardok in winter 1909. A report in the local press stated:

> Last Friday, January 15, our town welcomed about seventy students from the Novardok kollel, which is under the auspices of the great and righteous rabbi, R. Yosef Yozel Horowitz. The reason for this move is that at the moment there are disruptions and embarrassments because of the matter of the rabbis, disturbing the yeshiva's daily routine and studies. The rabbi [i.e., R. Yozel] therefore decided to transfer a large part of the group from Novardok to the nearby town of Dzyatlava. Our townspeople received them respectfully, with warmth [...] and our town has really taken on a new demeanor since these venerable guests arrived.[72]

This was not the first time that Yeshivat Novardok moved to nearby Dzyatlava. In May 1908 the yeshiva was forced to be there for a short while following a fire in its building in Novardok.[73] Now, however, the move was because of the dispute. R. Yozel's yeshiva received indirect support from the neighboring town (which already held R. Yozel in high esteem) in its struggle against Novardok's new rabbi and the local leadership that had elected him.

R. Nakritz later described the events in a similar fashion:

> As R. Yosef Yozel feared trouble and wasting Torah-study time, he decided to transfer most of the yeshiva's students [...] to nearby Zhetl. [...] Only the older ones of the group, about whom he did not worry that they would be harmed by the controversy in the town, remained in Novardok.[74]

R. Nakritz does not clarify what trouble R. Yozel feared and why. We can interpret the move in two ways. First, that some younger students were more zealous for R. Yozel's honor than he himself desired, and took steps that were too extreme, damaging the study routine of the yeshiva. R. Yozel therefore chose to distance

72. *Hed HaZeman*, February 16, 1909 (3:29), 4. The rabbi of Dzyatlava at the time was R. Barukh Avraham Mirsky (d. 1911). R. Mirsky was a Zionist, a fact which negates the claim that R. Yozel's opposition to some of the new rabbis in Novardok stemmed from their moderate stance on Zionism. R. Yozel's first stay in the area was in the forest close to Dzyatlava, a fact that can also explain its choice as a suitable place for the yeshiva during the present episode.
73. See the report in *Hed HaZeman*, May 11, 1908 (2:93), front page, and two more that month.
74. *Yeshivot Bet Yosef D'Novardok*, 254. Nakritz adds that the students returned to Novardok after about six months, perhaps once R. Burstein had left the town.

them from the center of the dispute in order to enable the yeshiva to operate properly. The second possibility is the reverse: R. Yozel himself led the campaign against R. Burstein, and moving the yeshiva was a way of exerting pressure upon the town's leadership.[75]

If the latter interpretation is correct, what precisely did R. Yozel fear [as per R. Nakritz's description], and why separate the younger students from the senior students? Perhaps the feelings about R. Burstein were a matter of discord in the yeshiva itself, and R. Yozel wished to distance the younger students from what were, in his opinion, negative influences. One can deduce this with caution by analyzing an ostensibly surprising announcement of "the yeshiva of the Novogrodek community" published in the press at the time:

> We, the undersigned, announce in the name of our community, that since there has been a group of young men learning Torah here for the last ten years; and since a famous rabbi [i.e., R. Burstein], well known among Torah giants, has been hired here; and he knows how to run the yeshiva according to the Torah and fear of God; therefore, our community has decided with the agreement of the rabbi, Rabbi Avraham Aharon Burstein, to make every effort to support the holy yeshiva, and strengthen the learning of Torah there. We will try to give as much material aid to the students as we can, and we hope that with the money raised we will be able to continue. Any talented young man with a recommendation of behavior pleasing to God and man, will be warmly welcomed in the coming summer.[76]

Despite the heading, which attributes the announcement (which appeared with no signatures at all) to the yeshiva administration, in fact the announcement could have been authored by anyone, from within the yeshiva or without.[77] What stands out in this notice is, first of all, the lack of mention of any sort of controversy surrounding R. Burstein's appointment as rabbi. Second, the yeshiva is pictured as an entirely conventional yeshiva. Third, and most noticeable, the advertisement sets down R. Burstein's role in the yeshiva [whose head, R. Yozel, was his fiercest

75. Ḥayim Zaks described the episode similarly in his memoir, *Der Alter fun Navardok*. R. Nakritz tended to explain it more according to the first possibility, from an apologetic point of view.
76. *Hed HaZeman*, February 15, 1909 (3:28), 4; and 17 Shevat/February 8 (3:22).
77. Another announcement, published at the same time by "the directors of the kollel and the yeshiva of the Novardok community," related that as a large part of the kollel was moved to Zhetl, prospective students should apply either to Novardok or to Zhetl" (*Hed HaZeman*, February 12, 1909 [3:27], front page). This announcement, and not the other, was written by the administration of the mussar yeshiva and signed Ейзель Гурвицуъ – Yozel Horowitz.

opponent]. It is likely that in the battle between R. Yozel and the new rabbi, there were those within the yeshiva who supported R. Burstein, and planned a split in the yeshiva, similar to what happened in Slobodka during the 1897 controversy.

Explicit confirmation of our hypothesis comes from an article that appeared in the press a year later, in June 1910. The article is sharply critical of R. Yozel and his yeshiva, and includes a rare, hostile and biased description of the yeshiva routine at the time. It presents the well-known stereotype of the Novardok approach, emphasizing the dominance of mussar study, the "bourse" rituals, etc. The anonymous writer claims that in contrast to the above,

> there is one group of young men, headed by the director's son-in-law, who do not submit to the director and his ways, distancing themselves from all this and immersing themselves only in Torah study [...] Among them are excellent students, and young men ordained as rabbis. They discuss any difficulties they have in their studies with the director's son-in-law. The director is not happy about this, and conflict sometimes breaks out between the two sides. It has occurred more than once that the director dismissed his son-in-law from the yeshiva, until the latter had to escape to Zhetl because he could not face R. Yozel's anger and jealousy.[78]

The said son-in-law is undoubtedly R. Alter Shmuelevitz, whose first clash with R. Yozel was mentioned above. He apparently continued to be in contact with the yeshiva and his father-in-law, and together with a group of older students served as an agitator who wished to promote the study of Talmud at the expense of mussar and preserve the yeshiva's original character. R. Shmuelevitz finally left the yeshiva about one and a half years following the events described here, taking with him scores of students.[79] His escape to Zhetl was not connected with the yeshiva's move to the town in 1909; however the whole description reinforces the assumption that the yeshiva's move stemmed from a fear of a split. The above notice seeking to institutionalize the relationship between R. Burstein and the

78. *Hed HaZeman*, June 27, 1910 (4:132), 3.

79. See R. Menaḥem Mendel Shok's testimony in *B'Derekh Etz HaḤayim* I:107. *Ḥayim* Zaks' memoir apparently also refers to this incident ("Der Alter fun Navardok"): "*Reb Yoizel hot azoi baleidigt zein eidem, az oych er hot gemuzt antloifen far herpa fun yeshiva, un mit im tzuzammen zeinen avek a groisser teil yeshiva-leit*" (translation: R. Yozel insulted his son-in-law to such an extent that he had to run away from the yeshiva in shame. A large group of yeshiva students left with him). It is difficult to assume that his leaving in both instances, 1908 and 1911, was as a result of public humiliation. Zaks' memory is probably confusing the mass departure of 1911 with the public shaming of 1908.

yeshiva was presumably part of preparing the ground for a split. Such a split was backed by forces in the yeshiva itself, as well as by the town leadership. The latter perhaps felt a sense of ownership of the yeshiva after having agreed to its establishment fifteen years earlier, and supporting it ever since. Be that as it may, a split never occurred. In the end, R. Yozel had the upper hand, and R. Burstein was forced to leave Novardok suddenly, probably in 1909.

If R. Yozel believed that his victory would bring about a change of attitude on the part of Novardok's leadership and their once again becoming supportive of the yeshiva, this never happened in practice. In January 1910, several months after R. Burstein's departure, R. Yitzḥak Yaakov Reines, the seventy-year-old leader of the Mizraḥi movement, and head of the Torah Voda'at yeshiva that he established in 1905 in Lida, some fifty kilometers northwest of Novardok, was appointed rabbi of Novardok. Avraham Klobak, a resident of Novardok wrote in the press:

> The question of the rabbinate in our town has been settled. By unanimous agreement, R. Yitzḥak Yaakov Reines, head of the Lida rabbinical court, has been chosen as the town's rabbi. The yeshiva in Lida will move to our town together with him. They will soon begin constructing a large building for the sum of 40,000 rubles ... This week R. Reines will come to live in our town.[80]

The people of Novardok reached an agreement with R. Reines that he would not only be appointed rabbi, but he would also move his yeshiva to Novardok. R. Yozel most likely opposed R. Reines' appointment, as is hinted at by R. Dov Katz: "R. Yozel also went to battle with the local residents over other candidates."[81] It is likely that R. Yozel's opposition was at least partly responsible for the long delay in R. Reines' assumption of the office of rabbi of Novardok. It was five months (!) after Klobak's report that Novardok's government-appointed rabbi, Sholom Eisenberg, announced R. Reines' arrival in Novardok: "Today, July 4, R. Yitzḥak

80. *Hed HaZeman*, January 27, 1910 (4:12), 3.

81. *Tenu'at HaMussar* 4:202. "Other candidates" – besides R. Burstein and R. Krakowsky (see below). R. Reines was among the thirty rabbis who had in the past written letters of support for R. Yozel's institutions (*Kuntres HaMikhtavim*, 17a). Nonetheless, there is no hint in R. Reines's early words that he would support the radical mussar regimen adopted by Yeshivat Novardok fifteen years later, when R. Reines himself would serve as town rabbi.

Yaakov Reines arrived here to accept the position of rabbi in our town. A large crowd of Jews met him with celebration and joy."[82]

But even after this long delay, it turned out that the celebration was premature. In the end, R. Reines' appointment never came to fruition, and this time the reason was unconnected to Novardok's internal affairs, but rather to R. Reines' position in Lida. According to R. Maimon (who was close to R. Reines), the appointment was canceled because the people of Lida did not want their celebrated rabbi to leave town. They refused to send his large library to Novardok, thus forcing him to forego the position and return to Lida.[83] Hints of such an occurrence appear in a notice published in the press by ten of Lida's dignitaries about six weeks after Eisenberg's report:

> There have recently been sporadic rumors in the press concerning our great rabbi, R. Reines, moving to Novardok together with his yeshiva. We, residents of Lida, [initially] did not take these rumors seriously.... However, we saw that there was indeed truth in these rumors, and the move was imminent. We turned to our great rabbi, and we learned that he had already promised the Novardok community to move there.... We put pressure upon our rabbi with word and deed to remain with us, but our rabbi did not retract his promise. **We then found means (in legal and honest ways) to compel our great rabbi not to leave us and to continue in Lida as rabbi** [...] The yeshiva also remains in Lida as previously, and nothing new has occurred.[84]

The episode of R. Reines' appointment as rabbi of Novardok lasted more than six months from mid-winter till the end of summer 1910. During that time and for a few more months, Novardok had no rabbi. Finally, at the end of 1910, R. Menaḥem Krakowsky, who had previously served in Khislavichi, was appointed rabbi of Novardok.[85]

---

82. *Hed HaZeman*, July 19, 1910 (4:150), front page.
83. *Sarei HaMe'ah* 6:155.
84. *Hed HaZeman*, August 29, 1910 (4:184), front page. The emphasis is mine.
85. R. Menaḥem Krakowsky, born in 1870, studied in Volozhin under Netziv. From 1895 he served as rabbi in Tsimkavichy (close to Slutzk, about a hundred kilometers southeast of Novardok) and then was appointed as rabbi in Khislavichi in northeast White Russia. He was the son-in-law of R. Eliyahu Feinstein of Pruzhany, and brother-in-law of R. Moshe, the son of R. Ḥayim Soloveitchik. Circa 1917 he left Novardok for Vilna, where he was appointed preacher, and where he lived until his sudden death in Ḥeshvan 1929.

YESHIVAT TORAH VODA'AT IN NOVARDOK

R. Menaḥem Krakowsky was not known as a militant foe of the Mussar Movement, but his relationship with R. Yozel and his yeshiva was similar to that of R. Burstein. The conflict was ignited by R. Krakowsky's decision in 1911 to establish a new yeshiva for youth in Novardok, and later one for young men.[86] Virtually at the same time, the mussar yeshiva also decided to establish a "preparatory yeshiva" (*mekhinah*), attached to the yeshiva for older students.[87] Even if this decision predated R. Krakowsky's move to establish his own yeshiva, the founding of two separate institutions competing for the same age group in the same place and at the same time was, without doubt, a recipe for friction between the two rabbis. This probably lay behind the fact that the mussar yeshiva's planned *mekhinah* was, in the end, established not in Novardok but in Baranowicze.[88]

The friction between R. Krakowsky and R. Yozel was heightened by the character of R. Krakowsky's yeshiva. Called Torah Voda'at, R. Krakowski's yeshiva was inspired by R. Reines' yeshiva in Lida of the same name. As in Lida, secular studies were part of the yeshiva day, resulting in a very different character from that of the mussar yeshiva.[89] A notice published in the press in spring 1912 by the board of the new institution described it as follows:

> Six months ago a yeshiva with a government license opened in Novardok (Minsk district). It has six classes which study: Talmud with Rashi and Tosafot, our national language [Hebrew], and general studies ... The

86. See Katz: "Finally R. Menaḥem Krakowsky was appointed as rabbi of the town [...] R. Yozel reached an agreement with him not to establish a second yeshiva in Novardok; but after R. Yozel denied him a foothold in his yeshiva, R. Krakowsky founded another yeshiva [...] to which many students were attracted." (*Tenu'at HaMussar* 4: 202–3).
87. See announcement by the yeshiva's administration, *Hed HaZeman*, February 10, 1911 (5:24), 4, and February 13 (5:26). The *mekhinah* was planned to include four grades, in which Torah would be studied in a fashion "faithful to Torah, and in a contemporary spirit." These *mekhinot* were the harbinger of today's age-based division between *yeshiva ketana* and *yeshiva gevoha*. Until the beginning of the twentieth century, this division did not exist, with all Lithuanian yeshivot including a certain number of youngsters (ages 13–17) together with young men. This change, as well as the division of the original *ḥeder* system into age-specific classes, undoubtedly reflects the internalization of pedagogical norms of educational institutions in the surrounding society, in general, and the *Haskalah* (Jewish Enlightenment) movement, in particular.
88. *Hed HaZeman*, April 4, 1911 [5:68], 4, and April 6 [5:70].
89. The name Torah Voda'at was not unique to the yeshiva in Lida; there were many schools of this name: in Bialystok, later in Lodz, Warsaw, Minsk, and elsewhere. At the same time as the yeshiva in Novardok opened, a yeshiva in Tauragė in northern Lithuania with the same name was founded. The name served as catchphrase for combining general education together with Torah study.

> yeshiva is under the supervision of our town's rabbi, M. M. Krakowsky, and R. S. Eisenberg. For details contact ...[90]

In practice, the yeshiva was in the traditional style, with classic Talmud study dominant, and a minimum of time devoted to secular studies, but operating with government approval.[91] R. Krakowsky was responsible for the yeshiva side of the new institution. R. Yitzḥak Mirsky, a resident of Novardok, was "pedagogical" principal.[92] On the eve of Passover 1913, they published a detailed educational program of the yeshiva integrating secular studies with traditional Torah studies – a model that became quite legitimate in Russia in the second decade of the twentieth century. Along with this came an announcement of the opening of a "*kibbutz*" of older, advanced students who would study only Torah.[93]

The establishment of this "*kibbutz*" created an arena of direct conflict with R. Yozel's older mussar yeshiva. Besides the ideological rivalry, they competed for the same pool of students, of the same age and from the same typical Lithuanian congregations. The tension is implicit in a notice addressed by R. Krakowsky's yeshiva to young candidates:

> In order to avoid any unpleasantness we encourage the students not to pay attention to the advice and suggestions of the members of the mussar group in our town, whom they will meet. They speak with only unfavorable intentions; do not take notice of them at all, or be led astray by them.[94]

---

90. *HaZeman*, April 7, 1912 (2:68), 6.
91. See the notice in *HaTzefira*, April 8, 1914 (40:73), 4, that the aim of the yeshiva is "to give its students Jewish education in the spirit of the ultra-Orthodox with all that that signifies, but at the same time to prepare them for the future when they go out into the world. [...] [The yeshiva] will ... introduce beneficial changes connected to education and improving the teaching methods. [...]" As an example of the yeshiva's relatively conservative character, P. Shapira points out in the 1912 report of the Society for the Spread of Enlightenment that the yeshiva's board disqualified the use of Simon Dubnow's history [book] because of a sentence regarding the splitting of the Red Sea, that "a great wind blew and the seawater dried up." Dubnow was switched to [Ze'ev] Yavetz ..." (Forman, *HaḤeder HaYom – HaḤeder B'Lita*, 319–20).
92. Yehoshua Yitzḥak Mirsky, a Zionist educator and author, born in 1870. His wife, Sara Retner, helped him manage the yeshiva. He perished together with the Jews of Novardok in 1942. See also Yaffa, *B'Ghetto Novogrodek*, 56–60, on R. Mirsky's activity in R. Krakowsky's yeshiva.
93. *HaZeman*, 1913 (3:82), 6.
94. *Hatzefira*, October 13, 1913 (39:222), 4, and again on October 21 (39:227), 6, and in the next day's issue. See a slightly shorter version in *HaZeman*, October 14, 1913 (3:218), 4, and October 22.

This announcement hints at attempts made by R. Yozel's students to transfer to their camp some of those headed for R. Krakowsky's yeshiva. R. Avraham Yoffen, R. Yozel's son-in-law, later wrote the following vivid description of the phenomenon:

> I remember that when the *Torah vehaskalah* [a play on the name Torah Voda'at, *haskalah* meaning enlightenment] yeshiva opened in Novardok, in the atmosphere of those agitated times, a very talented student came to that yeshiva. His father, a rabbi, had sent him, and in a letter he gave his son were these words: "My son has already tasted much from the Tree of Life, and now desires to taste also from the Tree of Knowledge...." However, the students of the Alter, who would spy after every new student who arrived in town, etc., preempted him and brought the student to the Rebbe [R. Yozel] [...] After a lengthy conversation and deep clarification, the student decided to stay in the Novardok mussar yeshiva and devote his whole being to mussar.[95]

R. Yitzḥak Mirsky published another documentation of the "kidnapping" of students, from the perspective of R. Krakowsky's yeshiva:

> The administration of Yeshivat Torah Voda'at in Novardok, Minsk district, hereby issues a general reply to the letters of complaint from parents received by the yeshiva, that they do not receive any information concerning their sons' progress despite our promises. It means that the students, their sons, are not in our yeshiva at all, but are in the "*kibbutz*" designated for mussar in our town. At the beginning of this term, the famed R. Yozel,

95. R. Avraham Yoffen, "*Ḥazitiha Me'aḥorai*," in Sara Yoffen [R. Yozel's daughter, 1884–1984], et al. (eds.), *Sefer Zikaron: Zekhor L'Avraham* (Bnei Brak, 1972), 7. The student was apparently R. Yitzḥak Waldstein (who later became R. Alter Shmuelevitz's son-in-law), who came to Novardok to study in R. Krakowsky's yeshiva but, as he himself relates, after he left his luggage at the rabbi's house, "out of curiosity went to visit and investigate the truth about the yeshiva run by the Rebbe [R. Yozel] ... He was attracted to stay in the Rebbe's yeshiva." R. Yozel even convinced him not to return to take his luggage from R. Krakowsky's house, lest the latter would influence him to retract his decision (Zeitchik, *HaMe'orot HaGedolim*, 229:162). Compare R. Avraham Rappaport's version, that R. Waldstein came to Novardok "to complete his studies in Russian and sciences..." (Rappaport, "*Kuntres Ḥasdei David*," 18. The identity of this booklet's author was discovered by Tikochinski, *Gadlut Ha'Adam VeShiflut Ha'Adam*, 228 footnote). He adds that R. Yozel promised him that if he stayed in the yeshiva he would find him a suitable teacher for those studies, but after a month, R. Waldstein himself did not want it.

> who heads that "*kibbutz*," rushed his front-guard to stations close to our town to welcome the youngsters coming to us. Using deceitful and veiled ruses, they attracted the most naïve students. For well-known reasons, we did not, in the past, accept students who had once joined the mussar "*kibbutz*," and for this reason after their misled sons understood their mistake and applied to us for admission – they were unable to join our yeshiva.[96]

This episode well illustrates the rivalry between R. Yozel and his institutions and R. Krakowsky and his institution. The conflict ended the chances that matters there would operate smoothly after R. Alter Shmuelevitz's final dismissal almost at the same time as R. Krakowsky's arrival. There were frequent clashes between the two institutions, which part of the time were even crowded together in the same study hall. This fact, according to R. Dov Katz, caused R. Yozel to consider putting an end to his life's work and "to take about a dozen of the best students in the yeshiva with him, and to move to Jerusalem."[97]

Confirmation that the new dispute motivated R. Yozel to attempt to leave Novardok again, and to transfer his yeshiva to another distant location, appears in a report in the press from spring 1912: "The mussar yeshiva in the town of Novardok is looking for another location because of its competitor; and only its creditors, to whom it owes two thousand rubles, are preventing the yeshiva from moving until it pays its debts."[98]

On the other hand, it seems that R. Krakowsky's yeshiva thrived during its short years of existence. In the fall of 1914 R. Krakowsky wrote: "In my yeshiva there is hardly any room to admit new students."[99] Eventually, each institution apparently recognized the other's right to exist.[100] R. Dov Katz relates that in light of

96. *HaTzefira*, September 23, 1913 (39:207), 4. Students who had visited the mussar yeshiva even once were not accepted to R. Krakowsky's yeshiva, probably out of a fear that they had been recruited as "double agents" who would be active in transferring additional students to R. Yozel.
97. *Tenu'at HaMussar* 4: 203.
98. *HaTzefira*, May 10, 1914 (38:36), 3.
99. *HaModia*, November 1, 1913 (5:3), col. 48. R. Krakowsky wrote that in light of the said overcrowding "I request that no boy should come without having first received a confirmation from me that he may come..."
100. See *Tenu'at HaMussar* 4:325, 204. Yaffe relates that R. Yitzḥak Mirsky helped the mussar yeshiva return to Novardok following the war (Yaffe, *B'Ghetto Novogrodek*, 58) and R. Dov Katz similarly relates that when R. Yozel's followers came to Novardok to reestablish the yeshiva there, R. Krakowsky, who was then in Vilna, gave them a letter of recommendation (*Pulmus HaMussar*, 281).

the damage caused by the dispute, R. Yozel agreed that when the erection of his yeshiva's new building would be completed (a project that began in 1912), his students would leave the large study hall where R. Krakowsky's students also studied.[101] However, the mutual rapprochement was cut short by the outbreak of the First World War in August 1914.[102]

The First World War, which caused R. Yozel's center of activity to move from Novardok to Gomel (and then to Kiev, where he died in Kislev 1919), changed the character of the mussar yeshiva once again. In fact, this was the factor that transformed "Novardok" into a veritable movement. Only from this period onward can one speak of a supra-regional network of yeshivot scattered over large parts of Eastern Europe with a center and orderly organizational hierarchy.[103] This is reflected in the opening of the first pamphlet of R. Yozel's teachings to be printed in 1918: "For reasons having to do with the times, the yeshiva has been divided between several locations [...] and, thank God, in each location, the number of students has grown."[104] An additional pamphlet published that year provides further details: "When, due to circumstances of the time, the yeshiva was divided and there are eleven locations conducting themselves in one spirit; nine yeshivot on this side of the border [Russia], and two yeshivot on the other side [Germany during the war], in Novardok and Baranowicze."[105]

Another period in the history of the Novardok yeshivot began in 1922, with the relocation of the center of activity to independent Poland as a result of persecution by the Communist regime in Russia. At this time, centers gradually opened

101. *Tenu'at HaMussar* 4:325.

102. R. Krakowsky left Novardok in 1917. It is likely that his departure from Novardok, in circumstances about which we know nothing, left hard feelings among the townspeople, which may be responsible for his and his yeshiva's virtual omission from Novardok memorial literature.

103. Before the war, the network of kollelim established in 1896 in northern Lithuania and in the area of Novardok had no real contact with each other. For the history of Yeshivat Novardok during the war and thereafter, see *HaYeshivot HaLita'iot*, 76–80, 93–95. See also: *Yeshivot Bet Yosef D'Novardok*, 255–60; *Tenu'at HaMussar* 4:210–12, 247–49; Silberg's memories in *Yeshivot Lita: Pirkei Zikhronot*, 370.

104. R. Y. Horowitz, *Madregat HaAdam B'Tekufot Ha'Olam* (Poltava, 1918), back cover. The initiative to print *Madregat Ha'Adam* is characteristic of the changes that turned "Novardok" from a local yeshiva to being a supra-regional movement. A short time after the printing of these booklets, a journal of the "Bet Yosef-Novardok" movement began to appear, *Ohr HaMussar*.

105. *Madregat Ha'Adam B'Tikkun HaMiddot* (Piotrkow, 1918), 2. See also the introduction to *Madregat Ha'Adam B'Yira U'v'Ahava* (Piortkow, 1911), 8, a pamphlet printed after R. Yozel's death: "As is known, during the war, in the midst of the storm, he would run like a deer, and opened more than forty yeshivot in Russia and the Ukraine."

in Bialystok under R. Avraham Yoffen, in Warsaw under R. Avraham Zalmans, and in Miedzyrzec Podlaski under R. David Bleicher, as well as centers in Pinsk, which belonged to Poland between the World Wars, under R. Shmuel Weintraub, and in Latvia, in Dvinsk, under R. David Budnik.[106] The expansion of the network, called Bet Yosef in R. Yozel's name, and consisting of tens of branches and thousands of students, led to a certain moderation of the radical tendencies that prevailed in R. Yozel's last years. However, its unique features and tight organizational structure left the network as a distinct and separate phenomenon from the other yeshivot in Eastern Europe of the time.[107] The network ceased to exist in 1939 with the German occupation of Poland.

EPILOGUE[108]

In conclusion, it seems that we can assert that even Yeshivat Novardok, considered the most anti-establishment institution in the history of Lithuanian yeshivot, was unable to develop without the strong backing of the rabbinate and communal establishment. Its moderate character during its first years of existence was what

---

106. For a discussion of the Novardok movement between the World Wars, see *HaYeshivot HaLita'iot*, 136–52, 262–67. See also *Yeshivot Bet Yosef D'Novardok*, 265–70; *Tenu'at HaMussar* 4, 227–29 (Katz wrote that a more extensive overview of the yeshivot of Novardok would appear in future volumes – but those were never published); Surasky, *Marbitzei Torah U'Mussar* 4:124–43; as well as information throughout (no editor given) *BeSufa U'v'Sa'ara*, 121–293; Rappaport, "*Kuntres Ḥasdei David*," 12ff.
107. See David Fishman, "The Musar Movement in Interwar Poland," in Y. Gutman, E. Mendelson, J. Reinharz, C. Shmeruk (eds.), *The Jews in Poland Between Two World Wars* (Waltham, 1989), 247–72 (in particular 266–70); "*HaRav Ḥayim Zaichik V'Likḥei HaShoa*," 135–38. At this point, we must comment on the words of Immanuel Etkes, who, in contrast to the testimony regarding the flowering of the Novardok yeshiva network between the World Wars, notes "that also at this time there were those who continued to disapprove of the yeshiva's ways. The most prominent and significant of them was R. Avraham Yeshayahu Karelitz" (Etkes, *Yeshivot Lita B'Re'i Sifrut HaZikhronot*, 24). In fact, besides there having not been any public expression at the time of the opposition of the Ḥazon Ish to the mussar yeshivot (his writings on the topic were published many years later), he did not yet have the status of being "most prominent and significant," in Etkes' words. This happened later in Eretz Yisrael. Compare Binyamin Braun, *HaḤazon Ish: HaPosek, HaMa'amin, U'Manhig HaMahapekha HaḤaredit* (Jerusalem, 2011), 80–82, 130–31, 168–70.
108. Ed. note: See the original Hebrew for a lengthy section detailing the economic consequences of the struggles engulfing Yeshivat Novardok following the passing of its patron Rabbi Epstein, and with the change in the yeshiva's character. They include a drastic reduction of funding sources, the cessation of aid on the part of the townspeople, an increase in debts, and accordingly, a reduction in the stipends distributed to its students, many of whom were literally on the verge of starvation. The shaky financial situation almost brought the yeshiva to closure, and ended only with the rapprochement with R. Krakowsky's faction.

garnered support from the surrounding society. Only this support allowed the yeshiva to establish itself to the extent that would afterward allow it to survive even during the time when its increasing radicalism kept previous centers of support at a distance. The bitter struggles during the second period of the yeshiva's existence, struggles that at times took place in its innermost circles, threatened it more than once with either partial or complete collapse.

On the other hand, with the decline in the yeshiva's material circumstances, and with the increasingly unbearable living conditions, the unique character, which gave the Novardok stream its fame for generations, became set.[109] This phenomenon illustrates yet again the close connection between the emergence of the Novardok ideology and the revolutionary movements that were prevalent in Russia at the time, and which also flourished under pressure and war conditions.

Paradoxically, one can say that the identity of the Novardok yeshiva network, as known today, could only have been formed once the parent yeshiva in Novardok, which gave its name to the entire stream, ceased to exist. Even the period in which the network of yeshivot in Poland thrived was only when R. Yozel, its great founder, was no longer alive. Nevertheless, the collective memory of the "defining period," when the yeshiva operated smoothly and peacefully in Novardok, and the lasting impression of R. Yozel, had an indelible influence on the course and Geist of the Novardok yeshivot and their leaders during their prime, between the World Wars.

109. R. Yozel's followers were already aware of the phenomenon of the flourishing of the yeshiva during the pressured days of the World War (discussed by Fishman); see R. Yisrael Yaakov Lubchansky's introduction in *HaMe'orot HaGedolim*, 217:135, 197:47.

Chapter 13

Arukh HaShulḥan and the Afflictions of the Censor[1]

A factor that delayed publication of *Arukh HaShulḥan,* especially in the first years, was the attention of the Russian censor, who, in that period, closely supervised the printing of Talmudic and halakhic works. In fact, this is the main reason that the second volume of *Arukh HaShulḥan Ḥoshen Mishpat* was printed almost a decade after the first volume. In a letter to his relative, R. Ḥayim Berlin, R. Yeḥiel Mikhel Epstein mentioned, "My book has been published through *siman* 188. Anything after that has not been printed yet. The manuscript is in Petersburg with my brother [R. Binyamin Beinush Epstein], to submit for review."[2] In another letter from that year (the winter of 1886–1887), R. Epstein wrote that the manuscript of the volume was already in the hands of the censor in Petersburg:

1. Translated by Rabbi Elli Fischer. This chapter initially appeared in the author's *Ta'arokh Lefanai Shulḥan* (Jerusalem, 2018).
2. *Kitvei Arukh HaShulḥan, siman* 56. The letter is dated 12 Nisan 5642 (April 1, 1882), but that is certainly a mistake, both because the first volume of *Ḥoshen Mishpat* had not yet been delivered to the printer by then, and because 12 Nisan of that year coincided with Shabbat. The earliest that this letter could have been written was 1884 (and in this case, we can suggest that those who attempted to decipher the letter confused the letter *dalet* with a *bet,* which are indeed similar in R. Epstein's handwriting). However, it seems more likely to me that this letter was written in 1887, because, as noted, the first volume of *Ḥoshen Mishpat* had already reached a broad public, *Even Ha'Ezer* was already completed, and we know from another source (see below) that the book was with the censor in that year.

> Regarding what the honored rabbi imagines, that all the volumes of *Arukh HaShulḥan* are completed and in print – unfortunately I still cannot publish it, due to lack of funds. Aside from that, the inspection of my work is in Petersburg; I was there, and they demand that I print the second volume only in Petersburg, where printing is very costly. Therefore, I have set this aside for now, until God shows me what is to happen.[3]

The fact that R. Epstein chose to first publish *Ḥoshen Mishpat* turned out to be a handicap, as the censor was far stricter about *Ḥoshen Mishpat* than he was about the other sections of *Shulḥan Arukh*. R. Yehoshua Mondshine describes "the special attention of the Russian censor to the *Ḥoshen Mishpat* section, which they viewed as the most 'dangerous' section of *Shulḥan Arukh*, because it clearly states that there can be a Torah law that is not compatible with the 'law of the regime' [*dina d'malkhuta*]. There is no greater act of sedition than this!"[4] R. Mondshine provides a long list of books that suffered from heavy-handed censorship when it came to *Ḥoshen Mishpat*, and particularly that they were forced to write that these laws are not to be practiced, that the law of the regime is the law, or to declare more generally that "these laws were practiced in the days of yore, always with the knowledge and license of the government under which they lived. Nowadays they are not practiced at all."[5] He adds that in several cases the censor was not content with this and actually prevented the publication of the "problematic" parts. For example, in the Jozefow edition of *Shulḥan Arukh HaRav* (1851–1855), the *Ḥoshen Mishpat* section was not printed at all (nor were the laws of interest in *Yoreh De'ah*). Similarly, whereas the title page of R. Yitzḥak Elḥanan Spektor's *Responsa Ein Yitzḥak* (Vilna, 1889–1895) states that the book covers all four sections of *Shulḥan Arukh*, in fact it does not include responsa on

3. *Kitvei Arukh HaShulḥan, siman* 104. See below regarding the ultimate circumstances of the publication.
4. Introduction to his publication of "*Teshuvah Avudah M'Kvod Kodsho Admor R. Shne'ur Zalman M'Liadi*," *Ohr Yisrael* 26 (2002), 9–10. Regarding the Russian censor more generally, see D. Elishevitz, "*HaTzenzurah HaMemshaltit al HaPirsumim HaYehudi'im B'Kesarut HaRusit*," *Toldot Yehudei Russia* 2 (Jerusalem, 2012), 63–72.
5. *Shulḥan Arukh HaRav* (Zhytomyr, 1847 edition, and similarly the Warsaw 1931 edition). Likewise, at the beginning of Rabbi David of Novardok's *Galya Masekhet*, published in 1844, it is written "all the laws branching out from matters were only practiced when they dwelled on their own soil or when kings allowed them to judge according to the law of the Talmud. However, in our time, these laws have been annulled, because judgment shall be in accordance with the laws of the kingdom and the state, and we must not second-guess the laws of the state." See also Rabbi Yisrael Meir Mendelevich's article about the author of *Galya Masekhet* in *Yeshurun* 12 (2003): 704–5.

Ḥoshen Mishpat. Another work of R. Spektor, *Naḥal Yitzḥak* (Vilna, 1872), which addresses only matters of *Ḥoshen Mishpat,* devotes an entire introductory page to praising the tsar and, of course, declaring that all of the laws in the book are not practiced nowadays:

> We must pray for the peace of his majesty, our lord, the righteous tsar, and the peace of all his advisers and ministers, from the greatest to the lowliest; may God uplift them all [...] and I encourage constant prayer for the peace and prosperity of our lord, his majesty, the tsar, in whose peace is the peace of all who take shelter in his shade.[6]

R. Yeḥiel Mikhel Epstein, whose books were printed in the same era and under the same regime, was likewise plagued by the same obstacles, especially in light of his having chosen to begin his work with *Ḥoshen Mishpat.* The publication of *Arukh HaShulḥan* was indeed plagued by concerns about harassment by the censor's officials and their ability to impede and even prevent the printing. This seems to be why a full page at the beginning of the *Ḥoshen Mishpat* section of *Arukh HaShulḥan,* entitled "The Glory of the King," is devoted to effusive praise of the tsar and his family – praise that is exceedingly similar to the preface to the aforementioned *Naḥal Yitzḥak.* After describing the loyalty of Russia's Jews to the royal family throughout the generations, and emphasizing the laws that benefit the king (such as the prohibition against tax evasion), the preface concludes with a grand call in honor of the incumbent Tsar Alexander III: "May God direct His grace to His anointed one, our king and lord, his majesty the tsar."[7]

It is possible, however, that these statements express, to some extent, R. Epstein's approach to the positive aspects of the regime, for without fear of it, people would devour one another alive.[8] Ultimately, however, there is no doubt that these

---

6. See other examples in the aforementioned article by R. Mondshine.
7. Cf. R. Yeḥiel Mikhel's introduction to his first work, *Or LaYesharim*:

   > Blessed be all the kings of the earth, along with their ministers and great men, in every generation, and especially our lord, the father of the country, his majesty, the pious [!] Tsar Alexander. We must never forget his grace and goodness for all generations. May all of Israel raise up a prayer and a hymn on his behalf and on behalf of his offspring, that he may succeed and cut down all who rise against him. For all the goodness of his deeds, may God extend the days of his reign.

   (This, of course, was written about Alexander II, who was considered relatively benign vis-à-vis the Jews.)
8. As he wrote in *Arukh HaShulḥan, Yoreh De'ah* 246:16 with respect to heretics:

   > Some of them, in their hearts, rebel against the earthly governments as well. This is not like those who immerse themselves in the Talmud, the codes, and the true wisdom; they

statements were written out of fear of the censor, for without them, the book itself would have been "devoured alive."[9] The description of Tsar Alexander III by R. Epstein's grandson, R. Meir Bar-Ilan, will suffice to demonstrate that the extravagant praise of that tsar could only have been said in an effort to conciliate the officers of the censor:

> The reign of Alexander III was one of the worst [...] The first pogroms, the expulsion from Moscow, the "temporary regulations" [the May Laws] of Ignatyev, and the unceasing decrees made Jewish life unbearable [...]. Everyone knew the wickedness of Alexander III.[10]

Given this background, it is not surprising that the Warsaw, 1911 edition of *Arukh HaShulḥan, Ḥoshen Mishpat,* printed after his death by R. Epstein's daughter and heir to his writings, **completely omits** the entire page of "The Glory of the King."[11]

> are wholeheartedly and willingly subservient to the earthly government, for so we have been commanded by our Sages, of blessed memory, in numerous instances. Thus said Shlomo: "My son, fear God and the king" [Prov. 24:21]. That is, one who fears God will also fear the king.

(*Arukh HaShulḥan, Ḥoshen Mishpat* 2:1 states similarly.) See also *Derashot Kol Ben Levi, derashah* 1, p. 2, where R. Epstein spoke in praise of the regime that protects the Jews from antisemites who wish to harm them, as well as in *Arukh HaShulḥan, Even Ha'Ezer* 7:1. See also what he wrote in the laws of Nedarim, *Arukh HaShulḥan, Yoreh De'ah* 248:27, namely, that there can be no communal bylaws against the king.

9. With respect to *Or Yesharim* as well, toward the end of the preface, after describing the travails of the Jewish people and declaring:

   > Thank God, we are now in a state of calm and tranquility, with no outcry and no outbreak [*peretz*]; may all the kings of the land be blessed, and may they merit the arrival of the son of Peretz [the Davidic Messiah]; and God shall be King over the whole earth [*eretz*]."

   R. Epstein adds: "Those who understand will understand all that your Levites sang." The "Levite" in question is obviously R. Epstein himself, who, in his books, regularly signed off as "the Youth of the House of Levi." It is possible, then, that these verse lines allude to the fact that the earlier praise of the regime was mere lip service. Either way, these lines were printed a year before the early pogroms against the Jews of Russia (Odessa, 1869); while the preface to *Arukh HaShulḥan, Ḥoshen Mishpat* was printed after the infamous pogroms of 1881.
10. *Mi'Volozhyn ad Yerushalayim* (Tel Aviv, 1971), 215–17. (The author was fourteen years old when this tsar died.) Even though R. Epstein's preface was written at the beginning of Alexander III's reign, pogroms had already taken place, and the nature of the tsar's attitudes toward the Jews was already known.
11. Nevertheless, new editions of *Arukh HaShulḥan*, published in our day, preface the volume with this paean to the tsar, as though we are still living under his heavy yoke. It was even printed without reservation in *Kitvei He'Arukh HaShulḥan.*

Yet despite all efforts to placate the Russian censor, he was heavy-handed with *Arukh HaShulḥan* in general, and especially the *Ḥoshen Mishpat* section, and the opening page to "The Glory of the King" was only a first indication of this.[12] R. Epstein himself, in a letter from 1903 on the authority of a local rabbi and communal regulations, referenced the relevant passage in the *Ḥoshen Mishpat* section of *Arukh HaShulḥan* and added: "I could not write at length about this due to the censor, of course."[13] Already at the beginning of the very first chapter, the following comment is added: "Everything explained in these laws is subject to the license of his majesty, the tsar, and '*the law of the regime is the law*.'" At the beginning of the *Dinei Mesirah*, in volume 2 of *Ḥoshen Mishpat*, an especially lengthy comment was added:

> It is known to all students of history that in days of yore and in distant countries no one was physically or financially safe, because of thieves and despoilers, who even held official titles – as is familiar even today from the plundering and robbery perpetrated by government officials in certain African countries. On the side of benevolence, we must mention the kings of Europe, and especially our lord, his majesty the tsar of Russia and his fathers, the tsars, and the kings of Britain, who spread the wings of their domain over distant lands so that the body and money of each and every person is secure, such that the wealthy need not hide themselves lest they be killed and their money plundered. All the laws in the Talmud and codes pertaining to a *moser*, an informant and a stool pigeon, hinge on this, for one who informs on his friend to such plunderers is considered a *rodef* in pursuit of his life and money, and therefore it is permissible to save [the victim] by taking the life [of the pursuer].[14]

---

12. Most of the comments written by the Gerrer Rebbe, author of *Pnei Menaḥem*, on *Arukh HaShulḥan* (printed in the back of each volume in the "Oz V'Hadar" edition) relate to changes made due to the censor. See, inter alia: *Ḥoshen Mishpat* 369:8 and 425:1; *Oraḥ Ḥayim* 55:16, 156:4, 8, 529:7, 545:25, and 670:2; *Yoreh De'ah* 81:34, 254, 265:18, 334:1, and 377:2; *Even Ha'Ezer* 129:93 and 154:18.
13. *Kitvei Arukh HaShulḥan, siman* 52. The passage in question is from *Ḥoshen Mishpat* 2:2, and indeed, at the end of this section we find ellipsis marks in the printed editions. The responsum deals with the authority of communal leaders to tax the sale of meat and the like in order to fund the salaries of religious functionaries. This taxation had been outlawed by the tsarist regime in 1844, so R. Epstein could not mention the practice in his book.
14. *Ḥoshen Mishpat* 388:7. The Gerrer Rebbe noted:

    This entire passage was inserted against the will of our rabbi [R. Epstein] because of the censor and out of fear of the Russian regime, may their name be blotted out. This is mistaken [...] Likewise, in many places in this work, it is apparent that the hands of the censor were in control.

The intrusions of the censor are easily discernible in other parts of *Arukh HaShulḥan* as well. Generally speaking, certain idioms are the obvious result of censorship – such as most comments that limit a particular law to "ancient times,"[15] and references to an "Egyptian" or a "despoiler" rather than a "gentile."[16] The effects of these intrusions are especially stark in certain particular areas of law. For instance, it is emphasized in the laws pertaining to conversion that "in our land we have no license to accept converts under the law of the regime," and that "even in ancient times, when we had license to perform conversion, we nevertheless should not incite any gentile to convert."[17] Or, for example, the laws of excommunication and ostracism are prefaced at length:[18]

> It is a great principle that the law of the regime is the law [*dina d'malkhuta dina*], and under the law of his majesty the tsar it is forbidden to impose any excommunication or ostracism. Such is the law in all the kingdoms of Europe. It is only in the lands of Ishmael, such as Turkey, Persia, and Morocco, that this is permitted under the law of the government. Therefore, all the laws that we clarify regarding excommunication and ostracism apply to those lands, but Heaven forfend that we would impose

---

See also what Rabbi Shaul Yisraeli wrote against those who understood these statements literally (*Ḥavot Binyamin* 1 [Kfar Darom, 1992], 184). It is worth noting the astonishing phenomenon of apologetics to the regime in books printed in countries where censorship was not an issue. See, for example, R. Menaḥem HaKohen Rizikow, *Palgei Shemen* (New York, 1939), 8: "Anywhere in my book where an *akum*, *goy*, or *kuti* is mentioned, the intent is gentiles who do not believe in the revelation of God, that is, the ancient gentiles. However, the gentiles of today believe in Divine revelation." It is possible that this was written so as not to increase enmity or the like. Alternatively, they follow the well-known opinion of Me'iri regarding such matters.

15. With certain exceptions, such as *Oraḥ Ḥayim* 329:9: "In ancient times, when the Temple stood." Based on 329:10, it seems that this was not affected by the censor. (And see *Mishnah Berurah* ad loc., in *Bi'ur Halakhah*, s.v. "*ela*," which includes a similar addendum about one who is liable for the death penalty in a properly constituted Jewish court.)
16. For example, see *Oraḥ Ḥayim* 329:2, which quotes Rambam on a "courtyard that has despoilers and Jews." The original, of course, has "*goyim*" instead of "despoilers" (though in the Vilna edition even Rambam's formulation was corrupted to "*akum*"). The same applies to the rest of that chapter (as well as *Mishnah Berurah* 329:8).
17. *Yoreh De'ah* 268:6. Likewise, anywhere else in *Arukh HaShulḥan* where converts are mentioned, it is qualified that this refers to "ancient times."
18. *Yoreh De'ah* 334:1. Cf. what R. Epstein wrote about the phenomenon of forced apostasy: "Know that none of this is relevant in our times, for the kings of the nations are gracious kings; Heaven forfend that they would force someone to convert" (*Even Ha'Ezer* 42:51). Likewise, regarding women captives: "This law does not pertain at all in our countries, for the kings are gracious and have no such despicable laws" (*Even Ha'Ezer* 7:27). A similar instance is *Yoreh De'ah* 251:21; regarding warfare, *Even Ha'Ezer* 141:168; on another matter, *Ḥoshen Mishpat* 156:13.

> excommunication and ostracism in our lands. However, it is incumbent upon us to know the laws of what is forbidden and permitted, so that we may refrain on our own from that which is prohibited to us. Therefore, it is necessary to write down all the laws that pertain to this.[19]

In the same vein, it is clear that the censor who oversaw the printing of the first volume (only) of *Arukh HaShulḥan, Oraḥ Ḥayim*, insisted, for some reason, that Tractate Avodah Zarah not be mentioned by its real name, instead replacing its name with *akum*, pagans, wherever it appeared.[20] The censors who reviewed the remaining volumes of *Oraḥ Ḥayim* did not have this hang-up, so in more than twenty mentions of this tractate, it is called by the usual name of Avodah Zarah – except in one solitary instance, where the censor caused a very strange corruption.[21]

Somewhat differently, the censor's oversight of the first volume of *Even Ha'Ezer* (published at the tail end of the tsar's reign) seems to have been more lax than that of *Ḥoshen Mishpat* and the other sections of *Arukh HaShulḥan*, for when R. Epstein discusses the principle that "we render judgment and execute by

19. Nevertheless, it is worth mentioning that in some places these notes have nothing to do with the censor. For example, with regard to Rabbenu Gershom's ban on polygamy, R. Epstein mentions that "all of the great latter-day authorities have written that this is not permitted except on the word of 100 rabbis and the **license of the government**." Later, again, one who seeks the permit of 100 rabbis requires "the license of the government for this" (*Even Ha'Ezer* 1:25; likewise, 119:22: "with the permit of 100 rabbis and license of the government"). It seems that this is also due to the censor; R. Epstein cites his source as *Ḥelkat Meḥokek* 1:12, but there, of course, government license is not mentioned. However, in a responsum about the permit of 100 rabbis, R. Epstein writes, "as long as it is done in accordance with the laws of his majesty's kingdom" (*Kitvei Arukh HaShulḥan, siman* 45). See also *Responsa Meshiv Davar* 4:2 and other responsa in which the permit is contingent upon government license.
20. See, for example, *Orah Ḥayim* 84:3, 187:9, and 224:3.
21. *Orah Ḥayim* 329:7 states: "That which **we say in *Akum*** that we are not concerned about short-term life...." This does not refer to a gentile, but rather to Tractate Avodah Zarah (as indicated by the reference to 27b). However, because that law deals with Jews, the censor apparently thought that *avodah zarah* in this context refers to a gentile, so he changed the language to the more distant *akum*. It should be noted that the censor was also very heavy-handed toward *Mishnah Berurah* in that chapter (besides the aforementioned change from "*goyim*" to "despoiler"). Thus, a note is appended at the end of 329:17, stating: "The Talmud has ruled that the law of the regime is the law." This is a serious corruption, because the "law of the land" alone is not grounds, Heaven forbid, to desecrate Shabbat (see *Mishnah Berurah* 656:9). Rather, the permit in question is to prevent enmity that entails risk of reaction from the regime (see *Ḥiddushei Rabbi Akiva Eger, Oraḥ Ḥayim* 330; *Responsa Ḥatam Sofer, Yoreh De'ah* 131). It is quite astonishing that contemporary publishers continue printing religiously this "novel insight" of the Russian censor.

stoning on the basis of presumptions [*ḥazakot*]"[22] and mentions the various punishments meted out by the court, not once did he have to limit the applicability of such matters in the present day, as he had to do on numerous occasions in other volumes.[23]

22. *Even Ha'Ezer* 19.
23. See also *Even Ha'Ezer* 16:20 and elsewhere. It should be noted that the last volume of *Yoreh De'ah* (*simanim* 240–403) was printed in Poland, after the end of the Russian tsarist regime. It would therefore seem that, unlike the preceding volumes, it did not have to undergo censorship. However, as we have seen, in fact it was affected by the intrusions of the censor as much as, and even more than, other volumes of *Arukh HaShulḥan*. The explanation for this is that the volume was arranged for print during the tsarist era (as is evident from *Yoreh De'ah, siman* 334), and it seems that they had already been prepared for the review of the censor. At that time, all of the changes made by an author preparing for eventualities (as we saw in n. 14 above) were inserted. For the same reason, even in the laws of vows, which were first printed recently from the manuscript, R. Epstein mentions (*Yoreh De'ah* 232:41) what he wrote in *Ḥoshen Mishpat, siman* 388 (above, n. 15) and continues in the same spirit.

Chapter 14

Zealotry Versus Tolerance in the Old Yishuv: The Case of R. Yeḥiel Mikhel Pines, His Excommunication in Jerusalem and Its Aftermath[1]

FOREWORD: BACKGROUND TO THE BAN ON R. YEḤIEL MIKHEL PINES

In the second half of the nineteenth century, the Ashkenazi community of Jerusalem's Old Yishuv felt itself under siege. The community had established itself in the early half of the century after disciples of the Vilna Gaon settled there and called themselves Perushim. The community grew and established synagogues, kollelim, yeshivot, and charitable institutions such as soup kitchens and orphanages. They were mainly supported by the *ḥaluka* system of charity, in which donations from all over the world were sent to Jerusalem by their

1. Translation and foreword by Michael Appel. This chapter is a consolidation of two longer Hebrew articles. Readers wishing further detail are referred to *HaMa'ayan* 49:2 (Tevet 5769), 19–38, and *HaMa'ayan* 50:2 (Tevet 5770), 68–84. The first article appeared as well in English translation in *Ḥakirah* 27. R. Eitam Henkin's original Hebrew article on R. Dovid Karliner was challenged by his good friend R. Betzalel Deblitsky, in an article entitled *"Emek Akhor"* in *HaMa'ayan* 49:4 (Tamuz 5769): 69–74, and R. Eitam responded in the same issue with an article entitled "*Petaḥ Tikvah,*" 74–78.

Jewish brethren to support their endeavors. The community was impoverished but prided itself on its Torah institutions and fidelity to the Jewish lifestyle and traditions of its European forbears.

By the late 1800s, however, this way of life was threatened by several developments. Waves of Jewish immigration brought a different sort of population to Palestine. These settlers of the "New Yishuv" were proponents of Jewish self-sufficiency and attacked the *ḥaluka* system. The Old City of Jerusalem was overcrowded, lacking in sanitation, and poor, so several projects were initiated to develop new neighborhoods outside the city walls. Philanthropists were donating funds for these neighborhoods and for education projects to teach Jewish youth the skills they would need to get jobs. The leaders of what was now known by contrast as the "Old Yishuv" dug in their heels and refused to compromise on its way of life. This meant a traditional *ḥeder* and yeshiva education for boys in which only Torah was studied. There was no room for secular subjects. Any hint of a breach was dealt with quickly and harshly.

In 1878, R. Yeḥiel Mikhel Pines arrived in Jerusalem as the representative of the Montefiore Trust. He was a Polish Jew from a rabbinic family, steeped in Torah but with self-taught secular learning alongside it. While still in Europe, he became a member of the Ḥovevei Tziyon movement and was thus a perfect candidate for his mission. He set out for Jerusalem to help build new neighborhoods outside the walls and to develop vocational programs. Almost immediately upon arrival, he was viewed with suspicion by the followers of R. Yehoshua Leib Diskin, one of Jerusalem's leading rabbis. In 1880, the first of two bans against R. Pines was proclaimed.

Contrary to the impression conveyed by the ban and by later ḥaredi books, R. Pines was far from the heretical *maskil* who intended to corrupt the youth of Jerusalem's Old Yishuv. R. Eitam Henkin carefully documents his standing in the Lithuanian yeshiva community. He uses documents, letters, and previously unpublished manuscripts to show that R. Pines was a well-regarded *talmid ḥakham,* a student of R. Mordekhai Gimpel Yafeh, and brother-in-law of R. Dovid Karliner, a highly regarded halakhic authority in Lithuania. Furthermore, he shows that Jerusalem's other leading rabbi, R. Shmuel Salant, as well as most of Jerusalem's rabbis firmly sided with R. Pines against the zealots clustered around R. Diskin.

R. Henkin's articles on this subject focus on the incidents that led to the bans as well as the wider communal battle lines that were drawn between the moderate faction and the zealots of Jerusalem. He documents the phenomenon of hagiographical biographies that attempt to erase the moderate voices from the history of the Old Yishuv, leaving the impression that the entire community embraced the minority's extremism, claiming it as the only expression of "Torah-true" Judaism to this day.

INTRODUCTION

In the years 1880–1882, R. Yeḥiel Mikhel Pines was subjected to two excommunication bans in Jerusalem. R. Pines was a rabbinic scholar and community leader who had come to Jerusalem several years earlier representing the Moses Montefiore Trust, which promoted Jewish settlement in the Land of Israel. This episode took place shortly after R. Yehoshua Leib [Maharil] Diskin arrived in Israel from Brisk and gathered a following around himself. It constituted the first significant struggle by the zealots of Jerusalem's Old Yishuv Ashkenazi community, and had a broad impact on the ongoing relationships within Jerusalem's Jewish community.

The activities of the Jerusalem zealots from that period onward can be characterized by three features: First, they were a minority of the city's population, Ashkenazim and Sephardim; second, they received the backing of a prominent Torah personality; and third, their activities were carried out against the will and positions of most of the city's rabbinic leadership. The excommunication of R. Pines was the first time in which all three of these factors converged, making it an important milestone in understanding the development, conduct, and influence of the community of Jerusalemite zealots, whose activity would be expressed again and again in the ensuing years: a few years later in the *shemitah* controversy; then in their famous war against R. Kook at the end of R. Yosef Ḥayim Sonnenfeld's lifetime; and ultimately, in the emergence of the modern-day *Edah Ḥaredis* as it is constituted today. Later on, this community would produce several historians, or perhaps more aptly, revisionist writers, who in an impressive literary undertaking, would transform the history of Jerusalem's zealots into the official and sole history of the entire scrupulously religious community of Jerusalem, by sweeping under the rug any mention of multiple positions, religious outlooks, or internal disagreements.

Someone whose historical knowledge is based on books such as *Mara D'Ara Yisrael* [a biography of R. Y. H. Sonnenfeld] by R. Menaḥem Mendel Gerlitz might feel uncomfortable reading our chapter. That book, with others like it, together have considerable influence on the historical consciousness that rules the day among those who consider themselves to be the rightful heirs of the venerable Jerusalemite rabbis. They feel compelled to follow the path of Jerusalem's zealots without knowing how vehemently the Torah giants of the time criticized them – even while professing allegiance to the path [of those selfsame Torah giants]. The ban on R. Yeḥiel Mikhel Pines is an ultimate example of the disparity between widely accepted notions and factual history.[2]

RESPONSE TO THE BAN: THE *EMEK BERAKHAH* PAMPHLET OF R. DOVID KARLINER

The story of the excommunication was covered in the past in several places.[3] We will focus mainly on the facts and our findings concerning the positions of the rabbis who were involved, beginning with the *Emek Berakhah* pamphlet of R. Pines' brother-in-law, R. Dovid Friedman of Karlin, author of *Yad David* and *She'eilat David*.

In the month of Av, 1880, several members of Maharil Diskin's circle enacted the first ban on R. Pines. The cause was R. Pines' association with Dr. Wilhelm Herzberg's orphanage, in which foreign languages were taught – proscribed by Jerusalem's rabbis twenty years earlier. A year and a half later, in Tevet 1882, an additional ban was imposed, this time at the behest of R. Diskin himself, after R. Pines founded a *bet midrash* for the youth of his neighborhood. The first half of the day was devoted to learning trades and the latter half to Torah study. According to R. Diskin and his followers, this would soon become a place of heresy and "*haskalah*."

When the first ban was declared in 1880, R. Dovid [Karliner] Friedman set out to defend his brother-in-law by composing a pamphlet entitled *Emek Berakhah*, consisting of a comprehensive halakhic investigation of excommunication bans and communal edicts, in which he assailed at length the possible arguments of the excommunicators. He completed the pamphlet in Av 1881 (p. 15a). The first excommunication had dealt with the teaching of foreign languages in Jerusalem.

---

2. R. Menaḥem Mendel Gerlitz first wrote about the excommunication in *Mara D'Ara Yisrael* 1 (Jerusalem, 1969), 265–69, and again with some small revisions in vol. 2 (Jerusalem, 2003), 122–26. He based much of it on *Amud Esh* (Jerusalem, 1954), 114–18, by his father-in-law, R. Yosef Sheinberger. R. Shlomo Zalman Sonnenfeld followed in their wake with *Ha'Ish al HaḤomah* (Jerusalem, 1975), 189–201, and added several details of his own. R. Gerlitz (as his father-in-law before him) relied on R. Yeḥiel Mikhel Pines' description of the excommunication by copying complete passages from his letter, *Shimu Harim Rivi* (See *Mara D'Ara Yisrael* 2:122) while expunging whatever was inconvenient for him. [A facsimile of the original is printed in Benjamin Kluger's book *Min HaMakor* 5 (Jerusalem, 1987), 17–18. The complete original manuscript, longer than what was publicized, was printed by Alter Druyanov in *Ketavim L'Toldot Ḥibat Tziyon* 3 (Tel Aviv, 1932), columns 366–82]. See appendix illustrating how R. Gerlitz systematically tampered with historical material, excising Netziv's language praising R. Pines.
3. For references, see my article in *HaMa'ayan* 49:2, n. 5.

R. Friedman therefore addressed this issue, concluding that the prohibition was not valid (p. 14a). After R. Friedman sent the manuscript to his brother-in-law, R. Pines prepared it for publication, and appended to it *Karnei Re'em*, a responsum of R. Eliyahu Mizraḥi regarding excommunication bans. He had prepared the title page with the Hebrew year of 5641 (using the numerically equivalent phrase, "the year of 'no ban or excommunication will arise in your camp' "). However, the printing was delayed for several months, and by then, in Tevet 1882, the second ban was imposed, referred to in the publisher's endnotes on the last page of the pamphlet. The delay in publication allowed R. Friedman to compose an additional letter concerning the *bet midrash* founded by his brother-in-law, in which he concluded that the excommunicators were guilty of an egregious error in an elementary and widely known halakhah (*to'im b'dvar Mishna*), and that there was no validity to the ban pronounced upon the *bet midrash* ("Responsum of the Author," 15b).

One can feel the sting in his words defending his brother-in-law against the onslaught of the Jerusalem zealots, whose inflated sense of their rabbinic standing enabled them to ignore the opposition of illustrious Diaspora rabbis:

> In these days, due to our many sins, the Torah sages of the Diaspora have diminished in number, until there remain only a scattered handful, like lonely grapes in a ruined vineyard. But in Jerusalem, I have heard that, thank God, they continue to multiply so much that, in one evening, 150 great sages were born(?).[4] However, even today, I am not mistaken in saying that they are nothing compared to the great sages of the Diaspora. And their [Jerusalem's] great sages are truly, in their full glory, relegated to their place alone. The Sages of Israel do not turn to them with their questions, do not ask for their advice, and those who crown themselves as "Rabbi of all Diaspora Jewry" are impugning the honor of the real Diaspora rabbis and will have to answer for this in the next world.[5]

4. The parenthetical question mark is printed in the original, apparently added by R. Pines. It seems that R. Friedman is hinting to rumors from Jerusalem that the ban on R. Pines' *bet midrash* was supported by "175 rabbis of Jerusalem" (according to R. Eliezer Mordekhai Altshuler in his notes, published by Druyanov in his monthly, *MiYamim Rishonim* 1, issue 6 [Tel Aviv, November 1934], 164–68). The reference appears to be about the number of rabbis certifying the ban.
5. *Teshuvat HaMeḥaber*, 15b:1. See also p. 9a: "And specifically in the Holy Land...," etc.

Why was the pamphlet's publication delayed by half a year? We can unravel the mystery as R. Friedman's handwritten notes on *Karnei Re'em* appear in the margins of the original pamphlet.[6] This shows that after R. Pines prepared the manuscript of *Emek Berakhah* for publication together with *Karnei Re'em,* he sent them to his brother-in-law[7] and waited for his response before publishing. After several months, he received them back with comments on *Karnei Re'em* and numerous additions to *Emek Berakhah*[8] that he incorporated into the final version. R. Pines added his own content to this version: comments on *Karnei Re'em* (published on the final page), comments and edits on the entire *Emek Berakhah,* and most importantly, an extensive essay on bans in Judaism, published as an introduction to the pamphlet.[9]

THE *LUḤOT HA'EDUT* LETTERS

R. Pines himself responded to the excommunication by publishing a pamphlet entitled *Luḥot Ha'Edut,* a pamphlet small in both dimension (10 × 20 cm) and length (twenty pages), published without a title page or publisher's details, in

6. This is apparent as most of the notes begin with the Hebrew "N.B." or *nikhtav b'tzido,* "written in the margin," or the like. In the second note it says, "See what I noted above," i.e., on the page.
7. With regard to *Karnei Re'em* this is explicit, as R. Friedman notes up front, "Author's note: This is the first time in my life that I have seen the pamphlet *Karnei Re'em,* and I decided to elucidate it with a few comments." Regarding *Emek Berakhah,* see the following note.
8. These additions appear across the entire pamphlet, entitled "Author's comments," and prove that R. Pines sent him a copy of *Emek Berakhah* prior to its final publication, and received it back with comments. Many of the "publisher's objections" appear within the "Author's comments." In other words, R. Pines wrote his comments only after his brother-in-law returned the original copy of the pamphlet.
9. The introduction appeared anonymously, but Druyanov uncovered the author's identity based on a notation by A. Z. Rabinowitz on one of the pamphlets (*Ktavim L'Toldot Ḥibat Tziyon* 3, col. 367), as did Geula Bat Yehudah in her article "R. Yeḥiel Mikhel Pines," in *Notrei Moreshet* (Jerusalem, 1968), 214. However, they both missed the testimony of R. Pines himself in a letter to R. S. Y. Fin (Printed in *Ktavim L'Toldot Ḥibat Tziyon* 1 [Odessa, 1919], Letter 37): "I hope that you have already read the book *Emek Berakhah,* and the introduction appended to it that came from my pen." This source was verified by Yosef Klausner (*Historia Shel HaSifrut Ha'Ivrit HaḤadashah* 6 [Jerusalem, 1959], 86), and later by R. Bezalel Deblitzky, but both missed the fact that by 1912, the author's identity had been made known by R. Shmuel Noaḥ Gottlieb, secretary of R. Dovid Friedman. In the entry on R. Friedman in his book *Ohalei Shem* (Pinsk, 1912), 179, he notes that "a long introduction was added [to *Emek Berakhah*], with good taste and knowledge, by his brother-in-law, the rabbi, gaon, wide-ranging sage, R. Yeḥiel Mikhel Pines *shlit"a.*" (Parenthetically, R. Gottlieb sent a letter to R. Pines on December 6, 1911, asking him to send biographical material on R. Friedman in preparation for the entry in *Ohalei Shem.* See the Central Zionist Archives (henceforth: CZA), loc. A109/117, and an additional letter there from December 20, 1911).

Jerusalem mid-1882.[10] The pamphlet, whose credibility is not in doubt,[11] consists of fifteen letters relating to the ban,[12] containing important findings for any serious research into this episode.[13]

---

10. P. 1 mentions the letter *Shim'u Harim Rivi*, published in the winter of 1881–82. This letter, along with *Luḥot Ha'Edut* and *Emek Berakhah,* was almost certainly published in the Jerusalem printing house of his friend R. Yoel Moshe Solomon.
11. First, because the pamphlet was published in the lifetimes and the place of residence of most of the correspondents (and those who were far away were the brother-in-law and the mentor of the publisher, the latter of whom explicitly referenced the pamphlet in one of his own letters), and there is no greater "matter likely to be exposed" than this. Second, R. Pines was never suspected of any forgery. Even in this affair, he conducted himself honorably (see below, n. 42). Even R. Gerlitz and the like relied on his words (see n. 2). Third, and most important, there is no evidence (in language, style, content, or facts) that would suggest a forgery. Fourth, there is ample corroboration in contemporary newspapers and writings (see nn. 28, 33, etc.) to confirm the contents of most of the letters. Finally, some of the original handwritten letters – or copies thereof – have been found in various archives. Not surprisingly, their contents match exactly the text found in *Luḥot Ha'Edut.* This all goes without saying.
12. They are: **Letter 1:** From R. Pines to R. Diskin, inviting him to adjudicate the ban in the Sephardi religious court of Jerusalem. Several witnesses and judges from the Sephardi court signed in the margins endorsing its content. **Letter 2:** From R. Mordekhai Gimpel Yafeh to R. Shmuel Salant. **Letter 3:** Response of R. Salant to R. Yafeh. **Letter 4:** From R. Friedman to R. Salant. **Letter 5:** R. Salant's response to R. Friedman. **Letter 6:** From prominent Ashkenazi rabbis of Jerusalem to R. Diskin. **Letter 7:** Text of the ban's release, by Jerusalem *gedolim.* **Letter 8:** Additional letter from R. Yafeh to R. Salant. **Letter 9:** Addition of the names of R. Rafael Meir Panigel and R. Yakov Elyashar to the release of the ban on R. Pines. **Letter 10:** From an anonymous rabbi (according to the publisher, a great and well-known rabbi). **Letter 11:** From R. Hillel of Shklov. **Letter 12:** From the trustees of the Minsk-Pinsk-Karlin Kollel in Jerusalem to R. Friedman. **Letter 13:** From the notables of Mohilev to R. Moshe Neḥemiah Kahanov (providing stellar character testimony on behalf of R. Pines). **Letter 14:** Letter to R. Pines from thirty-seven family members of Kollel Reisen (except for R. Eliezer Dan Ralba"g, who supported his relative Maharil Diskin, according to the publisher, *Luḥot Ha'Edut* and in *Shim'u Harim Rivi*: "The gaon R. Shmuel Salant and the trustees of the kollelim of Vilna, Zamut, Minsk, Pinsk, Grodno, and most of Kollel Reisen support me. The trustees of the kollelim of Warsaw, Hungary, Austria, and R. Eliezer Dan Ralba"g – close relative of the rabbi of Brisk [R. Diskin] – are aligned with the zealots against me. And the rest of the people are perplexed"). R. M. N. Kahanov is added in the margins. **Letter 15:** R. Friedman's joining with those who repealed the ban. Citations and summaries from most of the letters will be brought later.
13. The pamphlet was so rare that Druyanov notes that he was unable to find it (*Ketavim L'Toldot Ḥibat Tziyon* 3, note to col. 367). However, most of those who looked into the incident later on were familiar with it and mentioned it briefly (Klausner, Kressel, et al.), but none dedicated the attention it deserves besides, perhaps, Geula Bat Yehudah (see her article referenced in n. 9, pp. 218–19). A single original copy is housed at the National University Library in Givat Ram.

We will begin with the second letter in *Luḥot Ha'Edut,* sent by R. Mordekhai Gimpel Yafeh of Ruzhinoy (Ruzhany) to R. Shmuel Salant on January 13, 1882, two weeks after the second ban was imposed. R. Pines had grown up in Ruzhinoy, the town of R. Mordekhai Gimpel Yafeh. He grew close to R. Yafeh, eventually seeing him as his *rav muvhak,* rabbinic mentor. R. Yafeh, in turn, considered R. Pines his disciple, and a rare tie developed between the two.[14] R. Pines' estate contains close to three hundred notebook pages comprising almost seventy letters received from R. Yafeh over a twelve-year period, from when R. Pines first departed their hometown, until R. Yafeh joined him in Israel.[15] These letters are a treasure trove of information about their era, surroundings, and the social circles and acquaintances of the two, especially as regards the Ḥibat Zion movement, settlers, and settlement in Eretz Yisrael, as well as a wide range of Torah material, starting with a discussion of *etrogim* of Eretz Yisrael, mitzvot applying in Eretz Yisrael, laws of *kitniot* (legumes) on Pesaḥ, as well as matters related to *agunot* (abandoned wives).

R. Mordekhai Gimpel felt that the best response to the attacks was to ignore them, "and let God fight his battles."[16] He advises R. Pines not to rock the boat, to any possible extent, because many Jerusalemites supported him:

---

14. Two representative incidents: When the Montefiore Testimonial Fund was established, with R. Pines as its Jerusalem representative, R. Yafeh sent a letter to R. David Friedland, saying: "It is admirable that they have appointed him the bearer of their standard, a man head and shoulders above the rest, outstanding in Torah and worldly knowledge, with exemplary character, my good friend R. Yeḥiel Mikhel Pines. I know my friend from his youth..." and he continues to praise his love of the Land of Israel (printed in R. N. Friedland, *Yosef Ḥen* 1, [Warsaw, 1878], 156–57). Later on, R. Yaakov Lifshitz related that R. Yafeh was the first to recommend R. Pines for this position (*Zikhron Yaakov* 2 [Kovno, 1884], pp. 180–81). Second: When R. Yafeh arrived in Israel in 1888, R. Pines stood at the head of the welcoming party, as R. Yafeh described: "As I disembarked from the ship in the port of Jaffa, the great rabbi and sage, R. Y. M. Pines, came out to greet me, together with his brother-in-law, R. Zev Wolf Yavetz" (letter from April 8, 1889 to his son-in-law, R. Z. H. Wolk, *Keter Kehuna* [Jerusalem, 2004] 56). R. Pines then helped R. Yafeh find an apartment in Yehudiya (see the letters of R. Yafeh to the Aderet, *Igrot LaRa'ayah* [Jerusalem ed., 1990], 543, 549). Also note R. Pines's eulogy for R. Yafeh, copied "letter for letter" by R. Yafeh's son, R. Tzvi Hirsch Yafeh, in his letter to his brother-in-law, R. Z. H. Wolk, December 21, 1891 (CZA AK189/2).
15. These writings are preserved in the Central Zionist Archives. These are copies of original letters from the private collection of Raphael Malachi, biographer of R. Pines (see the introduction to *HaRav Mordekhai Gimpel Yafeh – Mivḥar Ketavim* [Jerusalem, 1978], 3 [henceforth: *Mivḥar Ketavim*]). There are additional letters that R. Pines received from him earlier. See, for example, *Yaldei Ruḥi* 2 (Mainz, 1872, 117–19); *HaMelitz*, September 1, 1887 [Yr. 7, issue 34]; *HaLevanon,* May 20, 1869 [Paris, Yr. 6, issue 20] cols. 153–56.
16. Letter from January 6, 1881, CZA A109/184, p. 184.

> My friend, it pains me greatly to see your name besmirched for naught, when they slander and sully your reputation. But, my friend, many stand with you, including the gaon R. Shmuel Salant who stands by your side, and undoubtedly, many others with him. [With this support] you can withstand the slings and arrows, saying "all this is for the good." In the end, the truth will win out, and your righteousness will shine. Therefore, my friend, be strong and patient. This is how you will overcome those who malign you.[17]

However, despite expressing distress at the attacks suffered by R. Pines, R. Mordekhai Gimpel also laid out his position regarding the study of foreign languages in the Jerusalem orphanage. Here, he disagrees with R. Pines, who believed that this would help extricate the youths from poverty. He writes, "Jerusalem will not benefit from this, it will not solve the problems of poverty…The Arabic language will not help the poor people, who have no money with which to do business with the Arabs."[18] Similarly, R. Mordekhai Gimpel expresses concern lest these studies weaken the students' fear of Heaven. He wrote that his heart told him that this was a dangerous idea, and that it would be best to stay away from such a step (p. 147). On the other hand, R. Mordekhai Gimpel criticized the zealots and wondered why R. Pines lost his patience this time, after heeding his advice and ignoring the first ban… [and] sums up by saying, "Let the innocent man go on his way, praying and teaching Torah, and the truth will take care of itself."[19]

17. Letter from September 12, 1880 (after the first ban), CZA A109/183, p. 148.
18. P. 146. In reality, R. Pines' opinion on the matter was similar to R. Yafeh's, as he wrote to his brother-in-law R. Z. Yavetz three days earlier in a long letter in which he rejected criticism of his part in the founding of "schools": "… Education of the poor Jews will not raise farmers who work the earth, will not build factories, and will not launch ships out to sea… I too, like the zealots, am not pleased with these schools, but for different reasons" (letter from September 9, 1880, CZA A109/120). A similar thought is expressed in his diary entry about the Herzberg orphanage, that the students "did not succeed because of the lack of practical learning and excess of theoretical learning. And not even theoretical learning about working the land, but theoretical learning about the French language which will not help them at all in securing employment." He concludes: "The French language should be eliminated completely in favor of Hebrew and Arabic alone" (*Sefer HaYovel L'Melot Ḥamishim Shana L'Yesud Petaḥ Tikvah* [henceforth: *Sefer HaYovel*] [Tel Aviv, 1929], 310).
19. Letter from February 5, 1882, CZA A109/184, p. 185 (published partially in *Mivḥar Ketavim*, p. 92); among other things, it mentions the letter he sent to R. Salant, the letter sent to R. Meir Anikester, and the protest against R. Yeshaya Orenstein. See also his letter from March 7, 1882 (CZA, ibid.), in which he advises R. Pines again to keep the matter quiet.

R. Yafeh was surprised that R. Salant permitted the excommunication to happen; and suggests that perhaps R. Salant believed that the followers of R. Diskin knew R. Pines better than R. Yafeh did; and therefore, they must be correct in whatever faults they found with R. Pines. However, this was not so. R. Yafeh continues heaping praise upon R. Pines, his personal history and activities,[20] and stating what, in his opinion, brought Maharil Diskin to take action against R. Pines:

> When I received a letter yesterday from my friend, the incisive and illustrious rabbi, the sage R. Mikhel Pines, may his light shine, that this haughty decree had been issued by the gaon and saintly rabbi from Brisk, may his light shine.... I am expressing my love for only him [i.e., R. Pines] as I have known him since his youth, and I have never met the sage from Brisk, even though I have heard of his reputation, good name, righteousness, and holy countenance. I also know that he undoubtedly acts for the sake of Heaven. So I must conclude because he is immersed in isolation in his Torah studies, that those who surround him must have slandered R. Pines in front of him.... (p. 3). Therefore, I am surprised that His Honor [i.e., R. Salant] sees iniquity and did not look to dispute the matter, that they tarnished the reputation of R. Pines in the name of the sage of Brisk. (p. 5)

At the same time, R. Yafeh also wrote to R. Ḥayim Berlin, son of Netziv, who was then rabbi of Moscow. The entire letter deals with the ban. Besides praise for R. Pines and sharp criticism of the zealots – as in the letter to R. Salant – it contains additional details about the incident, including his correspondence with both R. Pines (that was cited earlier) and R. Salant. The letter appears in print here for the first time:[21]

---

20. He refers to R. Pines' years in Ruzhinoy, where he grew in Torah. He then married and lived in his father-in-law's home where he continued to advance in both Torah and secular studies, following "the path of the famous gaon R. Menashe of Iliya *ztz"l*, who was beloved by R. Shemaryahu Luria *ztz"l* (R. Pines' father-in-law)" (p. 3), who was a righteous man, "although he [R. Menashe Iliyer] held freewheeling beliefs regarding several kabbalistic practices" (p. 4). R. Yafeh continues to say that, although he did not always agree with this approach, "R. Pines was always dear to me because he was righteous and always focused on Torah..." (ibid.) He continues to heap praise upon R. Pines, his Torah knowledge, piety, and character, "even though I sometimes disagreed with certain beliefs, and my personal practice is to follow the sages of Volozhin, whose customs have the force of Torah law and it is forbidden to doubt them. Still, I never stopped loving R. Pines, then and now, seeing his honest practices..." (p. 4). Finally, he asks R. Salant to show the letter to R. Pines.
21. CZA A109/142; The existence of the letter was mentioned by R. Moshe Zeira (*Yeshurun* 9 [2001], 788, n. 15), and later by R. David Kaminetzky, who quoted a short excerpt (*Yeshurun* 20 [2008], 781, n. 134). My thanks to R. Zeira who helped me locate the letter and secured a copy for me.

> Monday, 15 Adar 5642 [March 6, 1882],
> Ruzhinoy
>
> Greetings to ... my friend, the renowned gaon, known by every honorific, my master R. Ḥayim Berlin.
>
> I am anguished by the necessity to exchange letters regarding matters that mortify the soul of all rational people. Ever since the people of Jerusalem welcomed the sage R. Yeḥiel Mikhel Pines to Jerusalem, malicious people – ḥasidim from Hungary, Poland, and some from White Russia – took upon themselves the mantle of zealots, to wage a fierce battle against all those who do not think as they do. And now, the astute sage, R. Pines, bears the brunt of their anger, as is evident in his manifest, *Shim'u Harim Rivi.*

R. Yafeh writes that while he counseled R. Pines to ignore the zealots' attack, he himself immediately wrote R. Shmuel Salant, a friend from the days of his youth, presuming that he had some role in the proceedings, and petitioning him to publicly rein in the zealots:

> These ruffians, sons of Tzeruyah, continue to stoke the flames with whatever material they can use, defaming, slandering, and writing outright lies. They take cover beneath the shadow of the holy gaon from Brisk [Maharil Diskin], who is blameless, as they hide from him what they can and defame his name by using it in their attacks. They are in immediate need of sharp blows on the head. If you would please save the day, please send a decree against them, and act with the power of your stature for the sake of peace and honor in Jerusalem, the Holy City, that has been defiled by these rogues.
>
> I described R. Pines to our friend, the gaon R. Shmuel Salant, not as a saint who sits all day, fasting, wrapped in tallit and tefillin. Rather, I described him as he is, a man who loves both Torah and secular wisdom. From early on, he studied and taught students Gemara, Rashi, Tosafot. When he became wealthy, he took care of the yeshiva and its leaders. He was a good friend, colleague, and well known to the regulars who together studied Talmud, Bavli and Yerushalmi, here, also spending his days and nights in the *bet midrash*. He learned here and prayed here, even though the *bet midrash* of his fathers was closer to his neighborhood, only because the Talmud study group was based here.

> He also dealt in scientific study. But he was self-taught,[22] never seeing the inside of a [secular] school. His philosophy in these matters is similar to the approach of his father-in-law, R. Shmaryahu Luria *z"l*, who followed the opinions of the gaon R. Menashe of Ilya *z"l*, whom he supported; and his sons-in-law also accepted this path. When he read many of the new books, he closely followed the approach of R. Menashe of Ilya, but I hereby testify that he never issued any halakhic ruling without seeking my approval. And we discussed these matters together after his readings. It is clear that his approach departs from that of our fathers who walk in the ways of my grandfather, the saintly gaon R. Ḥayim of Volozhin. On this, I argued with him, but I was always honest with him. With all this, he was a beloved friend to the Torah and its students. The greatest Torah sages and God-fearing men were regular guests at his table, on Shabbat and weekdays.
>
> One of the *maggidei shi'ur*, lecturers, in the *bet midrash* founded by R. Pines in Jerusalem is your relative, R. Zissel [Alexander Ziskind] Shaḥor, who receives one and half rubles per week to teach there – this is the "heresy" that they claim will arise from this *bet midrash*.[23] And they continue to heap lies upon lies to strengthen their evildoing, increasing desecration of God's name in Jerusalem, at a time when the entire Land of Israel is in dire economic straits, awaiting Divine Judgment... Therefore, I beseech you to take upon yourself the mitzvah to do whatever you can in this matter. From one who asks after your well-being for all days,
>
> M.G.

R. Ḥayim Berlin's position regarding the ban is not entirely clear. The critical words of his father, Netziv, on the topic are well known, based on his letter to their relative, R. Alexander Ziskind Shaḥor. Of course, this does not prove that his son felt

22. R. Pines in his autobiography, tells the story of how, at age nine, he picked up books of literature and *haskalah*, reading them in secret [*Kitvei Yeḥiel Mikhel Pines* 2, book 1 (Tel Aviv, 1939), 10]. When he was twelve, several community leaders came to evaluate his suitability for marriage prospects. One of the evaluators was "a young man, not yet thirty, an intelligent and deep thinker, who paced back and forth across the room with hands clasped behind his back, humming a pleasant tune. He was the famous *ilui* R. Dovid'l Kaminitzer... today a well-known gaon, elder sage of the rabbis in the Diaspora, our master R. Dovid Friedman *shlit"a*..." (ibid., p. 12).
23. This last sentence is written with irony. The "heresy" in R. Pines' *bet midrash* that the opponents feared were the lectures of R. Shaḥor....

the same way.[24] Yet we do have evidence that R. Ḥayim Berlin did, in fact, fulfill R. Yafeh's request and sent a letter of support to R. Pines. This is explicit in an additional letter written by R. Mordekhai Gimpel to R. Pines after the publication of *Luḥot Ha'Edut*. Among other topics, he suggests that R. Pines publish an additional pamphlet to include letters that were not published in the first one:[25]

> I don't know if what I have already written on this matter has reached you: The letter to you from Moscow, the posters that I have in my possession, the thank-you letter from notable rabbis that I received for my letter to R. Salant.[26] But I have not received any letter – the troublemakers obviously removed it from the post [...]
>
> I do not know which rabbis were silent and did not defend you. According to your letter, there are more of them on your side than against you, thank God. I, myself, sent many letters to the places that I felt needed to be reached most urgently: The letter to Moscow[27] took precedence over the letter to R. Salant, and he [R. Berlin] responded as per my request.

In an additional letter sent by R. Yafeh to R. Salant, on February 14,1882 (Letter 8), he adds an admonishment about "the travesty perpetrated against our friend, the precious and well-known rabbi, R. Mikhel Pines." He writes that he was

24. A hint, but not necessarily a proof, can be cited from a letter sent by R. Ḥayim Berlin to R. Pines dated 14 Kislev 5641 (November 17, 1880) – several months after the first ban – dealing with the passing of a childhood friend and concern for his children and their inheritance. He turns to R. Pines in a friendly and respectful tone: "Let the mountains bear greetings like rivers from all sides for the upright precious ones, to His Honor, the rabbi and sage, complete in Torah and the sciences, whose fear of Heaven precedes his wisdom, the gaon, Yeḥiel Mikhel Pines, may God strengthen him, may God protect him and grant him long life..." (CZA A109/141).
25. CZA A109/143. R. Pines himself wrote something similar in a letter from March 13, 1882 to the editor of *HaMelitz*: "... When you see *Luḥot Ha'Edut* in which I am publishing the letters that reach me one at a time, and I am also prepared to publicize with this letters from other notables, *ge'onim*, and rabbis from Russia, Poland, and Germany related to this matter, all of whom have rallied to my support. And those who defend me are not only in the Diaspora, but also in Jerusalem itself, including most of its population, the majority in number, and in standing..." (*HaMelitz*, April 18, 1882 [Yr. 18, issue 13], and again in *Kitvei Yeḥiel Mikhel Pines*, vol. 2, book 2 (Jerusalem, 1939), 140–41).
26. This is the letter printed in *Luḥot Ha'Edut*. Apparently, the aforementioned notable rabbis saw it there.
27. This refers to the previously cited letter to R. Ḥayim Berlin in Moscow. Therefore the "letter to you from Moscow" mentioned in the previous paragraph refers to the response from R. Berlin to R. Yafeh, to be cited presently.

happy to read in R. Salant's response (see below) what he had suspected from the beginning, that R. Salant had no part in the ban (p. 12). Similarly, he writes, "For many years now, I have considered my friend [R. Salant] to be the leading rabbi of Jerusalem, and he should be the decisor."[28] R. Yafeh's hypothesis, that R. Diskin's followers took advantage of his isolation from worldly affairs to sway his opinion against R. Pines, was validated by R. Salant's response on January 31, 1882 (Letter 3), in which R. Salant unequivocally and sharply declared:

> That this entire incident with R. Pines happened without me and against my opinion… due to our many sins, among the men who come and go from the Rabbi of Brisk's house, there are men of…[29] and those who foment quarrels and strife, who invent lies and seek out sins among righteous men…. I told this to the sage from Brisk so that he would know to be careful and not to listen to them. However, to my great dismay, and to the distress of all who fear God, this man[30] still comes and goes with his friends to the great sage's house. The great righteous sage refuses to see iniquity in them because they put on a pure disguise. For this reason, my friend R. Pines has been ensnared by their wickedness, as they have fabricated lies about him every day.[31]

28. Two letters from R. Yafeh to R. Salant and R. Salant's response were republished by Benjamin Yafeh in his book *HaRav Mordekhai Gimpel Yafeh – Mivḥar Mikhtavim* (Jerusalem, 1978) 88–92. See the expanded treatment of these letters in Henkin, "*Kishrei Harav Mordekhai Gimpel Yafeh V'Talmido Ri"m Pines B'Aspaklaryat Parshat HaḤerem B'Yerushalayim*," *HaMa'ayan* (Tevet 5770).
29. The ellipses replacing a deleted name appear in the original.
30. Referring to someone close to R. Diskin, whom R. Salant chastised earlier without mentioning his name. In his letter in *HaTzefira*, R. Salant mentions this person again, adding several details: Twenty-five years earlier, he had distributed *pashkevilim* (broadsides) against "*HaRav HaGaon HaTzaddik R. Yeshaya (Bardaki) ztz"l* with lies and falsehoods, as is his practice. Then, several years later, he did the same to *HaRav HaGaon HaTzaddik*, the well-known R. Meir Auerbach *ztz"l*, rabbi of Kalish. And this is what he always does…"
31. Pp. 5–6. At the time, this letter was copied and distributed widely: R. Salant also sent it to R. Friedman (see below, n. 43); R. Yafeh sent it to R. Ḥayim Berlin (see n. 27); R. Pines sent it to R. Ze'ev Yavetz – a brother-in-law from another side of the family (see his letter from February 10, 1882, CZA A109/120), and also to R. Yafeh's son-in-law, R. Yosef Zekharia Stern from Shavel, adding in the margins: "To His Honor, my friend, the well-known gaon, R. Yosef Zekhariah Stern, *av bet din* of Shavel! Please take note of these published writings. I implore you out of our long-standing friendship, for the honor of God and His Torah, for the love of His land and His people, please join the battle to save me from my oppressors, who have embittered my life endlessly. Peace be with you, from your friend, Yeḥiel Mikhel Pines." (This letter had circulated among the descendants of R. Stern. It is currently held by R. Ḥayim Stepansky, who graciously allowed me to copy it. A sixth copy sits in the National University Library. It is still not catalogued, but I have a photocopy. Thanks to Mrs. Rivkah Plesser for her help in locating it.

Further on in the letter, R. Salant describes how the zealots tried to involve him in the ban's proceedings, but he rebuffed them.[32] Still, he did not wish to publicly confront R. Diskin for fear that those gathered at the proceeding would not understand that both had pure intentions. And, "ever since the great sage R. Diskin arrived in Jerusalem, I have acknowledged him as a sage and I defer to His Honor." However, "the great sage unwittingly trusts the liars who surround him, who have convinced him that he is fighting a holy war" (p. 6). Later, he writes in a note to Letter 7 (p. 11), "And the great R. Diskin was not accepted by the city elders as a rabbi and community leader. Since his arrival, he does not leave his house or the four cubits of halakhah" (p. 11).[33]

R. Salant even joined with R. Yafeh as a character witness on behalf of R. Pines, writing: "In truth, since our friend R. Pines arrived in Jerusalem, I have spent much time with him on many matters, and have never observed any strange or heretical beliefs" (p. 7). He adds that if anyone has questions or concerns regarding R. Pines' writings, he should ask R. Pines directly.[34]

The pamphlet also contains a letter sent by several of Jerusalem's leading Ashkenazi rabbis to R. Diskin, among them R. Salant and his *bet din*, on February 23, 1882 (Letter 6). They ask him "to regard with his pure heart and

32. His words match R. Yafeh's description in his letter *Shim'u Harim Rivi*: "And the great gaon R. Shmuel Salant also encouraged me, as did R. Akiva Yosef Shlesinger, known by his book *Lev Ha'Ivri*, who prayed in my *bet midrash*. However, this was a thorn in the sides of the devil's craftsmen among the zealots… who convened a group in Jerusalem… without inviting those steadfast men who would remain unswayed, except for R. Salant, whom they hoped to outweigh by their numbers – yet he was wise and foresaw the outcome, so he declined to participate…."
33. Regarding this, see the letter published at that time by R. Tzvi Hirsch Salant, grandson of R. Shmuel Salant (who was then in Jerusalem), in which he contradicted some rumors printed in a certain article, writing: "All that he wrote concerning a split, God forbid, between the Sage of Brisk (R. Diskin) and my grandfather (R. Salant) was drawn from a dry spring…" He adds that both men were equally opposed to the teaching of foreign languages in Jerusalem, except that "they differ slightly in the methods to achieve this goal. This is because there are young men who frequent the house of R. Diskin who have attracted other young men from the Kollel Ḥabad Hungary/Warsaw. They make a racket demonstrating at night, blowing shofars and terrifying the people with their cursing and screaming against people they believe to be tolerant of secular studies in Jerusalem…. They lie and make up stories to smear them in periodicals – thinking that this will stem the tide. They justify their actions by claiming that the great Sage of Brisk is with them and agrees to their actions…." [*HaLevanon*, September 7, 1841 (Mainz, 18:7) 55].
34. Regarding this: On p. 16, R. Pines mentions that R. Yehoshua of Kutna told his son-in-law R. Ḥayim Elazar Waks, in public, that there is no heresy in the book *Yaldei Ruḥi*. On the contrary, "it contains many good and pleasant things," but one must have attained a high proficiency in Hebrew to understand them.

respond with a clear answer, written and signed by his hand"[35] (p. 9). They write that the ban on praying and studying "in the *bet midrash* founded by R. Pines was not accepted by the masses, and the prayer quorum has continued there every day, and many God-fearing men enter there. Many outstanding men are bitterly protesting this ban," even among those who participated in the ban's proceedings. "Also, we have received many letters from great sages of Israel and from community leaders in the Diaspora, screaming like a crane" (p. 10). Subsequently, they describe how ten rabbis joined to nullify the ban on behalf of anyone who had not accepted it upon himself, and they ask R. Diskin to join them as well. The letter is signed by: R. Shmuel Salant, R. Moshe Neḥemia Kahanov, R. Avraham Eisenstein, R. Binyamin Wolf of Kavidian, and R. Mordekhai son of R. Aryeh Leib.[36] The following Sephardi rabbis joined the aforementioned nullification: R. R. M. Panigel and R. Y. Elyashar (Letter 9).[37] Even R. David Friedman joined the nullification (Letter 15) and wrote that "there is no place for this type of ban on individuals, promulgated by a sage such as R. Diskin" (p. 20).[38]

---

35. Apparently to avoid charges of forgery. However, their request went unfulfilled. The publisher notes that the letter was sent to R. Diskin, who responded on the same day, via messenger, saying that "there is no reason to release the ban."
36. As the publisher notes (p. 11), the latter was one of the three *dayanim* who originally signed the ban, and who now retracted his signature. A few details of his life are in *Encyclopedia L'Toldot Ḥakhmei Eretz Yisrael* 2, col. 277. Biographical details on R. Binyamin Wolf of Kavidian are also scant [ibid., vol. 1 (Jerusalem, 1975), col. 243]. More information exists on R. Avraham Eisenstein, one of the elder judges in Jerusalem (ibid. cols. 24–25, and see Gliss, *MiGedolei Yerushalayim* [Jerusalem, 1967], 65–70).
37. The text of the ban's nullification by the rabbis of Jerusalem, headed by R. Salant, is brought in Letter 7. This text, along with the letters of R. Panigel and R. Elyashar, was published at the time as a public announcement that was apparently circulated prior to the publication of *Luḥot Ha'Edut*. A single copy survives in the Pines archive. Similarly, there is a handwritten copy in the archive on Montefiore Trust letterhead, along with a copy of the letter from the rabbis asking R. Diskin to join them in nullifying the ban.
38. An item regarding the letters from R. Yafeh and R. Friedman to R. Salant was published at the time in *HaLevanon*, March 13, 1882 [Mainz, 19:10], 76–77. It included a section from R. Friedman's letter (even before its publication in *Luḥot Ha'Edut*). It also reported on the gathering of ten rabbis to nullify the ban, and on the messenger sent to R. Diskin asking him to join them, along with his refusal (including the name of the messenger, Avraham Telzer). These last details had been previously reported in brief, in *Ḥavatzelet*, March 3, 1882 (Jerusalem, 12:20), 154–55. The same details are corroborated in *Emek Berakhah* itself, in R. Friedman's description of the second ban: "... some Ashkenazi sages of Jerusalem got together and banned him ... but the leading sage of the city [R. Salant] along with ten distinguished Torah scholars annulled the ban, and the Sephardi leaders and their rabbis agreed with them, as did most of the population" (Author's Response, p. 15b).

To conclude this section, let us cite one more letter from R. Salant, from May 1882, published in one of the newspapers of the day, and similar in content to the other letters previously cited:[39]

> Our friend R. Pines has shown us defamatory writings that evildoers sent from here to several destinations.... When I saw these writings and the lies they contained, I was not surprised, as these men are well known to us, and they are famous for inventing lies that never happened and disseminating them through posters... God-fearing men did not push him [R. Pines] away, only the evildoer and those like him have stung him with thorns and maligned him in front of R. Diskin. And he, in his pure innocence, believed their lies because they appear before him as God-fearing, while our sages have warned us against charlatans....
>
> In truth, it was difficult for me to get involved in this matter against the great R. Diskin, and I worried that this would create a schism between me and R. Diskin, whose honor is extremely important to me, as he is a great sage and Torah scholar who acts for the sake of Heaven. In my opinion, his only mistake is in listening to treacherous men who foment discord, whom he holds to be God-fearing. However, I could no longer stand idly by and see R. Pines' blood spilled on the ground. I had to uphold the commandment not to stand by while one's brother's blood is spilled. So when the many Torah scholars who are listed, along with R. Moshe Neḥemia, the rabbi of Haslovich, declared that this ban is not binding on those who do not voluntarily accept it, as explained in all the writings that were published with my signature and signatures of the other rabbis, since then, thank God, the fire is almost quenched.[40]

---

39. The letter was published in *HaTzefira*, May 30, 1882 [Warsaw, 9:19] 147–48. It is cited by Geula Bat Yehudah in her article (see above, n. 9), p. 219. A copy is preserved in the Pines archive, CZA A109/74. There is an interesting testimony corroborating the description in these letters – that R. Salant, even while greatly respecting R. Diskin, felt that he had been swayed by evil slander. Yehudah Aharon Weiss, as a child, attended R. Diskin's funeral with his father. He relates how, before the funeral procession, R. Salant "said a few parting, conciliatory words, in order to dispel the notion that he and R. Diskin feuded 'not for the sake of Heaven.'" He adds, "I heard that R. Salant said roughly as follows: 'Now that the venerated Rabbi of Brisk is in the World to Come, he knows how many times gossip and slander were brought before him'" (*B'Sha'arayikh Yerushalayim* [Jerusalem, 1949], 90).
40. "The writings that were published" are, apparently, the public nullification of the ban that was circulated in Jerusalem (see n. 37) and/or the entirety of *Luḥot Ha'Edut*. In the rest of the letter, R. Salant refutes each claim against R. Pines, point by point: The claim that he associated

FURTHER COMMUNICATIONS OF R. DOVID (KARLINER) FRIEDMAN

As noted, Rabbis Yafeh and Salant were united in their opinion that Maharil Diskin's saintly and aloof personality caused him to trust the zealots who surrounded him. Just like Netziv before them, they chose to honor R. Diskin although they considered him to be gravely mistaken. R. Dovid Friedman, on the other hand, had quite a different attitude toward R. Diskin, as we have seen. He expressed this in a letter to R. Salant on January 16, 1882 (Letter 4), in which he bluntly admonishes R. Diskin and the "evil cabal" that surrounded him. He even called for a counterban in response:

> How can he turn a blind eye to the evil and injustice taking place in the Holy City [Jerusalem], perpetrated by one of its leaders, who garbs himself as if he were a Heavenly angel with a club in hand, as if guarding the Tree of Life. And with the demons who are with him – Lilith[41] and her coterie – they hurt all that is good, and will bring, God forbid, destruction upon the people of Jerusalem, reveling in their shame as they watch my brother-in-law wallowing in his own righteous blood. The honorable Torah scholar Yeḥiel Mikhel Pines is most upright of men, representing the righteous Sir Moses Montefiore, may he live a long life… (p. 7)
>
> When this matter is brought before our rabbis, the sages of the Diaspora, may God protect them, I will certainly not stand by while innocent blood is spilled. I call upon all the rabbis, and those remnants who still have some fear of God remaining within them, to rise up and protect the victim, who is entitled to a defense, even at the cost of his pursuers' lives. Excommunicate them, as is appropriate for those who excommunicate the innocent…. Let His Honor reflect upon how much damage this will cause to the needy souls of Zion and Jerusalem who will be burned by the

---

with frivolous individuals upon his arrival in Jerusalem "is a falsehood without evidence. In truth, upon his arrival here, he attached himself to God-fearing men, wise and intelligent…." The claim that he was disseminating *Yaldei Ruḥi* among the youth "is also false [and] I am sure that the book was not distributed in Jerusalem, and the zealots had to search long and hard to acquire a copy. Perhaps they did not understand the contents, and I have expressed my honest opinion that they should ask R. Pines himself about the details that they have difficulty with…" And so on.

41. This harsh expression seems to be directed at Rabbanit Sarah (Sonia) Diskin, wife of R. Diskin, known as the "Brisker Rebbetzin." Many, apparently including R. Dovid Friedman (Karliner), blamed her for various disputes and controversies surrounding R. Diskin in Shklov, Brisk, and Jerusalem.

> coals of the one who violates the peace of the city.... Theft and bribery infest the walls of Jerusalem from this accursed gang! (p. 8)

Through the harsh rhetoric of R. Friedman, written with great agitation following the ban,[42] we learn of his admiration for his brother-in-law R. Pines, praised as a tzaddik, righteous man, and "most upright of men" who was persecuted for no reason. R. Friedman fought with all his might to restore R. Pines' trampled reputation.[43]

R. PINES' STANDING AFTER THE BAN

Based on the facts presented here, given the extensive array of contemporary evidence and documents, it is no surprise that influence of the bans never extended beyond the circle of Maharil Diskin and his followers. After the excommunications, R. Pines remained an accepted personage by most of the Old Yishuv[44] until

---

42. It should be noted that R. Pines himself shied away from the accusations directed at R. Diskin. With extraordinary integrity, he published a stinging rebuke of a certain critic:

> I must declare that it is a terrible thing in my eyes that he chose such language to heap scorn and disgrace upon a great and exalted man, esteemed beyond thousands of sages of Israel for his Torah and his character. While I have suffered greatly at his hand, and I continue to suffer, as he does not cease his pursuit of me, and at his behest they hire men to slander me and hang vilifying wall posters... with all that, I am pained to see his honor and name tarnished to this degree. Because all that has befallen me through his hand has not blinded me, and I would never suspect him of duplicity, God forbid. I know that he believes he is acting for the sake of Heaven, and this can even be called an "innocent error" [ed. note: i.e., not intentional evil], as his zealousness [for God] has weakened his vision... When we see all this, we can only feel the pain of the Torah, but Heaven forbid that we hear vilification of a Torah scholar and remain silent!" [*HaMelitz*, June 6, 1882 (Petersburg, 18:20)], 388.

This letter was also cited by Geula Bat Yehudah (see n. 9), p. 219. In her words, "This letter is a badge of honor to Pines the man, and demonstrates his exemplary character." We should also mention R. Pines' letter to Alexander Cederbaum (Erez), editor of *HaMelitz*, protesting Cederbaum's call to cease contributions to the *ḥalukah* in order to deter the zealots: *Hamelitz*, April 18, issue 13, p. 241.

43. The pamphlet goes on to bring R. Salant's response to R. Friedman, dated 10 Adar 5642 (March 1, 1882, Letter 5). His words are brief, ignoring the complaints, implicit and explicit, against R. Diskin. But he reiterates his support for R. Pines, and summarizes what he had written at length to R. Yafeh (about how the zealots had tried to include him, but he refused). He appended a copy of his letter to R. Yafeh to this letter, along with the text of the ban's nullification. He also writes that it was untrue that the ban was placed on R. Pines personally, but only on his *bet midrash* (p. 9). This is corroborated by a notice in *HaLevanon*, January 12, 1882 (Mainz, 19:2), 15–16.

44. This despite the fact that R. Pines was mostly associated with the New Yishuv, and rightfully so. He was notably different from most of the Old Yishuv, specifically during his early years

his death. This is expressed not only in his continued friendly ties with many of the Torah leaders in Eastern Europe[45] and in his articles in Torah periodicals in Eretz Yisrael and abroad[46] but also in his well-established position in Jerusalem itself. Nothing prevented the "excommunicated" R. Pines from being appointed to various public roles with several central Old Yishuv institutions, such as *Bikur Ḥolim*, the *Va'ad Klali*, and *Moshav Zekeinim*.[47]

---

in Jerusalem, in his unique, sometimes exceptional, positions; in his worldly knowledge; and most importantly, in his willingness to establish social ties with people who had departed from a Torah way of life. On this, see the response of R. Bezalel Deblitzsky to my first article, and my response to him (*HaMa'ayan* 49:3 [Nisan 5769]: 69–78).

45. Besides the evidence presented here, I will cite the lengthy letter to R. Pines from R. Ḥayim Eliezer Waks from March 4, 1885, regarding settlement in the Land of Israel (Published in *Ketavim L'Toldot Ḥibat Tziyon* 3 [Tel Aviv, 1932], cols. 934–38, and again in *Shem V'She'erit L'Nefesh Ḥaya* [Jerusalem, 1961], 73–76), the letter from R. Azriel Hildesheimer from July 18, 1895, one of many regarding the Gedera issue (*Ḥavatzelet*, August 2, 1895 [Jerusalem, 25:43], title page), etc. Also, see the letter from R. Pines to R. Yom Tov Lipman of Mir from September 9, 1888 regarding the Land of Israel, in which he mentions a letter he received from him on August 17, 1888 (*Kitvei Yeḥiel Mikhel Pines* 2, 121–23). His continued close relationship with R. Shmuel Salant goes without saying. We'll just cite one example in R. Salant's letter to him from July 9, 1884, in which he recommends his son, R. Binyamin-Beinish, an *etrog* dealer in Israel (CZA A109/146), and R. Salant's letter to R. Dovid Friedman from November 20, 1900: "I have seen from your brother-in-law, our good friend R. Yeḥiel Mikhel Pines, a letter regarding the prohibition of establishing funds..." (*Torat Rabbenu Shmuel Salant ztz"l* 1 [Jerusalem, 1998], 162). R. Pines was also a welcome guest of R. Rabinowitz-Teomim. We find in R. Teomim's responsa notebook: "R. Yeḥiel Mikhel Pines, may his light shine, asked me about a certain *Pri Megadim*..." (*Shelosha Sefarim Niftaḥim... Oznei Yerushalayim* [Jerusalem, 2006], 93). An interesting story which requires further confirmation is told by R. Meir Bar-Ilan, regarding a charity collector from Jerusalem who came to Brisk for a time, and spoke badly about R. Pines. The young students of R. Ḥayim Soloveitchik, who believed that their rabbi "greatly respected R. Pines as a scholar and God-fearing man," argued with the collector and then brought the matter to R. Ḥayim Soloveitchik. He scolded the man, calling R. Pines "a God-fearing Jew and Torah scholar." The collector mentioned the ban imposed by Maharil Diskin, who was known to have R. Ḥayim's respect. R. Ḥayim responded, "If so, it's a difficult dilemma. But Pines is a kosher Jew!" (*MiVolozhin ad Yerushalayim* 1, 261).

46. See *HaPeles*, 2:12 (Berlin, 1902): 712–14, and his articles in *HaMe'asef*, 2:3 (Jerusalem, November 4, 1897); *Kedushat Ha'Aretz*, *siman* 3; 8:6 (Jerusalem, Adar 1903), *siman* 51; 8:7 (Nisan) *siman* 62; 8:8 (Iyar) *siman* 70; 8:9 (Sivan) *siman* 78; 8:11 (Av) *siman* 94; 14:6 (Adar 1909) *siman* 34, 14:7 (Nisan) *siman* 41; 14:10 (Tamuz) *siman* 55, 14:11 (Elul) *siman* 61, and others.

47. See A. R. Malakhi, *Talpiot* 6:3–4 (New York, Iyar 1956): 754. Most members of the *Va'ad Klali* were nominated by close friends. We'll specifically mention R. Yosef Rivlin and R. Yoel Moshe Solomon (see A. R. Malachi, ibid., 753; Y. Y. Rivlin, *Meah She'arim* (Jerusalem, 1947), 59–60; *Sefer HaYovel*, 175–77, 314–15, etc.). To illustrate, we'll cite a newspaper item written by R. Salant's secretary, R. Mikhel Mikhlin, when R. Shmuel Mohilever visited Jerusalem: "On Friday, all the guests assembled at the house of the *Va'ad Klali* together with most of the kollel leaders, to discuss recommendations regarding the city's poor. Joining them was the gaon

A story that illustrates R. Pines' standing in Jerusalem's Old Yishuv and in the Diaspora is his active involvement, together with his friends from the *Va'ad Klali,* in bringing R. Eliyahu David Rabinowitz-Teomim ("the Aderet") to Jerusalem as the designated successor to R. Shmuel Salant. As R. Salant aged and searched for a suitable successor from Europe, he assigned R. Pines the task of writing letters, "turning to all the great rabbinic leaders in Russia to ask for their attention."[48] As a first step, R. Pines turned to his brother-in-law, R. Dovid Friedman, to suggest appropriate candidates.[49] After the first round of discussions with several rabbis did not fare well, R. Friedman and R. Pines contacted R. Ḥayim Ozer Grodzenski, who ended up recommending R. Rabinowitz-Teomim.[50] After additional contact on behalf of R. Salant,[51] R. Pines

R. Shmuel Salant, the gaon R. Mordekhai Gimpel Yafeh [who was visiting Jerusalem for the Shavuot holiday], and the rabbi and scholar R. Yeḥiel Mikhel Pines" (*HaTzefira*, June 17, 1890 [Warsaw, 17:125], reprinted in *B'Re'i HaDorot* [Tel Aviv, 1950], 57).

48. Attested to by R. Gedaliah Naḥman Broder, *Ish Yerushalayim* (Jerusalem, 1938), 49–50. The specific details of the story are well documented there, but there is another important source: R. Shmuel Noaḥ Gottlieb, confidant of R. Dovid Friedman, who handled his correspondence in Eastern Europe related to bringing R. Rabinowitz-Teomim to Jerusalem to succeed R. Salant. From his letters to R. Pines that have not been published until now, many new details emerge to fill the blanks in R. Broder's story.
49. Besides R. Broder's details, see the letter from R. Gottlieb to R. Pines from March 19, 1900, when the leading candidate at that time was still R. Eliyahu Feinstein of Pruzhany: "I saw your endorsement to our master regarding the appointment. I immediately sent him a copy of your letter and a copy of the letter from the gaon R. Ḥayim Ozer of Vilna, together with a copy of R. Shmuel Salant's letter to R. Feinstein. And this serves as an answer to the Gaon's [R. Salant's] letter that I received yesterday, complaining to me that he received letters from the heads of the kollelim that reveals that they are not considering him. When the letter of appointment reaches me, I will send a copy together with the letters from our master [ed. note: R. Ḥayim Ozer] to the Ḥabad rabbis to seek their endorsement. I cannot give advice myself as to whether or not to ask for endorsement from R. E. H. of Lodz…" (CZA A109/117).
50. As R. S. N. Gottlieb wrote to R. Pines on October 7, 1900: "I have written to Vilna twice, asking the master to sign his approval to the letter that is circulating about the rabbinate in our Holy City, and have not yet received a reply from R. Ḥayim Ozer. This week, I received a letter from the Rabbi of Pruzhany who revealed that he removed himself from consideration only due to his fear of rejection by the Ḥasidim. However, he now realizes that his fears are unfounded. I answered him immediately that, in light of the facts on the ground, it's already too late…" (CZA, ibid.). It is attached to a previous letter from R. Gottlieb to R. Ḥayim Ozer Grodzenski in which he tells of his visit to R. Feinstein, who agreed to take on the role of "*av bet din,* aide to the gaon and authority for Eretz Yisrael R. Shmuel Salant *shlit"a,* leader and head of the kollelim, lecturer in Yeshivat Etz Ḥayim." However, he conditioned this upon the full agreement and desire of R. Salant, and on certain salary issues, the letter of appointment, etc. (ibid.)
51. R. Salant himself, in a letter dated 28 Av 5660 (August 23, 1900) to R. Yaakov Meir Kaminetzky of Vilna (who collaborated with R. Ḥayim Ozer on this), wrote that "I have already sent word to my friends R. Yoel Moshe Solomon and R. Yeḥiel Mikhel Pines to reply to His Honor…" (*Aderet Eliyahu,* [Jerusalem, 2003], 91).

reported to R. Gedaliah Naḥman Broder in a letter dated 3 Elul 5660 (August 28, 1900) that he had received word from R. Grodzenski that R. Rabinowitz-Teomim had finally accepted the position, and he (R. Pines) was busy preparing the official document of rabbinic appointment.[52] And so, the document that appointed the Aderet was signed by R. Shmuel Salant together with twenty Jerusalem rabbis. Three were members of his rabbinic court, and among the other seventeen appears the name of R. Pines.[53]

An additional story illustrating R. Pines' standing in the eyes of his contemporaries, even after the ban, is his appointment as the representative of Ḥovevei Tziyon in Israel and as the *mashgiaḥ ruḥani* of the Bilu'im in Gedera. When the first reports surfaced regarding a religious breach in Gedera, a vigorous discussion ensued among the leadership of Ḥovevei Tziyon as to the best way to combat the problem. At the same time, R. Shmuel Mohilever wrote R. Yafeh seeking a way to convince Baron Rothschild to appoint R. Pines as rabbi in one of his settlements, because R. Pines' work with the Montefiore Testimonial Fund had ceased. R. Mohilever wasn't able to accomplish this, but wrote, "Be assured that I will do everything in my power for the sake of R. Pines."[54] This is how, in early 1888, R. Pines was suggested as a candidate for supervision of the people of Gedera to guide their ways. In a letter to the director of Ḥovevei Tziyon, Yehudah Leib Pinsker, R. Mordekhai Eliashberg of Boisk wrote, "Regarding Pines – his brother-in-law the gaon Friedman from Karlin wrote to me in the name of Baron Hirsch, who is inclined toward appointing him in the colony of Gedera."[55] Subsequently, R. Mohilever informed

52. Published in *Ish Yerushalayim*, p. 75. See also pp. 51–52, describing an early meeting of the leaders of the Ḥasidim and Perushim, including R. Pines, convened to settle their differences regarding the rabbinate. It also mentions a notebook that presented R. Salant's views on the topic written by R. Pines, who also prepared announcements of R. Rabinowitz-Teomim's arrival. An additional letter from R. Gottlieb to R. Pines, from March 10, 1901, reads: "The gaon, R. Hayim Ozer, promised me that the day the Aderet departs on his way, he will inform me immediately...," and talks about newspaper publicity about this (CZA, ibid.).

53. *Ish Yerushalayim*, pp. 82–84. A striking fact is that among the twenty signatories – the heads of the *Va'ad Klali*, the Etz Ḥayim yeshiva, *Bikur Ḥolim*, and the rabbinic court of the Perushim – there is not one disciple of the Maharil Diskin (such as R. Yosef Ḥayim Sonnenfeld, R. Yaakov Orenstein, R. Moshe Naḥum Wallenstein, etc.) This is not by chance. R. Moshe Blau has already pointed out that Kollel Shomrei HaḤomot (Ungarin) refrained from supporting the Aderet, due to a fundamental opposition to the appointment of any [chief] rabbi of Jerusalem (*Al Ḥomotayikh Yerushalayim* [Tel Aviv, 1950], 88, and compare to *B'Tokh HaḤomot – Yovel Shanim* [Jerusalem, 1948], 237–38). Also, see the sharp language of R. Rabinowitz-Teomim regarding Maharil Diskin's disciples, in my article, "*Mitosim V'Uvdot B'Pulmus HaShemitah*," *Alonei Mamre* 121 (Kiryat Arba, 2008): 57–58.

54. Letter from July 11, 1887, CZA A109/141.

55. Letter from November 6, 1887, *Ketavim L'Toldot Ḥibat Tziyon* 2 (Tel Aviv, 1925), col. 358. On R. Pines' activities in strengthening religious life in Gedera, see his letter to Pinsker from February

R. Pines, "I have already written to Dr. Pinsker to give you a position of authority in Gedera, to be the director and overseer of both its spiritual and physical needs."[56]

While they were dealing with the Gedera issue, the need arose for a representative and contact person on behalf of Ḥovevei Tziyon over all the settlements. At this point, Netziv of Volozhin got involved, as he had been appointed in Elul 1887 as senior adviser to Ḥovevei Tziyon (alongside R. Shmuel Mohilever and R. Mordekhai Eliashberg). Pinsker would send him reports on the activities of the movement.[57] Netziv felt they should appoint a "rabbi" in the full sense of the term to deal with the settlement issue. He also expressed support for the appointment of R. Pines as representative of Ḥovevei Tziyon in Israel. He wrote to Pinsker:

> It seems appropriate to mention R. Naftali Hertz from Bialystok, currently the rabbi of Jaffa. He should be on the committee advising regarding the needs of the Yishuv, together with R. Pines. And he, R. Hertz, should be appointed as overseer.... Regarding the request to appoint R. Pines as secretary of Ḥovevei Tziyon and to sit in Jaffa on the committee – my humble opinion agrees to this, because I know he is wise and knows how to wield his pen at the right time. He also knows the feelings of our brethren in Russia as well as the variety of opinions of our French brothers. His wisdom will help to harmonize all the opinions, with God's help.[58]

10, 1888, ibid., col. 488.

56. Letter from November 13, 1888, *Ketavim* 2, col. 384. A short time after, R. Shmuel Mohilever sent to R. Eliashberg: "When [Dr. Pinsker] notified me that he already appointed the rabbi and scholar, R. Y. Pines, as overseer and director in Gedera, specifically for its religious direction ..." (letter from first day of Ḥanukkah 1887, published in *Ha'Olam*, June 4, 1925 (London, Yr. 24), 386). Also see in *Ketavim*, ibid., Pinsker's letter, and in col. 386, his letter to Netziv on the same subject, and in col. 394, an additional letter from R. Mohilever to Pinsker, blessings on R. Pines' appointment, "as overseer for religious affairs," in Gedera.

57. This is how Netziv became involved with the Gedera issue. See his letter to Pinsker from November 17, 1887: "I received a letter from one of the great rabbis of Jerusalem [R. Shaḥor], who is well-known to our friend R. Pines, and [R. Shaḥor] is no zealot and speaks kindly of the settlements. But yet, he still condemns the residents of Gedera ..." (*Ketavim*, vol. 2, col. 377). Also, see his letter to Pinsker from December 5: "Our friend R. Pines would like to appoint a ritual slaughterer [*shoḥet u'bodek*] for the residents of Gedera ..." ibid., cols. 390–91.

58. Letter from 6 Ḥeshvan 1887, *Ketavim* 2, cols. 341–42. To appreciate the significance of Netziv's support of R. Pines' appointment, contrast that with another letter in which Netziv was reluctant to support another man because he was unfamiliar with, "him and his conversation," and whether or not he was honest "with God and man." Also see his letter to Pinsker from December 24, 1888 (ibid., col. 442) in which he asked to allocate settlers in Safed in order to show the public that they did not support only the people

Indeed, even R. Naftali Hertz, a close confidant of Maharil Diskin, did not abstain from participating with R. Pines in building the New Yishuv. Although Netziv's advice was not implemented, R. Hertz and R. Pines later sat together on the Jaffa city council. According to the council's secretary, Yaakov Goldman, "On 8 Sivan 5650 [May 27,1890], the first council was elected in the city of Jaffa.... Among those elected were the famous sage R. Pines... and the rabbi of the city, the gaon and sage, master R. Naftali Hertz, president of the council. And R. Pines established parliamentary procedures for conducting council business."[59]

CONCLUSION: THE DIVERSE APPROACHES OF JERUSALEM'S GREAT RABBIS

We now return to the focus of our discussion – the various ways in which the sages of Jerusalem in that era behaved and how the excommunication affected the Old Yishuv from then on. The episode brought about a new situation in the Ashkenazi community of Jerusalem: For the first time, the Torah leadership split into two adversarial streams, arguing over fundamental questions related to conduct and leadership. On one side was R. Shmuel Salant, considered the heir of his predecessor, R. Meir Auerbach. Most of Jerusalem's community, including the institutions and kollelim, saw themselves as subject to his rulings; and on the other side, the venerated Maharil Diskin, who acted independently with his own separate rabbinical court. A portion of the community and some institutions now detached themselves from the *Va'ad Klali* and the influence of R. Salant, and would now answer to Maharil Diskin alone.[60]

The friction between R. Salant's ways and Maharil Diskin's faction began from the moment R. Diskin arrived in Jerusalem. However, until the ban episode and

---

of Gedera: "It seems that you are unaware of the feelings of our observant brethren in Lithuania and Zamut. Therefore pay attention to R. Pines' advice, as he is familiar with and knows much about this. And you [ed. note: Pinsker] will realize that I am not just speaking for myself..."

59. *Bnei Asher* (Jaffa, 1924), 108–9. Also see *HaMelitz*, April 6, 1893 (33:69), 7, which published a letter from R. Hertz calling for support of Torah schooling in Jaffa. In the margins, R. Pines added: "I wholeheartedly agree with the wise sage, that is our teacher, the gaon, the head of the rabbinical court in our camp..." Moreover, see the letter from R. Hertz to, "His Honor, the rabbi and scholar, our teacher R. Yeḥiel Mikhel Pines," from July 21, 1895, in which he accords him great honor and advises him not to do public battle with the enemies of the Old Yishuv, because this would only strengthen them (*Ḥavatzelet*, July 26, 1895 [25:42], 349, and R. Pines' response).

60. This is not the place for a lengthy discussion of the relationship between R. Salant and Maharil Diskin. We will emphasize just that, despite the tension between them over the question of leadership and over various matters, the two greatly respected each other and participated together in many activities.

its related incidents, the split was not official and public. Here is how R. Y. D. Fromkin described it: "In the *bet midrash* of R. Pines, the question of rabbinic leadership and religious courts for the Perushim congregations in our city was renewed.... The founding of this *bet midrash* [and the ban placed on it] was the cause for awakening this question from its slumber and hastening its solution."[61] Eventually A. M. Luntz would write the following:

> That year [1882], when the leaders of the Ashkenazi-Perushi community saw that the gaon Maharil Diskin *ztz"l* sought to impose new decrees and edicts that the community would not abide, and arguments and dissent broke out over it in the Ashkenazi community, many respected rabbis gathered in one building and signed into law: That all the decrees issued by Maharil Diskin without the approval of our master and gaon, R. Shmuel Salant, and the gaon R. Moshe Neḥemiah Kahanov (rosh yeshiva of Etz Ḥayim), or the reverse, will not be accepted by the community. Moreover, the religious court will always sit in the meeting house of the Ḥurva of R. Yehudah HeḤasid. This agreement effectively made the gaon, R. Shmuel Salant rabbi of the Ashkenazi community.[62]

Thus, after the ban episode, the Ashkenazi community in Jerusalem split, to some extent, into two factions with clear behavioral differences. The zealot historiography depicts its revered rabbis as paragons of extreme zealotry.[63] Opposed to this

61. *Ḥavatzelet*, January 13, 1882 (12:14), title page. It should be emphasized that during that time, Fromkin was equally hostile to both sides.
62. Addendums to *Tevu'at Ha'Aretz* (Jerusalem, 1900), 502 (mentioned in a letter by R. Pines from March 13, 1882). The original text of this decision, from January 8, 1882, alongside a description of the circumstances, was published in *HaTzvi*, November 16, 1885 (Jerusalem, 2:7), 26:

    > To keep the Torah's honor and the honor of the kollelim of the Perushim... We agreed fully and unanimously to situate the place of the rabbinic court of the Perushi kollelim in the courtyard of Rabbi Yehudah HaḤasid *ztz"l*, beside the home of the gaon R. Shmuel Salant. He will keep a watchful eye over the halakhic decisions and all the court's major activities. Any decrees or edicts and prohibitions or pronouncements without the signatures of both great rabbis, R. Yehoshua Leib Diskin and R. Shmuel Salant, is hereby not granted any force over the community.

    Twenty-five years ago, this declaration was republished from the original text (in the anthology *Har HaMor* 2 [Jerusalem, Tamuz 1982], 66–67), including the names of the signatories, among them, R. M. N. Kahanov and R. Yehoshua Betzalel from Melitsch, as well as the heads of the *Va'ad Klali* and some of the kollel representatives. Absent from the list are the close followers of Maharil Diskin and representatives of the kollelim associated with him.
63. For example, R. Yosef Sheinberger tells the story about the time a *gabbai* of the Hurva synagogue was deathly ill. Maharil Diskin was asked to pray on his behalf, but refused because this

stands the more measured approach of R. Shmuel Salant, R. Rabinowitz-Teomim, R. Avraham Yitzḥak Kook and other great rabbis of Jerusalem. The words of R. Salant, in a letter regarding the Aderet's arrival in Jerusalem, are illuminating:

> My main goal in seeking out a true friend and successor was my concern for peace of my holy congregation. Because I feared that after my time, the leadership would, God forbid, pass to men, who despite their greatness and wisdom in Torah, would not possess in sufficient measure the necessary character to lead the public in a city with a population of diverse approaches as in our Holy City, may it be rebuilt, in order to maintain its peace and tranquility.[64]

The great effort to hide the fact that most of Jerusalem's rabbis (and the Diaspora rabbis who spoke out on the matter) forcefully objected to the ban on R. Pines and opposed the actions of Maharil Diskin and his faction is aimed toward nothing less than denying historical confirmation of the way of the

---

gabbai had in the past declined to announce his ban "*Alot HaBrit*" in the Ḥurva (*Amud Esh* [Jerusalem, 1954], 129–131 – without any references). A marginal note is that the *gabbai* had acted in compliance with a strict directive from R. Shmuel Salant (according to the British Consul from 1879; see R. S. Z. Sonnenfeld, *Ha'Ish Al Haḥomah* 1 [Jerusalem, 1971], 167–68). R. Sheinberger also tells the story of a noted rabbi from Berlin who wrote an article against the Jerusalem zealots following their attacks upon R. Ḥayim Hirschenson. Following this, one of the zealots published a response that, according to R. Sheinberger, "was written with acrimonious language." The zealot was not satisfied until he forged the signature of a Jerusalem rabbi on the notice. When the notice reached the rabbi in Berlin to whom it had been sent, he turned to the Jerusalem rabbi whose name had been forged. The rabbi was incensed by the forgery and wanted to publicly denounce it. However, when R. Diskin heard about the matter, writes R. Sheinberger, "he arose and sent his messenger to rule in his name that this denial should not be publicized!" R. Sheinberger hides his source and all the names of the parties involved. But the source is in *Ḥavatzelet*, December 4, 1887 [18:8], 57–59. There, it identifies the Berlin rabbi as R. Azriel Hildesheimer, and the rabbi whose signature was forged is none other than R. Shmuel Salant and the members of his *bet din*. It also contains additional details, including the claim – adopted with a significant change by R. Sheinberger – that R. Diskin had ruled to refrain from protest because the forgery ostensibly had been carried out with his knowledge! (See also the issue from Rosh Ḥodesh Tevet, and *HaTzvi*, December 16 [4:3], 1–2, revealing that the forgery had been exposed by R. Shmuel HaLevi Zuckerman, and December 30, p. 1 which published the denial of R. Salant, and *HaMelitz*, January 24, col. 2977.)

64. *HaMelitz*, June 6, 1901 [Peterburg, 41:112], 3. Following this, he hints to the words of the Sages, "A man who possesses the spirit – who can walk against [ed. note: who can stand up against] the path of each and every person" (*Sifrei* Bemidbar, 140, and see the formulation in *Sifrei Zuta* 27, 18 – "That he can conduct himself with the strong-armed ones in their fashion and with the moderates in their fashion").

moderate leadership, with a measured, gentle approach ("pushing away with the left hand, while bringing close with the right hand"), and is diametrically opposed to, and opposes, those who seize upon zealotry as a way of life.

APPENDIX – ON ḤAREDI HISTORIOGRAPHY

Let us illustrate how R. Gerlitz dealt with the story of the ban, and with historical material in general, using the following example: After the ban was placed on R. Pines' *bet midrash*, R. Alexander Ziskin Shaḥor of Jerusalem – who knew R. Pines and befriended him in Ruzhany[65] – turned to his uncle, Netziv of Volozhin, asking him to intervene on behalf of the victim ("to fight his battle"). Netziv answered with a lengthy response, complex and balanced.[66] On the one hand, he declined to impugn the decisions and direction of R. Y. L. Diskin, whom he was quick to praise:

> I cannot imagine how one could reproach the gaon and tzaddik R. Yehoshua Leib *shlit"a*. Does a man of his stature need to be reminded how discord is abhorrent and how much we must be concerned for the desecration of the Almighty's name? And that he carefully balanced the cost of strife against the benefit?

On the other hand, he praises R. Pines and dismisses the personal charges leveled against him. With that, he goes on a lengthy criticism of R. Pines' activities in Jerusalem, and determines that R. Pines must move the institution he founded from Jerusalem – even while defending him.

On the whole, Netziv's letter displays support for R. Diskin's position (and not with the ban itself). However, R. Gerlitz seems to feel that Netziv showed too much respect for R. Pines. Therefore, he systematically censored any sign of Netziv's respect for R. Pines. For example, in the sentence "With respect to his [R. Diskin's] making me aware of his conflict with the scholarly and pure Rabbi M. Pines, may he live and be well," he changed the reference to, "the scholar Mikhel Pines." The sentence "I have never met the upstanding gentleman

---

65. See Eliezer Rafael Malakhi, *"Mishpaḥat Berlin V'Hayishuv," Talpiot*, 5:3–4 (New York, Tevet 5711/1950), 399. We will add an important but little-known fact: From a letter by R. Mordekhai Gimpel Yafeh to R. Pines on May 10, 1882, we see that R. Pines appointed R. Ziskind Shaḥor as a *maggid shi'ur* (lecturer) in his *bet midrash* – the very *bet midrash* that was placed under the ban by the zealots!

66. Letter dated 14 Nisan 5642 (April 3, 1882), first published in *Ketavim L'Toldot Ḥibat Tziyon*, op cit., cols. 382–86. The editor notes at the beginning of the letter that this was apparently a first draft or copy, as it lacked a signature.

R. Mikhel Pines, may his light shine," is revised to, "The gentleman Mikhel Pines." The sentence "They wisely chose the upstanding gentleman Rabbi Mikhel Pines, may he live and be well," is revised to, "The gentleman Mikhel Pines." And so forth.[67] The gist of this project of R. Gerlitz and his colleagues is self-evident from the above chapter, in which the story of the ban against R. Pines, or more exactly, the attitude of the rabbis of Jerusalem and the Diaspora toward him in light of this episode, is a historiographical litmus test.

67. I have many more similar examples. For the sake of brevity, I will cite just one significant one: In *Mara D'Ara Yisrael* (vol. 1, pp. 258–59, vol. 2, pp. 114–15) R. Sonnenfeld's letter from 1886 to R. Ḥayim Hirschenson, editor of *HaMisdrona*, is published. In it, he sharply criticizes "the heretic Pines" over an anonymous article written in the previous issue of the monthly publication, whom he identified as R. Pines. R. Gerlitz knows to note that the letter was published in *HaMisdrona* with omissions (1:5 [Jerusalem, 1888], 240). So he must also know that, in the same issue, R. Hirschenson published a response clarifying that the author of the article in question was not R. Pines ("he knows nothing of this article") but R. Hirschenson himself! Therefore, when R. Gerlitz writes, "Mikhel Pines, albeit anonymously, had already warranted criticism from R. [Sonnenfeld] on his article and research about the word '*apikoros*'" (*Mara D'Ara Yisrael*, (vol. 1, pp. 258–59, vol. 2, pp. 114–15), he is deliberately misleading his readers.

Chapter 15

The *Shemitah* Controversy: Myths and Facts[1]

INTRODUCTION

The appearance of an article entitled "*Heter Mekhirah* or Imported Vegetables?" in the journal *Alonei Mamre*[2] has provided me with the opportunity to discuss prevalent assumptions, assertions, and views held by various groups within the religious community about the *shemitah* controversy. It is not my intention to deal here with the halakhic aspects of the *heter mekhirah* [permissibility of selling the land] in our time but rather with the historical component of the article, which describes the controversy surrounding the *heter mekhirah* between the *shemitot* of 1888–89 and 1909–10. Although the article makes use of many sources, in my humble opinion it suffers from a certain imprecision, which is often found in articles written nowadays about *shemitah*, which would seem to result from the authors' agenda, and sometimes on an overreliance on a particular source.

I believe that this imprecision could be avoided if the writers – many of whom attempt to find justification in the events of the past for their outlooks in the present – would avoid reinventing the wheel. For there are readily available, balanced, and relatively complete summaries of the *shemitah* controversy, written by well-known, reliable Torah scholars such as R. Shlomo Zalman Auerbach in *Ma'adanei Aretz* (Jerusalem, 1944, introduction, 1–3) and R. Yeḥiel Mikhel Tucazinsky in his *Sefer HaShemitah* (Jerusalem, 1951, 59–62). Were people to

1. Translated by Yocheved Cohen. This chapter initially appeared in *Alonei Mamre* 121 (2008).
2. Summer 2008.

make proper use of these summaries, they would avoid many common pitfalls. What we shall write can serve as a useful prototype for a critique of articles and works of this sort.[3]

Another important note before beginning our deliberation is that the blanket usage of the phrase "*heter mekhirah*" can be misleading. It makes it seem as if what is being discussed is a single permission and a single sale. In fact, there are often differences among the various permissive authorities. They differ in their motivations, their halakhic reasoning, and even the details of applying the *heter*. This is also the case when it comes to those who forbid the sale. It follows that when we are exploring the details of a specific *heter* or trying to extrapolate from what happened then to what should be done today, sweeping generalities must be avoided. Nevertheless, since there is one key point which all agree is subject to disagreement – selling land or produce in order to allow agricultural work in the Land of Israel to continue during *shemitah* – we will use the general term *heter mekhirah* for the ease of the reader.

OPPONENTS AND PROPONENTS OF THE *HETER*

Based on the description of the controversy in the aforementioned article, one might come away with the impression that it was those who "threw off the yoke," i.e., left Orthodoxy, who sought the *heter mekhirah*. The author writes: "Then members of the First Aliyah began to publicize and spread falsehoods.... The colonists did not wish to observe *shemitah*.... A number of Eastern European rabbis were contacted." The statements of Moshe Leib Lilienblum are the primary support for this theory. He later testified that his efforts to make sure that fields were not left fallow stemmed from his desire to avoid setting a precedent

3. R. Kalman Kahana's "*Shemitah B'Mahalakh Hazemanim*," originally published in his booklet *Hilkhot Shemitat Karka'ot* [Jerusalem, 1944], and reprinted in his book *Shnat HaSheva* [Tel Aviv, 1965], 188–206 (see especially sections 5–9) deserves its own treatment. The piece is important and comprehensive; but it is also flawed and far from being balanced. As the overview in the article we are commenting on is largely based on this [i.e., R. Kahana's] article, therefore most of our comments apply to it as well. Contrast this with the noteworthy, comprehensive article of R. Moshe Tzvi Neriyah, "*L'Toldot Kiyum Mitzvat HaShemitah*" (originally published in his booklet *Dvar HaShemitah* [Jerusalem, 1938], and reprinted in his book *Tznif Melukha* [Kfar Haro'eh, 1992], 274–88; see especially sections 11–16). One might say that R. Neriyah's topic is that of the ***heter*** *mekhirah*, while the subject of R. Kahana's article is the **opposition** to the *heter mekhirah*; in other words, each author writes extensively about his topic, and gives very short shrift to the opposing side. This actually leads to the articles complementing one another. Nevertheless, it should be noted that R. Neriyah's article generally avoids making subjective and biased judgments, which are prevalent in R. Kahana's article. A few of the comments below are based on the statements of earlier scholars, as I note.

for *shemitah* observance. Lilienblum's own statements, though, make it clear that he would equally have opposed any *heter* containing any type of limitation or qualification; his efforts and those of his colleagues were dedicated to eliciting across-the-board permission for all agricultural work during *shemitah*.[4] It is patently clear that the people who needed and wanted the *heter* were the Torah-observant farmers. Given this, it is unclear how the article can state as fact that R. Yitzḥak Elḥanan Spektor's permission was given due to the "tricky machinations" of the irreligious. This claim relies on the opinion of Ridbaz (R. Yaakov David Wilovsky) and others who forbid the *heter*, but it is not accepted at all by those who permit it,[5] and its factual basis is extremely shaky (as we will demonstrate below).

The article also leaves the reader with the impression that R. Spektor became involved in the matter only due to the request of the three permissive rabbis [R. Shmuel Mohilever, R. Yisrael Yehoshua Trunk of Kutna, and R. Shmuel Zanvil Klepfish]. However, R. Spektor himself wrote that he was asked about the issue earlier, in 1888 (before the coming *shemitah* year), by a representative of Baron Edmond de Rothschild.[6] When R. Spektor investigated the issue, he

4. Accordingly, some attempted to create the impression that R. Yitzḥak Elḥanan Spektor was a supporter of a sweeping *heter* with no qualifications. (See the quote from R. Rabinowitz-Teomim [Aderet] below.) There were even false reports printed in newspapers, which R. Yehoshua of Kutna complained about (*Responsa Yeshu'ot Malko, Yoreh De'ah* 59; see also the letter of R. Yosef Dov HaLevi Soloveitchik in *Shnat HaSheva*, 187–88). It should be noted that once the New Yishuv was well-established, the goal of those who had left Orthodoxy changed. Now they would have preferred for the rabbis to prohibit the sale of the land categorically, which would have allowed them to sever relations completely with the rabbinic establishment. R. Kook described this around 1910: "I saw that the wicked would like no one at all to be permissive... so that they would be able to publicly announce, with heads held high, that the Yishuv needs to cast off the burden of mitzvot entirely" (*Igrot HaRa'ayah* 2, 154). Elsewhere he wrote, "The freethinkers actually want the rabbis to prohibit. This would be a great victory for them, for they would be able to show everyone that if they listen to the rabbis, the land would be destroyed" (ibid., vol. 1, 258).
5. R. Kook hinted at this when speaking of Ridbaz: "I do not agree with him in his fundamental objection to the *heter*, which comes from great Torah scholars of yore" (*Igrot HaRa'ayah* 1, 294; see also p. 258). Similarly, he wrote, "I was not the first to be permissive; this path has already been trodden by the gaon R. Yitzḥak Elḥanan of Kovno and the Sephardi gaon R. Yaakov Shaul Elyashar. My father-in-law R. Rabinowitz-Teomim (Aderet) also agreed to it during the last *shemitah*" (ibid., p. 334). R. Kook wrote directly to Ridbaz: "The *heter* was already published and publicized without me, by R. Yitzḥak Elḥanan, the Sephardi Rabbi Elyashar, and a few other famous rabbis" (ibid., vol. 2, pp. 154–55).
6. Baron Rothschild lived in France, and therefore his representatives turned first to French rabbis with the question about *shemitah*. However, due to the seriousness of the question, the French rabbis preferred not to decide by themselves. Rather, they passed the question on to R. Yitzḥak

found that it "could involve saving hundreds of lives." In light of this, "I saw fit to get involved in this important matter and suggested being permissive." R. Spektor wrote a pamphlet devoted to the topic, "but I did not want to publicize this ruling, because I did not want to be the sole permissive voice." It was afterward that the permissive rabbis turned to him. He adds that "I felt gratified and pleased when this happened, as I realized that I was not the lone voice on this important matter."[7]

The list of names which the article mentions, under the heading "In Europe too, a number of rabbis came out publicly against the *heter mekhirah*," is also riddled with imprecisions. For example, R. Yeḥiel Mikhel HaLevi Epstein is mentioned among them, based on what he writes in *Arukh HaShulḥan He'Atid*. However, that work was only printed in 1938, thirty years after R. Epstein had died. It is thus impossible to include him among those who came out publicly against the

---

Elḥanan Spektor, as R. Yehudah Lubetzky of Paris testified: "When Baron Rothschild founded settlements in the Land of Israel, I was asked by R. Erlanger in the presence of my master and teacher R. Tzadok Kahn about working the land during *shemitah* nowadays. I responded that I was not worthy of answering such a momentous question, and that I would ask someone greater on their behalf. We chose the gaon R. Yitzḥak Elḥanan Spektor and two other great rabbis of the generation" (*Ein Tnai B'Nissu'in* [Vilna, 1930], 9; see the supporting testimony of the Baron's representatives in *HaMaggid* 32:47 [Lyck]: 372–73). See also the testimony of R. Yehoshua Leib Diskin stating that in the winter of 1888–89, the representatives of the Baron turned to him too with questions about *shemitah,* but he did not wish to respond (letter dated 14 Adar 5648 (February 26, 1888), published first in *HaMelitz* 28:237 [November 13, 1888], and later in Alter Droyanov, *Ketavim L'Toldot Ḥibat Tziyon V'Yishuv Eretz Yisrael* [henceforth: *Ketavim*] 2 [Tel Aviv, 1925], col. 614; for a mention of the visit of Baron Rothschild's representatives to the rabbis of Jerusalem, see *HaTzvi* 4:5 [Jerusalem, December 30, 1887], p. 19).

7. R. Spektor's letter of permission is cited in a number of places, including *Sefer HaShemitah,* p. 67. R. Spektor wrote similarly on that very day (February 15, 1888) in a letter to R. Shmuel Mohilever. He attached his letter of permission and added: "... Until now, I did not know if other current great rabbis would be in agreement with the permission for the colonists, especially given that I received a letter from the Land of Israel claiming that the rabbis there are opposed to this, and I did not want to be the lone dissenting voice. But now that I have received the precious letter [of the three rabbis] permitting this, I would like to conclude the matter..." (*Oraita* 9 [Netanya, 5747], 231–32). The context was clarified by a resident of Kovno, R. Isser Baer Wolf, who testified that it was R. Spektor who initiated turning to the great rabbis of Jerusalem "out of respect, and fear of controversy" (letter dated Tevet 22, 5648 [January 6, 1888], published in *Ketavim* 2, col. 442). In another letter, R. Wolf added that as a result of R. Spektor's receiving the letter opposing the *heter,* he had decided "not to go to war about this with the *ge'onim* of Jerusalem" (letter dated 14 Shevat 5648 [January 27, 1888], published ibid., p. 477). Accordingly, R. Spektor had initially written a hesitant letter to the Baron's representatives. (See *Oraita,* above, 228–29.) This position changed with his receipt of the permissive letter from the three rabbis.

heter, even though it is true that he opposed it. The same applies to R. Eliezer Gordon of Telz, who is also mentioned in the article; true, at the end of 1889 he wrote a long letter opposing the *heter*, but the letter was only printed in 1936, by a third party – Yehudah Appel in his book *Betokh Reishit HaTeḥiyah*. R. Gordon's negative opinion concerning the *heter* was not expressed publicly during the 1889 *shemitah*, nor during those that followed.[8]

A more conspicuous error, if a common one, is the article's including R. Samson Raphael Hirsch among the opponents of the *heter*. In fact, there is no substantive proof of this claim, and the article offers no source whatsoever for it. Presenting R. Hirsch as opposed would seem to be based on two short letters which he wrote a few weeks before his death in December 1888. In the letters, he expresses

8. For more about this letter, see R. Amihud Levine, "*Mikhtav HaGaon R. Eliezer Gordon ztz"l al Heter HaMekhirah B'Shmitat 5649*," *Oraita* 9 (Netanya, 5747), 238–47. An additional rabbi who opposed the *heter* then was R. Malkiel Tzvi HaLevi Tannenbaum, the head of the rabbinical court in Lomza. He wrote a responsum about it in 1895. There he begins by saying that he does not want to decide between the sides. However, he goes on to speak at length about the prohibition of *lo teḥonem* and concludes, "It would seem that the primary position is that land in Israel should not be sold to the Arabs in order to bypass the *shemitah* laws, as it involves transgressing the prohibition of *lo teḥonem*." He goes on to say that in his opinion, even without that issue it is not proper to search for halakhic leniencies in this area (*Responsa Divrei Malkiel* 7:49). However, as with the positions of R. Epstein and R. Gordon, this responsum too was not published until many years after it was written (R. Malkiel Tzvi HaLevi Tenenbaum, "*Mekhirat Karka'ot B'Shvi'it L'Nokhri*," *Torah She'be'al Peh* 15 [Jerusalem, 1973], 164–67). Therefore, it did not play a real role in the *shemitah* controversy. See too the letter that R. Simḥa Bamberger sent to R. Shmuel Salant in the winter of 1887–88 (*Responsa Zekher Simḥa* [Frankfurt am Main, 1925], no. 216).

The same fate befell the positions of a number of those who were permissive. For example, R. Yehoshua Lang, head of the rabbinical court of Stawiski, expressed his support of the *heter* in a letter he wrote R. Yitzḥak Yaakov Reines in 1903: "People already have been accustomed to be lenient and sell the fields to non-Jews during *shemitah*, and they have authorities to rely upon..." There was a large delay before this letter was published in 1944 (in R. Shmuel Mohilever's responsa *Ḥikrei Halakhah U'She'elot U'Teshuvot* [ed. R. Yehudah Leib Maimon], 45–46, and later in *Responsa of R. Shmuel Mohilever*, 42–43). Another example is R. Yaakov David Rappaport, who was the son-in-law of R. Yosef Zekharia Stern of Shavli/Šiauliai (and who took over from R. Kook as head of the rabbinical court of Zeimel). He expressed his support of the *heter* in a letter he sent to his grandfather-in-law R. Mordekhai Gimpel Yafeh around 1889. However, it was published only recently (*Moriah* 23:10–12 [Jerusalem, Adar 5761]: 77–90). For some reason, the article there implies that R. Rappaport opposed the *heter*, perhaps because of his family background or his sharp language at the beginning of the letter. There he writes: "The permission to sell to a non-Jew, which was made up by some of the schemers who wish to break boundaries." However, in the body of the letter he expresses support for the *heter* clearly and unambiguously! There he writes: "... Based on this, the permission to sell to a non-Jew is defensible" (see there, section 8).

his support for the initiative of Jerusalem rabbis to collect money for those who were not working the land. In his words: "The rabbinical courts in the Holy City of Jerusalem are asking for donations for farm workers who are observing *shemitah* in the Land of Israel and are not working their fields this year."[9] Does this allow us to draw conclusions as to his opinion of the *heter*? Even prominent rabbis in favor of the *heter* took part in initiatives which offered support to those who chose not to work the land during *shemitah*. These included R. Yehoshua of Kutna during that *shemitah*, and R. Kook during later ones.[10]

It should also be noted that even R. David Friedman of Karlin, who is considered one of the leaders of the opposition to the *heter*, and who is represented by the article as someone who participated in the public controversy of 1889, was involved only behind the scenes. He expressed his opinion only in personal letters (similar to R. Ḥayim Elazar Wax and R. Yitzḥak Yaakov Reines; see below). R. Friedman's position on the matter was not published until after the controversy of 1910![11]

9. The original is in German. The Hebrew translation is taken from the collection of his letters, *Shemesh U'Marpeh* (New York, 1992), 217.

10. See the list of donors in *Ḥavatzelet* 20:22 (March 21, 1890), 175, where the donations of R. Yehoshua of Kutna and his son-in-law R. Wax appear. As for R. Kook, see *Igrot HaRa'ayah* 1:196, 251.

11. It would seem that the pamphlet *Ḥidushim B'Inyanei Shvi'it*, where R. Friedman detailed his opposition to the *heter*, was written in 1888 but not published until 1913 (in Pietrkov at the end of *She'elat David* 1 [pp. 27–43]). His involvement in the 1889 controversy was expressed only in his letters to Eliezer Ben-Yehudah, R. Yeḥiel Mikhel Pines (his brother-in-law), and others. Two of these letters were published by Binyamin Rivlin, "*HaGaon R. David Friedman ztz"l U'She'elat HaShvi'it*," *Sinai* 58:351 (December 1966), 143–49. There is no real basis for presenting R. Friedman as a staunch opponent of *heterim* regarding *shemitah*. It is true that he did not accept the *heter mekhirah* ("This permission should be swallowed up and never again said," because of *lo teḥonem* and trickery), and he sharply opposed a sweeping *heter* without limitations. On the other hand, fundamentally he was supportive of the search for leniencies: "How wonderful it would be if the most senior of the rabbis, the gaon R. Yitzḥak Elḥanan, rabbi of the holy community of Kovno, would call upon all the rabbis and learned people whom he knows. They could study the laws intensively for a number of months, and then all gather together in Tamuz to reach a joint decision about this matter. They could include leniencies that are for ordinary circumstances, as well as leniencies that are limited to pressing circumstances. This *shemitah* is certainly a case of very pressing circumstances, as the discerning are well aware" (letter to Eliezer Ben-Yehudah, dated 23 Shevat 5648 (February 5, 1888); published by Rivlin, ibid., p. 145). In accordance with this approach, R. Friedman raised a number of his own ideas for leniencies. For example, in pressing times, Jews can work the fields of non-Jews: "This should not be permitted barring great need, relying on those great rabbis when circumstances are pressing" (letter to R. Pines, January 21, 1894; ibid., p. 146). Alternatively, the majority of contemporary Torah scholars could agree that even without the land being sold, Jews could work the land in ways that would normally be rabbinically prohibited during *shemitah*. Non-Jews might even be

Even though the article admits that R. Yosef Engel[12] and Avnei Nezer[13] supported the *heter* (as publicized after the 1910 controversy), he fails to note that there were other, well-known European rabbis who had supported the *heter* in 1889. These included R. Alexander Moshe Lapidus of Raseiniai[14] and R. Mordekhai Eliashberg of Boisk,[15] who both allowed room to be lenient even without selling the

---

permitted to engage in working the land in ways that would normally be biblically prohibited during *shemitah*: "It is possible to allow recent arrivals, who were not able to prepare for *shemitah* by putting away some food in previous years, to perform certain types of work that even in Temple times were prohibited only rabbinically. If we do not permit this, it will lead to the destruction of the Yishuv, forcing them to sell their fields to non-Jews… Nevertheless, people should do this only with the agreement of all the sages… Therefore, if most of the rabbis agree (as a large group) to permit rabbinically prohibited actions, at least during the current *shemitah,* people may rely on this. The rabbis might even permit the new colonists, who are unprepared for *shemitah,* to hire non-Jews to work the land."

12. *Otzrot Yosef – Kuntres Shvi'it BaZeman HaZeh* (published in Vilna in 1928, but written in 1914), 90–102. R. Engel, like the rabbis we will cite below, was of the opinion that permission to work the land could be granted even without a sale. The purpose of the sale is to provide additional basis for the leniency. (See there, pp. 94, 100, and 102.)
13. R. Avraham Borenstein, *Responsa Avnei Nezer* 2 (Warsaw, 1913), *Yoreh De'ah, siman* 458. For what lay behind his permission and the possibility of applying it to current realities, see *Responsa Tzitz Eliezer* 6:32. The subject deserves a more thorough treatment, but this is not the place for it.
14. As early as the *shemitah* of 1881–82, R. Lapidus had publicized his view that it was possible to be lenient even without a sale (*HaLevanon* 19:15 [Mainz, April 27, 1882], 119). R. Shmuel Salant and R. Neḥemia Kahanov of Jerusalem publicly objected to this (*Ḥavatzelet* 12:29 [Jerusalem, May 21, 1882], 228). Later on, R. Lapidus publicized the letters he received from them and wrote: "Since such *ge'onim* (may there be many among the Jews) disagree with this, we must invoke the rule that we follow the majority, especially if they are the majority both qualitatively and quantitatively. Therefore, I subordinate my opinion to theirs" (*HaLevanon* 19:22 [Mainz, June 15, 1882], 173–74). Nevertheless, R. Lapidus' recanting of his ruling was not because he had changed his mind, but because he wanted to avoid disagreement, and he felt uncomfortable being a lone opinion at odds with the majority. Accordingly, he kept to his position privately, and even publicized it again before the 1889 *shemitah* in a letter to his colleague R. Mordekhai Eliashberg, who was of the same mind (*HaTzvi* 4:14, Jerusalem, March 9, 1888], 3–4). In the letter, R. Lapidus declares that "I have already made it known that I am not relying upon this in practice; I will gain by speaking of it theoretically.… I am presenting all this theoretically, and I will not act upon conjecture." However, his introduction to the letter makes it clear that making his opinion public was meant to test whether other rabbis would share his opinion. Later on, he published an article (*Knesset HaGedolah* 1 [Warsaw, 1890], 39–42) in which he argued with other rabbis who had objected to what he had said. In that article, R. Lapidus writes that "certainly, one who is stringent should be blessed, as the holy Torah promises us… But for others it is proper to search for possible leniencies." He goes on to say that in any case, one should not object to those who are lenient and permit selling the land.
15. R. Eliashberg agreed with R. Lapidus and went a step further, writing that the risk to life and the danger to the Yishuv superseded the *shemitah* prohibitions, which are only rabbinic nowadays: "When the permission was granted by the great rabbis of Poland and Russia for the colonists

land. R. David Judah Leib Silverstein, head of the rabbinical court of Weitzen, maintained a similar position, although unlike them, he did not actively participate in the *shemitah* controversy. As early as 1880, he wrote that when circumstances are pressing, it was possible to be lenient regarding *shemitah* (without the need to sell the land), at least as long as the market for fruit in the land was under the control of non-Jews.[16]

Another rabbi who was part of the permissive group was R. Ḥayim Elazar Wax of Kalish, son-in-law of R. Yisrael Yehoshua of Kutna. None of his writings about the *heter* have been preserved, but his involvement has been proved conclusively, as we see from the following passages written by R. Shmuel Mohilever:

> First I met in Warsaw with the righteous gaon, my teacher R. Yehoshua *z"l*, head of the rabbinical court of Kutna. We invited the gaon, R. Shmuel Zanvil [Klepfish of Warsaw] to form a rabbinic court of three. We permitted working the land during *shemitah* that year, based on a sales contract which would be drafted by the rabbinic court in Jerusalem. Afterward, others agreed with us, including the great gaon from Kovno; R. Ḥayim

to work the land ... I was honored to be approached by my colleague, who is greater and better than me ... the exalted gaon R. Shmuel Mohilever, head of the Bialystok rabbinical court. He asked me to join those who permitted the *heter* in one way or the other, as there were slight differences between the recommendations of most of the great rabbis and those of the most senior among them [R. Yitzḥak Elḥanan Spektor]... [But] it seemed to me unnecessary to find dubious ways to be permissive as did these Torah giants, as I think the Torah view completely permits working the land in the upcoming *shemitah* year..." (*HaMelitz* 28:268 [December 19, 1888], and reprinted in the book by Eliyahu Moshe Ganhovsky, *Rabbi Mordekhai Eliashberg* [Jerusalem, 1937], 83–84). In the same article, R. Eliashberg sharply criticized the rabbis and leaders of the Old Yishuv. He asserted that their support of those who did not cultivate the land during *shemitah* stemmed from a desire to bring about the collapse of the New Yishuv and thus avoid a reduction in *ḥaluka* payments. In response, the rabbis of Jerusalem attacked him furiously and viciously, claiming that the content and style of his accusation placed him on the same side as the formerly Orthodox. R. Shmuel Salant joined the opponents of R. Eliashberg. R. Shmuel Mohilever, though, defended him, writing a letter supporting him and attacking his opponents. (For more on this episode and references to most of the important sources, see Israel Klausner, *MiKatovitz ad Basel* 2 [Jerusalem, 1965], 340–46. There is more to say, but this is not the place.)

16. In R. Silverstein's words: "However, the common practice is not to observe *shemitah* in our Holy Land nowadays ... as it is a matter of life and death. If we disallow this, what will our brethren living there do? They are unable to gather grain and food from last year, and they are unable to import from abroad... Certainly, in such a case, [the Sages] did not prohibit, and it is close to being a danger to life, so it is impossible to forbid it. However, buying and selling *shemitah* produce should not be permitted" (*Shvilei David* 4 – *Yoreh De'ah* [Przemyśl, 1880], *Klalei Ḥovat Karka*, ch. 3, *siman* 13 [p. 29a]).

> Elazar Wax, head of the rabbinical court of Kalish; and the great gaon R. Mordekhai Eliashberg *z"l* of Boisk... [17]
>
> Don't you know that our brothers too – the righteous gaon, my teacher *z"l*, the head of the rabbinical court of Kutna; his gaon son-in-law *z"l*, the head of the rabbinical court of the Holy City of Kalish; the righteous gaon, the head of the rabbinical court of the Holy City of Boisk; I (whose signature is below); many *ge'onim*, whose pamphlets I have from 5648 [1888] as well as from last year, and particularly a printed *heter* from the chief rabbinic leader of the Sephardim in Jerusalem – we would not have been lenient, God forbid, about such an important matter, if the permission were not obvious to us.[18]

R. Yitzḥak Yaakov Reines, head of the Lida rabbinical court, should also be counted among the behind-the-scenes supporters of the *heter* in 1889. He began exploring the question after the Ḥovevei Tziyon organization turned to him during the previous winter. R. Reines went so far as to say that "the beginning of my work on *shemitah* gives me hope that with the help of God, a *heter* will be forthcoming which will benefit the pioneers." However, when he heard that R. Yitzḥak Elḥanan Spektor had already issued a *heter*, he halted his research, as "the words of the rabbi from Kovno require no further support."[19]

---

17. This is from R. Mohilever's letter of permission for the 1896 *shemitah*, which is dated 18 Tamuz 5655 (July 10, 1895; published by Menaḥem Friedman in his article, *"L'mashmauto HaḤevratit Shel Pulmus HaShemitah 5649–5670"* in *Shalem: Meḥkarim B'Toldot Eretz Yisrael V'Yishuva*, 1 [Jerusalem, 1973], 476–78). Of the seven letters on the subject published by R. Yehoshua of Kutna in his book, four are addressed to his son-in-law R. Wax. They too attest to R. Wax's active participation in the debates about the *heter* – which he undertook at the request of R. Mohilever (as is mentioned in *Responsa Yeshu'ot Malko, Yoreh De'ah*, end of *siman* 55; see also *siman* 58).
18. This is a letter by R. Mohilever to Jacob Broide, which appears in Eliyahu Ze'ev (Wolf) Lewin-Epstein, *Zikhronotai* (Tel Aviv, 1932), 201. See too R. Yitzḥak Nissenbaum, *Igrot HaRav Nissenbaum* (Jerusalem, 1956), 36. We must also note that in 1889, Jewish laborers continued working the *etrog* orchards in Kfar Ḥittim owned by R. Wax. This is further proof that in practice he relied on the *heter* (as pointed out by Klausner, *MiKatovitz ad Basel* 2, p. 336).
19. This was reported by his son Moshe Reines in *HaMelitz* 28:21 (February 7, 1888), cols. 210–11 (see further there). See also Moshe Leib Lilienblum's account of the end of the winter of 1887–88: "The gaon Reines from Lida promised me when he was here a few weeks ago that he would encourage well-known rabbis to be permissive for next year's *shemitah*" (*Ketavim* 2, col. 328). The support of R. Reines for the *heter* was also expressed in the run-up to the *shemitah* of 1903, in a letter to Aderet in which he addressed the issue of whether the *heter* was still necessary (*Igrot LaRa'ayah* [Jerusalem edition, 1991], 552–54).

Since the author chose to mention R. Tuvia Rosenthal of Jerusalem, an opponent of the *heter* who printed a pamphlet in Warsaw in 1895 called *Halakhah Mevoreret* (see especially pp. 3–6), he should have also mentioned R. Yehonatan Abelman, a *posek* in Bialystok and R. Yisrael Salanter's nephew, a supporter of the *heter* who printed a pamphlet in Vilna in 1889 called *Torat Yehonatan* (see especially the end of ch. 10, pp. 80–82). There were others as well.[20]

---

20. While we are on the subject of pamphlets, we should note several more. R. Yeḥiel Mikhel Wolfson, head of the rabbinical court of Yanishok, opposed the *heter* and published a pamphlet, *Kuntres Zekher L'Shvi'it*, in Vilna in 1888. It appeared as part of his *Responsa Sefat HaYam* 2; see especially *simanim* 65–72 (pp. 36–41). (For additional letters by R. Wolfson relating to the *heter* of 1895 [before the 1896 *shemitah*], see *Nezer HaTorah* 8:3 [Jerusalem, Tevet 5768], 31–32.) At the same time and place, R. Yehoshua Heschel Margaliot, head of the rabbinical court of Vishnyeva, published a pamphlet, *Kol HaTor*, in which he strongly objected to a sweeping, unqualified *heter* for *shemitah*. At the same time, he showed willingness to discuss various possible *heterim* that were qualified (a non-Jew working a Jewish field, or a Jew working an ownerless field). On the other side of the issue, R. Meir HaLevi Levine of Pinsk defended the continued validity of the *heter* in a pamphlet, *Ma'amar al Inyan HaShvi'it BaZeman Hazeh*, which he published in Berditchev in 1889 under the name "Rama." Similarly supportive was R. Ḥayim Yaakov HaKohen of Tzefat, who published the pamphlet *Ḥok HaShemitah* in Cracow in 1889 (as part of his *Imrei Shabbat*, 163–75). There he objected to rabbis who permitted Jewish labor, but he did permit the sale of the land.

    In addition to these pamphlets, a number of others appeared in Jerusalem in 1888–89. These included those who permitted the *heter* (*Devar HaShemitah* by R. Yitzḥak Hirschensohn) and those who prohibited it (*Davar Be'Ito* by R. Yaakov Orenstein; *Kedushat Eretz Yisrael BaZeman Hazeh* by R. Ḥayim Eliezer Hausdorff; *Devar HaShemitah* by R. Eliezer Wallenstein; the first two are responses to Rama). The authors of most of these pamphlets were generally young rabbis who had not yet made names for themselves. Some were children or relatives of better-known rabbis. In this connection, we should mention two rabbis who were involved in arranging the *heter*: R. Tzvi Hirsch Rabinowitz (son of R. Spektor), who was then the head of the rabbinical court of Mitau (later Jelgava), and R. Yehonatan Eliashberg, head of the rabbinical court of Vilkaviškis. (See *Ketavim* 2, columns 401–402, 442, 486). Most of the pamphlets are considered only of secondary importance.

    Besides the pamphlets, we should mention a number of rabbis who published newspaper articles in 1888 supporting the *heter mekhirah*. The most important figure was R. Yaakov Mordekhai Hirschensohn of Jerusalem (*HaTzvi* 4, issues 5–7, 9–12, 15 [December 1, 1887 through March 16, 1888], pp. 21–24, 27–28, 35–36, 39–40, 43–44, 47–48, 58–60; some of these pieces were reprinted in the pamphlet cited above by his son, R. Yitzḥak Hirschensohn; see also the article of his other son, R. Ḥayim Hirschenson in *HaTzvi* 4:8 [January 27, 1888], pp. 31–32). Another important author was R. Yom Tov Yisrael (Ḥerezli), head of the rabbinical court of Egypt (*HaTzvi* 4:7 [January 13, 1888], 28; *Torah MiTzion* 1:4 [Tevet–Adar 5648], *siman* 8 [pp. 16–17] and *siman* 17 [p. 28]). Other rabbinic authors included R. Meir Levin, Rabbi of Vilkija/Wilki (See *HaMelitz*, 28:26 [February 13, 1888], col. 266); R. Yitzḥak Wolf (Zev) Olswanger of St. Petersburg (*HaMelitz*, 28:23 [February 9, 1888], cols. 229–30, and issue 33 [February 21, 1888], cols. 345–46); R. Avraham Dov HaKohen of Jerusalem (*HaMelitz*, 28:18 [February 3, 1888], cols. 178–79). The opposing camp included R. Yaakov Salant, whose article objected to the

It is appropriate to mention here that, to our dismay, then as now, part of the Ashkenazi ḥaredi community displayed a dismissive attitude toward Sephardi rabbis. This was reflected in the *shemitah* controversy by those who ignored the fact that the greatest Sephardi rabbis of Jerusalem – R. Yaakov Elyashar and his *bet din*, as well as Chief Rabbi Raphael Meir Panigel – supported the *heter* and were the ones who put it into practice in 1889[21] (as the article mentions). We must cite here a statement which normally we wouldn't quote because of its sharpness, but since none other than R. Yehoshua of Kutna said it, quote it we will:

> ...especially since the greatest Sephardi rabbis, **whose fingernails are thicker than the bellies of the Ashkenazi scholars**, permit non-Jews to work the land during the seventh year by means of a sale... How can we disdain their Torah. The truth is that Ashkenazi rashness would cause great damage.[22]

In an earlier letter which R. Yehoshua of Kutna sent to R. Shmuel Mohilever on the tenth of Sivan, May 20 1888 (but which was not printed in his book and therefore is not widely known), he expressed himself in a manner that is no less sharp:

> Thank God, He did not deny a redeemer and rescuer for the poor, since the great Sephardi sages of our Holy Land came to their rescue, enabling

permission of R. Elyashar (*Ḥavatzelet* [Jerusalem], 18:23 [April 18, 1888], 178–79). These articles too are generally considered only of secondary importance (similar to some of the names signed on the Jerusalem rabbis' pronouncement of prohibition).

21. The first account of their *heter* was published in *HaTzvi* 4:15 (Jerusalem, March 16, 1888), p. 1 of the appendix. The permissive responsum itself was published in *HaTzvi* 4:16 (March 23, 1888), second appendix and later in *Responsa Simḥa L'Ish* (Jerusalem, 1893), *Yoreh De'ah, siman* 26 (pp. 107a–109b; R. Elyashar entitled it "*Kuntres Shnat HaSheva*"). Appended to the end of the responsum is a paragraph by R. Panigel lending support: "I am not afraid to say that the halakhic conclusion is correct, in accordance with everything that our master [R. Elyashar] has ruled... I lend my support to him in both theory and practice, and his words need no further reinforcement." See also the front page of *HaTzvi* 4:29 (July 27, 1888), which announces "the sale of all the settlements – both in the secular courts (as a formality) as well as in the great rabbinical court of the Sephardim in our holy city of Jerusalem (may it be rebuilt) – was done in full accordance with Jewish law." For an additional letter of R. Elyashar about the *heter*, see the front page of *HaTzvi* 4:18 (April 27, 1888).
22. *Responsa Yeshuot Malko, siman* 53, my bolding. When R. Binyamin Zilber came upon this quote at a later date in a responsum of R. Ovadiah Yosef, it disturbed him greatly (even though he acknowledged that R. Ovadiah was simply quoting it from *Responsa Yeshuot Meshiḥo*). R. Zilber expressed his disquiet: "How is it possible to write such disparaging words ... about Torah giants, supremely knowledgeable men, the very mention of whose names leaves people awestruck? And who is qualified to declare one greater than the other?" (*Responsa Az Nidberu* 4:45 [p. 122]).

> them to remain in our Holy Land. As I wrote in my earlier letter, this is their only option. Your Honor hemmed and hawed on the subject, maintaining that Ashkenazi rabbis took issue with this [*heter*], and that Ashkenazim care only about what their own rabbis have to say. I am surprised, as this attitude is relevant only when dealing with practices which were followed in the Diaspora ... but not when dealing with something that did not exist there at all ... Certainly, [the rabbis of the Holy Land] are permitted to rule based on what they see as right and based on the majority, **not to mention that anyone with even a smidgen of knowledge knows that Sephardi sages are more authoritative. Enough said ...**[23]

Based on what we have written, if we count up the positions of the greatest halakhic decisors actively involved in the controversy of 1889, we find that the numbers of proponents and opponents are almost equal; this was the case in the next two *shemitot* as well. Periodically, the position of an additional *posek* comes to light. However, a unique situation arose in the 1910 *shemitah*. At that time, the efforts of Ridbaz (alongside R. Naḥum Weidenfeld) led to the publicizing of the position of some fifteen European rabbis (among them important *poskim*) who opposed the *heter*, together with the reiterated position of the rabbis of Jerusalem forbidding the sale. R. Kook was close to the lone dissenting voice. If not for his strong and stubborn perseverance, it is reasonable to assume that the *heter mekhirah* would have become a dead letter. In any case, a survey of the position of the great *poskim* who expressed their opinions about the controversy between 1888 and 1935 (from the beginning of the controversy until the death of R. Kook) shows that the ratio of opponents to proponents was approximately 3:2. Thus the widespread claim that "Torah giants of the previous generation opposed the *heter* almost unanimously, with only a few dissenters" (*Shnat HaSheva*, p. 210) is simply incorrect.

An additional fact which the author ignores pertains to R. Kook's father-in-law, R. Eliyahu David Rabinowitz-Teomim (Aderet). After he moved to Eretz Yisrael, he began to support the *heter*, declaring in 1903 that it could be used wherever it had been used during the previous *shemitah*. This ruling was approved by R. Shmuel

23. Quoted by R. Mohilever's secretary R. Yaakov Bakhrakh in *HaMelitz* 29:158 (St. Petersburg, July 30, 1889), 2. It should be emphasized that R. Yehoshua of Kutna visited Jerusalem for about a month in the summer of 1886, so he was familiar with the main players there. This knowledge is reflected in his *Yeshuot Malko*; see *Oraḥ Ḥayim*, *siman* 42, which is addressed to R. Elyashar; *Even Ha'Ezer*, *siman* 2, which is addressed to the Ashkenazi high rabbinic court; and *Yoreh De'ah*, *siman* 65, which is addressed to R. Shmuel Salant.

Salant, and based on the *heter* of none other than R. Yehoshua Leib Diskin. During the 1896 *shemitah,* he had permitted R. Naftali Hertz HaLevi, rabbi of Jaffa, to sell the land. True, this *heter* was much more limited than that of R. Spektor, but it was still a *heter,* as opposed to the categorical prohibition of 1889. R. Rabinowitz-Teomim (Aderet) wrote to R. Kook about it:

> The head of the rabbinical court of Jaffa (R. Naftali Hertz HaLevi) wrote to me that already during the previous *shemitah,* R. Yehoshua Leib Diskin *z"l* ruled that it was acceptable to rely upon [those who are permissive], and that no one could object to a person doing so. And this was followed. I [R. Rabinowitz-Teomim, Aderet] too responded simply that they had already ruled permissively... followers of R. Diskin ganged up on me, as all they know is that he publicly prohibited it in 5649 [1889] to prevent sinners from completely uprooting the commandment of *shemitah.* Their opposition is also based on the position of R. Spektor *z"l.* Even though I argued at length at the meeting in my home that [R. Diskin] would have permitted it nowadays as well (and in fact, the Rabbi of Jaffa wrote to me that he *had* permitted it), they unanimously refuse to believe it. All they care about is the proclamation signed by twenty great rabbis, including him, opposing the *heter*... And if the Yishuv is destroyed (God forbid), and three hundred Torah-observant families have nothing to live on, that is not their problem.[24]

---

24. *Eder HaYakar,* 84; compare *Igrot HaRa'ayah* 1, 377. Also see p. 258 there, as well as the pamphlet *Hora'ot Sha'ah* written by R. Yosef Tzvi HaLevi (son-in-law of R. Naftali Hertz HaLevi) and published in Jerusalem, 1909 (pp. 115–16 and 121–22). (See also the letter by R. Rabinowitz-Teomim that was first published in the issue of *Nezer HaTorah* cited above in n. 20 [Tevet 5768/2008], 33–34.) This testimony as to the limited *heter* which R. Diskin approved can be supported by a letter that the Ashkenazi rabbis of Jerusalem sent to R. Naftali Hertz HaLevi in the summer of 1895. There they requested that he fight against the scuttlebutt that claimed "the rabbis of Jerusalem permitted violating *shemitah,*" meaning they gave a sweeping *heter* with no restrictions. In this letter, they made mention of "**what we permitted on a temporary basis to avoid the collapse, God forbid, of the Yishuv's institutions**" (*Mara D'Ara Yisrael* 1 [Jerusalem, 1969], 183; R. Diskin added his name to this letter). R. Rabinowitz-Teomim further testified that R. Yosef Ḥayim Sonnenfeld agreed that the pronouncement forbidding the *heter* in 1889 was not relevant to the *heter* of R. Diskin in 1896:

> They have a proclamation signed by the gaon R. Diskin *ztz"l,* the gaon R. Shmuel Salant (may he have a long life), and a whole army of rabbis and laymen, stating that no work whatsoever of any way, shape, or form should be done, even by a non-Jew ... **Later the gaon rabbi, R. Ḥayim Sonnenfeld, who is one of the signatories there, after careful deliberation responded that the prohibition agreed upon in the proclamation did not apply to the permission of those great rabbis.** Since I would like everyone to agree, I decided to explain the law (*Kuntres Hora'ot Sha'ah,* 121).

At a later point R. Rabinowitz-Teomim (Aderet) returned to the subject, and his statements about the zealots in Jerusalem were cutting and sharp as tacks:

> Your Honor is quite correct in your letter, pointing out that it is not my job to supervise others, etc. However, if you were here, you would see that things are not as you imagine. R. Yehoshua Leib Diskin's admirers shut their ears like a deaf snake. On Ḥanukkah, I made myself hoarse arguing with them… despite the fact that the rabbis of Jaffa (R. HaLevi *ztz"l*) and Petaḥ Tikvah (R. Aharon HaKohen Orlanski) and others (may they live and be well) explicitly attest that in the previous *shemitah*, R. Yehoshua Leib Diskin agreed to it, and R. Shmuel Salant himself pointed to [the lenient opinion of] the Maharit. These fanatics are too fierce for me. God forbid I should draw their ire. Even R. Diskin suffered at their hands at the end of his life (may it not happen to us); there is no end to the deeds of the wicked.[25]

It should be unnecessary to point out that this testimony completely disproves the claim of the author that "R. Diskin was sharply opposed to the *heter mekhirah*, and the support he granted was on a one-time basis." According to R. Rabinowitz-Teomim, the sharp opposition in 1889 was only "to protect [*shemitah*]," as people wished to uproot its observance entirely. Fundamentally, though, R. Diskin did not reject the possibility of using certain permissions during *shemitah*

25. *Eder HaYakar*, 87. Similarly, R. Rabinowitz-Teomim (Aderet) wrote about the zealots in a third letter: "Complex discussions do not register with them at all. They are united in saying 'their signature is right here [in the proclamation].' This proclamation means more to them than fundamental Torah principles…" (*Kuntres Hora'ot Sha'ah*, 121). R. Rabinowitz-Teomim went on to explain how he continued to apply the ruling of R. Diskin in the 1903 *shemitah*: "Since he already ruled in 1896 to sell when there is no choice, we can certainly do the same now – selling only the trees with the soil they need to grow, and requiring the non-Jews to cut them down [a condition that will not be met – transl.]. This is how R. Diskin said to do it. **Even if this decision was not meant to apply for all time, in any case he allowed it because of the pressing circumstances then. It is even more necessary for the upcoming *shemitah*, taking into account the current situation of the workers (may God have mercy)**" (ibid.). R. Kook too, in the 1910 *shemitah*, continued relying upon the *heter* of R. Diskin, but he kept it secret from the zealots. As he explained: "In no way would it have been effective at all to announce and publicize that R. Diskin *ztz"l* agreed to the *heter*, because they would have been prepared to issue a public denial. Since we don't have a handwritten letter from him specifying his consent, it would be easy for them to deny it. My father-in-law R. Rabinowitz-Teomim (Aderet) suffered as a result of this denial…" (*Igrot HaRa'ayah* 2, 1–2).

as needed at the time.[26] Therefore, R. Rabinowitz-Teomim was convinced that he would have permitted it in 1903 as he did in 1896. Additionally, as mentioned above, R. Shmuel Salant withdrew his staunch opposition of 1889 and agreed that it was possible to rely on the *heter* of R. Diskin. R. Rabinowitz-Teomim testifies to this elsewhere:

> I spoke with the honored, revered, and holy R. Shmuel Salant as to how we can be lenient regarding *shemitah* due to the danger to life... I told him about the discussions I had with your father-in-law (R. HaLevi)... concerning the details of the *heter* to which the gaon of Brisk (R. Diskin) agreed. [R. Salant] nodded and said that I was right to advise your father-in-law that what he had done in the previous *shemitah* [1896] he should do now as well.[27]

26. This position receives further support from an additional oral tradition in the name of someone close to R. Diskin: "I heard from the Rabbi of Teplyk, the gaon R. Shimshon Polansky *ztz"l*, who heard from R. Moshe Shoḥet [Frankenthal] – R. Diskin's right-hand man – that there is value in searching for a *heter* for farmers who are not up to the challenge of keeping the mitzvah. At the same time, there is also a need to publicize objections to giving such a *heter*. This way, it will not become entrenched, and people will remain aware that such permission is granted only due to pressing circumstances and the needs of the hour" (R. Avraham Shapira, "*Kedushat Shvi'it*," in *Torah She'baal Peh* 28 [Jerusalem, 1987], 2). There is more to be said about the various rumors surrounding the position of R. Diskin, but this is not the place for it.
27. *Kuntres Hora'ot Sha'ah*, 125. By the way, everything cited above completely contradicts the claim of the Satmar Rebbe (R. Yoel Teitelbaum, *Kuntres Shalosh Teshuvot* [Brooklyn, 1953], 75–76) and others that R. Diskin rescinded his permission; but this is not the place to elaborate. As for R. Shmuel Salant, on the one hand, he supported the *heter* of R. Diskin. (He even permitted more than R. Diskin did, as detailed by R. Naftali Hertz HaLevi, "*Piskei Dinim B'Hanhagat Avodah BaShvi'it*," in *Kuntres B'Tzet HaShanah* [n.p., 1959], 78 and *Har HaMor – Shvi'it* [Jerusalem, 1994], 110.) On the other hand, R. Salant also vehemently opposed a sweeping *heter*, as for example that of R. Spektor. He went so far as to tell R. Kook that it did not fit into the category of "Better that they eat the meat of a slaughtered animal even if it was dying, rather than eat unslaughtered animals" (*Kiddushin* 22a); instead, "This *heter* is an unslaughtered animal" (*Ḥavatzelet* 40:52 [Jerusalem, August 15, 1910], 2). Apparently, those present at that conversation included Ridbaz, R. Ḥayim Berlin, R. Yitzḥak Winograd, and his brother R. Yosef Eliyahu Winograd. And yet, we should note that when R. Ḥayim Berlin suggested to R. Shmuel Salant that he publish a proclamation for those in the Diaspora to support those shutting down for *shemitah*, he made it conditional upon R. Kook joining the effort (letter by R. Winograd dated 8 Iyar 5669 [April 29, 1909] and published in *Igrot LaRa'ayah*, 87). In fact, R. Kook did join, as is mentioned in a letter he wrote to R. Ḥayim Berlin and R. Shmuel Salant (cited above in n. 8).

SPECULATIONS ABOUT R. YITZḤAK ELḤANAN SPEKTOR'S POSITION

Later in the introduction, the article describes R. Kook's conduct during the *shemitah* controversy of 1910:

> While he lived in Russia, he opposed the *heter mekhirah* – "My opinion then tended toward those who prohibited." With the approach of *shemitah* in 5670 [1910], he was pressured to permit selling the land. The pressure was so strong that he remarked that if some yeshiva in Jerusalem were to give him a... monthly stipend, he would leave his position (as rabbi of Jaffa) on account of the *shemitah* issue and join the yeshiva students. Nevertheless, in light of the severity of the economic situation in the Land of Israel, he permitted the sale.

This description, which relies upon Ridbaz (as does the claim in the previous section), is certainly distorted.[28] R. Kook explained in detail the reasons and motivations for his support of the *heter* as a necessary temporary measure, in **dozens** of letters and essays found throughout his extensive writings. This is so well known that there is no point in discussing it further. Certainly, his writings do not support such speculative claims.[29]

The source of these claims is the introduction of Ridbaz to his work *Bet Ridbaz*, a commentary on *Pe'at HaShulkhan* (Jerusalem, 1912). On the surface, relying on Ridbaz would seem to be proper. After all, this is the personal testimony of an illustrious rabbi, so it must be correct. Sadly, though, an examination of Ridbaz's introduction reveals a number of problems, making it difficult to consider it a reliable source regarding what happened in 1889 and R. Kook's conduct in 1910.

---

28. Why doesn't the author cite the continuation of the quote which begins with "My opinion then tended toward those who prohibited"? R. Kook goes on to explain that this opinion stemmed from a lack of complete familiarity with the situation (*Igrot HaRa'ayah* 1, 258). We should also note that the above-quoted statement seems to be referring to the first two *shemitot* (1889 and 1896). By contrast, with the approach of the third *shemitah*, R. Kook's opinion tended to permit, even while he was still in Boisk. He wrote this explicitly in 1900: "Now, if the circumstances are so pressing that the survival of the Yishuv depends upon it, it seems it can be permitted..." (*Mishpat Kohen, siman* 58).
29. For further reading on the subject, I recommend the article of our colleague Shaul Avdiel, "*Heter HaMekhirah O Otzar Bet Din? Shitat Maran HaRa'ayah Kook ztz"l*," in *Alonei Mamre* 120 (Kiryat Arba, 2007), 51–60. See also the booklet by Dr. Ḥagi Ben-Artzi, *HaRa'ayah Kook B'Fulmus HaShemitah* (Jerusalem, 2007), which is devoted to an analysis of the halakhic introduction to R. Kook's *Shabbat Ha'Aretz* and the correspondence between R. Kook and Ridbaz.

First, here is how Ridbaz describes the involvement of R. Yitzḥak Elḥanan Spektor in the controversy of 1889:

> Using trickery and deceit, they misled the gaon R. Yitzḥak Elḥanan of Kovno *z"l* by suggesting to him that observing *shemitah* would jeopardize lives... Some Jews from Kovno [who later moved to the Land of Israel] asked him how he could have permitted it. He responded that the heretics misled him into believing that danger to life was involved. In any case, his ruling explicitly stated that it was only a temporary measure. Even this temporary permission sparked the opposition of all the great rabbis of the time. These included the holy gaon R. Yehoshua Leib Diskin, the gaon R. Yosef Dov [HaLevi Soloveitchik] *z"l*, the gaon Netziv *z"l*, and all the other great rabbis of the time, whose pinkies were thicker than his hips...[30] These wicked people made the Rabbi of Kovno their flag-bearer, as if he were the Rabbi of the entire Diaspora. The impure journals did not accept the words of the great rabbis of the generation (may their merit protect us), and they went and permitted [the violation of] *shemitah*.

What Ridbaz heard from the people from Kovno reflects the scuttlebutt prevalent in the community of those in the land who were opposed to the *heter mekhirah*. They maintained that not only was R. Spektor's approbation received only because he was misled, but also that after the fact he himself admitted it. It would seem that there was a certain amount of truth to these rumors, even if it was very limited.[31] Nevertheless, if someone wishes to claim that R. Spektor ultimately concluded that his support for the *heter mekhirah* was a complete mistake, and

30. See Melakhim 1 12:6.

31. It would seem that the source for these rumors was R. Yeshaya HaLevi Horowitz, a student of Ridbaz in Tzefat, who heard about the meeting with R. Spektor from his father, R. Asher Yeḥezkel Horowitz. He recounted: "My master, father, and teacher *z"l* told me that when he was abroad, he traveled to Kovno to see and meet the great rabbi of the generation, R. Yitzḥak Elḥanan *z"l*... He spoke with him about matters pertaining to the Land of Israel (may it be rebuilt). R. Spektor confessed that he had been tricked into giving a *heter* to sell the land to a non-Jew; they told him that if the Jews did not work their fields for a year, the government would confiscate them" ("*Sippurim MiKitvei Yad HaRav HaGaon Moreinu HaRav R. Yeshaya Horowitz ztz"l, Av Bet Din Kehilat Tzefat,*" published by his son-in-law R. Avraham HaLevi Mehudar in *Likutei Avraham* [n.p., 1987], 208–9). As one reads the collection of stories where this appears, it becomes clear that they are not very precise, to put it mildly. Additionally, they were put into writing only decades later. Nevertheless, despite these reservations, the testimony is firsthand. Keep in mind, though, that the idea that R. Spektor felt tricked does not appear explicitly or implicitly anywhere in all his writings on the *heter*.

that he admitted that "the heretics misled him into believing that danger to life was involved" (when, as Ridbaz maintained, in fact it was not) – that person must presume that when this mistake came to light, R. Spektor took back his support of the *heter*. Is this what actually happened? If we ask R. Spektor himself, the answer is **a resounding no**! In Tishrei 1896, a few months before his death, he wrote in a letter to R. Naftali Hertz HaLevi of Jaffa: "In terms of your question as to my opinion about *shemitah*, **I have not changed my views at all, and my current position is identical with the one I expressed during the last *shemitah*. Nothing new at all**."[32] In another letter from the same period (June 3, 1895), which was sent to the settlement supervisor who had been appointed by Baron Rothschild, R. Spektor elaborated on his continued support of the *heter*:

> In 5648 [1888], before the previous *shemitah*, I was also asked about this. At the time, we saw that the *heter* was necessary to avert a life-threatening situation. For many poor and destitute people would either perish or be forced to leave their holdings in the Holy Land, Heaven forbid. Therefore, I and other rabbis agreed to permit in the following manner… Even though in 5648 [1888] the *heter* was explicitly limited to 5649 [1889], in the meantime many more of our brethren have come to settle in our Holy Land, thank Heaven. Thus, it is still a matter of life and death, and the *heter* is still necessary so that the people will not suffer from famine, Heaven forbid. Therefore, we are of the opinion that the *heter* with all its particulars should be applied again in the upcoming *shemitah* of 5656 [1896]. My opinion now is the same as my opinion then.[33]

This letter, where R. Spektor repeats the reason for his *heter* – jeopardy to life for the settlers – clearly contradicts the claim of Ridbaz that R. Spektor came to

32. *Hora'ot Sha'ah*, 125. R. Rabinowitz-Teomim (Aderet) was aware of this as well. He wrote: "The gaon of Kovno *z"l* responded to sell the land… We did not know his reasoning, only the short ruling that he issued **for two *shemitot***" (*Eder HaYakar*, 85). It should be noted that R. Naftali Hertz HaLevi asked R. Spektor not to go public again with his *heter*, as he had already elicited a limited *heter* from R. Diskin. But R. Spektor did not honor this request (*Hora'ot Sha'ah*, 125; see the account of R. Yitzḥak Nissenbaum on June 14, 1895 that states that R. Mohilever had just received a letter from R. Spektor informing him that "he reiterates and confirms his previous permission" (*Igrot HaRav Nissenbaum*, 32).

33. *Oraita*, issue 19 (1996), 355. At the end of this letter, R. Spektor repeats his declaration that "this permission is valid only for the upcoming *shemitah* year of 1896" (as he had declared in 1889), so that people would not consider the permission to be permanent and timeless. On the same day he wrote that letter, he sent out an almost identical letter to the head of the Ḥovevei Tziyon movement in Odessa. (See *Oraita*, issue 9 [5747], 236–37.)

believe that the *heter* he gave in 1889 was mistaken.[34] Even if R. Spektor admitted to R. Horowitz that he was originally in possession of mistaken information about some detail or another (note 31 above), it is clear that his primary reason for granting the *heter* was not based on disinformation. Evidently, he felt that the danger to life was real even without that detail, and thus in his opinion the *heter* was entirely justified and remained so.

If one looks only at the letter of the *heter*, he might get the impression that R. Spektor's knowledge of what was going on in the Land of Israel was somewhat vague. Perhaps that is why many claim that he was misled. Nevertheless, his vast correspondence regarding the *heter* shows that he was in contact with writers representing a very diverse range of opinions.[35] This very much minimizes the credibility of the claim that R. Spektor was working with only partial or incorrect information.

It is also difficult to understand the claim that he was misled, as the question of whether an agricultural shutdown would jeopardize people's lives was the subject of disagreement between the proponents and opponents of the *heter*. It is possible that the opposition believed that if the permissive Europeans lived in the land, they would change their minds. An example is R. Mordekhai Gimpel Yafeh, whose opposition to the *heter* became stronger after he immigrated to Eretz Yisrael at the end of Elul 1888. But an opposite example is R. Rabinowitz-Teomim (Aderet), whose unhesitating support for the idea that lives were at stake began after he arrived in the land and saw the reality with his own eyes: "My opinion now is very different from my opinion in 5656 [1896], at which time I argued in Dobele with the head of the rabbinic court of Bialystok ..."[36] R. Elyashar as well,

34. Ridbaz makes a number of claims about various ways in which R. Spektor was misled. Besides the one mentioned above about danger to life, he mentions in his introduction a second way in which R. Spektor was misled: "The sinners and heretics misled the Rabbi of Kovno by saying that in the Land of Israel, it was unnecessary to have a court-approved sales contract ..." Toward the end of the introduction, Ridbaz mentions a third area where R. Spektor was misled: "If a tree misses being pruned once or twice, that will not kill it, what the sinners told the Rabbi of Kovno to the contrary notwithstanding."

35. This diverse group included: R. Mohilever, his secretary R. Yaakov Bakhrakh, and their fellow Bialystoker R. Yehonatan Abelman; Chief Rabbi of France R. Tzadok Kahn and R. Yehudah Lubetsky of Paris; R. Dr. Judah Elyakim Goldberg and Eliyahu Scheid, representatives of Baron Rothschild; Michael Erlanger and Avraham Greenberg of Ḥovevei Tziyon; R. Naftali Hertz HaLevi of Jaffa; rabbis of Jerusalem, most prominently R. Shmuel Salant; and others.

36. *Igrot HaRa'ayah* 1, 377. See R. Kook's testimony to this on p. 258. It should be noted that R. Mohilever visited the Land of Israel in 1890 and this did not lead to his rescinding the *heter*, which he supported again for the 1896 *shemitah*. (See, for example, his letter of June 30, 1895 that was published first in *Hayehudi*, issue 26 [1910] and later in R. Moshe Tzvi Neriyah's *Tznif*

who was a resident of Jerusalem, noted in 1889 that one of the reasons he permitted was "lest the settlement be destroyed by landowners deserting their holdings ... The whole Yishuv would be destroyed."[37] The disagreement, apparently, did not necessarily stem from location-based perceptions of reality.

As for R. Spektor himself, a letter which he sent to R. Mohilever on May 14, 1888, a number of months after he penned the *heter*, makes it clear that he was well aware that Ashkenazi rabbis in the Land of Israel, led by R. Shmuel Salant and R. Diskin were opposed to the *heter*. He exchanged letters with them, listened to their reasoning, and was even aware of the claim that he had been provided with misinformation! Nevertheless, R. Spektor forcefully rejected the accusations and continued to support the *heter*:

> I want to inform you that a letter from the gaon R. Shmuel Salant has reached me. In it he writes that Dr. [Judah Elyakim] Goldberg has come to Jerusalem on behalf of the generous baron of Paris, requesting that [R. Salant] write a sales contract for *shemitah* in his rabbinic court. The gaon R. Salant is withholding his consent, as a contract which is not drawn up in the secular courts is worthless. Accordingly, the sale must be done through the secular courts. I replied that a sale through a rabbinic court in the Land of Israel is good enough, as I explained at great length in my pamphlet with the Almighty's help ... Afterward, letters reached me from all the rabbis of their central committee (Kollel Perushim) and their high rabbinical court (*Badatz*). There are seventeen signatories, all loudly screaming at me and arguing with me, maintaining that there is no threat to life involved ... On the contrary, [they claim that not selling the land] is what is best for the Land and their community. They carry on in their usual fashion when it comes to such matters, and I did not respond to them at all.

Melukha, 285. See also *Responsa of R. Shmuel Mohilever, Yoreh De'ah, siman* 22.) In fact, even without living in the land, R. Mohilever was well aware of what was going on in the New Yishuv in general (see *Sefer Shmuel – Zikaron L'HaRav Shmuel Mohilever* [Jerusalem, 1923], especially pp. 24–69 and 73–86), as well as what was going on in Petaḥ Tikvah and Ekron in particular. (See the article by Aḥiezer Arkin, "*HaRav Mohilever U'Mazkeret Batya*," *HaMa'ayan* 33:2 (Tevet 5753]: 24–37.) It is thus impossible to put forward the claim that R. Mohilever was "not an expert in the matter," which was a claim leveled against other Ḥovevei Tziyon rabbis. In any event, the fact is that of those rabbis who had ruled permissively in 1889 and were still alive in 1896, not a single one rescinded his *heter*.

37. *Responsa Simḥa L'Ish, Yoreh De'ah, siman* 26 (p. 107b).

> Then R. Dr. Goldberg wrote to me that the Ashkenazi rabbinic court will not agree to have the *heter mekhirah* drawn up there. They feel that it must all be done in a secular court. Only the Sephardi rabbinic court is willing to take care of the sale. The aforementioned doctor asked if we Ashkenazim would go to the Sephardi court, given that we would normally rely only on the Ashkenazi court. I have not responded to him yet, since it seems that doing so would be very divisive, Heaven forbid, and this pains me. I never imagined such a thing.
>
> The signatories of the above-mentioned long letter include those who claim to represent R. Yehoshua Leib [Diskin], may he live and be well. They write that in his opinion it is forbidden, and he is among the opponents. The long letter also misconstrues reality, saying that there is no pressing need, and that those who asked for a *heter* based on need were lying. All this is in the letter too, and in their usual way everything is presented angrily and divisively.[38]

As an aside, it should be noted that Ridbaz's attitude toward R. Spektor is a bit odd. Of particular interest is his use of the expression "whose pinkies are thicker than his hips." Of course, the rabbis to whom Ridbaz compared R. Spektor – Netziv, Bet HaLevi [R. Yosef Dov HaLevi Soloveitchik] of Brisk, and R. Diskin – were top-tier rabbis. Nevertheless, it is common knowledge – then as now – that R. Spektor was closer to being considered "the decisor of the generation" than they were, and almost no one of his caliber then was responding to practical halakhic questions. This is not the place to prove this, nor is it necessary.[39] Furthermore,

---

38. R. Spektor continued in his letter to R. Mohilever: "I wanted to inform Your Honor of all this. Please let me know what Your Honor's response is to the above, as well as the response of our colleague, the gaon Rabbi Yehoshua of Kutna, as these letters must have been sent to you and him as well. I find all of this greatly distressing, may God have mercy…" (*Oraita* 9, 233–34). In fact, R. Mohilever immediately contacted R. Yehoshua of Kutna, who responded with a sharp letter on the tenth of Sivan, part of which is quoted earlier in this chapter. In a letter soon afterward, on the twelfth of Sivan, R. Yehoshua of Kutna addressed R. Spektor's question: "I thought I would write further and let you know that I did not write anything to Jerusalem about the ruling and the decree… But certainly, if the farmers wish to rely upon the opinions of the Sephardi scholars in the Land of Israel, that is fine." (This is excerpted in the issue of *HaMelitz* cited above in n. 23.)
39. It goes without saying that the permissive rabbis, who were themselves among the most senior rabbis of the time, turned to R. Spektor for approbation (and not to R. Yosef Dov HaLevi Soloveitchik, for example). Netziv himself, when he was originally asked by Leon Pinsker about *shemitah*, responded: "We have become aware that the gaon, the head of the rabbinic court of Kovno, *shlit"a*, **who is older and greater than I am, was asked about this. Therefore, I do not**

even someone who believes otherwise would never think of actually saying "their pinkies are thicker than his thighs"! Another surprising sentence by Ridbaz is "These wicked people made the Rabbi of Kovno their flag-bearer, as if he were the Rabbi of the entire Diaspora." In fact, R. Spektor was frequently described as "the Rabbi of the entire Diaspora" during his lifetime, and even more so after his death. This is common knowledge and requires no proof.[40] It seems that no other rabbi in recent times (with the possible exception of R. Ḥayim Ozer Grodzenski) was considered by the masses to be "the Rabbi of the entire Diaspora" in the way that R. Spektor was.[41]

There is yet another fundamental problem with Ridbaz's description of the 1889 controversy. For the only players he mentions are the "wicked people" who came to convince R. Spektor on the one side, and the opposing rabbis on the other side. Where did the other permissive European rabbis disappear to? Where did the Chief Rabbis of Jerusalem, R. Elyashar and R. Panigel, disappear to? Instead of hearing about these rabbis and additional ones, we hear twice that "all the great rabbis of the time" except for R. Spektor opposed the sale – as if no permissive authorities existed. It is possible that Ridbaz believed this, in light of the incomplete information at his disposal. However, in light of the fuller picture, his opinion cannot be relied upon.

---

want to put myself forward, especially since the *ge'onim* of Jerusalem, may it be rebuilt speedily in our days, Amen, are right there, and better equipped to examine the details of the agricultural work than I am" (letter dated 20 Kislev 5648 (December 6, 1887), published in *Ketavim* 2, col. 393). R. David Friedman of Karlin (cited above in n. 11) writes something similar. However, it is important to clarify that some people tried to claim that R. Spektor issued a sweeping *heter* with no limitations. In order to advance their own cause, they presented him as someone who was willing to ignore all the rulings of all of the sages of his times. R. Kook expressed his reservations about this: "Had I not granted a *heter*, some people would have said that no *heter* is necessary, because they are fond of saying that R. Spektor *z"l* was greater than all the rabbis of the generation, so who can oppose his *heter*? Then they would have found someone or another to arrange some sort of sale…" (*Igrot HaRa'ayah* 2, 191).

40. To give the reader just a taste, I will give a single example, chosen at random. R. Tzvi Hirsh Shapira of Munkacz in volume 1 of his well-known book *Darkei Teshuvah* (Vilna, 1893) publicized letters of approbation from a number of important rabbis, but only upon one of them did he bestow the title "the Rabbi of the entire Diaspora." Of course, that was R. Spektor.

41. Ridbaz's strange attitude toward R. Spektor becomes a little clearer in light of what he writes in one of his letters to R. Kook: "Is this really possible, that the old rabbi who permitted (R. Spektor) was greater than Your Honor in either Torah knowledge or fear of God? My heart says no" (*Igrot LaRa'ayah*, 84; see further there). It still remains to be clarified what Ridbaz had against R. Spektor. But in any case, it is clear that Ridbaz was expressing his opinion of R. Spektor and his alone.

RIDBAZ ON R. KOOK

As mentioned above, Ridbaz goes on to assert that R. Kook's support for the *heter* was also brought about by pressure and force exerted by the secular:

> Their power extended so far that they pressured the Rabbi of Jaffa, "holding the mountain over him like a barrel" to coerce him to permit *shemitah*. [And I testify, with heaven and earth as my witnesses, that the Rabbi of Jaffa sobbed in front of me – not merely sniffles but hot tears] and said, and I quote, that if some yeshiva in Jerusalem were to give him six napoleans a month, or even five, he would leave his position and join the yeshiva students, but what could he do now that he is standing on a narrow path, where there is no space to deviate, neither right nor left. [Now, when a person is surrounded and under attack, sometimes he does something that he would rather not do.] I have a clear indication that this is the case. The head of the rabbinical court of Paterson, whose name is R. (A.) [J.] L. Seltzer, told me that he spoke with him about this matter, and he told him that he is very happy that the Torah scholars opposed him so vociferously; this way, the practice would not become rooted, Heaven forfend, and people would not say that *shemitah* is truly no longer operative, God forbid. However, little by little, he began to fool himself and to defend the *heter*. It is not befitting for him to hand down distorted rulings far from the truth, God forbid, thus delaying the Redemption of Israel.

At first glance, it seems that Ridbaz is testifying that he personally heard a very strange and disturbing statement from R. Kook – that if he only had the means of a kollel student in Jerusalem, he would quit his job as rabbi of Jaffa and the settlements, and stop dealing with *shemitah*. This testimony, of course, does not fit in with anything we know about R. Kook and his activities as rabbi of Jaffa and the settlements. In truth, a careful reading of Ridbaz reveals that he is not claiming that he himself heard what he reported. First, without providing a source, he recounts that the heretics forced R. Kook to rule permissively. He then adds a sentence in brackets: "And I testify, with heaven and earth as my witnesses, that the Rabbi of Jaffa sobbed in front of me – not just sniffles but hot tears." In other words, R. Kook told him about the pressure he was under. The ending of the bracketed sentence indicates that here, Ridbaz's personal testimony – that which is bracketed – ends. What follows the bracketed sentence is a story that is unattributed, about the pressure brought upon R. Kook. This is how the letter should be read: "They pressured the Rabbi of Jaffa, 'holding the mountain over him like a barrel' to coerce him to permit *shemitah.* [Ridbaz's conversation with R. Kook is described here in brackets.] And he said, and I quote, that if some yeshiva in Jerusalem were to give him..." That statement was not heard by Ridbaz himself, but rather was based on what he heard from others. An uncontestable proof of this is found in the continuation: "I have a clear indication that this is the case, as the head of the rabbinical court of Paterson told me...." If the entire earlier statement was heard by Ridbaz himself and was the subject of his phrase "I testify with Heaven and earth as my witnesses," why would he need to bring a clear indication that it was correct? Rather, there is no doubt that Ridbaz heard the statement from someone or other, whose authority and reliability remain unknown. Only in parenthetical sections does Ridbaz attest to what he personally witnessed ["the Rabbi of Jaffa cried in front of me"] and add his opinion about the matter ["that explains why"].

Now we must examine the proof Ridbaz brings for the statement's reliability – the testimony of R. Judah Leib Seltzer. A close friend of Ridbaz in Tzefat, he would later become the secretary of Agudas Harabonim, the Union of Orthodox Rabbis of the United States and Canada. R. Seltzer told him [Ridbaz] that R. Kook said that he was happy about the strong opposition to him, as it prevents people from mistakenly thinking that *shemitah* is now a dead letter. Only afterward did R. Kook begin to "fool himself," eventually becoming convinced that the *heter* was truly correct. At first glance, this is reliable testimony. However, according to a recently published letter, when R. Seltzer saw Ridbaz's introduction citing him, he quickly sent a letter of apology to R. Kook and told him it was a misunderstanding. R. Seltzer wrote as follows:

> If Your Honor saw the introduction of our friend the gaon Ridbaz to his recently published book *Shulḥan Arukh L'Shvi'it,* you must have found some confused statements in my name, claiming to be quoting you. Your esteemed Honor will certainly understand, but just to be certain I am saying to you explicitly: **The blame is not mine, neither concerning the publication of these statements nor the confused rendition.** I, in my fashion, and due to my desire to make peace between you and the abovementioned gaon, was very precise when I told him what you had said, to make sure it would not cause any later problems. At the same time, I explained how deeply you felt about the situation concerning *shemitah.* This was in order to remove any animosity from the heart of the gaon Ridbaz, who deep down feels respect and admiration for you. Besides, how long must we be smeared and denigrated? But **he used it as a support for**

> **figments of his imagination, changing them somewhat so they ended up confused.** If Your Honor is upset about this, I ask that you let me know.[42]

The bottom line is that this letter of R. Seltzer is sufficient to prove our claim that it is impossible to accept Ridbaz's introduction as a reliable source, for a depiction of the events in general and the attitude of R. Kook in particular.

As an aside, we should also comment on what Ridbaz quotes at the beginning of this same introduction. It is based on a letter by R. Eliyahu Guttmacher that is printed in R. Wax's book *Nefesh Ḥayah*. According to Ridbaz:

> [R. Guttmacher] wrote in his letter that it is clear to him that if the Jewish people in the Land of Israel – 130 Jews (in his time) – were to keep *shemitah* properly, they would rectify the sin of our ancestors when they lived in the Land. Disregarding *shemitah* is the first reason given for the exile of the Jews from their land, as the Torah explicitly tells us. With this sin rectified, our righteous Messiah would arrive. But Satan will do his very best to interfere with it.

We are forced to say that Ridbaz's citation of R. Guttmacher's words was from memory rather than from R. Wax's book, as the connection between them is very weak. First of all, R. Guttmacher does not speak about the coming of the Messiah, but rather the beginning of the Redemption. He maintains that this

42. *Igrot LaRa'ayah*, 113. R. Kook's response to R. Seltzer was brief: "As for my close friend Ridbaz, I did not see the book, but there is no place for grudges between lovers of truth like us" (*Igrot HaRa'ayah* 2, 125). Compare his letter to Ridbaz: "I did not see what you wrote in the introduction to your book, as I have not been honored with a copy and it has not come my way. But if Your Honor is suffering because these people are angry at you for speaking up in my defense…" (ibid., p. 155). At the same time, R. Kook's letters to Ridbaz include subtle rebuke for too readily accepting slander against him and unfairly judging him harshly. For example: "I am very surprised that people attribute sordid motivations to me, and accuse me of somehow forcing my will upon those who do not agree with me about the *heter*" (*Igrot HaRa'ayah* 1, 346; see further there). "I have heard that Your Honor speaks badly about me behind my back. I am taken aback by this, as you are such a faithful friend, who knows me so well. How did it come to this?" (ibid., 286). In the draft of a letter to Ridbaz that ultimately was not sent, R. Kook expresses this even more explicitly: "I do not know why you hurt me like this. The Holy One knows that my intentions are good and for His sake. If Your Honor wants to pursue me, do whatever you want… But God should forgive you for saying that I am flattering the Jewish Colonization Association" (*Igrot HaRa'ayah* 1, 295). This draft was written immediately after R. Kook received a letter from Ridbaz. However, later on that day, he drafted a new letter which was less harsh and which he actually sent (p. 296). Comparing the two versions is informative, but this is not the place to elaborate.

would take place on account of the settling of the land, even if the nation does not deserve it. He does not write that the exile was for disregarding *shemitah*, but rather for distaining the land. Furthermore, what Satan would try to interfere with was the settling of the land. There are additional differences as well, as can be seen in the actual letter:

> It is already clear to me that if the Jews begin working the Holy Land with 130 families, this will be the beginning of the Redemption, even if the Jews do not deserve it. In this letter, we will explain it only a little: We find in Tehillim 102 [verses 14–15], "It is the time to have mercy, for the time has come, for Your servants desire its stones," etc. See Sforno there, who says that they were taken into exile on account of disdaining the land, so when that is rectified, the Redemption will come.

Only later does R. Guttmacher mention *shemitah*, as part of a paraphrase of R. Moshe Alshikh, that was a basis for Ridbaz's words: "'And I will remember the land' [Vayikra 26:42] – They insulted the land unforgivably by not observing *shemitah* or offering the tithes." R. Guttmacher immediately explains what Satan would try to prevent: "Therefore the land must be appeased. Common sense charges us to take action to redeem the land. It must be started by us, and then it will be finished by God. We must see the great purpose of this, for the husks defeat even the most righteous to nullify this goodness…"[43]

Now that we have reached the conclusion of this chapter, it is worth noting that although the disagreement between R. Kook and Ridbaz was stormy, when all is said and done it was a disagreement for the sake of Heaven. The Sages say that such a disagreement ends in love (*Kiddushin* 30b). Ridbaz testified to this in an emotional letter to R. Kook at the height of the 1910 *shemitah*:

---

43. *Nefesh Ḥaya, Oraḥ Ḥayim* (Piotrkow, 1877), 10 [page 16 in the version at hebrewbooks.org – trans.]. Absurdly, many writers past and present have chosen, for obvious reasons, to copy Ridbaz's garbled version instead of copying R. Guttmacher's actual letter from *Nefesh Ḥaya*. (See, for example: R. Yaakov Ḥayim Sofer, *Torat Yaakov* [Jerusalem, 2005], 276; R. Reuven Sofer, *Kuntres al Issur HaMekhira BaShvi'it* [Jerusalem, 1987], 59; R. Yosef Efrati [ed.], *Min HaShoresh* [Jerusalem, 2007], 27; R. Yitzḥak Halberstam, *Shoshanat Ha'Amakim – Shemitah* [Bnei Brak, 1979], 54; R. Shalom Krauss, "*B'Inyan HaPulmus B'Heter HaMekhira U'be'Inyan Alei Ḥassa HaGedelim B'Ḥamamot B'Gush Katif*," *Or Yisrael* 6:4 [Monsey, Tamuz 5761/2001], 123; R. Menachem Meir Weissmandel, "*Birur L'Issur B'Nidon Tavlinim Shonim She'gidlu B'Eretz Yisrael B'Kibbutz Sde Eliyahu Shel Shnat HaShemitah Im Heter Mekhirah Prati She'assu LiSdoteihem*," *Or Yisrael* 7:2 [Monsey, Kislev 2002], 137; R. Yeḥiel Mikhel Stern, "*Sipurei Shemitah*," *Kol HaTorah*, issue 49 [Tishrei 5761], 55; and more.)

> What can I say to you, my dear friend, about my pain, anguish, and suffering during my time living in the Holy City, may it be rebuilt speedily in our days, Amen. Perhaps Your Honor can stop the evil journals from butting into debates between Torah scholars? … On the subject of *shemitah*, these journals degrade the rabbis of Jerusalem and the high rabbinic court. Yesterday, R. Yehoshua Kasovsky showed me a wall poster, full of endless, worthless slander and curses against Your Honor… What can I do? Your Honor is dear to me, and *shemitah* is beloved of me, and I am very confused. When it is just the two of us, we debate words of Torah; my pamphlet about *shemitah* and yours are both Torah. You raise difficulties with what I say, and I raise difficulties about what you say. We coexist peacefully, lovingly, and as friends, thus fulfilling the verse "*love truth and peace*" [Zekharia 8:19]… From me, writing with tears, Yaakov David Ridbaz.[44]

44. *Igrot LaRa'ayah*, 94, letter dated "Wednesday of *Parashat Shlaḥ*," which was June 23, 1910. The two of them later went through other rough patches. But these twists were eventually worked out, as R. Kook wrote in March 1913: "At the end of your letter, Your Honor mentions the renewal of our friendship. From my perspective, our friendship was continuous and unbroken. The statement of our holy Sages (*Avot* 5:16) applies to us: 'Love which is not dependent on anything never disappears'" (*Igrot HaRa'ayah* 2, 155–56). Similarly, R. Kook wrote to Ridbaz in Sivan 1910 in his now-famous letter no. 555: "You, the gaon, my beloved master, write that I should believe you when you say that your love for me is hard to quench. I truly do believe this, for faces reflect each other just as water does. I feel the holy flame of your holy love in the depths of my heart and soul; even large amounts of water cannot sweep it away. As far as all the disagreements between us concerning *shemitah*, our intentions are pure and for the sake of Heaven" (ibid., p. 196). Three months later, in Tishrei 1913, Ridbaz passed away. It seems he did not manage to respond to R. Kook's letter. (See further there, letters 605 and 609.)

Chapter 16

The *Shemitah* Controversy: More Food for Thought[1]

INTRODUCTION

During the last *shemitah* year, I published an article dealing with various aspects of the *shemitah* controversy across the generations – specifically that of 1888–89 – that contradict "common knowledge" in various quarters.[2] In this article I wish to revisit the same topic, to fill in a number of details regarding matters that I dealt with in the prior article and to add new comments and sources on additional matters.

MORE ON THE DESCRIPTION IN THE INTRODUCTION TO *BET RIDBAZ*

In 1912, the book *Pe'at HaShulḥan,* on the laws of *shemitah,* with the commentary *Bet Ridbaz* by Rabbi Yaakov Dovid Wilovsky (Ridbaz) was published in Jerusalem. Ridbaz led the battle against the *heter mekhirah* of 1909–10. In his introduction, Ridbaz deals with various topics in the history of the *heter,* specifically the involvement of R. Yitzḥak Elḥanan Spektor of Kovno in the *heter* of 1888–89 and the involvement of R. Avraham Yitzḥak HaKohen Kook in the *heter* of 1909–10. Over time, the descriptions in this introduction significantly influenced the historical picture of the *shemitah* controversy, especially among opponents of the

1. Translated by Michael Appel. This chapter originally appeared in *HaMa'ayan* 214 (5775).
2. *Uvdot U'Mitosim B'Pulmus HaShemitah, Alonei Mamre* 121 (Kiryat Arba, 2008), 48–69.

heter mekhirah. In the previous article, I addressed this introduction in some detail.[3] Here, I will fill in an additional piece.

One of Ridbaz's arguments is that, in his opinion, a land sale has no effect without the approval of the government courts. Yet "**the sinners and heretics misled the Rabbi of Kovno by telling him that in the Land of Israel, they do not require court approval for legal acquisitions and that a Jewish document alone suffices to transfer ownership in this country. This is an outright falsehood.**"[4] However, similar to other charges leveled against R. Yitzḥak Elḥanan, we know now that the truth lies exactly in the reverse: First, the legal facts prevailing in the Land of Israel had already been conveyed to R. Yitzḥak Elḥanan in a letter from R. Shmuel Salant on January 4, 1888. He writes that, "The sale of land without formal, legal government approval is worth nothing. And to sell land to non-Jews with formal legal government enforcement is something that is impossible at the present time."[5] Second, with respect to the halakhah itself, R. Yitzḥak Elḥanan's position was that there was no need to effect the sale under secular government auspices; it was enough to perform the sale in a Jewish *bet din* alone, without registering the sale in the land registry. He responded to R. Salant on May 6, 1888: "I wish

3. See previous chapter. Also see comments by R. Tzvi Yehudah Kook on the Introduction of Ridbaz, *HaTorah V'ha'Aretz*, vol. 8 (2008), 354 and on. Added to this material is the testimony of R. Asher Zev Werner in his book, *BiNarenu U'viZkenenu* (Jerusalem, 1957) 54: "There was a terrible controversy regarding *shemitah*. But the aforementioned *ge'onim* only fought with each other to clarify the Torah's law. Otherwise, they loved each other very much. I heard great compliments from the Ridbaz *ztz"l* about R. Kook *ztz"l*, in keeping with the spirit of "love truth and peace."
4. Ridbaz also wrote concerning this matter: "In truth, we wanted to do this through a government land registry like in Russia, or the *tabu* that we have here. But the attorneys have informed us that the sum will be more than one and half million francs. Because this is an exorbitant sum, it will be impossible to remove the land from Jewish ownership." The meaning of his words is unclear to me at this point, for he himself wrote shortly thereafter that it is forbidden to sell land in Eretz Yisrael to non-Jews. Presumably, even were it not cost-prohibitive, he would not have personally assisted in arranging the transaction.
5. *Torat Rabbenu Shmuel Salant* 1 (Jerusalem, 1998), 275. Compare this to the letter of R. Yaakov Elyashar, dated 6 Iyar 5648 (April 17, 1888):

   > How can we legally effect a sale? To this I respond as follows. If it were possible to arrange the sale according to official government regulations, that would be best because there could be no possible doubt [as to its effectiveness]. But, if this proves impossible, there is another way. The representative, who has power of attorney from the one whose name is on all the official settlement documents, will sell it to a non-Jew in front of four or five Ishmaelites, who will sign as witnesses to the bill of sale. The great rabbi, the *Rishon LeTziyon* (Ḥaham Bashi) will also sign the sale document with the seal that he uses for official government business. A bill of sale of this sort will have validity close to that of an official government transaction. (*HaTzvi* 16 [April 1888], front page)

to notify you of my opinion that it is sufficient to effect the sale through a document in a Jewish *bet din* alone. I explained this fully in my treatise, and I do not have the strength presently to copy my words in this letter."[6] R. Yitzḥak Elḥanan mentions this exchange in a letter sent to R. Shmuel Mohilever on May 14, 1888:

> I received a letter from R. Shmuel Salant…that he disagrees with me because any document that is not executed in the civil courts has no effect at all, and therefore, the sale must take place in their courts. I responded to him that it's sufficient to complete the sale in a Jewish *bet din,* as I explained in great length in my treatise.[7]

If so, then not only was R. Yitzḥak Elḥanan **not** misled at all regarding the local legal statutes, but even had it been so, it would have made no difference to him based on his halakhic position on this issue.

THE CONNECTION BETWEEN R. YITZḤAK ELḤANAN'S *HETER* AND THE *SHEMEN HAMOR*

In the letters cited above, as well as others, R. Yitzḥak Elḥanan mentioned a comprehensive treatise that he had authored to buttress the *heter mekhirah* in 1887–88.[8] We were not fortunate enough to actually see it. The treatise was not published in R. Yitzḥak Elḥanan's later years, nor in the lifetime of his son and successor, R. Tzvi Hirsch Rabinowitz.[9] It appears to have been lost along with his other writings in the chaos of World War I.[10] Therefore, our knowledge of the details of his *heter* comes mainly from his letters – among them the *heter*

6. *Torat Rabbenu Shmuel Salant,* Jerusalem, p. 276.
7. *"MiKitvei HaGaon Rav Yitzḥak Elḥanan ztz"l," Orayta* 9 (Netanya, 1987), 233.
8. See also his letter to R. Zadoc Kahn from January 30, 1888, in which he mentions that, "I have spent two months delving into the broad question of *shemitah*…. After much toil and careful study of this question…," he briefly outlined the fundamentals of his position to allow a limited sale to the Ishmaelites. He added that he had wanted to call upon other rabbis to weigh in with their opinions. However, once he heard that there were voices in protest, "I have therefore gone back and carefully considered their words" (ibid., 228).
9. R. Tzvi Hirsch Rabinowitz also dealt with the matter of the *heter,* as mentioned by R. Yitzḥak Elḥanan in the above referenced letter. He himself authored a treatise on this topic (see *K'tavim L'Toldot Ḥibat Tziyon* 2, col. 442).
10. No edited works of R. Yitzḥak Elḥanan Spektor were published at all after his death in 1896. In the introduction to his last work, *Ein Yitzḥak* 2, published a year before his death, he writes that, "May God help me to publish the rest of my responsa and novellae, and to arrange them in a pleasing manner." Similarly, at the end of the book: "May God continue to help me, in His goodness and loving-kindness, to publish the rest of my responsa and the novellae for which He bestowed knowledge upon me. They are here with me among my papers."

document itself – alongside other textual witnesses preserved in various sources. One such document to be cited presently notes that "he found creative leniencies to allow them [non-Jews] land rights." This brings us to the question of R. Yitzḥak Elḥanan's reasons behind the *heter* as it related to the prohibition of *lo teḥonem*.

According to well-known testimony delivered by Rabbi Ḥayim Yaakov Shapira, a *dayan* in Kovno and, late in life, one of the *gedolim* of Jerusalem, "The basis of his [R. Yitzḥak Elḥanan's] teaching relied on the *Shemen HaMor* that is cited in *Ikarei Dinim*, but was not to be found in Kovno. They sent it to him from Berlin (I believe)."[11] In light of this testimony, R. Eliyahu David Rabinowitz-Teomim (Aderet) also believed that "it appears that he only went as far as permitting that which was written in *Responsa Shemen HaMor*." Indeed, from that point onward, it was claimed on multiple occasions that the *heter* of R. Yitzḥak Elḥanan was dependent and conditioned upon that which was written in *Shemen HaMor*. So if the reasoning of *Shemen HaMor* no longer applies today, then R. Yitzḥak Elḥanan's *heter* would likewise have no basis.[12]

However, in light of the facts we have today, we can establish that this claim is also incorrect. In R. Yitzḥak Elḥanan's first letter to R. Shmuel Salant on December 8, 1887, he explains that not only was he convinced of the *heter* prior to receiving a copy of *Shemen HaMor*, but he had already concluded writing his treatise in support of the *heter*. He did, in fact, know about the existence of a responsum on the issue by *Shemen HaMor*, as it was referenced in *Ikarei Dinim* ("*Ikarei HaDat*" of R. Daniel Tirani of Florence). This is why he went to great lengths to acquire a copy of the book in order to see the responsum himself and to bolster his own *heter* with it. As he writes in the *heter* document, "I do not wish to stand alone in this innovation, as is my custom regarding these types of issues."[13] But at the

11. Letter from Aderet, 1902, cited in R. Yosef Tzvi HaLevi's *Hora'at Sha'ah* (Jaffa, 1910), p. 123. This also appears in the monograph *Shabbat LaHaShem* by Rabbi Moshe Naḥum Wallenstein, printed at the end of the book *Bnei Moshe* (Jerusalem, 1990), 175: "The great gaon and tzaddik, Rav Ḥayim Yaakov Shapira *ztz"l* has already testified that the gaon from Kovno *ztz"l* relied on the *heter* of the *Shemen HaMor ztz"l*, namely, the temporary sale that the gaon allowed."
12. This was most recently reiterated by R. Zev Weitman, who was so bold as to claim that, "The explicit responsum by Rav Mordecai Rubio, author of *Shemen HaMor*... created the basis which was relied upon by those who established the *heter mekhirah*" (*HaMa'ayan* 55:2 (Tevet 5775):70.
13. Cited, amongst others, by R. Yeḥiel Mikhel Tukachinsky, *Sefer HaShemitah* (Jerusalem, 1952), 67. Parenthetically, I will point out something that I haven't seen mentioned. R. Yitzḥak Elḥanan's exact formulation in his *heter* letter clearly repeats verbatim the text of the *heter* by the three rabbis in almost every detail. Apparently, he did this for the same reason, so as not to stand alone, etc.

time he decreed and wrote up the *heter*, he still did not have *Shemen HaMor* in front of him. And from the brief citation in *Ikarei Dinim* there was insufficient detail to learn much about the reasoning behind it:[14]

> With the help of the Almighty I found a friend. *Ikarei Dinim, Yoreh De'ah, siman* 32, paragraph 400, cites *Shemen HaMor*.... I do not have this book *Shemen HaMor* in my possession, but I saw *Sefer Shem HaGedolim* [of R. Ḥayim Yosef David Azulai, Ḥida] mentioned him.... Perhaps it will be found in the Holy City of Jerusalem, as the *Ikarei Dinim* only provides a brief citation and I do not know his basis and reasoning. In truth, with the Almighty's help, I have already explained it sufficiently.

According to all the evidence before us, the main factor in R. Yitzḥak Elḥanan's position that the prohibition of *lo teḥonem* does not apply, is the fact that the sale would be temporary:[15] "I have decided to allow it based on the suggestion to sell the fields and vineyards to the Ishmaelites, both the land and the produce, for the two-year duration only. After that time, the fields and vineyards will revert to their owners."[16] This is how R. Shmuel Salant understood him:

> It appears that his opinion is that a temporary sale is not included in the prohibition against providing them [non-Jews] with any land rights. Without a doubt, his treatise (which I have not seen) explains his reasoning.... If he has a chance, perhaps he will copy the treatise for me.[17]

---

14. *Torat Rabbenu Shmuel Salant* 1, 274.
15. A similar reason (a sale conditioned upon its future reversal) is one of the two main reasons for the *heter* of R. Yisrael Yehoshua Trunk from Kotna (see *Shu"t Yeshuot Malko, simanim* 55–59). This, obviously, has no connection to the *Shemen HaMor*.
16. This is the sole reason of all the reasons given by *Shemen HaMor* that is mentioned in *Ikarei HaDat*, ibid.:

    > And see the author of *Shemen HaMor* in *siman* 14, regarding one who purchases a vineyard in the Land of Israel and how he should conduct himself during the *shemitah* year.... He should sell his vineyard to a non-Jew, an absolute sale of the land itself, with a written deed, for two years, the year prior to *shemitah* and the *shemitah* itself... the land and the trees to be controlled by the buyer like one who makes a permanent acquisition, but will then return it after the *shemitah* year.

17. *Torat Rabbenu Shmuel Salant* 1, 274. He also writes on p. 275: "I hereby notify his excellency that I have obtained a copy of *Shemen HaMor*, who was the Sephardi rabbi of Hebron over one hundred years ago." He briefly described the details of the *heter* for a temporary sale, adding that, in his opinion, the matter was impractical. Parenthetically, it should be noted that it was unnecessary to seek a copy of *Shemen HaMor* from as far as Berlin. A copy existed in Vilna,

Also, he added the opinion that the prohibition of *lo teḥonem* does not apply to Muslims – "The sale should be only to the Ishmaelites" – which is not mentioned in the *Shemen HaMor* or in the *Ikarei Dinim*. (See also section 4 below regarding Netziv.)

To summarize, the innovations of R. Yitzḥak Elḥanan, "who greatly innovated in order to reach a lenient opinion regarding giving gentiles land rights" (according to the testimony cited below), are not based on the specific considerations of *Shemen HaMor* and do not rely upon it. He did include it to strengthen his case ("I found a friend"), and in light of it, he delineated his requirement that the sale be for the two years in which the *shemitah* is included (it appears that this is the inference in R. Yitzḥak Elḥanan's words, "according to his suggestion"). But this is the extent of his connection to *Shemen HaMor*. The basis of his *heter* and his treatise were completed before *Shemen HaMor* reached him. Therefore, it is utterly impossible to claim that the *heter* depends on the conditions described in that responsum.

THE QUESTION OF R. YAAKOV LIFSHITZ'S INVOLVEMENT IN THE *HETER*

We know from several sources that R. Yonatan Eliashberg, son of Rabbi Mordekhai Eliashberg of Boisk, himself the *av bet din* of Wolkowysk, and formerly of Mariampol, was one of those who intervened with R. Yitzḥak Elḥanan Spektor on behalf of the *heter mekhirah*.[18] Several years ago, I found first-person corroboration of this in a letter from R. Eliashberg himself to R. Yeḥiel Mikhel Pines on December 29, 1887. His words are published here for the first time from the manuscript:[19]

> We have already dealt with the *shemitah* question. When I arrived in Kovno, I came before the gaon R. Yitzḥak Elḥanan and found that he had been asked about this by Rabbis Erlanger and Lubetzky and Tzadoc Kahn. After much discussion, he promised me that he would write a responsum the following day to fully permit the sale to non-Jews. This would enable our brethren to go up [i.e., to immigrate] to Eretz Yisrael. **He innovated in**

which R. Yeḥiel Mikhel Wolfson of Einshok consulted when authoring his own treatise on *shemitah*, *Shu"t Sefat HaYam* 2 (Vilna, 1888), 36, 40.

18. See the letter from Shmuel Yosef Fine to Yehudah Leib Pinsker, dated 23 Kislev 5448/December 9, 1887, *Ktavim L'Toldot Ḥibat Tziyon* 2 (Tel Aviv, 1925), cols. 401–2. Also, see letter dated February 10, 1888 (ibid, col. 486), and additional letters there, col. 669 and cols. 423–24.
19. Central Zionist Archives, A109/141. Toward the end, he writes: "In my opinion, it would be proper for the residents of Ekron to inquire of the Gaon of Brisk. I have no doubt that he, too, will come out leniently and not forbid it."

> **order to reach a lenient opinion regarding giving gentiles land rights.** After I left there, R. Yaakov Lifshitz came and told him that the rabbis of Jerusalem would be angry with this. Therefore, he wrote to me here that he himself – the gaon *av bet din* of Kovno – would write to the Jerusalem rabbis that he has a *heter* and that he wishes to hear their opinion.

This testimony completes the picture about what we know regarding R. Yitzḥak Elḥanan's turn to the Jerusalem rabbis. Conversely, it also adds to the rejection of a strange rumor that R. Yaakov Mark related about R. Yaakov Lifshitz, a confidant of R. Yitzḥak Elḥanan Spektor. According to this:[20]

> He revealed a secret to me, that he played a big part in the *heter* promulgated by R. Yitzḥak Elḥanan, because he had pressured R. Yitzḥak Elḥanan to give it. And if you will ask me: How does it make sense, that Yankel Lifshitz would try to help the Zionists? ... Evaluate for yourself, if the students from Kharkov [the men of Bil"u] returned and observed the commandment of *shemitah*.... I imagine that they would heap upon Yankel Lifshitz all the stones to be found in the streets of Kovno, for daring to speak ill of these great righteous men.... But their evil nature has pushed them into the mud and I have helped with that.

There are numerous problems with this bizarre, twisted story.[21] But in essence, the testimony of R. Eliashberg completely refutes it. It proves that R. Yaakov Lifshitz did try – as expected – to prevent the *heter*, not to support it in some kind of strange "reverse psychology." Even if Mark had heard something to that effect from him,[22] it should be viewed, at most, as a type of ironic joke, or perhaps, as

20. Yaakov Mark, *B'Meḥitzatam Shel Gedolei HaDor* (Jerusalem, 1958) 104. First published in Yiddish in the 1920s.
21. A more straightforward and trenchant idea was set forth by R. Zevulun Leib Britt, *av bet din* of Pelongian, in a letter printed in *Shivat Tziyon* (Warsaw, 1892), 51:

> Some *ḥaredim* disassociated from the Ḥovevei Tziyon group because they permitted work during *shemitah*. But in truth, if one is to complain about this, he can only do so by upholding the view that the Yishuv represents the beginning of the Redemption [*atḥalta d'geula*]. Only then could this be considered unworthy even if permissible, as the Torah explicitly states that the destruction came about through the sin of violation of *shemitah* by its inhabitants. However, for those who oppose this view and claim that the [danger to] the Yishuv is purely economic, it would certainly be proper to show concern for the poor and request the *heter*.

22. We can learn about Mark's credibility in these matters from another assertion of his, that "the tens of thousands of letters that emanated constantly with the signature of R. Yitzḥak Elḥanan

an expression of disappointment of one who realizes that behind his back, a dish was cooked not to his taste.

NETZIV'S OPINION ON SELLING LAND TO MUSLIMS

In a short article in the wake of the previous *shemitah*,[23] I mentioned the fact that the second half of Netziv's treatise on *shemitah* (*Shu"t Meishiv Davar* 2, *siman* 56, part 2) is not his own. It is a separate essay of R. Yehoshua Heschel Margaliyot, *av bet din* of Vishniev, published in 1888 in a corrected edition under the title *Kol HaTor Nishma B'Artzenu*. The fact that these were not the words of Netziv first came to light in 1984. Before that, it was assumed to be the work of Netziv, for after all, it was printed with his responsa. This was presumed even by the great rabbis who knew both men personally, such as R. Kook.[24] Even recently, various authors continue to attribute these words to Netziv, ignoring the newly available facts.

The most cited passage from R. Margaliyot that is attributed to Netziv is found in the introduction. In vivid language, he describes the difference between the weight of *shemitah* today versus the biblical prohibition of *lo teḥonem*:

> In reality, the aforementioned gaon escaped the wolf, only to be snared by the lion. He attempted to avoid the prohibition of *shemitah*, which most *poskim* hold to be rabbinic today, and was ensnared in the prohibition of selling land in Israel to idolaters, which all agree is a biblical prohibition.[25]

It has already been pointed out that the first part of this quote does not fit with the well-known position of Netziv regarding the applicability of *shemitah* laws

---

were almost all written by R. Yaakov Lifshitz. Many that were not worthy of being signed directly by R. Yitzḥak Elḥanan were signed by R. Lifshitz" (ibid., 102). Over the years, I have had the opportunity to see hundreds of letters and photocopies of letters from R. Yitzḥak Elḥanan Spektor, and I can count the number of them that were NOT in his handwriting on one hand. The letters we have regarding the *shemitah* are all written in his handwriting.

23. "*Ḥatzi Shel Kuntres HaShemitah Shel HaNetziv Eino Shelo*," *HaMa'ayan* 50:3 (Nisan 5760): 102–4. See also corrections in *HaMa'ayan* 50:4 (Tamuz 5760): 71–72.
24. See *Shu"t Mishpat Kohen*, *siman* 61. On his familiarity with Rav Margaliyot, see *Ḥavazelet* issue 83, (7 Iyar 5759/1999), 443. Similarly, R. Kook's disputant in the *shemitah* controversy, Rav Moshe Naḥum Wallenstein (who did not personally know Netziv) cited in his own work on *shemitah* from the same section of *Meshiv Davar*, and in parallel, a citation from Rav Margaliyot. See the treatise *Shabbat LaHaShem* at the end of *Bnei Moshe* (Jerusalem, 1990), 175.
25. In the original quote from *Kol HaTor Nishma B'Artzenu*, 22, it is clear that the "aforementioned author who escaped the wolf" was R. Alexander Moshe Lapidot. See his response to the objections of Rav Margaliyot in the compilation *Knesset HaGedolah* 1 (Warsaw, 1890), and now available in *Torat HaGaon Rabbi Alexander Moshe* (Lakewood, 2006), 128–29.

today, which he asserts is biblical, not rabbinic.[26] But the second part, regarding the prohibition of *lo teḥonem*, which prevents the land sale strategy, was already noted by those who negated the *heter mekhirah*, led by Ridbaz. In his *shemitah* treatise, he mentioned those who rely on the opinion that Ishmaelites are not considered "idolaters" in order to validate the sale. He writes that, "This opinion has already been nullified by the great gaon, Netziv *ztz"l*, and he is correct that they [Muslims] are not included in the category of *ger toshav*."[27]

However, in truth, not only is the first half of the quote incompatible with Netziv's opinion, but the second half, regarding *lo teḥonem*, is almost diametrically opposed to the true opinion of Netziv. In the continuation of his deliberations on the *heter mekhirah* in the original *shemitah* essay of his (i.e., the first half of *siman* 56 II), he agrees in theory that selling land to Muslims would not fall under the prohibition of *lo teḥonem* because they are not idolaters – a possibility that would be raised soon after by his student, R. Kook.[28] However, because Netziv held that working the land during *shemitah*, even today, would be considered biblically prohibited, this leniency would be useless, as the prohibition would extend even to working the fields of a non-Jew: "Even to sell to a non-Jew, **where it is possible to hold that the prohibition of *lo teḥonem* does not apply, because the Arabs are not idolaters**, in any event, a Jew is prohibited from plowing any land, even that owned by a non-Jew."

We see from here that, contrary to the accepted view, Netziv fundamentally accepted the possibility of selling the land to a non-Jew who is not an idolater in order to avoid the prohibition of *lo teḥonem*.

THE QUESTION OF *PIKUAḤ NEFESH* CONSIDERING THE SITUATION OF EKRON RESIDENTS DURING THE *SHEMITAH* OF 1888–89

One point of contention between those favoring the *heter mekhirah* and those opposed during the *shemitah* of 1888–89 was the question of whether or not

26. To be more precise – working the land is biblically prohibited. However, the sanctity of the *shemitah* produce is rabbinic: "It is impossible to marshal more voices unless we say that it is rabbinically prohibited, and not like our approach, in which it is prohibited biblically. However, with regard to the prohibition of the produce, we can marshal voices…" (see inside). *Or Same'aḥ* leans in a similar direction, in his responsa, vol. 2, *siman* 1.
27. *Kuntres HaShemitah L'Ridbaz* (Jerusalem, 1909), 12a. Even *Ḥazon Ish* eventually hinted at these words attributed to Netziv in his treatment of the subject of *lo teḥonem*: "On the contrary, the *shemitah* prohibition today is rabbinic and the sale is not biblical[ly prohibited] like a *treifa* or a milk/meat mixture, etc., as seen in *Meshiv Davar*, *siman* 56" (*Ḥazon Ish, Shevi'it, siman* 24:4).
28. Regarding R. Kook's opinion on this topic, see what I have previously written: "*Al Mekhirat Karka L'Goyim U'Michtav HaRabbanim,*" *HaMa'ayan* 52:2 (Tevet 5772): 113–15.

the settlements that would have to forego agricultural activity would be in life-threatening danger, even to the point of the collapse of the New Yishuv. This was the well-known opinion of those in favor from the Diaspora, led by R. Yitzḥak Elḥanan Spektor, as mentioned in the documents permitting the *heter*. Against them was the claim that this opinion was based on lack of knowledge as to the true facts on the ground in the Land of Israel. To quote Ridbaz: "With trickery and deceit, they led astray the great gaon R. Yitzḥak Elḥanan of Kovno *ztz"l* by suggesting to him that if they were to observe the *shemitah*, it would endanger lives."[29] Therefore, when R. Mordekhai Gimpel Yafeh made aliyah in 1888 and lived in the agricultural settlement of Yehud, his opposition to the *heter* intensified. He wrote that now it was clearly evident to him that there was no impending life-threatening danger: "The din of lying voices cried out that observing *shemitah* would lead to life-threatening danger. It was only for this reason that many great *ge'onim* of the Diaspora found ways to be lenient due to their faraway location."[30] On the other hand, there were rabbinic authorities in Eretz Yisrael who held that this was a life-and-death question for the settlements, as R. Yaakov Elyashar wrote: "The settlements might be destroyed because of their owners abandoning them... and the whole Yishuv will be destroyed." In general, it is difficult to find proof for the claim that the *gedolim* of the Diaspora who were involved in the *heter* were not fully updated on the happenings in the Land of Israel.[31]

In practice, within those settlements that observed the *shemitah* prohibitions, the first being Mazkeret Batya (Ekron), there did arise grave life-threatening circumstances. These were a result of the conflict between settlement families who wanted to observe *shemitah* according to the rulings of the Ashkenazi Jerusalem rabbis, and the representatives of Baron Rothschild, who expected them to rely on the *heter*.[32] This illustrates, on the one hand, that the concerns of those favoring the *heter* for life-threatening conditions and the destruction of the Yishuv were well-founded. On the other hand, it is reasonable to argue – as did the

29. Introduction to *Bet Ridbaz*. Compare to R. Yaakov Orenstein at the end of *Davar B'Ito* (Jerusalem, 5449/1889), p. 16: "Even though the fools of this generation tricked the gaon [R. Yitzḥak Elḥanan] *shlit"a* and suggested to him that there was immediate danger to life if he did not permit working the land during *shemitah*..." (This detail is not the only one shared by the two accounts. Enough said for now.)
30. See article by R. Bezalel Landau, "*Igeret Rabbi Mordekhai Gimpel Yafeh MiYehud L'Ḥatano HaRi"z Stern BiDvar HaShemitah,*" *HaMa'ayan* 13:1 (Tishrei 5773): 9–18.
31. For specifics, see previous chapter (the quote from R. Elyashar is to be found there as well). There is more to add to the article regarding R. Yisrael Yehoshua Trunk of Kutna, author of *Yeshuot Malko*.
32. See Aḥiezer Arkin, *Naḥshonei HaShemitah* (Mazkeret Batya, 1994).

prohibiting side – that the danger could have been averted had all the effort been focused on convincing Baron Rothschild to increase his support for the settlements, along with encouraging all Jews to increase their donations to the Yishuv during the *shemitah* year.[33]

Either way, we are publicizing a letter that appears here for the first time (as far as I know) from R. Naftali Hertz HaLevi, *av bet din* of Jaffa, that describes in vivid color the existential crisis and life-threatening conditions that prevailed during the course of the 1889 *shemitah*:[34]

> *B"H,* Monday of *Parashat Va'era,* 5649 [29 December 1888], Jaffa
>
> Greetings to the great gaon, Shmuel Mohilever, *n"y*
>
> After inquiring as to your well-being, the men bearing this letter from …[35] were afflicted by God in leaving their homes in Russia and coming to settle the Holy Land. Before they even took their first steps on their land and before tasting the nectar of its fruits and the produce of the fields, a spirit of mistrust reigned between them and the administration. To this day, they stand naked, with nothing, with some of them on the brink of starvation as they will describe to His Honor. They are around two hundred men, many of whom risked their lives just in order to observe the *shemitah*. For this reason, they beg of Your Honor to advise them what to do. Please strengthen their spirits, which have fallen as a result of the crushing pressure and poverty, and perhaps God will provide Your Honor with the correct guidance for them, because a sage such as yourself has the advice and resourcefulness.

---

33. As described by Netziv at the end of his treatise. Those who sided with the *heter* believed, apparently, that it would be imprudent to rely on such means to sustain the communities and settlers for a full year (It is possible that they also held that it would be improper to ask Baron Rothschild et al., to fund the strict interpretation of law when there was a viable option in place, in the form of the *heter* – a form of "*kim li*" [a halakhic argument in which a disputant cannot be forced to spend funds when he can claim to hold by a halakhically viable side to a dispute] – see *Shu"t Ḥatam Sofer, Yoreh De'ah, siman* 334). Also see letter from R. Yitzḥak Elḥanan Spektor to R. Tzadoc Kahn from the winter of 1888 (see above, n. 8), dealing with the idea to convince the Baron to support the settlements instead of relying upon the *heter*. This topic requires a full treatment of its own.
34. The letter, in R. Hertz's handwriting on ordinary paper, was recently displayed at a public auction.
35. The word is not clear in the manuscript.

> I also traveled to Yehud to confer with the gaon R. Mordecai [Yafeh] because the danger to the colonists is dire, God have mercy. But after returning here, I decided not to persevere further for several reasons. And I leave it to Your Honor to consider and offer advice, to them and also to the other colonists. Perhaps, if I see there is hope, I will journey to Jerusalem, *bli neder*.
>
> Signed – Naftali Hertz HaLevi of Jaffa

It seems that this is what R. Kook meant when he wrote to Ridbaz, that "during the first *shemitah*, when the strict opinion prevailed in Ekron, I saw that they wrote a letter begging for support because there were actual cases of deaths by starvation, God forbid, there."[36]

REGARDING THE *HETER* DUE TO PUBLIC WELFARE CONSIDERATIONS

As explained above, the *heter* was first initiated to address the fear of the viability of the Yishuv and its population if they had to survive through an entire year of refraining from agricultural work. According to those who permitted it, this fear extended throughout the years of the British Mandate, when the Yishuv was far from economically independent and there were many whose entire livelihood depended on agriculture.[37] Over the years, especially after the founding of the State, conditions in Eretz Yisrael changed several times. Nevertheless, the permitting group pointed out various reasons for continuing the *heter* as warranted by the new conditions.[38]

---

36. *Igrot HaRa'ayah* 2, p. 190 (Letter 555, Sivan 1913).
37. Prior to the *shemitah* of 1931, R. Kook again wrote, "The basis of the *heter mekhirah* is only in the context of a *hora'at sha'ah* [temporary ruling] and pressing circumstances, in order to save our settlements from destruction, God forbid" (*Shu"t Mishpat Kohen, siman* 73). R. Reuven Katz wrote something similar prior to the *shemitah* of 1938: "In truth, the *gedolim* only permitted it during a time of pressing circumstances. And there is no time of pressing circumstances greater than what we face today" (*Kuntres Erekh Shevii't* [Jerusalem, 1937], 41; also see R. Ben Tziyon Meir Ḥai Uziel, ibid., 27). At the start of the following *shemitah*, in 1944, R. Tzvi Pesaḥ Frank wrote: "Only in recent years has it become apparent that today we are faced with tremendous *she'at hadeḥak*,, to the point that we do not have the wherewithal to uphold the commandment of *shemitah* as written" (marginal note in his approbation to *Ma'adanei Eretz* [Jerusalem, 1944]; compare this to R. Shemayah of Zlichov regarding "Times of stress and emergency, such as what we currently face in the Holy Land, may God have mercy" in *Moriah* 30:5–7 [Nisan 2010]: 52).
38. For a list of those who permit it in the generation following the establishment of the State, see "*La'Amitah Shel Shemitah,*" *Alonei Mamrei* 121 (Kiryat Arba, 2008), 42–45 in the footnotes. Regarding R. Shaul Yisraeli, one should take into account his responsa in *Shu"t Sho'alin*

One reason that was mentioned throughout the years was the need to keep people from sinning or stumbling. There is a well-known Talmudic dictum[39] that it is better to permit meat of a ritually slaughtered dying animal (although unsavory),[40] than to permit the meat of an animal that was not ritually slaughtered and died of itself. In the earliest *shemitah* years, this reasoning was directed toward the farmers. Without the *heter*, they were likely to work their fields as usual, thereby violating an absolute Torah prohibition. But in the later years, this reasoning was directed to the general public, consumers of the agricultural produce, who were, for the most part, not observant. At a time when a large portion of the public is not observant, and with many farmers violating the prohibition anyway, the produce flooding the country without the continued use of the *heter mekhirah* would inadvertently cause the masses to sin. This was expressed in our generation by R. Ovadiah Yosef:

> Had the Chief Rabbinate not used its authority to permit the sale of the land, they [ed. note: the farmers] would have conducted themselves sinfully, as they did all the years. They would have worked their fields without the sale and sold their produce throughout the land, thereby causing the innocent to sin. By utilizing the sale to non-Jews we save the masses of Israel from stumbling on *shemitah* prohibitions.[41]

It is clear that this reasoning was not born with the founding of the modern State of Israel. It was brought up during the Mandatory years against the backdrop of the expansion of Jewish farming and distribution of Jewish produce throughout an increasingly Jewish consumer population. Perhaps the first to proffer this line of reasoning was R. Ze'ev Wolf Twersky of Rachmastrivka in reservations to his 1937 approbation of *Bnei Tziyon* by Rabbi David Shapira:

> And he cited all the foundations of the *heter* from all the great rabbis and refuted them with clear proofs.... And he generally came out against it.

V'Dorshin 3, *siman* 67; also "*Sefikhei Shevi'it*," *Alonei Mamrei* 122 (5769/2009), 206 in a footnote. In addition to all those mentioned there, R. Hanoch Zundel Grossberg, who participated in the *heter* for the *shemitah* of 1966 – see *HaTorah V'ha'Aretz* 8 (5768/2008), 313.

39. Kiddushin 22a.

40. Ed. note: Meat of a dying animal is technically permitted, although unsavory, because of the chance that the animal might recover with proper medical treatment. See *Seridei Esh* 2:4.

41. *Shu"t Yabia Omer* 10, *Yoreh De'ah, siman* 38 (before that, he mentions the reason based on supporting the farmers). Before him, Rav Yeḥiel Mikhel Tukachinsky wrote in the same vein, *Sefer HaShemitah* 2, ch. 3:20, "Most farmers will not submit to the rulings of the rabbis.... They will transgress and perform all the work in the fields, causing the community to sin by eating *shemitah* produce." (See also ch. 5.)

> However, I do not agree. Rather, let the great rabbis reinforce the *heter* that is still in place, selling the land to the non-Jews, legally or otherwise, after reading [what I have written in] *Bnei Tziyon.*[42] There might be a slight violation in the selling of the land, but this is what the Sages meant when they said (Eruvin 32b) that it is better for a scholar to violate a minor prohibition than let the ignorant violate a major one. **Because the kibbutzim and the settlers on the lands of the JNF who are irreligious will not listen to the rabbis and will plant without *heterim,* and this will cause the public to unwittingly sin with fruits of the sabbatical year.** In pressing circumstances (*she'at hadeḥak*), we can rely on a minority opinion to be lenient.[43]

Rabbi Twersky finished by saying, "But one who wishes to observe *shemitah* properly has performed a great thing and has sanctified God. God is sure to reward him doubly... In the merits of those who observe *shemitah* even in today's times, may He bring the complete Redemption soon."

CONCLUSION

The reader might ask himself, "What is the upshot of all this? For or against the *heter mekhirah?*" That question is irrelevant to this discussion. The personal opinion of this writer as a matter of public halakhic policy matters not a whit. The message here, as with the previous articles that I wrote on this topic, is different: One must clarify the facts honestly to the fullest possible extent, and be careful not to misrepresent them one way or the other, consciously or otherwise, in order to buttress the desired outcome. This is what has occurred, sadly, in a great many of the materials that have been written (and continue to be written) on the topic of *shemitah.* The real world tends by nature to be nuanced, for which reason the tendency to describe historical data as if they all, from beginning to end, support a specific contemporary position is a far cry from the pursuit of truth.

---

42. Apparently, he means that after the rabbis read *Bnei Tziyon* against the *heter mekhirah,* which contains a compelling argument, they should still feel obliged to promulgate the *heter* in one form or another in order to save the masses, etc.
43. *Shu"t Bnei Tziyon* 2 (Jerusalem, 1955), introduction. (See, in contrast, the approbation of R. Shlomo Zalman Ehrenreich of Simleu [the Shimloyer Rav].) Subsequently, he added another reason: "In the current prevailing conditions, there is a concern that if they don't plant, it is possible that the Arabs will steal the land and plant; and afterward, it will be difficult to recover the land from them. Even according to the author of *Bnei Tziyon,* this would be permissible according to most *poskim.*"

Chapter 17

The *Arukh HaShulḥan* and His Rabbinic Ordination of R. Avraham Yitzḥak HaKohen Kook[1]

Many people are ignorant of the fact that not only did R. Yeḥiel Mikhel Epstein ordain R. Avraham Yitzḥak HaKohen Kook but that he was the only rabbi who did so. For this reason, as we shall see, this *semikhah* played a central role in R. Kook gaining his first rabbinic post. This lack of awareness is no surprise since anyone who leafs through Simcha Raz's popular book about R. Kook, *Angel Among Men*, will discover that not only does R. Epstein's ordination go entirely unmentioned but also the individual seemingly involved in R. Kook's appointment to the rabbinate in the town of Zeimel [Zeimelis] was none other than R. Yisrael Meir HaKohen from Radin (*Ḥafetz Ḥayim*), the author of the *Mishnah Berurah*. Raz writes as follows:[2]

1. Translated by Meshulam Gotlieb. This article was written on 22 Adar Bet [5768], one hundred years after R. Y. M. Epstein's demise (1829–1908). This chapter was published in the author's *Ta'arokh Lefanai Shulḥan* (Jerusalem, 2018).
2. S. Raz, *Angel Among Men* (Jerusalem, 1994), 13.

> When they were sitting together, the illustrious rabbi, the author of *Ḥafetz Ḥayim,* turned to him.... "My request," said *Ḥafetz Ḥayim,* "is for you to become a rabbi among the Jewish people." "Your work as a rabbi" – continued the *Ḥafetz Ḥayim* – "is even more important to me than your work in the Laws of *Kodashim.* **There is a rabbinic position available in the town of Zeimel, please allow me to put in a good word, and I hope they will accept you with love and respect."** Several days after his meeting with *Ḥafetz Ḥayim,* the community of Zeimel approached the Rav [R. Kook] and offered him the rabbinic post.

The story that Raz bases himself on – according to which *Ḥafetz Ḥayim* asked R. Avraham Yitzḥak HaKohen Kook not to reject a rabbinic post – is admittedly based on R. Tzvi Yehudah HaKohen [Kook]'s testimony: "He had no desire whatsoever to accept the rabbinic position; however, he was forced to do so by the request of the illustrious sage, R. Yisrael Meir HaKohen, *Ḥafetz Ḥayim ztz"l* who happened to visit Ponevezh in 1887 and spoke with him about committing to studying the laws of *kodashim,* who persuaded him to accept it."[3]

However, the bolded passage, which records that *Ḥafetz Ḥayim* himself reported that he advised R. Kook to serve as the rabbi of Zeimel, is baseless.[4] The true story of R. Kook's appointment to the rabbinate in Zeimel appears in the journal of his father-in-law, R. Eliyahu David Rabinowitz-Teomim ("Aderet"). He provides an entirely different rationale for R. Kook's motivation to search for a rabbinic post:

> At that time my son-in-law recognized my penury and realized that there was insufficient room in my household for him; therefore, he decided to accept a rabbinic post in whatever city happened to turn up.... For this

---

3. *Kuntres L'Sheloshah B'Elul* (Jerusalem, 1938), 7. See also *Shivḥei HaRa'ayah* (Jerusalem, 1979), 54.
4. *Ḥafetz Ḥayim* himself, in a letter he wrote to Aderet on this matter, writes: "I received a letter from my friend... who wrote me that his son-in-law, the rabbi and illustrious sage [R. Avraham Yitzḥak Hakohen Kook] was appointed as rabbi and head of the *bet din* in the town of Zeimel, and my heart rejoiced greatly over this. May HaShem grant that he goes ever upward. for he is a true Torah giant" (*Tal HaRa'ayah* [Kfar Haro'eh, 1985], 100–101). *Ḥafetz Ḥayim* doesn't even hint at the fact that he took part in the appointment process. We should note, however, that Raz was probably not the source of the fabrication. Two months after R. Kook's demise R. Ḥayim Karlinski wrote a brief biographical article, in which he related that R. Avraham Yitzḥak HaKohen "was appointed as rabbi of Zhoimel through the influence of *Ḥafetz Ḥayim*" (*HaYehudi,* 1 [New York, Tishrei 1935], 22).

> purpose he sent a messenger to the city of Zeimel, which had no rabbi. This man implored us both to travel there as soon as possible, and so we did.[5]

In a following passage, R. Rabinowitz-Teomim relates that when they reached Zeimel they proceeded to the house of the communal leader, R. Matityah Ḥayut and spoke with him at length. The following day, R. Kook delivered a public sermon. This is also recounted in a book by R. Aharon Ḥayut, the son of the community's head,[6] who provides a lengthy description of the extent to which R. Rabinowitz-Teomim went to convince the community members of R. Kook's worthiness, for while impressed by R. Kook, they were concerned he was too young for the position.[7] R. Rabinowitz-Teomim describes the incident thus:

> And he impressed them, and they were satisfied with my assurances that he was worthy of deciding Jewish law, and I also showed them the *semikhah* he received from the illustrious sage of Novardok when he was still unmarried, which he had never even shown me. And… I told them that they could be certain that in a few years… their own standing would be elevated by his standing. They immediately appointed him rabbi with pomp and circumstance… and I wept bitterly that my sins had forced him to accept a rabbinic post in the spring of his days because of my duress and penury.

---

5. From this we may conclude that R. Rabinowitz-Teomim probably did not know the story told by R. Tzvi Yehudah Kook about *Ḥafetz Ḥayim*'s request, even though the story apparently took place in his house in Ponevezh! "Therefore, he decided to accept a rabbinic post in whatever city happened to turn up" – because R. Rabinowitz-Teomim could not support him any longer, not because the *Ḥafetz Ḥayim* had previously asked him to enter the rabbinate…. R. Moshe Tzvi Neriyah already sensed this contradiction and he reconciled the two stories by explaining that, at first, R. Kook acceded to the *Ḥafetz Ḥayim*'s request that if he was offered a rabbinic post, he would not reject it, while later he actively searched for a rabbinic post, as R. Rabinowitz-Teomim relates (*Tal HaRa'ayah*, 90). Whatever the case may be, clearly R. Rabinowitz-Teomim did not know anything about his son-in-law's conversation with *Ḥafetz Ḥayim*, so he was distraught by the fact that his son-in-law had to take the heavy yoke of the rabbinate on his shoulders because of his own poverty.
6. *Shishim V'Shalosh Shana B'Yerushalayim* (Jerusalem, 1953), 10, and *Shivḥei HaRa'ayah*, 57–58.
7. R. Aharon Ḥayut even exaggerated, writing that his father "was the one who initiated and implemented the appointment of R. Kook" – a claim that contradicts his own testimony in *Shivḥei HaRa'ayah*, and also does not fit in with R. Rabinowitz-Teomim's remarks in his journal. Apparently Ḥayut was writing as a son praising his father, and the kernel of truth at the heart of the story is that his father was the key player in persuading Zeimel's other communal leaders to accept R. Kook notwithstanding the concerns.

Thus, we see that two factors helped R. Kook receive the rabbinic post in Zeimel. Firstly, his father-in-law's persuasion, and secondly the *semikhah* he had received in his youth from R. Epstein, which until now he had even hidden from his father-in-law due to his tremendous humility. Shouldn't the fact that R. Epstein's *semikhah* helped R. Kook receive his first rabbinic post be worthy of mention in books like *Angel Among Men*? Apparently Raz and others preferred to enhance the story by associating the ordination with the more famous and revered figure of the *Ḥafetz Ḥayim.*

Now, let's address the very nature of R. Epstein's *semikhah,* in and of itself. Exactly when and how did R. Kook receive it? Here too, we find two conflicting versions, and as we will see, R. Rabinowitz-Teomim's version may again help us verify the correct one.

The first version, brought by R. Moshe Tzvi Neriyah in a work based on "oral accounts and written remarks" gives no source (*Siḥot HaRa'ayah* [Tel Aviv, 1979], 103–4). According to what is told, in the winter of 1885, R. Epstein came to Volozhin to visit his brother-in-law, Netziv (R. Naftali Tzvi Yehudah Berlin). The latter hastened to introduce him to his cherished student, R. Kook. R. Epstein proceeded to engage him in halakhic give-and-take and was very impressed by him. R. Neriyah adds that R. Kook was wholly immersed in the world of learning and it never occurred to him to ask for ordination; however, the guest thought otherwise: it was not every day that there appeared before him a young Torah scholar who was so deserving of being ordained with two hands. However, he did not grant the ordination immediately, preferring to invest the matter with a festive air – and in keeping with this [decision] he chose to surprise him [R. Kook] by sending him "a novel *mishloaḥ manot*" on Purim: rabbinic ordination empowering him *ladun u'lehorot* [to judge and to rule upon halakhic matters].[8]

Pinḥas Hamburger relates an entirely different version, ascribing the story he tells to what is presumably the most authoritative source – R. Kook himself.[9] He relates that he heard the following from R. Kook in the winter of 1931:

8. R. Neriyah even quotes ostensibly the words "*yoreh yoreh, yadin yadin* etc., as one of the illustrious rabbis" from the rabbinic ordination certificate; however, we should not conclude that he actually had the document in his possession, for if that were the case, he would have published it in one of his books. This "quote" was probably taken from the same anonymous source the story was found in.

9. "*Zikhron Ra'ayah,*" *Sinai* 97 (Jerusalem, 1987), 246.

> I will tell you something that no one knows, for if you go to Jaffa Street tomorrow and ask whether R. Kook has rabbinic ordination and how many ordinations he has, doubtless they will tell you that he certainly has been ordained several times. However, this is not the case, for I never received rabbinic ordination, but when I went to be appointed to my first rabbinic post in Zeimel, my father and teacher and my other acquaintances told me that it was not fitting to be appointed to a rabbinic post without *semikhah.* So on my way to Zeimel, I stopped in Novardok and received my one and only ordination from the illustrious sage R. Yeḥiel Mikhel Epstein *ztz"l* the author of the *Arukh HaShulḥan* – and [I received] no other.

First of all, this version attests to the fact that R. Epstein did not himself initiate giving *semikhah* to R. Kook; rather, R. Kook, at his father's behest, approached him and asked for it. Second, and most importantly, according to Hamburger's testimony, R. Kook did not receive the ordination in his youth; rather, he got it on the way to his appointment as rabbi in Zeimel. Note that R. Rabinowitz-Teomim clearly attests in a journal written at that very time that the ordination was granted when he "was still a *boḥur*" – that is to say, before he was married, and certainly not during his journey to Zeimel.[10] Furthermore, the journey from Ponevezh to Zeimel passes nowhere near Novarkok. If so, how can we reconcile Hamburger's version? Presumably, R. Kook told Hamburger something about R. Y. M. Epstein's ordination helping him obtain the rabbinic post in Zeimel – as R. Rabinowitz-Teomim wrote – but since Hamburger only transcribed this conversation decades later, he mixed up the details and recorded them inaccurately.

On the other hand, R. Neriyah's story about R. Y. M. Epstein initiating the ordination and ensuring that it arrived precisely on Purim as *mishloaḥ manot* is far too romantic a tale to be believed, and, as we have mentioned above, the tale has no source. Here too, we may assume that the kernel of the story is true, and that after meeting R. Kook in Volozhin, R. Epstein sent R. Kook a certificate of *semikhah* in the mail – that may have even arrived on or near Purim – but not because R. Epstein intended to surprise R. Kook and/or send him the ordination as a form of *mishloaḥ manot.*

10. It should be noted that several other rabbis born in Griva – R. Kook's birthplace – were ordained by R. Epstein, among them R. Shmaryahu Leib Horowitz (see *Kitvei He'Arukh HaShulḥan, siman* 89) and R. Yaakov Binyamin Ze'ev Yakimowsky (see ibid., *siman* 94). This suggests that asking R. Yeḥiel Mikhel Epstein for *semikhah* was quite common in R. Kook's milieu "when he was an unmarried youth" – another clue to the circumstances in which he received *semikhah.*

We should note that *Oholei Shem,* which was written in R. Kook's lifetime, reports that R. Kook received rabbinic ordination from Netziv too. However, this is incorrect. R. Kook certainly studied with Netziv, who was perhaps the Torah personality with the greatest influence upon him, as R. Neriyah heard from him;[11] but he never asked for, nor ever received, rabbinic ordination from him, as he related to Hamburger.

In closing, I will note two explicit mentions by R. Kook of the rabbi who ordained him, R. Epstein. Firstly, on the tombstone of Batya Miril Berlin – R. Epstein's daughter and the second wife of Netziv. The language, which was composed by R. Kook, mentions "the true gaon, our master Mikhel HaLevi Epstein *ztz"l,* the illustrious sage, the head of the rabbinic court of Novardok."[12] Secondly, in one of his responsa, R. Kook wrote about R. Y. M. Epstein: "And behold, the esteemed Torah scholar relied upon the ruling of the author of the *Arukh HaShulḥan,* who was lenient in this matter even without the presence of two poles and he, *z"l,* is worthy of being relied upon in pressing circumstances."[13]

11. *Tal HaRa'ayah,* 66.
12. *Siḥot HaRa'ayah,* 109.
13. *Shu"t Oraḥ Mishpat* (Jerusalem, 1985), end of *siman* 78.

Chapter 18

R. Kook's Attitude Toward Keren Hayesod – United Israel Appeal[1]

The philosophy of R. Elḥanan Bunem Wasserman, may HaShem avenge his blood, follower of the Ḥafetz Ḥayim and rosh yeshiva of the Baranovich Yeshiva in Lithuania, and among the most extreme anti-Zionists of Eastern European Torah leaders between the two World Wars, is still considered today as having significant influence on the prevalent "Lithuanian" ḥaredi attitudes toward Zionism and the State of Israel. In this respect, he constitutes almost an antithesis to the first Chief Rabbi of Eretz Yisrael, R. Avraham Yitzḥak HaKohen Kook, in whose philosophy religious Zionism found its main ideological footing.[2]

1. Translated by Rachelle Emanuel. The chapter has been abridged by the author's mother. Readers wishing greater detail, including a rebuttal of Prof. Menachem Friedman *z"l*'s assertion that R. Kook supported Keren Hayesod, are referred to the original article, published in *HaMa'ayan* 51:4 (Tamuz 5771).
2. It is interesting to note that R. Wasserman, as a youth, was privileged to learn from R. Kook for a while. In 1890, R. Wasserman's family moved to Bauska (Boisk), where five years later R. Kook was appointed as rabbi of the town. At the time Rabbi Wasserman was a student in Yeshivat Telz, and when he returned home during vacation, he would participate in the classes given by R. Kook. See R. Zev Aryeh Rabbiner, "*Shalosh Kehilot Kodesh,*" *Yahadut Latvia: Sefer Zikaron* (Tel Aviv, 1953), 268; Aharon Surasky, *Ohr Elḥanan* I (Jerusalem, 1978), 30.

A rare statement of R. Wasserman, aimed apparently at R. Kook, found resonance with a portion of the ḥaredi public, and is used to justify rejecting R. Kook and his teachings. The words appear in a letter from June 25, 1924 to R. Yosef Tzvi Dushinski, who took over R. Yosef Ḥayim Sonnenfeld's position as head of the Edah Ḥaredit:

> A proposal has been made to combine the ḥaredi *bet din* with the Chief Rabbinate. It is well known that he who heads [the Chief Rabbinate] has written and signed on a manifesto calling on Jews to contribute to Keren Hayesod. It is also known that the funds of Keren Hayesod go toward educating intentional heretics. If that is the case, he who encourages supporting this organization causes the public to commit the worst sin. Rabbenu Yonah in *Sha'arei Teshuvah* explains the verse "The refining pot is for silver, and the furnace for gold, and a man is judged by his praise" (Mishlei 27:21), that the test of a person is what he praises. If we see that he praises the wicked, we know that he is an utterly evil person, and it is clearly forbidden to associate with such an individual.[3]

As far as R. Wasserman was concerned, because the head of the Chief Rabbinate publicized statements calling for support of Keren Hayesod, which among other activities, funded the secular-Zionist education system, he was causing the public to sin and it was forbidden to be associated with him.[4]

---

3. *Kovetz Ma'amarim V'Igrot* I (Jerusalem, 2001), 153; previously in *Kuntres B'Ein Ḥazon* (Jerusalem, 1969), 92. Concerning R. Wasserman's dealing with issues in Eretz Yisrael, R. Ḥayim Ozer Grodzenski, R. Wasserman's brother-in-law, wrote less than two months later in a reply to R. Reuven Katz's complaint regarding the open letter published by R. Wasserman to Poalei Agudath Israel in Eretz Yisrael, calling on them not to accept help from Zionist organizations: "I, too, am surprised at what [R. Wasserman] saw that he publicized his personal opinion without consulting us, and I did not know of it. He also exaggerated. The matters of the Yishuv in Eretz Yisrael cannot be compared to private matters in the Diaspora for several reasons, and certainly it is impossible to give a ruling on so serious a matter from afar without knowing the details" (*Aḥiezer – Kovetz Igrot* [Bnei Brak, 1970], 1:299. For R. Wasserman's open letter and more material on this subject, see *Kovetz Ma'amarim V'Igrot* I, 133–52).
4. This statement is based on the words of Rabbenu Yonah Gerondi (*Sha'arei Teshuvah*, 3:148), and R. Wasserman's interpretation of them elsewhere (*Ikveta D'Meshiḥa, siman* 36, translated from the Yiddish by R. Moshe Schonfeld and printed as a pamphlet in 1942, and in *Kovetz Ma'amarim* [Jerusalem, 1963], 127–28). However, it seems that there is a substantive difference between the words of Rabbenu Yonah and R. Wasserman's interpretation (compare with a parallel commentary of Rabbenu Yonah to *Avot* 4:6, and the way his words were interpreted by Rashbatz, *Magen Avot* 4:8, and R. Yisrael Alnekave, *Menorat HaMa'or*, Enlau edition, 310–11), and let this suffice. For an example of the reverse position, see: R. Tzadok HaKohen, *Pri Tzaddik*, Vayikra (Lublin, 1922), 221.

However, it seems that R. Wasserman's biting assertion is based on a factual error.[5] According to R. Kook's son, R. Tzvi Yehudah Kook, his father supported, and called upon others to support, Keren **Kayemet** L'Yisrael, but not Keren **Hayesod.**

> As a result of [his] demands and complaints about their behavior regarding religion ... [R. Kook] put on hold expressing support for Keren Hayesod; and none of the entreaties and efforts of Keren Hayesod's activists could move him. By contrast, although he constantly protested concerning those same claims and complaints, he never hesitated giving words of support to Keren Kayemet. None of the entreaties and efforts of those who opposed Keren Kayemet could change ... his support and encouragement for Keren Kayemet considering its projects as mitzvah of redeeming and conquering the land.[6]

If these words are correct, R. Wasserman's protest loses ground. In light of the above we would have to say that R. Wasserman's biting statement about R. Kook relies on a rickety foundation of rumors ("It is well known ...") that were rife in certain localities in Eastern Europe.[7] However, precise research shows that despite Rav Tzvi Yehudah Kook's clear testimony, for which we will bring below explicit

---

5. See R. Yitzchak Dadon, *Imrei Shefer* (Jerusalem, 2008), 273.
6. "*LiShelosha B'Elul*" (Jerusalem, 1938), *siman* 24 (p. 22). See also *Siḥot HaRav Tzvi Yehudah – Eretz Yisrael* (Jerusalem, 2005), 84. On the other hand, R. Shmuel HaKohen Weingarten, who also heard from R. Tzvi Yehudah about his father's refusal to call for support of Keren Hayesod, pointed out an item in the newspaper *Dos Idishe Likht* (May 23, 1924), according to which R. Kook adamantly refused to support a proposal raised at the Agudas Harabonim convention to boycott Keren Hayesod (*Halikhot* 33 [Tel Aviv, Tishrei 1966], 27). Compare with R. Kook's reasons for not waging a public war against the Gymnasia HaIvrit high school, despite his vehement opposition to the school (*Igrot HaRa'ayah* 2, 160–61).
7. The falsity of rumors about R. Kook was mentioned already in 1921 by the Gerrer Rebbe, R. Avraham Mordekhai Alter, in his well-known letter written on the boat:

   > What is imagined abroad is unlike the reality. According to hearsay [abroad], the gaon R. Kook was considered an enlightened rabbi who ran after bribes. He was excommunicated and cursed. Even the newspapers *HaYud* and *HaDerekh* sometimes published these one-sided reports. But this is not the correct way – to listen to one side, no matter who it is (*Osef Mikhtavim U'Devarim* [Warsaw, 1937], 68).

   R. Moshe Tzvi Neriya's description is typical:

   These rumors even made their way into sealed Russia. They said: "He's close to the high echelons and has an official position." This automatically excluded him from being seen as a great rabbi. And then again it was said, "He's close to the Zionists"... All those figments of the imagination melted away on seeing him. (*Likutei HaRa'ayah* [Kefar Haro'eh, 1991], 1:13–14).

   A strikingly similar description was written by R. Yitzchak Gerstenkorn, founder of Bnei Brak: "I imagined R. Kook *ztz"l* as a modern rabbi [...] and how thunderstruck I was, on my first visit

references from R. Kook himself, R. Wasserman's words were not based on rumor alone. It turns out that even while R. Kook was alive, propaganda attempts were made to attribute to him support for Keren Hayesod. In one case, at least, it was intentional fraud, upon which it seems R. Wasserman unwittingly based himself.

BETWEEN KEREN KAYEMET L'YISRAEL (JNF) AND KEREN HAYESOD (UNITED ISRAEL APPEAL)

Whatever the case may be, the reader will ask: What's the big difference between Keren Kayemet and Keren Hayesod? Perhaps in R. Wasserman's opinion they both were "abominations," since both organizations were headed by "heretics"; and although Keren Kayemet did not deal with education, nevertheless it enabled freethinkers to settle on its land. If that were the case, supporting Keren Kayemet would fall into the category of lauding the wicked, etc. However, one cannot ignore the fact that R. Wasserman was talking about Keren Hayesod in particular, on the grounds that its funds were "going toward raising willful secularists" in the educational institutions – something not relevant to the activity of Keren Kayemet. Keren Kayemet had been founded at the beginning of the century for very specific, broadly accepted goals – redeeming land from the hands of gentiles, while Keren Hayesod was established in the early twenties in a very different political climate, and with a broad mandate. R. Kook himself, in a response from winter 1925 to the famous letter from four ḥasidic rebbes (Ger, Sokolov, Ostrovtza, and Radzhin) who had heard that "Your Honor is indignant over our opposition to giving aid to the Keren Kayemet and Keren Hayesod," gave his reasons in full for supporting Keren Kayemet, and only Keren Kayemet.[8] In an earlier draft of

---

to R. Kook, when I saw before me a holy tzaddik, among the few in our times" (*Zikhronotai al Bnei Brak* I [Jerusalem, 1942], 74).

8. See *Igrot LaRa'ayah*, 303–6. See also his 1923 declaration in support of Keren Kayemet in which he emphasizes that "it is meant *only* for redemption of the land" (Raz, *Malakhim Kivnei Adam* [Jerusalem, 1994], 238) – i.e., not for educational and other purposes like those of Keren Hayesod. It should be noted that there were sometimes strained relations between Keren Kayemet and Keren Hayesod because of the impression that the latter also dealt in redeeming lands (see *Protokolim Shel Yeshivot HaKeren Kayemet L'Yisrael*, Central Zionist Archives, Jerusalem, 4:109, 498/33 – protocols from March 31 and July 7, 1922; see also the arrangement between the two funds, *HaOlam* 10:14 [January 27, 1921], 16). Keren Kayemet's standing among substantial parts of the rabbinical world is brought home by the resolution of Agudas Harabonim's thirty-second annual convention in the US and Canada, 1937, stating: "Agudas Harabonim imposes a sacred debt on all Orthodox Jews to generously support Keren Kayemet L'Yisrael." It should be noted that the majority of America's great rabbis of the time participated in this convention. (See *HaYehudi* 2:10 [New York, Iyar 1927], 195. Previous conventions too passed similar resolutions; see, for example, *HaPardes* 5:3 [Sivan 1931], 31, *siman* 7; *HaPardes* 6:3 [Sivan 1932], 25, *simanim* 5–8.)

his response, in his handwriting, preserved in his archive, he writes regarding the difference between the two organizations:

> I... gave credentials for aid to Keren Kayemet alone [...] which is busy transferring land from the hands of gentiles to Jewish possession.... Keren Hayesod... does not deal in redeeming land, but rather in settling it and in matters of education. I have never yet given them a recommendation [and will not do so] until the matter will, please God, be put right, and... at least a significant part of the funds will be allocated to settling Eretz Yisrael in the way of our holy Torah.[9]

In fact, there exists a wealth of information on R. Kook's ties with Keren Kayemet, most of which involved ongoing support for its efforts to redeem land, all the while keeping his eye on, and immediately protesting, any deviation from Torah perpetrated on its grounds.[10] On the other hand, in all writings of R. Kook published to date, the few mentions of Keren Hayesod all demonstrate reservations about the organization.[11] Only one who is fed by rumors and presents R. Kook as one who "lends his hand to evildoers" will assume that he similarly called for support of Keren Hayesod. By contrast, for someone who is familiar with R. Kook's life story, his work, and his letters, the idea that he would be capable of

---

9. This draft is quoted by R. Yaakov Filber, *Kokhav Ohr* (Jerusalem, 1993), 21–22 (with slight stylistic changes, according to a photocopy in my possession). R. Kook's actual letter omitted criticism of Keren Hayesod, leaving only praise of Keren Kayemet. R. Filber posits that, based on the letter that R. Kook sent to his son, Rav Z. Y. Kook, about a week later (ibid.), that the reason for the omission was R. Kook's concern lest the negative sentences be used to lambaste the Zionist funds in general. In my opinion, taking into account R. Kook's style, it is unlikely that he had such a concern, but rather probably wished not to take part in a public boycott of Keren Hayesod (see above, note 6).
10. See R. Neriyah Gutel, "*Hilkhot V'Halikhot HaKeren HaKayemet L'Yisrael V'Haḥug HaHityashvuti B'Ma'arekhet Hitkatvuyotav Shel HaRav Kook*," *Sinai* 121 (5758/1998), 103–15; Ḥayim Peles, "*Teguvotav Shel HaRav A. Y. Kook al Ḥilulei HaShabbat al Admat HaKeren HaKayemet L'Yisrael*," *Sinai* 115 (5755/1995), 180–86; see also R. Kook, *Ḥazon HaGe'ula* (Jerusalem, 1937), 220–30; ibid., 33–34, et seq. I have expanded on R. Kook's relationship with Keren Kayemet elsewhere. [Ed. note: The author is referring to his book *Lehakot Shoresh*.]
11. In a letter from winter 1924 to R. Dov Arye Leventhal of Agudas Harabonim about a trip to America, R. Kook writes that one of the questions that his trip depends upon is "whether there will not be a tendency to confuse the funds he would raise via [Agudas Harabonim] with Keren Hayesod" (*Igrot HaRa'ayah* 4 (Jerusalem, 1984), 177. In a letter from winter 1925 to R. Akiva Glasner of Klausenburg, he urges him to make use of "the Zionist funds of Keren Hayesod" for purposes such as *sheḥitah* and *mikva'ot* in settling Transylvanian immigrants in Eretz Yisrael. He comments that when all is said and done, in most places the donors are religious Jews; but of course he should ensure that everything is done according to the Torah (ibid., 216).

calling for support for an organization which directly causes *ḥilul Shabbat*, secular education, and so on, is ludicrous. Even his support for Keren Kayemet was not unconditional, but with conditions, restrictions, and even warnings attached. The following examples suffice to prove the point:

In a letter to Menahem Ussishkin, chairman of Keren Kayemet, from February 4, 1927, concerning violations of Shabbat in the Borokhov neighborhood located on Keren Kayemet land (by the residents, not by Keren Kayemet itself), R. Kook warned "that if they do not take the necessary steps to correct these wrongdoings that have exceeded all limits, I will be forced to publicize the matter in an open letter… to the whole Jewish people."[12]

In a letter to Tnuva from March 2, 1932, that was sent following a report concerning *ḥilul Shabbat* on Kibbutz Mizra, R. Kook announced that so long as the kibbutz members did not mend their ways, their milk would be considered as *ḥalav akum* (milked by a non-Jew) and Tnuva would be forbidden from using it.[13]

In a letter to Ussishkin from April 3, 1929, R. Kook complained about the fact that Keren Kayemet had stepped beyond its mandate by publishing literary pamphlets, an abuse of funds donated for redemption of the land: "I hope… [this] obstacle will be removed without delay, so that we will all together, as one, be able to carry out the sacred work of redeeming the land with the help of Keren Kayemet L'Yisrael."[14]

THE FORGERY IN THE 1926 PUBLIC LETTER

Because of the weight of his opinion, over the years many attempts were made to ascribe to R. Kook outright support of the fund. The most flagrant case occurred in the winter of 1926 (about a year after R. Kook's letter to the ḥasidic rebbes on the difference between Keren Kayement and Keren Hayesod). Several months previously, a severe economic crisis hit the Yishuv, resulting in unemployment of a third of the workforce, a decrease in aliyah, and a steady outflow of Jews from the country.[15] This crisis, the worst during the British Mandate, was the first time

12. *Sinai* 115 (1995), 181; the full letter was printed in *Mikhtavim V'Igrot Kodesh* (ed. R. David Avraham Mandelbaum [New York, 2003], 588). R. Kook hints that if they do not take the necessary steps, he will stop supporting Keren Kayemet, and even publicize the matter.
13. *Sinai* 115 (1995), 183.
14. R. Moshe Zuriel, *Otzarot HaRa'ayah* I (Rishon Lezion, 2002), 487.
15. See, inter alia, Dan Giladi, *HaYishuv B'Tekufat HaAliyah HaRevi'it: Beḥina Kalkalit U'Politit* (Tel Aviv, 1973), 171–92. The cause of the crisis was twofold: on the one hand, the especially large number of new immigrants in the two years prior to the crisis, for which the economy was unprepared; on the other hand, the strict limit on taking money out of the country imposed by

that the impetus of the Yishuv's development, which had been increasing since the end of the First World War, was brought to a standstill. The Zionist leadership galvanized in an emergency campaign, via Keren Hayesod, for the unemployed in Eretz Yisrael. Because of the severity of the situation, R. Kook, too, sought to encourage contributions to improve the economic situation in Eretz Yisrael, and when R. Moshe Ostrovsky (Hame'iri) left for Poland on behalf of the appeal, R. Kook gave him a general letter of encouragement to the Jews in Eastern Europe.[16] At the same time, on November 8, 1926, R. Kook wrote a public letter calling for support of the Zionist leadership's initiative, in which he wrote, inter alia:

> [I] raise my voice with the call, "Help us, now." Our holy edifice, the national home for which the heart of every Jew holds great hopes, is facing a temporary crisis which requires the help of brothers... to endure.... I am convinced that the great call which the Zionist leadership is issuing throughout the borders of Israel, to make every effort to come to the aid and relief of this crisis, will be heard...; and that, besides all the frequent donations for all the general matters of holiness which our brothers wherever they live will give for the sake of Zion and Jerusalem, all the sacred institutions will raise hands for the sake of God, His people, and His land, to give generously to the appeal to relieve the present crisis, enabling the needed sum to be promptly collected.

Although the appeal was made through Keren Hayesod, R. Kook avoided mentioning the name of the fund because of his principled refusal to publicize support for it (as he explained in his letter to the ḥasidic rebbes). The version quoted above was published in the newspapers of Eretz Yisrael, under the title "For the Relief of the Crisis."[17] However, amazingly, it becomes apparent that in the version published some weeks later in Warsaw [Jewish] newspapers, the words "the

---

the Polish government in an attempt to fight the hyperinflation of the zloty, which disrupted both donations to Eretz Yisrael, and the ability of new immigrants to bring their possessions with them to Eretz Yisrael.

16. For details of R. Ostrovsky's trip see *HaTzefira* 66:30 (March 6, 1927), 8. For the *berakhah* that he received from R. Yeḥiel Moshe Segalovitz, head of the Mława *bet din*, see ibid. 66:34 (March 11, 1927), 3. R. Kook's letter to Polish Jewry was published in *HaOlam* on April 3, and again in Zuriel, *Otzarot HaRa'ayah* 2 (1998 edition), 1075.
17. See the monthly *HaHed*, Kislev 1926, p. 12, and the weekly *HaTor* 7:16 (November 19, 1926), front page. This version was printed later in *Ḥazon HaGe'ula*, 180. The version quoted here is based on minor corrections of mistakes in one of the sources. In the description attached to the public letter in *HaHed* the following was written: "In honor of Keren Hayesod's special aid program for the unemployed in Eretz Yisrael, our master R. Kook published a special public letter...."

Zionist leadership" were altered to read "the head office of Keren Hayesod," and accordingly, the words were presented as nothing less than "R. Kook's public letter in favor of Keren Hayesod"![18]

Even if we had nothing before us other than the two versions of this public letter, there could be no doubt that the authentic version is the one published by R. Kook's acquaintances, the editors of *HaHed* and *HaTor* in Eretz Yisrael, which would be seen by R. Kook. On the other hand, when Keren Hayesod circulated R. Kook's letter in Poland's Jewish press, they would not have been concerned that the author would come across the version they had published far away. Furthermore, they had a distinct interest to insert into R. Kook's words a precedential reference to Keren Hayesod. Even if we only had before us the "Eastern European" version of the letter, it would not be difficult to perceive that unauthorized hands had tampered with it. This is not only because of R. Kook's letter to the ḥasidic rebbes from about a year earlier, but because of a letter that R. Kook sent to the heads of Keren Hayesod a few weeks following the public letter on behalf of the appeal. In this letter to Keren Hayesod, he informs them in brief that he is prevented from cooperating with the directorate of the fund or even visiting its offices (!) until they comply with the demands that he had presented them with regarding religious matters. The background to this letter is a request sent to R. Kook on December 7, 1926, after the inauguration of Keren Hayesod's offices in the new national complex in Jerusalem. The directors of the head office of Keren Hayesod had written that "it would give us much joy and be a great honor if our master would be so good as to visit our office – the world headquarters of Keren Hayesod."[19] In reply, R. Kook wrote a letter – published here for the first time – to the heads of Keren Hayesod, (Arye) Leib Yafeh and Arthur Menaḥem Hantke:

> 8th Tevet 5687 [December 13, 1926], To the honorable Dr. Yaffe and A. Hentke,

18. *HaTzefira* 65:50 (Warsaw, November 9, 1926), 3. The accompanying cover letter reads: "On 2 Kislev [November 8, 1926], the Chief Rabbi of Eretz Yisrael, R. Avraham Yitzḥak HaKohen Kook sent the following public letter to the head office of Keren Hayesod . . . ." A few days later the letter was also published in *HaOlam* 14:50 (London, December 3, 1926), 944, with the same headline and description as in *HaTzefira*, but without the insertion of "Keren Hayesod" in the body of the letter; see also *HaOlam* 14:48 (December 9), 906, where it was reported that "R. Kook published a call to world Jewry to aid Keren Hayesod to ease the crisis in Eretz Yisrael."
19. Central Zionist Archives, KH421036. As is explained in this file, R. Kook's colleague, Chief Rabbi Y. Meir, visited the offices of Keren Hayesod.

> I received your invitation to visit your esteemed office. I hereby inform you that I will be able to cooperate for the benefit of Keren Hayesod, and I will, *bli neder*, also visit Keren Hayesod's central office, after Keren Hayesod's leadership and the Zionist leadership will fulfill my minimal demands concerning religious issues in the kibbutzim and in education.
>
> Yours, with all due respect ...[20]

Over time, R. Kook nonetheless came into contact with members of Keren Hayesod in several instances, mainly in connection with allocations for religious needs.[21] However, as this letter illustrates, even such limited cooperation was dependent, from R. Kook's point of view, on the demand to change the fund's conduct with respect to religion.[22] What were these demands, in order for Keren Hayesod to be considered as having "put things right" (as he wrote in his letter to the ḥasidic rebbes)? We can clarify this from a document which is also being published here for the first time. This document, whose heading is "R. Kook's answers" to Keren Hayesod, was apparently written after the previous letter, in reply to a question by Keren Hayesod concerning his attitude toward them, probably against the backdrop of rumors that R. Kook forbade (!) support of Keren Hayesod.[23] We only have a copy of the document in our possession, written in the first person, meaning that R. Kook wrote it himself, and the person who copied

---

20. From a copy of the letter in the possession of R. Ze'ev Neuman, to whom I am grateful. It should be noted that Leib Yafeh was a relative of R. Kook: his paternal grandfather, R. Mordekhai Gimpel Yafeh, was R. Kook's paternal grandmother's brother. Nevertheless, at the opening of the letter, R. Kook does not show any family sentiment, but opens with an altogether neutral tone.
21. About two years before the above letter, in 1925, R. Kook, together with other rabbis, participated in a meeting with Keren Hayesod where sums were allocated for religious needs, and recipient groups were decided upon (Yehoshua Redler-Feldman [R. Binyamin], *Otzar Ha'Aretz* [Jerusalem, 1926], 72–73; see also n. 11 above).
22. The reader should note the letter of both the chief rabbis from March 27, 1927 – about two months after the above letter – which was sent, among others, to the secretary of Keren Hayesod, Mordekhai Helfman, with the demand to prevent desecration of Shabbat and kashrut in settlements on Keren Kayemet lands, or supported by Keren Hayesod. In his reply from March 30 (quoted in Motti Ze'ira, *Keru'im Anu* [Jerusalem, 2002], 172), Helfman justified himself saying: "The leadership of Keren Hayesod is only a mechanism for collecting money [...] We are, of course, ready to help with moral support, and we hereby promise His Honor, that we will use our influence at every opportunity to emphasize that which is wrong."
23. The document can be found in the Central Zionist Archive KH1/220/2. I am grateful to Mr. Yitzḥak Dadon, who made me aware of the document's existence and gave me a photocopy. Most of the demands in this document were repeated, with different emphases, in a declaration publicized by R. Kook in the spring of 1931.

it apparently chose to copy just the body of the letter without the opening and closing including signature:

1. I have never expressed any prohibition, God forbid, against Keren Hayesod. On the contrary – I am very displeased with those who do so.
2. Concerning my attitude toward the Zionist funds: my reply was that I unreservedly support Keren Kayemet at every opportunity. However, concerning Keren Hayesod, at the moment I am withholding my letter of support until the Zionist leadership corrects major shortcomings that I demand be put right, as follows:
    a. That nowhere in Eretz Yisrael will education be without religious instruction, not just as literature, but as the sacred basis of the Jewish faith.
    b. That all the general religious needs be immediately taken care of in every *moshav* and kibbutz. For example, *shoḥet*, synagogue, mikveh, and where a rabbi is needed – also a rabbi.
    c. That there will be no public profanation of that which is sacred in any of the places supported by Keren Hayesod, such as *ḥilul Shabbat* and *ḥag* in public.
    d. That the kitchens, at least the communal ones, will be kosher.
    e. That all above provisions which concern the settlers in Keren Hayesod's *moshavot* and settlements, will be stipulated in the contract as matters hindering use of the property by the resident, and his right to benefit from the land is contingent upon his adhering to these basic principles.

    And because I fervently hope that the leadership will finally conform to these terms, I therefore am postponing my support of Keren Hayesod until that time. I hope that my endeavors for the benefit of settling and building our Holy Land will then be complete.

It should be noted that these terms are, in essence, similar to those that R. Kook set before Keren Kayemet. However, while the latter's dealings were with redeeming the land, the areas referred to in R. Kook's demands were at the heart of Keren Hayesod's work. For that reason, R. Kook did not make compliance with his demands into a condition for cooperation and support for Keren Kayemet; but he certainly did so with Keren Hayesod.[24]

Whatever the case may be, if R. Wasserman did indeed see the public letter of 1926, without doubt he saw the falsified version published in the Polish newspapers, reinforcing in his mind the opinion that "it is well known that he who heads [the Chief Rabbinate] has written and signed on a declaration calling on Jews to contribute to Keren Hayesod."[25] However, as has been shown, these words have no foundation.

THE SIGNIFICANCE OF SUPPORTING KEREN HAYESOD

R. Kook's words that he could not support Keren Hayesod until "at least a significant part of the funds will be allocated to settling Eretz Yisrael in the way of our holy Torah" seem to give the impression that were a significant part of the fund's functions directed to activity in the spirit of the Torah, then R. Kook would give his support even if another part was still directed to secular education. However, in practice, there is no doubt that R. Kook's demand was much stricter. In Keren Hayesod's bylaws, it was stipulated to allocate only about 20% of its resources to education[26] (and only a certain portion of that budget would be directed to "questionable" education) – and despite this, R. Kook refused to call for its support. It must be emphasized that this paragraph in Keren Hayesod's bylaws was strictly applied. A summary of the fund's activity between the years 1921 and 1930, indicates that 61.4% of its resources were invested in aliyah and settlement (aliyah training, aid for refugees, agricultural and urban settlement,

24. Even though R. Kook repeated in this letter that he was not announcing a prohibition of support of Keren Hayesod, later, when in 1932 the Jewish Agency did not honor its pledge to transfer a sum earmarked for religious affairs, R. Kook warned in a sharp letter that if at least part of the promised sum was not transferred, he would be forced to turn to rabbis in America and to Mizraḥi in Poland, with the demand to prevent support of the Keren Hayesod appeal (letter from April 6, 1932, Central Zionist Archive S255894–419).
25. News of R. Kook's supposed support of Keren Hayesod, based on the Eastern European forgery of the public letter, quickly reached R. Kook's opponents in Eretz Yisrael and even in America. In a letter from December 29, 1926, Meir Heller-Semnitzer, one of Jerusalem's most extreme zealots (around whom, that same summer, a major scandal erupted, concerning a brazen wall-poster of his defaming the Gerrer Rebbe and R. Kook), informed R. Tzvi Hirsch Friedman of New York (who, a year previously, had been expelled from Agudas Harabonim because of attacks on R. Kook that he had published in one of his books), that R. Kook issued a proclamation calling for support of "the baseless fund" [play on words: *yesod* means base]. See Friedman, *Tzvi Ḥemed – Mishpati im Dayanei Medinat Yisrael* (Brooklyn, 1960), 67.
26. As R. Yitzḥak Yehudah Trunk pointed out already in 1921 (see n. 28 below).

housing, trade, and industry), 19.6% in public and national services (security, health, administration), and only 19.0% in education and culture – from which a certain portion was allocated for religious needs: education; salaries for rabbis, *shoḥatim,* and kashrut supervisors; maintenance of *mikva'ot, eruvim,* and religious articles; aid for the settlements of Bnei Brak, Kfar Ḥasidim, etc.[27] In light of this data, it seems that R. Wasserman's reproach of those who backed support for Keren Hayesod, and his defining them as "utterly wicked" people, is not essentially different from reproach of those who back the paying of compulsory taxes to the State of Israel – a call heard today only from extreme marginal groups within the ḥaredi sector.

Indeed, not surprisingly, it transpires that in fact some of the illustrious rabbis of that generation did call to contribute to Keren Hayesod, despite the problematic nature of some of its activity.[28] Just several months before the publication of R. Kook's aforementioned public letter, another public letter was published, calling for support of Keren Hayesod, and signed by more than eighty rabbis from Poland and Russia. Among them were well-known personalities such as R. Ḥanokh Henokh Agus, author of *Marḥeshet*; R. Meshulam Rata (Roth); R. Reuven Katz, and more.[29] Moreover, in several locations, particularly in America, there was a

27. A. Elitzur, "*Keren Hayesod Be'Mivḥan HaZeman*" in *Luaḥ Yerushalayim – 5706* (Jerusalem, 1945), 259–68; see also *Otzar Ha'Aretz,* 70–76.
28. In this connection it is customary to mention R. Meir Simḥa HaKohen of Dvinsk, author of *Ohr Same'aḥ,* who acceded to the request of an emissary of the World Zionist Organization in preparation for the appeal of Keren Hayesod in Latvia, and wrote his famous letter calling for support of the Yishuv in Eretz Yisrael (printed in *HaTor,* 3, 1922, and also in R. Ze'ev Arye Rabiner, *Rabbenu Meir Simha Kohen* [Tel Aviv, 1967], 163–65, and elsewhere). However, although the historical context of the letter was the Keren Hayesod appeal, the letter itself deals with general support for settling Eretz Yisrael, with no explicit mention of Keren Hayesod or any other Zionist organization. Hence it is difficult to see in the letter a statement concerning the fundamental question of whether to support Keren Hayesod despite the fact that a portion of its allocations went to secular education. The same applies to a similar letter written in the same year and in the same connection by R. Eliezer Don Yiḥye of Lucyn (See *Otzar Ha'Aretz,* 84–86). By contrast, R. Yitzḥak Yehudah Trunk of Kutno, the grandson of the *Yeshu'ot Malko* and one of the rabbis of the Mizraḥi in Poland, authored a lengthy letter that same year, explicitly calling for support of Keren Hayesod, and rejecting arguments against contributing to the fund (see *Sinai* 85 [Nisan–Elul 5739/1979], 95–96). See also the footnotes which follow.
29. See *Otzar Ha'Aretz,* 78–82. It should be added that the Chief Rabbi of Tel Aviv (later the *Rishon LeTziyon*), R. Ben Tziyon Meir Ḥai Uziel, participated personally in the activity of Keren Hayesod (*Mikhmanei Uziel* 4 (Jerusalem, 2007), 31–32, 283–84, and in 6: 297–99, and elsewhere), as did R. Ostrovsky (as mentioned above), and others.

rabbinic consensus on support for Keren Hayesod,[30] and even R. Kook's colleague in the Chief Rabbinate, R. Yaakov Meir, called for support of Keren Hayesod.[31] Would R. Wasserman have defined all of these scores of rabbis as evil men "who cause the public to sin on the most terrible level"?[32] Whatever the case may be, it transpires that it was specifically R. Kook who stands out as being the most forceful among them, and he consistently agreed to publicize support only for Keren Kayemet. In light of all we have written, one wonders whether R. Wasserman's zealous words to R. Dushinski[33] were only written in order to deter him

30. In an issue of *HaOlam* (18:46 [London, November 11, 1930], 911) in honor of Keren Hayesod's tenth anniversary, a "declaration of Eretz Yisrael's rabbis concerning Keren Hayesod" from September 1930, was published. Hundreds of rabbis – the majority from America, and others from Eretz Yisrael, Europe, and Eastern countries – signed the declaration calling explicitly to strengthen Keren Hayesod, "which for the last ten years has borne on its shoulders the esteemed task of building our sacred inheritance, and faithfully supporting all projects that bring us close to that great aim." It seems that there is not one well-known rabbi who was active in Agudas Harabonim who did not sign this declaration: R. Yehudah Leib Graubart, R. Elazar Preil, R. Ḥayim Fischel Epstein, R. Yosef Kanowitz, R. Yosef Eliyahu Henkin, R. Eliezer Silver, R. Ze'ev Wolf Leiter, R. Ḥayim Yitzḥak Bloch, R. Yehudah Leib Salzer, etc., etc. (Nevertheless, in light of the scope and unusual diversity of the signatories, one wonders whether this was a resolution approved by majority vote at the conference of Agudas Harabonim, such that the weight of the opponents was not reflected, and therefore the names of all the Agudas Harabonim members were given as signatories).
31. See *Otzar Ha'Aretz*, 77, his letter from December 8, 1925 calling for support of Keren Hayesod. See above n. 19, and more below.
32. A most interesting fact in this connection is that R. Wasserman's relative by marriage from 1929 (the father-in-law of his son R. Elazar Simḥa), R. Meir Abowitz, head of the rabbinical court of Novardok and author of *Pnei Me'ir* on Talmud Yerushalmi, not only was an avowed member of the Mizraḥi movement, and in 1923 even signed a call to join the movement (see *Encyclopedia of Religious Zionism* I [Jerusalem, 1958], cols. 1–2), but also was one of the signatories on the aforementioned declaration in favor of Keren Hayesod! (*Otzar Ha'Aretz*, 81). The fact that R. Wasserman was involved in R. Abowitz's younger daughter's marriage, is testimony to the good relationship between the families (see R. Wasserman's daughter-in-law's testimony in the photocopied edition of *Pnei Me'ir* on the tractate Shabbat [U.S.], at the end of the introduction. R. Abowitz's letters to his son-in-law are published at the end of R. Wasserman's *Kovetz Shi'urim* 2 [Tel Aviv, 1989], 117–19).
33. It is instructive to compare these words with R. Yosef Ḥayim Sonnenfeld's moderate language in a letter to his brother written in 1921, in which he gives the benefit of the doubt to the donors of Keren Hayesod:

    Those pure-hearted ones, who contribute to Keren Hayesod out of unblemished love in order to ensure the viability of settlement in our Holy Land, certainly have a mitzvah. I do not know to what purpose they will actually put the money of Keren Hayesod, but if it is given to faithful hands, who will use it honestly for settling the land, this is in all respects a great mitzvah. However, as has been said, it must be in such hands that will use it for build-from cooperating with the Chief Rabbinate (which he strongly opposed); and perhaps this is the reason that he avoided mentioning R. Kook explicitly by name.[34]

CONCLUSION

R. Kook's path was falsified many times, both during his lifetime and after his death, sometimes unintentionally and sometimes intentionally. In what we have written here, it is proven beyond all doubt that R. Elḥanan Wasserman's claim that R. Kook called for the support of Keren Hayesod – a claim through which he explained his opposition to cooperation between the Edah Ḥaredit and the Chief Rabbinate – is based on a mistake. The historical truth is that R. Kook, in his dealings with the institutions of the Yishuv, more than once took a more aggressive and stringent stand than did other rabbis of his generation, as is expressed in the issue at hand.

---

ing and not for destruction [...] "and because of our sins we were exiled from our land" (translated from Yiddish, S. Z. Sonnenfeld, *Ha'Ish al HaḤomah* 3 [Jerusalem, 1975], 436).

34. Although R. Yaakov Meir, who explicitly backed Keren Hayesod, was also one "who heads the above [i.e., the Chief Rabbinate]," nevertheless, it is accepted to take R. Wasserman's words as addressed specifically to R. Kook. On the other hand, it is interesting that in a letter that R. Wasserman wrote to his brother on July 30, 1935, the following sentence appears: "What is R. Kook's illness, and how is he feeling now?" (*Kovetz Ma'amarim V'Igrot* 2, 124).

Chapter 19

R. Hutner's Testimony on R. Kook and Hebrew University[1]

INTRODUCTION

It is well known that R. Yitzḥak Hutner recorded, both in writing and orally, the circumstances surrounding R. Avraham Yitzḥak HaKohen Kook's participation in the opening ceremonies for Hebrew University on Mount Scopus (on April 1, 1925), and the developments that followed. In this chapter, I will analyze the two versions we have of his testimony, comparing and contrasting their sources and the corresponding details elsewhere, with the aim of determining, so far as is possible, the facts as they took place.

TWO VERSIONS OF THE STORY

R. Hutner's testimony appeared in two unrelated places, the first based on an oral communication of his, and the second on an account he himself penned. The words were first printed in R. Shlomo Zalman Sonnenfeld's *Ha'Ish al HaḤomah* 3 (Jerusalem 1975), where the author writes that he noted down the story "from the mouth of the Rosh Yeshiva [R. Hutner], the whole story also having been recorded on tape by R. Yosef Buxboim."[2] Just over a decade

1. Translated by Perry Zamek. This chapter initially appeared in *HaMa'ayan* 52:2 (Nisan 5773).
2. *Ha'Ish al HaḤomah*, part 3, (Jerusalem, 1975), 412. A further version of the testimony was published in Ḥayim Lifshitz's *Shivḥei HaRa'ayah* (p. 198), but it is clear that this was based on the version in *Ha'Ish al HaḤomah*.

later, R. Moshe Tzvi Neriyah's *Bisdeh HaRa'ayah* was published (Kfar Haroeh, 1987), including an edifying chapter on relations between R. Hutner and R. Kook. Printed there is a letter sent by R. Hutner to R. Neriyah twenty-five years previously, in 1962, in which R. Hutner himself wrote the essentials of his testimony.

Although published later, R. Hutner's letter to R. Neriyah was written [and sent] many years before R. Shlomo Zalman Sonnenfeld heard the story from R. Hutner. Furthermore, the letter is in writing, which by nature is to be preferred over an oral recounting. Nonetheless, our discussion will begin with the version in *Ha'Ish al HaḤomah,* since it is this version that first brought the topic to the attention of the public. I would preface this by saying that, although R. Shlomo Zalman Sonnenfeld wrote that the story was "taken down by the writer of these lines from [R. Hutner's] mouth," this clearly does not mean that the report was written down verbatim; the whole of the story (originally recounted in Yiddish) is presented in the third person – that is, not only was it translated, but it was also edited for style by the author:[3]

> Following Pesaḥ, in Nisan 5685 [1925], when [R. Hutner], as a young man, came to study in the Ḥevron Yeshiva, he went to visit R. Kook, to whom his family was distantly related. [...] In the course of their conversation, R. Kook was called away to an urgent telephone call in an adjacent room. On his way back from the office [i.e., the room with the phone] to his room, R. Kook overheard a conversation between his nephew, R. Raphael Kook, and another person, at the end of which R. Raphael burst into raucous laughter. To R. Kook's question, "What is the meaning of this laughter?" R. Raphael replied: The young man with whom I was speaking just came from the university on Mount Scopus, where he heard a lecture from Prof. Torczyner (Tur-Sinai), head of the Department of Biblical Criticism [...]
>
> Upon hearing the foolishness of that "learned" member of the university faculty, R. Kook's demeanor turned serious, and he returned sadly to his room, sat in his armchair, and sank in thought. "Why are you so saddened?" asked the young guest [R. Hutner]. "My dear young man," replied R. Kook, "you should know that when Chaim Weizmann came to invite me to the inauguration ceremony for the university, I firmly

3. *Ha'Ish al HaḤomah,* 411–12.

> refused the invitation. And when Weizmann persisted, pleading with me to participate, I told him that, as Chief Rabbi and spiritual leader of the Jewish community in Eretz Israel, I could not participate in the dedication of a Hebrew college which would also include a chair for the study of Biblical Criticism. It was only after Weizmann solemnly promised me that the Hebrew University would not have a chair in Biblical Criticism, that I consented to attend the university's inauguration. And now it turns out that Weizmann deceived me...." The gaon [i.e., R. Hutner] concluded his recounting of the incident thus: At that time I was so bold as to say to R. Kook: Please don't be offended if I say this to you: I am certain that Weizmann would not have been able to deceive Rabbi Ḥayim Sonnenfeld.... "You may be right," responded R. Kook, with sorrow and disappointment.

Now we will quote, in full, what R. Hutner himself wrote in his letter to R. Neriyah, dated 28 Elul 5722 (September 27, 1962). The background to the letter, as described by R. Neriyah,[4] is that, during his visit to the United States in the summer of 1957, he heard from R. Hutner that "[R. Kook *ztz"l*] knew well the roots of this or that individual's soul, but he did not know where their body stood...." R. Neriyah published these comments following his return to Eretz Israel (without mentioning who was being quoted), and challenged them. Later, in the summer of 1962, R. Hutner visited Eretz Israel, and among other things met with R. Neriyah. Upon returning to the United States, R. Hutner sought to provide him with the broader context for his statement regarding R. Kook:[5]

> I saw what you wrote, in connection with what you heard from me when you were in America. Now, you should know that those statements that you heard from me, I had said in my youth to our teacher (R. Kook), may his soul rest in Eden ("I was childish, and I was emboldened" etc.). But here I wish to tell you what actually transpired. I had arrived in the land for the first time a few days before the opening of the university on Mount Scopus, and that was when I first became acquainted with our teacher, of saintly memory. At the time, he spoke with me at length of all the reasons for his decision to be present at the inauguration, as he moved from one realm of thought to another, as was his holy way, with

4. *Shivḥei HaRa'ayah*, 431–33.
5. Ibid., 435–37.

> the flow of his majestic words. One of the main elements of these conversations was the promise that had been made to him, that there would be no place in this university for a chair in Biblical Criticism. Sometime later it happened that I was present in our teacher's room, when someone entered and reported on the content of Prof. Torczyner's lecture, which he had delivered at the university the previous evening. Of course, the entire lecture was filled with biblical criticism of the worst sort. Our teacher, of saintly memory, gave me a penetrating glance that conveyed disappointment, bitterness, and pain. To this day I still feel that look in my heart, as though it were a hundred needles stabbing me all at once. I was astounded and shaken by that look, and then, unthinkingly, my lips let out the words: "Apparently, apart from the soul, one needs to know the body as well." I find it appropriate to recount the above facts to you.

CONFRONTING THE FACTUAL DATA

A comparison between R. Hutner's written language, and the spoken words attributed to him, raises a long string of inconsistencies, most significantly one at the beginning of the reported words and two at the end: First, according to R. Sonnenfeld's version, the entire story took place after Pesaḥ 1925, while R. Hutner's letter indicates that there were two separate instances – the first, which took place around Nisan 1925, was when R. Kook spoke with him regarding his participation in the university's inauguration, while the second took place "a long time afterward," with R. Hutner being present when the content of a lecture delivered at the university was reported to R. Kook. Second, according to R. Sonnenfeld's version, what R. Hutner said "impudently" to R. Kook was "Weizmann would not have been able to deceive R. Ḥayim Sonnenfeld," whereas R. Hutner's letter states that what he said was, "Apart from the soul, one needs to know the body as well." Third, according to R. Sonnenfeld, R. Kook quietly acknowledged R. Hutner's comment, while there is no hint of this in R. Hutner's letter.

In any event, a close examination of the details appearing in *Ha'Ish al HaḤomah*, proves that **the story described there could not have occurred.** R. Sonnenfeld describes that, following Pesaḥ 1925 – toward the end of Nisan or during Iyar – a young man came to R. Kook's home, and reported on the content of the lecture delivered by Professor Naftali Herz Torczyner (Tur-Sinai), who, according to the account, served as "head of the Department of Biblical Criticism." The fact is, however, that Tur-Sinai was at that time at the Hochschule für die Wissenschaft des Judentums in Berlin, Germany. He only came to Eretz Israel in 1933, and began to teach at the university in 1934;[6] hence, prior to that date it was not possible to discuss the content of his lectures in Jerusalem.[7]

Is it possible that this was merely a minor error, and that the matter involved not Prof. Tur-Sinai, but some other professor? This too cannot be said, in light of the fact that (as we shall see below) Bible studies at the Hebrew University did not take place at all prior to the **middle of 1927**![8] The required correction to the details of the story is, thus, not to the name, but to the date, with the incident apparently occurring in early 1934 – at which time R. Hutner was indeed back in Jerusalem.[9] This conclusion is consistent with what is stated in R. Hutner's letter, that a great deal of time had passed since the university's inauguration till the incident in question took place. There is no doubt, therefore, that the version offered by R. Sonnenfeld suffers from substantial corruptions (even though it was published during R. Hutner's lifetime), and that the succinct description written by R. Hutner himself is reliable and to be preferred in all respects (as will be demonstrated again below).

However, once we adopt this logical conclusion, the testimony before us will need to address a further fact, which to a large extent takes the sting out of the whole story: R. Kook had already expressed objections to the study of biblical criticism at the Hebrew University in **the spring of 1927** (as we shall see below),

---

6. And even then not as a professor of Bible (he was never a member of the Department of Bible) – his lectures on the Book of Job were in the framework of his holding the Chair in Hebrew Language (see *Do'ar Hayom*, issue 69 [December 19, 1935], 4).
7. A further difficulty in dating the incident to 1925 is that it is unthinkable that a young lad of 19, albeit a distant relative (a second cousin of R. Kook's daughter-in-law; his grandfather and the grandfather of R. Tzvi Yehudah Kook's wife, Chava Leah, were brothers), would dare say such a thing to R. Kook, certainly not at their first meeting. Nine years later, on the other hand, R. Hutner already had a long-standing acquaintance with R. Kook, and was also known as a *talmid ḥakham* and author of an important book (*Torat HaNazir*, [Kovno, 1932] – with an approbation from R. Kook, of course).
8. Moreover, in R. Sonnenfeld's amazingly detailed description of R. Hutner's report, there is also a footnote that expands on the nature of the urgent telephone call to which R. Kook (according to the story) was called. According to the report there, R. Kook spoke with Dr. Ḥayim Yaski, then Director of Hadassah Hospital, and demanded that he prevent the autopsy of someone who had died. Now, Yaski was only appointed to his first administrative position at Hadassah in 1928, while in 1925 – which is when the incident occurred, according to R. Sonnenfeld – he was still an itinerant eye doctor (see, inter alia: *Do'ar Hayom*, issue 211 [June 11, 1928], 4).
9. After leaving for a stay in Europe from the winter of 1929 to the summer of 1930, and again from the winter of 1931 to the spring of 1933; in the spring of 1934 he left for the United States, where he remained for many years (see the biographical article written by his daughter, *Sefer Hazikaron LeMaran HaPaḥad Yitzḥak*, Jerusalem, 1984, 16–27).

a full seven years prior to his being "surprised," as it were, by that young man's report regarding Tur-Sinai's lecture!

THE EVENTS AS THEY TOOK PLACE

In order to place matters in their proper sequence, let us for the moment set aside the testimony in question, and describe in chronological order the events associated with the inauguration of Hebrew University and the study of Bible there.

The inauguration ceremony for the university took place on Mount Scopus, as we said, on April 1, 1925. Even prior to that, at the beginning of Ḥanukkah 1925, came the dedication of the University's Institute of Jewish Studies, but in both that year and the following year, **no** framework for Bible study was yet established, and the Institute focused primarily on Talmud and Jewish History.[10] The reason for the absence of Bible as a field of study at the university during those first two years was the stormy public debate, both within the university's leadership and in the press, over the desired nature and character of Bible studies at the university: Should such studies be conducted in keeping with the spirit of Jewish religious belief, or should there be unqualified "academic freedom," meaning of course biblical criticism?[11] During its first year, most of the lecturers at the Institute of Jewish Studies were observant (among them Professors Yaakov Naḥum Epstein, Shmuel Klein, and Simḥa Assaf), but this changed the following year with the appointment of additional lecturers (prominent among them being Prof. Yosef Klausner and Prof. Gershom Scholem).[12]

R. Kook was well aware of all these developments taking place in Jerusalem. As early as the **winter of 1926**, R. Kook expressed chagrin over the emerging character of the University's Institute of Jewish Studies in letters to R. Joseph Hertz of Great Britain, R. Aharon Teitelbaum in the United States, and others, and was markedly pessimistic regarding the chances that biblical criticism would not be taught there in the future:

> Regarding the Institute of Jewish Studies, even were its character to be fixed without a dramatic retreat from the path of Judaism, it would not provide

10. For example, see the Institute's schedule for the summer of 1925: *Do'ar Hayom*, issue 164 (April 19, 1925), 2, and issue 167 (April 24), 7. See also *Yediot Hamakhon Lemada'ei Hayahadut*, Booklet 1 (Jerusalem, April 1925), 49ff.
11. See, inter alia, *HaTzefira*, issue 68 (March 20, 1927), 2; *HaTzefira*, issue 72 (March 25), 3; *Haynt*, issue 68 (March 21), 4.
12. Compare the content of the newsletter from the Institute for Jewish Studies, n. 10 above, with the book *Mada'ei Hayahadut* 1 (Jerusalem, 1926).

> us with the full spiritual capital – the sanctity of the Torah and the wholehearted belief in its holiness and purity. All the more so as that there is no hope of inoculating it against enormous propellers sweeping it into the maelstrom of the foreign, poisonous circle that rules the secular world.[13]

Indeed, the university's leadership slowly began to lean in the direction of offering biblical criticism, and two years after the university's establishment, on May 2, 1927, Bible studies commenced there for the first time.[14] It was only a few weeks thereafter that R. Kook publicly expressed his displeasure over the nature of these studies. This was at a press conference held at R. Kook's home, upon his return from his "tour of the *moshavot*" in May 1927. After recounting his impressions from the tour, R. Kook was asked by the journalists a number of questions, one of which touched on the issue of biblical criticism that had begun to take hold within the university. According to the journalistic documentation, published the following day, R. Kook stated that "it was only after having been approached, at the time of the university's opening, by Rabbi [Prof. Israel] Levy, the Chief Rabbi of France, and Rabbi [Dr. Joseph] Hertz, the Chief Rabbi of England, and promised by them that the college would not be non-religious, that he consented

13. Letter to R. Teitelbaum dated November 9, 1925 (22 Ḥeshvan 5686); quoted by R. Ari Yitzḥak Shevat, "*Te'udot Ḥadashot B'Inyan Gishat HaRav Kook L'Hakamat HaUniversita Ha'Ivrit,*" *HaMa'ayan* 47:4 (Tamuz 5767): 22–24.

14. See *Do'ar Hayom*, issue 201 (May 9, 1927), front page. Note that, at this stage, a separate Bible Department was not set up; rather, a professor (Shlomo Pereles from Germany) was appointed to teach the subject in the Institute of Jewish Studies. Furthermore, this professor returned to Europe after less than a year, and so, in effect, the *status quo ante* was reinstated! Bible studies within the university framework were only reinstated in 1933, and a Department of Bible was only opened in 1940. As described by the chroniclers of the Hebrew University, this extended delay in the establishment of the Bible Department stemmed from tensions within the administration of the Institute of Jewish Studies, between those who supported biblical criticism and those who opposed it:

> This tension was well reflected in the nuanced approach adopted by R. Joseph Hertz, Chief Rabbi of London, who chaired the advisory board of the Institute of Jewish Studies: Despite his view that, in principle, the Institute should be an academic institution, the teaching of Bible was not assigned to any instructor who might be suspected of the taint of "criticism." Not just a researcher such as Torczyner, but even Tzvi Peretz Chajes [of Vienna] was considered too radical, and did not pass this hurdle (Sarah Yefet, "*Yisudo V'Reshit Toldotav Shel HaḤug L'Mikra,*" in *Toldot HaUniversita HaIvrit Birushalayim – Hitbasesut Utzmiḥa* [Jerusalem, 2005], 300, where there is additional extensive material on this issue).

Actually, biblical criticism as a separate field of study commenced at Hebrew University at a relatively late juncture: According to Yefet (ibid., pp. 302–3), the full critical freedom became dominant in the Bible Department only following the establishment of the State of Israel, over twenty years after the university's founding, and many years after the death of R. Kook!

to speak at the opening ceremony. And when he spoke then, he wanted to speak fully, paying no attention to the notes and comments from Dr. Weizmann, or the mutterings around him, until he had finished saying all that he had to say.[15] But now he sees that in the Jewish Studies Department they are analyzing the Bible and criticizing it, and so on, contrary to the promise of the 'enlightened' rabbis of France and England."[16]

This is most instructive. On the one hand, there is a clear similarity between this and the upshot of R. Hutner's testimony:[17] R. Kook's consent to participate in the university inauguration was tied to the promise that he received regarding the nature of the studies that would take place there.[18] On the other hand, R. Kook already made his views known as early as 1927, and even prior to that

---

15. Indeed, R. Kook's speech lasted about three-quarters of an hour, leading some to complain in the next day's newspapers about its length. Among other things, R. Kook stressed in his speech the demand that

> **the instructors for Jewish studies, from the Book of Books, the Bible – the light of our lives – and on to all branches of the Talmudic literature, the wisdom of Israel and its history, should be people who, apart from their enormous knowledge in their respective fields, should also be faithful to the traditions of Israel in their views, their feelings and their whole way of life.** (*Ma'amarei HaRa'ayah* [Jerusalem, 1984], 300)

As Israel Bartal summarized it: "In particular, R. Kook was concerned about the teaching of the sacred Jewish texts in a scientific-critical way, and so, first and foremost, he warns [in his speech] against biblical criticism…" ("*Ne'umo Shel HaRav Ay"ah Kook: Divrei Parshanut*," in *Toldot HaUniversita HaIvrit Birushalayim – Shorashim Vehatḥalot* [Jerusalem, 1997], 316–17. This is not the place to dwell on the speech and the reactions to it).

16. *Do'ar Hayom*, issue 221 (May 31, 1927), 4 (see also *Davar* of the same date, issue 611, front page). In the ironic statement with which R. Kook closed, he intimated that even the enlightened rabbis, with the titles of professor and PhD from France and England, were opposed to the nature of these studies.

17. And contrary (again!) to R. Sonnenfeld's version, it turns out that it was not Weizmann who gave the promise to R. Kook, but rather the rabbis from England and France (who were members of the directorate of the Institute of Jewish Studies). For a mention of their (separate) visits to R. Kook's home, some days prior to the ceremony, see: *Do'ar Hayom*, issue 145 (March 29, 1925), 3. The corresponding portion of Weizmann's recollections of the university's opening, in *HaUniversita HaIvrit Birushalayim – Kaf-Heh Shana* (Jerusalem, 1950), 21–24, has no mention of any such matter.

18. In R. Shevat's previously mentioned article (n. 14), proofs are gathered "from the remains on the threshing floor" in an attempt to demonstrate that R. Kook felt greater exultation than trepidation at the establishment of the university, to the extent that he writes of "a sense of satisfaction […] from the university's opening ceremony" (ibid., p. 16) – this despite the fact that in the entirety of R. Kook's correspondence on this topic, without exception (I am not referring to documents penned in English by an associate of R. Kook, for example), his concern regarding the university was expressed vastly more than his happiness over its establishment. To think that R. Kook might take a positive view of an academic institution within whose walls

he was closely following events within the university – as well as subsequently.[19] In other words, there is no escaping the conclusion that the description of R. Kook's allegedly being "surprised" or "disappointed" seven years later, when he supposedly heard for the first time that biblical criticism was being taught at the university – cannot be correct.[20]

Now let us return to R. Hutner's report, and examine its details in light of the facts cited here. When that young man in 1934 informed R. Kook about Tur-Sinai's lecture, R. Kook reacted with clear chagrin – the appropriate response to hearing of such nonsense, contrary to the sanctity of the Torah. He subsequently turned to R. Hutner, who was present on that occasion, and again told him the story – which he had already recounted at the press conference in 1927 – regarding the connection between his consent to participate in the university's inauguration and the promise that he had received at that time regarding the nature of the studies at the university. R. Hutner, who apparently was under the impression that this was the first time that R. Kook had become aware of the university giving a platform to biblical criticism, interpreted R. Kook's chagrin, from what he heard, as "a penetrating glance that conveyed disappointment, bitterness, and sadness," because of the "discovery" that the promise had been broken,[21] and so blurted out the statement, "apart from the soul, one needs to know the body as well."

---

biblical criticism is taught is absolutely unfounded; R. Shevat would certainly agree with this, but his article lacks a clear statement of such reservations.

19. See, for example, his letter to Prof. Avraham HaLevi Frenkel, dated 30 Sivan 5688 (June 29, 1928), in which he agrees that the latter should accept an appointment at Hebrew University, since "as many as the university's shortcomings are, you cannot ignore our duty to fight to seize a proper place within it for the benefit of faithful Judaism" (*Otzarot HaRa'ayah* 1, 479).
20. To amplify this point: No one, at any date, could have "surprised" R. Kook with a report on the existence of biblical criticism studies at the university, since R. Kook had already anticipated that this would be the case, some time before such studies actually commenced there.
21. According to R. Sonnenfeld's version, R. Kook even added ingenuously: "And now it turns out that Weizmann deceived me…" The problem is that there is no basis to this "deception," unless one assumes that this incident took place following Pesaḥ 1925, that is, that it was only a few weeks after the opening ceremony that the promise had already been broken and lectures in biblical criticism delivered at Hebrew University. In fact, as noted above (particularly in n. 15), Bible was not even taught at the university for some years following its opening, and when the university began to do so, it was only following stormy debate. That is, the promise given to R. Kook was not an act of deception or trickery, and from the outset it was indeed kept, but after an internal power struggle within the university administration, those who sided with biblical criticism gained the upper hand. Furthermore, as shown above (in the note cited), the public opposition to the study of biblical criticism served to moderate the nature of Bible studies at the university for a period of two decades or more! Thus, the efforts of R. Kook and of others indeed continued to have an influence for a significant period.

A FINAL COMMENT

To close, I would like to comment briefly regarding the claim that "the Rav [R. Kook] *ztz"l* was well acquainted with the root of this or that individual's soul, but did not know where their body stood," and that "apart from the soul, one needs to know the body as well": In an encompassing study that I recently published along with R. Avraham Wasserman, on R. Kook's relations with Keren Kayemet L'Yisrael (the Jewish National Fund),[22] we described at length, inter alia, R. Kook's relentless efforts to check the widespread decline in religious observance in Eretz Israel, and his perpetual struggle for Shabbat and kashrut observance in settlements on Keren Kayemet lands in particular. There are some who were acquainted with R. Kook's multi-faceted personality primarily as a rabbi who spoke or taught in the *bet midrash*, who was a *posek* for those who consulted him, or who delved into the intricacies of the Torah, both revealed and esoteric; however, the complete historical picture of R. Kook's life and work as Chief Rabbi of Eretz Israel (significant parts of which were surveyed in the previously mentioned book) clearly demonstrates that R. Kook definitely knew "where [the secularists'] body stood," had a close understanding of the situation of all his contemporaries, and worked energetically – and with quite some success – to prevent decline and to correct failings in matters related to observance of Torah and mitzvot in the public arena in Eretz Yisrael.

22. In *Lehakot Shoresh – HaRa'ayah Kook Vehakeren Hakayemet L'Yisrael* (Jerusalem, 2012). See also previous chapter.

Chapter 20

Did R. Kook Believe that Eliezer Ben-Yehudah Repented?[1]

In religious-Zionist lore, there is a fairly well-known tale that on that the day before his death on Shabbat, December 16, 1922, Eliezer Ben-Yehudah visited R. Kook at home while he was studying with his disciple R. Yitzḥak Arieli. Ben-Yehudah asked several questions about the Hebrew language and near the end of the conversation, R. Kook said to him: "Ben-Yehudah, maybe the time has come for you to repent?" Ben-Yehudah responded, "Perhaps..."

That very Friday night, Ben-Yehudah passed away. As the story goes, "upon hearing of his death, R. Kook's eyed brimmed with tears and he said, "That 'perhaps,' which he uttered Friday morning, is considered a *hirhur teshuvah,* a thought of repentance, and thus he left this world in a righteous state. May he be remembered solely for the renewal of the Hebrew language and not for the damage he did." From that point on, R. Kook was careful not to speak ill of Ben-Yehudah, for, as he had said, his words contained the sparks of repentance."[2]

---

1. Translated by Meshulam Gotlieb. This chapter was written in 2009 and published in the internal publication of Yeshivat Nir.
2. One kollel fellow told this story almost verbatim, and when I asked what his source was, he claimed that his father had related it to him or he had read it in a book. Space considerations

This tale of Ben-Yehudah's reversal prevails, in one version or another, throughout the *dati-leumi* educational system.[3] It functions both as a foundation for the posthumous "rehabilitation" of Ben-Yehudah's image and as a testament to R. Kook's love of all Israel, in that he managed to find a spark of good even in a dedicated enemy of religion like Ben-Yehudah. The source of this tale is Dr. Naḥum Arieli, whose father, R. Yitzḥak Arieli, was, as mentioned above, a witness to the episode. Dr. Arieli related the story dramatically and at length in a special edition of *HaTzofeh*, published to mark the fiftieth anniversary of R. Kook's passing.[4] The words were then copied in an abridged fashion by Simcha Raz in his popular volume *An Angel Among Men*:[5]

> The door opened and Eliezer Ben-Yehudah entered and took a seat... Ben-Yehudah began to ask the Rabbi [Kook] questions about the Hebrew language. When the questioner fell silent, R. Kook spoke with brevity, saying only the following: "Mr. Ben-Yehudah, maybe the time has come for you to repent?" And he answered: "Perhaps"... Fifteen hours after this encounter with the Rabbi, [Ben-Yehudah died], **and my father interpreted the conversation saying that Ben-Yehudah's response to R. Kook of "perhaps" fell under the rubric of *hirhur teshuvah*, which is deemed to be like repentance itself.**

In fact, however, the end of the story as told by Dr. Naḥum Arieli, is precisely the reverse of what transpired. The true version is readily available to us from the only witness, in R. Yitzḥak Arieli's own words:[6]

---

do not allow me to cite all the folk references, but he is not the only person whom I heard speak of, or whom I saw in possession of, a similar version. See following footnotes.

3. Author's addition: Since this piece was written, Ben-Yehudah has been featured quite a few times in the *national-religious* press (especially in the various Shabbat flyers), in columns with names like "Our Nation's Outstanding Figures," in keeping with the best tradition of secular-Zionist historiography. This year the National-Religious Public School system is slated to highlight Ben-Yehudah's work – and, presumably, him as well – in light of a similar decision made by the Public School System. As we will see below, this decision flies in the face of R. Kook's true legacy.
4. *Musaf HaTzofeh*, September 15, 1985, 16. Most of Dr. Arieli's material is based on his father's notes, so he clearly knew the truth. This notwithstanding, a comparison of his article with his father's notes reveals that Dr. Arieli must have written from memory, for there are many inaccuracies regarding details (for instance, the story about learning *Guide for the Perplexed* was really about the *Kuzari*). Perhaps, the story about Ben-Yehudah also became garbled in his mind over the years.
5. 2005 edition, 131–32.
6. First printed by Shaul Schiff, *HaTzofeh*, November 23, 2003, Letter 24 (one of fifty-two memorial paragraphs of R. Arieli about R. Avraham Yitzḥak HaKohen Kook).

> Once Ben-Yehudah burst in on a Friday morning while [R. Avraham Yitzḥak HaKohen Kook] was studying our daily quota of five-Talmudic-folios with me (during which time, no one was allowed to interrupt), and he [Ben-Yehudah] inquired about some matters concerning his dictionary. The Rav turned to him and said, "Ben-Yehudah, perhaps the time has come for you to think about repentance?" He responded: "Perhaps" (and one might have thought that he had ruminations of repentance).

Up to this point, R. Yitzḥak's version matches his son's, but pay attention to the next few sentences:

> (And one might have thought that he had ruminations of repentance – **but, as everyone knows, that was not the case**). On that Shabbat eve he [Ben-Yehudah] passed away, **and they came to him [R. Kook] and pressured him to attend the funeral, but he did not accede to their request and said: "There is no way I am going to his funeral!"**

Thus, not only did R. Arieli never claim that Ben-Yehudah's "perhaps" might have implied a yearning to repent; he said exactly the reverse: "As everyone knows, that was not the case." Furthermore, not only did this incident fail to usher in a new era in which R. Kook looked benevolently upon Ben-Yehudah, but he adamantly refused to attend his funeral, notwithstanding the pressure put on him!

Dr. Naḥum Arieli did not wish to recount all this, so instead he wove a tale that still resonates today. Perhaps history will forgive him, but the truth – with all its educational and religious significance – needs to be made public.[7]

---

7. For further insight into the relationship between the two, see R. Neriyah Gutel's article "*Bein Teḥiyah L'Ḥidush: HaRa'ayah Kook V'E. Ben-Yehudah*" in *Kovetz Merḥavim* 6. R. Gutel reviews their correspondence concerning the Hebrew language (which was a result of Ben-Yehudah's requests for advice, and notes, among other things, that R. Kook took the unusual step of never opening any of his letters to Ben-Yehudah with greetings or salutations – that is to say, a *derishat shalom*). Cf. M. Godfrey's article entitled "Rabbi Kook's War on Eliezer Ben-Yehudah," *Perakim*, December 1958. Prof. Yosef Lang recently published a comprehensive, two-volume biography of Ben-Yehudah, which contains no mention of our story. Apparently Lang did not thoroughly investigate the nature of Ben-Yehudah and R. Kook's relationship.

Chapter 21

The Ḥaredi/National-Religious Dichotomy in Israel I: Three Case Studies in Historical Revisionism by the Families of R. Kook's Disciples[1]

INTRODUCTION

Three famous rabbis with personal connections to R. Avraham Yitzḥak HaKohen Kook, to his inner circle, and to his yeshiva, are discussed in this chapter. While these rabbis never denied their connections to R. Kook, their descendants – for various ideological and educational purposes – did everything possible to rewrite their forbears' histories by eliminating all references to R. Kook and his yeshiva, Merkaz HaRav.

This revisionism is tightly correlated with the split of the Orthodox population in Israel into a ḥaredi community on the one hand and a national-religious community on the other.[2] This split, which became pronounced in the middle third of

1. Translated by Michael Appel. This chapter was mostly written in 2009, and was first published *Assif* 3, 2016 in commemoration of the 80th anniversary of R. Kook's passing.
2. See Benjamin Brown, *"M'Hitbadlut Politit L'Hitbatzrut Tarbutit: HaḤazon Ish V'Kviat Darkah Shel HaYahadut HaḤaredit B'Eretz Yisrael,"* in Mordekhai Bar-On, Tzvi Zameret (ed.), *Shnei Evrei Hagesher* (Jerusalem, 2002), 400–408.

the twentieth century and which solidified a decade later after the Six-Day War,[3] is reflected amidst the inner circle of R. Kook's followers.

R. YITZḤAK ARIELI

The most famous rewrite, judging by its publicity at the time, was perpetrated on R. Yitzḥak Arieli, author of *Einayim LaMishpat* (1896–1974). R. Arieli, Jerusalem-born, learned in the yeshivot of the Old Yishuv and became close to R. Kook upon the latter's return to Israel in Elul 1919. When Yeshivat Merkaz HaRav was founded, he was appointed its *mashgiaḥ* and later functioned as a member of the yeshiva's administration. In 1941, he was appointed Rav of the Knesset Yisrael neighborhood, and later functioned as the official *posek* for Bikkur Ḥolim Hospital. Simultaneously, his involvement with Merkaz HaRav waned, and he ceased his administrative role due to events beyond the scope of this article.[4] He maintained, however, an active role in the yeshiva until the early 1950s, and continued afterward for several more years to serve in an unofficial capacity. Until his death, R. Arieli represented the face of the yeshiva to its students.[5] One could argue that most of the rabbis who received *semikhah* from R. Arieli in the last twenty years of his life were students at Merkaz HaRav who had come to learn with him.[6] He himself referred to Merkaz HaRav as *yeshivateinu hakedoshah,* our holy yeshiva,) using the definite article,[7] and he continued to participate in the yeshiva's important ideological ceremonies such as the celebrations of *Yom Ha'atzma'ut* and *Yom Yerushalayim*.[8]

3. My dear friend, Yair HaLevi, will shortly finish a doctoral dissertation entitled "*Mahapekhat HaḤaredit HeḤadashah B'Shnot HaShivim Shel HaMe'ah Ha'Esrim*" See also his thesis, "*Teguvot HaZerem HaḤaredi HaMerkazi L'Milḥemet Sheshet HaYamim,*" (2010).
4. See the next chapter for a biography of R. Arieli, his ties to R. Kook, his role in the history of Merkaz HaRav, and the reasons he was forced out of Merkaz HaRav.
5. See R. Moshe Tzvi Neriyah, *Bisdei HaRa'ayah* (Kfar HaRo'eh, 1987), 373–74. Compare to the interview conducted with him in 1966 upon his receiving the Israel Prize in rabbinical literature: "Even after he left the yeshiva, his students flocked from all over Israel to visit his home in Jerusalem in order to hear Torah from his mouth" (*Maariv*, 4 Iyar 1966, 19).
6. Among others, it is worth mentioning: R. Uzi Kalkheim, R. Moshe Dimentman, R. Eitan Eisman, R. Isser Klonski, R. Aryeh Horowitz, R. Zephaniah Drori, R. Yaakov Ariel, R. Yisrael Ariel, and others. Of course, the list can include additional *musmakhim* of Merkaz HaRav from earlier years, including R. Yeshayahu Meshorer.
7. As the term appears on the *semikhah* of R. Eisman, from 27 Iyar 1967[!] (*Bisdei HaRa'ayah* 375).
8. At the *se'udat hodaya* (thanksgiving meal) held at Yeshivat Merkaz HaRav to commemorate the first anniversary of *Yom Yerushalayim*, on 28 Iyar 1968, R. Arieli sat in a seat of honor between R. Tzvi Yehudah Kook and the Nazir and even delivered a speech (*Bisdei HaRa'ayah* 372). The prior year, R. Arieli participated in a *Yom Ha'atzma'ut* banquet hosted by the yeshiva on 5 Iyar

In the introductions to the early volumes of *Einayim LaMishpat* published by R. Arieli between 1936 and 1948, he acknowledges the deep influence of R. Kook during the sixteen years in which they were close, as well as his own role in the establishment of Yeshivat Merkaz HaRav. Here, greatly summarized, is how it is described in the introduction to his first volume, on Tractate Kiddushin, as published in 1936:

> Avraham [Kook] was unique, a giant among giants, sent by HaShem to sustain renewed generations in the Land of the Living. Pillar of fire, holy crown, wise one of the generation and its leader, our master and teacher, R. Avraham Yitzḥak HaKohen Kook *ztz"l* [...] The chosen few in the Holy City of Jerusalem were drawn to him through bonds of strong love and fidelity. [...]
>
> Praise and thanks to HaShem who has enabled me to be one of the few who gathered this aforementioned group, and one of the early founders of the holy yeshiva. After much hard work and investment of spiritual and material energy, HaShem willed that our efforts be rewarded and develop into a great and wonderful yeshiva that serves today as a flagship of our glorious Holy City, by the name of Yeshivat Merkaz HaRav. And here I am, a bearer of the holy ark, standing in service from its founding until today. May HaShem grant me the opportunity to continue in this holy work, to learn and to teach, etc. And I owe him [R. Kook] a debt of gratitude for bringing me close to this holy work, and I had the merit to stand before him for sixteen years, to listen to his holy words and to meditate upon his holy ways. And he even recruited me to contribute to his massive work, *Halakhah Berurah,* of which two tractates, Ketubot and Makkot, were compiled by me, with HaShem's help [...]
>
> Our only remaining comfort is the light hidden within his holy books and his spirit which infuses this yeshiva, the embers of his holiness, the beautiful yeshiva, his soul's work and his life's joy, which grew and was cultivated with great effort and influence of his splendor[...] And we can only grasp at his coattails and attempt to walk in his footsteps.[9]

1967, and delivered remarks on *inyanei d'yoma,* the topics of the day (as cited by R. Yitzḥak Shilat in his journal, *Arba'im L'Binah* [Ma'aleh Adumim, 2007], 13). There are photos corroborating both of these events.

9. *Einayim LaMishpat,* Kiddushin (Jerusalem, 1936), introduction, 2–3.

Twelve years later, R. Arieli wrote concisely, but in a similar vein, in his introduction to the second volume, on Berakhot, published in 1948:

> Some of these *ḥidushim* were said before the *gedolim* of our holy yeshiva, Merkaz HaRav, the yeshiva brimming with the spirit of its founder, the Gaon and Saint of Israel, our master and teacher, R. Avraham Yitzḥak HaKohen Kook *ztz"l* [...] And through the grace of HaShem I was among those who were privileged to found and erect the holy yeshiva through hard work, with spiritual and material investment. And the great Rabbi *ztz"l* bestowed upon me administrative duties and various jobs. I was a bearer of the holy ark during all the days of its establishment.[10]

And yet, in 2006, several descendants of R. Arieli published a new edition of *Einayim LaMishpat* on Berakhot, omitting the end of the introduction that was just quoted above. Moreover, they appended a biography of R. Arieli to the introduction with no reference whatsoever to R. Kook or Yeshivat Merkaz HaRav. This was immediately discovered and vilified by the national-religious press[11] amidst calls to flood the publisher with complaints and to boycott the new edition.[12]

It is easy to understand the protest, as this type of censorship is wrongful and its intent is to erase history. Moreover, it serves to diminish the stature of R. Kook. What is more difficult to comprehend is that this protest took place in complete ignorance of a much greater omission in the introduction to *Einayim Lamishpat* on Kiddushin, published a decade earlier in 1994 and prior to that in 1989. More than half the introduction, including all the descriptions cited above

10. *Einayim LaMishpat,* Berakhot (Jerusalem, 1948), introduction, p 2.
11. See R. Eliezer Melamed's column in *Revivim* 207, August 31, 2006; and the following footnote. [Translator's note: see https://www.inn.co.il/Besheva/Article.aspx/6057.]
12. R. Neriyah Gutel, "*Meḥa'ah al Kevod HaRav*" in *HaTzofeh – Musaf Sofrim U'Sefarim,* August 25, 2006. Later, R. Gutel testified that after exposing the revisionism, he received threatening calls from the publisher (Letter to the Editor, *Makor Rishon,* August 21, 2009). Ultimately, as told by R. Melamed, after the publisher heard the criticism, he sought the advice of R. Yosef Shalom Elyashiv, who ruled that his actions were improper. The books were returned to the publishing house, the first page was corrected, reprinted, and inserted in place of the censored page, "And this is how the book is sold today" (*Revivim* 216, November 9, 2006). In the letter from R. Gutel cited above, there is one correction: It was not the publisher himself who turned to R. Elyashiv, but the donor who commissioned the publication, R. Eliyahu Mordekhai Sonnenfeld (great-grandson of R. Yosef Ḥayim Sonnenfeld). We should point out that the publisher's introduction was not corrected, and still contains no reference to R. Arieli's ties to Merkaz HaRav. [Translator's note: see https://www.inn.co.il/B'Sheva/Article.aspx/6191.]

regarding R. Kook and Yeshivat Merkaz HaRav were omitted as if they had never existed. Moreover, the first edition to contain this drastic omission – to our great distress – is the 1967 edition published by R. Yitzḥak Arieli himself![13]

If so, it was R. Arieli himself who decided, by the end of the 1960s, to omit from his introduction all mention of R. Kook and Yeshivat Merkaz HaRav. Why would he do this? One would expect an ideological shift, or a concern for his public image, or something similar. However, apart from this being anachronistic,[14] and not reflecting the very close relationship between R. Arieli and R. Kook,[15] it is impossible to accept this in light of the above cited facts regarding the very public relationship during those very same years between R. Arieli and Yeshivat Merkaz HaRav. A more plausible explanation is that R. Arieli wanted this volume to be accepted by the growing community of yeshivot and institutions that did not look kindly at works that emphasized the persona of R. Kook.[16] The ultimate proof is that when R. Arieli republished the volume on Berakhot three years later, he retained, toward the end of the introduction, the very language praising R. Kook and Yeshivat Merkaz HaRav (which would later be omitted in 2006), as they do not stand out as much as those in the introduction to the volume on Kiddushin. This explains why even in the text of the Kiddushin volume, R. Kook's name is not entirely absent.[17] Nor did R. Arieli remove the reference to his position at

13. *Einayim LaMishpat,* Kiddushin, New Edition with Revisions and Supplements (Tel Aviv, 1967). This is photocopied from the 1936 edition. Appended to the end of the book is a letter from R. Menaḥem Zemba and fifteen additional pages of corrections and additions. Erased from the introduction are the words beginning from "Avraham was unique..." until the end, including the passages describing the composition of *Einayim LaMishpat* – except one sentence about the erasure of the author of *Ein Mishpat.*
14. Later in this article, we will encounter a similar claim, specifically around this period immediately following the Six-Day War.
15. If this were the case, then on the contrary, we would have expected R. Arieli to emphasize the true nature of his revered teacher.
16. There are many examples of this. The most famous one is the book *Torat HaNazir* by R. Yitzḥak Hutner, first printed in Kovno in 1932. In the photo offset copies produced during the author's lifetime, in 1965 and 1980, the approbations of R. Kook were erased (as was that of R. Avraham Dov Ber Kahana Shapira). R. Hutner's son-in-law, R. Yonatan David, claims that distribution considerations were behind this move. Moreover, similar incidents took place during R. Kook's lifetime, when multiple editions of books were published, first with R. Kook's approbation, and later without it. Examples include *Sefer HaMa'aseh V'haMidrash* (Jerusalem, 1937), and *Sefer Yabi'a Omer* (Jerusalem, 1924). I have written at length about this elsewhere, and will return to the topic in the future.
17. See the errata section to *Daf* 70b.

Merkaz HaRav. These references were also retained in the rabbinic approbations printed at the end of the volume[18] – just as in the original version.

Either way, the evidence suggests that the omissions from the new edition of 2006 were not simply business considerations. Even more so, there is a fundamental difference between revisions by the author himself, and others who tamper with his writings. Who is this descendant of R. Arieli responsible for this publication? Investigation leads us to a known personality from the family of R. Mordekhai Ilan, the oldest son-in-law of R. Arieli. Because this individual subjected his own father's writings [R. Mordekhai Ilan's] to even greater revisionism than those of his grandfather [R. Yitzḥak Arieli], we will now move on to the case of R. Mordekhai Ilan.

R. MORDEKHAI ILAN

R. Mordekhai Ilan (Ilander) was born in Suvalk in 1915. From 1930 and on, he studied in the yeshiva of Ramailes in Vilna with "the gaon, tzaddik, our teacher R. Raphael Ḥayim Shlomo Hyman *ztz"l*, who nurtured me with great love in my youth." He also studied with "the great R. Ḥayim Ozer Grodzenski *ztz"l* and the well-known R. Ḥannokh Henoch Eigis *ztz"l Hy"d*, the author of *Sifrei Marḥeshet*, who enlightened me with the light of their Torah and drew me close during the years I found myself in their domain."[19] When he moved to Eretz Yisrael in mid-1935 he first learned in Merkaz HaRav with "the great gaon, our strength, the holy master of Israel, R. Avraham Yitzḥak HaKohen Kook *ztz"l*." In the yeshiva he also met his future father-in-law, "the great gaon R. Yitzḥak Arieli *shlit"a*, founder and *rosh metivta* of Yeshivat Merkaz HaRav, and one of the great rabbis of our generation in the Holy City," and married his daughter, Sara Rivka.

Subsequently, R. Ilan studied in Bet Midrash Ohel Torah, "led by the great rabbi, our strength, master of Eretz Yisrael, R. Yitzḥak Isaac HaLevi Herzog *shlit"a*, who

---

18. Especially in the approbation of R. Yaakov Moshe Ḥarlap: "He is the blessed fruit of the Torah of the great gaon and holy man of Israel, our master R. Avraham Yitzḥak HaKohen Kook *ztz"l*. Ever since he appeared in Jerusalem with his great vision to establish a central, world yeshiva in the Holy City, he [R. Arieli] was one of the exalted few who was roused to implement this lofty and holy concept, and became one of its key founders…" (p. 166). Had there been serious ideological opposition, these words would also have been omitted. But because we are only speaking of "distribution concerns" it was enough to omit the more obviously problematic material at the beginning of the book.
19. R. Ilan on the back of the title page to his *Torat HaKodesh* 1 (Jerusalem, 1949). The letters he received from R. Shlomo Hyman were published in *Ner Mordekhai*, included in *Shitta Mekubetzet*, Tractate Tamid (*Makhon Knesset Ha'Rishonim* edition, Bnei Brak, 1982), 268–69.

kept me close to him from the day he arrived."[20] Along the way, R. Ilan became close to "the gaon and master, R. Yitzḥak Ze'ev HaLevi *ztz"l*, the Brisker Rav, master of the Talmud, with whom I discussed many details of my book." He was also close with "the gaon R. Isser Zalman Meltzer *ztz"l*, who published my comments to his book *Even Ha'Azel* on the laws of sacrifices."[21] In 1956 he was appointed *dayan* of the Tel Aviv *bet din*, where he eventually became *av bet din*. In addition to his work *Torat HaKodesh*, he published many important works during the course of his life, from novellae of *Rishonim*, and participated in Torah undertakings of the Harry Fishel Institute, the *Encyclopedia Talmudit*, and others. He also participated in many conferences of Mossad HaRav Kook until his death in 1981.

From this impressive background, it is plain to see the breadth and diversity of great rabbis whom R. Ilan counts as major influences on his life. Among all these, between his youth and his later rabbinic career, he did not fail to mention Rabbis Kook, Herzog, and his father-in-law, R. Arieli. However, as we shall see, what was eventually done to R. Arieli by some of his grandchildren was also done to R. Ilan in the very year of his death – by some of his own sons.

In Bnei Brak in 1982, R. Ilan's sons, headed by R. Yaakov David Ilan,[22] released his work *Torat HaKodesh* – the second edition, volumes 1 and 2. In the book's foreword, the sons provided a short biographical sketch of their father. It describes how he studied with R. Shlomo Hyman, R. Ḥayim Ozer Grodzenski, and the author of *Marḥeshet*. It then immediately skips to "his marriage and arrival in Eretz Yisrael, and entering the house of his illustrious father-in-law R. Yitzḥak Arieli," with no mention at all of Yeshivat Merkaz HaRav or R. Kook, nor of Ohel Torah

---

20. R. Ilan in his introduction to *Torat HaKodesh*, vol. 1. Compare this to a letter of recommendation on behalf of R. Ilan sent by R. Isser Zalman Meltzer to the administrators of Ohel Torah, October 19, 1938: "... The Rav HaGaon, the paragon of excellence, R. Mordekhai Ilander, son-in-law of my dear friend HaRav HaGaon R. Yitzḥak Arieli *shlit"a*, has received a stipend of two lira per month from Yeshivat Merkaz HaRav from the time he was a young man prior to marriage. And knowing well the situation of my friend R. Arieli, and knowing the awesome potential of R. Mordekhai his son-in-law, I strongly request the honorable institution Ohel Torah to accept him..." (Catalogue of the Kedem Auction House, Summer 2011, Auction 16, Lot 469)
21. Language of R. Ilan, at the end of his introduction to *Torat HaKodesh* 2 (Bnei Brak, 1969).
22. Born 1954, resident of Bnei Brak, *rosh metivta* at Yeshivat Knesset Yitzḥak in Ḥadera, son-in-law of R. Moshe Meir HaLevi Pereg, who was rosh kollel of Shomrei HaḤomot in Jerusalem. He authored *Masa Yad* (3 volumes); *Kovetz al Yad* on *Shas*; edited various works of *Rishonim* (as part of the project *Knesset Rishonim*, and with the *Machon LeHotza'at Rishonim V'Aḥaronim* of Mossad HaRav Kook, etc.), and serves as one of the lead editors for the Schottenstein Talmud. He was awarded the Rav Kook Prize in Rabbinic Literature in 2008 by the municipality of Tel Aviv (ironic, considering the events we are about to describe).

and R. Herzog. Several lines earlier, the sons mention that their father published his book "with the encouragement and approval of the *gedolei hador* of that time, R. Isser Zalman Meltzer and the Brisker Rav *ztz"l*." Rabbis from a different circle, who were also considered *gedolei hador* by R. Ilan, disappeared without a trace.[23]

In addition, several passages authored by R. Ilan himself were omitted. A comparison between the introduction to the 1982 edition – entitled the "Introduction from the First Edition" – and the actual introduction to the 1949 edition reveals that the final third was omitted. In it, R. Ilan describes how some of the topics in his book were reviewed "before the *gedolei Torah* of the Holy City of Jerusalem":

> Several topics were discussed and elucidated through *pilpul* and exchanges with exalted Torah scholars in the centers of Torah in which I sat during the compilation of this work – that is, the great yeshiva, the central world institution, Yeshivat Merkaz HaRav, founded by the exalted gaon, the holy master of Israel, R. Avraham Yitzḥak HaKohen Kook *ztz"l*, may his memory protect us, whom I merited to stand before; and the great institution Ohel Torah under the leadership of our great Rabbi, the gaon, our strength, master of Eretz Yisrael, R. Yitzḥak Isaac HaLevi Herzog *shlit"a*, who brought me close to him from the moment he arrived in this holy place (may he merit to speedily see the ultimate salvation on this holy ground, with the rebuilding of the Temple, speedily in our days) [...] And I hereby am pleasantly obliged to mention with special blessings my father-in-law, the great gaon, R. Yitzḥak Arieli, *shlit"a*, founder and *rosh metivta* of the holy Central Yeshiva [i.e., Merkaz HaRav] and one of the great rabbis of the Holy City of Jerusalem, who is responsible for a large portion of this book. May he merit the continuation of his holy work in spreading Torah with peace of mind, and to complete his great Torah work, *Einayim LaMishpat* on *Shas*.[24]

With respect to these types of omissions, his descendants could argue that their father himself cut his ties with the aforementioned rabbis and the institutions "of

23. Indeed, in his introduction to *Torat HaKodesh* 2, R. Ilan singles out these two rabbis (as described above) and even writes that, "These two *geonim* were most responsible for shaping my learning style." But he then goes on to qualify, "in addition to the instruction from my previous teachers, as I mentioned in volume 1."

24. Of course, also omitted are the concluding lines from the introduction, in which R. Ilan expresses, "Thanks and blessings to Mossad HaRav Kook, at whose heads stands the great Minister of the State of Israel HaRav HaGaon Yehudah Leib HaKohen Maimon *shlit"a*." (And instead, several *Divrei Torah* were inserted into the empty spaces in the new edition.)

his past" during the course of his lifetime. The "past," in our opinion, would seem to be the period of time before R. Ilan entered into the orbit of the Brisker Rav (R. Yitzḥak Ze'ev Soloveitchik). However, in this case, it is impossible to make this claim in light of the fact that in the beginning of *Torat HaKodesh* Volume 2, published in 1969, R. Ilan chose to republish two approbations that he received for *Torat HaKodesh* Volume 1, one of which was from R. Herzog.[25] His sons, not surprisingly, omitted this approbation from their version and kept only the second one (from R. Isser Zalman Meltzer). Besides this, R. Ilan's connection to the Brisker Rav began even before he published Volume 1 of *Torat HaKodesh*,[26] yet this did not cause him to deny his earlier rabbinic influences or to completely adopt the positions of the Brisker Rav. It certainly did not cause him to downplay the honor of great scholars from other rabbinic circles.[27] The sons, of course, see things differently.[28]

Moreover, it is clear that this case departs from a simple case of omitting "uncomfortable" passages that would potentially harm sales of the book among certain segments of the ḥaredi public. It rises to a level of revisions and erasures within sentences across the entire introduction, even where the intent of the author is materially changed, or the passage rendered nonsensical. For example, the second sentence of the original reads:

---

25. This was a decade after the deaths of R. Herzog (1959) and the Brisker Rav (1960). The significance is reinforced by the fact that the relationship between the two men was tense in the last years of their lives when they fought over the establishment of Hekhal Shlomo, the seat of the Israeli Chief Rabbinate, which was then headed by R. Herzog. See also the letter from R. Ilan to R. Shalom Nathan Ra'anan, from the end of 1959, eulogizing his son, R. Avraham Yitzḥak, in which he signs it, "Your friend, and friend of the Yeshiva" (*Laḥai Ro'i* [Jerusalem, 1961], 72–73).
26. Comments by "Our master, the gaon, HaRav Yitzḥak Ze'ev HaLevi *shlit"a* of Brisk," are cited numerous times throughout the book: Pages 14b, 25a, 41a, 47a, 69b (where a responsum is cited), 72b, 94b, 96b, 104b. See also the following two footnotes.
27. To wit, in *Torat HaKodesh* (1949 edition), pages 87b–88a, the Brisker Rav is cited. Shortly afterward, in a footnote on 89a, he cites, "a great question posed by the Chief Rabbi of Israel, our great gaon, master R. Yitzḥak Isaac HaLevi Herzog *shlit"a*..." Further, in the errata at the end of the book (page 104b), n. 5 cites, "the novella from the gaon R. Yitzḥak Ze'ev HaLevi [the Brisker] *shlit"a*." Several lines later, n. 7 mentions, "I saw that, in *Mishpat Kohen*, the Chief Rabbi of Israel the gaon and master R. Kook *ztz"l* dealt with this issue, and look there to see his beautiful words in this matter."
28. In *Torat HaKodesh*, section 1, letter 8 (p. 6a), R. Ilan added parenthetically, "And see *Mishpat Kohen* by our master, the Rav *ztz"l* in *Hilkhot B'hab* where he dealt with a contradiction in between two Tosftot." In the edition published by the sons (p. 81), this note is omitted. We should note that R. Ilan himself had begun to prepare a second edition of his book, as the sons mention in their introduction. However, this fact cannot be used as a blanket cover-up for omissions of this sort.

> And if on the one hand, God's justice was revealed through the horrific bloodletting in the body of Israel, extending like bottomless depths; on the other hand, emerging before us is a sign of the beginning of the appearance of God's righteousness, whose peak is like "the mountains of the Lord." [...] And therefore, praise for the current generation that is closer to the Redemption must come from the deep realization of God's activity here in our world.

In other words, parallel to the horrific devastation of the Holocaust, the rise of the Jewish nation in its land is a sign that we are approaching Redemption. However, in the introduction published [by the sons] in 1982, the words "emerging before us" are missing. According to R. Ilan's sons, the Holocaust itself was both "like bottomless depths" and also "like the mountains of the Lord!"

Similarly, in the next sentence, R. Ilan writes in the original: "[God's] appearance and revelation will be correlated with the increased pace of yearning [for it]. The current generation is beginning **to 'clothe' itself in the 'attire of action' envisioned by generations of Israel.** This is in the merit of the unceasing yearning of the past generations." The sons omitted the bolded line (my emphasis) in the 1982 version. The author continues, "And appearing before our eyes – **with the hope that these are the first sprouts of the flowering of the Redemption of our Holy Land and His nation** – they are the fruits of the fire of passion." Again, the bolded line has been omitted.

We find similar conduct in the new version of *Torat HaKodesh* Volume 2, published in Bnei Brak, 1985. Besides certain additions taken from the author's original manuscript (in this case, annotated correctly), many changes were again made in the content. Here too is an obvious intent to erase any hint of R. Ilan's relatively positive attitude toward the events of that era.[29] It goes without saying that the second foreword to the book, which was entirely colored by the events of the Six-Day War (which occurred two years before the original version), was completely removed.

In this last instance, perhaps the author's sons will justify their actions with the claim that the "current events" discussed in the original introductions were only appropriate for their time (a mere fifteen years prior), but not for posterity. But

29. The sentence, "In light of the events of our generation, it is our hope that we are taking great strides toward the Messianic age," is erased. And the words that immediately followed, "And we have come ever closer to 'speedily shall the Temple be rebuilt'" were revised to, "we look forward to speedily rebuilding the Temple." And so on.

this claim can't cover up the historical revisionism: the rewriting of sections; the omission of R. Herzog's approbation; eliminating R. Kook and his institutions from the biography; and the other changes described above. It is also not credible, in light of the fact that other sections which can also be classified as "current events," but with less disturbing content from the sons' hashkafic perspective, seem to have been left alone.[30]

R. YITZḤAK SCHULZINGER

Now we come to the most drastic example of a man's life and works being completely recast by his sons. R. Yitzḥak Schulzinger was born in Siemiatycze, Poland, in 1904. As a youth, he studied in the Radin Yeshiva. He made aliyah in 1924 and studied in Merkaz HaRav for ten years, receiving *semikhah* from R. Kook and R. Ḥarlap. In the winter of 1934, he married and became rabbi of Kfar Ganim. In 1935, we find his approbation on the compilation, *MiPninei HaRambam*, alongside those of his teachers R. Kook and R. Ḥarlap. From 1936, R. Schulzinger served as a *posek* in Haifa, supervised the local slaughterers, and was also the rabbi of the local synagogue. He continued in these roles until his sudden death in the winter of 1956.[31]

In Jerusalem in 1950, R. Schulzinger published *Imrot Yitzḥak* on Bereshit – a compilation of weekly *drashot* (sermons) delivered during his tenure as rabbi in Haifa. In the first pages of the book, alongside his *semikhot* from Rabbis Kook, Ḥarlap, and Abba Yaakov Borokhov, he included approbations from: R. Ḥarlap; R. Yitzḥak Arieli; R. Shalom Natan Ra'anan, the son-in-law of R. Kook and director of Yeshivat Merkaz HaRav; and the Chief Rabbis of the time, R. Herzog and R. Ben Zion Meir Ḥai Uziel. He even included a letter from the director of the Chief Rabbinate, R. Yaakov Barukh. In his introduction (p. 2), R. Schulzinger describes how

> I was fortunate to bask in the holy shadow of our teacher, the holy light of Israel, its chariot and riders, crown of the generation, my master and teacher, rabbi of all Israel, the first Chief Rabbi in Eretz Yisrael, the great gaon, R. Avraham Yitzḥak HaKohen Kook *ztz"l*, the priest and judge of the Holy Place [...] Our teacher *ztz"l* led and judged the entire nation

30. For example, R. Ilan mentions that, "The awakening of the last generation has caused *gedolei haTorah* to revive the practice of studying the halakhot of *Seder Kodashim*." Can "the last generation" really be referencing the new edition's publication date?
31. For further reading on R. Schulzinger, see R. M.Z. Neriyah, *Bisdei HaRa'ayah*, 465–72; Eliezer Tosh in *Sefer Kehilat Siemiatycze* (Tel Aviv, 1965), 251; and in his sons' books, see below.

> righteously, dedicating his life for what is just and viewing the entire nation favorably [...] For many years I was privileged to serve his holy presence, to listen to his teachings on halakhah, aggadah, mussar, theology, and philosophy. And all of it was delivered "from the mouth of the High Priest in holiness and purity."

Further on, R. Schulzinger continues to praise Yeshivat Merkaz HaRav and to quote the teachings of R. Kook. Similarly, he describes the personality of R. Ḥarlap and cites his teachings as well, writing as follows (p. 3):

> God granted me the singular privilege of becoming close to the Rosh Yeshiva, the great gaon, R. Yaakov Moshe Ḥarlap *shlit"a* [...] who drew my soul close with both of his holy and faithful hands. I was a constant guest in his home on Shabbat and weekdays.

Later in the introduction, R. Schulzinger expounds upon the virtues of Torah, the Jewish people, and the Land of Israel, declaring explicitly (p. 11): "We must give thanks to HaShem, who blessed us – after the horrific, devastating Holocaust in Europe, after this great tragedy – with the beginning of the Redemption, the establishment of the State of Israel and the government of Israel, and the beginning of the ingathering of the exiles." In conclusion, he notes the many lives lost "on the altar of the holiness of the nation and the land" during the War of Independence, including two of his own nephews.

At the end of the book, R. Schulzinger returns to the subject of his nephews' activities in the Israel Defense Forces,[32] constantly repeating the refrain that the establishment of the State of Israel is the beginning of the Redemption:

> The fallen have brought us, with God's help, to the beginning of the Redemption, bringing the Yishuv to the Redemption of a Jewish State (p. 286).
>
> We are approaching the era of the War of *At'halta di-Geula,* the Beginning of Redemption [...] and through the spirit of the holy Torah, he [that is, his nephew] arose as a hero with all his soul, to go out heroically

32. Amongst other places, he writes (p. 282), when detailing the activities and heroism of his nephew, Amiḥai, in the Hagana and Tzaha"l until his death on the battlefield, "We have reached, thank God, the beginning of the Redemption. Yet we are still tense and on alert before our enemies, as we are still far away from the complete Redemption..."

> to fight for the Sanctification of the Name and the land, and he played a significant part in the war against the enemy – the War of Independence. (p. 289)

> Our enemies did not want us to go from destruction to rebuilding, from exile to freedom. Against this evil and cruel desire of the enemy, he fought resolutely, with no hesitation. And at the beginning of Adar, when the light of the *At'halta di-Geula,* Beginning of Redemption, began to shine [...] his life was cut short. After all the hardships he endured, and all his toil on behalf of the nation's independence, he did not merit seeing its establishment, dying the death of a hero on its very doorstep. (p. 291)

The entire book is embedded with similar expressions in this vein, declaring the State of Israel's establishment to be the beginning of the redemptive process.[33] The author even dedicated a *drashah* in honor of the day on which "the United Nations accepted a Jewish State in the Land of Israel," an anniversary that became known as "29 November" – and in it (pp. 205–6) he writes:

> What occurred then, when the United Nations decided to give the Jews a Jewish State in the Land of Israel, for which we have waited almost two thousand years, is a great, historic moment. We are obligated to view it as a miracle from Heaven [...] Our precious and holy blood has been spilled in the war to redeem our land, God have mercy, but we will not fear nor despair [...] Now, with the beginning of the Redemption, we fight as a nation defending its territory and homeland.

These words were written at the time of the State of Israel's establishment. Within the next two years, during elections for the first Knesset and in the course of its term, the government's secular goals regarding the judicial and political character of the State began to take shape. The Zionist establishment wanted the Yishuv's institutions to continue operating as they had under the Mandate. This conflicted with the hopes of many members of the observant community who believed that a Jewish State would be characterized by a greater fealty to traditional Jewish values. The government's policies caused many rabbis of the national-religious community, with Chief Rabbi Herzog at the forefront, to fight to strengthen the religious character of the State and protest against secular trends in lawmaking. This, alongside their praise for the

33. See pages 62–63, 89–90, 110–11, 135, 171, 227–28, 268.

State.[34] R. Schulzinger was part of this group and delivered many *drashot* on the subject, writing (pp. 153–54):

> The protest rallies of today are, to our great distress, not against foreign rulers or invaders, but against our own ministers, our Jewish brethren. We are full of thanks to God for the miracles He performed for us. We merited establishing the State of Israel and a Jewish government after two thousand years of exile and tribulations. Now we protest against the government for feeding the Jewish people under its auspices forbidden foods [...] It is foolishness on the part of this heathen-like government to violate the Torah's commandments [...] We must ask the question: Is it feasible to have two different kitchens, two tables? [...] We are one nation, we must be united in the home, in the family, at the table, in the one Torah and land, one state, the State of Israel. We should not be separated.

R. Schulzinger expresses the same sentiment, in fiery language, in an additional *drashah* (pp. 245–49) prior to the vote for the first Knesset:

> We face a grave danger, the establishment of laws and character in the State of Israel and the Nation that lives in Zion that contradict the Torah!! We must ask: Is this what we prayed for all these years, suffered in exile, kept the nation of Israel from assimilating, [...] that after we finally merited the Beginning of Redemption, there are those who want to simply cross out the glorious past of the Jewish nation of God's Holy Torah [...] Let us all rise up and vote for representatives loyal to the Divine mission [...] to establish the law of the land and character of the State in accordance with a Torah way of life.

---

34. Compare R. Schulzinger's comments with those of R. Herzog:

> It is inconceivable in the mind of the truly religious Jew, for the Jewish State to abandon its source of water, our Holy Torah, and to dig empty wells with laws of another nation [...] We always thought that, immediately upon declaration of a State, those in power would confer with the religious representatives of the nation [...] Who will save us from this disgraceful, painful situation!" (*HaTorah V'haMedina* 7 (Tel Aviv, 1957), 10.

See also R. Shaul Yisraeli, introduction to volumes 1–4 (Tel Aviv, 1949–52). Also, see R. Tzvi Pesaḥ Frank's approbation to *Sefer Mishpat HaTzava B'Yisrael* [Jerusalem, 1949]). Of course, the emergent ḥaredi camp did not view the State of Israel as the beginning of the Redemption and so reacted differently. They found it much easier to retreat from overt support of the State that they had expressed in the immediate aftermath of the Declaration of Independence and to advocate a separation from the rest of the Jewish community in the State.

In summary, we can characterize the two previous cases of revisionism – that of R. Arieli and of R. Ilan – as erasing personal connections between the subjects and R. Kook and Merkaz HaRav and with other Torah greats of this community, but not at all connected with any particular pro-religious-Zionist ideology (even if one can detect such ideology between the lines, especially in the case of R. Arieli). However, in this case, *Imrot Yitzḥak* is unequivocally a religious-Zionist text, both in its content and in its intended audience. The author is tightly wedded to the idea that the State of Israel represents the beginning of the Redemption, and from this position, he fights for the religious character of the State.

However, here too, neither R. Schulzinger's biography, nor his ties with R. Kook's circle, nor his book, published just seven years before his death – none were enough to save him when his sons proceeded to get involved with his life and writings. In Bnei Brak, in 1974, fifteen years after his death, a second publication of *Imrot Yitzḥak* was released by his sons, led by R. Moshe Mordekhai Schulzinger.[35] In the introduction, R. M. M. Schulzinger published a biography of his father,[36] in which he describes at length how his father studied in the yeshivot of Europe, mainly in Radin, where he gained the favor of the Ḥafetz Ḥayim.[37] He quotes at length from the introduction to *Imrot Yitzḥak* and from a letter his father received from R. Naftali Tropp. Yet when he reaches the year 1924, when his father came to Israel and entered Merkaz HaRav to study under R. Kook, not a word is mentioned, other than this laconic sentence: "And he learned in

35. Born 1941 and learned as a youth in Yeshivat Merkaz HaRav (see further, n. 46). From 1959 and on, he learned in various yeshivot in Bnei Brak, and in 1964, became the son-in-law of R. Shlomo Cohen, a close disciple of the Ḥazon Ish. He published dozens of books in his lifetime, most notably *Sidrat Mishmar HaLevi* on the Talmud. He was known as a great Torah scholar and influential lecturer. He was close with the Lithuanian ḥaredi leadership. He died in the summer of 2010. A book about him was recently published: *Rav Moshe Mordekhai* 1 (Modi'in Illit, 2013).

36. This article was previously published in his introduction to *Mishmar HaLevi* on Tractate Yoma (Bnei Brak, 1971), and was published in many of the subsequent volumes of *Mishmar HaLevi*, including: Temurah (Bnei Brak, 1999); Ketubot (Bnei Brak, 2000); Megillah (Bnei Brak, 2000); Sukkah (Bnei Brak, 2002); Rosh Hashanah (Bnei Brak, 2003); Shabbat/Eruvin (Bnei Brak, 2003); and also in the introduction to *Shalmei Sarah* (Bnei Brak, 2000).

37. With this, R. M. M. Schulzinger attempts to portray the Ḥafetz Ḥayim as his father's main teacher and mentor, even though R. Schulzinger only studied briefly in Radin during his youth. However, in Merkaz HaRav, he studied for a full ten years, beginning at age twenty, and those rabbis conferred his *semikhah* to the rabbinate. This is why R. Schulzinger himself, in the introduction to *Imrot Yitzḥak*, gives R. Kook much more gravitas than he does the Ḥafetz Ḥayim.

Jerusalem for ten years until he married."[38] The son makes no mention of, nor even hints at, which yeshiva his father studied in, whom he learned from, which rabbis he was close to, who gave him *semikhah,* who gave approbations to his books, and whom he valued most over all other rabbis.

In a later instance, we find tampering not just with the biographical details of R. Schulzinger, but also with the content itself. In the introduction to *Mishmar HaLevi* on Bekhorot (Bnei Brak, 1997), p. 1, R. M. M. Schulzinger quotes a passage from his father's introduction to *Imrot Yitzḥak* in the following fashion: "From time to time, I would go to Jerusalem to greet my rabbis, where I would also exchange written articles and responsa with them. Due to lack of funds, I hereby publish at this time only on Sefer Bereshit." One who looks at the source (p. 10) will find that after the word, "responsa," there appears another sentence: "And two responsa directed to me from the Rabbi *ztz"l* were published in his book *Da'at Kohen*" – of course referring to R. Avraham Yitzḥak Kook.[39] It goes without saying that R. M. M. Schulzinger declines to mention in any of his books all references to the fact that his grandfather – the father-in-law of R. Schulzinger – R. Avraham Ḥayim Chechik, was extremely close to R. Kook from his tenure in Jaffa, and was known as his *meshamesh,* aide, during the entire time that R. Kook resided in Jerusalem.[40]

38. Later on (p. 6 of the introduction), R. M. M. Schulzinger quotes his brother, R. Shmuel Schulzinger, describing his father's practical rabbinic training. He mentions only R. Shimshon Aharon Polonski from Teplik, and adds innocently, "After his death, I heard that he also trained with great rabbis in Jerusalem."
39. At the end of the introduction to the aforementioned book (where R. Schulzinger's biography was published a second time), R. M. M. Schulzinger mentions again that his father arrived in Israel in 1924. Here again, he does not mention where his father learned. So too, in an article printed in *Mishmar HaLevi* on Berakhot (Bnei Brak, 2005), p. 7, eulogizing his mother, he relates that his father brought with him a letter signed by the Ḥafetz Ḥayim "on a promise that, immediately upon disembarking at the port, he would go to yeshiva." Again, no mention is made of the yeshiva's identity. Parenthetically, it should be noted that R. Schulzinger did not travel to Israel as a young, single yeshiva student, as implied by the article. In fact, he arrived with his family (see the description of his niece, in *Sefer Kehilat Siemiatycze,* 248–49).
40. See, for example, R. Chechik's memories of R. Kook, brought by R. Neriyah in *Likutei HaRa'ayah* 2 (Kfar HaRo'eh, 1991), 358–60. Compare to what R. Chechik wrote in 1966 (several years after his grandson's ideological turnabout, described below): "Heaven granted me the opportunity to actively serve [...] the great rabbi, master of Israel, who, when I uttered his holy name my bones would shudder in awe and fright, our master and teacher R. Avraham Yitzḥak Kook *ztz"l*" (R. Neriyah, *Ḥayei HaRa'ayah* [Tel Aviv, 1983], 337). R. M. M. Schulzinger published a memorial volume to his grandfather, *Ḥayei Avraham* (Zikhron Meir, 1982). In the introduction, he lists a short biographical sketch, which of course, mentions nothing about R. Kook. It just says that his grandfather was born during the lifetime of the Maharil Diskin and grew up together with his son, R. Y. Y. Diskin, etc.

The force behind these historical revisions, and the underlying motivations, are clear. There is no need to explain why, even though R. M. M. Schulzinger published dozens of books over the years, he never republished the one book that his father published during his lifetime, *Imrot Yitzḥak*. Nor did he publish additional *drashot* from the manuscripts of *Imrot Yitzḥak*, that his father wrote in his introduction that he had "on all five books of the Torah," but was unable to publish for lack of funds, only succeeding to publish the volume on Bereshit.[41]

R. Moshe Mordekhai's Schulzinger's younger brother, R. Elazar Schulzinger, born in 1945, followed in his footsteps. Among other roles, he served as a community *askan* and was the son-in-law of MK R. Shlomo Lorincz. In Bnei Brak in 1988, he published the book *Al Mishkenot HaRo'im*, devoted to the clash in outlooks between the national-religious community and the Lithuanian ḥaredi community. The book's first chapter, "The Son Respects the Father" (15–23), describes his father's personality in greater detail and more systematically than his brother's article. But here too, there is no mention of R. Kook or Merkaz HaRav. However, unlike his brother's revisionism, in which he omits material in passing, R. E. Schulzinger decided to mention the omission explicitly and to justify his brother's actions (16–17):

> In 1971 my brother, the gaon R. M. M. Schulzinger *shlit"a*, published his first book, *Mishmar HaLevi*, and mentioned that our father studied in Jerusalem for ten years without mentioning that he studied in Yeshivat Merkaz HaRav. R. Moshe Tzvi Neriyah *shlit"a* approached my cousin and asked him, "R. Yitzḥak Schulzinger was a true *talmid* in Merkaz HaRav. He learned there for ten years straight. Why did his son remove the name of the yeshiva from his book?"

41. The deep ideological chasm between the father and the son is further illustrated in the eulogy that R. Yitzḥak Schulzinger delivered in 1949 for his brother, R. Moshe Simḥa, who died in 1921 (*Imrot Yitzḥak*, 281–82) – and for whom the son, R. Moshe Mordekhai, was named: "In these recent years, the Nation of Israel and the Land of Israel have experienced a cataclysmic turnabout... I want to tell you that God has granted us the great miracle of the beginning of the Redemption. The great ideals of the Love of Zion and the return of Israel to its land that you lamented over in your heart with a burning flame... has borne fruit... and in this past year the State of Israel was founded and a Jewish government rules over it, as it begins to sprout and illuminate the light of Redemption. This is what you had so yearned to see... But this miraculous wonder bestowed from on high has not come without sacrifice. Many have fallen, young heroes who died martyr's deaths in the heroic conquest of the land. Your two sons who grew up to make you proud... served loyally in the Hagana and the IDF for several years now."

> My brother, R. M. M. *shlit"a*, said to my cousin, "Answer him as follows: Yeshivat Merkaz HaRav is no longer what it was. If I were to write that my father *ztz"l* learned in Merkaz HaRav, people would think he wore short sleeves, short pants, sandals without socks, and was a farmer in the hills of Hebron. If Yeshivat Merkaz HaRav of today were like it was when my father *ztz"l* learned there, when the overwhelming majority of the students educated their children in the way of the holy Torah, and not like these distorted ways, I would have written in bold letters that he studied in Merkaz HaRav. I published this book in his memory and for the benefit of his soul. To say today that he learned in Merkaz HaRav, and to have to explain that this was the Merkaz HaRav of fifty years ago, has no relevance. They are two different worlds. Today, Merkaz HaRav educates [students] to become pioneers, but they do not teach that the main purpose in life is to learn Torah and live a life of Torah. Rather, one who dresses as a pioneer and works the land is better than one who sits all day learning Torah and performing mitzvot."

These lines, besides revealing the colorful stereotypes common among part of the ḥaredi community regarding the nature of Merkaz HaRav, testify to the unwillingness of R. Schulzinger's sons to recognize how far their path diverged from their father's.[42] We are not just talking about the disappearance of the name of the yeshiva where Rav Schulzinger studied, as the son claims, but about the systematic erasure of all of his (and his father-in-law's) tie to R. Kook and his inner circle, and with it, any mention of his approach to the establishment of the State of Israel.

AFTERWORD

Over the course of this article, we have surveyed blatant examples of how descendants, firmly grounded in the ḥaredi world of our time, dealt with the fact that their forbears were personally, and sometimes ideologically, actively associated with R. Kook, his circle, and Yeshivat Merkaz HaRav. Sometimes, they took relatively minor steps, such as omitting approbations from republished books.

---

42. There is a single reference in the book (p. 86), where R. E. Schulzinger mentions R. Kook respectfully. By contrast, in the one place I was able to find R. Kook's name in the numerous publications of his brother, R. M. M. Schulzinger, it was in the context of a story that contained more than a nugget of disrespect toward R. Kook (see "*Simḥat HaLevi B'Hakarat Ha'Emet*" in *Kuntres Simḥat HaLevi* [Zikhron Meir, 2009], p. 50). However, I have heard from people who were close to R. M. M. Schulzinger that he did, in fact, speak respectfully of R. Kook in conversation.

In some cases, they took bolder steps, such as eliminating important biographical details of their fathers' histories. And in other cases, as we have seen, they took drastic measures to tamper with and revise the actual bodies of work that appeared in print.

This behavior is consistent with the general attitude toward revisionism as an accepted historiographical tool in the ḥaredi world. It arises from the combination of a desire to maintain ideological hegemony – in which little legitimacy is accorded to the existence of differing approaches to modernity in general, and to the State of Israel in particular; with an accepted norm that prefers the bending of historical details for the sake of pedagogical concerns.[43] Yet, on the other hand, one can still wonder: What drives these descendants, in so many instances, to distance themselves from the fundamental paths of their forbears, to the point where they are unwilling to lay out the true facts as they occurred, making it impossible to relate to the fathers themselves?

In certain circumstances, we can ostensibly find answers within the family dynamics. In the case of R. Yitzḥak Schulzinger, for example, it is plausible that the matter is entwined with his early, untimely death in 1956. His son, R. M. M. born in 1941 was sixteen years old at the time. Shortly before his father's death, he began to learn at Merkaz HaRav, but was forced to leave after a year and a half (in 1958) because he disrespectfully protested one of the rulings of the rosh yeshiva, R. Tzvi Yehudah Kook.[44] In early 1959 he began to study in the Yeshiva of Slobodka in Bnei Brak under R. Yeḥezkel Abramsky. Even prior to this, he came under the influence of his uncle, R. Ze'ev Dov Chechik, who was close with the Brisker Rav.[45] As described by his brother, R. Menachem Mendel Chechik, in a letter dated 5745

43. Ḥaredi historiography has benefited from much scholarly research over the last twenty years, even though it is not specifically related to the Zionist/Anti-Zionist axis. See, among others, David Assaf, *Ne'eḥaz Ba'Svakh: Pirkei Mashber U'Mevokha B'Toldot Ha'Ḥasidut* (Jerusalem, 2006), introduction (19–49). Also see the recent book by Marc Shapiro, *Changing the Immutable: How Orthodox Judaism Rewrites Its History* (Oxford 2015), especially ch. 5.

44. A description of the incident, with the student's name deleted, is brought by R. Ḥayim Steiner in Hilah Walberstein's *Mashmi'a Yeshu'a* (Merkaz Shapira, 2010), 109. R. Steiner told me the fully detailed story (private conversation, 7 Elul 2011), he being R. M. M. Schulzinger's *ḥavruta*, at the time. The general details are also confirmed by additional rabbis who studied in Merkaz HaRav at the time. For another version of the incident, which is deficient in several respects (this is not the place to discuss them), see *Rav Moshe Mordekhai*, 92–96.

45. His story was eventually published in *Torat Ze'ev* (Zikhron Meir, 2000). (This was a combination of the third edition of *Peninim V'Igrot Torat Ze'ev* (Zikhron Meir, 1987, with the second edition of *Torat Ze'ev* on Tractate Zevaḥim [Zikhron Meir, 1985]). The title page describes R. Ze'ev Dov Chechik as one who "lights up the eyes with God's Torah and with pure fear of Heaven."

(1985) and printed in the introduction to *Torat Ze'ev*, "Did he not bring you in under the shadow of the great and holy rabbi, the Brisker Rav, during bitter and difficult days, when the splendor of our family, your sainted father, fell ... ?" The timing and circumstances of this ideological shift, therefore, are abundantly clear. So too with the second brother, R. E. Schulzinger, who was even younger when his father died. In the introduction to his book, *Mishkenot HaRo'im* (p. 10), we learn that even he underwent a similar shift after his father's passing, upon arriving to study in Slobodka in 1961, following in his brother's footsteps. By contrast, their older brother R. Shmuel Schulzinger was twenty-two when his father died, and was educated under his tutelage for a more significant time span, including the early years of his studies in the yeshivot of Bnei Brak.[46] Despite the fact that he identifies with the same ḥaredi community as his brothers, he did not take part in the public ideological debates or in revising the family history.

But in truth, the breadth and diversity of this phenomenon prevents us from attributing it solely to personal characteristics and behaviors of these and other descendants. The causes are far more complex and broader in nature. This is where we reach the point with which we began: the separation of the Orthodox community in Israel into two distinct communities. This is a topic that I hope to explore in depth in a separate article, with particular emphasis on how it is reflected within R. Kook's inner circle.

46. R. Shmuel Raphael Schulzinger was born in 1925 (it is rumored that R. Kook was the *sandek* at his *brit mila*). He studied in Yeshivat Ponevezh and became the son-in-law of R. Yehudah Aryeh Leib Gefen, the Rabbi of Kfar Ata (known today as Kiryat Ata). After the untimely death of his father-in-law in 1957, he was chosen to fill the position (at the behest of R. Dov Berish Weidenfeld of Tshebin), at the age of twenty-three. He served in that capacity for forty-seven years until his death in the winter of 2004. See the article by his son, R. Tuvia Schulzinger, *Yeshurun* 16 (5764/2004), 207–14. Some of his Torah thoughts are also cited there (215–32). Recently, his books, *Atarot Shmuel* (Kiryat Ata, 2005), *Gilyonei HaGra"sh* (Bnei Brak, 2008), and others, have been published posthumously.

Chapter 22

The Ḥaredi/National-Religious Dichotomy in Israel II: R. Yitzḥak Arieli and his Disappearance from the Circles of R. Kook and Merkaz HaRav[1]

Editor's Note: *In the author's opinion, the split within the circle of R. Kook's closest followers, and the events transpiring within the walls of Yeshivat Merkaz HaRav during the 1950s and 1960s, were symptomatic of the differentiation of the religious*

1. Translated by Michael Appel. Ed. note: Footnotes of this chapter have been abridged. Readers wishing greater detail are referred to the author's original Hebrew article, in *Assif* 4 (2017). This chapter is a continuation of the previous chapter, on historical revisionism by the families of R. Kook's disciples. The author worked on the present article in several stages, but we did not merit seeing his completed work. We are publishing the material as is, because of its importance and interest. From the author's words, it appears he intended to delve into the split in the Orthodox community in Eretz Yisrael into two separate camps, and to draw conclusions about the aspects of R. Kook's legacy that the proponents of the various positions sought to foster in his yeshiva. A file on the first topic, the split in the Orthodox community, was found on the author's computer, and is appended to this chapter. We did not find material related to the second topic; this work is left to the reader. In the second-to-last section, entitled "Leadership of Yeshivat Merkaz HaRav in the Generation following R. Kook," the author collected several passages that it seems he was preparing to analyze. Here too, we have not completed the work save connecting words or sentences.

community in Eretz Yisrael into separate streams. By force of his immense stature in Torah coupled with his multi-faceted personality, R. Kook had been a magnet for members of a very broad spectrum of ideologies and camps, which he hoped to bring under one central umbrella. Fascinating in and of itself, this chapter sheds light on the ḥaredi/national-religious dichotomy in Israel.

INTRODUCTION – R. ARIELI'S PLACE IN THE R. KOOK CHRONICLES

At the end of 5766 (summer 2006), the religious-Zionist press erupted in protest over censorship by descendants of R. Yitzḥak Arieli, one of R. Kook's greatest disciples and long-time *mashgiaḥ* in Yeshivat Merkaz HaRav. These descendants published an updated version of Tractate Berakhot of their grandfather's monumental work on the Talmud, *Einayim LaMishpat*, and chose to eliminate the final section of the introduction in which R. Arieli described his reverence for R. Kook and his own involvement in the founding and, over many years, in the administration of Yeshivat Merkaz HaRav. Moreover, the descendants added their own biographical introduction of their grandfather that completely ignored any ties between him and R. Kook or Merkaz HaRav. "But this was the focus of his life!" protested R. Eliezer Melamed in his weekly column in *B'Sheva*.[2] Similar indignation was expressed by R. Neriyah Gutel, who called upon readers of *HaTzofeh* to flood the publisher with complaints and even to boycott the new edition.[3]

The protests were, of course, justified. Censorship of facts and revisionist history are unacceptable, especially when they impugn the image of R. Kook for ideological purposes. On the other hand, the question begs: Did R. Arieli receive his due recognition in the historical consciousness of Merkaz HaRav circles and those who continued the path of R. Kook?

2. *Revivim, B'Sheva,* no. 207, 7 Elul 2006.
3. *"Meḥa'ah al Kevod HaRav"* in *HaTzofeh – Musaf Sofrim U'Sefarim,* 1 Elul 2006. An even greater omission by several orders of magnitude was made in the edition of *Einayim LaMishpat* published in Jerusalem in 1989 (and again in 1994). In it, the publisher erased almost half (!) of the introduction to Kiddushin in order to omit any reference to R. Kook and Merkaz HaRav (although a letter from R. Ḥarlap, in which the bond between R. Arieli and R. Kook and his yeshiva were not omitted, appears at the end of the book; the volume on Berakhot as well left this letter intact). It is surprising that the uproar erupted only in connection with this small omission from the Berakhot volume, almost two decades later!

Let's take, for example, a wide-ranging article on the history of Merkaz HaRav by R. Yitzḥak Shilat, who studied in the yeshiva during the 1960s.[4] R. Shilat goes through all the prominent personalities who took part in the yeshiva's founding: Starting with the founder himself, R. Kook and the brief era of R. Avraham Aharon Burstein, the Gaon of Tavrig, through the tenure of R. Ḥarlap as rosh yeshiva following R. Kook, ending with his own days in the yeshiva under the stewardship of R. Tzvi Yehudah Kook and, at his side, R. Shalom Natan Ra'anan the *menahel*, and R. David Cohen (the Nazir). Also studying there at the time were young rabbis including R. Mordekhai Frum, R. Shaul Yisraeli, and R. Avraham Shapira. R. Shilat even mentions the well-known story in which R. Kook supposedly invited R. Shimon Shkop, head of the yeshiva in Grodno, to serve as rosh yeshiva of Merkaz HaRav,[5] and also mentions additional young students from the time of R. Kook. Only one person is conspicuously absent from this version of the yeshiva's history: R. Yitzḥak Arieli.

R. Professor Neriyah Gutel did the same thing. A popular contemporary researcher on R. Kook's writings and teachings, he writes the following in his introduction to his book, *Mekhutavei Ra'ayah*:

> Four men continued "the Path [of R. Kook]." They were constantly in his close orbit and were appointed in his lifetime to positions in the yeshiva he founded. It seems that **no one would argue** that these four are: His son, R. Tzvi Yehudah; R. Yaakov Moshe Ḥarlap; his son-in-law, R. Shalom Natan Ra'anan; and R. David Cohen, the Nazir.... The appointment of these four, his entrusting his writings and his yeshiva to them, and even their "self-abnegation" to his persona, speaks for itself.[6]

---

4. "*HaMahapekha HaMerkazit*," *Nekuda* 181 (1995), 20–24. It is clear that R. Shilat's descriptions of personalities in the yeshiva before his own time were greatly influenced by R. Tzvi Yehudah Kook and things he said (or did not say) about them.
5. In his article "*Ad Asher Emtza Makom B'Mishkenot L'Avir Ya'akov*," *HaMa'ayan* 50:1 (Tishrei 5770): 79–96, my good friend Shemaryah Gershuni proved that although R. Shkop was interested in the position, his request was denied by the yeshiva's leadership!
6. *Mekhutavei Ra'ayah* (Jerusalem, 2000), 30–31; emphasis mine. On the same page, R. Gutel protests the omission in a certain article of R. Ḥarlap and R. Ra'anan as disciples of R. Kook – without realizing that he himself has fallen into the same trap. It should be noted that R. Gutel's words are similar to Ḥagai Segal's in his article, "*Orot Ba-Ofel*": "Four men were considered heirs of R. Kook's spiritual legacy [...] R. Yaakov Moshe Ḥarlap was appointed rosh yeshiva of Merkaz HaRav, R. Tzvi Yehudah was charged with publishing the estate's halakhic and aggadic writings, the Nazir, with the philosophical writings, and R. Shalom Natan Ra'anan-Kook, the son-in-law, was appointed *menahel* of the yeshiva." (*Nekuda* 113 [1987], 17).

And R. Yitzḥak Arieli? What happened to him?

The question is astounding: Why wasn't R. Arieli worthy in R. Gutel's eyes to be included alongside the others on the list of those who "continued the path," those who were constantly in R. Kook's closest inner circle? After all, he specifies criteria for inclusion. And, even if one could argue with some of them,[7] there is no doubt that R. Arieli fulfills them no less than the others, as will be proven shortly. And if R. Gutel wants to limit his list to four men, there is sufficient evidence to claim R. Arieli's inclusion over that of R. Ra'anan.[8]

We're not talking about an isolated incident. Erasures of the bond between R. Arieli and R. Kook and of R. Arieli's place in the history of Merkaz HaRav can be found in books, articles, and other publications about R. Kook and his yeshiva.[9] Sometimes, this is even found in official publications, such as the annual calendar of Merkaz HaRav, under the auspices of R. Yaakov Kahane-Shapira – today's rosh yeshiva. In the 2007–2010 calendars, and even in some earlier calendars, the yahrzeits of the yeshiva's rabbis are marked and emphasized, including R. Kook, R. Tzvi Yehudah, R. Ḥarlap, the Nazir, and R. Ra'anan. R. Shaul Yisraeli merited

7. For example, responsibility for his writings: As far as we know, R. Ḥarlap never himself prepared R. Kook's writings for publication, although he was among the principal assistants of the Nazir in editing *Orot HaKodesh*. See *Mishnat HaNazir* (Jerusalem, 2005) 90–91, and also p. 95. This does not detract from his rightful status as R. Kook's prime disciple.
8. Whose only "advantage" in this respect, is the fact that he was R. Kook's son-in-law. Let us compare their functions in Merkaz HaRav in R. Kook's lifetime: R. Ra'anan came to the yeshiva as a student in 1924. Four years later, he married R. Kook's daughter, and additional time elapsed until he took on a significant role in the yeshiva. By contrast, R. Arieli was appointed to the senior staff of the yeshiva from the moment of its founding, and throughout all of those years. In *Mekhutavei Ra'ayah*, 30–31, R. Gutel cites numerous letters that R. Ra'anan received from his father-in-law, R. Kook. However, I have already pointed out (together with Shemarya Gershuni, in our article "*Mekhutavei Ra'ayah U'Michtavei HaRa'ayah*" (*Alonei Mamre* 122 [Kiryat Arba, 2009], 151, footnote), that most of these letters dealt solely with family matters.
9. Additional examples abound. To mention one amongst many: The monumental entry on R. Kook in the *Encyclopedia of Religious Zionism* 5:269 (Jerusalem, 1983), states that after the yeshiva's founding, "Appointed at R. Kook's side were his son, R. Tzvi Yehudah, R. Yaakov Moshe Ḥarlap, and the Nazir, R. David Cohen" – and R. Arieli is missing without a trace! It is almost certain that the authors of this entry were following R. Menaḥem Mendel Porush's "Within the Walls – a Jubilee" (Jerusalem, 1948), 290, which mentions the three men without reference to R. Arieli. By contrast, R. Kook's leading biographer, R. Moshe Tzvi Neriyah, who was a student of R. Arieli in Merkaz HaRav (and is always careful to call him – and only him – "my master and teacher") is one of the very few to recognize R. Arieli's rightful place (see *Shaḥar Oro* [Jerusalem, 2002], 95 and elsewhere), as does Simḥa Raz in his popular work *Malakhim Kivnei Adam* (Jerusalem, 1994), hereafter *Malakhim*.

inclusion, as did R. Mordekhai Frum, and of course, R. Avraham Shapira *ztz"l* – but they did not note the yahrzeit of R. Arieli.[10]

In this chapter, I hope to address the question as to why R. Arieli does not, today, merit his rightful place among those who seek R. Kook's legacy. As a foundation for this discussion, I will build a broad platform describing R. Arieli's persona, his work, his connection to R. Kook, and his position in Merkaz HaRav using the four criteria of R. Gutel as a yardstick to measure those who "continued the path" of R. Kook: (1) presence in his innermost circle; (2) reverence for R. Kook and "self-abnegation" toward him; (3) responsibility for R. Kook's writings; (4) a significant position in the yeshiva.

BIOGRAPHY IN SHORT

Before we broaden our view onto his relationship with R. Kook, I will start with a brief biography, review of publishing activity, and family.[11]

R. Arieli was born in Elul 1896 in Jerusalem. He studied in Yeshivot Torat Ḥayim and Etz Ḥayim, receiving *semikhah* from R. Ḥayim Berlin. During the First World War, he moved to Petaḥ Tikvah to escape possible conscription into the Ottoman army.[12] After the war, he returned to Jerusalem. When Merkaz HaRav was founded in 1923, he was appointed rav and *mashgiaḥ*. In 1941, he was appointed rabbi of the neighborhoods Knesset Israel, Betzalel, and Mazkeret Moshe (the eastern section of Naḥla'ot), at the behest of R. Yosef Gershon Horowitz[13] among others. His letter of appointment was presented to him by his neighbor and fellow worshipper at the

10. In the 5769 (2008/9) calendar, R. Arieli is mentioned on the back of the calendar alongside other rabbis of the yeshiva. However, the anniversary of his death is not marked on the calendar itself. Another example of the prevalent historical consciousness in the yeshiva today: there was for many years an impressive collage on the wall of the dining room, half of which portrayed the *rashei yeshiva*, while the other half portrayed its past rabbis. All the noted rabbis appear, with no trace of R. Arieli. [Ed. note: The collage has since been replaced by photographs, with R. Arieli's nowhere to be found.]
11. The survey is based, among others, on the *Encyclopedia of Religious Zionism* 6 (Jerusalem, 2001), 113–16. I will cite additional sources in subsequent footnotes.
12. For the same reason, he went by the name "Rivlin" during the war years. See his signature in a letter sent in 1916 to R. Tzvi Pesaḥ Frank: *Kovetz Har Hamor* 5 (5744/1884), 49. R. Ḥarlap also referred to him by this name in a letter from the same year. (A copy of the letter was provided to me by R. Arieli's descendants.)
13. In a letter to the members of the *Va'ad Klali* dated 7 Tevet 5701 (January 6, 1941), Rabbis Y. G. Horowitz and Tzvi Pesaḥ Frank recommended R. Arieli for the position as "one of the *gedolim* of Jerusalem." (I received a copy of the letter from his family.)

same synagogue, R. Isser Zalman Meltzer,[14] and his installation was keynoted by his friend R. Tzvi Pesaḥ Frank.[15] Over time, he became the *posek* of Bikur Ḥolim Hospital, and in the 1960s, he was a member of the government committee on autopsies.[16] All along, he was involved in communal affairs, including the building of Jerusalem neighborhoods[17] and matters of the Jerusalem rabbinate,[18] and more. He passed away on 13 Nisan 1974 at the age of seventy-seven.

In 1936, he published the first volume of his monumental work on the Talmud, *Einayim LaMishpat.* Over the years, he published novellae on seven tractates of the Talmud Bavli along with portions of the Talmud Yerushalmi, the Tosefta, the Minor Tractates, and notes on the entire *Shas.* In 1966, he was awarded the Israel Prize for Jewish Literature by a panel of judges including R. Shlomo Yosef Zevin, R. Shaul Yisraeli, and R. Avraham Shapira. He also wrote *Shirat HaGe'ulah,* a commentary on the Passover Haggadah (Jerusalem, 1956), and a collection of *drashot* on the month of Tishrei, *Yeraḥ HaEitanim* (Jerusalem, 2001). Several additional volumes of *Einayim LaMishpat* as well as a two-volume work on the Torah called *Midrash Ariel* were published posthumously.

R. Arieli and his wife, Chaya Leah (nee Tannenbaum, d. 1965), had five sons and two daughters. His sons – R. Gershon Arieli, author of *Torat HaMelekh*; R. Ḥayim Yaakov Arieli, author of *Be'er Yaakov*; R. Shemaryahu Arieli, author of *Mishpat HaMilḥamah*; the writer Dr. Nahum Arieli; and R. Moshe Leib Arieli. His daughter Sara Rivka married R. Mordekhai Ilan, *av bet din* in Tel Aviv and

14. In a letter from January 12, 1941, he congratulated R. Arieli on his appointment, saying that although the position did not measure up to R. Arieli's eminent Torah stature, R. Meltzer anticipated that R. Arieli's greatness in Torah would serve the public, and his addressing practical issues would birth great numbers of *ḥidushim*, novellae. (I received a copy of the letter from his family.)
15. *HaPardes* 2:15 (May 1941), 18.
16. Alongside R. Avraham Kahane-Shapira. See his article in *Torah SheBe'al Peh* 6 (Jerusalem, 1964), 40–60, and the booklet of R. Kalman Kahane, "*B'Ma'avak Neged Nituḥei Meitim*" (Jerusalem, 1967), 10–11.
17. The well-known photograph of him with R. Kook is from the dedication of the Kiryat Shmuel neighborhood in 1929. See *Otzar HaḤesed Keren Shmuel* (Jerusalem, 1940), 89, 107. Another photograph of him on the same occasion, beside R. Kook, was published in *Malakhim*, 300.
18. Two examples: R. Arieli chaired the committee of Jerusalem rabbis in the summer of 1948 that dealt with the proposal to internationalize the city (*Or Hamizraḥ* 25 [New York, 1980], 277–78). And, in a conference of Jerusalem rabbis in the winter of 1950, initiated by the Chief Rabbinate with the intent to present a united front against participation in a coalition with Mapai in the Jerusalem municipality as the status of Judaism in the country worsened, it was decided that R. Yitzḥak Nissim and R. Arieli would be responsible for implementing the conference's resolutions (*Har Hamizraḥ* 8:9 [29 Kislev 5711/December 8, 1950], 2).

author of *Torat HaKodesh*; and his daughter Ḥasida married R. Tzvi Kahane, rosh yeshiva of Harei Yehudah in Bet Meir. One of his in-laws was R. Moshe Sternbuch, head of the Edah Ḥaredit, whose sister, Shulamit, married R. Arieli's son, R. Ḥayim Yaakov.

IN R. KOOK'S INNER CIRCLE

The personal relationship between R. Yitzḥak Arieli and R. Kook was formed upon the latter's return to Israel in 1919, at the reception arranged in his honor at the Lydda Station.[19] This relationship deepened quickly, and a few months later, in the winter of 1920, R. Arieli was included among the small group of twelve *avrekhim*, scholars, who gathered in R. Kook's home every afternoon, and soon became known as Merkaz HaRav.

R. Arieli enjoyed a singular closeness with R. Kook, expressed in a daily one-on-one *ḥavruta* in Talmud that continued almost unbroken for fifteen years until R. Kook's passing.[20] During those hours, R. Kook uncharacteristically kept his door closed, allowing no disturbances,[21] and the two were able to complete the study of the entire Talmud together.[22]

19. According to R. Neriyah, *Bisdei HaRa'ayah*, 352. R. Arieli himself wrote of the encounter: "When he reached Lydda, it was worth gazing upon his radiant face, lost in thought," and added that it was he who delivered to R. Kook the letter of welcome, "in lieu of an official rabbinic appointment," as representative of "all the great pillars of the yeshivot" (Shaul Shiff, "*Reshimot HaRi"a*," *HaTzofeh* Supplement, October 24, 2003, section 23).
20. Dr. Naḥum Arieli, "*Sipurim SheSiper Li Avi*" (hereafter: "*Sipurim*"), *HaTzofeh* Supplement, September 15, 1985. According to his description, "Not a day passed where they did not sit to learn [...] and this continued for sixteen years until they completed the entire Talmud ... [to] the day of R. Kook's passing." However, this is hyperbole. During those years, there were many periods in which R. Arieli was not with R. Kook, including R. Kook's visits to the agricultural settlements in Eretz Yisrael over the years, his lengthy trip abroad in 1924, vacations in Motza and the Carmel, etc. It is also doubtful if the study sessions began immediately when they met. Apparently, the description is based on R. Arieli's words, referring to the period: "I had the merit to stand before him for sixteen years, to listen to his holy words and to meditate upon his holy ways" (*Einayim LaMishpat*, Kiddushin, p. 2). Their daily personal connection is one explanation for the paucity of written letters between the two (based on current knowledge). As R. Arieli lived in the same neighborhood and sat in the same yeshiva as R. Kook all those years, there was no reason for any extensive written communication between them.
21. *Shivḥei HaRa'ayah* (Jerusalem, 1995), 168, quoting R. Arieli; see Naḥum Arieli's expanded testimony in "*Sipurim*," 16; it is also cited in brief in *Malakhim*, 80–82. R. Arieli mentions it in his notes: "In the morning, when he learned with me five pages a day (and during that time, would not let anyone else into the room)," "*Reshimot HaRi"a*," section 24. He also notes that they learned for a minimum of two hours per day (sections 24 and 36).
22. Dr. Naḥum Arieli in *Malakhim*, "*Sipurim*." Their studies may have been connected to the *Halakhah Berurah* project, in which R. Kook was involved for the last twelve years of his life.

His son, R. Gershon Arieli, describes it thus:

> When he came close to the Rav [Kook], he was entranced by the fullness of his personality, and literally clung to him as a loving student does to his teacher. Every conversation with the Rav was precious to him, and he recorded every word on scraps of paper. He was forced to defend the Rav's honor from the attacks of zealots and suffered greatly from the strife.[23]

Many anecdotes testify to the depth of this connection between the two over the years: The Hebraization of R. Yitzḥak's family name from "Zombrover" (after his grandfather's town) to "Arieli" in those early years, was with "the advice and encouragement" of R. Kook.[24] When R. Kook traveled to the United States in 1925, R. Arieli sought the choicest *etrog* from Eretz Yisrael for his teacher who was abroad.[25] Over the years, R. Kook often included him in visits with Torah sages, such as R. Yosef Ḥayim Sonnenfeld, the kabbalist R. Shlomo Elyashiv (author of *Leshem Shvo V'Aḥlama*), and the Gerrer Rebbe;[26] And at R. Kook's funeral, R. Arieli was among the eulogizers before the procession, delivering his eulogy beside the Aron Kodesh.[27]

R. Arieli wrote that he was one of the first to become involved in *Halakhah Berurah*, under the auspices of R. Kook (see below, n. 34).

23. *Bisdei HaRa'ayah*, 367. An illustration of R. Arieli's defense of R. Kook from attacks by zealots is a wall poster from January 1933 protesting slander of R. Kook by Tze'irei Agudath Israel, signed by R. Arieli along with the Nazir on behalf of Merkaz HaRav (Benjamin Kluger, *Min Hamakor* 2 [Jerusalem, 1980], 94; reprinted in *Malachim* 210). A decade earlier, R. Arieli published a response in the Jerusalem newspaper *Kol Yaakov* 2:23 (1923), 2, to a stinging attack upon R. Kook elsewhere, written "with unprecedented brazenness against the great rabbis of the Chief Rabbinate and its head, the great rabbi, R. Kook *shlit"a*." Also, see Nahum Arieli's description of his father's saving R. Kook from stoning by zealots: "*Sipurim*," 17, and also *Malakhim*, 212.
24. R. Neriyah, *Bisdei HaRa'ayah*, p. 353.
25. See the introduction of R. Yehudah Zoldan to *Etz Hadar Hashalem* (Jerusalem, 1986), 34, n. 23.
26. Dr. Naḥum Arieli, "*Sipurim*," 17. Regarding the visit with R, Shlomo Elyashiv, see "*Reshimot HaRi"a*," *siman* 17.
27. After the eulogies delivered in the yeshiva by R. Ḥarlap, R. Tzvi Yehudah, and R. Kook's brother R. Dov Kook (*Sha'arei Tziyon* 15 (Jerusalem, Tamuz–Elul 1935), 31). At the first gathering of the students in the *bet midrash* two days later, R. Ḥarlap spoke first, followed by the *mashgiaḥ*, R. Arieli, and then R. Ra'anan (ibid., p. 34). He apparently also spoke at the *sheloshim*, alongside R. Ḥarlap, R. Tzvi Yehudah, and R. Isser Zalman Meltzer (see the notice in *Malakhim*, 425).

REVERENCE FOR R. KOOK AND "SELF-ABNEGATION"

We can learn of R. Arieli's reverence for R. Kook in his lengthy encomium in the introduction to the first volume of *Einayim LaMishpat,* written during the first year after R. Kook's passing. It stands as a testament to the void R. Kook's passing left in his dedicated disciple's life:

> Avraham [Kook] was unique, a giant among giants, sent by HaShem to sustain renewed generations in the land of the living. Pillar of fire, holy crown, genius of the generation and its leader, our master and teacher, Rabbi Avraham Yitzḥak HaKohen Kook *ztz"l*... The chosen few in the Holy City of Jerusalem were drawn to him through bonds of mighty and faithful love. Those great in spirit saw in him the source of life, an ever-flowing river. He organized in his home an important group of great and accomplished scholars who heard his lectures on halakhah and aggadah. Our teacher saw in them the seed of the realization of his holy aspiration: the establishment of a central world-yeshiva in the Holy City... and he bestowed great affection upon me, bringing me close to this holy task, and I was privileged to stand before him for sixteen full years, to listen to his holy words and to ponder his holy ways....
>
> At the beginning of this past summer – 1935 – the Crown of Israel was already on his final sickbed, and we hoped that he would soon return to his former vigor and repose amidst us as before. But to the dismay of all Israel, who followed his condition with grave concern, our prayers went unheard, and his condition worsened with each passing day. And the tragedy was so great that the crown of Israel suddenly fell and the sun was darkened at noon. "*We were as orphans*" – we realized that even when he lived in our midst, we were like orphans who didn't know how to hold the crown fast on our heads and how to use this treasure of treasures. "*With no father*" – the wellspring that flowed over us, even without our knowledge, that sustained and watered us with its pure waters. Our only remaining comfort is the light hidden within his holy books and his spirit which infuses this yeshiva, the embers of his holiness, the majestic yeshiva, his pure soul's work and his life's joy, which was cultivated with great effort and influence of his splendor.... We too will grasp our master's coattails, to walk in his footsteps.[28]

28. *Einayim LaMishpat,* Kiddushin 2–3.

This quote is far from unique. It is just one of the many places in his writings where R. Arieli expresses his reverence for and self-abnegation vis-à-vis R. Kook.[29] We will cite but one example from one of his letters, to provide a feel:

> To the holy majesty, my master and teacher, *shlit"a,* shalom! After inquiring after our dear master's well-being... we yearn for our master's return. Please inform us when he thinks to return to us. From his servant and student, Yitzḥak Arieli...[30]

These examples should be sufficient to provide the feeling that he too, like his other colleagues who were closest students of R. Kook, drew the world of his spirit from R. Kook, and was influenced by him more than by any other individual.

PUBLICATION OF R. KOOK'S WRITINGS

Nobody disputes the fact that the two most central figures in disseminating R. Kook's writings were his son, R. Tzvi Yehudah, and the Nazir. However, R. Arieli also had a certain role: In the winter of 1924, he and his friend R. Uri Segal Hamburger, began work to republish R. Kook's first work, *Ḥevesh Pe'er* (Warsaw, 1891), "with permission of the author *shlit"a.*"[31] This was not a routine copy of the original work, but included at their urging new material which, upon his return from abroad, R. Kook wrote for the volume, as well as material "from our master's manuscripts." The latter included, most importantly, aggadic and exegetic material from the first volumes of *Ein Ayah* and *Olat Ra'ayah* – works that were now revealed to the public for the first time, at the loyal hands of R. Arieli.[32] The volume also included

---

29. See 1961 interview in *Hed HaMo'etza HaDatit* (Jerusalem), 17–18 (reprinted in *Bisdei HaRa'ayah,* 367–71). Several years ago, sixty-two vignettes and practices of R. Kook which R. Arieli had recorded in his notebook were published, and from which his closeness to his *rav muvhak* is apparent ("*Reshimot HaRi"a,*" see n. 19 above). Even his remarks at the installation of R. Tzvi Pesaḥ Frank as *av bet din* of Jerusalem, within a year of R. Kook's death, were dedicated to expressing "melancholy and grief within this joyous occasion, like one who marries the sister of his departed first wife. Had we merited, our teacher, R. Kook *ztz"l,* would be here with us." ("*Seder Hakhtarat HaRabbanut,*" [Jerusalem, 1936], 26).
30. Letter dated 11 Sivan 5684 (June 13, 1924), *Bet HaRav* archive, box 176. Written on R. Kook's personal stationery, the letter deals mostly with the yeshiva's budget and ends with a report on communal matters and councils in Jerusalem. Toward the end, he mentions, "comments I sent in my last letter," regarding halakhic matters, and signs it, "Warm regards from all the students."
31. *Hevesh Pe'er* (Jerusalem, 1925), 3.
32. The more active of the two, as mentioned several times: "The publisher [Y.B.A.]" (pp. 3–4, p. 57, etc.), read as "Yitzḥak Ben Avigdor." The editor's notes throughout the book are his, and R. Arieli himself writes: "When I revealed to him that I wished to republish it, he told me that

comments from the great scholars of Jerusalem who were close to R. Kook – R. Ḥarlap, R. Frank, and R. Tukachinsky – and R. Kook's responses to them. Beyond this, the entire work, including the scholarly rabbinic comments, is replete with the notes of R. Arieli, who went to great lengths to defend the words of R. Kook and to add his own commentary on the topics.[33] All in all, this new book of R. Kook's, published by R. Arieli, is over three times thicker than the original work.

Moreover, at the behest of R. Kook, R. Arieli was among the first to join in the monumental undertaking of *Halakhah Berurah*, and even annotated two of the first volumes: "He even recruited me to contribute to his massive work, *Halakhah Berurah*, of which two tractates, Ketubot and Makkot, were compiled by me, with HaShem's help."[34]

After this project, R. Arieli began work on *Einayim LaMishpat* – also encouraged by R. Kook, who was able to see the first volume in the series:

> And when I presented the material [from *Einayim LaMishpat*] before our teacher *ztz"l* [...] he told me then that before us is another monumental work, unique in its kind....[35] Tractate Bava Batra was completely edited and corrected with commentary and many novellae for our master R. Kook to see.[36]

HIS PLACE IN YESHIVAT MERKAZ HARAV

Merkaz HaRav was officially established in the summer of 1923. R. Arieli played a major role in its founding, as described by his friend and partner, R. Yaakov Moshe Ḥarlap:

---

it was his gift to me. And when it was ready with the numerous annotations that I added, he was delighted and wrote a new introduction." ("*Reshimot HaRi"a*," *siman* 29).

33. He even intended to add an afterword of his own, as written in the introduction (p. 3). In the end, it did not appear. R. Neriyah surmised that this was due to excessive printing costs (*Shivḥei HaRa'ayah*, 364).

34. *Einayim LaMishpat*, Kiddushin p. 3. It is almost certain that *Einayim Lamishpat* was a product of his earlier involvement in *Halakhah Berurah*, based on the *Ein Mishpat* marginal glosses to the Talmud (which these *Einayim LaMishpat* come to correct and complete). This is pointed out by R. Ḥarlap in his letter printed in *Einayim LaMishpat*, Kiddushin, 166: "Blessed fruits of our holy master's Torah [...] once R. Arieli entered his [ed. note: R. Kook's] perfume shop, he internalized the light, regarding connecting the Talmud with the *Poskim*."

35. This might refer to a comment that R. Arieli made elsewhere: "When he saw my additions to the notes that were in *Einayim LaMishpat*, he said, 'If so, my work [*Halakhah Berurah*] has been superseded [because it added so many additional notes], and said that he would attempt to produce a second edition with addenda" ("*Reshimot HaRi"a*," *siman* 12).

36. *Einayim LaMishpat*, Kiddushin 166. He concludes: "I was unable to print it all because of its length." This is why he printed Kiddushin first).

> Our master, the holy Gaon of Israel, our teacher, Rabbi Avraham Yitzḥak HaKohen Kook *ztz"l* appeared in the gates of Jerusalem with his immense vision to establish a central world-yeshiva in the Holy City of Jerusalem. His Honor [R. Arieli] was one of the select individuals who was moved to realize this great and holy idea, and had a major role in its founding and establishment.[37]

Upon the yeshiva's founding, R. Kook appointed R. Arieli to serve as its *mashgiaḥ ruḥani*[38] – a task that he fulfilled from then on.[39]

R. Kook also involved him in day-to-day administration, as he wrote: "Our master, the Rav [Kook] *z"l*, placed the yeshiva's administration upon me with its various tasks."[40] During R. Kook's entire tenure, R. Arieli maintained his position as head administrator of the yeshiva, alongside his three colleagues – R. Ḥarlap, the Nazir, and R. Tzvi Yehudah Kook. The four constituted the top administration that met weekly in the office or in R. Kook's home for most decisions, save exceptional circumstances that they brought to R. Kook.[41] R. Kook himself often referred to this foursome as a unified team in his letters.[42] The four also appear alongside R. Kook in two iconic photos from the years 1927–29.[43] The

37. Ibid., 166.
38. *Bisdei HaRa'ayah*, 354. The role of *mashgiaḥ* in Merkaz HaRav differed from the standard in the mussar yeshivot and their ilk. It did not include policing the students' lifestyles, delivery of talks on timely issues, etc. Its essence was to be a presence and mentor for the students, mostly regarding their learning, but also for personal advice, as well as oversight of the daily learning schedule in the study hall (see *Ḥayim Shel Yetzira*, 171–72).
39. R. Arieli signed a letter from 1926 to R. Ra'anan's parents as "*mashgiaḥ hayeshiva*" (*B'Shemen Ra'anan* 2 [Jerusalem, 1991], 16). From an exchange of letters in the years 1928–31 between R. Ra'anan and R. Yosef Aryeh Nandik, the *mashgiaḥ* of Ponevezh, who was interested in aliyah, it would seem that the *mashgiaḥ* position was open (*B'Shemen Ra'anan* 1, 20–21). However, R. Neriyah, who arrived in 1930, describes at length R. Arieli's persona as *mashgiaḥ* (see *Bisdei HaRa'ayah*, 351). It is plausible that R. Ra'anan meant to describe a "supervisory role" of some sort in the yeshiva, and R. Nandik assumed that he meant the (senior) "*mashgiaḥ ruḥani*."
40. *Einayim LaMishpat*, Berakhot, end of introduction. Elsewhere, R. Arieli describes how R. Kook pressed him to travel abroad on behalf of the yeshiva, but he didn't want to leave Israel ("*Reshimot HaRi"a*," *siman* 21).
41. This, according to R. Y. Rudik, *Ḥayim Shel Yetzira* (Jerusalem, 1998), 130, based on the protocols preserved from *Bet HaRav*. R. Arieli was the youngest of the four (R. Ḥarlap was born in 1882, the Nazir in 1887, R. Tzvi Yehudah in 1891, and R. Arieli in 1896). His youth, both in absolute terms and relative to the other three, further emphasizes the degree to which R. Kook held him in esteem.
42. See *Bet HaRav* Archive, no. E293, and elsewhere.
43. See *Likutei HaRa'ayah* 2 (Kfar Haro'eh, 1991), 176; *Bisdei HaRa'ayah*, 448. R. Rudik (*Ḥayim Shel Yetzira*, 129) describes "dusty minutes from 1926 found in the archives of *Bet HaRav*" in which

first notes their positions: R. Kook is the *rosh hayeshiva* and *menahel*, R. Ḥarlap is *rosh metivta*, R. Arieli is *mashgiaḥ*, R. Tzvi Yehudah Kook is *menahel*, and the Nazir is *maggid shi'ur*.

HIS ROLE IN THE YESHIVA DURING R. KOOK'S TENURE

We have abundant information on R. Arieli's role in the yeshiva during R. Kook's years. The yeshiva's protocols reveal his extensive activity, mainly as *mashgiaḥ*:

> R. Yitzḥak Arieli asks for a raise in salary, now that he is working every day in the role of *mashgiaḥ*, and has been forced to abandon his other work."[44]

In parallel, he was also greatly involved in the management of the yeshiva from the outset.[45] This included activities such as obtaining books for the yeshiva's library,[46] or hiring secretaries,[47] but mostly its financial management, as described across all the protocols:

> R. Yitzḥak Arieli accepts responsibility for ensuring that salaries are paid [...]. R. Yitzḥak will visit the secretaries' office twice a week to supervise, motivate and manage the work.[48]

> R. Tzvi Yehudah contends that it is too difficult for him to continue managing the yeshiva's receivables, and suggests that the job be turned over to R. Arieli and R. Natan Ra'anan. They will organize the receipts and sign for all expenses.[49]

---

the yeshiva staff is described otherwise. However, the strange job descriptions he brings do not correlate well with their actual activities.

44. The protocols were found and preserved by R. Yoḥai Rudick.
45. For example, the letter cited above n. 30, provides a picture of his participation in minute details of management and finances.
46. See the letter from R. Arieli to R. Ḥayim Hirschenson from the US, dated 17 Tevet 5685 (January 13, 1925), where he writes at the end: "It would be appropriate for His Honor to send some exemplars to our yeshiva's library, 'Merkaz HaRav'" (*Ḥidushei HaRav Ḥayim Hirschenson* 3 [New York, 1926] *siman* 11, p. 16).
47. In summer 1926, R. Arieli concerned himself with hiring Rav Shabtai Shmueli as a secretary in the yeshiva, mainly in order to keep him from having to leave the country due to financial pressure (Yitzḥak Goldberg, *HaRav Shabtai Shmueli – Ohev Tziyon, Ish Ha'Oz V'ha'Anava* [Jerusalem, 2008], 55).
48. Protocol from Monday, 25 Feb. 1929 (*Hayim Shel Yetzira*, p. 146).
49. Protocol from April 1, 1929, ibid., p. 147.

GRADUAL SEPARATION FROM A ROLE IN THE YESHIVA

From an outsider's perspective, it would seem that R. Arieli's role in Merkaz HaRav continued unchanged during R. Ḥarlap's tenure as rosh yeshiva. He expresses this in his introductions to his writings from that period. In the introduction to *Einayim LaMishpat* on Tractate Kiddushin, published in 1936, he writes of his role in founding and sustaining Yeshivat Merkaz HaRav:

> And with thanks to the Almighty, I am a bearer of the holy ark, standing in service from its founding until today. May HaShem enable me to continue in this holy work, to learn and to teach, etc.

R. Arieli, remarkably, writes almost the exact words twelve years later, at the end of his introduction to the volume on Berakhot, printed in 1948. Here too, we hear of his continuing role in Yeshivat Merkaz HaRav:

> Some of these *ḥidushim* were said before the *gedolim* of our holy yeshiva, Merkaz HaRav, the yeshiva brimming with the spirit of its founder, the Gaon and Saint of Israel, our master and teacher, Rabbi Avraham Yitzḥak HaKohen Kook *ztz"l* [...] Through the grace of HaShem I was among the founders the holy yeshiva through hard work, with spiritual and material investment. The great Rabbi *ztz"l* bestowed upon me running the yeshiva in various roles. **I was a bearer of the holy ark ever since its establishment. So too should [I] merit to continue in this holy work to learn and to teach, etc.**[50]

However, practically speaking, tracing R. Arieli's actual work in the yeshiva during those years reveals that his physical presence in the yeshiva markedly declined. Just prior to R. Ḥarlap's death, he stopped teaching regularly in the yeshiva, even though he continued to visit often enough that, throughout the 1950s, his designated place in the *bet midrash* was maintained.[51] It is difficult to precisely pinpoint

50. See also a letter from R. Meltzer from December 1947, printed in the front of the photo offset version of *Einayim Lamishpat*, Berakhot, vol. 1, Tel Aviv, 1970, in which he described R. Arieli as, "One of the leaders and founders of Yeshivat Merkaz HaRav." (And earlier in his section of *Even Ha'azel*, 4 [Jerusalem, 1945], in the addenda. A similar description is in a letter of greeting from 1936 printed in *Einayim Lamishpat*, Kiddushin, p. 164. Also see the words of R. Frank in his letter, ibid., p. 162.) Similar language was used by R. Arieli's son-in-law, R. Mordekhai Ilan, in the introduction to his *Torat HaKodesh*, vol. 1, Jerusalem 1949: "My father-in-law, the great gaon R. Yitzḥak Arieli *shlit"a*, founder and *rosh metivta* in Yeshivat Merkaz HaRav and one of the great rabbis of the Holy City."
51. I learned (on 24 Adar 2, 2008) about the overall picture from R. Dov Lior, who began learning in Merkaz HaRav around 1953. This is also the recollection (23 Adar 2, 2008) of R. Eliezer

the exact time that R. Arieli's official role in the yeshiva ceased. However, the self-described moniker that he used in his books, "*Rosh Metivta* in the central world-yeshiva Merkaz HaRav," appeared for the last time in *Einayim LaMishpat* on Tractate Makkot, published in 1959.[52] By contrast, in the "Complete *Einayim LaMishpat*," published in 1963, this description is already eliminated in favor of the more generic, "Rav and *Rosh Metivta* here in the Holy City of Jerusalem." This self-description continued in all his published books until his death.[53] His final resignation from any official position on the staff of Merkaz HaRav happened sometime during the intervening years, most likely in the autumn of 1960.[54]

But this is just an arbitrary official date. In practice, R. Arieli ceased any significant role in the yeshiva at least a decade earlier, and this is puzzling. It is conceivable that he wanted to devote his time to his *Einayim LaMishpat* project.[55] However, this is not a sufficient reason to explain so noticeable an absence from an institution where he was a pivotal figure (according to his own testimony). Examination of documents heretofore held in private yields a complicated picture regarding R. Arieli's standing within the yeshiva and his relationship with the other yeshiva leaders following R. Kook's death. This is tightly connected to the gradual diminution of R. Arieli's role as the years progressed – and, as I will claim – also to his neglected place today within the consciousness of the Merkaz HaRav community.

Waldman, who learned there from 1957 onward. I heard about his fixed place in the *bet midrash* from R. Ḥayim Steiner (on 7 Elul 2010), a student from 1955 onward, who recalled that, although R. Arieli had ceased teaching in the yeshiva, his *shtender* remained there.

52. Similarly in all the prior volumes: Kiddushin (1926), Berakhot 1 (1947), Berakhot 2 (1952), Bava Batra 1 (1957). Also, his son R. Gershon Arieli refers to his father in Adar 1958 in his book, *Torat HaMelech*, 7, as, "Founder and *Rosh Metivta* in Yeshivat Merkaz HaRav."

53. Nedarim (1965), Yerushalmi and the Minor Tractates (1966), Makkot, second edition (1967), Berakhot, second edition (1970), Sanhedrin (1971), Nedarim, second edition (1972), Yevamot (1973). There is speculation, anachronistic in my opinion, that this change was to market his books in the wider ḥaredi yeshiva world. In fact, he made a corresponding change on his personal stationary. Despite this, it is notable that he left the phrase, "Founder and *rosh metivta* in the Central Yeshiva" on his stamp (along with "Rabbi of the Knesset Yisrael neighborhood") until his last years.

54. Although in fall, 1960, he signed a proclamation of Jerusalem rabbis and yeshiva leaders regarding internal strife within the religious world as "*Ra"m* in Yeshivat Merkaz HaRav, and rabbi of the Knesset Yisrael neighborhood" ("*Kri'ah LeShalom*," *Ma'ariv*, issue 4876, 6). In 1966, in an interview held upon his receiving the Israel Prize, it was reported that, "Six years ago, he left the yeshiva, in order to spend more time in his home in the Knesset Yisrael neighborhood, to dedicate himself to writing and serving the religious needs of his community" (*Ma'ariv*, April 24, 1966, p.19).

55. R. Lior (above) once asked R. Arieli why he did not write any novellae on Seder Zera'im in *Einayim LaMishpat*. He answered, "Because I did not have the time…".

Before I lay out the case, I must emphasize that R. Arieli's association with the yeshiva continued after this separation of 1960–61. Until his last days, he was a sought-after personality by the yeshiva's students. Many would regularly visit his home to learn with him. Some even served their rabbinic apprenticeships under him and received rabbinic ordination from him.[56] He continued to refer to the yeshiva as "our holy yeshiva," using the definite article (*heh hayediyah*).[57] And he continued to participate in the yeshiva's ceremonies including ideological functions such as *Yom Ha'atzma'ut* and *Yom Yerushalayim* celebrations.[58] This was not a thunderous parting of the ways, a turning of his back, or an ideological about-face. Rather, as we shall see, it resulted from a painful conflict within Merkaz HaRav, principally regarding the main lines of R. Kook's legacy and the future direction of the yeshiva.

LEADERSHIP OF YESHIVAT MERKAZ HARAV IN THE GENERATION AFTER R. KOOK

In the first meeting of the yeshiva's administration after R. Kook's death, on 21 Elul 5695 (September 19, 1935), it was decided that all the administrators would remain in their respective roles, in light of the appointments by R. Kook in his lifetime: R. Ḥarlap would continue to be "*menahel ruḥani* and rosh yeshiva"; R. Tzvi Yehudah, *menahel* and lecturer; the Nazir, lecturer; R. Ra'anan, lecturer and treasurer; and R. Arieli would continue as *mashgiaḥ ruḥani*.[59] Apparently, this division of responsibilities continued in force throughout 1936.[60] From then

56. See *Bisdei HaRa'ayah*, 373–74. The interview (above, n. 54) from 1966 noted: "Even after his departure from the yeshiva, his former students continue to visit his home in Jerusalem from all over the country to hear words of Torah from his mouth." Those who received *semikhah* from him include: R. Yeshayahu Meshorer, R. Uzi Kalkheim, R. Moshe Dimentman, R. Eitan Eisman, R. Aryeh Horowitz, R. Zefaniah Drori, R. Yakov Ariel, and R. Yisrael Ariel.
57. As in his language on the *semikhah* of R. Eisman, from 27 Iyar 1967 [!] (*Bisdei HaRa'ayah*, 375).
58. At the first annual banquet to commemorate the anniversary of *Yom Yerushalayim*, R. Arieli sat in a seat of honor between R. Tzvi Yehudah Kook and the Nazir and even delivered a speech (*Bisdei HaRa'ayah*, 372. The prior year, he spoke at the yeshiva's *Yom Ha'atzma'ut* banquet (*Arba'im LeBinah* [Ma'aleh Adumim, 2007], 13). He also was present at the cornerstone dedication for Merkaz HaRav's new building, August 28, 1960, sitting in the second row among the yeshiva's rabbis (see photograph in R. Yoḥai Rudik's *Eretz Geulah* [Jerusalem, 1989], after p. 96). He was also one of the eulogizers for R. Avraham Yitzḥak bar Shalom Natan Ra'anan, who passed away in 1959 (*Lahai Roi* [Jerusalem, 1961], 91).
59. From the meeting's minutes, *Ḥayim Shel Yetzira*, 265.
60. At a reception in honor of R. Dov Aryeh Leventhal of Philadelphia, in the home of R. Frank in the summer of 1936, R. Arieli spoke as a representative of Merkaz HaRav (*Sha'arei Tziyon*, 16: 9–12 [5696/1936], 55).

on, R. Arieli began to sign his correspondence as *ra"m and menahel* in Yeshivat Merkaz HaRav.[61]

[However,[62] within two years of R. Kook's death, differences of opinion began to arise between R. Arieli and the rest of the leadership. A hint to this tension is given] in a letter dated November 13, 1936 to R. Yaakov Leib Moinester.[63] In it, he dismisses the invitation to leave Israel for a time to travel to the US. R. Arieli [mentions] his pressing "economic situation" (and his thoughts about "bringing in a full complement of Torah scholars, working and helping to formulate and sharpen for publication the vast material that was collected"). Among his reasons for declining the invitation, he writes that he is concerned lest leaving the yeshiva for any length of time cause unpleasantness afterward ("no more needs to be said"). His hint is clear: He was worried that if he left the yeshiva even for a short time, he would not be ensured of his position when he returned.

[A protocol dated 27 Nisan 5698 (April 28, 1938)] of a meeting in R. Harlap's home,[64] established that] "the five members of the administration [R. Ḥarlap, R. Tzvi Yehudah Kook, the Nazir, R. Ra'anan, and R. Arieli] have equal say, and all matters of the yeshiva must be conducted through the entire group."[65] [But, in summer 1938, only three years after R. Kook's death, the tensions between the group's members boiled over, resulting in a decision by the rabbinical court of the Chief Rabbinate[66] in favor of R. Arieli. In a stinging letter] dated 5 Av 5698 (August 2, 1938) to R. Harlap and the Nazir, R. Isser Zalman Meltzer strongly protested the yeshiva's retaining an attorney in a bid to overturn in a secular court the Chief Rabbinate's decision regarding the matter of R. Arieli's dispute with the yeshiva's leadership.[67]

---

61. Per his expression in *Einayim LaMishpat*, Kiddushin. Similarly, in *Keter Torah – Seder Hakhtarat HaRabbanut* [cited above, n. 29], 29, he signs as, "*Menahel* in Yeshivat Merkaz HaRav." R. Moshe Tzvi Neriyah, also described him thus, in his article in *HaHed*, 1939, "One of the *rashei yeshiva* of Merkaz HaRav and its leaders" (*Bisdei HaRa'ayah*, 359).
62. Everything to this point is as penned by the author himself. From here to the end of this chapter, minor gaps in the composition were filled in by the author's parents from his writings. These are indicated by square brackets.
63. Provided to me by the family.
64. R. Yoḥai Rudik, *Yeshivat Merkaz HaRav: Hitpat'ḥuta U'Magamoteha HaḤinukhiyot (5681–5742)*, doctoral thesis, Haifa University, 1995 [henceforth: *Yeshivat Merkaz HaRav*], 140.
65. R. Rudik notes a similar announcement in *HaBoker*, June 9, 1941, signed by R. Tzvi Pesaḥ Frank and others.
66. [These minutes are unfortunately missing from the Chief Rabbinate archives, so further details are unavailable.]
67. The letter was in the estate of R. Ḥarlap, and was sold at an auction in December 2010 by the auction house, Asufa, lot number 508.

[From] 1948 and on, R. Arieli's place in the yeshiva began disappearing.[68] In parallel, [these were] years of significant decline in the yeshiva itself, which by then comprised several dozens of students in small cliques of different ages and backgrounds, with little social cohesion as a student body.[69] This waning of the yeshiva also caused R. Arieli to turn his attention primarily to his writings.

THE SOCIAL COMPOSITION OF THE YESHIVA AND ITS LEADERSHIP

In our humble opinion, in order to understand these events, it is not enough to investigate what transpired within the walls of Yeshivat Merkaz HaRav during the 1950s and 1960s. Rather, we must examine the socio-ideological character of the pre-Holocaust yeshiva world, and what replaced it afterward – while focusing on Merkaz HaRav's roots and R. Arieli's background. Using the following broad survey,[70] we hope to illuminate the causes for R. Arieli's dissociation from Merkaz HaRav, and consequentially, his elimination from the yeshiva's historical memory.

Yeshivat Merkaz HaRav was founded in the summer of 1923. By mid-1925, it already had fifty students, and by 1927 and on, the number remained close to eighty.[71] If we analyze the makeup of the student population, we find three broad groups, separated by social and ideological characteristics, most notably by their relative open- or closed-mindedness to the current zeitgeist:

---

68. Ed. note: In 1948, discord erupted in Merkaz HaRav over the military drafting of yeshiva students. R. Arieli and R. Ḥarlap were opposed, and R. Tzvi Yehudah in favor. A file on this gathered by the author included a passage by Prof. Naḥum Rackover in *Shma'atin* 184 (2013), "R. Arieli related his entries from *Einayim LaMishpat* on Bava Batra, on "Rabbis do not require security" to the issue of the yeshiva draft, while R. Tzvi Yehudah brought his own sources to refute."

69. R. Rudik (*Yeshivat Merkaz HaRav*, 139) entertains the possibility that R. Kook's stature with government officials enabled him to obtain many certificates [ed. note: immigration certificates, from the British Mandatory government] for yeshiva students. After his death, the yeshiva lost its ability to bring over many students from Eastern Europe. Besides which, when four years later World War II broke out, the stream that had dwindled to a trickle ceased altogether. [Ed. note: He does not consider the leadership struggles as a factor in the yeshiva's decline, but] on pp. 124–42 he writes that "a struggle broke out between R. Tzvi Yehudah Kook, the Rav's son, and the family of R. Ḥarlap. However, the relative gap in age and authority, and the scope of Torah greatness, decided in favor of R. Ḥarlap." Also: "During the war, the yeshiva was almost empty of students. Even afterward, not many returned, only around ten or twenty" (ibid., p. 157).

70. Ed. note: Which, sadly, we did not merit the author's completing.

71. For sources of this data, see Gershuni, "*Ad Asher Emtza Makom B'Mishkenot L'Avir Ya'akov,*" *HaMa'ayan* 50:1 (Tishrei 5770): n. 34.

The first group, encompassing the majority of the students, was Eastern European in origin, from Russia and Poland, the world center of Jewish life at that time. This group was characterized, among other things, by the broad spectrum of its members, a measure of openness, and the modern norms of the mussar yeshivot.

The second group, comprising a small minority of students, was from the Old Yishuv, specifically in Jerusalem and the other "holy cities." This group was characterized by a strong Orthodox tradition concerning preserving past traditions. It was heavily influenced by the "Hungarian" ideology that had a strong presence in Jerusalem at that time.

The third group, by far the smallest in size and influence, was from the New Yishuv in Eretz Yisrael – both those who lived it in practice, and those who identified with it and saw themselves as part of it (the Mizraḥi). This group was characterized by strong nationalism and identification with the Zionist movement.[72]

During those years, the relative sizes of these groups established the yeshiva's character and public image. Because the overwhelming majority of students came from Eastern Europe – as this was the source of most yeshiva students at the time – the yeshiva took on an external character similar to the yeshivot of Slobodka-Hebron and Lomza-Petaḥ Tikvah, whose students also were drawn from the same pool.[73] This division, to a certain measure,[74] and its implications, also applies to the four personalities who comprised the faculty of Merkaz HaRav:

72. There is another important population, geographically separate, that is the Jews of the United States, who also came to learn in Merkaz HaRav. However, we have chosen not to list them as a distinct sociological group, because, on the whole, those Americans coming to learn in Merkaz HaRav, were part of an immigrant population in the US that had not yet coalesced into a distinctive population. Practically speaking, it is possible to assign them to the three other groups: Some were similar in style and character to the Eastern Europeans; some took up the call of the Zionist New Yishuv; and some – very few – closely resembled the Jews of the Old Yishuv and Hungary.

73. Even the number of students in those yeshivot was strikingly similar. As opposed to the yeshivot in Eastern Europe, the yeshivot in Eretz Yisrael during that time were unable to accommodate large numbers of students, primarily for economic reasons. Another factor contributing to the similarity between Merkaz HaRav and other yeshivot was the noted Eastern European rabbi who led Merkaz HaRav for a short time: R. Avraham Aharon Burstein from Tavrig, who served as rosh hayeshiva from the winter of 1924 until his death from illness in Kislev 1925. For details regarding his tenure in the yeshiva, see Gershuni, "*Ad Asher Emtza Makom B'Mishkenot L'Avir Ya'akov.*"

74. With full awareness that sociological categorization of this sort is simplistic and limited by nature. Nevertheless, there is truth in it and it can serve a great purpose here.

1. R. Ḥarlap: He was, without a doubt, a product of the Old Yishuv. His father was a *dayan* in the rabbinic court of R. Yehoshua Leib Diskin, and his teacher (R. Tzvi Mikhel Shapira) was also a student of R. Diskin. Later on, as a young kollel fellow, he met R. Kook, grew close to him and became his prime student. However, his decision to walk in R. Kook's path did not change his basic nature, which was formed in his childhood home.
2. The Nazir: Though he grew up in a Lithuanian yeshiva environment, attended yeshivot in Radin and Slobodka, and followed the general path of the aforementioned Eastern European group, he later turned toward academia and forged an iconoclastic path for himself. It is impossible to fit him into any categorical box. Nevertheless, on the open- versus closed-minded spectrum, he was similar to the New Yishuv group.
3. R. Tzvi Yehudah Kook: Defining him is a complicated task. He grew up in Latvia, where in addition to the traditional studies, he also learned European languages. He then made aliyah with his father and learned for a time in Yeshivat Torat Ḥayim in Jerusalem, well known as an Old Yishuv institution. However, he spent his most formative years in Jaffa, a center of the "New Yishuv." In some sense, we can place him on the continuum between the Eastern Europeans and the New Yishuv.
4. R. Arieli: Like R. Harlap, he is most readily identified with the Old Yishuv in Jerusalem. The major turnabout in his life took place when R. Kook arrived in Jerusalem in the summer of 1919.

As for R. Kook himself, his greatness lay in his ability not only to encompass and absorb all these different social groups, but also to serve as a magnet for students so varied from each other, as evidenced by the many circles of his followers.

[Unfinished][75]

ADDENDUM[76]

R. Kook's personality and activities as a Torah giant and public figure reflected, on the one hand, the preservation of the glorious tradition of classic spiritual

---

75. See n. 1, above.
76. Ed. note: This addition, dealing with the split of the Orthodox community in Eretz Yisrael into two separate communities, was found on the author's computer following his ascent to the Heavens. It seems to have been intended for an additional article that would explain historical revisionism in the families of R. Kook's disciples as a key to understanding the ḥaredi/national-religious dichotomy in Israel. It contains a broad analysis that will clarify the causes of R. Arieli's diminished relationship with Merkaz HaRav, and with it, his disappearance from the yeshiva's historical memory. Therefore, we have chosen to append it to the current chapter.

leadership of generations past, including an emphasis on the Torah-yeshiva primacy. On the other hand, he lent a certain legitimacy and showed favor to the *ḥalutzim* and the youth movements that had sprung up in Eastern Europe and in Eretz Yisrael. All of this was based on his unique worldview of the new generation and the implications of the events that were unfolding throughout the Jewish world.

The idea of "encompassing unity" developed by R. Kook found expression in his activities: He supported and cooperated with, at one and the same time, opposing parties, Agudath Israel and Mizraḥi, while refraining from declared identification with one specific group. He hoped to unite the entire Orthodox camp under a single umbrella movement, "Degel Yerushalayim." Similarly, Merkaz HaRav, at its inception, served as a common address for a wide variety of students spanning the ideological spectrum, more than any other yeshiva of that time. In the *bet midrash*, learning side by side, were students from the Old Yishuv and New Yishuv; from America and Eastern Europe; Zionist pioneering youth alongside members of venerable Jerusalemite families; children of ḥasidic courts with those of *mitnadgim*. With all this diversity, the yeshiva managed to maintain a social balance, despite the fact that the lion's share of students hailed from Russia and Poland. Their profile, no matter how you slice it, is identical to their peers in the yeshivot of Ḥevron and Lomza, who arrived in Israel from Lithuania during the same years.[77]

A similar cultural and ideological diversity existed, as pointed out, among the rabbinic staff of Merkaz HaRav during R. Kook's lifetime. The head *ra"m*, R. Ḥarlap, was a product of the Old Yishuv in Jerusalem, with a kabbalistic side to his personality. R. Yitzḥak Arieli, the *mashgiaḥ*, was also raised in the Old Yishuv and displayed its classic analytical learning style. R. Kook's son, R. Tzvi Yehudah, who was a *ra"m* and *menahel*, was multi-faceted, soaking up a variety of influences during his years in Latvia, Jerusalem, and mainly, the New Yishuv city of Jaffa. The remaining *ra"m*, R. David Cohen, the Nazir, had a unique personality all his own. He was educated in Lithuania, but then pursued an academic and philosophical path, forging his own esoteric way. R. Avraham Aaron Burstein, who served for a

77. There has yet to be a comprehensive sociological study conducted on the students of Merkaz HaRav during the R. Kook era. However, my friend Shemaryah Gershuni has already shown, in his article "*Rav Shimon Shkop ztz"l U'Kehunat Rosh Yeshivat Merkaz HaRav – Mesorot V'Uvdot*" (*HaMa'ayan* 50:1 [Tishrei 5770]: 79–96; see especially n. 44), that there was a regular flow of students between Merkaz HaRav and the other Lithuanian yeshivot of the time. It should be noted that there were sporadic examples of students in other yeshivot who came from outside the normal groups. But in Merkaz HaRav this was a widespread and notable phenomenon. See *Ḥayim Shel Yetzira*, 259–61.

time as a senior *ra"m*,[78] was a perfect example of classic Lithuanian yeshiva world. To all this, was added of course, the personality of R. Kook himself.

We can say that Merkaz HaRav, its teachers and students, similar to parallel institutions such as the Harry Fischel Institute (est. 1933), and other groups close to R. Kook's circle, succeeded in reflecting his multi-faceted personality. This holds true even more for the wider circle of R. Kook's supporters who hailed from different social and religious groups in Europe, Eretz Yisrael, and Jerusalem itself. Among them were *ḥalutzim*, academics, and people with a modern orientation on the one hand; and on the other hand were many from the Old Yishuv. The latter group's identification with R. Kook came, not from internalizing his innovative thinking or a Zionist activist outlook, but from his spiritual charisma, greatness in Torah, and his activities in support of Judaism in Eretz Yisrael. R. Kook, in his lifetime, succeeded in embracing within his circle, many and diverse – and even opposing – components of Orthodox existence.

THE CRYSTALLIZATION OF PARTY IDENTIFICATION IN R. KOOK'S IMAGE

However, not long following R. Kook's passing, the situation changed, and a significant shift was becoming apparent: Within a few years, R. Kook's legacy and teachings began to be identified more and more with the Mizraḥi movement and its branches in Israel.[79] While R. Kook had a close and positive relationship with Mizraḥi and its leaders in his lifetime, it was a complicated one. Alongside mutual appreciation, there existed ideological and practical differences of opinion.[80] Mizraḥi leaders found R. Kook to be an exemplary Torah and national leader,

78. See my article, "*Od B'Inyan HaRav MiTavrig U'Merkaz HaRav*," *HaMa'ayan* 51:3 (Nisan 5771): 85–89.

79. I use the term "Mizraḥi" more broadly than just the political organization. I use it because there is no better choice in the absence of a term to refer to the larger group affiliated with religious Zionism. One must be careful, generally speaking, not to map the Jewish community of that generation onto stereotypical party divisions. A significant percentage have a social profile consistent with a particular party in the view of modern historiography, but nevertheless held ideological positions that were not necessarily those of the said party. As mentioned, the thesis of this chapter is that, prior to the establishment of the State of Israel, the boundaries between camps within Orthodoxy were more fluid.

80. See, among others: Yossi Avneri, "*HaRav Avraham Yitzhak HaKohen Kook V'Zikato HaMa'asit LaTzionut Hadatit*," in *Meah Shenot Tziyonut Datit* 1 (2003), 41–77; Dov Schwartz, *HaTzionut HaDatit: Toldot U'Pirkei Ideologia* (2003), 56–66; Shulamit Eliash, "*HaRabbanut HaRashit V'haMizraḥi Bitkufat HaMandat*," *Katedra* 37 (1986), 123–48; Menachem Friedman, *Ḥevra VaDat* (Jerusalem, 1978), 161–67.

but most of them did not see themselves bound to his opinions or approach.[81] By contrast, in the generation after his death, the Mizraḥi movement and its offshoots – Hapo'el HaMizraḥi, Bnei Akiva, and others – took hold of R. Kook's image and legacy (as they proceeded to fashion it), and crowned him as their venerated spiritual leader while downplaying their former ambivalence toward him.[82] This was not a directed, methodical process, but an inherently intuitive one at its core. But as a result, the gaps and differences of opinion between R. Kook's path and the Mizraḥi that existed during his lifetime were quickly forgotten with his passing. This is how, in less than a decade, a narrow political identification emerged, something that R. Kook strove to avoid his entire life![83]

The circumstances by which R. Kook's image became so quickly identified with the Mizraḥi are wrapped up, among other circumstances, with the failure of R. Kook's vision for a "Degel Yerushalayim" movement, formulated during his London years. During its numbered years of existence, Degel Yerushalayim did not succeed in becoming the umbrella organization for Orthodoxy, as its founder had dreamed.[84] As a result, R. Kook left no organized group to express his unique approach and give it over to the next generation. The institutions that formed around him during his Jerusalem years, such as the Chief Rabbinate and Merkaz

81. Other than when his teachings comfortably fit with their own outlook. One well-known example is the confrontation between R. Kook and the Mizraḥi over women's suffrage in the 1920 elections. Friedman (*Ḥevra VaDat*, 166) and Avneri (*"HaRav Avraham Yitzhak HaKohen Kook V'Zikato HaMa'asit,"* 56) quote sharp language from R. Yehudah Leib Maimon, which they claim was directed at R. Kook: "With regards to [ritual] permissibility, we'll ask the rabbis, but for day-to-day activities, we'll ask ourselves." However, examination of the source (*Do'ar HaYom* 2:160 [April 19, 1920], 2) reveals that R. Maimon's words were directed at the "ḥaredi zealots." See R. Maimon's conciliatory words regarding the establishment of the Chief Rabbinate in 1921 (Geula Bat Yehudah, "*Yisud HaRabbanut HaRashit – V'haMizraḥi*," in *Sefer HaTzionut HaDatit* 1, 410). Nevertheless, this gives some indication of the gap between R. Kook and R. Maimon. In any event, clear criticism of R. Kook was heard from a segment of the religious Zionists of the day (see Friedman, and Avneri, p. 65).

82. This is captured well in words penned later on by none other than R. Maimon: "What a mysterious connection he had with the Mizraḥi. He was our teacher, and we were his students. We drank up his words thirstily" (*HaRa'ayah – R. Avraham Yitzḥak HaKohen Kook* [Jerusalem, 1965], 115). In practice, although the religious Zionists at that time embraced R. Kook's general thought, many did not feel obligated to follow his practical teachings and leadership unless the latter comfortably matched their own outlook.

83. Typical of this is the following passage from R. Meir Bar-Ilan in summer of 1940: "Degel Yerushalayim, the organization that R. Kook *z"l* conceived of but was never realized, and its entire program as described in "*Matarat Degel Yerushalayim*" is implemented today by the Mizraḥi organization"! (*Ḥazon HaGe'ula* [Jerusalem, 1941], 10).

84. See, among others: Yosi Avneri, "Degel Yerushalayim," in *Bishvilei HaTeḥiya* 3, 39–58.

HaRav, expressed his personality and philosophy so long as he remained at the helm. But that was not enough to make a broad-band [religious] current into a permanent leadership presence.[85]

In addition, of all the different groups that had been under the influence of R. Kook, the Mizraḥi and its branches were, without a doubt, the most organized and active. An overwhelming majority of those who labored to preserve R. Kook's legacy, via publishing and setting up research institutes and educational institutions, came from the ranks of Mizraḥi or its supporters. The many initiatives include R. Maimon's establishment of Mossad HaRav Kook in 1936; the founding in 1940 of *Ḥug HaRa'ayah,* whose participants were mostly religious Zionists;[86] and the educational activities of R. Moshe Tzvi Neriyah, R. Kook's famous "ambassador" to Bnei Akiva, who in 1940 founded Yeshivat Kfar Haro'eh in his name. By contrast, there was a vacuum among other groupings of R. Kook's followers when it came to furthering his legacy, especially among those from the Old Yishuv in Jerusalem. They remained within their traditional frameworks, with little appetite for joining new movements and modern initiatives.

This is how R. Kook came to be identified with the official institutions of religious Zionism. This left no room for R. Kook's staunch followers from the Old Yishuv, unless they were willing to actively identify themselves with religious Zionism. As long as they remained passive in the face of the burning issues of the day, as a significant group of Jerusalemites did, they lost their ability to be counted among the ranks of R. Kook's followers.

ABSORPTION OF SOME R. KOOK FOLLOWERS INTO THE ḤAREDI CAMP

In parallel, in other segments of the Orthodox community, an opposite course was underway. In R. Kook's time, the European Agudath Israel (as opposed to the Jerusalem faction) under the spiritual leadership of R. Avraham Mordekhai Alter, the Gerrer Rebbe, took a careful, conciliatory approach to the ideological struggles between opposing camps in Israel. However, later on, as the center of gravity of the Jewish people tilted toward Eretz Yisrael, the Eastern European

85. This is besides the many conflicts that broke out over personal and ideological issues: The splitting of duties of the Chief Rabbi of Israel and the Rabbi of Jerusalem, strife within Merkaz HaRav in 1937, and others. These conflicts had clear origins in the ongoing fragmentation within R. Kook's circle that we have described.

86. Ḥayim Lifshitz (ed.), *B'Ma'agalei Ḥug HaRa'ayah* (Jerusalem, 1946), 47. See also: R. Neriyah Gutel, "*Protocol HaAgudah L'Hotza'at Kitvei HaRav Kook – Mismakh,*" *Sinai* 126–27 (Jerusalem, 2001), 340–53.

ḥaredi community that identified with Agudath Israel came under the influence of the followers of R. Yosef Ḥayim Sonnenfeld, considered the main adversary of R. Kook in Israel.[87] Another indication of this shift is the traction gained by the anti-Zionist thought of Rav Elḥanan Bunim Wasserman, specifically in the generation following his death (*al kiddush HaShem*), while during his lifetime, he often represented a minority view.[88]

By the 1940s, the ideological differences between the camps became more externally visible. It became increasingly untenable for someone to identify socially and culturally with one camp while, at the same time, identifying with the philosophy of someone seen as the founder of the other camp. When faced with a stark choice between a pro-Zionist ideology, or at least a measured approach to the nationalist stirrings within the Jewish people in the spirit of R. Kook on the one hand, and, on the other hand, the conservation of the old-world traditional way of life that was being preserved only in the ḥaredi community, many of R. Kook's fervent supporters chose the latter approach. Only a few chose to cling to the Zionist ideology while still functioning within the "Lithuanian" ḥaredi community, or the reverse: to operate within the religious-Zionist community while maintaining a ḥaredi lifestyle. This complex choice generally did not succeed in holding its ground through two or three generations.[89] For this reason, many of

87. The discussion of this part of the process is outside the parameters of this article. See, among others: Friedman, *Ḥevra VaDat*, ch. 5, especially p. 145, dealing with the weakening of the moderate faction in Israel in the face of the strengthening of the Yerushalmi Agudath Israel faction. A clear description of this phenomenon is expressed by R. Menaḥem Porush, a scion of a Jerusalemite family that during R. Kook's lifetime was divided between pro- and anti-R. Kook factions: "Only after R. Kook's passing did things slowly change. With the founding of the State of Israel and due to the problems that arose, a single outlook developed, and soon, any remnant of those who followed R. Kook was forgotten" (*Sharsheret HaDorot Bitkufot HaSo'arot* 1 (Jerusalem, 2001), 209; see also 3:430).
88. We should briefly mention the stinging rebuke at the hands of his brother-in-law, R. Ḥayim Ozer Grodzenski regarding his meddling from afar in affairs in Eretz Yisrael; his dispute with the Ḥazon Ish and R. Isser Zalman Meltzer regarding participation of rabbis in the National Council (Va'ad Leumi); his minority position in the third Knessiah Gedolah of Agudath Israel on the question of the establishment of a (mitzvah observant) Jewish State.
89. It will suffice to mention several Jerusalemite families who counted themselves among R. Kook's staunch supporters during his lifetime, but by the 1940s and 50s were no longer considered part of this circle: Auerbach, Elyashiv, Waldenberg, and more. Members of those families who knew R. Kook personally did not abandon their reverence for him and his work, or even occasionally, part of the philosophy identified with him. But the public expression of this waned over the years – in equal measure with their legitimacy in ḥaredi public life – so that this virtually disappeared from their descendants. A similar development occurred in the second or third generations in most of the Zachs, Frank, Tukochinsky, Levine, and other families.

the personalities close to R. Kook in his lifetime (including R. Mordekhai Ilan and R. Yitzḥak Arieli who were profiled in my previous chapter) sent most of their sons to learn in Yeshivat Ponevezh in Bnei Brak or in Yeshivat Ḥevron in Jerusalem, and not in Merkaz HaRav or other religious-Zionist yeshivot such as Kerem B'Yavneh (est. 1953). Nor did they even consider intermediate options, such as Yeshivat Kletzk/HaDarom in Pardes Ḥana/Rehovot (est. 1947).[90]

This is the key to understanding the phenomenon that we have presented, of individuals whose current identification with the ḥaredi camp prevents them from coming to terms with the fact that their fathers and grandfathers, in their day, were counted as part of the circle of supporters and associates of R. Kook. This is also the key to understanding a long string of historical phenomena on the seam between the ḥaredi and religious-Zionist camps. It explains the decline of Merkaz HaRav during the era of R. Yaakov Moshe Ḥarlap's leadership.[91] It explains the creation of middle-of-road political options, such as Poalei Agudath Israel, and their subsequent collapse. And it can also explain the edifying case of Germany's Orthodox Jews. Upon the aliyah of many during the 1930s, they split almost evenly into the religious and ḥaredi camps, sometimes even within families. To use stereotypical terms, when these Jews, who grew up with the ideology of "Torah and *Derekh Eretz*," landed in Eretz Yisrael in the 30s and 40s, they were forced to choose between a camp that claimed sole ownership of "Torah" and a camp that claimed sole possession of "*Derekh Eretz*." A decade earlier, in the days of R. Kook, this dichotomy did not yet gain traction, certainly not in R. Kook himself. Yet later on, he would become identified with only one political, social, and cultural camp.

---

90. Of course, one can give other reasons, such as the size of the yeshivot, the breadth of staff, their age, and the prominence of their *rashei yeshiva*. However, the fact remains that the ideological-nationalist factor was clearly de-emphasized, in a manner one would not have expected from R. Kook's closest students.

91. This topic has not yet been covered with the broad academic research it deserves. (For an initial work, see *Ḥayim Shel Yetzira* [Jerusalem, 1998], 138–69). In general, it can be described as follows: On the one hand, its main stock of student recruits – Eastern European Jews – was destroyed in the Holocaust; on the other hand, the yeshiva's identification with the legacy of R. Kook as fashioned by Mizraḥi discouraged potential students from the ḥaredi camp that was taking shape; and on a third side, a gap opened up between the conservative persona of the rosh yeshiva together with some of the staff on the one hand, and the character of the yeshiva's diminished religious-Zionist student population on the other.

Part III

Rabbi Yosef Eliyahu Henkin

Chapter 23

America's Rabbi[1]

"I was certain that he would live to welcome mashiaḥ for us. Now, who will welcome him on our behalf?" (R. Yaakov Kaminetzky, in his eulogy for R. Y. E. Henkin).

On the afternoon of Shabbat Naḥamu, August 11, 1973, the elder *posek* of the United States, R. Yosef Eliyahu Henkin, passed away peacefully. Tens of thousands attended his funeral, among them nearly all the *gedolim* of the US, most of whom delivered eulogies: R. Moshe Feinstein, R. Yaakov Kaminetzky, R. Yaakov Yitzḥak Ruderman, R. Shneur Kotler, R. Yosef Dov Soloveitchik, R. Gedaliah

1. Translated by Michael Appel, and abridged by the family. Readers seeking greater detail are referred to the Hebrew article in *Yeshurun* 20 (2008), 125–220. [Ed. note: This chapter is based in part on an essay by the author's father, R. Yehuda Herzl Henkin, on his grandfather and teacher, the saintly R. Y. E. Henkin. See *Responsa Bnei Banim* 1 (Jerusalem, 1981), 166–72.]

   Ed. note: The author *Hy"d* intended this chapter to document the historical background and biography of his great-grandfather, the gaon and tzaddik R. Yosef Eliyahu Henkin *ztz"l*, who, although legendary amongst *poskim*, is less known in many circles. This chapter does not deal with R. Henkin's halakhic methodology, originality, and the sweep of his legacy. From the vast mass of material on his computer, it would appear that R. Eitam had planned to write about this. Sadly, the task will now await others. A collection of R. Henkin's *piskei halakhah* on Oraḥ Ḥayim and *Yoreh De'ah*, annotated extensively by R. Doniel Asher Kleinman with the assistance of R. Eitam, can be found in two volumes of *Shu"t Gevurat Eliyahu* that were published in recent years. Hopefully, the volumes on *Ḥoshen Mishpat* and *Even HaEzer* will be published in forthcoming years. This collection, annotation, and publication of R. Henkin's *teshuvot* was undertaken by R. Doniel Osher Kleinman with the encouragement of R. Shmuel Kaminetzky.

Schorr, the ḥasidic Rebbes of Bobov and Ciechanow, and others. R. Yaakov Yisrael Kanievsky, the "Steipler," wrote from Bnei Brak mourning the passing of "the great tzaddik, tremendous gaon, pillar of loving-kindness, R. Yosef Eliyahu Henkin, may the memory of the righteous be a holy blessing." We will attempt, to the best of our abilities, to give an account of R. Henkin's life and activities, his piety, and his greatness as a Torah scholar and *posek*.

EARLY DAYS, LEARNING IN SLUTSK, AND ORDINATION AS A RABBI

R. Yosef Eliyahu Henkin was born on Rosh Ḥodesh Adar I, in Klimavichy, a town of 2,500 Jews situated in the district of Mohilev in White Russia (Belarus of today), to R. Eliezer Kalonymos and Fruma Shifra, the middle child of seven siblings. At age three, he was known as a *wunderkind* who knew much of Tanakh.[2] According to his journal, he began to study Torah at age five with "R. Yitzḥak the *melamed*," and at age six, with his great-grandfather, who lived to an advanced age. At age seven, he began to study Talmud and other books with his father, the local rosh yeshiva. After three years of study with his father, he entered the yeshiva of R. Tzvi Hirsch Lifshitz, the rabbi of Klimavichy, and at the age of eleven, he moved to the yeshiva in nearby Kritshov, headed by the town's rabbi and his future father-in-law, R. Yehudah Leib Kreindel.[3]

Following his bar mitzvah, he returned to Klimavichy and studied on his own for two years while attending *shi'urim* of the local rabbis and taking on several local boys as study partners. During those two years, he completed *Seder Mo'ed* of the Talmud four times.[4] In 1896, at the age of fifteen, he traveled to study in Mir. However, as he records in his journal, he continued on to the neighboring town of Karelitz, studying there for a year "with members of that community." During his year in Karelitz, he completed the tractates of Shabbat and Eruvin alone close to forty times, in addition to his other studies.[5]

What forced him to bypass Mir and continue to Karelitz? R. Moshe Roginsky heard the story decades later:

---

2. Ibid., 168.
3. Born in 1854. A Ḥabad ḥasid, he first taught in Klimavichy and then moved to Kritshov, where in 1890 he was appointed rabbi of its ḥasidic community (*Oholei Shem* [1912], 189). When the Communists came to power, he was forced to flee and left all his writings behind. A lone surviving responsum was published by his son-in-law in *Lev Ivra* (p. 79). He passed away in 1933. R. Henkin described him as, "excellent in probing the depths of Torah and halakhah, with outstanding righteousness" (ibid.) and referred to him several times in his halakhic writings.
4. *Responsa Bnei Banim* 1:168.
5. As reported by R. Moshe Eliezer Margolin (introduction to *Kitvei Hagaon Rav Yosef Eliyahu Henkin* 2, p. 4) and others. See below.

> He [R. Henkin] once told us a story of his youth. When he was fourteen, his mother wished to send him to yeshiva. She was destitute and had to sell (or pawn) her featherbed to pay the wagon driver to take him to Mir. When he arrived, they turned him away as being too young. What could he do? He had no money to return home, so he went to nearby Karelitz and, as per the custom then, slept in the *bet midrash* and "ate days."[6] During that year, he completed the study of Eruvin forty times, along with the tractates Pesaḥim, Sukkah, Beitzah, and others. When I told this story to one of the *gedolim*, he said to me: I understand how someone could study Eruvin forty times. However, I will never understand how he was able to complete it the *first* two times within a single year.[7]

In 1897, R. Isser Zalman Meltzer established a yeshiva in Slutsk together with fourteen students from Slobodka[8] at the behest of Ridbaz, the rabbi of Slutsk, and with the blessing of R. Nosson Tzvi Finkel, the Alter of Slobodka. When R. Henkin arrived in Slutsk to apply as a student, R. Meltzer tested him on Tractates Shabbat and Eruvin. R. Henkin responded with the names of the individual Sages of the Talmud on every page, with all their statements, and the commentaries of Rashi and Tosafot, and more. By the end of the test, R. Meltzer exclaimed in astonishment: "This child knows these two *masekhtot* better than I do!"[9]

R. Henkin studied in Slutsk for six years, during which he became known as the *iluy*, young genius, of the yeshiva.[10] He became the close friend and *talmid*

---

6. Ed. note: On the custom of "eating days" ("*essen teg*"), wherein a yeshiva *bochur* would be matched with a family or several families for meals for "days" or for the week, see E. Etkes and S. Tikochinski eds., *Yeshivot Lita, Pirkei Zikhronot*, 314–16.
7. *HaPardes* 48:10 (1974), p. 30. His younger brother, Dr. Yitzḥak, wrote about his parents' dire straits in a letter from July 22, 1976 to his nephew, Professor Louis Henkin: "We were raised and educated in poverty, with nothing, with poor parents, and we suffered greatly. To understand our economic situation then, I'll describe our Friday night Sabbath meal: We all sat around the table, hungry and half asleep. Together with Father, we sang the *zemirot* tunefully – 'This day is the most glorified of all the days'..."
8. Who were later known as "the *Yad HaḤazaka*" (trans. note: a play on the numerical value of *yad*: 14). Most went on to become Torah sages of the first order, including: R. Eliezer Yehudah Finkel, rosh yeshiva of Mir in Lithuania and Jerusalem; R. Yosef Kanowitz, son-in-law of the Ridbaz and President of Agudas Harabonim in America and Canada; R. Reuven Katz, rabbi and *dayan* in Petaḥ Tikvah; R. Pesaḥ Pruskin, the *mashgiaḥ* of Shklov, rabbi of Kobrin, and a leader of Agudath Israel in Poland; and others.
9. According to R. Naftali Tzvi Yehudah Rif, *HaPardes* 48:1 (1974), 34. Also see *Responsa Bnei Banim* 1:168.
10. As he innocently answered a kollel student who asked him if he was the yeshiva's greatest genius: "Did they say that about me? Of course it was true" (*Responsa Bnei Banim* 2, 1:4). This

muvhak, disciple, of R. Meltzer, who was eleven years his senior. When R. Meltzer would travel on yeshiva business, he would leave R. Henkin in charge of the yeshiva.[11] When R. Henkin left Slutsk for his first rabbinical appointment, R. Meltzer presented him with a copy of '*Levush Mordekhai*' (on *Bava Batra*) by his brother-in-law R. M. M. Epstein, with a handwritten inscription:

> I gift this volume to my dear and beloved friend, fountain of Torah, outstanding in learning, future leader of Israel, His Honor R. Yosef Eliyahu Henkin, may his light shine, who studied for six years in this great yeshiva that is proud of having nurtured so great a scholar. May it be God's will that he take his strengths and grow to become a Torah giant who will increase the glory of Israel. From one who greatly values and appreciates him, Isser Zalman Meltzer, rabbi of this town.

At twenty years of age, R. Henkin received *semikhah* from three of the *gedolim* of the previous generation in addition to R. Meltzer: R. Yeḥiel Mikhel Epstein, head of the rabbinical court in Novardok and author of *Arukh HaShulḥan,*[12] R. Yaakov David Wilovsky, rabbi of Slutsk and author of *Bet Ridba"z* on the Talmud Yerushalmi,[13] and R. Barukh Ber Leibowitz, rosh yeshiva in Kamenitz and Slobodka and rabbi of Halusk.[14]

---

was despite the fact that his peers (the *Yad HaḤazaka*) were all accomplished, and many were considerably older than him. R. Rif added: "Lest you think that he became haughty regarding his knowledge? No way! He was extremely humble from his youth... and this humility took root and grew over his lifetime. Although he had expert knowledge in both Talmuds, all sections of *Shulḥan Arukh,* and responsa with all the later commentaries, he never glorified himself to show off his knowledge" (*HaPardes* 48:1 [1974], 34).

11. *Responsa Bnei Banim* 1, 165.
12. *Oholei Shem* (1902), 177. R. Henkin knew the author of *Arukh HaShulḥan* quite well. Once, when visiting him, Arukh HaShulḥan repeated a page of Talmud from Tractate Shabbat by heart without even intending to (*Responsa Bnei Banim* 2, 1:12).
13. During his years in Slutsk, R. Henkin spent much time attending to Ridbaz and frequented his home. In one article, he repeated a homily that he heard from Ridbaz after the Kishinev pogroms of 1903 (*Teshuvot Ivra, siman* 126). Seventy years later, he remembered the melody to "*Ḥassal Siddur Pesaḥ*" that he had learned from Ridbaz, and sang it to his grandson and his wife (*Responsa Bnei Banim* 1:172). R. Henkin related in praise of Ridbaz that it was difficult to converse with Ridbaz during his studies, so as not to interrupt the flow of his memory, as he studied everything by heart (ibid).
14. R. Henkin mentioned that the exam from R. Leibowitz took several days, after which R. Leibowitz said that he would write the *semikhah* document with great joy (*Responsa Bnei Banim* 2, 1:8).

HIS YEARS IN GEORGIA AND CORRESPONDENCE WITH *GEDOLEI HADOR*

In 1903, at the age of twenty-two, R. Henkin married the daughter of his former teacher, R. Y. L. Kreindel. After a year's residence with his father-in-law in Kritshov, R. Henkin returned to Slutsk to be near R. Meltzer. During that time, a community leader from the Caucasus, David Bazov, reached out to him. Bazov had studied in Slutsk and was searching for a suitable rabbi to join him in the Georgian town of Uni, 1,400 kilometers from White Russia with a population of 19,000 Jews, mostly of eastern origin. R. Henkin accepted the position with the blessing of R. Ḥayim Soloveitchik of Brisk,[15] joining the line of Ashkenazi rabbis trained in Lithuanian yeshivot and serving in the Caucasus. In 1904, R. Henkin became rabbi of Uni.

The Jews of Georgia had singular practices. They would not remove anything from the home of a sick person, so as not to anger the demons. They would eat sweets and perform other activities in the cowsheds "to bring blessing to the animals." They referred to Purim as "Rosh Hashanah" and would draw water in the middle of the night, so that "the new year would be blessed." And they would decorate the dead and place money and food in their graves, and recite the *Sheheḥeyanu* blessing at the burial.[16] R. Henkin endeavored relentlessly to uproot these practices. On the other hand, he discovered local praiseworthy customs related to prayer, many of which he mentioned in his responsa decades later, particularly that their Hebrew pronunciation was preserved from earliest times without European influence, and is correct.[17]

R. Henkin dealt with many aberrations by Georgian Jewry in marriage and divorce. For example, upon "engagement" the groom publicly presented his intended bride with money and property, after which she was referred to as his "wife." Despite this, were the "engagement" to be called off, the community believed that return of the gifts and property would be sufficient. R. Henkin protested that their practices constituted *kiddushin,* betrothal, under Jewish law, requiring a *get.*[18] There were also divergent customs regarding writs of divorce. They would write only the Jewish names, which were not used on a daily basis, without writing the common names into the divorce document. Here too, R.

15. According to *Responsa Bnei Banim* 2, article, 1 *siman* 30, and based on the editors' comments in *Responsa Har Tzvi* 1, *Even Ha'Ezer, siman* 100.
16. These quotes are taken from a letter that R. Henkin sent to R. Malkiel Tzvi HaLevi Tenenbaum of Lomza, whose answer was published in *Responsa Divrei Malkiel* 4:100–109.
17. *Teshuvot Ivra, siman* 10, section 2.
18. See his extensive discussion in his letter to R. Ḥayim Berlin from 1911, printed here (from which the following quote was taken).

Henkin worked to correct this custom in order to conform to halakhah.[19] Besides the difficulty in changing a widespread custom, R. Henkin had to deal with the added suspicion of an Ashkenazi rabbi coming to alter time-honored practices:

> I had to contend with their leaders who refused to listen, saying, "This is how our ancestors always did it." And how much worse it was when I came out against customs that were not expressly forbidden by stating, 'This is how the Sages ruled.' They would suspect me of leading them away from religion. And this especially applied when I attempted to bring a precedent from Ashkenazim, whose very name was invalid in their eyes, because of the numerous secular Ashkenazim in adjacent lands. Even though they are aware of great Ashkenazi sages, their rulings are not acceptable to the masses.

However, slowly, over time, his efforts began to bear fruit.

R. Henkin's activities brought him, as a young man of twenty-five, into correspondence with the leading rabbis of his generation, including R. Malkiel Tzvi HaLevi Tenenbaum of Lomza, author of *Divrei Malkiel*;[20] R. Ḥayim Soloveitchik of Brisk;[21] R. Yosef Rosen of Dvinsk – the Rogotchover;[22] R. Yehudah Leib Tzirelson, head of the rabbinical court in Kishinev;[23] and R. Isser Zalman Meltzer[24] along with leading rabbis of Eretz Yisrael such as R. Ḥayim Berlin and R. Tzvi Pesaḥ Frank.[25] R. Henkin sought their thinking across all areas of Jewish law, and

19. See the letter of R. Isser Zalman Meltzer in *Yagdil Torah*, 1900, printed here.
20. See *Responsa Divrei Malkiel* 5: 100–109, 249–51; 6:37, 41; 7:29. R. Henkin records additional correspondence between them in his journal.
21. As recorded by R. Henkin in his *Perushei Ivra, siman* 5, section 13, and elsewhere.
22. See *Responsa Bnei Banim* 2, 1:28–29. [Ed. note: The previously unpublished correspondence of R. Henkin and the Rogotchover is appended to R. Eitam Henkin's article in *Yeshurun* 20.] R. Henkin said that the Rogotchover's encyclopedic knowledge made him unique not only in his own generation but also among earlier generations. He also said that even though the Rogotchover dismissed all the other rabbis verbally, he did not take those feelings to heart – it was just his nature to speak that way (*Responsa Bnei Banim* 2, 1:28–29).
23. See *Responsa Atzei Halevanon, siman* 92, as well as the previous responsum.
24. See the anthology *Yagdil Torah* 2 (Slutsk), 22:71. In this letter, R. Meltzer wrote: "My friend R. Eliyahu Henkin was correct in all his ways," adding that he had showed R. Eliezer Rabinovitch, the *av bet din* of Minsk, the words of R. Henkin and he also agreed with them. Another letter to R. Meltzer is published in *Responsa Minḥat Shlomo Tinyana* (2–3), *siman* 26.
25. R. Henkin himself mentioned in one letter: "And I remember that forty years ago, I wrote this to R. Ḥayim Berlin *ztz"l*" (R. Y. Y. Greenwald, *Sefer Kol Bo al Aveilut* 2, 20). Also see the editors' comments to *Responsa Har Tzvi, Even Ha'Ezer* 1:100: "In 1911 R. Ḥayim Berlin *ztz"l* – rabbi of Jerusalem – was asked a similar question by R. Henkin *ztz"l*, who was then serving as rabbi of

raised numerous issues requiring practical rulings. Years later, he would say that his sojourn in Georgia is what made him conversant with *psak*.[26]

During this period he began to disseminate his first halakhic writings.[27] In a letter from that time he described the standing of a rabbi among the Jews of Georgia, opening a window into the challenges he faced there:

> The rabbi among our brethren in Georgia is mostly a *ḥazzan* with responsibility for the synagogue service, a ritual slaughterer, and a teacher... The simple and pure-hearted folk assume that he knows everything... Each rabbi also ordains other rabbis. Requirements for *semikhah* are several paragraphs in the laws of *sheḥitah*, an oral lesson on checking the lungs, and slaughtering three chickens before the ordaining rabbi. The *semikhah* includes severe warnings against those who would contest it. There is no specialized ordination in matters of marriage and divorce or ritual law; and these rabbis use the power of their ordination to officiate in divorce and marriage, as well as ritual law... Many of them will be so bold even today as to officiate in divorce and marriage, and to rule in areas in which they are clueless regarding the pertinent halakhot.[28]

R. Henkin spent four years in Uni, after which he briefly taught in Tskhinvali in the yeshiva of R. Avraham Khrolis.[29] In 1910, he moved to Kulashi, where he taught Talmud for three years and served as a *posek*. Toward the end of his time in Kulashi, around 1913, R. Henkin had a strange encounter in which he shared a wagon trip with one Josef Vissarionovich Jugashvili, who would come to be known as Josef Stalin, tyrannical ruler of the USSR. They were traveling between two cities:

---

several communities in Georgia at the behest of R. Ḥayim of Brisk *ztz"l*. R. Berlin also turned to R. Frank..." R. Henkin and R. Tzvi Pesaḥ Frank shared written correspondence for many years. See *Responsa Har Tzvi Oraḥ Ḥayim* 1:123; 2:14, 40; *Yoreh De'ah* 2:174; *Even Ha'Ezer* 1:53, 65, 137, 143, 148 section 11, 161, 204. Also in *Teshuvot Ivra, siman 29, HaPardes* 20:3 [1946], issue 3, pp. 28–30.

26. Introduction to *Responsa Bnei Banim* 1, article 1 (p. 169).
27. See the anthology *Yagdil Torah* (Slutsk) 2:22, 71; *Kovetz Sha'arei Torah* 5:3.
28. Printed in *Oholei Shem* (1912), 177. An additional letter written by R. Henkin during that period, expanding on these themes, is printed in the anthology *Har Ha'mor* 2.
29. A highly regarded rabbi who was born in Lithuania in 1857, studied in Kovno, and was sent to the Caucasus by R. Yitzḥak Elḥanan Spektor. He became the rabbi of Tskhinvali and founded Torah and charitable institutions there and in other cities. He passed away in 1931. In 2006, the Georgian government issued a commemorative stamp in his honor.

> [Stalin] engaged R. Henkin in conversation. First he praised the Jews, even expressing sympathy for the persecutions they suffered under the tsar and elsewhere. He spoke this way until he began to drink. When they stopped at an inn along the way, he descended from the wagon and drank several shots of vodka whereupon his mood changed. Then he opened his mouth and spoke in a different vein: He cursed the Jews and heaped scorn and derision upon them. He blamed them for everything: being bourgeoisie, exploiting people, and responsible for all the world's ills. During one of these rants, Stalin invited R. Henkin to join him in a shot of vodka. Looking at the murderous face, R. Henkin feared for his life. Even today, when R. Henkin remembers that strange encounter, he feels compelled to recite *birkat hagomel* again.[30]

After three years in Kulashi, the government canceled R. Henkin's residence permit and he moved to Akhaltsikhe, where he was chosen as rabbi. However, this too was short-lived, as the local authorities did not allow him to take the position. After several months in which he served as rabbi in the large city of Kutaisi, R. Henkin was forced to leave the country, returning to White Russia in 1913.

The nine years that R. Henkin spent in Georgia left a significant impression on the Jews there, and his influence was still recognized after many years.[31] When the first Georgian immigrants arrived in the US in the 1960s, they hurried to visit R. Henkin, falling on their knees and kissing his hand. Many had been born

---

30. *Keshet Giborim* 1, p. 78. The author, R. Aharon Ben Zion Shurin, was close to R. Henkin (who invited him to join the trustees of Ezras Torah, as recorded in *Keshet Giborim* 1 [2002 edition], 11) and conversed with him often (see, for example, *Keshet Giborim* 2, 239; he even received the photograph at the beginning of the chapter [vol. 1, 77] from him), and he almost definitely heard this story directly from R. Henkin – as evidenced by the concluding words. This is further evidenced by the fact that in 1965, after his book was published, R. Shurin presented a personally signed copy to R. Henkin, so that he knew for sure that the story – which had been previously published in the *Forvertz* – would be read by the eyes of its protagonist.
31. Heard directly by his grandson, R. Yehuda Henkin, from Georgian Jews who immigrated to Israel. For decades, a sign hung in the Uni slaughterhouse with instructions to the ritual slaughterers, "by the orders of R. Eliyahu Yosef Henkin" (*Responsa Bnei Banim* 2:236). R. Tuvia Preschel recounted that, "R. Henkin loved to talk about these pure, poor Jews. He often described how they made do with little and had extremely generous hearts" (*Or Hamizraḥ* 23 [1974], booklets 1–2, p. 152).

after R. Henkin had left their country, but they knew of him from their fathers and had been instructed to honor him anywhere.[32]

MEETING ḤAZON ISH, AND HIS RABBINATE IN SMOLYAN

R. Henkin's first stop in White Russia was the home of his mentor, R. Isser Zalman Melzer, who had, in the interim, become rabbi of Slutsk. R. Melzer joined R. Henkin in a lengthy journey in the hopes of his securing a rabbinic post in one of the cities along the way. In late 1913, R. Henkin was appointed rosh yeshiva in Stoiptz, under the leadership of R. Yoel Sorotzkin, the city rabbi.[33] R. Melzer sent students from Slutsk to strengthen the yeshiva.

That year, R. Avraham Yeshaya Karelitz – Ḥazon Ish – also arrived in Stoiptz. R. Sorotzkin, under government pressure to leave, asked him to take over as the city's rabbi. In this fashion, the two great leaders met one another. Their first meeting, in R. Sorotzkin's home, was described by R. Henkin in his eulogy for the Ḥazon Ish:

> I entered the rabbi's house (R. Yoel Sorotzkin *ztz"l*) and saw a young scholar pacing back and forth, not dressed in rabbinic garb. I asked who he was. His answer: The son of the rabbi of Kosava! What does he do? A storekeeper! I asked if he sets aside time to learn Torah, and he answered: When there's time. I asked what he was doing in the rabbi's house. He answered: The rabbi summoned me. I thought: He must be involved in some dispute in his trade. Later, I learned that this young scholar had authored a work of genius but didn't want to profit from the community, and the rabbi [R. Sorotzkin] had summoned him to take his place while he traveled for his health.

That year, R. Henkin and the Ḥazon Ish sat together in the *bet midrash* and studied together:

> During that half a year, we covered Talmud, *halakhah l'ma'aseh,* [laws of] *eruvin, mikva'ot,* and other subjects. In every area, it was as if the table was set before him and he would work to clarify each matter according to the Torah's Truth, without seeking novellae for their own sake.

---

32. According to his grandson (*Responsa Bnei Banim* 2:236). R. Moshe Roginski also tells: "Two or three years ago, when the first group of Georgian immigrants reached New York, and visited 'their rabbi' R. Henkin *shlit"a*… R. Henkin suggested setting up a 'Georgian Immigrants Fund' as he foresaw an increase in immigration from Georgia every day" (*HaPardes,* 47:7 [1973], 35).
33. *Responsa Bnei Banim* 1, article 1, pp. 168–69. Also see the introduction to *Kitvei R. Y. E. Henkin* 1.

R. Henkin also added a rare description of the Ḥazon Ish's personal practice as he directly observed it:

> His conduct and caution were holy. Although he prayed silently, it was apparent that he would cry during the *amida*. When the rabbi was away, he performed the rabbinic functions and included others in his rabbinic rulings. But when the rabbi was home, he involved himself in nothing, focusing only on Torah learning. He would answer those who came to him with questions in learning, and would test the students who came to his home.[34]

Later that year, R. Henkin moved to teach in Shklov, in the yeshiva founded by R. Meir Schwartz. At the same time, he sought out a rabbinic position that would suit his disposition and leaning. In late 1914, at the age of thirty-three, he was appointed rabbi of Smolyan (near Vitebsk, most of whose residents were Ḥabad Ḥasidim) by the outgoing rabbi, R. Yeḥezkel Abramsky, who chose him from a field of twenty-five candidates.[35]

During his eight-year tenure as rabbi of Smolyan, R. Henkin's renown spread as a halakhic authority, answering questions from the rabbis of the region. His journal records many dozens of questions regarding ritual law and business decisions that he rendered as head of the religious court.[36] He also strove to stabilize the lives of the Jews of the region during the tumultuous years of World War I and the Russian Revolution. To that end, he instituted various rules and practices to regulate economic activities between Jews and

---

34. *Lev Ivra*, 91–92. Also see R. M. Yashar's *Ḥafetz Ḥayim*, 2:478, and *Responsa Bnei Banim* 2, 1:14–16.
35. Surasky, *Melekh B'Yofyo* 1 (Jerusalem, 2004), 118. R. Henkin himself helped R. Ḥayim Yaakov Levin, son of R. Aryeh Levin, to win the rabbinic position in Agudas Shalom of Jersey City in 1949 out of dozens of applicants: *Ish Tzaddik Haya*, 350. In several rabbinic rulings that R. Henkin recorded in his journal from 1915 to 1916, R. Abramsky is mentioned again, as he remained in contact with R. Henkin, who was his senior. Later on, the two kept in touch through letters. One example is from a letter sent by R. Abramsky to R. Henkin on November 28, 1950: "The honorable friend of He Who Abides Above, and my dear friend, the great rabbinic genius praised with all manner of praises, R. Henkin *shlit"a*, after inquiring as to your health; in response to your question regarding the *get* in the possession of R. Yaakov Hellerstein, secretary of Agudas Harabonim ... Deepest friendship, Yeḥezkel Abramsky. P.S. Did you receive the book I sent you?" (handwritten).
36. Most are printed in *Teshuvot Ivra*, *simanim* 100–101. Some of his decisions regarding the laws of kosher meat are printed there in *siman* 37:3. A few short notes were not published, and are in my family's possession.

with the surrounding gentile populace.[37] In one example, from April 27, 1919, R. Henkin collected the signatures of the leaders of a neighboring village in which they committed to participate with Smolyan and follow all the community regulations:

> We the undersigned, men of Okovzin, that was always considered within the environs of Smolyan, hereby renew our commitment to bear the communal responsibilities together with Smolyan, in supporting the poor, hiring rabbis, [maintaining] the synagogues, cemetery, mikveh and all things necessary, like residents of the city. We also commit to abide by the city's enactments and take upon ourselves... not to sell produce purchased in Smolyan and its environs except for feeding our families, so long as there isn't a regulation in this respect in the city.

In 1920, an epidemic spread through Smolyan. His wife, mother of his children, Rebbetzin Freida Rivka, daughter of R. Yehudah Leib Kreindel, was in her eighth month of pregnancy when the epidemic reached the city, and no one was prepared to bring food to those who were ill. When she went out to care for them, she herself contracted the disease and passed away shortly after giving birth, at the age of thirty-eight. Her husband wrote in his journal:

> My best friend and life partner, the apple of my eye, my crown, a "woman of valor who can find," who dedicated her life to all our household needs, who loved me with all her heart, who attended to all my needs and the needs of the home, traveling near and far and toiling to the ends of her strength, passed away after delivering a seventh child. She hemorrhaged and was afflicted by dysentery, and her soul returned to its Maker on the Holy Sabbath, September 2, 1920. May her soul be bound by God in the bounds of life, and may her merit guard over all her offspring, whom she was not privileged to raise and educate in comfort and fear of God.

---

37. These were also recorded in his journal, as well as the list of marriages and divorces that he performed, birth and death records of the community, other communal data, and details about life in that era. I heard from his son, Professor Louis Henkin, that during those years, he was also a member of Agudath Israel in Russia (although in the US he did not join any party [*Responsa Bnei Banim* 2, 1:23]; however, he participated in and spoke at several conventions of Agudath Israel in America).

Her daughter, Rivka, born before her passing and named for her, also passed away, three weeks later.[38] A year later, R. Henkin married "the woman presented to me by God (as per his journal), Ḥayah Ḥannah daughter of R. Yaakov Leib Kozakov, who was also born near Klimowitz.[39]

JOURNEY TO AMERICA

In 1921, after the Bolshevik Revolution, half of White Russia was annexed to Soviet Russia, including Smolyan. From then on, the government made trouble for the local rabbis. At one point, they tried to conscript R. Henkin into manual labor, relenting only when the Jews demanded that the local priest receive the same treatment.[40] At that point, R. Henkin concluded it was time to leave and immigrate to America. At the beginning of Ḥanukkah 1922, he left Smolyan together with his family and his wife's family. Her brother, Ḥayim Tzvi Kozakov, returned to Europe to facilitate their move. He secured visas to the United States and official invitations from their relatives there, and purchased tickets for the ship.[41] Diplomatic relations between the US and USSR in those years precluded direct travel between the two countries. They traveled to Riga, Latvia; from there to Paris; and after one and half months, reached Cherbourg, where they boarded a ship to the US. On February 8, 1923, R.

38. In a chilling journal entry that R. Henkin wrote,

> On the eve of the Sabbath, 6 Elul, my daughter was born, and named for her mother, my wife Rivka, who was plucked from us before reaching the age of forty. May her memory guard us all, and watch over the baby Rivka, whose name is within her, may God merit that I be able to raise her to a life of good deeds.

Later, on the continuation of the line he added: "Passed away, eve of the Sabbath, 28 Elul."

39. He wrote about her in the dedication page of *Edut L'Yisrael* (p. 3):

> I extend my blessings to my distinguished and wise partner, Ḥayah Ḥannah, may she live and be well. She enabled our household to escape the war zone and arrive to this blessed country… May God grant her long years of marriage with physical and mental health, and the ability to continue her charitable works until 120.

Rebbetzin Henkin was well-known as a pious woman of *ḥesed*. She would go to the market on Thursdays with Rebbetzin Ḥanna Karlinsky, where they would purchase at their expense a great deal of provisions for Shabbat, and distribute these secretly to the poor early Friday mornings. She passed away in 1964 and was buried in Jerusalem according to her wishes. Many great rabbis participated in her funeral, including R. Moshe Feinstein, R. Yaakov Kaminetzky, R. Shmuel Kotler, R. N. Telushkin, and others. "The final eulogizer was her husband who, in a weak voice, described her greatness and her sacrifices for Torah, the extent of her charity and hospitality that she displayed to all who entered her home, which enabled him to dedicate himself to the holy work of Ezras Torah" (*HaPardes* 38 [1964], issue 9, p. 41).

40. *Responsa Bnei Banim* 1, article 1 (p. 170).
41. As R. Henkin described in a letter from *Erev Shabbat Ha'azinu*, 1945 (unpublished), from which the other details are taken.

Henkin and his family arrived at Ellis Island outside New York City. They were detained there for five weeks until they succeeded in obtaining immigration papers with the help of a local New Yorker, R. A. Levi, whose mother-in-law was formerly from Smolyan.

In New York City, R. Henkin lived on the Lower East Side of Manhattan, the center of Jewish life in the city at the time. He was appointed rabbi of the Anshei Shechuchin and Greive Synagogue, and also frequented New York's two large yeshivot, Yeshivat R. Jacob Joseph and Yeshivat Rabbenu Yitzḥak Elḥanan. During this time, mid-1925, at the age of forty-four, he published his first work, *Perushei Ivra.*[42] Its first section contains five lengthy articles of halakhic exposition and a great many novellae in areas of matrimonial law. The second section was a compilation of *drashot,* aggadic material, and Jewish thought. Some had been composed in Smolyan and earlier, while the rest seem to have been delivered in the synagogue in New York.

During that era, most of the rabbis – no matter how great – served as pulpit rabbis for local synagogues. This did not exhaust R. Henkin's time,[43] and he began to initiate projects to aid the Jews from his homeland. At this time, he joined Agudas Harabonim, becoming involved in all the burning issues affecting Torah Jewry in the US. In 1924, for example, he headed a group from the Agudas Harabonim to standardize kashrut and supervision of the slaughterhouses and butcher shops in New York City and its surroundings.[44]

On July 7, 1925, two and a half years after arriving in America, R. Henkin was chosen by Agudas Harabonim of America and Canada to fill the place of R. Barukh Epstein (author of *Torah Temimah*) as director of "Ezras Torah" of the Agudas

42. Ivra [איברא], acronym of his Hebrew name **E**liyahu **Y**osef **B**en **R**abbi **E**liezer. This was his given name at birth, and how he began signing his name. In 1914, he began to write Torah thoughts in his journal under the heading *Likutei Ivra* – but there were some who called him "Yosef Eliyahu," and this was the name that fell into use when arriving in America (as evidenced by his stationery from that period).

43. As he wrote to his father-in-law, R. Kreindel, "I do not have enough to do to fill up my time" (*Responsa Bnei Banim* 1, article 1 [p. 170]). During that era, there were almost no advanced yeshivot or Torah institutions in New York and its environs. Most of the rabbis – no matter how great – served as pulpit rabbis for local synagogues.

44. As he described it himself at great length in 1931. See *Teshuvot Ivra, siman* 45:1 (and see further below). Also see *Tzvi Ḥemmed,* booklets 28–29 [*HaShabbat K'hilkhato, Oneg V'gam Simḥa*] 75, which has a photograph of the Agudas Harabonim convention in Lakewood, 1923, including R. Henkin, who had just recently arrived in the US several months earlier.

Harabonim.[45] This appointment happened almost by chance, as told by his assistant, R. Moshe Eliezer Margolin, who later succeeded him:

> R. Henkin *ztz"l* told me innocently how he became director of "Ezras Torah." There was a meeting of Agudas Harabonim and he entered to seek help for needy Jews in Russia, just as they were raising the question of whom to appoint… When R. Henkin appeared at the meeting, they recognized him and offered him the position.[46]

HEAD OF EZRAS TORAH

How was it that one of the great *poskim* of his time came to head a charity organization? The answer may lie in understanding the tribulations and upheavals of the times. The story of Ezras Torah begins during World War I. The war, which broke out in 1914, reached its full catastrophic effect in Poland and Russia, the greatest Jewish population centers at the time. Hundreds of communities were wiped out as tens of thousands of Jews were forced from their homes before the advancing armies. When news of the scope of the devastation reached the US, and when the Ḥafetz Ḥayim and R. Ḥayim Ozer Grodzenski turned to American Jewry, Agudas Harabonim and Mizraḥi set up a "Central Relief" organization. However, as the misery spread, it became apparent that the yeshiva world, its students and teachers, and rabbis across the globe, were in danger of complete collapse. R. Grodzenski urged Agudas Harabonim to take on a special relief effort to support the Torah scholars. Thereafter, the work was split in two: "Central Relief" for communities, and "Ezras Torah, Torah Relief" for Torah scholars and yeshiva students. The founders were led by R. Israel HaLevi Rosenberg[47] and

---

45. R. Epstein arrived in the US circa 1923 and lived in New York (see *Barukh HaLevi Epstein*, p. 21). In 1925, the original leader of Ezras Torah, R. Yaakov Iskolski, vacated the position and R. Epstein was apparently chosen to fill the role. However, he did not hold the appointment for long, and by the end of that year, he left for Chicago in order to raise funds to publish his books – while leaving the door open to return to his position at Ezras Torah (see the quote from R. Moshe Margolin in the sources from the following footnote). In 1926 he returned to Europe, and in 1928 he published *Mekor Barukh* in Vilna.
46. *HaPardes* 57:2 (1983), 23 (corresponding to the introduction to *Kitvei R. Henkin* 2, p. 5). R. Margolin also added in the *HaPardes* article that R. Henkin's appointment was supported by R. Yosef Kanowitz, one the leaders of Agudas Harabonim, who knew him from their time together in Slutsk (for written correspondence between R. Henkin and R. Kanowitz, see *Responsa Divrei Yosef* 2, *siman* 15 [section 7]).
47. Born in Lomza, 1875. At the age of fourteen he traveled to study in Slobodka at the behest of R. Noaḥ Yitzḥak Diskin (brother of Maharil Diskin). He received *semikhah* from R. Yeḥiel Mikhel HaLevi Epstein, author of the *Arukh HaShulḥan*. At age twenty-six he moved to New York and was shortly appointed rabbi of Bayonne, NJ. Two years after arriving in the US he

R. Eliezer Silver,[48] together with dozens of well-known American rabbis who served as leaders and trustees.[49]

Like R. Henkin in the US, the leaders of Ezras Torah in Europe were neither wealthy community leaders nor professional fundraisers, but rather the leading rabbis of their generation who gave their imprimatur to the organization and performed most of the work. For example, the director of Ezras Torah in Vilna was none other than the great sage R. Ḥayim Ozer Grodzenski; the director in Latvia was R. Meir Simḥa HaKohen of Dvinsk; the director in Minsk was R. Eliezer Rabinovitch; the director in Austria was R. Meir Arik, etc.[50] Others included R. Yisrael Meir HaKohen of Radin, the Ḥafetz Ḥayim;

---

joined the Agudas Harabonim and soon became one of its leaders, while still maintaining rabbinic pulpits in various New Jersey communities. At the outbreak of World War I he was appointed vice president of the Central Relief fund, and from 1925 until his death, close to forty years, he served as President of Ezras Torah. In 1927 he was also elected President of the Agudas Harabonim. In 1929 he resigned that position despite the pleadings of his colleagues, but remained as chairman of the board. Through these and other activities, he became well known as one of the great rabbinic leaders of American Jewry alongside his friend R. Eliezer Silver. He passed away in 1956.

48. As he describes in the Ezras Torah memorial volume, p. 16:

> The day I left Vilna in the summer of 5675 [1915] ... the gaon R. Ḥayim Ozer asked me ... that when I return to America, the first thing I should do is to recommend that the Agudas Harabonim establish an Ezras Torah branch here in the US. Thank God, when I got here I discovered that the rabbis were already discussing the matter, like two prophets prophesying in tandem. They had already established an organization named Ezras Torah and it is already recognized for its good works.

He also told the story in his introduction to *Anfei Erez*, 1, p. 9:

> During the First World War, I arrived here in the name of R. Ḥayim Ozer.... I notified my good friend R. Rosenberg, *z"l*, as to the request of R. Ḥayim Ozer to establish a committee to assist Torah scholars in the name of Ezras Torah. R. Rosenberg told me that he had already planned to do this. So we established it together and I suggested that he be the head of the organization and I would serve as his assistant (see also p. 14).

49. At first, the working committee consisted of twenty-four rabbis, twelve of them selected by the Agudas Harabonim and twelve selected by the Mizraḥi. Among the early members of the committee were: R. Dov Ber Abramowitz, R. Yehudah Levin, R. Moshe Shimon Zivitz, R. Yitzḥak Segal, R. Eliezer Silver, R. Yosef Kanowitz, R. Eliezer Friel [then a *ram* in Yeshivat Rabbenu Yitzḥak Elḥanan], R. Dr. Dov Revel, R. Azriel Epstein, R. Aaron David Burak, R. Ze'ev Gold, and others. R. Rosenberg was the president and R. Dr. Hillel Klein was the chairman. The secretary was R. Yaakov Iskolski (Ezras Torah Memorial Volume, p. 5).

50. See *Zikaron BaSefer* (1922), 346–47. Once postal communications were in place and the activity was centralized, distributions were made directly from New York. Only Eretz Yisrael kept a local Ezras Torah branch headed by R. Isser Zalman Meltzer and R. Yehoshua Zimbalist (see Ezras Torah Calendar [5696/1936], 15).

Rashab of Lubavitch; R. Ḥayim Soloveitchik of Brisk; R. Rafael Shapira; R. Avraham Dov Ber Kahane-Shapira of Kovno; and R. Moshe Naḥum Yerushalmski, *av bet din* of Kiltz. These men did not serve as figurehead "honorary presidents" but performed the lion's share of the work. In 1921 alone, Ezras Torah distributed over $75,000 in Eastern Europe, including $4,600 in Vilna by R. Ḥayim Ozer Grodzinski, $3,000 in Kovno by R. Ḥayim Dov Ber Kahane-Shapira, $1,000 in Pressburg by R. Akiva Schreiber, etc.[51] R. Isser Zalman Meltzer wrote in 1927: "I have received an invitation from my good friend, R. Henkin *shlit"a* to get involved ... If we attempted to count the great deeds they have performed, the thousands of souls they have saved ... there would not be enough ink to describe the great acts of kindness."[52]

For forty-eight straight years, over half his life, R. Henkin served as director and leader of Ezras Torah. Under his direction $6 million was distributed (worth ten or twenty times that amount in today's dollars). Under his leadership, Ezras Torah served as the main force in reestablishing the Torah world that was destroyed in the Holocaust. During the years of the Holocaust, it distributed $1.3 million, and in the eight years afterward, another $1.5 million, mostly in Israel and the US.[53] Under his leadership, Ezras Torah became the most well-known charitable organization in the Jewish world. A popular saying of the time was that, "All the charities are holy – but Ezras Torah is the holy of holies."[54] During the dark times in Europe, all the Torah leaders, ḥasidic rebbes, and yeshiva heads turned

51. *Zikaron BaSefer*, 351. The letters compiled in this book describe the activities in detail. In a letter from 1920, R. Eliezer Rabinovitch from Minsk wrote: "It has been three months since I received ten thousand dollars from you that was distributed by committee... R. Ḥayim Ozer from Vilna informed me that he receives every month from New York and London, which he holds for Vilna, Grodna, and others..." (ibid., p. 98). R. Shapira of Kovno wrote during that year: "I received your letter from 12 Nisan with the check for the Slobodka yeshiva. I have sent the funds to the directors of the yeshiva and enclosed is a receipt for this amount and also for the previous 20,000 marks..." (ibid., p. 214). There are many more letters like these from the great sages.

52. Ezras Torah calendar, p. 10. Something else that set Ezras Torah apart was that the funds it raised did not just come from wealthy donors; rather, they were collected from thousands of small donations made by ordinary Jews, especially rabbis. In its early days, it was Ezras Torah's policy to solicit only from rabbis and other religious functionaries (ibid.). It is also well known that Ezras Torah never employed paid fundraisers or collectors, both to minimize overhead costs (which were only 6 or 7 percent) and also because of a deep conviction that this was the correct way to manage the fund. In the words of R. Henkin: "It does not raise funds using bombastic techniques. It makes do with simple requests through letters or from supporters" (*HaPardes*, 17:11 [1944], 12).

53. See the summary tables at the end of *Edut L'Yisrael* and in *She'erit Yisrael*, English edition, p. 5.

54. *Responsa Bnei Banim* 1, article 1, p. 170.

to Ezras Torah, to the point that there was almost no Torah institution that was not being supported by Ezras Torah. Its name spread far and wide, and with it, the righteousness of its leader, R. Henkin.

R. Henkin transformed Ezras Torah into an institution of *ḥesed* in every area in which help was needed. He would try to find jobs for those who arrived in the US after the war, help with matchmaking, and, when needed, conduct divorces, which he considered also a great act of kindness.[55]

The tireless devotion of R. Henkin to Ezras Torah became legend during his lifetime. Over forty-two years, until he reached the age of eighty-six (!), he worked full days in his office. Even afterward, he continued to work for several hours a day. In his later years, when he had trouble climbing the stairs to his office, he worked out of the Agudas Harabonim office on the first floor. When that, too, became difficult for him, he worked from home, where his deputies would join him and conduct meetings there.[56] He never took a vacation, going into the office even on fast days and Ḥol HaMo'ed. On Shabbatot, he would make his way to New York synagogues, great and small, to deliver *drashot* and appeals on behalf of Ezras Torah, sometimes speaking two or three times in a single Shabbat. He would travel several times a year to other cities, some remote, to collect funds for Ezras Torah.[57] R. Shmuel Aharon HaLevi Pardes describes thus the sight of R. Henkin at work:

> When you arrived to visit the office (of Agudas Harabonim), the first room you pass is the Ezras Torah office where you will find its director, R. Henkin *shlit"a,* completely engrossed in his work all day. His eyes display the pain of Jews the world over, which he bears. In his face you can read the hundreds of depressing letters that reach him every day from all corners of the world.[58]

Another document reads:

> I was recently in New York where I met the director, the well-known gaon R. Henkin *shlit"a,* sitting at a table. On the table were hundreds and thousands of terrible letters written in blood… He began to read them to me, reading and weeping, reading and weeping…"[59]

R. Henkin himself wrote in his will:

55. Introduction to *Kitvei R. Henkin* 2, p. 5.
56. As told by R. Moshe Eliezer Margolin, *HaPardes* 57:2 (1983), 23.
57. For all this, see *Responsa Bnei Banim* 1, article 1, p. 170, and see his will below.
58. *HaPardes* 5:4 (1931), 3.
59. *HaPardes* 5:12 (1929), 1.

> I worked for this institution as secretary and director from 15 Tamuz 5685 [July 7, 1925]. I worked day and night, in the Ezras Torah office and in my home, almost every Shabbat I went to conduct appeals. In the summers and sometime the winters, I traveled to various places for Ezras Torah, especially to Baltimore, Rochester, and the bungalow colonies in the mountains, and I always suffered hardships. I neglected my family for my work and did not properly oversee my household. I also abandoned my studies. When I sent *teshuvot,* responsa, to both scholars and laymen, I always tried to find a way that it would benefit Ezras Torah. I donated my meager salary to Ezras Torah. I tried to answer the best I could, but all my interest was for Ezras Torah, until it became a part of my soul, and my heart aches to support it, to see it grow and blossom.

A telling story illustrating R. Henkin's dedication to Ezras Torah was related by R. Avraham Aaron Preiss, author of *Mishnat Avraham*. It was a winter morning, beset by a snowstorm which, according to R. Preiss, "If not for the fact that a man had to recite *kaddish* he would not have left his home." In a small New York synagogue, that could barely gather a *minyan* due to the weather, the door opened and in walked R. Henkin, there to make an appeal on behalf of Ezras Torah. R. Preiss asked in surprise, "*Rebbe,* for a few dollars, did you have to come out in this weather?" R. Henkin answered him, "This is my job. Should I take a salary for doing nothing?!'"[60]

R. Yehudah Altusky, vice president of Ezras Torah, summed up R. Henkin's activities in an article published upon the fortieth anniversary of Ezras Torah:

> Who has ever seen such a thing, who has heard of an institution with so many areas of focus being managed by a single great rabbi, who is already aging, who performs his holy work from morning until late at night, every day, six days a week, every week of the year, without a summer vacation. On the contrary, during the summer, he redoubles his efforts to take day trips to all the vacation sites and to recruit other rabbis to his cause. Those rabbis want to rest and take a breath of fresh air, but when this most honored rabbi appears, they get up and travel in his entourage without eating, drinking, or resting. How can they show weakness in the face of the man who doesn't know weakness? What is rest? What is fatigue? From his spirit, indomitable as a rock, residing in a broken body, he influences

60. Brought in *Responsa Bnei Banim* 4, article 1, p. 92.

> everyone who comes into contact with him, rabbis and laymen … to have mercy on the abandoned and downtrodden … because he is the symbol to whom you can point with a finger: Just as I receive no compensation, you should also shoulder the burden of Ezras Torah for no reward … [He] lives in the neighborhood where the poor live, in a dark cramped apartment [and] has not worn new clothing in many years … The spirit of an angel, giant in halakhah and in good deeds, R. Yosef Eliyahu Henkin *shlit"a* … is asked all manner of halakhic questions, and who answers in every area of Jewish law and practice to all those who inquire of God's law and all who seek genuine help.[61]

"On rare occasions has a charitable institution been under the complete authority of one of the greatest rabbis in the world."[62] Such was written about R. Henkin. Indeed, it is hard to find another example in our generation of this unique combination: a man considered to be in the first tier of *gedolim* and *poskim*, but whose primary occupation was not one of rabbi or rosh yeshiva – but the *menahel* of a worldwide charitable organization. R. Henkin once admitted that, "in his youth, it is true that they foresaw a great future for him if he continued his studies. But, upon reaching this country and spending all his energy on Ezras Torah, he did not progress in his Torah knowledge to his full potential. He abandoned his entire future for the sake of Ezras Torah."[63]

His words are surprising: If this is what R. Henkin said about himself during a time when he only managed to study for three or four hours per day, who can imagine the heights he might have reached had he dedicated his full time to study? However, he decided that the Jewish people would be better off with thousands of scholars and their families rather than one great genius – and to this he dedicated most of his life.

AMERICA'S HALAKHIC AUTHORITY

R. Henkin's reputation was not derived from his work for Ezras Torah. It arose only from his status as a gaon and halakhic authority *par excellence*.

---

61. *Hegyonei Yehudi* 5 (Devarim), 180–82.
62. R. Shimon Finkelman in *Rabbi Moshe Feinstein*, 94.
63. Written by R. Moshe Margolin on a gathering in his honor in 1956 (*Kitvei Rav Henkin*, introduction to vol. 1). R. Moshe Roginski also related:

    > We once asked him how it's possible to remember so much of his early studies from his youth when His Honor only studies 3–4 hours every day during these forty years of service to Ezras Torah. He answered, "Oy, if I only remembered what I had learned, I'd be in a completely different situation" (*HaPardes* 48:10 [1974], 30).

Over the course of a generation he became recognized as the leading *posek* in the US. To properly set the stage, we must begin with a short historical introduction to the circumstances R. Henkin encountered upon his arrival in America.

At the beginning of the twentieth century, the world of Torah Judaism began to make inroads in the US with the growth of Jewish immigration from Eastern Europe. Agudas Harabonim was founded in 1902. Almost all the rabbis who arrived in the US served as congregational rabbis, and the number of yeshivot in the entire country could be counted on one hand. Rabbinical courts were rare and very few American rabbis were known outside the country as halakhic authorities. Among the few were R. Avraham Aharon Yudelewitz, author of *Bet Av*, and several others. Observant Jews found obstacles in their path in every area of religious life: Sabbath observance, kashrut, *eruv*, mikveh, marriage, divorce, etc.

In the 1920s, amidst these circumstances, R. Henkin arrived in New York. The city had the largest concentration of Jews in the country. It is therefore not surprising that he dedicated his first book, in 1925, to bringing a Torah lifestyle to American Jewry, starting with the subject of marriage and divorce[64] – an area on which he had previously focused in Georgia. He also devoted energies to organizing the rabbinate in the US.

> He later wrote in *Perushei Ivra*: My conclusions, summarized in this introduction, are as follows:

1. That every synagogue should hire a rabbi. Those that cannot afford to do so should band together with other groups to hire one, because in the current environment, most people are not affiliated with a rabbi. When a serious question arises they turn to charlatans who take on the question for money […].
2. In areas with many rabbis, they should get together to create rabbinical courts for difficult matters. [But when an outstanding scholar is present in a city, matters pertaining to the city should be referred to him.] Rabbis should band

64. As he wrote to R. Yosef Rosen, the Rogotchover:

> The book (*Perushei Ivra*) is very relevant here in New York where the notion of "marital annulment" has spread like a scab. When a woman has trouble receiving a *get* from her husband, her advisors come to the rabbi and claim that so-and-so officiated at the wedding and all the participants were Sabbath violators. On this basis, they allow a married woman to remarry. In my book, I refute all these claims… alacrity in this matter is praiseworthy as this is the way things are here. (Letter from Feb 2, 1925)

together to organize kashrut supervision and Sabbath observance, Torah education, and operation of *mikva'ot* [...].

3. The large rabbinic institutions, such as Agudas Harabonim and Knesses Harabonim, should not compete with one another. Each should operate in its own community to raise the banner of Torah. They should establish a central rabbinical court for disputes [...].
4. It would be desirable to establish a rabbinic journal where all questions could be raised for discussion. They could also clarify the kashrut of ingredients, discuss the operation of *mikva'ot,* and encourage the rabbis to approach difficult issues with gravity, and to turn in those instances to the great *gedolim* of Eretz Yisrael and Europe.[65]

These ideas, today self-evident, were revolutionary at that time. R. Henkin applied himself to the solution of these problems upon arrival on American shores.[66] Many rabbis played an active role during those lean years of Torah Judaism in America – some in communal leadership, some in kashrut supervision, marital laws, education, Torah institutions, and yeshivot. However, R. Henkin was the first halakhic authority in the US whose influence spread across *the entire country.* There had already been *poskim* in America, but most had only local influence in their hometowns and states. R. Henkin, however, was the first whose address became the place where the entire country turned with their questions. By 1924, a year and a half after his arrival, the venerable, aged R. Gavriel Ze'ev Margaliot, president of Knesses Harabonim, gave his imprimatur. About a certain matter of kashrut, he proclaimed that, "if R. Henkin will accept the supervision upon himself, I will concur – but I will not rely on anyone else in this matter."[67] In a few short years, he was recognized as one of the great *poskim.* When his young colleague, R. Moshe Feinstein, arrived in New York in 1936, R. Henkin was

---

65. Introduction to *Perushei Ivra,* section 26, 16–17. Note that most of R. Henkin's suggestions were carried out. For example, less than two years after he called for the establishment of a new rabbinic journal, the periodical *HaPardes* was founded in the US by R. Shmuel Aharon HaLevi Pardes, who had previously published in Europe. From its establishment until his death, R. Henkin used *HaPardes* as his platform for his articles on halakhah, Jewish thought, and communal issues.
66. As later described by R. Shlomo Aaronson:

    > He was one of the few on the American scene who succeeded – though his purity of action, genius in halakhic teachings, idealistic endeavors, and abundant ethics – in raising the American rabbinate to the highest possible level. The American rabbinate found its salvation in the great strides made by R. Henkin, who restored the rabbinic crown to its glory, and crowned it with Torah and fear of Heaven. (*HaPardes* 30:9 [1956], 21)

67. As told by R. Henkin himself, *HaPardes* 5:10 (1921), printed in *Teshuvot Ivra, siman* 45:1.

already established as the *mara d'atra* of America – as would soon be expressed by R. Yosef Shalom Elyashiv. This was well-expressed by R. Efrayim Zalman Halperin, founder of the Center for Family Purity, who said to his son-in-law upon arrival in Israel: "There is one rabbi in America to whom you can turn with questions – that is R. Henkin!"[68]

Over several decades, especially after the Holocaust, R. Henkin was the greatest *posek* in the US. There was no greater halakhic authority than he during those years: "He was the *posek* of the generation, and from his home, his decisions spread throughout America."[69] During the 1980s, his grandson traveled to communities across the US and Canada, and related:

> In every city, I heard the same thing from rabbis and elders: "R. Henkin answered thus. R. Henkin established the correct way to name our city, enabling the writing of a *get*. R. Henkin answered this, and taught that." More than once, I heard that in the 1940s and 50s, the rabbi whose name was invoked in thousands of American homes was R. Henkin.[70]

Rabbis from across the country considered R. Henkin to be their rabbi, to be called whenever they had a pressing question.[71] People would come to him from far and wide for *gittin*, hundreds of which were performed in his home and office.[72] His Luaḥ Ezras Torah containing synagogue customs and laws is still in widespread use today in the US (like the calendar of R. Yeḥiel Mikhel Tikochinsky

68. *Responsa Bnei Banim* 1, article 1, p. 171, based on a letter by R. M. Galinski, who testifies that, "I heard these words many times from my sainted father *ztz"l*" (son-in-law of R. Halperin).
69. Anthology *Kol Tzvi* (New York, 2000).
70. *Responsa Bnei Banim* 4, article 1, p. 92.
71. *Responsa Bnei Banim* 1, article 1, p. 171. In many yeshivot in the US, it was customary to include R. Henkin's telephone number with every *semikhah* certificate.
72. Ibid. It is also told that dozens of rabbis gathered in his home every year to sell ḥametz before Pesaḥ. His home was likewise the venue for *ḥalitzah* ceremonies. His grandson relates that, "I researched and found that there are two forms of shoe used in *ḥalitzah*, even though they are not explicitly mentioned – and then I found that he had the two types" (ibid.). The contract for *eruvin* in New York between the local officials and the rabbis was prepared according to his instructions (*HaPardes* 34:8 [1960], 34). In the well-known controversy surrounding the Manhattan *eruv*, his opinion was the deciding factor together with R. Tzvi Pesaḥ Frank and R. Y. Steif (*Responsa Mishneh Halakhot* 8:89, 91, 147, etc., and the introduction to the pamphlet *Tikkun Eruvin B'Manhattan* by R. Y. D. Moskowitz [New York, 1959] and on p. 6, and in the pamphlet of R. Menaḥem Mendel Kasher that was printed at the end of *Divrei Menaḥem* 2: in the summary on pp. 323–24, and in the pamphlet itself on pp. 14–16, 38, 134–35; see *Teshuvot Ivra. siman* 25).

in Israel) and many set their halakhic practices based on his word.[73] In all the American halakhic works – *She'arim Metsuyanim B'Halakhah, Taharat Mayim, Yesodei Yeshurun, Mishnat Avraham, Mishneh Halakhot, Rivevot Ephrayim, etc.*, and above all R. Feinstein's *Igrot Moshe* – R. Henkin's rulings are cited dozens of times. His rulings in many areas of halakhah are still followed in many places, especially in the laws of divorce, where he is considered the final authority and greatest expert of the generation.[74]

R. Henkin authored many articles on *hashkafah* over the years, on topics germane to his generation. He was widely known for his integrity, staying aloft of all partisan frictions and not bending his views to conform to social pressures. When asked regarding his organizational affiliation, he would say: "I am a Jew. What does that mean? I study *Ḥumash*, Talmud, and I live. That's a Jew."[75]

From 1963 until his passing, R. Henkin served as honorary president of Agudas Harabonim of America and Canada.[76] Many stories illustrate how greatly R. Henkin was esteemed by the great rabbis of the generation, in America and throughout the world. [77] One rabbi related that he asked R. Yosef Yitzḥak Schneerson of Lubavitch a halakhic question and the Rebbe avoided answering,

73. According to R. Mordekhai Genut, *Luaḥ Davar B'ito*, 5755, 153. See also R. M. Klein on the same calendar: "I recall that even here in America, the great rabbi R. Henkin *ztz"l* invested all his strengths into publishing the Ezras Torah calendar every year and making sure every detail was correct. Even after his death, they are diligent and careful with it every year" (*Responsa Mishneh Halakhot,* second edition, 5:142).
74. Over the years, he received hundreds of letters concerning divorce matters – for clarifications, questions, requests, etc. – from every corner of the world: from the religious courts of R. Tzvi Pesaḥ Frank, the Jerusalem rabbinate, Tel Aviv, Petaḥ Tikvah, Ashkelon, London, Zurich, Toronto, and every part of the US (dozens of them were preserved in his estate). The great R. Ḥayim Kreizwirt of Antwerp trained in *gittin* with R. Henkin (*Moriah* 134, 24:10–12, p. 77) as did R. J. David Bleich, head of the *Kollel L'Hora'ah* at Yeshiva University (*Or Hamizraḥ* 39, 140:1 [5751/1991], 278), and many others. R. Dov Burstein, *av bet din* in Tel Aviv brought many of R. Henkin's decisions while he was still living, in his book, *Gufo Shel Get* (see the pamphlet, pp. 223–38, also previously published in *Mazkeret Am*, 433–66).
75. One could not trick him, either in general or specific matters, as related by his grandson: "Once, someone phoned him to ask about avoiding travel tax using a certain ploy. After concluding the call, he [R. Henkin] turned and said, "This person wants to sin and wants me to participate?!" *Responsa Bnei Banim* 1, article 1, 171.
76. *HaPardes*, 37:4 (1963), 34.
77. *Teshuvot Ivra, siman* 113 (In a letter to R. Unterman and R. Nissim). An example of the high esteem in which R. Henkin was held is provided by R. Yeḥiel Yaakov Weinberg wrote to him: "It is the duty of *HaPardes* to publicize a protest in the name of the great American rabbis: R. Eliezer Silver, R. Yosef Eliyahu Henkin, R. Moshe Feinstein, etc, etc., and you can also sign my name…" (*HaPardes* 40:9 [1966], 39).

saying, "Go ask a rabbi." When asked whom he considered to be a rabbi, he answered, "A rabbi like R. Henkin!" In matters of divorce, one great European rabbi maintained a certain practice, but "here, R. Henkin does not allow that."[78] Once, R. Aharon Kotler was asked whether or not a tune without words was considered an interruption in prayer. R. Kotler answered in the negative, but when informed that "R. Henkin forbids it," he immediately retracted: "If so, then I also concur."[79] R. Yaakov Kaminetzky told a *mohel* not to circumcise a baby with a certain bilirubin level, adding that once before, a baby in that condition was circumcised and died. When the *mohel* told him that R. Henkin permitted circumcision under those conditions, R. Kaminetzky replied: "R. Henkin is a Jew who merits Divine assistance," and allowed the circumcision to proceed.[80]

This high regard for R. Henkin was expressed not only anecdotally, but also in print. R. Yeḥiel Yaakov Weinberg, author of *Seridei Esh*, wrote: "R. Henkin in New York has already ruled that letters which are mispronounced in Ashkenazi pronunciation should be sounded with the Sephardi pronunciation, but the other letters should not be changed from one pronunciation to another."[81] R. Henkin has ruled – no further discussion is necessary! The Sanz-Klausenberg Rebbe, R. Yekutiel Yehudah Halberstam, wrote regarding prayer formulation (*nusaḥ*): "This is Torah and I must learn it, so I ask that you please clarify the matter with the elder, R. Henkin *shlit"a*."[82] R. Shlomo Zalman Auerbach, in the conclusion of a letter to R. Henkin, requested: "I very much wish that you closely look at page

78. *Responsa Bnei Banim*, vol. 1:171. R. Henkin cooperated with Ḥabad in several endeavors. For example, in Kislev 1941, he participated in a meeting in Ḥabad headquarters ("770") regarding construction of a new building for the yeshiva *Tomkhei Temimim* (see his signature in the minutes in *Toldot Ḥabad B'Artzot HaBrit*, 192).
79. *Responsa Bnei Banim* 2, article 1:31–33. For correspondence between R. Kotler and R. Henkin, see *Responsa Mishnat R. Aharon*, 2:59–60. For the eulogy delivered by R. Henkin, see *HaPardes* 37:3 (1963), 39.
80. As told by R. Shlomo Breslauer, in *R. Yaakov – Toldot Ḥayav U'Fo'alo Shel HaGaon R. Yaakov Kaminetzky*, 444. We will also mention the description of R. Yosef Dov HaLevi Soloveitchik of Boston, who, upon seeing R. Henkin for the first time, said that now he can describe what Adam looked like before his sin and banishment from the Garden of Eden (from the OU website, entry of R. Henkin). The story is also told in *Responsa Bnei Banim* 4, article 1 (p. 92) about a gathering in RIETS in memory of a deceased rabbi. During the speeches, R. Henkin entered through a side door – and when R. Soloveitchik, sitting on the stage, realized who had walked in, he jumped to his feet to escort R. Henkin to the stage.
81. *Responsa Seridei Esh*, 1:15. This decision is also cited in *Responsa Yabi'a Omer* (*Oraḥ Ḥayim* 6:11). Similarly, R. Eliezer Waldenberg writes in his *Tzitz Eliezer*: "And I see that my reasoning is consistent with that of the established halakhic decisors, such as R. Henkin in his book" (*Responsa Tzitz Eliezer* 14:39).
82. *Responsa Divrei Yatziv, Even Ha'Ezer* 104.

32 (of *Me'orei Esh)* and on, and send me your opinion – *da'at Torah* – on what I wrote there."[83] Many other examples abound.[84]

The extent to which R. Henkin's opinion held sway in the US, was recognized by the great *poskim* of Israel. R. Yeraḥmiel Fried, author of *Yom Tov Sheni B'Halakhah,* who was close to R. Yosef Shalom Elyashiv for many years, was invited to serve as rabbi in an American congregation, subject to *semikhah* from a well-known rabbi. When R. Fried asked this of R. Elyashiv, R. Elyashiv tested him with the following question: "When you get to the US and encounter twin boys requiring circumcision, would you rule that two blessings on circumcision are required? Or just one?" R. Elyashiv continued to answer: "R. Henkin lives in America and is the leading halakhic authority. Until R. Feinstein arrived, he was the sole authority. R. Henkin ruled that when circumcising twins, the blessing is only recited once – and you must rule in accordance with the halakhic authority [*mara d'atra*] of America!"[85]

83. *Responsa Minḥat Shlomo* (1999), 2:18; *Minḥat Shlomo Tinyana* (2000), *siman* 26. For additional correspondence between them regarding civil marriage, see *Responsa Minḥat Shlomo* 3:100, and *Perushei Ivra, siman* 75:3. It is also interesting to note the story told by R. Auerbach's son, R. Barukh Auerbach, about his father's practice to recite the blessing "The Redeemer of Israel" aloud: "It was his opinion and practice for the leader to conclude the blessing aloud together with the congregation… and he would always say that R. Henkin *ztz*"l tried hard to end the practice of concluding the blessing quietly and he was quite vocal about it" (*Halikhot Shlomo – Tefila,* p. 94).

84. For example, R. Avraham Ḥayim Na'eh writes with joy: "Soon my dear friend, the famous gaon R. Henkin *shlit"a,* the *menahel* of Ezras Torah, will publish his book *Edut L'Yisrael* – and he positively cites my book, *Shi'urei Torah*!" (*Shi'urei Torah,* vol. 2 [*Shi'ur Mikveh*], 162, referring to citation in *Edut L'Yisrael,* 193). Similarly, R. Dov Ber Rivkin, head of *Mesivta Torah Vodaas,* writes: "When I recently met my dear friend R. Henkin *shlit"a,* I told him this idea of mine… and I was happy to hear from the *gadol* that my idea was correct" (*Ashkavta D'Rebbe,* 78). R. Menasheh Klein told the story of a difficult question that he was struggling with. In the meantime, he received a call from the Cheshinover Rebbe, who told him that he had just been to the home of R. Henkin and had asked a similar question. R. Henkin had answered the question in the same manner in which R. Klein was inclined. When R. Klein heard this, he was filled with great joy at arriving at the same conclusion as R. Henkin: "And I was as happy as could be, because I saw that Heaven had arranged for R. Henkin to rule leniently in the same situation" (*Responsa Mishneh Halakhot* 9, end of *siman* 278) – and there are many more examples.

85. As told by R. Elyashiv's grandson to R. Yeḥiel Sternberg (I thank him). For that ruling by R. Henkin, see *Teshuvot Ivra, siman* 60. Another anecdote: When R. Ovadiah Yosef was Chief Rabbi of Israel, he received a recommendation from R. Henkin (April 13, 1973) regarding his grandson, R. Yehuda Herzl Henkin, upon whom he had bestowed *semikhah.* Shortly thereafter, the younger R. Henkin was appointed rabbi of the Bet Shean valley.

R. HENKIN AND R. MOSHE FEINSTEIN

At this point we come to the account of R. Henkin's relationship with his younger colleague, R. Moshe Feinstein, the preeminent halakhic authority in the US both beside and after R. Henkin. When R. Feinstein reached New York in 1936, R. Henkin was already considered America's foremost *posek*. Over several decades, this remained the case, even as R. Moshe Feinstein became recognized as one of the great *poskim* and Torah leaders. R. Feinstein's prominence rose in the 1960s, when the first three volumes of *Responsa Igrot Moshe* were published between 1959 and 1960. From then on, he became the *posek* of his generation, alongside R. Henkin.[86] After R. Henkin's passing, R. Feinstein stood alone as the leading authority in America and beyond.

These two giants were close friends, living alongside each other in New York for decades. R. Moshe Feinstein's Mesivta Tiferet Yerushalayim and R. Henkin's office at Ezras Torah were close-by on East Broadway on the Lower East Side of Manhattan, where they both lived. Although R. Henkin was fourteen years older than R. Feinstein, there were remarkable parallels in their two life stories. Both studied in Slutsk with R. Meltzer. Each lost his eldest son, almost at the same time – Pesaḥ Ḥayim Feinstein passed away on August 15, 1926, while Ḥayim Shimi Henkin passed away on February 25, 1927. Each lived in the US for exactly fifty years. Just as R. Henkin served as director of Ezras Torah for forty-eight years, so did R. Feinstein serve as rosh yeshiva of Tiferet Yerushalayim for forty-eight years (and also was named honorary president of Ezras Torah). Both lived long lives and passed away at almost the same age – R. Henkin at ninety-two and a half; R. Feinstein at ninety-one.

86. Many have described it this way, some in the ensuing years – "Rabbis Eliyahu Henkin *ztz"l* and Moshe Feinstein *ztz"l* were the two pillars of halakhic decision making in twentieth-century America" (R. Ḥayim Jachter, *Teḥumin* 25, p. 176) – and some during that era: "Take a close look with your eyes and see, who is the greatest rabbi in America? R. Yosef Eliyahu Henkin, who is not the spiritual leader of a specific congregation, R. Moshe Feinstein, who maintains no official rabbinic position, or R. Yosef Soloveitchik who also holds no pulpit?" (R. Simḥa Elberg, *HaPardes* 40:5 [1966], 2); "This ruling was given then [1967] by R. Barukh Shapira *ztz"l*, the venerable rabbi of Seattle, who was a dedicated student of the *Or Sameaḥ* in Dvinsk – and he regularly consulted with R. Moshe Feinstein *ztz"l* and R. Yosef Eliyahu Henkin *ztz"l*... R. Henkin taught me to assist R. Barukh Shapira in clarifying the facts and details" (R. Shalom Rivkin, in the anthology *Torah Shebe'al Peh*, 31 [1990], 145–46), and many more such references.

They often worked on halakhic issues together, both in print and in person.[87] They frequently sat together in *din Torah* sessions, both those involving disputes between private parties, and those involving rabbinic disagreements, such as a 1963 question regarding kashrut of the mikveh in Rochester. They jointly headed the Agunot Commission which Agudas Harabonim established following the Shoah.[88] R. Feinstein was the first to eulogize R. Henkin at his funeral, and later wrote about "the passing of a great man, one of the last few whom God summoned, our master R. Yosef Eliyahu Henkin *ztz"l*, who is a great loss in the world of Torah and loving-kindness... signed in honor of the Torah and in honor of R. Henkin *ztz"l*."[89]

R. Shimon Finkelman described the relationship between the two:

> They frequently consulted one another on halakhic questions. They did not always agree, but there was always affection and mutual respect between them...Occasionally, R. Henkin would ask R. Moshe to act on behalf of Ezras Torah, sometimes requiring walking long distances on Shabbat or holidays. R. Moshe never refused, out of respect for the holy mission of Ezras Torah and the great man who stood at its head...Once, R. Moshe Margolin, a senior assistant to R. Henkin, arrived at his behest in R. Moshe's home. R. Moshe was ill at the time and the rebbetzin did not want to disturb him. R. Margolin waited while R. Moshe rushed to

---

87. As R. Feinstein notes in many of his responsa (see below), and illustrated by the following story from his disciple R. Mikhel Zalman Shurkin: "One winter morning, when the streets were covered in snow, I saw R. Moshe *ztz"l* approach a young man who had a car and asked him: 'Could you do me a favor and take me to R. Henkin, as I need to discuss a question with him" (*Megged Givot Olam* 1, 29). The two often served together on a three-judge panel to rule in *dinei Torah*. Examples include: In 1957, they ruled on the question of reinterring the remains of the Stoliner Rebbe in Israel (see a summary of the events in *Kovetz Bet Aharon V'Yisrael* 7:6 [1992], 147–48). In 1963, they ruled on the kashrut of the mikveh in Rochester, which had been challenged by several rabbis (see their ruling in *HaPardes* 37:10, 33). They both served at the head of a committee on *agunot* of the Agudas Harabonim after the Holocaust in 1946 and ruled together on hundreds of cases that came before them from all over America (see *HaPardes* 21:9 [1947], 14). They also sat together on many other committees of the Agudas Harabonim over the years.

88. *HaPardes* 21:9 [1947].

89. *HaPardes* 48:8 [1974], 2. R. Henkin, in turn, praised R. Moshe using the following rabbinic saying: "Is fear [of Heaven] a small matter? Yes! For **Moses** [Moshe] it is a small matter" (Berakhot 33b). As he explained to R. Shurkin: "It means that those who come near to Moshe, when they see the great rabbis of Israel – the fear of Heaven is a small matter" (*Megged Givot Olam* 1, 65).

> the kitchen, saying: "The gaon R. Henkin requests something of me for Ezras Torah – how can I refuse?"[90]

The extent of R. Moshe Feinstein's regard for R. Henkin is evidenced by the dozens of times he cites him in *Igrot Moshe* – far more than other contemporary *poskim*; and he never explicitly takes issue with R. Henkin on any subject, with the one well-known exception of whether civil and Reform marriages require a *get*.[91] This esteem recurs time and again in every volume of *Igrot Moshe*, both during and after R. Henkin's lifetime. [92]

In several places, R. Moshe Feinstein cites R. Henkin's rulings as *halakhah pesukah*, the authoritative final ruling. In other words, once the ruling has been issued, no further discussion is appropriate: "I spoke with R. Henkin *shlit"a* and this fowl is unknown in this country. Therefore, it should not be slaughtered because we do not have a tradition [to eat it]."[93] And: "The question of permitting opening a refrigerator [on Shabbat] has many components. But R. Henkin has already ruled that it is permitted to open it when the motor is running – and this is the preferred method. There is no reason to write any further on the matter."[94]

---

90. *Rabbi Moshe Feinstein*, 94–95. R. Ephrayim Greenblatt, author of *Responsa Rivevot Ephraim*, relates that many times, R. Feinstein "would tell me stories about R. Henkin's greatness" (*Responsa Rivevot Ephraim*, 4:420).
91. To be discussed below. In his eulogy for R. Henkin, R. Moshe mentioned this: "And so in regard to civil marriage, in which we had a halakhic debate as is customary for Torah scholars, where one permits and one forbids, we remained friends. Even though I wrote a responsum against his arguments, he, in his righteousness, did not leave it at that. In his concern lest he be responsible for any harmful consequences, he sent a personal messenger with an outright protest against my ruling." (*HaPardes* 61:1 [1987], 9–10). Even though R. Moshe strongly disagreed on this with R. Henkin, he tried his best, in many responsa, to prove that in certain situations, even R. Henkin would have concurred with his leniency; see *Responsa Igrot Moshe, Even Ha'Ezer*, 4:76–77, 112; 1:30, 77; 2:19; 3:23, 45; 4:81, etc. Also see *Responsa Bnei Banim* 2, 145–46. In another case, as related by R. Aharon Felder of Philadelphia, R. Feinstein visited the aged R. Henkin as he ruled that a child born following induced labor should not be circumcised on Shabbat, similar to the law of *yotzei dofen*, a child delivered by caesarean section. After departing, R. Feinstein remarked to R. Felder that in his opinion, induction applies to the period before birth, and that the birth itself was natural, for which reason the brit is held on Shabbat – but that he had refrained from voicing his opinion before R. Henkin out of respect for his stature.
92. *Rabbi Moshe Feinstein*, p. 94.
93. *Responsa Igrot Moshe, Yoreh De'ah*, 1:34. In other responsa, he presents his ruling alongside that of R. Henkin: "This question has been discussed for over two years, and twenty people have already brought it to me…and they also brought these questions to R. Henkin, and we still hesitate to respond because it is very difficult to be lenient" (ibid., *siman* 93).
94. Ibid., *Oraḥ Ḥayim* 2:68. Previously, he wrote on the same topic: "I do not wish to respond because there are valid arguments on both sides – please refer to the *Sefer HaYovel* of Ezras

Many times, R. Moshe Feinstein would add to the rulings of R. Henkin, or would cite him in support of his own rulings: "This is the reason I chose to permit, and R. Henkin agreed with me, but his ruling was oral and not printed, until I have now written it down."[95] "I have discussed this … with R. Henkin and we do not see a reason to prohibit this."[96] "His Honor can rely on R. Henkin, whom I heard to say…."[97]

R. Feinstein valued the opinions of R. Henkin so highly that he often analyzed his exact phrasing, as if R. Henkin were an authority of generations past, in order to buttress his own rulings:

> When R. Henkin used the phrase "It is proper to rule strictly," he does not mean that there are good reasons to permit, yet he wishes to be strict regardless. If so, he would have mentioned them [the reasons]. And he also did not write that the matter should be discussed. Therefore, he means that it is proper to be strict either because there are no clear reasons for leniency, or because he simply wishes to rule strictly. After all, he put into writing only the bottom-line conclusion on how to behave.[98]

Similarly, in another responsum, he found, inter alia, a logical reason for a specific ruling by R. Henkin: "Perhaps this is R. Henkin's reasoning, that one should not change [the purpose of the contribution] until after the Torah scroll is presented to the synagogue, then they can sell it."[99] And: "R. Henkin gave a different reason … and I think there is some support in Tractate Yevamot, for his words would not have been arbitrary."[100]

Torah of R. Henkin *shlit"a*" (ibid., 1:128).

95. Ibid., *Yoreh De'ah* 2:58. Also: "The gaon, R. Henkin *shlit"a* has also agreed with this ruling" (ibid, *Even Ha'Ezer* 1:30), and similarly phrased there in *siman* 135. Also see *Even Ha'Ezer* 1:132: "Therefore, the letter *shin* is not required to be written. I believe that R. Henkin also does not write the *shin*."
96. Ibid., *Yoreh De'ah* 3:44. Also: "I agreed to allow it in accordance with His Honor, R. Henkin, *shlit"a*" (ibid., *Yoreh De'ah* 2:58). There are many other similar examples.
97. Ibid., *Yoreh De'ah* 4:44. And when R. Moshe Feinstein gave approbation to new ritual slaughterers, he sent them to be examined by R. Henkin:

    > Regarding the *shoḥet* who behaved improperly, according to multiple testimonies … he should be removed and banned from ritual slaughtering and from serving as a kashrut supervisor [*mashgiaḥ*] … until 15 Elul of this year … and after 15 Elul he should be examined by R. Henkin … and should receive new credentials from R. Henkin, and only then will he be permitted to be a *shoḥet* and *mashgiaḥ*." (ibid., *Yoreh De'ah* 3:3)

98. Ibid., *Oraḥ Ḥayim* 5:20. He is referring to *Edut L'Yisrael* (see above, n. 76).
99. Ibid., *Yoreh De'ah* 1:164.
100. Ibid., *Even Ha'Ezer* 1:28.

HIS BOOKS AND WRITINGS

R. Henkin's dedication to Ezras Torah led him to incorporate his writings (other than his first, book, *Perushei Ivra,* published in 1925 before he assumed leadership of Ezras Torah) into the Ezras Torah Jubilee volumes. He wrote in one of the introductions: "The books that only have Ezras Torah content, the recipients briefly gloss over them once, after which they are stored away and forgotten. But when a book has practical content for rabbis and Torah scholars, we hope these will remain on their tables, reminding them of Ezras Torah."[101]

Edut L'Yisrael: In 1936, R. Henkin published in the Ezras Torah Jubilee volume a collection entitled "Fundamental Laws and Practices of the Synagogue" together with fifteen short articles on various matters of Jewish law. In 1946, he expanded the section on laws and practices by fifty percent and added another thirteen articles, publishing it as a halakhic section of the jubilee volume entitled *Edut L'Yisrael,* which then became the name of the collection.[102]

***Lev Ivra*:** In 1957, he published his third book, *Lev Ivra,* incorporated into the Ezras Torah yearbook *She'erit Yisrael.*[103] It contained thirty-two articles that had previously been published in various periodicals, half of them concerning Torah

101. Twentieth annual yearbook, 5.
102. At the end of the volume, he wrote: "All this was prepared by the head of Ezras Torah. If anyone finds an incorrect practice, he should contact me, I will either justify it or admit my mistake." In the introduction to the halakhah section of *Edut L'Yisrael,* he added:

    Although we generally do not learn halakhah from digests, and any halakhic decisor must be mindful of the early sources to the best of his ability, and one who has not reached the level of a decisor must ask his rabbi, despite this, the digests have value, because they are like a key ring with many keys hanging from them. One who reads the digest can remember all the laws that are hanging from it. And this also helps the scholar as well as someone less learned who needs immediate help and has nobody to ask in the heat of the moment.
103. The previous book, *Edut L'Yisrael,* was named in honor of R. Yisrael Rosenberg, to whom the volume marking Ezras Torah's thirtieth jubilee was dedicated. The fortieth jubilee volume was dedicated to R. Henkin, and should have been named in his honor. However, R. Henkin would not allow this in any form. Finally, because R. Rosenberg had passed away that year, it was decided to also name this volume for him. In the introduction, R. Henkin wrote:

    I beg forgiveness from those who wanted to wish me well in this yearbook, as I have not published the accolades that they have written. As it is known from the Talmud Yerushalmi, Makot 2, "When a scholar who only knows one tractate comes to a city and they want to honor him like one who knows two tractates, he must admit that he only knows one." In my humble opinion, this refers to a monetary honorarium, in which their erroneous assumption could lead to potential theft, but when it comes to mere accolades, we do not worry. However, that just pertains to one who listens [to the excessive praise] and remains silent. But to publish these exaggerated praises would certainly be inappropriate. Therefore, I have been forced to omit them.

and Jewish law, and the other half concerning Jewish thought and timely matters. He added sixteen articles on Jewish thought in Yiddish and a treatise on proper spelling of names in Jewish divorce documents.

Teshuvot Ivra: Over the years, R. Henkin wrote thousands of responses to questions from all over the world, but he never made copies of them. He was repeatedly approached to collect these letters and publish volumes of *She'elot U'teshuvot,* but

> ... he never agreed to this, because he felt that most of his answers were in the category of post facto (*bedi'avad*). In a few instances, he characterized some of his answers using the phrase, "better they commit a lesser act than a more severe sin." He felt that his answers should be limited to a specific time and place, and would not agree to publish them for the public as *l'khatḥilah* rulings.[104]

In fact, shortly before his death, he said, "It is not my way to publish [theoretical] *ḥiddushim,* but there are certain halakhic behaviors that I would like to correct."[105]After his passing, some of his staff at Ezras Torah worked diligently with his family to collect many of his articles from over the years and responsa that he had sent to private individuals, publishing them in a book called *Teshuvot Ivra* – similar to the name he had used for himself in earlier publications.

These four books were published together in two volumes entitled *Kitvei HaGaon R. Yosef Eliyahu Henkin* (Vol. 1 –1981; Vol. 2 –1989) by Ezras Torah in New York and Israel. [Ed. note: Subsequently, *teshuvot* of R. Henkin were collected by R. Doniel Osher Kleinman and published as *Gevurot Eliyahu* under the auspices of Machon Harav Henkin in Lakewood, NJ.][106]

---

104. According to R. Moshe Eliezer Margolin in his introduction to *Kitvei HaGaon R. Henkin* 1.
105. As noted by my father *shlit"a* [*ztz"l*], in his annotations on the manuscript. R. Margolin also heard R. Henkin say that he "did not write many responsa – but regarding those that he *did* write, he would not be ashamed to state them in public, even before the gaon Maharam Schick" (introduction to *Kitvei R. Henkin* 2, 4). In his introduction to his guidelines for writing English names in *gittin,* which he wrote in 1957 and published more fully in *Lev Ivra,* he added:

    > Based on many requests, I am writing this pamphlet on how to write English names [in *gittin*] ... Many rabbis already base themselves on "*Dikdukin B'Shmot Gittin*" in *Edut L'Yisrael,* on pages 178–90, which is a concise rendition of complex matters, and those who arrange *gittin* should read it, and perhaps also review it several times.
106. Vol. 1, *Oraḥ Ḥayim,* 2013. Vol. 2, *Yoreh De'ah,* 2016. [Ed. note: R. Kleinman relates that R. Eitam was a crucial partner in producing *Gevurot Eliyahu,* literally completing the volume on *Yoreh*

When R. Henkin's third book was published in 1957, R. S. A. Aharoni reviewed it in *HaPardes*:

> A common thread runs throughout the entire book from beginning to end. The halakhic responsa, the polemical articles, and the philosophical essays are all infused with pure fear of Heaven [and] absolute integrity... R. Henkin speaks with clarity. His conclusions are not veiled and he does not quit the battlefield in the midst of a conflict. He deals with each and every question to its full depth and breadth. And after citing those who came before him, he expresses his own opinion... without fear or hesitation, and resolves the issue.[107]

FAMOUS HALAKHIC DECISIONS

R. Henkin's writings eschew casuistry in favor of studying the *sugya* in terms of the halakhic bottom line. Regarding yeshiva curricula, in which Nezikin, Nashim, and Kodashim were commonly studied, he emphasized the paramount importance of study of halakhah, and particularly of Seder Mo'ed. He felt that in-depth study should be focused on the tractates in Mo'ed:

> One should not study principally those areas of Gemara without practical application, with halakhah studied haphazardly. After all, this is the main goal of study – learning in order to perform the mitzvot. A *talmid ḥakham* must not resort to *sifrei kitzurim,* abbreviated works; he must immerse himself in depth in tractates such as Shabbat, Eruvin, Pesaḥim (half of it), and Beitzah... It is difficult to imagine that they would study new tractates in the yeshivot when it is hard enough to keep up with the old ones. But this is only because they have emphasized casuistic methods of analysis, which are meant to spice up the learning. Yet these are like pepper and spice, where a little is good, but too much is not... The yeshivot should begin with tractates that deal with practical topics. Even those who have studied their fill of Nashim, Nezikin, and Kodashim – which are not of practical benefit other than for *poskim* – are obliged to study tractates of practical halakhah and the related *poskim*.[108]

De'ah immediately before the murder. Among other tasks, the two spent long hours on the phone deciphering R. Henkin's handwriting, and working together through R. Henkin's *psak.*]

107. *HaPardes* 31:7 (1957), 34. See also R. Betzalel Landau's summary of *Teshuvot Ivra*: *HaPardes* 64:1 (1990), 22–24.

108. *Teshuvot Ivra, siman* 56: 1; see there for an extended discussion.

R. Henkin behaved this way all his life, as R. Moshe Roginsky describes: "R. Henkin's studies were always as if he had to rule on a halakhic question right there and then. In every discussion, from the Talmudic passage until the modern *poskim,* he always arrived at the practical ruling."[109] His grandson wrote:

> This was our teacher's method in halakhah and *hashkafah,* with no embellishments. When he wrote at length, he did so as needed for the ruling. In *Perushei Ivra* there are one hundred pages on one intricate topic – and he carefully weighed everything according to its practical significance, whether in Torah or in his charitable activities.[110]

To illustrate R. Henkin's Torah legacy, let us lay out for the reader several well-known rulings that are known throughout the Torah world in his name:

Ruling in Disagreements Between *Arukh HaShulḥan* and *Mishnah Berurah*

R. Yeḥiel Mikhel Epstein, author of *Arukh HaShulḥan,* was R. Henkin's final authority in matters of halakhah. The *Arukh HaShulḥan* was published around the same time as the *Mishnah Berurah* of R. Yisrael Meir HaKohen Kagan of Radin, so the question naturally arose according to which of the two to rule in a dispute between them. R. Henkin greatly valued the *Mishnah Berurah,* learned it regularly, and knew it almost by heart. On the other hand, he knew the author of *Arukh HaShulḥan* quite well and considered him unique in his generation, saying that he was "the most significant of the later *poskim.*" Therefore, he ruled, "The authority of the *Arukh HaShulḥan* is greater than that of the *Mishnah Berurah,* and when they dispute, one should decide according to *Arukh HaShulḥan.*"[111] Many of his students reported this directive in his name, including R. Menashe Klein,[112] R. Naḥum Eliezer Rabinowitz,[113] and his grandson, my father and mentor, R. Yehuda Herzl Henkin.[114] Such was

109. *HaPardes* 48:10 (1974), 30.
110. *Responsa Bnei Banim* 1, article 1, p. 167.
111. *Responsa Bnei Banim* 2, article 1, pp. 10–12; see also section 13.
112. *Responsa Mishneh Halakhot* 8:107, and see below.
113. Introduction to *Arukh HaShulḥan,* with the commentary *Tzafo HaTzafit,* n. 1. Also see his entry in the Encyclopedia Judaica Yearbook (1974), 415. When he was a young rabbi in the US, R. Rabinowitz turned to R. Henkin with many of his questions, many of which he published in various Torah journals. See, for example, *HaDarom* 10, 77–81, issue 15, 74–77; issue 26, 79–81.
114. *Responsa Bnei Banim* 1, section 6, p. 22, and vol. 2, section 8.

also the opinion of his friend and colleague R. Moshe Feinstein.[115] R. Eliezer Yehudah Waldenburg, author of Responsa *Tzitz Eliezer,* also felt that *Arukh HaShulḥan* is the final authority in our generation.[116]

My father and mentor, the author of *Responsa Bnei Banim,* R. Henkin's grandson, provided an additional reason: The first two volumes of *Arukh HaShulḥan* on *Oraḥ Ḥayim* (through *siman* 428) were published after the corresponding sections of *Mishnah Berurah.* Therefore, the author of *Arukh HaShulḥan* had seen the relevant sections of *Mishnah Berurah* and disputed with it many times, both explicitly and implicitly.[117] Since he had clearly seen the *Mishnah Berurah* and disagreed, he had advantage of being ruled as *batrai,* "the latter" decision maker, the one who is normally followed.[118] On the other hand, many important *poskim,* led by Ḥazon Ish[119]

---

115. As heard from him by R. David Kahn and others (*Or HaMizraḥ* 31, 108:1, p. 324). This was also the opinion of additional rabbis, including R. Gedaliah Felder, author of *Yesodei Yeshurun* (cited in *Responsa Bnei Banim* 4, 107), R. Moshe Zev HaKohen, author of *Tiferet Moshe* (*Or HaMizraḥ,* ibid.), and others.

116. Therefore, he often referred to him as the "final great *posek*" [*haposek hagadol haaḥaron*]. See *Tzitz Eliezer* 10:25, ch. 6; 13:66; 13:99; 18:59; and more. R. Waldenberg did not refer to anyone else, including Mishnah Berurah, by this appellation aside from Arukh HaShulḥan, with the exception of one instance where he calls Ḥazon Ish the "final *posek* in time, but first in quality" (19:32). R. Waldenberg arranged his book, *Ramat Raḥel,* about medicine, according to the order set forth in *Arukh HaShulḥan.* Throughout the work, he frequently cites and discusses the *Arukh HaShulḥan*'s positions.

117. See *Arukh HaShulḥan, Oraḥ Ḥayim* 11:22, 14:5, 275:2, 319:22, and in close to thirty additional places where he explicitly disagrees. For implicit disagreements, see *Oraḥ Ḥayim* 55:20 against the *Mishnah Berurah,* ibid., n. 52; *Oraḥ Ḥayim, siman* 370:13 against *Mishnah Berurah,* ibid., n. 27, and there are many more like this. Note that *Arukh HaShulḥan* rarely cited halakhic authorities of his own generation. Therefore, the fact that he explicitly cites the *Mishnah Berurah* dozens of times shows the value and esteem that he placed upon the work almost from the beginning. It may also attest to his recognition of the importance already accorded to the *Mishnah Brurah* at the time it was published.

118. *Responsa Bnei Banim* 2:8. With this, it should be stated that all the arguments by the *Arukh HaShulḥan* against the *Mishnah Berurah* are organized around two topics: The laws of the morning routine (tzitzit, tefillin, and prayer: *simanim* 1–127), and laws of the Sabbath and *eruvin* (242–395), the only two volumes of the *Mishnah Berurah* to be published before the parallel volumes of *Arukh HaShulḥan.* Therefore, it is possible that the principle of "ruling according to the latter" might only apply in these two areas, while in all other areas of *Oraḥ Ḥayim,* the principle of "the burden of proof is on the one who, *motzi meḥavero,* changes the status quo" might apply; this would specifically relate to volume 6 of the *Mishnah Berurah* (529–697), which was first published in 1907, after the *Arukh HaShulḥan* section on *Oraḥ Ḥayim* had already been published. Ed. note: For further information, see the author's *Ta'arokh Lefanai Shulḥan,* pp. 311–13.

119. See *Kovetz Igrot* 2:41: "The accepted ruling that we live by, according to our rabbis such as *Bet Yosef, Magen Avraham, and Mishnah Berurah,* are definitive like the word of the Sanhedrin in their Temple office," and these words are well known.

and R. Kook[120] viewed the *Mishnah Berurah* as the final word in halakhah for our generation, and this was widely accepted. It is important to note that R. Henkin's ruling was only stated "in the case where *Arukh HaShulḥan* and *Mishnah Berurah* argue evenly based on their own opinions or in explaining the opinions of others."[121] However, R. Henkin's words were not intended to apply to circumstances wherein the majority of *poskim* were inclined toward one direction or if there is another good reason. Therefore, each situation must be treated on its own merits.

The Prohibition Against Eating Prior to the Blowing of the Shofar

R. Henkin ruled that, other than those who are ill, one may not eat before listening to the first thirty shofar blasts on Rosh Hashanah, because of the Talmudic ruling that one may not eat before fulfilling a biblical commandment. Therefore, the custom of making kiddush prior to the shofar blasts is "a complete mistake." Those who are weak should wait until after the first thirty blasts (*tekiot d'meyushav*), as the custom not to interrupt from there to the end of the shofar blasts is only a custom and *hidur mitzvah,* enhancement of the commandment.[122] He publicized this every year in the Ezras Torah calendar, and "he did not refrain from rebuking any great rabbi who criticized him regarding this issue," even in his later years.[123] However, some *poskim* did not agree. R. Yitzḥak Yaakov Weiss, author of *Minḥat Yitzḥak,* argued with R. Henkin, writing that, "he greatly exaggerated by writing this."[124] Indeed, in Jerusalem and additional communities and yeshivot, it is customary to have kiddush prior to the shofar blasts, according to the position that is more concerned with interruption between all one hundred blasts, even though many agreed that one should not eat excessively.[125]

---

120. See *Ma'amarei HaRa'ayah,* 132. In his halakhic works, he often quotes the *Mishnah Berurah* with great reverence.
121. In the words of his grandson in *Responsa Bnei Banim* 2:8, 31.
122. *Teshuvot Ivra,* 45–48, and see the next note.
123. *Responsa Bnei Banim* 1:15, 55. See there and *siman* 14, also vol. 2, p. 233. R. Mikhel Zalman Shurkin relates that a few days before his wedding, he visited R. Henkin to receive his blessings. R. Henkin – who was already an elderly man – "said that I should inform R. Moshe [Feinstein] of his ruling that it is forbidden to eat prior to the shofar blasts" (*Megged Givot Olam* 1, p. 65). R. Kalman Epstein related that every year, before Rosh Hashanah, he would visit R. Henkin to wish him a *ketivah vaḥatimah tovah* and receive R. Henkin's blessing. Each time, R. Henkin would entreat him not to eat before shofar-blowing. "The year before he passed away, he entreated me to promise with a handshake that I would not eat before shofar-blowing, and I did, and such is my practice ever since" [related to me by R. Epstein].
124. *Responsa Minḥat Yitzḥak* 5:111, and see his response in *Responsa Bnei Banim* 1:14, 54.
125. See extensive discussion in *Responsa Tzitz Eliezer* 6:7; 8:21; 20:23.

Requirement of a *Get* from a Civil Marriage

One of R. Henkin's most famous rulings is that a woman who was married in a civil ceremony, or a Reform Jewish ceremony, has the halakhic status of a married woman and requires a *get* before being permitted to remarry.[126] Other *poskim* also held thus,[127] but in the world of halakhah, this position became established in R. Henkin's name. He first publicized it in his 1925 work, *Perushei Ivra,* and reiterated it in responsa and articles over the next decades. R. Yeḥiel Yaakov Weinberg wrote: "The greatest of the prior generations disagreed in this matter. Even in our current generation, some are strict and some are lenient – among them is the great R. Henkin *shlit"a,* head of Ezras Torah in New York."[128] Although R. Moshe Feinstein is known as the most lenient on this issue, and according to his position we can dispense with a *get* in the case of civil marriage – nevertheless he ruled that *l'khatḥilah,* we should be concerned for R. Henkin's opinion, and should, from the outset, try to require a *get l'ḥumra,* as a stringency: "If it is possible to obtain a *get* then it would be appropriate to rule strictly in order to comply with the opinion of R. Henkin *shlit"a.*" R. Feinstein was only willing to forego the *get* if it would create a situation of *mamzerut* or leave the woman chained as an agunah.[129]

Even though most contemporary *poskim* rule permissively according to the opinion that the woman does not require a *get* at all,[130] R. Henkin's resolute position

126. See extensive discussion in *Perushei Ivra, simanim* 4–5; *Lev Ivra, siman* 2; *Teshuvot Ivra, simanim* 74–76.

127. *Responsa Tzofnat Paneaḥ* [Dvinsk] *simanim* 1–4; *Responsa Zkan Aharon, Mahadura Tinyana, siman* 103; *Sefer Ma'arkhei Lev, siman* 87; *Responsa Yam Hagadol,* end of *siman* 75; *Sefer Mishnat Avraham* 2:24. Also see *Responsa Bnei Banim* 2, 145–46, and the works cited in the note there.

128. *Kitvei HaGaon R. Yeḥiel Yaakov Weinberg, siman* 24 (p. 52). Similarly in *Seridei Esh* 1:117. R. Ḥayim Fishel Epstein wrote something similar in attempting to counter R. Henkin's arguments (*Responsa Teshuvah Sheleimah* 2, *Even Ha'Ezer, siman* 17 [pp. 43–55]). Before this, R. Avraham Dov Ber Kahana Shapira, in his responsum on civil marriage, mentioned that "I have seen from those who rule stringently on this (I believe R. Henkin from New York), who explained…" (*Responsa D'var Avraham* 3:29 [1946 edition, p. 62]).

129. *Responsa Igrot Moshe, Even Ha'Ezer* 1:74. He also wrote in a different responsum: "But in civil courts where this rationale does not apply, there is room to say that a *get* is required *l'khatḥilah* to conform to R. Henkin's opinion. But in the case of an agunah, here too we can be lenient" (ibid., *Even Ha'Ezer* 3:25). Also see the description of R. Moshe Feinstein's sons and sons-in-law: "Nevertheless, our Rabbi greatly honored R. Henkin *ztz"l.* Since he was strict with civil marriages and Conservative and Reform marriages, our Rabbi [R. Moshe Feinstein] taught that, when possible, one should initially strive to obtain a *get*" (introduction to *Igrot Moshe* 8 [*Oraḥ Ḥayim* 5, *Yoreh De'ah* 4], p. 27).

130. *Responsa Mishpatei Uziel, Even Ha'Ezer, siman* 29; *Responsa Heikhal Yitzḥak, Even Ha'Ezer, siman* 31; *Responsa Ḥelkat Yaakov* [1992 ed.], *Even Ha'Ezer, simanim* 71–72 (in the old edition,

carries so much weight that every rabbinical court in Israel, the US, and elsewhere has adopted as normative practice to insist on a *get* unless the woman would become an agunah, in accordance with R. Moshe Feinstein who showed concern *l'khatḥilah* for the ruling of R. Henkin. As formulated by R. Binyamin Be'eri, head of the rabbinical court in Ashkelon: "In practice, even with civil marriages… we arrange a *get* to be strict – mainly because of the opinion of R. Henkin."[131] And we have a letter from R. Isser Zalman Meltzer, who wrote to R. Henkin, that even though he himself was not quick to prohibit the woman from remarrying, "Even so, you have done a good thing by protesting and writing several times contradicting those who permit it – so that at least, a rabbi who is God-fearing should not find it so easy to permit."[132]

HIS RIGHTEOUSNESS

> There are those whose greatness in Torah and wisdom are recognized in the course of conversation and extensive contact. But there are some whose greatness in Torah and spirit is recognized at first glance, with nothing said. R. Henkin was one of the latter. His holy countenance, deep eyes burning with the fire of Torah, and noble appearance express his shining character. Anyone meeting him would stand before him in awe and reverence that cannot be expressed in words.[133]

R. Henkin was not only known as a gaon, but also as a tzaddik. As described by R. Avraham Hafterman: "In this generation… when any rabbinical novice is adorned with titles …, R. Henkin alone among the great rabbis of this country is known as 'gaon and tzaddik,' a pair of honorifics rare even in this era of inflated titles."[134] His modesty and humility were legendary. Although known as a *gadol*

2:184–85); *Responsa Yabi'a Omer 6, Even Ha'Ezer, siman* 1. Some even opposed the requirement of *get* as a matter of stringency because, in their estimation, it would be "a stringency that will lead to a leniency."

131. Ruling of the *bet din* from Dec. 4, 2005, case number 2578-21-1; ruling from Nov. 17, 2005, case number 2484-21-1. Also see *Responsa Seridei Esh*, 1:117; *Responsa Bet Av"i* 4:156 (section 21 and the conclusion); *Responsa Mishneh Halakhot* 2:28; ibid., 12 [second edition, vol. 2]: 331. All write that they specifically are concerned about the position of R. Henkin in cases where the woman will not become an agunah. R. Moshe Sternbuch also writes: "We must be stringent with a *get* and only be lenient in the case of an agunah. This is what R. Henkin *ztz"l* from America raised in his pamphlet dedicated to these issues – that the woman requires a *get*" (*Teshuvot V'Hanhagot* 1:353).

132. Letter from circa 1937.

133. R. S. Aharoni, *HaPardes* 31:7 (1957), 34.

134. *HaPardes* 30:9 (1956), 23.

hador, he did not consider himself such. When he was asked why the righteous fear death – after all, the Garden of Eden awaits them – he answered: "Who says that I'm a tzaddik?" Another time, he opined that perhaps it was a good thing that he had never visited the Land of Israel, "as they might expect me to deliver a *drashah*, and perhaps it would disappoint them."[135]

"When it came to charity, R. Henkin behaved like one of the Sages of old," said R. Moshe Feinstein.[136] R. Henkin would purchase an average *etrog* for Sukkot, "because he could not afford an expensive one." Yet in the same month, he would secretly donate hundreds of dollars that he had saved up over the course of the year to Torah institutions in Israel. After all, "how can we enhance our personal mitzvot and deprive the charities of their funds."[137] When he reached the age of seventy-five, Agudas Harabonim decided to present him with tickets to visit Eretz Yisrael. However, he conditioned his acceptance on the donors' also sending thousands of dollars above the cost of the trip for him to distribute to needy Torah scholars there. And since they were not in a position to do so, he declined the offer and did not make the trip.[138] One who leafs through the fortieth anniversary journal of Ezras Torah that year (*Shearith Yisrael*, 1957) will find a small, modest ad on page 36 in memory of his family members – signed by "Yosef Eliyahu Henkin."[139]

---

135. *Responsa Bnei Banim* 1, article 1, p. 172. He specifically chose to be buried in the US, so that American Jewry would not be bereft of the graves of its rabbis (ibid.). Regarding the *tzaddik's* fear of death, he said: "It is because they are worried that they are not truly righteous." (*Responsa Bnei Banim* 2, article 1:43). In his will, he requested a simple grave with a simple headstone and without exaggerating descriptions. His wishes were carried out exactly.
136. Detailed in *HaPardes* 61:1 (1987), 9. He added: "R. Henkin *ztz"l* was well-known for his great work, his total dedication and complete faith, managing charity funds like R. Ḥannina b. Tradyon" (ibid., p. 10). R. Henkin even donated his personal fees from arranging divorce documents and other religious court proceedings in his home to Ezras Torah (told in *Keshet Giborim*1, 80).
137. Told by R. Moshe Roginski many years later (*HaPardes* 48:10 [1974], 30). This matter was kept so privately until his close friend R. Rif, president of Ezras Torah, said in his eulogy for R. Henkin: "He never revealed to a soul which families he was supporting. Other than government audits of Ezras Torah's books, nobody ever knew" (*HaPardes* 48:1 [1974], 33). A receipt was found in his estate papers, noting his contribution of a sum no less than $245, which he was careful to distribute among all higher Torah institutions in Israel at the time – sixty-seven in all.
138. As told in *Responsa Bnei Banim* 1, article 1, p. 170, and elsewhere.
139. That year, Ezras Torah organized a conference in his honor. There was unanimous consensus at the meeting of Agudas Harabonim, except for R. Henkin himself (*Keshet Giborim* 1, 81) – yet in the end, he agreed to the conference, because he knew that it would help Ezras Torah. The writer Hillel Zeidman described:

    R. Henkin made more than one sacrifice for his job at Ezras Torah; backbreaking work, long office hours, tedious work for tedious Jews, going to the office in the cold and rain when his health was failing. Yet the greatest sacrifice of all was when he agreed, after much protest, to a dinner in his honor, which afforded people an opportunity to praise him in

R. Moshe Feinstein also said about him: "This man derived no benefit whatsoever from this world, even to the slightest extent."[140] When R. Henkin began working for Ezras Torah, his salary was $25 per week, which had to support a family of eight. Over the course of many years, he turned down repeated requests by the trustees to raise his salary despite the rising cost of living. More than a few times, he would "forget" to draw part, or all, of his salary. In 1961, when he turned eighty and became ill, forcing him to cut back on his hours, he decided to take a cut in his already low ($70 per week) salary, out of concern that he was stealing from Ezras Torah. Because he signed the paychecks, including his own, no one was the wiser. During the annual audit, an unexplained profit appeared on the books. Upon investigation, it became clear that R. Henkin had not cashed all his checks in order to reduce his salary. There was a hue and cry when this became known during the annual meeting of Agudas Harabonim, but R. Henkin waived aside the rabbis' protests that one is not permitted to harm himself. He answered, "The recipients need the money more than I do," adding that only the recipients could decide if R. Henkin needed the funds more than they did.[141]

A story of R. Henkin's rectitude was told by R. Naftali Tzvi Yehudah Rif,[142] who worked at R. Henkin's side in Ezras Torah for close to forty years:

> I always noticed the gaon R. Henkin using a small notepad and didn't know what it was for. I was deeply curious about it until one day I discovered that he used it to write down all the minutes that he deducted from his work at Ezras Torah. And if you ask me, "What was he doing? Conducting some other business?" The answer is, "Of course not." But when someone came to the Ezras Torah office to discuss Torah matters with R. Henkin, or when he received a call with a halakhic question from

---

speeches and articles. He, who always fled from honor, who tried to do all his work humbly and quietly, agreed to a dinner when they convinced him that Ezras Torah would benefit. (*HaPardes* 30:9 [1956], 24)

140. *Rabbi Moshe Feinstein*, p. 94. His son Professor Louis Henkin described thus to me: "Being poor was a *madregah* for him. Not being wealthy was an ideal for him. His home contained no luxuries, he slept in a plain bed, and contented himself with basic necessities. He lived a very simple life."

141. Introduction to *Kitvei R. Henkin* 2, 5–6; For a detailed version of the story, see *HaPardes* 69:5 (1995), 28–30.

142. Born in Babruysk in 1895 and named for his great-grandfather, Netziv [R. Naftali Tzvi Yehudah Berlin]. He lived in America for almost fifty years, serving as vice president of the Agudas Harabonim, and in 1958, was appointed president of Ezras Torah (see *Keshet Giborim* 2, 237–40).

> American rabbis, from Los Angeles, New York, or from Israel, R. Henkin would look at the clock and notate how many minutes he "stole" from Ezras Torah, and immediately wrote down on the notepad how much he had to make up.[143]

Another time, R. Rif went to R. Henkin's house after midnight in order to consult him regarding a complex question. R. Henkin greeted him while fully dressed, with a smile: "I had a feeling that His Honor would surprise me."… R. Rif spied a *Tikkun Ḥatzot* on a stool in the corner of the room."[144] In his eulogy for R. Henkin, R. Rif related:

> He was very private, not just from the world, but he managed to hide himself from his household and close family. All those years, it never dawned on me that this frail man would recite *Tikkun Ḥatzot,* and I only discovered it by chance… From then on I would see him, night after night, sitting at home, reciting *Tikkun Ḥatzot* in tears over the destruction of the Torah and the exile of the *Shekhinah,* and immersing himself in the pain of Israel. Indeed, this was only one of a thousand character traits that he succeeded in hiding from everyone.[145]

---

143. *HaPardes* 48:1 (1974), 33. He concluded: "Because R. Henkin held that not only is it forbidden to engage in frivolous matters during 'company time' of Ezras Torah, but even words of Torah are forbidden to interrupt Ezras Torah." His intense care to avoid any hint of theft or misappropriation shows up in his journal from Smolyan, which is full of notes with exact sums that he received and documentation of repayment. For example:

    R. Tzvi Leflier, father of Shabtai, deposited seventeen rubles with me on Wednesday of Shabbat *B'ha'aloetkha.* He received it back from me on Friday of Shabbat *Ḥukat.* He then deposited another twenty rubles with me on Friday of Shabbat *Pinḥas* and I returned them on Sunday of Shabbat *Shoftim.*

    R. Yitzḥak Fleiss, married to his niece, daughter of R. Eliezer Dr. Fleiss, deposited one hundred rubles with me, to be used in the event that his wife wishes to divorce him, after Sukkot 5678 [1917]. I returned the money to him.

144. As described by R. Moshe Roginsky, *HaPardes* 48:10 (1974), 4.
145. *HaPardes* 48:1 (1974), 33. R. Henkin followed many pietistic customs. He always prayed *vatikin* [at sunrise], and was scrupulous in *tevilat Ezra, Tikkun Ḥatzot,* and more. He was conversant in Jewish mysticism, as told by R. Yehudah Altusky: "The whole world knew that he was an expert in the 'revealed' Torah and halakhah. But only a few know that he was well-versed in the 'hidden' Torah, as this is not meant to be publicized. 'Hidden' means hidden" (*HaPardes* 48:10 [1974], 4). R. Henkin quotes from the *Zohar* and other mystical works in his books:

    The *Zohar* explains that the man who 'gathered wood on the Sabbath' hints that he was contemplating the Tree of Knowledge and the Tree of Life to see which was better; it seems

R. Moshe Eliezer Margolin wrote about him:

> To me, his defining characteristic, which stood out constantly, could be summed up as integrity to the furthest extreme. This was always his guiding principle, beginning with his studies in yeshiva, where his diligence was exceptional. He once described how the *mashgiaḥ* of the yeshiva in Slutsk (Rav Sheftel *ztz"l*) would criticize him: "What will you end up as, if you continue to review *Ḥoshen Mishpat, Even Ha'Ezer, and Yoreh De'ah* incessantly? When will you have time to become a *lamdan*?..." And R. Henkin modestly said, "Perhaps he was correct" [...]. There was nobody as diligent and organized as he was: His routine for sleeping and awakening, study, davening – always *vatikin* – this helped him to develop all these qualities. I remember that one time, a visitor from Israel was praising R. Tzvi Pesaḥ Frank, the rabbi of Jerusalem, who was known for being phenomenally organized. R. Henkin said: "What's so surprising? If he weren't so organized, how could he have achieved such greatness?" R. Henkin was speaking from experience.[146]

R. Henkin's home was open not just to important rabbis and *gedolim*, but to simple men and women who called him or came to his house with questions or request a *brakhah*. He received everyone happily and took the time to answer all questions, simple or complex.[147] The author Dr. Hillel Zeidman wrote:

> Even more surprising was that whenever you turned to R. Henkin, whether in person or by telephone, he always directed his attention to you and

---

to indicate that the Tree of Life refers to *d'veykut* [clinging to God], which is the source of life (*Perushei Ivra*, Homiletic section, article 1, ch. 14).

146. *Kitvei R. Henkin* 2, introduction, p. 4. The quote from the *mashgiaḥ* in Slutsk was stated differently by R. Moshe Roginski: "Eliyahu Yosef! What will be your end? You review and review and review, is this a goal?" (*HaPardes* 48:10 [1974], 30). R. Rif also related that, "I never found him sitting home alone; he always had a book in his hand, either *Shulḥan Arukh Even Ha'Ezer*, or *Ḥoshen Mishpat*, or the responsa of the Ḥatam Sofer" (*HaPardes* 48:1 [1974], 33).

147. As told, for example, by R. Daniel Tropper:

> As a boy, I remember once asking R. Henkin a question. He took out an *Arukh HaShulḥan*, looked at it, and gave me an answer. Then he added: "You think I didn't know the answer? Of course I knew it. But I wanted you to learn that even when you know the halakhah, it's important to open a book and look inside. This helps you remember the halakhah." The great *posek*, venerated elder, answered me in a fatherly way, teaching me how to handle myself in the future. (*Akdamot* 11, [5762/2002], 80)

Once, a kashrut question arose from a *ba'alat teshuvah* visiting her parents for Pesaḥ. R. Henkin himself did not find a *heter*, but understanding that the situation would aggravate family relationships, directed that they phone R. Feinstein.

> fully listened to engage with your question. You would never hear the common refrains, such as, "he's busy," or "he's occupied," or "he's in a meeting," and the like.[148]

R. Henkin treated all those who came to him gently with great empathy.[149] If a caller declined to say his name, R. Henkin was careful not to ask, lest the person was embarrassed or had reason to remain anonymous.[150] R. Aharon Benzion Shurin described it this way:

> Why did so many people choose to turn to him? Because they would see in him an exemplar of the *poskim* of earlier generations.... Despite his great scholarship, no questioner felt belittled. He treated everyone as an equal and showed all who crossed his doorway great respect. His door was open to all, and one did not have to pass through a gauntlet of secretaries and aides. He was never "busy" when someone came to see him; he was happy to help another human being.[151]

---

148. *HaPardes* 30:9 (1957), 25. Adds R. Moshe Roginski: "Poor scholars did not just come to Ezras Torah to ask for his support. It was as if they were visiting a father to pour out their hearts." (*HaPardes* 48:10 [1974], 29). R. Rif also related:

> Nobody ever left without a proper sum of money. And when he offered an amount that the recipient was unhappy with, thinking it insufficient, he would not react... in anger saying, "You're not the only one. There are thousands like you." He would take his leave in tears, crying over the man's pain (*HaPardes* 48:1 [1974], 33).

149. R. Mikhel Zalman Shurkin lost his father when he was young. Prior to his wedding, he visited R. Henkin, who was already ninety, to ask for a *berakhah*:

> We talked Torah... and he gave me a warm heartfelt blessing and I returned home to Brooklyn. When I got home, my mother told me that R. Henkin's *gabbai* called to say that R. Henkin wanted to see me. I couldn't understand what he wanted, but I got on the train back to New York to his home. I came in and he said to me: "I forgot that your father passed away, and that you are a groom with no father to instruct you [regarding marital issues]. I will talk to you." And he proceeded to tell me that it was acceptable for him to discuss these topics because he was already an old, broken, and blind man. (*Megged Givot Olam* 1, p. 65)

150. Introduction to *Kitvei R. Henkin* 1. Despite this, it was R. Henkin's practice for many years to ask the caller if he had a local rabbi to ask. He sought to strengthen the position of community rabbi, and also because questions were best addressed face-to-face:

> It is not good that people ask their questions via telephone... in order to avoid the burden of complying with the rabbi, which they would have to do if they met him face-to-face. When you ask a rabbi in person, he has time to look up sources and to reflect. And if he changes his opinion, he can fix the mistake. (*Edut L'Yisrael*, 167, see further there).

151. *Keshet Giborim* 1, 80.

His simplicity won R. Henkin the love and admiration of the simple people, as told by R. Menaḥem Mendel Gettinger, the son-in-law of R. Rif:

> When I was in Safed, an old man approached me: "Are you from America?" he asked me. "I have a father there." "A father?" I wondered to myself, "This man appears to be over eighty!" The old man saw my confusion, "It's a father who cares about me and watches over me. His name is R. Eliyahu Henkin!"[152]

HIS FINAL DAYS

Toward the end of his life, R. Henkin's eyes dimmed, but he continued his work to whatever extent he was able.[153] Besides continuing his work for Ezras Torah, he continued paskening for the public, orally and in writing, answering simple and complex questions. When he could no longer write on his own, he dictated to his aides and they would also read to him from his books. Until his final days, he went on reading and writing in this manner, authoring letters and articles, both long and short, as he described himself in a letter in 1970: "I received your pamphlet regarding names in divorce documents, and two or three sections were read to me, because, unfortunately, my vision has dimmed and I must have others read to me, and I cannot impose excessively upon them..."[154]

During this time, his phenomenal memory served him well, as described by his assistant at Ezras Torah, R. Moshe Roginski:

152. "The Torah Personality," 296. His grandson, my revered father R. Yehuda Henkin related another anecdote:

> Once, two kollel fellows entered Bet Midrash Hagadol in Lower Manhattan, close to the end of Shabbat. He usually prayed in that synagogue, and was sitting and studying, waiting for the service to begin. They approached to speak with him. One mentioned that he was from Israel. My grandfather immediately stopped him and asked: "Do you need support from Ezras Toraḥ"... He didn't wait for people to ask for it. Some people are ashamed to ask and don't know how to ask ... My grandfather sought out and found those who need help and extended support first. (handwritten)

153. His vision began to fail around 1961. In 1963, he wrote to R. Gedalia Felder: "I received your important gift, your book *Yesodei Yeshurun*, vol. 4. I very much wanted to read it, but unfortunately, my eyes have dimmed. Even though I occasionally manage to write, reading is seven times more difficult" (*Gilyonei Yeshurun*, p. 50). There are full letters in his handwriting through circa 1966, when his eyesight worsened further. After that, his letters and articles were typewritten, and he would sign them by hand.

154. *Teshuvot Ivra, siman* 86:6.

> R. Henkin reviewed Torah all his days. It's not just that he knew the Talmud and early commentaries from memory, but down to the most recent responsa he knew by heart, including the text of the *Mishnah Berurah, Ḥokhmat Adam, Binat Adam, Arukh HaShulḥan,* and responsa of the *Aḥaronim.* All the rabbis who came into contact with him can attest to that.[155]

My revered father, R. Yehuda Henkin, who studied with him during that time, wrote:

> When his eyes dimmed, people would come and study before him, and he would correct their readings in Gemara, Rashi, Tosafot and refer to *poskim* and responsa that he hadn't seen in years. And he would also do this for Mishnah and Tanakh – because he knew them all by heart.[156]

One of those who assisted R. Henkin during this period was R. Avraham Shmuel Levin from Tel Aviv, who recorded the following in his notes:

> Between 1969 and 1972, when I worked for Ezras Torah in New York, I had the honor of studying with R. Henkin for half of each day. At that time, he was blind, so I read for him... Rabbis from across the US would turn to him with their difficult questions... in every area. I had the privilege of serving as the intermediary to answer the telephone and pass along the questions to him. I would read him the letters and he would dictate the answers. When he wanted to write an article for *HaPardes* or publish something in the newspapers, he would summon me and dictate his words.[157]

155. *HaPardes* 48:10 (1974), 4, 30. Also described by R. Rif:

    He was expertly conversant in both the Talmud Bavli and Yerushalmi and the four sections of *Shulḥan Arukh.* He could answer all difficult questions by heart. He once received an urgent phone call from Israel. Then they saw how clear-headed he was – when he answered questions from *Even Ha'Ezer* by heart. (*HaPardes* 48:1 [1974], 33)

156. *Responsa Bnei Banim* vol. 1, article 1, p. 172. Similarly, R. Yehudah Altusky wrote:

    Even when R. Henkin grew old and his vision dimmed, he saw in his mind's eye the entire Talmud and the four sections of *Shulḥan Arukh* spread out before him like a garment and he never missed the mark. Even in his old age, the greatest rabbis from across the world approached him with their halakhic questions. (ibid., 38)

    His grandson, Prof. David Henkin, who was seven years old when his grandfather passed away, told me that the image engraved into his memory more than any other from his grandfather's home was that of his father (Professor Louis Henkin) sitting and reading the Talmud to his grandfather, and his grandfather occasionally stopping him and correcting his reading from memory.

157. *Kfar Ḥabad,* issue 774 (5757/1997), 30. In the last months of R. Henkin's life, "His illness overcame him, affecting his legendary memory, and he suffered greatly," as told by a young man

When R. Henkin weakened toward the end of his life and it became difficult to go out, a *minyan* was established in his home for morning prayers, Shabbat, and holidays. The attendees were his neighbors, his *shamash,* and some of those who were close to him, one of whom was connected to the story of his passing. That was R. Eliyahu Moshe Shisgal,[158] son-in-law of R. Moshe Feinstein and rosh yeshiva of *Be'er Shmuel.* R. Shisgal had a deep bond with R. Henkin, who was forty years his senior. When the *minyan* in R. Henkin's home was established, R. Shisgal diligently came to daven with R. Henkin.[159] Years earlier, when R. Shisgal married off his daughter, he had sent a personal invitation to R. Henkin, who responded: "I know that many important rabbis and *rashei yeshiva* will be present at your daughter's wedding. I am happy to participate, but I do not want to be accorded any honors at the ceremony." R. Shisgal was unsure what to do, and asked his father-in-law, R. Moshe Feinstein, who advised him to ignore R. Henkin's request. And so, at the ceremony, R. Henkin was called upon to recite the first two *brakhot.*[160]

In 1973, R. Shisgal took seriously ill and was hospitalized in New York. On a summer Friday he was released to visit home for what turned out to be his last time. R. Peretz Steinberg, a student and aide to R. Shisgal, drove him to his home. On the way, he requested to be taken to R. Henkin's home. When they arrived, "R. Shisgal asked R. Henkin, who had passed his ninetieth birthday, and who was a very close friend, to bestow a blessing. R. Henkin blessed him and then asked – 'Now, *you* bless *me*!'"[161] R. Shisgal blessed him and soon afterward, on 3 Av, he

---

who studied with him for the last eight months of his life (handwritten). R. Moshe Margolin visited during the final days before his passing. He saw, "that his face had changed and he was groaning and calling out in a low voice, 'Gevald, Gevald.' I asked him why he was groaning. He replied that it hurt. I asked where it hurt and he replied, 'Where doesn't it hurt?'" (*HaPardes* 57:9 [1983], 27). Despite this, he continued to study and answer questions as best he could, with a clear mind until his last day (*HaPardes*, ibid. Also *Responsa Bnei Banim* 1, article 1 [p. 172]).

158. Born in Slutsk, 1921. In 1925, his family moved to the US. He studied in Torah Vodaas with R. Shlomo Hyman and R. Reuven Grozovsky. At the age of twenty-four, he married R. Moshe Feinstein's daughter, and soon after, began teaching at Torah Vodaas, later becoming rosh yeshiva of Yeshivat Be'er Shmuel, and one of the heads of the Tiferet Yerushalayim branch in Staten Island. He was known for his tremendously sharp intellect and his piety. He passed away after a serious illness in 1973 at the young age of fifty-two and was buried in Jerusalem. After his passing, R. Yaakov Kaminetzky remarked: "No one truly knew him.... His place was with the generations of old" (see *Rabbi Moshe Feinstein*, 169–83).

159. *Responsa Bnei Banim* 1, article 1, p. 172. R. Ḥayim Eliezer Sheinfeld also prayed with this group and the *gabbai* was Shmuel Morowitz.

160. *Rabbi Moshe Feinstein*, 181.

161. Ibid. (description of R. Shimon Finkelman).

passed away. Ten days later, R. Henkin also passed away. In his will, R. Henkin instructed that he be buried in a simple grave, with a simple gravestone, with the inscription: R. Yosef Eliyahu son of R. Eliezer Henkin, author of *Perushei Ivra* and *Lev Ivra,* formerly rabbi of various communities in Russia, and in this country in the Synagogue of Anshei Shechuchin and Greive, and director of the holy organization Ezras Torah; adding that "they should not embellish with additional titles."

To sum up, let us quote R. Henkin's grandson, my father and teacher, R. Yehuda Herzl Henkin *shlit"a* [*ztz"l*]:

> When I reached together with him the chapter of "The blue thread does not impede the white thread," he said that tzitzit are mentioned in two places: In Bamidbar it says, "They shall place a blue thread, *petil tekhelet,* on the fringe at thee corner." In Devarim it says, "You should make tassels on the four corners, *arba kanfot,* of your garments." The first reference mentions *petil tekhelet* but not four [corners]. The second reference mentions four [corners], but not *petil tekhelet.* This implies that the obligation to have the *petil tekhelet* is only on one corner. I said that this refers to him, and I vowed to say this after his long days and years, and HaShem assisted me… and I arrived in New York midway through the *hespedim.* Just as there are "tassels" (*gedilim*), so too there are *gedolim.* Each generation has many *gedolim* and each has his own special quality, but they are essentially alike. But once in a generation, or several generations, someone comes along whose character and unique qualities resemble the blue thread, which has no equal. Our rabbi, my teacher and grandfather *ztz"l* was that blue thread.[162]

162. *Responsa Bnei Banim* 1, article 1, p. 172.

Chapter 24

"This Is Politics, Not Halakhah!": R. Shlomo Goren, the Langer Affair, and R. Yosef Eliyahu Henkin[1]

In 1972, there erupted in Israel a public controversy unprecedented in the annals of the twentieth-century rabbinate. Known as the Langer Affair, the controversy involved almost all the great rabbinical figures of that generation to one degree or another. The public figure who caused the upheaval and stood at its center was R. Shlomo Goren, appointed Chief Rabbi of Israel in October 1972.

This article is composed of two sections. In the first, I discuss the development of the affair from the personal history of the Langer siblings up until R. Goren's rabbinical ruling on their behalf, and the commotion ensuing in its wake. In the second section, completed on the fortieth anniversary of the death of my great-grandfather R. Yosef Eliyahu Henkin on 13 Av 5733 (August 11, 1973), I focus specifically on his position with regard to this episode, as well as his opinion on the controversial rabbinical ruling, and his attitude toward

1. Translated by Simi Peters and the team at Academic Langauge Experts. This chapter originally appeared in *Assif* 1 (2014).

R. Goren. Among other sources, I make use of documents published here for the first time.[2]

THE LANGER AFFAIR: A BRIEF OUTLINE

The story of Ḥanokh and Miriam Langer, the brother and sister who gave this episode its name, began in 1923 when Ḥavah Ginsberg, a young Jewish woman from Lukov, Poland married a non-Jew named Bolek Borokovsky (1897–1983).[3] In 1924, Borokovsky was circumcised, his name was changed to Avraham, and he remarried Ḥavah Ginsberg in a Jewish ceremony. In 1931, the two emigrated to Israel and in 1941, Ḥavah left her husband without obtaining a *get* (Jewish divorce). In 1942, Ḥavah married Yehoshua (Otto) Langer. The marriage ceremony was performed by R. Yaakov Levitsky, the rabbi of Givat Rambam (today Givatayim).[4] The Langer's son Ḥanokh was born in 1945, and their daughter Miriam in 1948.

2. The first part of this article is based largely on familiar sources, most of which have been in print and accessible for some time. My contribution here is in consolidating and organizing the material systematically and clearly. New material and documents are found mostly in the second half of the article. For earlier research on the Langer Affair, see, among other sources, the following: For a historical perspective, S. Mishlov, *B'Ein HaSa'ara: Demuto HaTziburit V'Yetzirato HaToranit Shel HaRav Shlomo Goren B'Shanim 5708–5754/1948–1994*, doctoral dissertation (Ramat Gan, 2009), 37–52. For a halakhic-research perspective, see A. Hollander, *Dyokno HaHilkhati Shel HaRav Goren – Iyunim B'Shikulei HaPesika*, doctoral dissertation (Ramat Gan, 2010), 296–307. In the last few months, portions of the two works relevant to our discussion below have been published: S. Mishlov, "*Manhigut Datit No'ezet – HaPegi'ah B'Ma'amado HaTziburi Shel HaRav Goren B'Ikvot Parashat Ha'Aḥ V'ha'Aḥot,*" *Sefer Kenes Emdot* 5 (Elkana, 2012), 165–79; A. Hollander, "*Ne'emanut Kefulah L'Halakhah U'Medinah U'Fitronah: Pesikato Shel HaRav Shlomo Goren K'Mikreh Boḥan,*" *Ḥakirah* 15 (2012), 15–23. It is not my intention here to comment on these articles.
3. The facts recorded here, which are not generally disputed, are based primarily on the chronology printed at the end of R. Shlomo Goren's book *Psak HaDin B'Inyan Ha'Aḥ V'Ha'aḥot* (hereafter *Psak HaDin*), (Jerusalem, 1972), 184–91.
4. R. Yaakov Levitsky (1884–1947) was a veteran rabbi, alumnus of the Mir and Novardok yeshivot, ordained by the *Arukh HaShulḥan*, among others. From 1905 onward, he served as a rabbi in several small towns in Europe. In 1933, he emigrated to Israel, and in 1939, he was appointed rabbi of Givat Rambam, today Givatayim (*Ohalei Shem* [Pinsk, 1911], 6; *Dorot Ha'Aḥaronim* 1 [New York, 1913], cols. 211–13; *Anshei HaShem* [Tel Aviv, 1940], 52; *HaTzofeh*, February 10, 1948 [vol. 3075], 3; *Bet Aharon V'Yisrael* 149 [June–August 2010], 17–18). The two Chief Rabbis of Israel, R. Herzog and R. Uziel, are the signatories on R. Levitsky's certificate of appointment as Rabbi of Givat Rambam, dated August 5, 1940 (State Archives 2.8.1.8). The fact that Ḥavah's marriage to the man who would become the father of her children was performed by a recognized rabbi should have been halakhically significant, at least with regard to facts that were impossible to ascertain clearly later. Still, had R. Levitsky known that Ḥavah was considered married to Borokovsky, it is difficult to believe he would have decided independently that she did not need to obtain a divorce, without referring the case to a rabbinical court of law as would

In 1951 Borokovsky decided to marry again, and he and Ḥavah applied for a divorce which was arranged immediately by the rabbinical court in Tel Aviv.[5] Yehoshua Langer passed away in 1952, and three years later Ḥavah applied to the rabbinical court in Tel Aviv for permission to marry. In the course of approving the marriage permit, the rabbinical court (R. Eliezer Goldschmidt, R. Yosef Bebliki, and R. Shlomo Shimshon Karelitz) instituted proceedings to ascertain the legitimacy of Ḥavah's children by Yehoshua Langer. In October 1955, after a number of court sessions, the Tel Aviv rabbinical court (R. Mordekhai Jaffe Schlesinger, R. Yehiel Wilinsky, and R. Israel Sorotzkin) ruled that Ḥanokh and Miriam Langer were *mamzerim*. Following this ruling, the Chief Rabbi of Tel Aviv, R. Isser Yehudah Unterman, forwarded the information to all marriage registrars in the country, instructing them that the Langer siblings were forbidden to marry.

In April 1966, Ḥanokh Langer applied to the Tel Aviv rabbinate for a marriage license. Since his name appeared on a list of those blocked from marriage, he was referred to the rabbinical court. The rabbinical court declined to judge the case because of the prior ruling prohibiting the Langer siblings to marry; it did, however, leave open the possibility of appeal proceedings in the Supreme Rabbinical Court of Appeal. The brother and sister chose to appeal, and their case was transferred for another hearing to the rabbinical court in Petaḥ Tikvah, composed of R. Karelitz, R. Mikhel Zolty, and R. Shmuel Tanḥum Rubenstein (R. Yeshaya Schorer on occasion sat in for R. Rubenstein). The court began deliberations in September 1966, and in November 1967 it concluded that there was no possibility of reversing the original ruling.

In July 1968, the brother and sister filed an additional appeal in the Supreme Rabbinical Court composed of R. Yosef Shalom Elyashiv, R. Salman Ḥugi Aboudi, and R. Shaul Yisraeli, who agreed to return the case for further clarification to the rabbinical court in Petaḥ Tikvah. In January 1969, the rabbinical court in Petaḥ Tikvah began its additional hearing, with R. Naḥum Dov Kreisman replacing R.

---

have been customary. Compare this with the claim in an article published after the controversy broke out, that in testimony before the rabbinical court in Petaḥ Tikvah on September 26, 1966, Ḥavah testified that when she married a second time, she did not bother to give information about being already married (*HaModia*, December 1, 1971, 2). It is unclear, however, from her words whether she testified generally, "I did not tell that I had a husband" or whether she said explicitly "I did not tell the rabbi [Levitsky] that I had a husband." The words attributed to her vary depending on the source.

5. Apparently, even at this stage, for some reason there was still no discussion of the implications of Ḥavah's first marriage for her second marriage (and, by extension, the implications for her children's halakhic status).

Rubenstein. In June 1969, the court concluded once again that there was no possibility of changing the original ruling. A month later, in July 1969, the rabbinical court added that the brother and sister could appeal a third time before the Supreme Rabbinical Court. This decision followed a petition by R. Shlomo Goren, then Chief Rabbi of the Israel Defense Forces (IDF).[6] In November 1969, the Supreme Rabbinical Court began an additional hearing with R. Ovadiah Yosef replacing R. Aboudi. In February 1970, the court rejected the appeal. As far as the rabbinical courts of the Chief Rabbinate were concerned, the story was over.

Over a period of fifteen years, then, more than twelve rabbinical court judges in three separate rabbinical courts, including the Supreme Rabbinical Court, were involved in deliberations on this case. All came to the same conclusion: The two children of Ḥavah and Yehoshua Langer were *mamzerim* and forbidden to marry.

R. GOREN'S INVOLVEMENT IN THE CASE

R. Goren's involvement in the Langer Affair began in 1968, as the case was being passed back and forth between the rabbinical courts in Tel Aviv and Petaḥ Tikvah.[7] At the time, both siblings were in the army, with Miriam Langer serving near the office of the Chief Rabbi of the IDF. R. Goren began dealing with the case when the brother and sister turned to him for help. His first move was to contact the presiding judge of the Petaḥ Tikvah rabbinical court and the judges of the Supreme Rabbinical Court, as well as the presiding judge of the Supreme Rabbinical Court, Sephardi Chief Rabbi Yitzḥak Nissim. R. Goren's efforts did not succeed in changing the final ruling of the Supreme Rabbinical Court. In March 1971, at the request of R. Nissim,[8] R. Goren composed a halakhic opinion on the subject. In the process of writing his opinion, he obtained new evidence and documentation which led him to conclude that there was insufficient halakhic proof of Borokovsky's status as a convert.[9] Summing up, he wrote that

6. See *Psak HaDin,* 60.
7. As discussed in the introduction to *Psak HaDin,* 8.
8. And also at the request "of other senior personages in the State" (*Psak HaDin,* 8). R. Goren added that "after I had composed my halakhic opinion, the honorable R. Nissim made efforts to convene a special *bet din*...but his efforts in this direction did not yield results" (ibid., 9). For a description of R. Yitzḥak Nissim's inclination to leniency in the affair and the pressures brought to bear on him, see S. Maizlish, *Min HaHar el Ha'Am* (Jerusalem, 1973), 264–66.
9. Parenthetically, this is the main difference between the polemics surrounding the Langer Affair and the disputes about conversion in our generation. R. Goren's central argument was that there was insufficient basis for the presumption that Borokovsky had undergone a halakhically valid conversion. Only tangentially he added that if Borokovksy had converted, his subsequent actions testified that he had not truly intended to convert, and that his conversion was nullified retroactively. (Cf. with his words in *Mishnat HaMedinah* [Jerusalem, 1996], 184.) By contrast,

the possibility of permitting the siblings to marry was likely "on condition that a rabbinical court composed of three senior judges or at least a court composed of a presiding judge and two other judges would agree to this ruling." In June 1971, R. Goren ended his stint as Chief Rabbi of the IDF and shortly after was appointed Ashkenazi Chief Rabbi of Tel Aviv.

At this stage, the Langer case was already the focus of journalistic interest, having come to the attention of the press after the final verdict of the Supreme Rabbinical Court. The subject quickly became politically and socially charged. Both Langers had served in Defense Minister Moshe Dayan's office, and he began to pressure senior officials of the Israeli Rabbinate on their behalf, as did other public figures. For close to three years, the Langer case remained officially at a standstill, but behind the scenes, high-ranking politicians – especially Moshe Dayan and Golda Meir – exercised extremely strong pressure on the Chief Rabbinate to come up with a ruling to enable the Langer siblings to marry. Parliamentary activity added to the pressure as, for example, MK Gideon Hausner's proposal of a law to permit civil marriage for those who could not marry according to halakhah. The proposal touched off a political crisis. On the one hand, the situation aroused fears of potentially disastrous political intervention in halakhic matters, particularly those related to the boundaries of sanctity in Judaism. On the other, there was concern that secular parliamentarians would exploit the problem of *mamzerut*, children born of a prohibited relationship, to definitively separate religion and state and cancel the authority of the Chief Rabbinate in all matters related to marriage and divorce in the State of Israel.

Against this backdrop, at the beginning of 1972, elections for the Chief Rabbinate were being held, with R. Shlomo Goren competing for the seat against the incumbent Chief Rabbi Isser Yehudah Unterman. There were persistent rumors – denied by R. Goren – to the effect that an informal deal had been cut between R. Goren and senior officials in the government: Should he be chosen as Chief Rabbi, "the matter [of the Langer siblings] would be settled after the Chief Rabbinate elections."[10] Concerned that R. Goren might be

---

rabbinical courts that dealt with the case argued, among other things, that since Borokovsky was already publicly recognized as a righteous convert (and by the rabbinical court that arranged his divorce from Ḥavah Langer as well), there was no longer any halakhic significance to the doubts raised about his conversion process or evidence about his subsequent lifestyle.

10. From *HaMa'arakhah al Hatzalat HaRabbanut B'Yisrael* (Jerusalem, 1972), 4, published anonymously. The central thesis of this pamphlet was that R. Goren was playing into the hands of anti-religious elements and that his election as Chief Rabbi would endanger halakhah and its public practice in the State. Most of the arguments touched only tangentially on the Langer

elected Chief Rabbi, the ḥaredi community launched a broad propaganda campaign against him. In Av/August 1972, seven leading rabbis of the "Lithuanian" stream issued a proclamation on the subject. Formulated in general terms, it contained no explicit instructions and did not mention R. Goren by name, but its intent was clear – to prevent R. Goren's election as Chief Rabbi.[11] Among the signatories was R. Yosef Shalom Elyashiv, who was described in the proclamation as "a member of the Supreme Rabbinical Court." As we mentioned, he had been a member of one of the rabbinical courts that dealt with the Langer case.

It should be noted that rabbis outside the "Lithuanian" stream opposed R. Goren's candidacy as well, including some from his own circles, although their opposition was based on different considerations. In an announcement published in the press, R. Tzvi Yehudah HaKohen Kook declared that one is forbidden to stand for the post of Chief Rabbi against a current Chief Rabbi because doing so would mean ousting a rabbi from his position.[12] This was also the view of R. Shaul Yisraeli, [13] and the Lubavitcher Rebbe expressed similar thoughts in a personal letter to R. Goren.[14]

---

case, focusing primarily on R. Goren's worldview and his approach to halakhah. In response, a counter-argument was issued in the form of another pamphlet, *Oz V'Tiferet LaRabbanut HaRashit L'Yisrael*, which expressed support for R. Goren's candidacy.

11. "A spirit of frenzy now passes over our holy land... to permit forbidden things with no basis in reality and they are lies and falsehood. We declare that anyone who says thus has no place in halakhah and one should not rely on his teachings. And all who aid in disseminating this opinion will have to answer for this in the future" (*HaMa'arakhah al Hatzalat HaRabbanut B'Yisrael*).

    In addition to R. Elyashiv, the other signatories were R. Yeḥezkel Abramsky, R. Yaakov Yisrael Kanievsky, R. Elazar Menaḥem Man Shakh, R. Ḥayim Shmuelevitz, R. Moshe Ḥevroni, and R. Shlomo Zalman Auerbach. See also the description in *Responsa Yabi'a Omer* 9, *Ḥoshen Mishpat, siman* 9. It should be noted that the "Lithuanian" rabbinic leadership had already publicly expressed its opposition to R. Goren in 1970 in connection with Helen Zeidman's conversion. (See the proclamation by R. Shakh and R. Kanievsky in *Sha'aruriyat HaGiurim HaMezuyafim* [Jerusalem, 1989], 65.)

12. See, among other sources, his letter dated Rosh Ḥodesh Ḥeshvan 5733 (October 9, 1972), published in the newspapers on 5 Ḥeshvan.

13. Consequently, R. Yisraeli resigned from the rabbinical organization of HaPo'el HaMizraḥi (*Ḥever HaRabbanim Shel Hapoel Hamizraḥi*), whose members largely supported R. Goren's candidacy. Among other sources, see the letter of R. Katriel Fishel Tchorz, *HaModia*, October 13, 1972, last page. For more on HaPo'el HaMizraḥi's rabbinical organization and R. Yisraeli, see the articles of R. Neriyah Gutel and Aharon Kempinski in *Sugyot B'Ḥeker HaTziyonut HaDati* (Ramat Gan, 2011), 121–68.

14. Dated August 1972. *Igrot Kodesh* 27, 511–12. Sections of the letter were published in the press at the time.

In the beginning of October 1972, R. Shlomo Goren was chosen as Ashkenazi Chief Rabbi of Israel, with R. Ovadiah Yosef chosen as *Rishon LeTziyon* and Sephardi Chief Rabbi. Several days later, the Langer siblings turned to R. Goren in a letter requesting that he "arrange another hearing on the prohibition of our marriages."[15] In the period following the elections, there were occasional mentions in the press of R. Goren's efforts to assemble a rabbinical court to renew discussion of the Langer case, and likewise of attempts to persuade his colleague in the Chief Rabbinate, R. Ovadiah Yosef, to join a rabbinical court for this purpose.[16]

Five weeks after his election, on November 19, 1972, R. Goren convened "nine 'presiding judges' [*avot bet din*] and active judges in the official rabbinical courts of the State, Ashkenazi and Sephardi." Three were presiding judges, one a member of the Supreme Rabbinical Court, and one had been part of a rabbinical court that had ruled against the Langers. These ten *dayanim* overturned the decisions of the earlier rabbinical courts and ruled that Ḥanokh and Miriam Langer were permitted to marry.[17] That night, the weddings of the

15. These words are taken from their letter; *Psak HaDin,* 10–11.
16. Among other sources, see press reports from November 14–15, 1972. There were also reports of Borokovsky's application to the rabbinical court in Petaḥ Tikvah with a request that they affirm his status as a Jew. (This apparently accelerated R. Goren's efforts to implement the permissive ruling.) See also R. Ovadiah Yosef's letter to R. Moshe Weiss after the affair erupted, in which he writes, among other things, "And isn't it known and [hasn't it been] publicized, how hard I struggled with all my strength and laboring many nights in order not to join the special rabbinical court of R. Goren on this matter?" *HaModia,* November 28, 4. This was later reprinted in *HaPardes* 47:4 (December 1972), 15.
17. *Psak HaDin,* 22. It is unclear from the wording whether the ten were simultaneously present at one sitting, or – as seems more likely and in light of other details – that each of the ten offered his opinion individually. The opinions of the *dayanim* appear through p. 26 and the final ruling appears on pp. 152–55. In *HaPardes* 47:4 (December 1972), 22, it was claimed that the names of the nine *dayanim* were known to "our writer," and nine of the eleven were named, while at the same time the writer insisted that "last night, they emphatically denied that they had permitted the *mamzerim.*" However, even the editor of the journal that had published this questionable list did not himself rely on the report, and asked (p. 4) "Who are the nine?" In *Or HaMizraḥ* 23:2 (Tevet 5733/December 1972), 145, it was reported that "in Jerusalem, the names of one of the nine *dayanim* has been publicized." This was R. Shalom Mizraḥi, a Tel Aviv judge appointed at that time to the Supreme Rabbinical Court. According to the report, he agreed to the publication of his name. Over the years, there were rumors about the identities of the remainder of the *dayanim.* The most substantive among them were that one of the presiding *dayanim* was R. Yaakov Nissan Rosenthal, presiding judge of Haifa, and that the judge who had changed his mind about his previous negative ruling was R. Shmuel Tanḥum Rubenstein. Apart from these, there is no doubt that one of the ten was R. Eliezer Shapira, at that time a

Langer siblings took place. The Chief Rabbi of the IDF, R. Mordekhai Piron, performed Ḥanokh Langer's wedding ceremony, and Moshe Dayan attended both weddings. The names of the nine rabbinical court judges who joined R. Goren's permissive ruling were officially classified, with R. Goren explaining that this was "in order to protect them and their families from threats, harm, and slander from groups that terrorize, sow discord, and try to dictate [that others obey] their opinions."[18]

THE PUBLIC RESPONSE TO THE LANGER RULING

With the story's publication in the press the following day, the storm broke. The tone was set by the Edah Ḥaredit in Jerusalem, under the leadership of R. Yitzḥak Yaakov Weiss, who called for a mass protest rally "because the man chosen as Chief Rabbi of the Zionist Chief Rabbinate has gone out to uproot a prohibition of the Torah – 'a *mamzer* may not enter into the congregation of God.'"[19] A few days later, another rally was held in Bnei Brak. Several rabbinic leaders of the ḥaredi community participated, expressing themselves in very sharply worded statements against R. Goren and his permissive ruling. A message read at the rally in the name of R. Elyashiv (who had resigned in protest from the Supreme Rabbinical Court following R. Goren's ruling) stated that "he had seen the arguments behind R. Goren's ruling and said about them that 'they did not reach even the level of jesting.'"[20] In a letter from R. Yaakov Yisrael Kanievsky read at the rally, it was said that, "A man like this does not

---

judge in the rabbinical court in Jerusalem (see below). It is also almost certain that one of them was R. Shlomo Yeluz, serving at that time as presiding judge in the rabbinical court in Ashdod. His detailed responsum on the permissive ruling was published in *Responsa Asher L'Shlomo* (Bnei Brak, 1985), *Even Ha'Ezer* 4. In Mishlov's doctoral dissertation (p. 46), she verifies the identities of two more *dayanim*: R. Yosef Glicksberg of Givatayim, and R. Ḥayim Pardes of Tel Aviv.

18. Ibid., p. 23. Cf. the reports of verbal assaults on R. Goren on the day after publication of the permissive ruling, at the funeral of R. Yisrael Be'eri of Nes Ziona (*HaTzofeh*, November 21, 1972, front page) and against R. Eliezer Shapira (ibid., and in the following day's paper, front page). There was also the incident of a booby-trapped envelope which was sent to R. Goren. In response, it was claimed that this was a provocation intended to besmirch the reputations of R. Goren's opponents. (Cf. *HaTzofeh* and *HaModia*, November 29.)
19. *Otzarot Yerushalayim* 118 (1972), 277. For coverage of the rally, see ibid., 278–81. Obviously, there was nothing particularly surprising about the protest in itself, since the Edah Ḥaredit had always objected strenuously to the existence of the Chief Rabbinate and the Chief Rabbis. Parenthetically, it is interesting to note that in support of his conclusions, R. Goren made reference to a similar case adjudicated by R. Yitzḥak Yaakov Weiss in *Responsa Minḥat Asher* 1:121–122.
20. *Otzarot Yerushalayim* (ibid.), 283.

belong in the rabbinate at all... like the teachings of the Reform *ra-banim* ['evil sons', a pun on the Hebrew *rabbanim* (rabbis)] may the names of the wicked rot.... [R. Goren] has already taken himself out of the category of the faithful of Israel."[21] Simultaneously, notices signed by great rabbinical figures in the Israeli ḥaredi community announced that "all the teachings of this man are null and void and it is forbidden to rely upon [his rulings] at all."[22] In a short while, tens of rabbis from ḥaredi communities in Europe joined those who had issued the notices in Israel.[23]

On the eve of Ḥanukkah, about two weeks after the publication of the ruling, a new and important authority figure joined the protest. The president of Agudas Harabonim of the United States and Canada, R. Moshe Feinstein, announced in an open letter to the press:

> We also join *da'as Torah,* the Torah opinion, of R. Yeḥezkel Abramsky, may he live a long, good life, and the consensus of all the *gedolim* of the Land of Israel, that all the rulings of [R. Goren] are null and void; written and signed with great distress in the name of all the members of Agudas Harabonim of the US.[24]

At a protest rally of Agudas Harabonim held in New York, R. Feinstein expressed displeasure about R. Goren's decision to wait until his appointment as Chief Rabbi in order to issue the ruling; this raised suspicions of pressure and ulterior motives, i.e., that the ruling had been given in exchange

---

21. Ibid., 282.
22. Ibid., 288, and in vol. 119 (1972), 297–98. See also *HaPardes* 47:4, 24ff.; *HaModia,* November 24–December 6. The first proclamation was signed by R. Shakh, R. Kanievsky, R. Elyashiv, and R. Yisrael Weltz; the proclamation that followed was signed by R. Abramsky, R. Shmuelevitz, R. Ḥevroni, and R. Shlomo Zalman Auerbach; a later proclamation was signed by R. Shmuel Vozner, R. Yaakov Landa, R. Natan Gestetner, and others; a further proclamation was signed by R. Ḥayim Yosef Dinkels, R. Binyamin Mendelson, R. Moshe Sternbuch, and others. R. Gedalia Nadel, one of the heads of the Ḥazon Ish Kollel, wrote, "One should not relate to this ruling at all, and it is clear that [R. Goren] does not meet even one of the conditions that make a man fit to be a rabbi." *Otzarot Yerushalayim,* 119, 298.
23. Among them, R. Ḥayim Kreiswirth of Antwerp. See the announcements in *HaModia,* December 8, 1972, front page, and in *HaPardes* 47:4 (December 1972), 24–28. In her dissertation (p. 50), Mishlov points out that on the opposing side, some of the chief rabbis of Europe (such as R. Moshe Rosen of Romania) expressed support for R. Goren orally, although in some cases, (such as that of R. Immanuel Jakobovitz of England) the press reported otherwise.
24. *HaPardes,* ibid., p. 2 and *HaModia,* December 11, front page.

for his appointment.[25] The Lubavitcher Rebbe voiced similar concerns at a Lubavitch gathering.[26]

At this point, with the ruling issued but the reasoning behind it not yet published, the protests were couched in general terms. The objections of the ḥaredi community were directed primarily at the fact of the *heter* [permissive ruling], which was interpreted as straightforwardly permitting *mamzerim* to marry. Other objections related to R. Goren's general conduct in the affair and the questionable process by which the permissive ruling had been issued.[27] The heavy governmental pressure which had been brought to bear for so long a period, and the issuing of the ruling so soon after R. Goren's appointment as Chief Rabbi, created the impression that the ruling lacked a solid grounding in halakhah, and had been issued with ulterior motives. The impression of underhandedness was reinforced by the suddenness with which the ruling was issued, and the shotgun marriages immediately following.

Still, even these arguments are insufficient to explain the unprecedented ferocity of the attack on R. Goren. It is likely that beyond all this, the weightiness of the protest resulted from fear that the Langer Affair was only an introduction to the manner in which all future halakhic problems would be "solved" in the State of Israel, and that R. Goren's tenure as Chief Rabbi would be dedicated to additional

25. See coverage of the rally in *HaPardes* 47:5, January 1973, 32–46; also in coverage of an additional rally in Bnei Brak are further statements by the Lubavitcher Rebbe and others (ibid.). For the letter calling people to the rally, handwritten by R. Feinstein, see *Mikhtavim V'Igrot Kodesh* (New York, 2002), 672–73: "We are shocked by the terrible breach that has been made in the wall of religion in the Holy Land and from the new trend to falsify the Torah, to pervert the halakhah."

26. *HaPardes* 47:4, December 1972, 27. See also his cutting language in two Lubavitch gatherings following publication of the ruling. He summed up by saying, "After his resignation, it will be possible to begin to discuss his fitness for the rabbinate; but as long as he does not repent and cut himself off from the benefits of the government toward him, his disqualification from the rabbinate remains" (*Siḥot Kodesh* 1972, 1, unedited stencil [Brooklyn, 1985], 444–48). For more on the ḥasidic side, see the statement of the Kaliver Rebbe: "We lie down in our shame at the disgraceful and humiliating deed which to our great anguish the congregation of Israel was witness to in these days, woe to the eyes that see this" (*Kol Menaḥem* 1 [Rishon Lezion, 1974], 136). See also n. 29 below.

27. Even some of those who supported R. Goren in principle shared these qualms. Minister of Religion Zeraḥ Warhaftig, for example, wrote that "the main objection relates to procedure, and there is something to this objection," although he added that in an exceptional case like this, "there is sometimes – and we hope, rarely – [a need] that a rabbi, a *gadol hador*, may go on a special path and convene a special rabbinical court" (*Ba'ayot Dat U'Medinah* [Jerusalem, 1974], 136).

halakhic "reforms" in service of the government.[28] This impression was fortified by the mood of the previous three years during which the affair was repeatedly featured in the press and exploited by anti-religious personalities to batter the rabbinical world and halakhah. Under these circumstances, R. Goren's hasty *heter*, in opposition to the decisions of previous rabbinical courts, was interpreted as legitimizing the claims about "the insensitivity of the rabbinical establishment" and "the cruelty of the rabbis." Here, after all, was their "courageous antithesis" in the persona of R. Goren.[29]

Thus, in a press release published at the beginning of December 1972, the members of the *Mo'etzes Gedolei HaTorah* of Agudath Israel called upon "all rabbis serving as *dayanim* in the Holy Land not to submit to pressure from any personage in any manner and not to change the word of God, that is the law, in the slightest." They emphasized their fears concerning:

> the expression of the wish, and the actions, of secular personalities and public bodies who wish to harm, God forbid, the Holy of Holies of the nation and undermine [the institution of] matrimony – upon which all the house of Israel rests – by opening the gates to those who are disqualified from marriage.[30]

28. In response to the claim of the government having pressured him, R. Goren claimed that no less excruciating pressure was brought to bear over the course of three years by ḥaredi forces who tried to prevent the Chief Rabbinate's re-opening the case. The tendency of R. Yitzḥak Nissim to approve re-opening the case was mentioned above (note 8), and likewise that of his fellow Chief Rabbi, R. I. Y. Unterman, in an announcement in Tamuz 1972: "Chief Rabbi, the gaon R. I. Y. Unterman, announced that he would be prepared to preside over a *bet din* that would re-open the case of 'the brother and sister'" (*Or HaMizraḥ* 28:4, 245). It should be noted that among members of the earlier Supreme Religious Court that had heard the case, there was disagreement, with R. Elyashiv tending to prohibit, while R. Yisraeli suggested bases to permit (see their opinions in *Psak HaDin*, 156–74).
29. R. Goren's counter-argument was that without a halakhic solution to the problem, secular politicians would have exploited the Langer Affair and its attendant public pressure to separate religion and State and completely annul the authority of the Chief Rabbinate. Unfortunately, one cannot deny that there are indeed problems of *mamzerut* which cannot be resolved within halakhah. See in this connection, Hollander's dissertation, especially p. 307. His conclusions, written admiringly toward R. Goren, are likely to have the opposite effect on R. Goren's detractors.
30. *HaModia*, December 12, 1972 and *HaPardes* 47:5 (January 1973), 2. The following declaration was also repeated: "this ruling is null and void, and it is forbidden to rely upon any ruling or teaching of this man at all." In addition, there was an implicit request to the rest of the *dayanim* who had participated in the ruling to reverse themselves: "And those from whose hands this stumbling block has come, we beseech you to be courageous and sanctify the Name of Heaven

ARGUMENTS CONCERNING THE SUBSTANCE OF THE RULING

The Langer Affair entered a new phase in December 1972. After about a month of harsh criticism without a response from R. Goren or his supporters, R. Goren published a two hundred–page pamphlet entitled "The Ruling in the Matter of the Brother and Sister" (an expanded version of the halakhic opinion he had written in 1971). In it, R. Goren laid out the progression of events from his perspective, a detailed description of the ruling and the reasoning behind it, the conclusions of the nine rabbinical judges, the protocols of the earlier rabbinical court sessions, new documentation that came to light following the original verdicts, and more. The publication of the pamphlet transformed the protests and their orientation. The weightiest of the objections to the ruling was that it contravened halakhah. With the appearance of R. Goren's publication, his detractors would be required to deal with the substance of the ruling, presented in tens of pages of halakhic argumentation and evidence.

The first criticism regarding the content of the ruling came from the United States. R. Ephraim Eliezer HaKohen Yolles of Philadelphia presented a brief refutation of two points that had been presented in the press as reinforcement for the ruling.[31] Following him, R. Shmuel Tuvia Stern of Miami composed a pamphlet entitled "The Judgment of the Oppressed" on the Langer brother and sister ruling, and published an excerpt called "Some Notes on the 'Ruling' of R. Goren."[32] However, the most prominent attempt to refute the foundations of the ruling was written in Israel by R. Bezalel Zolty, one of the senior judges in the Supreme Rabbinical Court and a long-time opponent of R. Goren. He published a lengthy article with the goal of proving that "the words of the author of the pamphlet on the

---

and recant your position." Present at this meeting were the ḥasidic leaders of Gur, Vizhnitz, Mahanovka, Modzitz, Slonim, Strikov, and Erlau, as well as R. Shakh, R. Auerbach, R. Elyashiv, R. Ḥevroni, R. Barukh Shimon Shneerson, R. Yeḥiel Mikhel Feinstein, R. Moshe Shmuel Shapira, and others.

31. *HaPardes* 47:5 (January 1973), 6–7 and in *Responsa Divrei Efra'im Eli'ezer, siman* 219. Even before this, a section from one of the pamphlets was published by the Public Committee for Upholding of Torah in Israel, without attribution other than the note: "Those who study Torah will see for themselves and judge whether or not the author of this pamphlet (apart from other bases) is a reliable authority" (*HaPardes* 47:4, 28).

32. *HaPardes* 47:8 (April 1973), 9–11. He concluded:

> If R. Goren truly wishes to fulfill that which is written, "*vahev b'sufa*" [reconciliation among Sages], he should request of the rabbinical court in Petaḥ Tikvah to discuss the matter, perhaps with additional expert *dayanim*, according to new testimony investigated in a rabbinical court, and they will find the solution for the matter to do justice to the oppressed.

It should be emphasized that R. Yolles and R. Stern were **not** among the circles hostile to R. Goren, his path, or his point of view.

matter of the brother and sister are largely, if not totally, built upon distortion of facts and errors in halakhah." R. Zolty challenged various points in the ruling at great length, sharply denouncing R. Goren. R. Zolty refrained from using R. Goren's name, referring to him only "as one who dares to besmirch [others]" and one who "has removed himself from the category of rabbinic judges in Israel."[33]

R. Zolty's sense of grievance was particularly strong because of the accusations leveled by R. Goren against the rabbinical courts that had judged the case over the years. According to R. Goren, the judges of the rabbinical court in Petaḥ Tikvah "made erasures and changes contrary to what [the witness] had said"[34] and generally:

> One who studies the rabbinical court's questions to Borokovsky feels clearly that they were constantly seeking how to prohibit [the siblings]; and when they did not find fitting witnesses, they "kashered" invalid ones; and when they did not find those who were near they received those who were distant; and when they didn't have [valid] reasons, they prohibited without reason.[35]

These arguments, which cast doubt on the integrity of the rabbinical courts in the State of Israel, deeply offended the rabbinical court system. In response, thirty-one current rabbinical judges, including nine presiding rabbinical judges, issued a statement protesting accusations about "judges who deliberately falsify protocols of court sessions in order to prohibit and be stringent; [this is] a malicious libel, the likes of which have never been heard against the rabbinical courts."[36] Among those who signed this document – which did not mention R. Goren by name – there were also rabbinical court judges from circles considered close to R. Goren, such as R. Shaul Yisraeli and R. Yeshayahu Meshorer.

At this stage of the affair, the voice of R. Tzvi Yehudah HaKohen Kook, rosh yeshiva of Merkaz HaRav, was heard on the other side of the controversy. He published a letter in the press generally praising R. Goren on the permissive

---

33. *HaModia*, at the end of January 1973, continuing into vol. 7 (February); *HaPardes* 47:6 (February 1973), 6–12.
34. *Psak HaDin*, 128. And on the same page: "We can only assume with certainty that [the witness] did not speak the truth or that they distorted his words in the rabbinical court through erasures and similar [actions] and we have proof of this."
35. Ibid., 116. R. Goren also argued on the same page: "There were leading questions for the purpose [of obtaining] certain [types of] answers."
36. *HaPardes* 47:7 (April 1973), 33–34.

ruling.[37] Later, at the end of January 1973, following the content-based criticism of R. Goren's pamphlet, the first reasoned defense of the ruling by his supporters appeared.[38] Writing anonymously, one of the nine rabbinical judges published a response to R. Zolty's article. Shortly afterward, another response was published, by R. Eliezer Shapira (nephew of R. Avraham Elkanah Kahana Shapira), then a judge in the district rabbinical court in Jerusalem, and later in the Supreme Rabbinical Court.[39] In his response, R. Shapira agreed with some of R. Zolty's arguments but disputed others, and added that "the ruling is constructed of quite a number of clauses and apparently he [R. Zolty] found no more flaws than those he enumerated. From this we learn that, even according to him, the remainder of the ruling is justified." He also argued that R. Zolty did not approach the case objectively since he "is well known as an enemy of the Chief Rabbi." R. Zolty returned fire, countering with an article in which he replied to the critique, raising further points against the ruling. He also added that the argument about his lack of objectivity "is a base libel. I do not, God forbid, hate any Jew – I am indeed his 'opponent', but not his 'enemy.' And even as an 'opponent,' it is not, God forbid, on personal grounds, but because I disagree with his outlook and opinions and his path in adjudication of rabbinical law."[40] Furthermore, wrote R. Zolty:

37. "From the depth of my heart and my soul, I express my feelings of thanks and my blessings on the publication today of clarifications on the holy halakhic ruling to wipe out the slander against the souls of our brother and sister" (*HaTzofeh,* November 26, 1972, front page). To a certain extent, what was said in n. 19 above applies here as well, but from the opposing side. See also R. Tzvi Yehudah HaKohen Kook's letter of protest against someone who argued that R. Goren issued his permissive ruling under pressure from the government (*HaTzofeh,* December 13, 1972). During the same period, a letter from R. Natan Tzvi Friedman, the rabbi of Shikun Heh in Bnei Brak and author of *Responsa Netzer Mata'ai,* was published. He wrote that, "I publicly announce that I disagree with the defamatory wall poster which appeared in the streets of Bnei Brak against the Chief Rabbis of Israel" (*HaTzofeh,* December 8). The reference is apparently to the wall poster described in n. 22, issued by R. Vozner, R. Landa, and R. Gestetner, in which R. Friedman also appeared as a signatory. For some reason, R. Friedman does not refer to R. Goren by name.

38. "Open Letter," *HaTzofeh,* March 4, 1973, continued in issue of March 18 (p. 3).

39. *HaTzofeh* (February 9), 3, 6. In practice, R. Eliezer Shapira was the only supporter of the *heter* – or participant in it – who dared to come out in open halakhic debate against its detractors at the time. See R. Goren's letter of February 28 to [R.] Saul Lieberman in which he makes a pejorative reference to R. Zolty's article against him and adds, "I attach the important counter-argument by the gaon R. E. Shapira, member of the rabbinical court in Jerusalem and member of the Chief Rabbinical Council, who answered him properly" (Marc Shapiro, *Saul Lieberman and the Orthodox* [Scranton 2006], Hebrew section, p. 10).

40. *HaPardes* 47:7 (April 1973), 7–12. Toward the end of his statement, R. Zolty promised that "an analysis of the facts and testimonies, and a comprehensive halakhic clarification will be forthcoming, please God, in a special pamphlet, as I have announced"; he also pleaded with

> It seems that in all of Jewish history there has not yet been something like this, that all the great Torah personalities in the world are of one opinion in invalidating the rulings of a well-known rabbi, and that not even one great Torah personality who is [also] a great *posek* has come out openly to defend him."[41]

Up to this point, R. Zolty's claim was clearly accurate since there did not appear to be even one great *posek* of the generation willing to express support for R. Goren.[42] Unexpectedly, though, news arrived from abroad to the effect that R. Yosef Eliyahu Henkin, considered the elder *posek* in the United States, had let it be known that he supported R. Goren.

R. HENKIN AND HIS ATTITUDE TOWARD THE CHIEF RABBINATE

To understand R. Yosef Eliyahu Henkin's perspective on the Langer Affair, we need to know more about his background, his attitude to the State of Israel in general and his thoughts on the Chief Rabbinate in particular. R. Henkin (b. 1881) was a product of Lithuanian yeshivot and served as rabbi in a number of small towns in Eastern Europe. He arrived in the United States in 1922. Two years later, he was appointed director of the Ezras Torah organization established

---

the anonymous rabbinical judge to publicly withdraw his signature from the ruling (p. 12). According to rumor, the reason R. Zolty's pamphlet was never published (if indeed it was written at all) was due to concerns that spelling out the reasons for rejecting the *heter*, however strong they might be, would turn the episode into "yet another" halakhic controversy.

41. Ibid., p. 9. It is possible that the emphasis on "not even one great rabbinical figure who is also a great *posek*" (and not simply "one great rabbinical figure") was intended to exclude R. Tzvi Yehudah HaKohen Kook, known to be a great rabbinical figure – being a rosh yeshiva – but not necessarily a great *posek* (although this might also have been said about some of R. Goren's opponents). See the following footnote.

42. R. Goren was not, however, entirely alone in his permissive ruling. As noted, nine rabbinical court *dayanim* had joined him, some of them presiding *dayanim* and a few even well-known figures, such as R. Yaakov Nissan Rosenthal. Apart from these, there were other important rabbis who deliberately did not join the attacks against R. Goren, even if they didn't necessarily agree with his stance in the affair. (Among those who can be mentioned are the rabbis who served with R. Goren during his tenure in the Supreme Rabbinical Court: R. Avraham Shapira, R. Mordekhai Eliyahu, and others; similarly, the members of the Chief Rabbinical Council during the period of his tenure there, among them R. Menaḥem Yehudah Ushpizai, R. Ḥayim David HaLevi, R. Refael Kadir Tzaban, and others. See also, in this connection, an extremely friendly letter dated 16 Adar 5741 [February 2, 1981], sent by R. Ovadiah Yosef to his colleague R. Goren, cited by Mishlov in one of the appendices to her doctorate.) These facts were given very little weight at the time, however, since not even one of the personalities mentioned here expressed any public support for R. Goren.

by Agudas Harabonim of America (which for fifty years was considered the strongest rabbinical organization in America). With the passage of time, R. Henkin became one of the great *poskim* in America – in effect, the most important among them – even as his close friend and neighbor, R. Moshe Feinstein, was rising to prominence.[43] Apart from his greatness in Torah, R. Henkin was known as a non-partisan personality with an original outlook. On the one hand, until 1948, he was prominent among American rabbinic leaders who objected to the founding of a Jewish state. He sharply criticized both the leadership and the conduct of the Zionist movement, declaring that "Although I am close in spirit to the Agudah [Agudath Israel], I am not a member [of the organization], so that I will not be considered to have agreed with them in the establishment of the State."[44] On the other hand, after the State was established, he began to support it publicly using the same rationale for which he had objected to it – his concern that many Jewish lives would be lost. Now, with the existence of the State a fact, he felt obliged to support and strengthen it against its enemies to prevent the further shedding of Jewish blood. Consistent with this, he became a fierce opponent of Neturei Karta and their activities against the State.[45]

Throughout, R. Henkin was thoroughly involved in public matters pertaining to the State of Israel, and occasionally he expressed his opinions, publishing articles in Hebrew or Yiddish for the American rabbinic press. He continued to express his basic support for the existing State and even wrote that, in retrospect, its founding could be seen as a blessing:

> Everyone knows that I was one of the strongest opponents to founding an independent State; but now, in retrospect, I am obliged to say that the current government of Israel is democratic, and if [the number of] observant citizens will increase, it will be conducted according to Torah. And even now, as I will write in what follows, many of the foundations of the Torah are observed through them."[46]

43. For his biography, see previous chapter. As I write these lines, a new, expanded edition of his writings and responsa has been published, including tens of responsa and new rulings from manuscripts, under the title *Responsa Gevurot Eliyahu* (Lakewood, 2012).
44. *Teshuvot Ivra, siman* 109, 216–17. See also the articles and letters cited in the previous chapter, and in *Lev Ivra*, p. 93ff.
45. See *Teshuvot Ivra, siman* 106 (p. 208ff.). R. Henkin's singular outlook in these matters will not be described in detail here.
46. Ibid. See also the introduction to R. Henkin's book *Lev Ivra* (1956): "Throughout this time, many worlds of Jews and Judaism have been destroyed for our many sins – and in opposition to this, a sovereign state has arisen in Israel and the Land of Israel is continuing to be built."

In keeping with this perspective, R. Henkin accorded great importance to the institution of the Chief Rabbinate as the body responsible for matters of religion in the State, preventing it from becoming entirely secular. As he wrote, the rabbinate of the IDF played a significant role in this arrangement:

> The government founded the Chief Rabbinate and its subdivisions, and it aids and maintains houses of Torah, and **the armed forces conduct themselves with kashrut thanks to the supervision of a famous rabbi**, and all matters of divorce and marriage in the State are under the Chief Rabbinate and its subdivisions..."[47]

These words were written at the end of 1967, a few months after the Six-Day War, and the highlighted section about the famous rabbi who supervises matters of religion in the armed forces refers to R. Goren, then Chief Rabbi of the IDF.

Indeed, especially in the last fifteen years of his life, including the years when he was already blind (the end of the 1960s), R. Henkin intensified his involvement in public matters and wrote some of his longest articles explaining his perspective. At the beginning of the decade, around the "Who is a Jew?" controversy, he expressed his concerns about attempts to close the Chief Rabbinate.[48] A decade later, in 1971–72, he maintained correspondence on the subject of the religious character of the State with a number of public figures, including the Lubavitcher Rebbe, R. Menachem Porush, and even Prime Minister Golda Meir.[49] As we have stated, R. Henkin attributed great significance to the existence of the Chief Rabbinate in this context. In May 1968, he met with R. Yitzḥak Nissim, then *Rishon LeTziyon*, during the latter's visit to New York. In a follow-up to that meeting, R. Henkin sent a letter to the Chief Rabbis regarding the Conversion Law in which he expressed the position that, in principle, "the best solution and the first step

47. Ibid., p. 210; published first in *HaMa'or*, August–September 1967, and in the following months in *HaPardes*, *No'am*, and *Or HaMizraḥ*.

48. And even if Jerusalem alone will, God forbid, be handed over to the U.N., with this they will put a sword into the hands of those who ostracize us to do away with the Chief Rabbinate and with it any connection at all of rabbis and religion to the government. [...] And still they are attempting to do away with the connection [of the State] with the Rabbinate, and because of this, they have decreed to make non-Jews into Jews, which is a matter of the Rabbinate, and they hoped that the Chief Rabbis would resign because of this law, just as the religious mainstream withdrew, and this would serve them as an excuse to separate religion from the State. (*Teshuvot Ivra*, 222–23.)

49. About correspondence with the Lubavitcher Rebbe, see, among other sources, *Kfar Ḥabad* 774 (5757/1997), 30–31, and issue 1341 (5769/2009); *Igrot Kodesh* 27: 10/318–10/319; the remainder of the letters have not yet been published, and see *Yeshurun* 20, 148 in the footnote there.

to attaining peace between religion and state is precisely that all Jews who fall under the rubric "*dati*" [religious] be united, and that each political party not be separate unto itself."[50]

This, then, is the background to R. Henkin's position on the Langer Affair: a positive attitude toward the Chief Rabbinate, including the IDF Rabbinate and R. Goren, who stood at its head. As far as is known, R. Henkin never actually met R. Goren but, over the years, as someone who took pains to follow current events in the State of Israel, R. Henkin developed an appreciation for his activities.

R. HENKIN'S STATEMENT AND THE CONTROVERSY SURROUNDING IT

In the first months of the Langer controversy, R. Henkin made no public reference to the case, at least officially, although efforts were being made behind the scenes to elicit his opinion on the matter. Some of these efforts came from those who objected to R. Goren; others were initiated by his supporters, who saw R. Henkin not only as a non-partisan, non-political, independent personality, but also as someone who basically admired the Chief Rabbinate and its heads.

Thus, for example, in the middle of Ḥanukkah, R. Henkin received a letter from Mr. Max (Elimelekh) Schreiber. Schreiber was representative of American [Orthodox] Jews in lifestyle, but he had long-standing connections with rabbis in Israel (such as R. Yosef Shlomo Cahaneman and even the Ḥazon Ish) and was known to contribute generously to the cause of building *mikva'ot*. In his letter of December 5, 1972, Schreiber mentioned that he would be visiting Israel shortly. He had been close to R. Goren for twenty-five years, and on the other hand, in recent times was in contact with R. Moshe Feinstein, the Lubavitcher Rebbe, R. Yosef Dov Soloveitchik, and R. Henkin around the "Who is a Jew" issue. As such, Schreiber felt that he would be able to iron out the difficulties between R. Goren on his end, and R. Henkin and the other rabbis on theirs. Therefore, he suggested, "Please give me direction and with God's help, I am sure I can turn the tide and get him [R. Goren] to act according to your wish and thoughts."[51] In fact, though, we know of no involvement of R. Henkin in the case at that stage.

Matters changed later as the halakhic polemics around R. Goren's pamphlet on the ruling heated up in December 1972 and January 1973. Toward the end of January, rumors began circulating in New York about R. Henkin's positive attitude toward

---

50. *Teshuvot Ivra*, 223–24. See also Maizlish, *Min HaHar el Ha'Am*, 106–10.
51. From Mr. Schreiber's letter of December 5, 1972, in my possession.

R. Goren's *heter*. The first person to give public expression to these rumors was Rabbi Emmanuel Rackman whose statement was published in the American Jewish press in the beginning of February:

> R. Rackman praised a declaration by R. Yosef Eliyahu Henkin – whom he designated the leader of the Orthodox rabbinate in America – supporting R. Goren's ruling. R. Rackman added that R. Henkin's agreement "should silence once and for all those who reacted negatively" against the ruling.[52]

This announcement placed the leaders of Agudas Harabonim in an embarrassing position. As noted earlier, in the first months of the controversy, R. Moshe Feinstein, president of Agudas Harabonim, issued a strongly worded statement condemning the ruling "in the name of all the members of Agudas Harabonim" following which the organization held a protest rally in the spirit of the statement. All of this took place before there was even a hint that R. Henkin's position differed from that of his colleagues. It was problematic because, in addition to R. Henkin's importance as elder rabbi in the United States, he was also one of the honorary presidents of the organization. On the very same day of the press release, February 4, 1973, two representatives of the leadership of Agudas Harabonim hastened to R. Henkin's house to clarify his intent. The organization released the following official statement:

> We have determined that "Rabbi" Rackman's pronouncement does not accord with reality and is far from the truth. R. Henkin, may he live a long, good life, promised us that he never expressed an opinion about R. Goren's "ruling." Sadly, "Rabbi" Rackman uses improper means with the purpose of causing confusion in the Torah world which is united in its opinion, and has denounced R. Goren's *heter* in the strongest and clearest language possible. In a private discussion between R. Henkin and two of the important senior rabbis, on Monday, *Parashat Terumah*, R. Henkin said as follows: "I strongly object to those who publicize in my name that I agree with R. Goren's ruling, something which is not known to me and is completely foreign to me. I am not interfering, I cannot interfere, and I am not permitted to interfere...." The conversation with R. Henkin has been recorded in its entirety [and] a recording of the conversation has been sent to the president of the Agudas Harabonim, the gaon R. Moshe

52. From the original in English JTA, February 4, 1973.

> Feinstein, and to the Honorary President of the Agudas Harabonim, the gaon R. Yosef Dov HaLevi Soloveitchik.[53]

Knowing that an oral statement could be used tendentiously by interested parties – which is exactly what transpired – the leaders of Agudas Harabonim tried to elicit a written statement from R. Henkin. Indeed, at the end of that week, R. Henkin signed a letter about the ruling, the only one on the matter that he signed. An excerpt was published in the press; the full version appears for the first time below:[54]

> May God be blessed, 7 Adar 1, 5733 [February 9, 1973]
>
> With regard to the general question in the matter of R. Goren's *heter*, in my opinion, the matter is extremely difficult and requires the agreement of the great rabbinical leaders of our time, together with the agreement of the great rabbinical leaders in the entire world. And as long as no such court of law is convened, one should not rely on a *heter* such as this. And may God save us from obstacles so that no mishap comes through our hands.
>
> Y. E. Henkin

As noted earlier, R. Henkin had been blind for several years before the Langer Affair, and was not able to review R. Goren's pamphlet on his own. At best, he had access only to parts of it.[55] For this reason, the position he took in this letter does not address the intricate details of Borokovsky's status, and relates instead to the "general question" in the background of the affair. The nature of the "general question" can be understood in two possible ways: One, does a later rabbinical court have the authority to contradict a ruling agreed upon by a string of earlier rabbinical courts in a matter as serious as *mamzerut*? Alternatively, can a rabbinical court release someone from *mamzerut* by arguing that their mother's first husband was not converted according to Jewish law?

---

53. *HaPardes* 47:6 (February 1973), front cover.
54. From a photocopy in my possession. As noted above, R. Henkin, who was already blind during those years, would dictate the content of his letters to his secretary, but signed them with his own hand. (However, see below, on the question of the reliability of the above.)
55. In the manner which he describes in several of his letters and approbations from those years: "I have received [your] pamphlet... and they read for me two or three pages, because my eyes are heavy, ([may that] not [come] upon you) and it is [forced] upon me to listen from the mouths of others and it is impossible to burden them too much" (*Teshuvot Ivra, siman* 86:6, 1969).

Either way, in theory, it might be argued that R. Henkin rejected the validity of R. Goren's ruling, even if only after the fact. In practice, however, the Agudas Harabonim chose to quote only one sentence from the letter ("And as long as no such court of law is convened…"). Even this citation was in the margins of the press release. Why? Perhaps because of the preceding sentence mentioning "the general question, *hashe'elah hakhlalit.*" Quoting the whole letter would have allowed for an interpretation of R. Henkin's statement as leaving room to retroactively validate R. Goren's permissive ruling in connection with a **particular** question, *she'elah pratit.*[56] Perhaps another reason for not quoting the whole letter was the absence of the expected tone of sharp criticism of R. Goren himself.[57] In any event, as we will see, the fact that the complete letter was not quoted left ample room for those concerned with the affair to continue citing R. Henkin's opinion in defense of their own partisan positions.

At this point, the matter came to the attention of the Israeli press, with interesting results. Each side of the conflict – those who supported R. Goren and those who opposed him – chose to quote only those parts of R. Henkin's statement that were convenient for them to acknowledge. [The ḥaredi newspaper] *HaModia* cited the clarification issued by Agudas Harabonim,[58] presented as though it had been quoted in full, though part of R. Henkin's statement had been deleted, i.e., the words, "I am not interfering, I cannot interfere, and I am not permitted to interfere." As mentioned above, these words might have been taken to mean that despite his reservations about the ruling, R. Henkin did not want to come out against R. Goren personally. On the other hand, *HaTzofeh* [the national-religious daily] published a different statement entirely, repeatedly emphasizing what had been omitted by *HaModia* while ignoring the clarifications of Agudas Harabonim that did not serve its purpose:[59]

56. This, despite the conclusion of the letter, which makes it difficult to argue in favor of this possibility (unless one interprets it as relating to the possibility of connecting the permissive ruling to other cases). In any event, as will be shown below, this letter and its wording were far from R. Henkin's final word on the subject.
57. Indeed, the formulation of his words to representatives of Agudas Harabonim – "I am not interfering, I cannot interfere, and I am not permitted to interfere" – hint that in practice he refused their requests to join the public protest against R. Goren. See below.
58. *HaModia*, February 10, 1973, front page.
59. Another example of *HaTzofeh*'s efforts to bend the facts to fit their preferred stance is found in the front page report on November 28, 1972 and again on December 4, stating that R. Feinstein "refused to accede to pressure from the secretary of [Agudas Harabonim] R. Simḥa Elberg, an extremist ḥaredi activist, to protest against the ruling." Cf. R. Yehudah Altusky's clarification about R. Feinstein's opinion in *HaModia,* December 19.

> The gaon R. Yosef Eliyahu Henkin, one of the great rabbinical scholars in the United States and one of the heads of Agudath Israel [sic], expressed his opinion on the *heter* that the gaon R. S. Goren issued in the question of the "the brother and the sister," and said that one who speaks against him causes "bloodshed" – he spills the blood of a great rabbi in Israel and also spills the blood of the brother and sister. The gaon R. Y. E. Henkin spoke these words in a conversation with rabbis in the United States. His words were recorded on a tape recorder.[60] [...] After much thought, they sent a delegation of two important rabbis to the aged rabbi and requested of him nevertheless to join those who object to the ruling; however, the rabbi refused forcefully and returned and said to them, "I am not interfering, I cannot interfere, and I am not permitted to interfere...." In its embarrassment, Agudas Harabonim decided to publicize a public statement in response to the announcement publicized by R. Emanuel Rackman in the name of R. Henkin that he supports the ruling of the gaon R. S. Goren, in an attempt to contradict [R. Henkin's] words, but they did not succeed. In the public statement, spread over a full page, there was nothing for them to say against the announcement. The only thing they bring is the same sentence that he said: "I am not interfering and I am not permitted to interfere..."[61]

60. According to accounts on both sides of the controversy, R. Henkin's words were recorded on tape and even sent to well-known interested parties on both sides. However, as the recordings were never actually made public and no one knows where they are to be found, this claim does not have substantive implications. See below regarding whether R. Henkin consented to the recording of his words.

61. *HaTzofeh* (February 23, 1973), magazine, p. 2. In an item published later in the month, the following appeared:

> The gaon R. Y. E. Henkin discussed this topic with rabbis and great Torah scholars and said forcefully: "Whoever disagrees with this ruling is mistaken, it is forbidden to disagree with it, the gaon R. S. Goren is known as a great *posek* and God-fearing individual, I know him..." R. Henkin also rejected the argument that the ruling was given under pressure from government figures. "There is no substance in what they say, that the Chief Rabbi ruled in order to cull favor in the eyes of the government, and it is completely forbidden to say this, there is in this [kind of talk] defamation...," he said. [...] The president of *Histadrut HaRabanim*, R. Eliezer Bernstein, applauded these words, and also brought them to the attention of the heads of *Histadrut HaRabanim* at their convention. It is also known that the heads of religious Jewry in the United States sent to the Chief Rabbi of Israel, the gaon R. S. Goren, a reel of tape which contains the words of the gaon R. Y. E. Henkin (*HaTzofeh* [March 9, 1973], 2).

This, then, is how matters were described in the Israeli press, with the contradiction between the accounts in *HaTzofeh* and *HaModia* being interpreted by each side as a battle over differing versions of the same story based on the desire of "the other side" to portray reality in the manner most favorable to its own view. In any event, this attitude removed the necessity of contending with R. Henkin's actual statement.

Under the circumstances, with not even one great *posek* expressing public support for R. Goren and his permissive ruling, R. Henkin's position, as portrayed in *HaTzofeh,* clearly had a great impact on the religious-Zionist camp, and provided R. Goren's supporters with significant moral support. The elder statesman of *poskim* in the United States had not only refused to join the protest against R. Goren, but had also granted R. Goren his personal support, and approved his permissive ruling. R. Tzvi Yehudah Kook's words demonstrate the resonance of this among the supporters of R. Goren. He mentioned particularly how "in the midst of this, the announcement of R. Yosef Eliyahu Henkin of blessed memory was publicized, that one ought not doubt the teachings and rulings of the gaon R. Shlomo Goren, may he have a long, good life."[62] On another occasion, R. Kook expanded on this:

> The gaon R. Yosef Eliyahu Henkin *ztz"l* announced at the time that one ought not doubt the teaching of our master the gaon, R. S. Goren *shlit"a*. The power of the gaon R. Henkin *ztz"l* certainly is equivalent to and outweighs all those who signed on this offensive, fraudulent writ; and all their despicable words – they are certainly invalid and irrelevant compared to the ruling of this sage.[63]

NEW DISCOVERIES

Precisely what, then, was R. Henkin's view with regard to the *heter* in the Langer Affair, and with regard to R. Goren himself? Which of the two opposing versions of the story better accords with the truth, the account publicized by Agudas Harabonim or the one presented by *HaTzofeḥ?* The answer to these questions has not been settled to this very day.

There is, though, one piece of evidence, publicized recently, that unambiguously supports the account in *HaTzofeh*. This is the testimony of a kollel student who attended R. Henkin the year he died:

---

62. Letter dated October 20, 1977, *L'Hilkhot Tzibur*, p. 119.
63. Letter dated August 5, 1975, ibid., p. 73.

> In the matter of the well-known controversy that broke out between the Chief Rabbi of Israel, may he live a long, good life, and the rest of the great rabbinical figures of the generation, may they live long, good lives, it is incumbent on me to establish for posterity that my master and teacher the holy gaon whose righteous memory is a blessing, despite [the fact] that he never approved the ruling of the gaon R. S. Goren, may he live a long, good life (as is known [R. Henkin] was blind and therefore it was not possible for him to study the pamphlet composed by the Chief Rabbi and anyway, his great weakness did not allow him to study this complicated matter at all), in any event, he firmly placed himself on the side of the gaon R. S. Goren, may he live a long, good life, and ruled incisively that it is forbidden for any person to disagree with him since he was appointed to be the rabbi over all, and he was a great man ("one of *gedolim*" he called him); and all the arguments they made against him he dismissed with the flick of a wrist. (When I said to him that they claimed that the Chief Rabbi, may he live a long, good life, was in the category of one who takes a bribe, he answered forcefully and said "That's politics, not halakhah!") And it is incumbent upon me to add that he did not retreat from this opinion of his until he ascended to the heavens, despite the fierce pressures brought on him by various rabbis in the wake of the controversy.[64]

In theory, this testimony would suffice to dispel the uncertainty surrounding R. Henkin's position in the affair and verify that the description published in *HaTzofeh* faithfully reflects his opinion. However, there are a number of factors that call into question the absolute reliability of this evidence. First, the statement is attested to anonymously. The kollel student who wrote these words (and sent them to R. Henkin's family) did not sign his name to them, and his identity is unknown to this day. Second, the testimony is not completely independent and objective; it was written by someone who sided with R. Goren and who maintained a strong Zionist outlook.[65] Obviously, this in itself is no reason to doubt the trustworthiness of the witness. However, taken together

64. Cited in R. Yehuda Henkin, *Responsa Bnei Banim* 2:210. One sentence omitted in the citation appears here. The kollel student, as his handwritten words state, took care of R. Henkin "in the last eight months of his life," i.e., from December 1972, about a month after the controversy broke.
65. More than a quarter of the forty-seven paragraphs which the kollel student wrote in his record of R. Henkin's words deal with matters identified with the religious Zionist camp (e.g., R. Kook, R. Reines, R. Bar Ilan, Independence Day, and the Mizraḥi).

with the fact that some of his quotations of R. Henkin's words contain statements it is difficult to believe were uttered by R. Henkin as stated,[66] a question does arise regarding the precision with which the testimony was written. This is especially the case since the testimony was not written at the time of the events or immediately following, but only several weeks after R. Henkin's death at the end of that year.

While looking into writings from the estate of my grandfather, R. Henkin's son, Dr. Avraham Hillel, *z"l*, I found a handwritten note containing evidence of what he heard directly from his father about the episode. These words were written down on the same day that he heard them from his father, after a visit to his home on Sunday, March 4, 1973. Based on this evidence, it seems clear that R. Henkin did indeed express support and appreciation for R. Goren personally, being of the opinion that the affair did not undermine his "presumption of fitness" to be considered a great rabbi. Since this was the case, he added, the validity of the specific *heter* should not be questioned, although only the passage of time would show whether R. Goren's general conduct in the Langer Affair was justified. Additionally, this piece of testimony reveals extremely interesting information about R. Henkin's situation during that period, and about the nature of the pressures that were brought to bear on him. It casts doubt on the reliability of his signature on the letter mentioned above.

My grandfather's testimony was originally written in a combination of three languages – Hebrew, Yiddish, and English – and appears below in full.[67] It is important to emphasize that this evidence was not written for publication by someone who had a vested interest in the matter. The document is a private note whose sole purpose was a son's desire to permanently record his father's position – as heard from him on that day – within the family. This was the "motive" behind the writing of the document; in any event, its credibility is not subject to doubt.

---

66. Specifically the statement "that it is forbidden [!] for any person to disagree with him." Even fervent supporters of R. Goren did not make this claim. Also, the description of R. Henkin as "[firmly placing] himself to the side of [R. Goren]," etc. does not correspond with the general trend of the other sources, including the evidence below. It should be noted that in the introduction to his handwritten testimony, the kollel student commented "that to my great sorrow, I did not preserve the words in their form and there are many defects of omission and excess."
67. A photocopy of the original document appears at the end of the article.

March 4, 1973

Father said to me today:

1. He did not sign any letter.
2. He did not consent to be recorded.[68]
3. "I 'hold from' [have respect for] Rabbi Goren, he is a great rabbi and fitting for the position of head of the rabbis... [69] And [as] one who holds the position of head of the rabbis (as regards the permissive ruling), meanwhile, that is the ruling...." [70] In general, one rabbinical court cannot cancel [the ruling of] another rabbinical court, but Rabbi Goren can... [71] "But as to how right he was,[72] they will not know for a long time." It will take a long time to establish this, perhaps even years.

Among those who spoke with him for hours, in an attempt to move him from his position in favor of Rabbi Goren, were Rabbi [Naftali Tzvi Yehudah] Riff, Rabbi [Moshe] Feinstein, and Rabbi [Yehudah] Altusky.[73]

Mr. Berger[74] insists that someone by the name of Rabbi L.,[75] an employee of Agudas Harabonim, tried to force him [R. Henkin] to sign a partially empty paper, with the intention of filling in the content afterward, but Father refused, with [Mr. Berger's] help, understanding that he was being deceived. Dora[76] says that Rabbi [Moshe Eliezer] Margolin[77] got a signature out of him by means of a trick.

68. I.e., if indeed there were recordings made of his statements, they were done without his consent.
69. Ellipses as in the original throughout.
70. The two excerpts in quotation marks are written in Yiddish (in first-person speech) and reflect R. Henkin's original language.
71. Meaning, apparently, in his capacity as Chief Rabbi and president of the Supreme Rabbinic Court (as above.)
72. I.e., whether he was correct (in his conduct during the affair).
73. R. Rif was president of Ezras Torah from 1956 onward (in parallel with R. Henkin's tenure as administrative head) and R. Altusky (father of R. Ḥayim Dov Altusky) was then vice president of Agudas Harabonim.
74. R. Henkin's personal attendant in his home at that time.
75. I have omitted the rabbi's full name as he is currently alive in Israel.
76. R. Henkin's daughter, Ḥasha Devora, wife of R. Shimon Weber, who lived near her father in those years and helped him in his home.
77. R. Henkin's secretary in Ezras Torah, and the person who replaced him after his death as administrative head of the organization.

This document reinforces most of the details in the anonymous kollel student's testimony, and removes the contention that R. Henkin thought R. Goren's *heter* invalid. Beyond that, though, this testimony casts a shadow on the reliability of the single letter signed by R. Henkin mentioned above. In his testimony, R. Henkin's son passes on his father's statement that, "He did not sign any letter." How can this be reconciled with the signature displayed on the letter dated 7 Adar 1 [February 9], approximately three weeks earlier? The end of the testimony provides the answer: The signature was extracted from R. Henkin by some means, without his necessarily knowing that he was signing a letter about the matter of R. Goren or that this letter would be publicized.

Does this definitively rule out attributing the contents of the letter to R. Henkin? In my opinion, the answer to this question is complex. Howsoever R. Henkin came to sign the letter, those involved in the matter were respected rabbis who cannot be suspected of forging his name on statements that totally opposed his true opinion. The main problem is that the letter reflects only limited aspects of R. Henkin's position on the affair. There are no expressions of his support for R. Goren, but only R. Henkin's accompanying reservations about the affair. The letter does not mention R. Henkin's personal admiration for R. Goren or his statement that the specific ruling should not be categorically rejected, but rather that it should be examined on its own merit – something which R. Henkin was unable to do himself at that time.

In truth, in light of the information available to us now, it seems that the assertion "as long as no such court of law [is convened], one should not rely on a *heter* of this sort" should definitely be interpreted as relating to the "general question" that stood at the heart of the controversy, as in the discussion above. In other words, R. Henkin's assertion referred to the possibility of relying on the precedent set by R. Goren's ruling for future cases, but not necessarily to the question of the retroactive validity of this specific ruling for the personal status of the Langer siblings.[78] Knowing most of the participants in the affair well, and accepting the general reliability of the letter, as well as the testimony of the yeshiva student, this is how my father, teacher, and master, R. Yehuda Herzl Henkin *shlit"a* [*ztz"l*] understood the matter:

78. Indeed, if we had nothing other than the letter, a simple reading of it would indicate that it refers even to the retroactive validity of the specific permissive ruling. Attributing this position to R. Henkin is impossible, however, in light of the rest of the sources. Since we know that he did not dictate the exact formulation of the words, his connection with them being more general, the interpretation given above is the most reasonable one of his position.

1. R. Henkin did not express an opinion on the halakhic decisions of R. Goren in the matter of the Langer siblings since he did not read the actual ruling, and was prevented from reading by his blindness in those years. In keeping with his way, he never interfered in the rulings of rabbis in Israel when he was not requested to so and when the matter did not affect the existence of the Jewish people.
2. He firmly rejected accusations against R. Goren, since he was a great rabbi and one should not reject his decisions or – even worse – slander him.
3. R. Henkin made a distinction between the specific ruling (which should not be doubted because the *posek* was a great rabbi) and the question of whether future halakhic decisions should be determined according to the considerations in the ruling, for which one would need the consensus of the rest of the great rabbinical figures of the generation. See a similar discussion in what he [R. Y. E. Henkin] wrote in *Otzar HaPoskim* 4, in the footnotes, (p. 354, second column).
4. At the time of the controversy, both sides made strenuous efforts to persuade the gaon R. Henkin to add to, or retreat from these positions – and he refused.[79]

In summary, this was R. Henkin's position in the Langer Affair: On one hand, he supported R. Goren on the basis of long-standing appreciation for his achievements; and as a result, he refused in principle to invalidate the *heter*. On the other hand, he refrained from determining that the *heter* in itself was necessarily justified from a halakhic perspective. Either way, it is clear that in his opinion, the matter should be judged not with regard to R. Goren (since R. Henkin forcefully rejected all attempts to delegitimize him as a rabbi), but in its own right.

79. From a private letter (handwritten), second half of the 1970s.

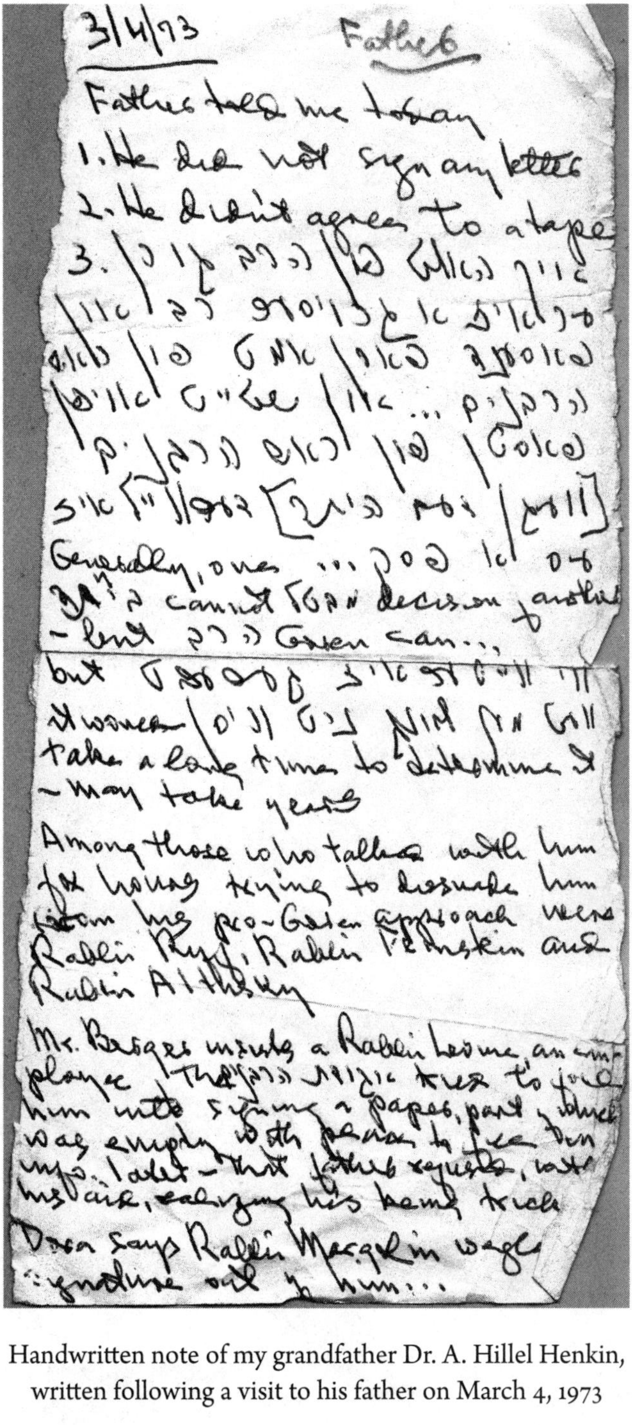
3/4/73 Father

Father told me today
1. He did not sign any letter
2. He didn't agree to a tape
3. [illegible]
[illegible]
Generally, one's ... [illegible]
cannot [illegible] decision of another
– but [illegible] Goren can...
but [illegible]
[illegible] it
take a long time to determine it
– may take years
Among those who talked with him for hours trying to dissuade him from his pro-Goren approach were Rabbi Ruff, Rabbi Feinstein and Rabbi Altusky
[illegible]

Handwritten note of my grandfather Dr. A. Hillel Henkin, written following a visit to his father on March 4, 1973

The fonts used in this book are from the Arno family

Maggid Books

*The best of contemporary Jewish thought from
Koren Publishers Jerusalem Ltd.*